FROM RAPHAEL TO CARRACCI

THE ART OF PAPAL ROME

General Editor
DAVID FRANKLIN

with essays by
SEBASTIAN SCHÜTZE
CARLO GASPARRI
INGRID D. ROWLAND

National Gallery of Canada
Ottawa 2009

Published in conjunction with the exhibition *From Raphael to Carracci: The Art of Papal Rome* organized by the National Gallery of Canada and presented in Ottawa from 29 May to 7 September 2009.

Catalogue produced by the Publications Division of the National Gallery of Canada, Ottawa

Chief of Publications: Serge Thériault
Editor: Lauren Walker
Freelance Editor: Usher Caplan
Photo editor: Andrea Fajrajsl assisted by Lindsay Sanford
Production manager: Anne Tessier
Translators: Michael Larrass, Donald Pistolesi, Käthe Roth

Design and typsetting: Fugazi, Montreal
Printing: Tri-Graphic Printing, Ottawa

Library and Archives Canada Cataloguing in Publication

From Raphael to Carracci: the art of Papal Rome.

Exhibition catalogue.
Issued also in French under title: De Raphaël à Carracci, l'art de la Rome pontificale.
Includes bibliographical references.

ISBN 978-0-88884-867-3

1. Art, Renaissance – Italy – Rome – Exhibitions. 2. Art, Italian – Italy – Rome – 16th century – Exhibitions. I. Franklin, David, 1961– . II. National Gallery of Canada. III. Title. IV. Title: Art of Papal Rome.

N6920 F73 2009   709.45'63209031   C2009-986006-6

Front cover: Raffaello Sanzio, called Raphael, *Allegorical Figure of Poetry* (detail), c. 1509–1510 (cat. 6). The Royal Collection © 2009, Her Majesty Queen Elizabeth II
Back cover: Bartolomeo Passarotti and workshop, *Portrait of Pope Pius V* (cat. 83). The Walters Art Museum, Baltimore, Maryland
Reproductions of papal portraits (pp. 65, 107, 155, 187, 221, 247, 261, 281, 313, 361, 401) from Alphonso Ciaconio, *Vitae et res gestae pontificum romanorum* ... (Rome, 1630). Bibliothèque nationale de France, Paris

Distribution
ABC Art Books Canada
www.abcartbookscanada.com
info@abcartbookscanada.com

CONTRIBUTING AUTHORS

CANADA

Nelda Damiano, Curatorial Assistant, National Gallery of Canada 44, 60

Una Roman D'Elia, Associate Professor and Queen's National Scholar, Queen's University, Kingston 88

David Franklin, Deputy Director and Chief Curator, National Gallery of Canada, Ottawa 9, 15, 16, 17, 32, 33, 36, 40, 43, 55, 67, 68, 76, 78, 84, 105, 113, 121, 125, 141, 142

Hilliard T. Goldfarb, Associate Chief Curator, Montreal Museum of Fine Arts 61

Stephen Gritt, Chief, Restoration and Conservation Laboratory, National Gallery of Canada, Ottawa 43

Graham Larkin, Curator, European & American Art, National Gallery of Canada, Ottawa 145

David McTavish, Professor, Department of Art, Queen's University, Kingston 31, 35, 51, 52, 64, 80, 85, 93, 117, 118, 140

Sebastian Schütze, Professor of Art History and Bader Chair in Southern Baroque Art, Department of Art, Queen's University, Kingston 23, 86, 91, 97, 109, 114, 127, 131, 132, 133, 134, 135, 136, 143, 144, 146, 147, 149, 150

FRANCE

Dominique Cordellier, Chief Curator, Département des arts graphiques, Musée du Louvre 14, 81

Philippe Costamagna, Art Historian, Paris 29, 62

Simon Legrand 20

HUNGARY

Zoltán Kárpáti, Curator of Early Italian Drawings and Prints, Szépmüvészeti Múzeum, Budapest 63

ITALY

Fiora Bellini, Director, Museo Nazionale di Castel Sant'Angelo 8

Alessandra Bigi Iotti, Art Historian, Reggio Emilia 100

Simona Capelli, Art Historian, Italy 59

Marzia Faietti, Director, Gabinetto Disegni e Stampe degli Uffizi 7

Lucia Fornari Schianchi, Superintendent for the Historic, Artistic, Ethnoanthropologic Heritage of Parma and Piacenza 90

Cristiana Garofalo, Art Historian, Gabinetto Disegni e Stampe degli Uffizi 13

Giorgio Marini, Curator, Gabinetto Disegni e Stampe degli Uffizi, Florence 6, 12

Raimondo Sassi, Art Historian, Gabinetto Disegni e Stampe degli Uffizi 3, 102

Anna Schreurs, Art Historian, German Institute of Art History (Max-Planck-Institute), Florence 95

Louis A. Waldman, Assistant Director for Programs, Villa I Tatti, The Harvard Center for Italian Renaissance Studies, Florence 42, 45, 58, 74, 87

Giulio Zavatta, Art Historian, Reggio Emilia 100

Alessandro Zuccari, Professor, Dipartimento di Storia dell'arte, La Sapienza 129

UNITED KINGDOM

Hugo Chapman, The British Museum 70

Florian Härb, Art Historian, London 53, 57, 65, 66, 94, 96, 121, 148

Paul Joannides, Professor of Art History, University of Cambridge 18

Arnold Nesselrath 46

Clare Robertson, Reader, The University of Reading 79, 126

Eike D. Schmidt, Director, European Sculpture and Works of Art, Sotheby's, London 82, 116

Rick Scorza, Independent Scholar, London 89, 115

Christian Tico Seifert, Senior Curator Early Netherlandish, Dutch and Flemish Art, The National Gallery of Scotland 138

Ben Thomas, Lecturer in History and Theory of Art, The University of Kent 69

Aidan Weston-Lewis, Chief Curator, Italian and Spanish Art, The National Gallery of Scotland 103, 104

Catherine Whistler, Ashmolean Museum, University of Oxford 5

UNITED STATES OF AMERICA

Carmen C. Bambach, Curator, Department of Drawings and Prints, The Metropolitan Museum of Art, New York 1, 2, 10, 41

Virginia Brilliant, Assistant Curator of European Art, The John and Mable Ringling Museum of Art 38

Julian Brooks, The J. Paul Getty Museum, Los Angeles 4, 25, 56, 71

David Alan Brown, Curator of Italian Paintings, National Gallery of Art, Washington 11

C.D. Dickerson III, Associate Curator of European Art, Kimbell Art Museum, Fort Worth, Texas 151

Rhoda Eitel-Porter, Charles W. Engelhard Curator and Department Head, Morgan Library & Museum, New York 30, 54, 106, 108, 110, 111, 112, 120, 122, 123, 124, 128

Larry J. Feinberg, Director and Chief Executive Officer, Santa Barbara Museum of Art 92

Jean Goldman, Independent Scholar, Chicago **72, 73, 119, 130**
John J. Marciari, Curator of Italian and Spanish
Paintings, San Diego Museum of Art **75, 77, 98, 99, 101, 107**
Sheryl E. Reiss, Department of Art History, University of
Southern California **19, 21, 22, 24, 37, 39**
Louisa Wood Ruby, Head, Photoarchives Research, Frick
Collection, New York **137**
Joaneath Spicer, The James A. Murnaghan Curator of
Renaissance and Baroque Art, The Walters Art Museum **83**
Linda Wolk-Simon, Curator, Department of Drawings
and Prints, The Metropolitan Museum of Art, New York
26, 27, 28, 34, 47, 48, 49, 50
Thomas DaCosta Kaufmann, Professor, Department of
Art and Archaeology, Princeton University, Princeton,
New Jersey **139**
Laura B. Zukerman, Curatorial Assistant, Department of
Drawings and Prints, Morgan Library & Museum **110, 111**

AUSTRIA
Vienna
Liechtenstein Museum **45**

CANADA
Kingston
Agnes Etherington Art Centre, Queen's University **31, 35,
51, 52, 140**

Montreal
The Montreal Museum of Fine Arts **61**

Ottawa
National Gallery of Canada **7, 43, 67, 68, 73, 77, 78, 84, 99,
101, 105, 121, 125, 135, 136, 141, 142, 145**

Toronto
Art Gallery of Ontario **118**

FRANCE
Paris
Musée du Louvre **14, 65, 81, 96, 107**

GERMANY
Berlin
Deutsches Historisches Museum **39**
Staatliche Museen zu Berlin, Kupferstichkabinett **17, 53, 76**

HUNGARY
Budapest
Szépmüvészeti Múzeum **47, 63, 95, 120, 123, 133**

IRELAND
Dublin
National Gallery of Ireland **29**

ITALY
Florence
Gabinetto Disegni e Stampe degli Uffizi **3, 13, 57, 79, 102, 126**
Galleria degli Uffizi **26**

Naples
Museo Nazionale di Capodimonte **88, 93**

Parma
Galleria Nazionale di Parma **90**

Rome
Church Santa Prassede **23**
Galleria Borghese **100, 115**
Galleria Colonna **28**
Galleria Doria Pamphili **86**
Museo Nazionale di Castel Sant'Angelo **8**

Sansepolcro
Museo Civico Sansepolcro **113**

Vatican City
Biblioteca Apostolica Vaticana **69**
Pinacoteca Vaticana **98**

NETHERLANDS
Haarlem
Teylers Museum **127, 129, 131, 143**

SPAIN
Madrid
Carmen Thyssen-Bornemisza, Museo Thyssen-
Bornemisza Collection **150**

UNITED KINGDOM
Chatsworth
Devonshire Collection **19, 21, 49, 80, 117**

Edinburgh
National Gallery of Scotland **33, 74, 103, 114, 138**

London
The British Museum **12, 18, 58, 66, 87, 149**
The Courtauld Gallery **144**
The National Gallery **59, 134**
Victoria and Albert Museum **24, 55, 82, 116**

Norfolk
Viscount Coke and Trustees of Holkham Estate, Norfolk **46**

Oxford
Ashmolean Museum **5**
Christ Church Picture Gallery **34, 37, 104, 110**
Her Majesty Queen Elizabeth II **6, 32, 40, 48, 91**

UNITED STATES OF AMERICA
Baltimore
The Walters Art Museum **83**

Boston
Isabella Stewart Gardner Museum **22**
Museum of Fine Arts **146**

Cleveland
The Cleveland Museum of Art **9, 132**

Forth Worth
Kimbell Art Museum **151**

Greenville
Bob Jones University Museum and Gallery **89**

Houston
The Museum of Fine Arts **36**

Los Angeles
The J. Paul Getty Museum **4, 20, 25**

New York
The Metropolitan Museum of Art **1, 2, 10, 41, 50, 71, 109**
Morgan Library & Museum **30, 54, 106, 111, 112, 122**

Providence
Museum of Art, Rhode Island School of Design **42, 128**

Sarasota
The John and Mable Ringling Museum of Art **38**

Seattle
Seattle Art Museum **62**

Washington
National Gallery of Art **11, 16, 27**

Private Collections
The Phillips Family Collection **44**
Mr. and Mrs. Marco Grassi **60**
Koelliker Collection **147**

Anonymous lenders **15, 56, 64, 70, 72, 75, 85, 92, 94, 97, 108,
119, 124, 130, 137, 139, 148**

Sun Life Financial is honoured to be the Presenting Sponsor of the National Gallery of Canada exhibit, *From Raphael to Carracci: The Art of Papal Rome.* Rarely has an exhibit of such magnitude been brought to Canada, with Ottawa, our nation's capital, as its sole venue. This extraordinary presentation of sixteenth-century art, garnered from the world's leading art galleries and museums, offers Canadians from all walks of life an unprecedented opportunity to see, perhaps for the first time outside the pages of a book, timeless masterpieces of some of the great artists of the era – Michelangelo, Raphael, Vasari, Carracci and others.

In keeping with our long-standing support of the arts in Canada, and our ongoing commitment to making the arts more accessible to a wider portion of our population, Sun Life Financial welcomes the opportunity to partner with our world-renowned National Gallery in presenting this unique collection. As an international financial services organization, we do business in many parts of the world. With the arrival of *From Raphael to Carracci: The Art of Papal Rome,* another world – a world of art – previously beyond the reach of many, has been brought to Canada for thousands to enjoy, making life a little brighter for all who experience its power.

We congratulate the National Gallery of Canada for organizing this once-in-a-lifetime experience, for bringing it to Ottawa, and by doing so, contributing greatly to our cultural environment and enriching us all.

DONALD A. STEWART
Chief Executive Officer

CONTENTS

The sixteenth century in Rome was a rich period in art history. Such celebrated masters as Raphael, Michelangelo, Salviati and Vasari practiced in the city during this time. Yet, although many exhibitions have celebrated Renaissance art in Florence and Venice, rarely has this period in Rome been so treated. Indeed *From Raphael to Carracci: The Art of Papal Rome* is unprecedented in its comprehensive examination of Renaissance Rome.

This careful selection of paintings and drawings represents a particularly ambitious and dramatic episode of cultural history in the "Eternal City." Arranged chronologically, from Pope Julius II to Pope Clement VIII, this linear approach reveals the remarkable diversity and affluent richness of work generated by a unique style of artistic patronage. The show probes the contradiction between the seemingly incompatible character of Rome both as the symbolic and administrative heart of the Catholic Church and as a location with extensive ancient art and architecture. The incredible tension between the religious present, serious and sumptuous, and the secular past, decadent and playful, emerges frequently in the art of this period.

Beginning with Raphael and Michelangelo, who together established a modern art tradition in Rome early in the century, this show traces their influence on the great many sophisticated and intriguing artists who followed, through to Annibale Carracci, a master of equal genius. Drawings are a natural focus because of the fundamental practice of developing original ideas on paper during this period – not only in Rome of course. And, it is through their drawings that many of these artists have been rediscovered.

Today this period is defined in such art historical style terms as the High Renaissance, Mannerism and early Baroque, yet by including major works from all three points of reference, this exhibition allows us to enjoy these artists on their own merit, without preconceptions. As well, this show will allow the public to discover a great number of "new" artists with styles of supreme originality and ambition.

An exhibition of this exceptional nature could not have been realized without the supreme generosity and vision of individual lenders. Particular thanks are due to Dr. Claudio Strinati, Superintendent for the Polo Museale in Rome, and to the various museum directors, curators and private collectors in that city who strongly supported this project from the start. The majority of these works have never before travelled outside of Italy, nor have they ever been seen together in one place. Given the value and rarity of the loaned objects, it was clear early on in the planning of the exhibition that only one venue would be possible.

I should like to thank David Franklin, Deputy Director and Chief Curator of the National Gallery of Canada, for undertaking the challenge of organizing this exhibition as a sequel to the highly successful 2005 exhibition on Renaissance art in Florence. He has been supported by his superb curatorial team, the distinguished scholars Rhoda Eitel-Porter, Sebastian Schütze, and Louis A. Waldman. We are especially proud of the catalogue – with contributions from more than forty scholars from Canada and abroad – which highlights considerable new research and a number of discoveries published here for the first time.

Special thanks are due to the dedicated team at the National Gallery of Canada for their professional contributions and personal commitment to this project, and to the Board of Trustees of the National Gallery of Canada for their support of the more recent acquisitions for the nation of some of the newly discovered works appearing in this show, including Francesco Salviati's *Virgin and Child with an Angel*.

Finally, I extend my sincere appreciation to Sun Life Financial for its most generous sponsorship of this exhibition and to Alenia North America who kindly supported the restoration of Perino del Vaga's *St. Julian Hospitaller* so that this enigmatic work could be exhibited in Ottawa.

MARC MAYER
Director
National Gallery of Canada

ESSAYS

FROM RAPHAEL TO CARRACCI:
AN INTRODUCTION

DAVID FRANKLIN

Rome's cultural and political history in the sixteenth century was linked inexorably to the popes, who were as respected, feared and, at times, corrupt as any European family dynasty. Indeed, these important families frequently influenced the power held by the papal office. For each consecutive pope – God's representative on earth, so it was believed, and leader of the Catholic Church – the sixteenth century was as event-filled and dramatic a period as any in the history of the church. The transitory nature of papal appointments and their correspondingly unpredictable lengths of term, created a climate of instability in daily life in Rome. The city's atmosphere could shift quickly from confident prosperity to despair depending on the politics of the Holy See. The emergence of Protestantism in northern Europe, rampant corruption and mismanagement in the Vatican, the ever-present menace posed by armies threatening the Papal States and even Rome itself, compounded by a frequently misjudged foreign policy, were among the factors troubling the papacy during the sixteenth century. Pivotal events such as the Sack of Rome of 1527 and the implementation of the decrees of the Council of Trent (1545–1563), the formation of new religious orders such as the Jesuits, and the workings of the Inquisition, naturally – and in some cases directly – had a profound effect on Rome, unparalleled elsewhere in Italy.

It was during the reign of Pope Julius II (fig. 1), elected in 1503, that Rome began its metamorphosis from a relatively shabby backwater to a true cultural capital. With his decision to vacate the Borgia apartments in the Vatican, Julius II initiated a new tradition of patronage and collecting that took visual form though the hands of artists like Raphael and Michelangelo. This is where the exhibition begins. By the time of the papacy of Clement VIII concluded with his death in 1605, Rome was unquestionably the jubilant centre of Christendom, thanks in significant part to the power of visual imagery, and moving into a new epoch, which in art historical terms is now referred to as the Baroque. A credible history of art in Rome during the sixteenth century can be traced via the papal projects concentrating on, but not exclusive, to the Vatican, Saint Peter's Basilica, the Castel Sant'Angelo, the Capitoline Hill and San Giovanni in Laterano. Art designed for all the major papal sites features in this exhibition.

Rome in the sixteenth century was marked by unrivalled ambition, monumentality and richness (and inevitably protracted execution). Popes were ostentatious and devoted to self-glorification, in part as a result of the intense pressure to represent a belief system throughout Europe and beyond. Having little choice but to build and to commission art, the popes competed consciously with the past, sometimes in homage or in deliberate opposition, and they were judged accordingly – often mercilessly – by their contemporaries. The enormous machinery of the Catholic Church, supported by military conquest, provided these rulers with considerable financial resources at their disposal. But their tenures – which ended only with their deaths – were naturally unpredictable, hence they governed within a dynamic instability that itself inspired creativity, especially among those artists who were confident, expedient and socially adept. The popes' tenured approach to patronage also distinguished Rome from other major centres in Italy, such as Florence or Venice where traditions and rivalries passed through generations of patrons and artists.

Patronage also came from the official papal administration, from members of the curia, and from the foreign embassies. In addition, their circle and supporters, especially the cardinals and immigrant bankers, mainly from Siena and Florence, such as the Altoviti, Chigi, Este, and Medici also provided luxurious patronage as they competed to create their own legacies in their chapels, palaces and villas. Often these wealthy patrons mirrored the ostentatious tastes of the popes as a deliberate means to engender greater loyalty and respect.

Rome more than anywhere else in Italy, with the possible exception of Venice, was a city of visitors, including pilgrims, diplomats, tourists, merchants and bankers, and this also directly affected artistic patronage and production. Art evolved to meet the demands of the ever-expanding tourist trade and to exploit the papal calendar of events, which also demanded an abundance of images. Those foreigners who died in Rome could become patrons of monuments, typically in their national church, and sometimes from an artist of shared nationality. Confraternities, as in other Italian cities and towns, were another important group who commissioned art but in certain instances they also took on a nationalistic character. The national communities settling there generally supported their own artists, providing additional opportunities for work. As well, the city rapidly expanded and contracted with visitors depending on the occasion; the Holy Years, for example provided further opportunity for ambitious artistic patronage. Rome had less of a neighbourhood character than did many Italian cities with their tightly knit families and enclaves. A city in the process of constant expansion and rebuilding, Rome underwent fairly

Fig. 1 Raphael, *Portrait of Pope Julius II*, 1512, oil on panel, 108.7 × 81 cm. The National Gallery, London

Fig. 2 Raphael, *The Transfiguration*, 1520, oil on panel, 410 × 279 cm. Pinacoteca, Vatican Museums, Rome

rapid growth during the sixteenth century, its population of about 50,000 around 1500 doubling to 100,000 by 1600. By the end of the sixteenth century Rome had become one of the most cosmopolitan, heterogeneous cities in Europe; its collecting patterns and the character of its art make it a fascinating subject for an exhibition.

Because of a marked decline in population in previous centuries, modern Rome had plentiful room in which to spread out and so ambitious building and town planning was possible, when the money and talent became available. The construction industry was vibrant throughout the sixteenth century and there was a consistent need for a large work force willing to relocate there. Naturally, the city also drew architects and artists who would design and decorate the new palaces and churches, inside and out, and restore and renovate the old, many of which had fallen into disrepair. A dramatic shift in attitudes towards ecclesiastical architecture in this period – not surprisingly, as Papal Rome was the locus for serious debates over the appropriate function of churches – also created work at an accelerated pace relative to anywhere else in Italy.

While Rome is far from marginalized in art historical scholarship, its artistic production has not been debated or examined as thoroughly as has that of Florence or Venice for example. What distinguishes art in Rome in the sixteenth century? Rome was unique for many reasons but most outwardly because of the tension between the very contemporary business of the international Catholic Church and how locals might deal with the conspicuous remains of Antiquity. Culture – and not just visual art – produced during this period can be studied with this opposition in mind and the various attempts to reconcile the religious and profane. In painting, by its sheer quality and novelty, the production of Raphael and Michelangelo in the Vatican established a new tradition that dominated the century. The reception of their contributions provides a lens through which the whole period can be viewed.

More than Michelangelo, Raphael exemplifies a new type of artist that developed in Rome in this period. His appearance and character, as much as his art, would become legendary and his premature death in 1520, at age thirty-seven, seems if anything, to have amplified his fame. Raphael's success was without precedent anywhere in Italy. He became almost untouchable, moving in elevated circles with a comfort and ease that few previous artists would have dreamed possible. Leo X reputedly even considered making him a Cardinal. His late painting of the *Transfiguration* (fig. 2) reveals as well as any other the drama and fertility of what would prove to be his final style. To truly appreciate the idealism and ethereality of his last contribution it is necessary to go beyond notions of Raphael as a universal and appreciate the variety, potential and even some of the more severe aspects of his art.

Fig. 3 Parmigianino, *Madonna and Child with Saints John the Baptist and Jerome*, called *Vision of Saint Jerome*, 1526–1527, oil on panel, 342.9 × 148.6 cm. The National Gallery, London

Fig. 4 Marcantonio Raimondi, *Holy Family with Young Saint John the Baptist*, called *Virgin with the Long Thigh*, c. 1520–1525, engraving, 41 × 27.4 cm. National Gallery of Canada, Ottawa

The artist himself died a "work in progress," with many major projects still incomplete, and it fell to his followers, with possession of the master's drawings, to promote all the options his style suggested into the 1520s. More prosaically, Raphael established the enduring model in Rome for a large, specialized and efficient workshop well suited to the demands of so much local art patronage. His own experience as a youth working with artists who also preferred collaborative enterprises like Perugino and Pinturicchio certainly inspired this approach. It was more far-reaching, however, in that many of his collaborators were not mere assistants but artists of genuine talent, whom he encouraged and trusted to use their own creativity within the group framework and push the house style in myriad directions. Artists who would themselves have major independent careers, including Giulio Romano, Giovanni Francesco Penni, Perino del Vaga and Polidoro da Caravaggio were all formed in this crucible, while others like Baldassare Peruzzi were impressed by Raphael's model in all its facets. Even a painter as talented as Titian working in distant Venice was aware of Raphael's Roman style, especially in portraiture. Unusually, it was an artist trained in a completely different tradition, Parmigianino, into whom it was believed that the spirit of Raphael passed at his death because of his graceful style – keeping in mind too that "grace" had a spiritual connotation in this period. The unconditional quality of Parmigianino's painting provides some justification for this view. His main public Roman work – the so-called *Vision of Saint Jerome* (fig. 3) in the National Gallery, London, unashamedly reveals its inspiration from Raphael's mature style for its vivacity, startling elegance and fluid, fluent technique, perhaps even as a challenge.

Raphael's designs (and eventually those of many other artists active in Rome) were also spread throughout the city and well beyond through the relatively new and original means of reproductive printmaking, which he in many ways inspired and then developed with his collaborator in this regard Marcantonio Raimondi (fig. 4). In part because of Raphael's initiatives, Rome became a centre for printmaking in this period and the production of images became part of the local tourist market in addition to serving the export market for images, both religious and secular. Printmaking and the designing of prints provided a stable income for many artists, often those who could find no other employment in the precarious work environment of the city. Prints also provided the first textbook of images from which artists and patrons could trace the history of art in Rome without even visiting the city.

Fig. 5 Sebastiano del Piombo, *Flagellation*, c. 1516–1524, fresco. San Pietro in Montorio, Rome

Fig. 6 Perino del Vaga, Decoration of the Sala Paolina, c. 1542–1545. Castel Sant'Angelo, Rome

To compete with Raphael's protracted legacy Michelangelo was himself forced, against his own tendency towards solitary creativity and drawn-out planning through successive drawings, to seek collaboration with such painters as the Venetian-born Sebastiano del Piombo (fig. 5), Daniele da Volterra and Marcello Venusti. At the same time, as a result of fierce controversy surrounding the nudity and severity of the *Last Judgment* fresco in the Sistine Chapel – part of which had to be over-painted because of the perceived lasciviousness of the male nudes in such a location – Michelangelo's style lost its broad appeal, especially for papal commissions. This was during the climate of Pius V, who, following his election to the papacy in 1566, closed the gallery of ancient sculptures in the Vatican to the public.

Raphael's late Roman style had been updated in countless ways following his death, but one of his early followers, Perino del Vaga in returning to Rome during the 1540s was most successful at doing so with regard to papal commissions (fig. 6). Perino thus impressed and inspired a whole new generation of talented artists born outside Rome, including the likes of Sermoneta, Agresti and Tibaldi who carried the torch forward past mid-century. More than any other artist of this period, however, it was Taddeo Zuccaro who most creatively developed Raphael's style. During the period of the Counter-Reformation when the church promoted by edict a style of art based on simplicity,

austerity, immediacy and official truth, in contrast to anything remotely pagan, Raphael's work in Rome could continued to inspire as a dignified, iconic prototype, even for sculpture. Indeed he remained an acceptable model throughout the sixteenth century in a way that Michelangelo, who outlived him by several decades, did not. Ultimately, it was Raphael's collaborative system of working creatively, and his refined, idealizing style, which Annibale Carracci would so sensitively codify by the turn of the seventeenth century.

With the exception of Giulio Romano and Giovanni Baglione, at opposite ends of the period under investigation here, there were no native-born Roman artists firmly upholding a particular tradition over generations against opportunistic intruders. The styles perpetrated by Raphael's followers and admirers were the closest approximation of this. Even referring to a "school" of Roman art is thus misleading and was certainly not a categorization used during this period.

Art in Rome was also conditioned broadly by a constant influx and exodus of artists from all over Europe. These artists quite often succeeded more easily, though not exclusively, depending on the birthplace of the particular incumbent pope, who during his reign would quickly assimilate the distinctive style of a native region to Rome, even if there existed no previous context for it. Rampant nepotism, with the placement of family members in

powerful positions within the administrations, enhanced this breed of patriotism. The rhythm of this influx accelerated as the century passed and artists were attracted increasingly, not only to seek patronage, but to study the famous achievements of Raphael, Michelangelo and myriad others, and, consistently, to stress, the art of the ancients. The continuous development and decoration of the city instigated by successive popes, who were generally motivated to compete with and surpass their predecessors whether they had artistic taste or not, also increased art patronage as the century advanced. Their support for art was taken for granted as a cultural and socio-economic driver of the city, yet some failed to meet expectations. Indeed, contemporaries commented negatively on Adrian VI's absence of interest in art and architecture; and the short papacies of Marcellus II (April–May 1555), Urban VII (September 1590), Gregory XIV (1590–1591), and Innocent IX (November–December 1591) did not realize any grand projects. But the city continued to draw artists, often young and without certain prospects or official introductions or contacts, to access and absorb the city's artistic greatness, past and present. Given the scale and depth of the art and city of Rome, this exercise was not without its perils; certainly many artists were frustrated by the experience. Not surprisingly, copy drawings form a crucial part of this exhibition. Whatever art was located outdoors or in churches had a particular significance for being easily accessible even to the most humble of artists, as did the many examples of antique architecture, art and sculpture. For certain artists, the availability of so much ancient art even encouraged an antiquarian tendency that could be supported by local humanists. Hence, a type of informal training became a distinctive aspect of the Roman experience as artists sought source material independently and at their own pace.

Yet the ease with which artists could access the contemporary internal decoration of the palaces, villas and the Vatican remains a matter for conjecture. Certainly copy drawings made by those fortunate enough to have had entrance to these privileged sites must have been coveted and lent (and recopied) with frequency. For those drawn to modern art, the facades – now sadly almost universally erased – by artists of the Raphael workshop, especially Polidoro da Caravaggio (fig. 7), who produced about fifty in collaboration with a mysterious Florentine painter named Maturino, as well as others like Baldassare Peruzzi, and later Pellegrino Tibaldi, were paramount for their development in drawing and design in copying. It should

be stressed that these works were not only outdoor but were executed solely in monochrome and on a monumental scale. The presence of so many fledgling artists on research visits to Rome will, in many instances, remain undocumented and can only be surmised. Federico Zuccaro's charming series of drawings (fig. 8) from the 1590s, now in the Getty, which recount the early experiences of his brother Taddeo in coming to Rome from the provincial Marche, provide the most vivid visual account of this obsession with Polidoro's facades as a training ground. The lessons learned from making these studies after Polidoro and Maturino could lead directly to commissions for a young painter, as in the case of Taddeo. Public facade paintings were significant too because they provided Rome with an external art historical tradition and thus became critical to the dispersion and maintenance of a recognizably local vernacular style. The style and subject matter of the facade frescoes were deeply inspired by the remains of ancient art, especially sculpture, and offered artists a chance to reconstruct anew the distant past, so outwardly Rome, past and present, had a tight symbiotic relationship in these images. Ironically, these external decorations, once so central to art practice in Rome of the sixteenth century, are now difficult to appreciate, though some reconstruction is possible mainly through the drawn copies themselves and prints.

The history of art in Rome provides evidence not only for individual stylistic development in making copies or studying prints, but also for a workshop practice that was relatively rare in terms of the collaborations that materialized between artists of different nationalities on ambitious projects that papal patronage frequently offered. The resounding scale and correspondingly tight deadlines of such commissions often provided great opportunities for younger artists arriving in Rome armed only with hope. This included ephemeral decorations, now completely destroyed, such as those for the triumphal entry of Charles V in 1536. Eclecticism is a distinguishing feature of the Roman art scene, as much as grandiose scale. Yet by virtue of their very monumentality these projects required a certain overall consistency of appearance to achieve some form of visual unity for the whole, which must have frustrated certain artists who might otherwise have sought to emphasize their difference. And so there was pressure for stylistic uniformity and concession, which created unusual working conditions for the artists involved. The sheer complexity and unpredictability, such that commissions, especially for sculpture, were often protracted or even entirely abandoned, also underscores the importance of the surviving drawings to unravelling the story of art in sixteenth-century Rome and reconstructing the original intentions of artists.

Conversely, artists from the same cities could quickly become enemies when in open competition for available commissions and shared nationality was no guarantee of cohesion. These larger projects were typically the responsibility of one artist, acting as the intermediary on behalf of the patron, who thus held enormous influence over his colleagues. In such a situation an artist would act virtually as a patron or power broker in assigning work to colleagues. Hence, in Rome the experience of many artists was contrary to a traditional apprenticeship or family workshop placement. To survive, they had to congregate into workshops depending on the availability and current progress of commissions. Unusual alliances often formed. Indeed, it is a wonder how these artists of different nationalities were able to communicate. No doubt they shared thoughts through their drawings as much as with words. This general situation also intensified rivalries and hostility could be raw, even life-threatening. The social world better known to us from the life of Caravaggio existed well before his time. The Popes had the power to starve artists as well as to outright banish them, as in the case of Federico Zuccari by Gregory XIII. Yet despite the potential for disappointment, the uncertainty, and the potential for peril, the temptations awaiting artists in sixteenth-century Rome were irresistible.

In fact, Federico Zuccari's temporary exile from Rome inspired him to create the first artist's academy in Rome – the Accademia di San Luca. The initial meeting was held in the house Zuccari designed, now the Bibliotheca Hertziana, where lectures on sound art practice were also given. This major initiative was not only the outward manifestation of the more civilized aspect of an artist's life in Rome, but part of the longstanding attempt, imported from Florence, to augment the respectability and social status of the artist with a textual underpinning. It was the moment of the codification of the tradition steeped in the achievements of Raphael and Michelangelo. The *Saint Luke Painting the Madonna* (fig. 9) with Raphael looking on in the Accademia di San Luca, attributed to Federico Zuccari, and possibly donated by him in 1593, is the key image in this regard, not only for the inclusion of the great master but because the style even approximates his.

Another decisive moment in the history of the period was the development of art history as a discipline as initiated by Vasari's *Lives of the Artists* published in 1550 and in an expanded edition in 1568, which buttressed a fledging art theory in the period. It is useful in the context of this exhibition that this great book was born not in Florence but in Rome in the circle of Cardinal Alessandro Farnese during the late 1540s. Vasari's stress on the overriding importance of Raphael for the recent history of art was decisive. Guidebooks too, required by the growing number of visitors, including artists, to the papal city, also memorialized art in an unusually self-conscious manner.

A career in Rome could breed success for artists in manifold ways. Art was frequently produced for export, as in the case of Giovanni de' Vecchi who supplied a set of altarpieces for his native town of Sansepolcro. There can be no doubt that the artist's reputation was enhanced enormously as a result of success in Rome and inspired commissions at home, even in the absence of any workshop in the native place. Sebastiano del Piombo's dispatch of his stringent and dignified religious paintings to Catholic Spain (fig. 10) is one of the richest and most durable examples of the export market from papal Rome, precedents for which can be traced to Raphael's career. Conversely, a few artists left Rome and continued their success. Among these, Federico Barocci sets the finest example. He abandoned the city after a relatively short sojourn, in part because of his aversion to the bitter competition and urban lifestyle, but continued to maintain links there and produced major commissions for the import market from a provincial base in the Marche. Titian provides a related instance of an artist who was attracted to Rome almost as an unavoidable temporary challenge – in the 1540s in his case – and then returned to Venice without making any significant impact on the local artistic scene.

In addition to the relevance of any artists of the day, the surviving art of ancient Rome provided a constant inspiration but also created an underlying tension of attraction and repulsion for artists and patrons throughout the period. Ancient art was also contemporary art in that much was being continually discovered through accidental finds and excavation, including major pieces linked to texts, such as the Laocoön. Nowhere else in Europe was there such a locus for a dynamic and stimulating pressure of the very alive past on the present. Unusually for a European city, its continuity and desire to renew was linked with distant Antiquity, as Rome had failed so miserably in its recent history. Of course, the miraculous

Fig. 9 Federico Zuccaro and Scipione Pulzone, *Saint Luke Painting the Madonna*, c. 1593, canvas transferred from panel, 220 × 160 cm. Accademia di San Luca, Rome

Fig. 10 Sebastiano del Piombo, *Descent into Limbo*, c. 1530, oil on canvas, 226 × 114 cm. Museo Nacional del Prado, Madrid

new pope would build his own power base by electing one or more nephews to the College of Cardinals and by installing other family members, relatives, clients and friends in key positions in the court and elsewhere in the Papal States or, more broadly speaking, by imposing his own network on the existing system. The process easily involved thousands of people directly and affected almost everyone indirectly. The election of the Medici popes Leo X and Clement VII early in the sixteenth century, for example, greatly enlarged the presence of Tuscan fellow citizens on the banks of the Tiber on many different levels: from the establishment of banking houses and the foundation of confraternities to the transfer of Florentine artists and artisans. The death of the pope and the election of his successor each time profoundly changed and dramatically challenged the social and political equilibrium, forcing individuals, families and social groups to adapt to new and somewhat unpredictable realities. Rise or decline, success or failure, fortune or misfortune, were largely dependent on their capacity to respond effectively to these circumstances. Compared with other societies of the *Ancien Regime,* the social structures of papal Rome can thus be described as extremely unstable, dynamic and competitive at the same time. Art and art patronage offered a powerful instrument, both for old and new elites, to affirm and represent family traditions and political alliances, their prestige, status and rank or the pretentions thereof.

The family palace and the family chapel, though by no means the only venues, provided ideal stages for such ambitions and absorbed the greatest economic and artistic resources. Location, size and architectural grandeur of the palace spoke eloquently to the wealth, status and prestige of its owners and positioned them, quite literally, within the social fabric of the city, as did the decorations of the palace and the collections housed therein. A highly ritualized protocol governed the reception of visitors of various ranks and meticulously defined their *parcours* through the palace and their point of encounter with the host, emphasizing the symbolic quality of the palace as a stage that represented and interpreted the finest nuances of hierarchical power relations. The Palazzo Farnese (fig. 24), located in the heart of Renaissance Rome, next to Campo dei Fiori and Via Giulia, offers a compelling example.[16] In 1513–1514 Cardinal Alessandro Farnese commissioned Antonio Sangallo to transform the pre-existing, late fifteenth-century building into a modern Renaissance palace, inspired by Bramante's Palazzo dei Tribunali on the Via Giulia. After his election to the papacy as Paul III in 1534, the original project was grandly amplified to meet the representational needs of a papal family and to project its fortunes and dynastic ambitions into the future. No less than four papal architects, Sangallo, Michelangelo, Vignola, and della Porta, contributed to its design and made it the most magnificent of all Roman Renaissance palaces. Generations of Farnese cardinals resided in the palace and continued to enrich its famed art collections with paintings and statues, tapestries, precious manuscripts and ancient gems, and to decorate its state rooms, from Francesco Salviati's Sala dei Fasti Farnesiani (fig. 25) to Annibale Carracci's Galleria. The palace represented the power, status and prestige of the Farnese family in papal Rome, promoting the ambitions of the dukes of Parma and Piacenza as well as those of the family cardinals, who regularly aspired to the Holy See.

Equally important was the family chapel. The chosen site alone could decisively speak to the national identity, the social rank, the political alliances and the religious beliefs of its owners, as did the choice of a specific type of decoration, of an iconographic program and of the artists involved. Considerations were plenty: would the chapel be located in a national church or in the church of a newly founded order?; along the aisle or in the transept?; which patrons owned the other chapels?; would an artist previously involved in papal projects execute the design?; would costly marble be employed in the decoration?; would the chapel be dedicated to a patron saint, to a popular Counter-Reformation cult such as the Immaculate Conception or the Madonna of the Rosary, or to a newly canonized saint? Contemporary sources indicate that all these aspects were observed carefully and interpreted as markers of distinction that positioned the family on the social map of papal Rome. Certainly Agostino Chigi, the famously wealthy banker of Julius II, for example, endowed his family chapel in Santa Maria del Popolo (figs. 26, 27) with the intent to underscore and strengthen his ties with the Rovere Pope and his family.[17] The Augustinian church, founded by Julius' uncle, Pope Sixtus IV, housed prominent Rovere and Riario tombs. Julius himself donated his famous portrait, executed by Raphael in 1511–1512 and today housed in the National Gallery in London, to the very same church. Strategically placed right inside the Porta del Popolo, through which most visitors to the papal city passed as they entered from the north, the church enshrined on its high altar the miraculous image of the *Madonna del Popolo* and enjoyed widespread popular devotion. The Chigi Chapel was attached to the left nave, where its greater size and octagonal plan distinguished it clearly from the existing side chapels. Raphael, the papal artist par excellence, designed its imposing centralized architecture around 1515 in clear reference to Bramante's crossing of new Saint Peter's. The walls were encrusted with ancient marbles and adorned with marble statues and

Fig. 26 Raphael, Dome of the Chigi Chapel. Santa Maria del Popolo, Rome

Fig. 27 Raphael, Chigi Chapel. Santa Maria del Popolo, Rome

bronze reliefs; the dome was covered with mosaics and the altarpiece by Sebastiano del Piombo was executed not on canvas, but on a wall specifically prepared with small marble pads. These precious, everlasting materials were to reflect the patron's magnificence, while giving material expression to his hopes for eternal life. They also allowed Raphael and Agostino Chigi to finally compete with the grandeur of the ancients not just by imitating their style, but by adapting their use of materials.[18] The Chigi Chapel set new standards for chapel decorations in Rome, followed decades later by papal chapels such as the Cappella Gregoriana in Saint Peter's or the Cappella Sistina in Santa Maria Maggiore, and only subsequently adopted for the most prestigious family chapels in Rome. The chapel's concept and design reflect a wide range of motivations, indistinguishably merging piety and devotion with more worldly representation.

If the constant need for distinction and the rivalry between old families and new elites were driving forces behind the Roman art production, other players contributed to make it an even more competitive field. Because of the unique role of the pope as sovereign spiritual ruler of the Catholic world, Rome was a very cosmopolitan city and the most important stage of international politics and diplomacy. The city's large communities of foreign residents, merchants and bankers, national cardinals, and diplomatic representatives of major and minor European courts were important patrons of the arts: from national churches and confraternities, palaces, private chapels and tombs to lavish processions and festival decorations.[19] Often these residents acted also as intermediaries and agents, commissioning prestigious Roman works for patrons throughout Europe, thereby promoting their circulation and further strengthening Rome's dominant role as cultural and spiritual capital. The same is true for old and newly founded religious orders, which established "headquarters" in the Eternal City, founding major churches and convents. Public presence in Rome was quintessential, when it came to papal favours and privileges, but also to stir popular support and to attract powerful donors. Fierce competition between the three most important Counter-Reformation orders, the Jesuits, Theatines and Oratorians, found its most eloquent expression in their Roman churches. All three orders erected their mother churches in close topographical proximity along the Via Papale (fig. 28), leading from Piazza Venezia to Ponte Sant'Angelo and the Vatican. The Jesuits were the first to realize their church, and the Gesù was erected between 1568 and 1584 by Jacopo Vignola and

Giacomo della Porta.[20] The Oratorian church, known as Santa Maria in Vallicella or Chiesa Nuova, was erected by Matteo da Castello and Martino Longhi in 1575–1594,[21] followed by the Theatine church of Sant'Andrea della Valle designed by Francesco Grimaldi, della Porta and Carlo Maderno in 1591–1620.[22] All three churches follow the same architectural type, with a central nave and accompanying side chapels, a large transept and a dome over the crossing, trying to surpass and outrival each other in grandeur.[23] Churches of this magnitude could be erected only with the support of wealthy benefactors. The Gesù was financed by Cardinal Alessandro Farnese, the Chiesa Nuova by Cardinal Pier Donato and Bishop Angelo Cesi, and Sant'Andrea della Valle by Cardinals Alfonso Gesualdo and Alessandro Montalto. The side chapels were entrusted to other patrons for their family chapels and while specific conditions for the concession varied greatly, their rich decoration was expected to contribute to the magnificence of the whole. The rivalry between Gesù, Chiesa Nuova and Sant'Andrea della Valle would continue for most of the seventeenth century, albeit in reverse chronological order when the Theatines commissioned Domenichino and Lanfranco, the Oratorians Pietro da Cortona, and the Jesuits Giovanni Battista Gaulli to decorate their respective churches. To endow an entire church or a chapel was indeed the perfect way to publically display personal wealth – a kind of church-sanctioned form of "ostentatious consumption" in honour of God and for the common good, for which Gregory XIII coined the term *carità pubblica*, "public charity."[24]

Papal patrons, Roman cardinals and foreign diplomats, old families and new elites, private and religious patrons alike all contributed decisively to the vibrant and extremely competitive Roman art market. Their need for visibility and social distinction fuelled the engine of a dynamic and innovative art production, attracting artists from all over Europe and pushing for constant change and rapid succession of styles. Both the supreme quality and the astounding spectrum of Roman sixteenth-century art are a grand collective achievement that might best be compared to a large symphony orchestra, where papal patrons provide the theme and conduct the ensemble, famous artists, cardinals and princes play the lead instruments, and myriad other major and minor players contribute to the volume and depth of the music that would resound in all of Europe.

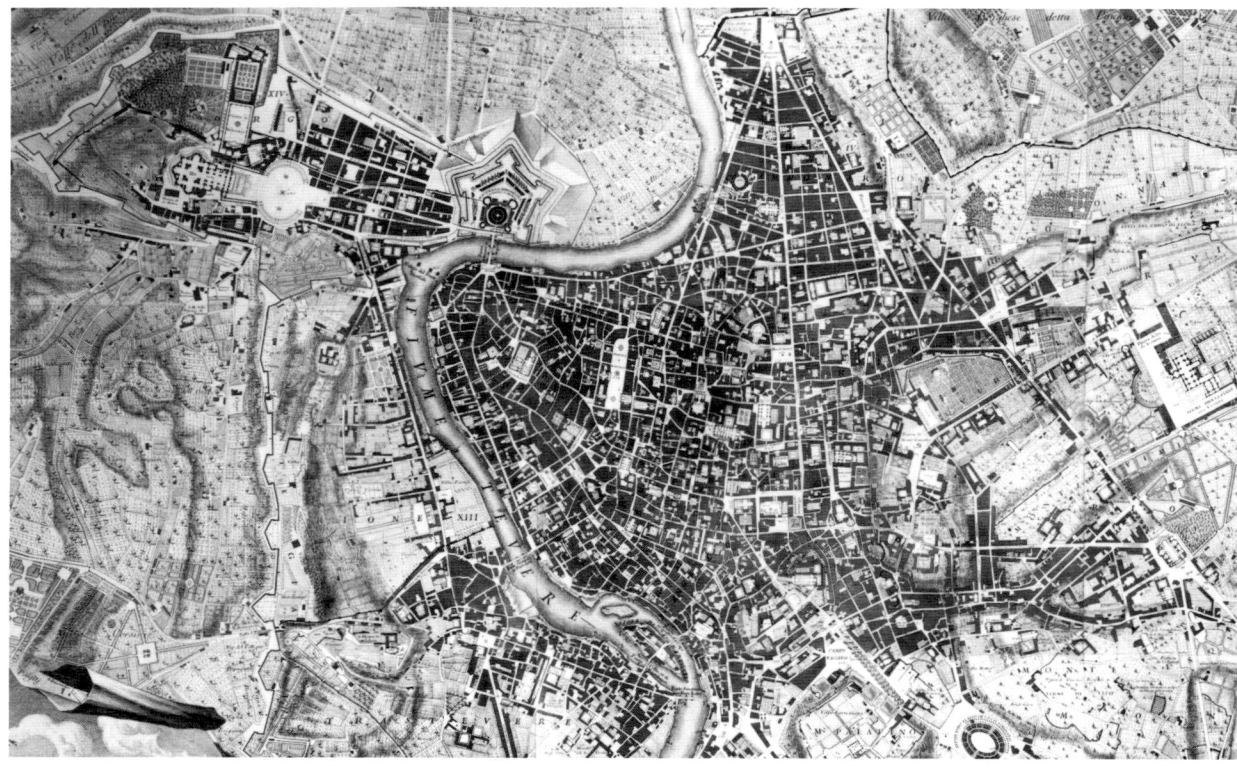

Fig. 28 Giambattista Nolli, *Map of Rome*, detail showing Via Papale, 1748. Museo di Roma, Rome

NOTES

1   In accordance with the essay format, no attempt is made in the foot-notes to reference the enormous historical and art historical literature on the subject. The most comprehensive treatment of the subject remain the relevant volumes in L. von Pastor, *The History of the Popes, from the Close of the Middle Ages,* 40 vols. (London, 1894–1961); recent surveys of art and art patronage in Rome in English include G.L. Hersey, *High Renaissance Art in St. Peter's and the Vatican* (Chicago and London, 1993); L. Partridge, *The Art of Renaissance Rome 1400–1600* (London 1996).

2   P. Prodi, *Il sovrano pontefice. Un corpo e due anime: la monarchia papale nella prima età moderna* (Bologna 1982) [English edition: *The Papal Prince, One Body and Two Souls: The Papal Monarchy in Early Modern Europe* (Cambridge, 1987)].

3   C.W. Westfall, *In this Most Perfect Paradise: Alberti, Nicholas V, and the Invention of Conscious Urban Planning in Rome, 1447–55* (University Park, 1974).

4   E.D. Howe, *Art and Culture at the Sistine Court: Platina's "Life of Sixtus IV" and the Frescoes of the Hospital of Santo Spirito* (Vatican City, 2005).

5   English translation from L. Partridge, *The Art of Renaissance Rome*, p. 12.

6   F. Buranelli and A. Duston, eds., *The Fifteenth Century Frescoes in the Sistine Chapel* (Vatican City, 2003).

7   C. Echinger-Maurach, *Studien zu Michelangelos Juliusgrabmal,* Hildesheim, 1991; J-M. Kliemann and M. Rohlmann, *Italian Frescoes: High Renaissance and Mannerism 1510–1600* (New York, 2004), pp. 88–181.

8   M. Winner, B. Andreae, and C. Pietrangeli, eds., *Il Cortile delle Statue: Der Statuenhof des Belvedere im Vatikan* (Mainz, 1998).

9   S. Ginzburg, *Annibale Carracci a Roma: Gli Affreschi di Palazzo Farnese* (Rome, 2000); Kliemann and Rohlmann, *Italian Frescoes,* pp. 452–475.

10   For a synthesis and recent contributions to the building and decor-ation of Saint Peter's see A. Pinelli, ed., *The Basilica of St. Peter in the Vatican,* 4 vols. (Modena 2000); *Barock im Vatikan: Kunst und Kultur im Rom der Päpste 1572–1676,* exh. cat. (Bonn, 2005); G. Satzinger and S. Schütze, *St. Peter in Rom 1506–2006* (Munich, 2008).

11   J. Pelikan and H.T. Hartmann, eds., *Luther's Work,* 55 vols. (St. Louis and Philadelphia, 1958–1967), for Luther's "Disputation on the Power and Efficacy of Indulgences (1517)," 31, pp. 17–33, for the citations from theses 50 and 82, pp. 30, 32.

12   Kliemann and Rohlmann *Italian Frescoes,* pp. 88–123; M.A. Kuntz, "A Ceremonial Ensemble: Michelangelo's 'Last Judgement' and the Frescoes in the Cappella Paolina," in *Michelangelo's Last Judgement,* ed. M.B. Hall (Cambridge, 2005), pp. 150–182

13   R. Zapperi, *Tiziano, Paolo III e i suoi nepoti: nepotismo e ritratto di stato* (Turin, 1990); Kliemann-Rohlmann *Italian Frescoes,* pp. 352–369.

14   T.J. Dandelet, "Financing New Saint Peter's: 1506–1700," in *Sankt Peter in Rom 1506–2006,* ed. G. Satzinger and Sebastian Schütze (Munich, 2008), pp. 41–48.

15   W. Reinhard, *Freunde und Kreaturen. "Verflechtung" als Konzept zur Erforschung historischer Führungsgruppen: Römische Oligarchie um 1600* (Munich, 1979); W. Reinhard, "Papal Power and Family Strategy in Sixteenth and Seventeenth Centuries," in *Princes, Patronage, and the Nobility: The Court at the Beginning of the Modern Age, 1450–1650,* eds. R.G. Asch and A.M. Birke (London, 1991), pp. 329–356; and contri-butions in *Art and Identity in Early Modern Rome,* eds. J. Burke and M. Bury (Aldershot, 2008).

16   C.L. Frommel, *Der Römische Palastbau der Hochrenaissance,* 3 vols. (Tübingen, 1973); *Le Palais Farnèse,* 3 vols. (Rome 1980–1994).

17   J. Shearman, "The Chigi Chapel in S. Maria del Popolo," in *Journal of the Warburg and Courtauld Institutes,* 24 (1961), pp. 129–160; E. Bentivoglio, *Raffaello e i Chigi nella chiesa agostiniana di S. Maria del Popolo: 1483 – 1983* (Rome, 1984); N. Riegel, "Die Cappella Chigi in Santa Maria del Popolo: eine kritische Revision," in *Marburger Jahrbuch für Kunstgeschichte* 30 (2003), pp. 93–130. After the sudden deaths of Raphael and Agostino Chigi, the chapel remained unfinished and was completed only in the seventeenth century by Bernini.

18   A concern that Raphael raised in his famous letter to Pope Leo X in 1519; F.P. Di Teodoro, *Raffaello, Baldassare Castiglione e la lettera a Leone X* (Bologna, 1994).

19   For the large Spanish community in Rome, for example, see T.J. Dandelet, *Spanish Rome 1500–1700* (New Haven and London, 2001).

20   R. Bösel, *Jesuitenarchitektur in Italien, Teil 1, Bauten der römischen und neapoletanischen Ordensprovinz,* 2 vols. (Vienna, 1985), I, pp. 160–179; C. Robertson, *Il Gran Cardinale: Alessandro Farnese, Patron of the Arts* (New Haven and London, 1992), pp. 181–196.

21   C. Barbieri, S. Barchiesi and D. Ferrara, *Santa Maria in Vallicella* (Rome, 1995).

22   S. Schütze, "Kardinal Maffeo Barberini, später Papst Urban VIII., und die Entstehung des römischen Hochbarock," in *Römosche Forschungen der Bibliotheca Hertziana* 32 (Munich, 2007), pp. 36–46.

23   In Santa Maria in Vallicella narrow side aisles were introduced in the final project.

24   For the concept of "ostentatious consumption" see N. Elias, *The Court Society* (New York 1983); for the concept of "public charity" see G. Baglione, *Le Vite de' Pittori, Scultori et Architetti dal Pontificato di Gregorio XIII fino a tutto quello d'Urbano Ottavo,* Rome 1649, p. 4: "Papa Gregorio XIII … fu un Principe molto liberale, e verso i suoi Popoli grandemente benigno; fece egli fare molte fabriche non tanto per sua gloria, quanto per pietà Christiana; perché soleva egli dire, che il fabri-care era una carità pubblica; e che tutti li Principi far la dovrebbono: perche con questa occasione al pubblico & al private si sovveniva."

ROME RESTORED:
VILLAS, COLLECTIONS, AND
GARDENS OF ANTIQUITIES IN
SIXTEENTH-CENTURY ROME

CARLO GASPARRI

Late fifteenth-century Rome must have presented an incomparably thrilling spectacle to all who flocked there searching out the vestiges of the city's past and tracing the clues provided by the ancient classics.

The close-knit fabric of medieval Rome – enclosed within the Aurelian Wall and characterized by towering ruins and massive churches connected to convents – was starting to open into broader avenues and squares lined with the palazzos of the prominent noble families and members of the papal court. These palazzos were modelled after architectural examples from a past that had always been physically present in the imposing, decaying walls of large public monuments, superb sculpted columns, plentiful bronzes, and colossal statues, presented in medieval Latin guides for pilgrims as *mirabilia urbis Romae*, the marvels of the city of Rome.

The people of Rome built their churches in the remains of these ancient monuments and temples, beneath the vaults of arches and theatres. There they lived, plied their trades, and conducted their business. Everywhere, countless ancient marble slabs carved with figures and inscriptions bore messages that awaited study and interpretation.

For centuries, the great mausoleums along the consular roads outside the walls had been despoiled of their decorated sarcophagi, which now served as fountains and drinking troughs in public squares and in the courtyards of houses and palazzos. In the basilicas, ancient columns and capitals were put to new use, supporting richly adorned lintels and mouldings; ancient altars and basins became stoups for holy water; vessels of precious marble supported altar tables and housed saints' relics; figurative reliefs encrusted ciboriums and pulpits; monumental sarcophaguses, often decorated with secular scenes, were mounted in the tombs crowding the naves and porches of churches. Ancient statues, reliefs, and architectural fragments adorned the homes of families wishing to give themselves noble origins. As in ancient times, huge bowls of rare marble served as basins for fountains in the middle of public squares.

There was no need for large-scale excavations to recover the image of the past. The past was already intensely present in everyday life, and new ruins would emerge daily, every time the earth was turned in vineyards and vegetable gardens or on the construction sites that were starting to change the face of the city.

Yet, much of what had been discovered was destined to disappear once again. Documents from the fifteenth century record a huge number of requests for excavation permits to extract material for use in new building, and throughout the next century a great deal of the marble that was recovered – including the remains of sculptures – would be reduced to lime in kilns or cut into slabs for use in new construction. At the end of the century, however, much would find its way into patrician collections, initially strewn in no particular order in courtyards and gardens. In the following decades, the many detached marble fragments and the material recovered from churches under renovation would fuel a true antiquities market. These pieces would be rearranged in new, systematic displays, just as in 1471 the Lateran bronzes – among the city's most illustrious witnesses of the past – were transferred to the Campidoglio by Pope Sixtus IV to form the basis of Rome's first public collection of antiquities.

Such artifacts had been the object of artists' and scholars' attention for some time, although the earliest sketchbooks and compendiums of inscriptions that have come down to us date from only the final decades of the century. In fact, it was the examination of inscriptions, together with the traditional study of gems, coins, and medals, and information found in the sources, that laid the scientific foundation for interpreting this huge and still incoherent wealth of images.

All this material inevitably attracted not only the interest of artists and scholars, but also the appetite of collectors, thus stimulating further specialized research.

It is perhaps to Alexander VI Borgia, whose personal approach to Antiquity is quite evident in the decor of his Vatican residence, that we owe the first large-scale excavation aimed at recovering classical sculptures. It took place at what would remain for centuries the richest collection of marble from the Roman world: Hadrian's Villa at Tivoli, whose colossal ruins, rising from the Tiburtine countryside dotted with the residences of many a noble family, had long been a magnet for artists and antiquarian scholars. The undertaking was a success. What we now know to have been the theatre of the so-called Accademia yielded a coherent group of statues – the Muses plus Apollo – as well as an abundant series of monumental marble masks, which shed new light on illustrated themes connected with the realm of theatre, literature, and poetry in ancient Rome.

The brief duration of Alexander VI's papacy precluded appropriate development of this assemblage, which was eventually dispersed among various collections (and which we will meet up with again below). But the search for and ownership of ancient sculptures continued to be a vital measure for his successors; beginning with Julius II

Fig. 29 Modern view of the Cortile delle Statue. Cortile del Belvedere, Rome

Fig. 30 *Laocoön*, 1st century AD Roman copy after Agesander, Athenodorus and Polydorus of Rhodes, marble, 210 cm high. Museo Pio Clementino, Vatican Museums, Rome

(Giuliano della Rovere), antique artifacts would become a means of expressing not only cultural but also moral and political values.

While still a cardinal, Giuliano della Rovere had already acquired important examples of ancient sculpture, including a statue of Apollo whose formal qualities were unequalled in Rome. But his elevation to the papacy was the prelude to one of the most astounding and complex endeavours of recovery and reinterpretation of ancient works: the Cortile delle Statue (fig. 29), built by Bramante in the course of extensive remodelling of the pope's Vatican residence.

In this limited, enclosed space behind Innocent VIII's old Belvedere Villa, Julius II added a sculptural group of unsurpassed value to his *Apollo* and the outstanding *Laocoön* (fig. 30) he had promptly purchased when it was discovered by chance in 1506. His intention was to convey a multi-layered allegorical message that combined the celebration of poetry and art (suggested by the presence of Apollo) and intellectual *voluptas* (personified by Venus) with the moral admonition implicit in Laocoön, who had been cruelly punished for attempting to oppose divine will. The political message conveyed by those same marble figures – openly referring to the sacrifice of Troy that was necessary for the founding of Rome under the protection of Apollo and Venus, mother of Aeneas and progenitrix of the *gens Iulia* – must have been equally clear, especially in light of Vergil's epic. Finally, Rome's imperial destiny, recalled by the colossal statue of the Tiber, was evoked in the superb image of the sleeping Ariadne that, at the time, was thought to represent Cleopatra committing suicide after Octavian's victory at Actium. The *restauratio* of a new Rome was precisely the program this second Julius was pursuing with his armies in the broader Italian political arena.

Fig. 31 Maarten van Heemskerck, *Garden Terrace at the Villa Madama*, 1532–1536, pen and brown ink, 13.6 × 21.1 cm. Staatliche Museen zu Berlin, Kupferstichkabinett

Fig. 32 Hieronymus Cock, after Maarten van Heemskerck, *Sculpture Court of the Cardinal della Valle*, 1553, engraving, 27.5 × 41.5 cm. Bibliothèque nationale de France, Paris

HÆC VISVNTVR ROMÆ, IN HORTO CARD· A VALLE, EIVS BENEFICIO, EX ANTIQVITATIS, RELIQVIIS IBIDEM CONSERVATA·

The two Medici popes who succeeded him, Leo X and Clement VII were more interested in enriching the family's wealth through the purchase of ancient sculpture – including the Muses from Hadrian's Villa – some of which were distributed throughout the splendid suburban residence on the slopes of Monte Mario – later known as the Villa Madama (fig. 31) – which Leo X had initiated and assigned to Raphael, and some went to his city palazzo. But this did not mean that they neglected the Vatican collection. The complex system of references in Julius II's Cortile delle Statue was enriched mainly by Clement VII, who, besides promoting the restoration of the Apollo and Laocoön, eloquently counterbalanced the Tiber with a similarly colossal statue of the Nile and placed atop the walls a series of theatrical masks, also from the Borgia pope's excavations.

Drawings by Maerten van Heemskerck, a Netherlandish painter who visited Rome from 1532 to 1536, provide valuable testimony of the ordering of Roman antiquities collections at this time; they reveal that under the two Medici pontiffs the architectural unity of the Vatican Cortile had not yet coalesced. Although this courtyard housed an array of sculptures that remains unequalled to this day, it still had the laboured feel of a disconnected conglomeration of figures. The merging of an architectural environment with antique sculptural furnishings was to be superbly achieved in another Roman courtyard completed in those same years by Cardinal Andrea della Valle (fig. 32), which adhered to the precedent of a *hortus conclusus* (enclosed garden) set by Julius II.

With the help of Lorenzetto, who had cultivated a thorough familiarity with the antique style in Raphael's school, the cardinal arranged several outstanding pieces within the elaborate architectural system of walls and loggias surrounding an open area in the mezzanine of his palazzo. In this case as well, they were chosen according to an exhibition plan with telling cultural and political implications that were more nuanced than those of his papal predecessor. Four statues of barbarian prisoners on high pedestals, in part decorated with Victories, framed a setting in which idealized figures of gods and heroes alternated with portraits of emperors in armour – among them the *optimi principes* Augustus, Trajan, and Marcus Aurelius – all standing in niches spaced at regular intervals between large panels representing "histories" in the form of processions, sacrifices, and triumphs created from reliefs taken from the Arcus Novus of Diocletian on Via Lata and broadly incorporated into stucco landscape backgrounds. The highest Olympic divinities – Jupiter and Neptune, and the protectors of the arts and poetry, Minerva and Apollo – were placed alongside the satyr Marsyas, condemned to be flayed, another moral *exemplum* of pride punished. The relief of Apollo and his sister Diana – goddess of the hunt, associated with woodlands – was echoed in plants climbing on the walls and trees growing in the centre of the courtyard. As at the Cortile del Belvedere, the latter were probably bitter orange trees, which, with their golden fruit, evoke the apples of the Hesperides and, by extension, the garden of the Muses. Here, too, there were large theatrical masks above, underscoring the intention to stage a world of images alluding to the historical past and its religion, while two facing rows of sarcophaguses with Dionysian processions, hunting scenes, and marine *thiasoi* celebrating some far-off age of happiness formed a border for the vegetation.

The political theme, allusion to the Empire's victories, is present in the series of historical reliefs embedded in the walls of the Valle courtyard and powerfully evoked by the figures of captured barbarian kings, three of which were in priceless Egyptian porphyry, a material that suggests the imperial colour purple and imperial dignity. In the years following the Sack of Rome, such political references became an obligatory commonplace for antiquities collections, which could no longer be contained in the closed space of a courtyard annexed to a palazzo. A larger natural setting became necessary.

In the garden that Cardinal Federico Cesi had begun arranging in 1537 behind his palazzo in Borgo, the theme of the celebration of the Empire – which had now become a transparent metaphor for the sovereignty of the Church – was spectacularly represented by a statue of Rome Triumphant (in fact a conveniently integrated image of a deity, perhaps a Ceres) seated on a pile of weapons, on a high pedestal decorated with the motif of the spoils of conquest. On the front, the theme was expounded in the relief of the grieving figure of a conquered barbarian woman, which would inspire Dürer. At the sides were two dark grey marble statues of barbarian prisoners, clearly alluding to both the religious and the political supremacy that the Church of Rome would re-establish in the years of the Council of Trent. And the addition of modern heads, made from the same dark marble, conveyed the increasing intensity of the fight against heresy, a battle the Church would wage against the Turks at Lepanto some decades later.

In Cardinal Cesi's pleasure garden – where the celebration of important political themes was combined with private family memories evoked through a collection of inscriptions of the *gens Caesia* – a new feature appeared: a pavilion located on the perspective axis of the garden's main alley. It was a *studiolo*, a small study, its interior richly inlaid with wood and marble, a place expressly built to house a choice collection of portraits of emperors and political personalities (among them the famous basalt "Scipio" today at the Palazzo Rospigliosi). They plainly reflected contemporary research on the portraiture of great figures of the past. The theme of *imagines virorum illustrium* found its first full-fledged scholarly definition in the second half of the century thanks to Fulvio Orsini and was to characterize the exhibition strategy for the major collections of the period.

At this time, the villa was the ideal setting for a collection of ancient sculptures, whereas smaller items such as inscriptions, gems, miscellany, and medals were destined for the *studiolo* or for the antiquarium.

A good example of this division is provided by Cardinal Rodolfo Pio da Carpi. In the large villa he built on the slopes of the Quirinal Hill between 1549 and 1564, he set out ancient statues and marbles according to a carefully conceived design. But at his residence in Campo Marzio he assembled a veritable museum of inscriptions, reliefs, portraits, small bronzes, medals, and even ancient painted vases, which became the subject of analysis and debate among a circle of international scholars. The jewel of his collection was the bronze portrait bust of Brutus, which was bequeathed to the people of Rome at the cardinal's death and added to the Capitoline collection of historical objects.

The Bolognese naturalist Ulisse Aldrovandi visited Rome in 1550 and left a valuable, systematic description of the collections of antiquities that he saw. *Delle Statue antiche che per tutta Roma si veggono,* published in 1556, devotes many pages to the Carpi "museum" and the villa on the Quirinal Hill, which he described as "not only the most delightful rural place in Rome and all of Italy, but in fact an earthly paradise." The Villa Carpi was in fact just one of the splendid mid-century creations built according to descriptions by Vitruvius, Varro, and Cicero in an obvious attempt to emulate and recreate the grand residences of the Roman emperors and aristocracy. Unfortunately for us today, they have all disappeared or been drastically altered.

Payment records are all that remains of the fleeting existence of the architectural and natural splendours of the villa built by Julius III del Monte during his brief pontificate from 1550 to 1555. It was there that, under the influence of the Florentine architect Bartolomeo Ammannati, a new component first appeared: marble encrustation and the use of ancient columns and marbles. The pontiff's collection of statuary was quickly dispersed after his death, but a crucial portion of it was later transferred to the Villa Medici on the Pincian Hill, including a large group of herms (all headless) representing famous men, with names inscribed, that had originally come from a villa in the countryside near Tivoli. These herms have long been included in compendiums of inscriptions, and now provide material for iconographic studies.

The culminating point was reached by Cardinal Ippolito d'Este who had already built a sumptuous villa on the Quirinal Hill. But in Tivoli, with the help of the Neapolitan architect and antiquarian Pirro Ligorio, he would create a villa beyond all comparison, exploiting the natural lay of the land and the unlimited availability of water, and reproduce the kind of theatrical effects that were suggested in the sources and attested by the ruins of the imperial residences on the Palatine and Pincian Hills and by the architecture of sanctuaries in Palestrina and Tivoli itself. The cardinal intended his new villa to rival the splendour of nearby Hadrian's Villa, where, taking advantage of his position as governor of Tivoli, he had obtained most of his ancient statuary. At the new villa, natural vegetation and the spectacular play of water combined with the sculpture to produce unique effects.

It is clear from Aldrovandi's text that at mid-century there were well-defined principles governing the distribution of ancient marble artifacts between the antiquarium or the *studiolo* and the patrician villa and palazzo, where the use of statuary as decor had by now become codified according to sanctioned concepts, with a fixed repertoire of subjects and figurative types that contributed to expressing these concepts. And only the unique and exceptional examples stood out from this repertoire, such as the Belvedere Apollo, Laocoön, Ariadne, Hercules, and the Farnese Bull – the exclusive pride of a few first-rate collections.

The extent of the Farnese family's plan for collecting materials from Antiquity would remain unequalled for the rest of the century, but like the Medici popes before them, the Farnese were less interested in enriching the Vatican collections than in celebrating the family name. Pope Paul III saw to completing the decor of Julius II's Cortile delle Statue and fulfilled Michelangelo's design for the Campidoglio (fig. 33) by transferring the equestrian statue of Marcus Aurelius there in 1538. But it was primarily his nephews, Duke Ottavio Farnese and Cardinals Alessandro and Ranuccio, who led this strictly private project over the

span of the entire second half of the century, largely through an abundant number of purchases and some remarkably successful excavations. In addition, they inherited significant assets, notably from Margaret of Austria, who had held title to Medici property, including the palazzo and the Villa Madama along with their sculptures, in addition to Lorenzo the Magnificent's former gem collection. At the very end of the century the Farnese came into possession of the large collection of gems, inscriptions, and portraits that had been assembled by the family's antiquarian, Fulvio Orsini (1529–1600), while conducting research for his *Imagines et elogia virorum illustrium* (1570), a seminal treatise for modern iconography. In addition to the family palazzo, the Farnese's wealth of art now included the gardens on the Palatine Hill, the residence in Caprarola, and the villa across the Tiber purchased from Agostino Chigi.

It was mainly after Ranuccio's death and through the efforts of Alessandro, known to his contemporaries as "il Gran Cardinale," that furnishing of the new Palazzo Farnese in the Campo dei Fiori took substance (spectacu-

larly introduced by a row of colossal statues under the courtyard's arcades) with the statues of Hercules from the Baths of Caracalla opposite the entrance, in an immediate and impressive suggestion of the ideal union of strength and moral virtue that defined the family. The theme, personified by the hero who, facing a difficult choice, resists the temptation of glory, was repeated inside the palazzo many times over. And according to a never-implemented plan, at the end of a long vista framed by the two Hercules, in a fountain in the garden across the Tiber, accessible by a specially built bridge, there was to have been the huge Bull sculpture (also recovered from the Baths of Caracalla): the ultimate moral *exemplum*, a complex theatrical illustration of the punishment of Dirce (fig. 34) for her cruel treatment of the innocent Antiope. The group of sculptures was of extraordinary value: the Hercules, by the Athenian Glykon, was one of few in Rome to bear the signature of its sculptor; the Bull is the only work besides the *Laocoön* that can be identified among those mentioned by Pliny. Alessandro's contemporaries would hail these marbles recovered from the excavations at the Baths as the "most beautiful thing in Christendom."

In the surroundings of the *appartamento nobile*, a pair of Barbarian Prisoners flanked the entrance to the Great Hall. Seized following a victory over the rival Colonna family – and thus a powerful reminder of the triumphs not only of the Empire but of the Farnese family – they introduced cycles of emperors' portraits that recalled the principle of dynastic continuity (a prerequisite for such triumphs), while a series of eighteen portraits of illustrious men evoked the moral and intellectual values on which ancient culture and government were founded. The collections of gems, coins, inscriptions, and manuscripts in the more intimate setting of the *studiolo* provided an overview of the elaborate cultural heritage that was now serving as model.

By the turn of the century, at the urging of Alessandro's great-nephew Cardinal Odoardo, the Galleria dei Carracci (fig. 35) was created to integrate a selection of the best pieces from the statuary collection with fresco decoration depicting a complex mythological program celebrating moral values, while in the palazzo's Great Hall itself, with the opportune addition of some of the more important sculptures from the Medici collections, a "Combat of the Gladiators" was composed to emphasize the family's military vocation. A foretaste of the Baroque, it can be seen as a precursor to creations of a few decades later, such as the one at the Villa Ludovisi.

The family's political and economic power enabled the Farnese cardinals to ignore the newly imposed dictates of the Council of Trent regarding the possession of antiquities. So, in parallel with an impressive program of family self-representation in the private sphere, Alessandro was able to exploit his collection of antiquities in order to carry out his plan to found a world public school in Rome.

During the same years, Gian Pietro Carafa (who would be elected Pius IV in 1559), of the Milan branch of the Medici family, resumed the deployment of Antiquity in the pontiff's residence, commissioning Pirro Ligorio to build a *casino* (little villa) decorated with ancient statues, reliefs, and stucco work patterned after Cardinal della Valle's courtyard. Moreover, in the lower part of the long courtyard designed by Bramante he built a theatre decorated with allegorical statues, busts, and inscribed herms of famous men. But this marked the close of the great sequence that had begun in 1503, during which the Vatican collections were amassed. His successor, the austere Dominican brother who was elected Pius V, immediately stripped both of Ligorio's creations of their statues and hid the masterpieces from the Cortile delle Statue collected by Julius II and the Medici popes. Pius V deemed possession of these "idols of false gods" inappropriate for a member of the clergy. The sculptures of the *casino* and Ligorio's theatre were added to the Campidoglio's collection of *mirabilia*, which would remain the city's most important public collection of ancient art until the eighteenth century.

At the deaths of the cardinals who had founded the great collections formed over the first half of the century and in the new cultural climate ushered in by the Council of Trent, with the exception of those of the Farnese family and the dukes of Parma, the great fortunes in antiquities that had made Rome's image unique (and which Ulisse Aldrovandi had so minutely described) would be scattered and disappear. A flood of ancient marble artifacts poured into a flourishing antiquities market and fed the appetite of foreign courts. During the years when the Savoia and Gonzaga collections and the great collections in Prague and Munich were being created, Rome registered no new instances of interest in classical art – with one stunning exception. Between 1576 and 1588, with sufficient economic means and the strength that came from the political independence that he too derived as a representative of the Grand Duchy of Florence, Cardinal Ferdinando de' Medici built a villa on the Pincian Hill. Located at the edge of the Aurelian Wall, on the border between the monumental core of the modern city and the open suburban spaces it enjoyed a superb view (fig. 36).

The appreciation of Antiquity that was characteristic of the Florentine court, together with Ferdinando's strong interest in astrology and nature as well as the artistic sensitivity and political spirit for which he was known, all gave rise to a creation that was unparalleled in the breadth and quality of its sculpture and governed by a complex web of ideas wherein all the most important themes essayed in the first half of the century were distilled into an organic whole.

The villa's design was organized on a tightly woven exhibition layout dominated by the figures of Apollo and Diana, the divinities of art, poetry, and nature, who kept watch over Ferdinando's domain. One end of the axis on which the villa was built called to mind Mount Parnassus, home of the Muses, and the Castalian Spring sacred to poets, in a natural wooded setting; the other told the story of Niobe and her children through the spectacular reassembly of a group of sculptures recovered from a villa near the basilica of San Giovanni in Laterano in 1583 and

Fig. 35 Galleria dei Carracci, detail of wall decoration with niches containing copies of ancient marble sculptures. Palazzo Farnese, Rome

Fig. 36 Villa Medici, Rome

SIXTEENTH-CENTURY ROME:
THE BIRTH OF A
CULTURAL CAPITAL

INGRID D. ROWLAND

The careers of Raphael and Annibale Carracci coincide neatly with the beginning and end of the sixteenth century, a century in which their adopted city, Rome, changed from a dangerous, somewhat provincial local centre to a capital of truly international stature. It was an eventful century, the twenty-third of Rome's long, turbulent history, ushered in by the Borgias and rounded off by the Jubilee of 1600, whose celebrations included burning the heretic philosopher Giordano Bruno at the stake. The sixteenth century was a time of artistic triumphs for Rome, with Donato Bramante, Bernardino Pinturicchio, Raphael and Michelangelo active in the first decade, and Annibale Carracci and Caravaggio blazing into action at the century's end. It was also a century of disasters, brought on by angry nature and human folly: devastating floods, outbreaks of plague and syphilis, the six-month sack of the city by German mercenaries in 1527. Above all, for the city of the Popes, this was the century that ushered in the Protestant Reformation and Catholicism's response, formulated officially in the decrees of the reforming Council of Trent and proclaimed not only in sermons, liturgy, and courses of study, but also in works of art, architecture, and music. Sixteenth-century artists therefore faced just about every possible human situation along with the inscrutable ways of God, and responded with a dizzying versatility. As Copernicus, Bruno and Kepler began to question the very structure of earth and heaven, artists made their own extravagant experiments in the arts. At the same time, however, experimentation was carefully regulated, justified, and counterbalanced by a thriving theoretical literature, which sought universal standards of quality and found them in God, nature and classical antiquity.

By any of these standards, divine or human, ancient or modern, both Raphael and Carracci shone forth as absolute masters, capable, in the eyes of their contemporaries, of distilling nature's divine harmonies with the same ineffable skill as the legendary artists who had worked for Alexander the Great or the emperors of Rome. For both artists, moreover, this strong link to the classical world stimulated rather than stifled their originality: however insistently artists and critics might speak or write about art as imitation, art's real business was transformation, shaping perceptions of the world. And in that sixteenth-century world of the here and now – never mind the shape of the cosmos – Rome stood at the centre of both a religion and a cultural movement, a place of ever-increasing real and symbolic importance.

Few pilgrims who came to Rome for the Jubilee of 1500 would have seen their destination as the Eternal City; the signs of decay were too obvious, an example of the ancient Romans' imperial pride brought low by time and chaos. By 1600, on the other hand, many visitors came carefully prepared with printed guidebooks that reminded them insistently of Rome's eternal significance. Magnificent new buildings suggested a vibrant modern city to rival its ancient predecessor, including a new Saint Peter's Basilica, a new Capitol, new churches, a new network of streets, new neighbourhoods, and old neighbourhoods renovated to a more opulent standard. With the return of Pope and Curia in the fifteenth century, the one- and two-storey houses of medieval Rome could no longer accommodate the city's multitudes. Taller and taller they rose, modest row houses with two windows to a floor and the magnificent palazzi of cardinals and nobility. From the mid-fifteenth century onward, the whole physical scale of the city changed to meet the needs of its burgeoning population, and expanded housing brought expanded needs for services, especially water and transport. By 1600, the building trades had become the city's chief industry, an essential element in the spiritual mission of the Church. But building Rome required vast amounts of money, and the best way to attract money was to attract visitors. Before the conception of advertising as we know it, papal Rome used the arts and the printing press to communicate the idea of the Eternal City and its apostolic mission in a campaign aimed at new residents and visitors alike; the phenomenal success of that campaign would be confirmed in the eighteenth century by the tradition of the Grand Tour, and in the twentieth by the vision of Rome as the romantic setting of *Roman Holiday*, the sexy metropolis of *La Dolce Vita*, and, not least, the spiritual destination of the pilgrims who have flocked to the city by the millions in the age of mass transport.

If Rome's ancient heritage was central to the image of its eternity, the sixteenth century understood that heritage in a particular way. Because the Gospel of Luke makes it clear that Jesus had been born during the reign of Augustus (specifically at the moment of the Augustan tax census), the birth of the Roman Empire and the birth of Christianity could be established as nearly contemporary events. In Rome itself, however, this connection in time was also experienced as a connection in space, for durable tradition held that the two most active apostles, Peter and Paul, were martyred in Rome during the reign of Nero.

Time and again, the New Testament shows how shrewdly the Apostles took advantage of the Roman Empire's centralized networks of travel and communication

Fig. 37 Interior of the Church of
Santa Maria in Aracoeli, Rome

to spread their gospel. In the Middle Ages, local Roman legends continued to emphasize the capital city's special role in the larger Christian mission. An ancient story held that the Tiburtine Sibyl had intercepted the Emperor Augustus en route to the Forum to give him a personal announcement of Christ's birth; ever afterwards the site of their encounter was known as the Ara Coeli, the "Altar of Heaven," and there the Franciscan order erected a splendid basilica in the thirteenth century, Santa Maria in Aracoeli [fig. 37] (at the top of whose steps Edward Gibbon conceived the idea for his *Decline and Fall of the Roman Empire*). Another basilica, San Pietro in Vincoli, recorded already in the eighth century, preserved the chains that had fettered Saint Peter in the Mamertine Prison; the Mamertine prison itself, a grim ancient cistern, still stands today at the edge of the Roman Forum. Churches eventually rose over the tombs of the martyred saints Peter and Paul, the city's official protectors, as well as many other sites associated with the actions of the apostles or early martyrs. A mosaic in the fifth-century basilica of Santa Sabina pays tribute to the two great traditions that built the early Church by portraying two dignified women, one labelled "the Church of the Jews" and the other "the Church of the Gentiles" (meaning the Greeks and Romans); these were the two groups who built the Roman Church in the years of Imperial Rome. Fifteenth-century theologians paid, if anything, a still more pointed tribute to these two early Church traditions: they

firmly declared that the wisdom of the Hebrews, like that of the sages and Sibyls of classical antiquity, had been essential to prepare the world for the Christian message.

Recalling that long tradition in the early fifteenth century from a papal court displaced to the fertile but uneventful hills of Provence, the Roman-born Pope Martin V, elected in 1417, concluded that the destiny of his native city could not, in fact, be separated from his office; the papacy should return to Rome. As it happened, Martin's decision to return coincided with the very moment when the Italian Renaissance had begun to burst into full flower in Florence, and in Florence the papal court was bound to stop on its route back from France. Indeed, Martin and his successor Eugenius IV actually spent a great deal of their reigns in Florence rather than Rome itself; the ancient capital remained their ideal more than their real destination. That protracted Florentine stay ensured that the fifteenth-century Church would associate the Renaissance revival of classical antiquity with a thoroughly contemporary mission: for reviving Rome meant transforming a medieval city, set within ancient ruins, into a modern Christian metropolis.

Several fifteenth-century Popes made huge strides toward turning Rome into a modern city, especially Nicholas V and Sixtus IV, whose interventions included large investments in the urban infrastructure and, simultaneously, in the Vatican Library, officially founded by Nicholas but extensively reorganized by Sixtus. (Although it is rare to think now of a library standing at the centre of a political and religious movement, we can certainly identify with their conviction that knowledge is a source, if not *the* source, of power). The Vatican Library's official title, Biblioteca Apostolica Vaticana, underlined the driving sense of Christian mission that guided all the papacy's efforts to recreate Rome as a capital city. But that mission was political as well. In 1453, with the papacy barely resettled permanently in Rome, Constantinople fell to the Ottoman Turks. After a cataclysmic siege, the ancient capital of the eastern Roman, and subsequently the Byzantine, Empire became the new capital of an empire ruled by Islam. The conquest sent a stream of Greek refugees into Italy and gave Rome's very survival as a Christian capital – let alone its revival – a more powerful symbolic charge than ever.

By now it may be hard to imagine that the renewal of Renaissance Rome could have been anything but an inevitable process. And yet this depressed medieval city turned into a European capital only by a colossal act of collective will, a will that gravitated at the time against nearly every law of economics and common sense. Given this extraordinary process, however, it is much less surprising to find that a city so dependent on the power of ideas became a cultural capital as it recovered strength; along with history, tradition, and faith, culture was one of Rome's chief natural resources.

As we have noted, by passing through Florence on its return to Rome, the papal court absorbed the new currents of Renaissance thought, and the Renaissance eagerness to bring classical elegance to a distinctively Christian culture. In 1427, the Florentines rewrote their city constitution in a Latin that sounded more like Cicero and less like medieval bureaucratic language; in essence, they wanted their speech, their writing, their art, and even their physical movements to be more beautiful, or, as we would probably put it, more engaging. This fascination with the classical past was never meant to become a wholesale revival of classical antiquity: the Tuscan city-states were merchant societies, entirely dependent for their livelihood on international trade. No one intended to give up modern innovations like the magnetic compass, brought from China in the eleventh century, or Hindu-Arabic numerals and algebra, brought from the Arabs to Pisa by Leonardo Fibonacci at the beginning of the thirteenth century, or the Christian faith that led one successful merchant, Leonardo Dati of Pisa, to head his ledgers with the phrase "In the name of God and of profit." But a little more style in their dealings, a little more beauty in their surroundings, a little more elo-

quence in their conversation could only help oil the wheels of business – and bring the contemplations of a Christian soul closer to the pure beauties of Heaven. The churchmen who brought the Curia back to Rome had every reason to believe that the ideas driving the Florentine Renaissance had a much greater physical reality, and a much greater missionary purpose, in Rome. It was fine for Heinrich Isaac to write a song declaring that Florence was "un paradiso," but Rome's purpose on earth was, through Christian salvation, to make the real paradise manifest to humankind.

THE 'HIGH RENAISSANCE'

If Rome's revival was an act of will, the most implacable will behind that revival belonged to the Pope who bribed his way into office in December of 1503. The new pontiff was a nephew of Sixtus IV, Cardinal Giuliano della Rovere, who took the name Julius II with Julius Caesar well in mind. As Cardinal, he had already been closely involved in his uncle's projects, from repairing aqueducts to supervising the Vatican Library. Like Sixtus, he was a Franciscan, and although he was not, like his uncle, a renowned theologian, Julius was a thoughtful man; surviving portraits of him by Botticelli and Raphael, executed thirty years apart, show him holding his head slightly downward with an abstracted expression (fig. 1, p. 19). Another portrait, by Melozzo da Forlì, shows the man we know from history, striding forward with terrifying energy and a look in his eyes that gave him the epithet *terribile*. Julius believed, following Augustine, that the human soul consisted of memory, intellect, and will, we can apply the same triple image to the soul of papal Rome, where historical memory combined catalytically with careful study – intellect – and the will to create. People as diverse as the painter, architect and musician Donato Bramante, the theologian Giles of Viterbo, and the banker Agostino Chigi, three of the Pope's closest friends, shared an extraordinary ability to see a larger picture in a wealth of incidental detail, and used their insights to forge a new idea of the Church and the specificity of its place, physically – that is, in Rome – and in the course of history. Bramante, by painstaking study, was finally able to penetrate the essential elements of classical style in architecture; his contemporaries praised him as the first modern to equal the architects of imperial Rome, and with Julius to support him he quickly revealed a sweeping ambition to match the Pope's – the two of them had no doubts that they were constructing a new capital city for Christendom. Together, they resolved to fix the longstanding structural problems of Saint Peter's

Fig. 38 Raphael, *The School of Athens*, c. 1510–1512, fresco. Stanza della Segnatura, Vatican Palace, Rome

basilica, and finally to replace the thousand-year-old building with a new church, one that would, in Bramante's words, combine the dome of the Pantheon with the majestic arcades of the Basilica of Maxentius in the Roman Forum. On a humbler scale, they outfitted some of the city's important *piazze* with pavements and drainage systems, as well as widening and straightening the labyrinth of streets that led to the Vatican. Giles of Viterbo, in turn, carried the Pope's message in sermons that drove his listeners through the whole range of human emotions – and convinced them to donate money in staggering amounts. With the banker Chigi to provide funds and advice, Julius and his Curia managed money with unusual competence; Chigi insisted in addition that Rome's economy should focus on tangible sources of revenue like alum and salt. The Pope therefore backed his epic plans for Church and city with more than enthusiasm and the power of his own driving will – he had the financial resources to make his plans concrete.

This was the Rome that Raphael entered in 1508, on Bramante's recommendation (they were distant relatives), one of a group of painters assigned to decorate the Pope's new suite of private apartments. The young man quickly demonstrated two superlative talents: an unrivalled mastery of fresco technique and an equally rare ability to put abstract ideas into tangible form. If Julius envisioned his Rome as a gathering of intellects, Raphael showed what

that gathering might mean in human terms. On the walls of the Pope's apartments (fig. 38), the books in the Vatican Library come to life as startlingly real people, from the squinting Pythagorean philosopher who peers over his master's shoulder, taking notes, to a sultry blonde version of the poetess Sappho. Epicurus is a chubby bon vivant modelled on Raphael's friend, the Vatican librarian Tommaso Inghirami, stern Dante looks on with Vergil as blind Homer sings, two thousand years of literature collapsed into a single shared moment – and because the works of these authors were all preserved in the Vatican Library, we still know what they are saying, half a millennium later.

As Raphael frescoed the walls of the Pope's private suite, Julius ordered Michelangelo to paint a far more public commission: the ceiling of the Sistine Chapel (fig. 17, p. 30). Michelangelo protested that he was only a sculptor, but Julius, as it turned out, was the one who saw farther. By 1512, with Saint Peter's rising from its new cornerstone, the Sistine Chapel unveiled and Raphael's work on the first room of the papal suite nearly complete, Rome could boast a Renaissance of its own, with a new, imposingly classical, style of architecture and a new classical style of painting, based on the monumental forms and dazzling colours of antiquity. Recent restorations in both the Sistine Chapel and the Raphael rooms reveal how strikingly the pigments of these frescoes depart from the traditional primary colours of the fifteenth century (visible, for example,

Fig. 39 Donato Bramante,
Tempietto, 1502. San Pietro in
Montorio, Rome

Fig. 40 Michelangelo, *Pietà*,
c. 1497–1499, marble. Saint Peter's
Basilica, Rome

in the wall frescoes of the Sistine Chapel, painted in 1481–1483); instead, deep, saturated pastels mix with dark ochre tones to give human figures an unprecedented depth and gravity. Both painters, well aware of Bramante's work in Saint Peter's, fill their frescoes with painted architecture, conducting bold experiments with perspective that would stand them both in good stead for the rest of their careers.

Julius II obviously adored taking risks, and rewarded bold creativity in the people around him. His successors, for the next three-quarters of a century, may have lacked his volcanic energy, but they continued to champion the Roman style that Julius ushered in for the arts and his strenuous defence of the Roman Church. Predictably, the Roman style in art and architecture emphasized historical continuity with the ancients: after Bramante, for example, architects were more likely to model their ornamentation on surviving fragments of ancient architecture than to invent their own capitals and mouldings, and to draw their proportional schemes from close examination of the ancient ruins. A distinctive combination of smooth Tuscan columns combined with a Doric triglyph-and-metope frieze became a kind of architectural symbol for the Roman papacy; Bramante tried it out for his 1502 shrine with the classical name *Tempietto* ("little temple") [fig. 39], used it again for the exterior of the new Saint Peter's, and thereafter the combination passed directly into local tradition. Sculpture also drew its inspiration from classical antiquity; statues of the Virgin Mary were modelled on Juno or Minerva, those of Christ on Apollo. Even a statue as profoundly Christian as Michelangelo's sublime *Pietà* (fig. 40) reveals its ancient pedigree in the heroic bodies and eternal youth that unite Christ and his sorrowing mother. If Mary and her son seem more like brother and sister than parent and child, more like ancient gods than real people, we hardly notice: for the Virgin's quiet mourning has an emotional depth, and a poignant humanity, that the blissful ancient gods never knew.

Raphael's frescoes for the papal apartments created a taste for monumental painted architecture, classical composure, and careful geometric composition – increasingly, he would fit his human figures into graceful abstract patterns of ovals, yet at the same time he rendered the textures of skin, cloth, hair, and metal with such skill that these abstractions, like his *Madonna of the Chair* of 1514, look more 'real' than the irregular (and realistic) incidental detail of his earlier work.

Fig. 41 Michelangelo, Partial view of the façade of the Palazzo dei Conservatori, Rome

Many of the pioneers of Julian Rome died not long after Julius himself, whose ten-year whirlwind of a reign ended in March of 1513: Bramante died in 1514, Raphael and the banker Agostino Chigi in 1520. The papacies of the Medici cousins Leo X (1513–1521) and Clement VII (1523–1534), sons, respectively, of Lorenzo il Magnifico and his murdered brother Giuliano, cemented the political and artistic connections between Florence and Rome for much of the sixteenth century, with profound results for the development of artistic style in Rome. As patriotic Tuscan popes, Leo and Clement fostered the careers of Florentines like Michelangelo, the architectural dynasty of the Sangallo, the architect and sculptor Bartolommeo Ammanati, the painters Francesco Salviati and Giorgio Vasari (born in Arezzo and therefore staunchly Tuscan), and sculptors like Benvenuto Cellini. By far the most influential member of this community was Michelangelo, a towering presence in all three arts, painting, sculpture, and architecture. As durable as he was versatile, Michelangelo remained as phenomenally active in his late eighties, when he redesigned Rome's Capitol, as he had been in his youth. In particular, Michelangelo's late architecture reflects his intensive study of Imperial Roman baths. One of his commissions involved transforming part of the colossal third-century Baths of Diocletian into a Christian basilica, and he applied the same monumental scale to the giant order of columns he had wrapped around Saint Peter's and used to bind together the facades of the Capitol. Late Imperial architecture combined riotously rich ornament with uninhibited experimentation: pile upon pile of intricately carved mouldings, columns stacked upon columns, flattened arches, spiral columns, concave walls, convex walls, domes and half-domes. Michelangelo tried many of these novel Imperial forms himself, but also, in a reversal of Bramante's 'archaeo-

logical' tradition, added elements of his own invention. Hence the Palazzo dei Conservatori on the Capitoline Hill (fig. 41) has columns that widen rather than taper from bottom to top, column capitals that turn into leering monster's heads, walls that seem to be made of jelly rather than stone and brick. At the same time, he experimented with sheer abstraction, stripping columns, mouldings, and other architectural elements of all their traditional ornament and turning them into pure geometries; this tendency can be seen on the Palazzo dei Conservatori and the ornamental gate of Porta Pia, designed by the ancient Michelangelo in the 1560s for yet another Medici Pope, Pius IV.

In painting, Michelangelo's muscular figures, pastel colours, and elaborately rhetorical poses set the standard for a generation of younger painters, like Daniele da Volterra, Francesco Salviati (whose splendid, newly restored *Descent from the Cross* in Santa Maria dell'Anima shows an especially close debt to Michelangelo), Federico and Taddeo Zuccari, and Giorgio Vasari, who could paint as swiftly as Michelangelo could carve – although nowhere near as skilfully – and distinguished himself more as an architect and biographer (his witty, gossipy *Lives of the Most Illustrious Painters, Sculptors, and Architects* has had a defining influence, for better or worse, but always entertainingly, on the assessment of Renaissance art). Under the patronage of Pope Paul III Farnese, who was close to Michelangelo's own age, the elderly painter went back to work in the Vatican Palace, on the back wall of the Sistine Chapel with the *Last Judgment* and on the neighbouring Pauline Chapel. Inspired by his example, the younger Tuscan artists continued to pour vibrant colour and an experimental spirit into Rome's classical style, an expressive freedom that continued to flourish under another Pius IV, and Julius III, a bon vivant who remembered the glory years of Julius II.

Fig. 42 Michelangelo, *Tomb of Pope Julius II* (detail), with figure of *Moses* in centre, c. 1513–1516, marble. San Pietro in Vincoli, Rome

Michelangelo's own activity as a sculptor slowed markedly as he grew older, especially in Rome, where he was haunted by the spectre of an unfinished project: the tomb of Julius II, first planned in 1506, interrupted when the Pope assigned him instead to the Sistine Chapel ceiling, and then by Julius' death. Rashly, he had projected no fewer than twenty-seven marble statues to decorate the tomb's huge architectural base; in the end, he completed only one, his *Moses* (fig. 42), a spiritual, if not a physical, portrait fully worthy of the *papa terribile*, a statue as marvellous as the *Pietà*.

THE PROTESTANT CHALLENGE

For much of the fifteenth century, calling a Church council was a risky business; not every cardinal was happy to move back to Rome from Provence, and a number of councils were called to elect alternative Popes in Avignon or Pisa. Julius II faced one of these renegade councils in 1511, and responded by calling a council to deal with the real problems that beset the sixteenth-century Church: corruption, dissent, and laxity. The Fifth Lateran Council began in 1512 with a rousing oration by Giles of Viterbo, reminding the delegates that "religion should change humanity; humanity should not change religion." The Pope's death in 1513 robbed Lateran V of its prime mover, and though it limped along under Leo X, the Medici Pope soon had a more urgent problem to contend with: a renegade Augustinian friar

named Martin Luther, who in 1517 announced his willingness to defend 95 different arguments against the claims to primacy of the Bishop of Rome.

Luther had come to Rome in the winter of 1510–1511, when Julius II was on military campaign in northern Italy. Like many northerners, he may have found the city's pervasive classicism less self-evidently Christian than the Romans did; certainly another visitor in the same period, Erasmus of Rotterdam, found Roman culture shockingly pagan, with its collections of ancient statues and its habit of calling the Pope "Jupiter the Thunderer" as well as Pontifex Maximus. Luther's excommunication in 1521 by the dying Leo X seems to have acted more as a stimulus than a deterrent to northern Europeans who objected to papal Rome's political and economic claims, while also reviving some longstanding controversies within the Church: the language of the liturgy, the celibacy of priests, the sale of indulgences (payments to reduce the time spent in Purgatory after death). It was clear early on that the protests were real, and that they had real economic impact. They also had a strongly regional, or national, flavour. When a band of German mercenaries descended on Rome in 1527 and subjected the city to a horrific six-month sack, they left Lutheran graffiti on the walls of the Vatican.

Ironically, the Pope who finally addressed the problem of reforming the Roman Church, Paul III, had been appointed cardinal after introducing his sister Giulia to

Fig. 43 Saint Peter's Basilica and Obelisk, Rome

59

Pope Alexander VI Borgia, who had promptly taken the beautiful young aristocrat as his mistress. As an old man, however, the formerly freewheeling cardinal Alessandro Farnese had become a sober statesman who called a general council in 1537. It would take eight years of wrangling before the council was seated in the Tyrolean city of Trent, strategically poised on the border between Italy and Germany, and nearly twenty more for the Council of Trent to issue its final decrees, which it did in 1563. Among these decrees were guidelines for the practice of art, architecture, and music. The guidelines themselves were more suggestions than prescriptions, so that artists, builders, and composers had to find their own way, but the general emphasis was clear: there should be no ambiguity about the Christian message. New churches should encourage the idea that worship was a common activity conducted in a single unified space, and Roman churches complied by eliminating or reducing side aisles and rood screens, and pushing the altar to the very back of the church; when the priest said Mass, he and the congregation faced the same direction. In painting, the riddling allegories and learned puzzles of the early sixteenth century gave way to dramatic presentations of well-known episodes, with Annibale Carracci and Caravaggio, in their very different ways, coming to rule the field.

Rome had always solicited pilgrims, but now the printing press was a powerful ally. Guidebooks became increasingly popular, and increasingly lavish with their illustrations. In them Rome's destiny could be spelled out clearly, so that there would be no doubt that the city of pagan ruins was still more emphatically a city of vibrant Christian faith. To drive home the Christian bent of Roman classical culture, Pope Sixtus V and his architect, Domenico Fontana, raised four ancient Egyptian obelisks to act as signposts for pilgrims in their journey through the city, beginning with the Vatican obelisk (fig. 43), which Fontana moved to the front of Saint Peter's. Sixtus exorcised each of these ancient monuments before baptizing and blessing it, and topped their spires at last with bronze crosses. The paintings he commissioned continued the pastel palette and ornate ornamentation derived from Raphael, Michelangelo and ancient Roman wall decorations, but they were more easily decipherable than the images of the earlier sixteenth century.

Architecture, after Michelangelo's wild experimentation in the 1560's, returned to a more conservative version of classical style, rooted in the sober sixteenth-century buildings of the Sangallo rather than the extravagant constructions, baths, especially, of the later Roman Empire. In part this conservatism in style and ornament may be compensating for the revolutionary changes that were taking place in the actual design of churches to reflect the concerns of the Council of Trent. The mother church of the newly founded Jesuits (approved by Pope Paul III in 1540), *Il Gesù*, used austere, traditional forms (hard to isolate now from eighteenth- and nineteenth-century alterations), but its floor plan, in which side aisles have been transformed into side chapels, and the placement of its altar at the very back of the apse, marked radical changes from the past.

At the very end of the sixteenth century, painting in Rome changed with three talented new arrivals, none of them from Florence. Federico Barocci came from the Marches on Italy's eastern seaboard, and trained in Bologna, where he learned to handle oil paint with exquisite delicacy. It is somewhat surprising to learn that he was the favourite painter of the austere Saint Philip Neri, but Neri was acutely sensitive to beauty, and there is nothing as pleasurably beautiful as Barocci's rendering of texture, whether of silk, or human skin, the fleece of a sheep, the feathers of a bird, the fur of a cat.

The other two painters, Annibale Carracci and Caravaggio, are often contrasted as the great classicist and the great realist to operate in Rome at the turn of the seventeenth century. In fact, however, they both mix classical and realist elements with tremendous subtlety. Both, like Barocci, were transplants to Rome: Carracci came from Bologna, Caravaggio from Milan, and both were moody, brooding souls, for whom creating art was often a supreme torment. If their religious paintings provide profound reflections on the impact of the Council of Trent, their secular subjects can be racy. Always, however, their figures observe a certain decorum, even Carracci's lowborn *Bean Eater*, Caravaggio's wickedly grinning *Love Triumphant* or the brutal executioners who torment Christ in a whole series of poignant images. In the Eternal City, every person has had a place in the endless pageant, a place that lends each one an inalienable dignity.

The Jubilee of 1600 provided Pope Clement VIII with the ideal opportunity to present Rome in its full glory as a Christian capital. His preferred architect, Giacomo della Porta, put the finishing touches on the Senatorial Palace on the Capitoline Hills, with Clement's Aldobrandini coat of arms prominent on the frieze. Della Porta had also completed the dome of Saint Peter's (figs. 44, 45), a taller, more slender shape than what Bramante and Michelangelo had envisioned, but a more graceful profile on the Roman horizon, visible from as far as Tivoli. In the streets, however, tensions between Catholic and Protestant erupted all too frequently into violence, a harbinger of the seventeenth century's Thirty Years' War. A few Protestant agitators had interrupted celebrations of Mass. The Pope responded with a show of intransigence that included the burning of a handful of heretics at the stake. The most famous victim was the philosopher Giordano Bruno, executed on Ash Wednesday of the Jubilee Year (17 February 1600) by burning alive. The international reaction to that event would quickly tell Clement, and all subsequent Roman popes, what they already should have known in contemplating the Early Christian martyrs: beautiful works and beautiful ideas were far more powerful instruments of persuasion than violence. Just as the message of ancient Rome had ultimately depended as much upon its educational system as on its military legions, so, too, the message of papal Rome made its greatest impact through the visible harmonies of its art, urban planning, architecture, and music. That was what visitors came to experience in the Eternal City, and what its residents came to love: what made a chaotic, unruly human community come close, on occasions, to a vision of Paradise on earth.

CATALOGUE

GIULIANO DELLA ROVERE

JULIUS II 1503–1513

1

MICHELANGELO BUONARROTI,
CALLED MICHELANGELO 1475–1564
DESIGN FOR THE TOMB OF POPE JULIUS II DELLA ROVERE c. 1505–1506

Pen and medium brown ink, brush and grey-brown wash, over extensive preliminary leadpoint and incised construction
51 × 31.9 cm
The Metropolitan Museum of Art, New York

Fig. 1.1 Jacomo Rocchetti, copy after Michelangelo, *Design for the Tomb of Pope Julius II*, 1513–1530, pen and brown ink, over incisions and construction, 56.8 × 38.6 cm. Staatliche Museen zu Berlin, Kupferstichkabinett

By 1505, eight years before his death, Pope Julius II had already begun contemplating plans to erect his grandiose tomb in the new Saint Peter's Basilica being constructed according to Bramante's design, and entrusted Michelangelo with the sculptural project. According to a first (lost) contract, the tomb project was to cost 10,000 ducats, was to be finished in five years, and was to be sited in Saint Peter's at a location that was yet to be determined.[1] Michelangelo alluded to these intentions in his letter of 2 May 1506 from Florence to his friend, the architect Giuliano da Sangallo in Rome,[2] for it was Giuliano who had encouraged the Pope in his choice of Michelangelo as the sculptor of the funerary program amidst the heated artistic jealousies of the papal court.[3] In his 1553 biography of the artist,[4] Condivi wrote the tomb of Julius II was to have been a three-storey freestanding monument and may have included as many as forty-seven large figures carved of Carrara marble, but Michelangelo's project was interrupted by other papal commissions, chiefly the frescoes on the ceiling of the Sistine Chapel (executed from 1508 to 1512), with which the early drawings for the proposed tomb share considerable stylistic similarities. Following the pope's death on 21 February 1513, Michelangelo signed a second contract to design a reduced version of the tomb to be finished in seven years.[5] The present drawing appears to reflect the first version of the Julius tomb project, around 1505–1506, as Hirst argued convincingly in 1988,[6] rather than that of the various designs produced after 1513, as has frequently been maintained in the literature. The work is much more subdued in design and scale than the recto of the comparably sized, nearly ruined drawing in the Kupferstichkabinett, Berlin,[7] the design that most likely reflects the contract of May 1513 and which is best understood through the faithful, if awkward, copy after it by Jacomo Rocchetti, preserved in the same collection (fig. 1.1).[8] To the present author's eye, Rocchetti's design appears to be a clean copy-drawing, in which the underdrawing was the result of a *calco* method of transfer from Michelangelo's sheet; in a process much like a carbon-paper copy, Michelangelo's original was placed on top of a sheet with a black-chalk-rubbed verso and another blank sheet underneath (Rocchetti's surface), and the outlines of the original were then incised with a stylus through the two layers of paper. Tellingly, the deriving copy is inscribed on the bottom of the sheet: "*questo disegno è di Michelangelo buonarota hauuto da M[aestro] Iacomo rocchetti*" (this design is by Michelangelo Buonarroti derived by Maestro Iacomo Rocchetti). The Berlin design by Michelangelo (as understood from

Fig. 1.2 Michelangelo, *Sketch of
a Pope in Profile*, 1505–1513, pen
and brown ink, 21.2 × 14.5 cm. Casa
Buonarotti, Florence

Rocchetti's clean copy) is also more subdued than that seen
of the lower part of the monument in the drawing at the
Uffizi, Florence,[10] once owned by Pierre-Jean Mariette and
which is perhaps a somewhat earlier version than the Berlin
drawing while being from the same 1513 campaign.

The diagrammatic clarity of form and precise construction of architectural elements in the large Metropolitan
sheet are typical of *modelli*, produced for a patron or to be
used for the execution of the design by members of the
workshop. As may be deduced from the present drawing,
the massive tomb ensemble was to be a three-sided structure attached to a wall and, in a daring departure from
tradition, Michelangelo designed the pope's effigy to be
seen frontally as, within the tall arched niche, two angels
raise it toward the Virgin and Child. A quick outline sketch
in pen and brown ink for the Pope's raised effigy, seen in a
side view facing left (fig. 1.2), best allows one to envision
the design of this main figure in elevation, as it were, in
the 1505–1506 monument.[11] The upper part of the wall
tomb with its monumental niche, or *cappelletta*, as it is
called in the Julius Tomb documents,[12] is of approximately
the same design, though squatter than in the Berlin drawings and the architectural detailing is in a style closer to
that of the quattrocento. Also similar to the solution evident in the Berlin drawings are the motifs of the Virgin
and Child in the mandorla (anticipating the design of
Raphael's *Sistine Madonna*, Gemäldegalerie, Dresden, of
1513), with the dead pope in frontal view being supported
over the sarcophagus by angels. But eliminated from the
Berlin drawings are the figures of the hirsute youths and
somewhat whimsical expression who flank and face the
niche in the Metropolitan sheet – that on the left with an
aspergillum and bucket of holy water, that on the right
with a censer; in the Berlin sheets, these figures are idealized and more schematic, and look outward.

It is the lower part of the Metropolitan drawing, however, that differs most radically from the designs in the Uffizi and Berlin sheets. It omits the classicizing figures of the slaves and herm pilasters seen in the latter, and the nearly square relief at centre offers an inventive portrayal of the Gathering of Manna (Exodus 16:11-36; Numbers 11:7-9), with acorns falling from an oak tree, in allusion to the heraldic device of the della Rovere family (in Italian, *rovere* means oak). The della Rovere acorns abound elsewhere in the design, filling a footed cup between two reclining river gods at lower centre, and decorating the finials of the thrones of the sibyl and prophet on the second storey of the monument. Allegorial figures of Charity and Faith stand within the niches to the left and right on the lower storey. The projection of the tomb from the wall is indicated by statues of standing figures seen in profile at extreme left and right, and the ensemble portrayed in the Metropolitan Museum drawing would have rested on a stepped base, as is seen in the Uffizi and Berlin designs, but which in this case is cropped by the lower border of the sheet.

The early date of the present sheet in 1505–1506 is confirmed by the style of the figures, similar to those in the small pen-and-ink jottings on the sheet connected with the *Battle of Cascina* in the Uffizi, Florence;[13] as well as further by the discovery, in 1990, of the fragmentary designs for the Julius Tomb, on the versos of two corresponding portions of the same sheet now in the Musée du Louvre, Paris, and of which the recto of one sheet depicts a nude seen from the back for the *Battle of Cascina*, begun in 1504.[14] "The tragedy of the tomb," as Condivi called Michelangelo's forty-year ordeal in producing the Tomb of Julius II, did not end until 1545, when the present, much scaled-down structure was installed in San Pietro in Vincoli in Rome, far away from the papal majesty of Saint Peter's Basilica (fig. 22, p. 33); the most in-depth study of the related drawings for the Julius monument is by Echinger-Maurach.[15] The gradual reinstatement of the large, carefully rendered Metropolitan Museum drawing in the Michelangelo literature is due to Hirst who, in 1976, published the first detailed analysis of it, also advocating for the authorship of Michelangelo himself (the Metropolitan Museum of Art had acquired the drawing fourteen years earlier, as a work by the school of Michelangelo.[16]) While the attribution to Michelangelo has met mostly with approval since 1976, it was not endorsed by Tolnay in his *Corpus* (1975–1980), who considered it a copy, with a style of outline-drawing too calligraphic, too soft, and less dynamic than Michelangelo's autograph studies. More recently, the drawing was also rejected by Zöllner, Thoenes, and Pöpper in 2007, without offering any reasoning.[17] Hirst's opinion in 1976 was that the Metropolitan sheet dated more or less to the time of the Berlin design of 1513, but in 1988 proposed the Metropolitan drawing as Michelangelo's original project of 1505 for the Julius Tomb.

Michelangelo's designs for the Tomb of Julius II offered meaningful visual sources (perhaps even normative ones) for artists of the following generation, as seen, for example, in the design produced by Antonio da Sangallo "The Younger" for the Tomb of Pope Clement VII (cat. 42).[18] Both drawings served as *modelli* – perhaps for the patron – precisely executed over a comprehensive construction with the stylus, compass, and ruler. While Michelangelo's working drawing is in good overall condition, the design has been roughly silhouetted and mounted onto a larger sheet, and the drawing surface seems sufficiently abraded for the underdrawing to have disappeared in several passages; the sheet also exhibits minor accretions, a horizontal crease at centre, and some brown stains.

CARMEN C. BAMBACH

RAFFAELLO SANZIO, called **RAPHAEL**
1483–1520
LUCRETIA c. 1508–1510

Pen and brown ink over soft black
chalk, or charcoal, outlines partly
incised
39.7 × 29.2 cm
The Metropolitan Museum of Art,
New York

This monumental study of *Lucretia* was rediscovered in a collection in Montreal, and was published by Stock in 1984, as by Raphael;[1] this attribution has been widely endorsed by subsequent scholars with one exception.[2] The autograph status of this drawing is amply confirmed by the numerous *pentimenti* evident especially in the vigorous, boldly reinforced under-sketch in soft black chalk, and the many precise comparisons of style and technique to Raphael's accepted pen-and-ink drawings for the Stanza della Segnatura frescoes in the Vatican Palace, particularly those for the *Parnassus* – the *Standing Man* on the recto and the *Drapery Study for Horace* on the verso, the god *Apollo*, the muse *Melpomene* on the recto and *Virgil* on the verso, as well as *Calliope*.[3] Typical is the use of emphatic, single contours and carefully descriptive manner of hatching with the pen, which in the sheets of greater size can create a somewhat dry overall effect (pen and ink do not naturally glide easily over large surfaces of paper, as a chalk or charcoal stick might). The head of *Lucretia*, seen in a three-quarter turn and in a slightly foreshortened perspective, as if viewed from below ("*sotto in sù*") recalls the beautiful design in black chalk for the head of the muse *Polyhymnia*, an auxiliary cartoon drawn on *spolvero* dots, also for the *Parnassus*.[4] This all suggests that the Metropolitan Museum sheet belongs in the early part of Raphael's Roman period, perhaps during the first two years of his arrival in the eternal city. He recast here a heroic early Roman legend to focus on the rhetorical gesture of Lucretia as a model of sublime virtue, which heightens the drama of her death. According to Livy's *History of Rome* (I:lvi.3 to lx.4) and Ovid's *Fasti* (II:711–852), the noble matron, Lucretia, committed suicide following her rape by Sextus, son of the tyrant Tarquin the Proud. Her husband, and later Junius Brutus, avenged her honour by leading a revolt that would help institute the republic as a form of government. Raphael chose to depict the dramatic moment when Lucretia is about to plunge a dagger into her chest, and his design reveals an arresting command of antique Roman sculpture and literary sources. The pose for the monumental female figure was clearly inspired by a Roman sculpture, for similar statue types can be recognized in the pages of Renaissance model books with copies after the antique, for example, in the *Codex Escurialensis* by the workshop of Domenico Ghirlandaio,[5] and in the *Rosenbach Sketchbook* by Girolamo da Carpi.[6] But the sculptural grandeur and monumentality of form evident in the *Lucretia* drawing speak freshly of Raphael's encounter with Roman antiquity in 1508–1510. The pro-

portions of the imposing idealized female figure appear to be those of the canon of antique sculpture, although she may not be based exactly on any single, identifiable Roman statue.

Stock first rightly connected the Metropolitan drawing with the well-known, though sometimes misread passage in the biography of Marcantonio Raimondi in the 1568 edition of Giorgio Vasari's *Lives*.[7] There, Vasari extolled Marcantonio's virtuosity as a printmaker by comparing him with Albrecht Dürer and Lucas van Leyden, adding:

> But to return to Marcantonio, on his arrival in Rome, he engraved in copper a most beautiful sheet by Raphael of Urbino, in which was [represented] a Roman Lucretia killing herself, [done] with such diligence and beautiful manner, that on its being immediately brought to Raphael by some of his friends, he was inclined to have some drawings of his things produced in print, and he took a drawing that was already made of Paris, in which Raphael had designed the chariot of the Sun, the nymphs of the woods, as well as those of fountains and rivers, with vessels, rudders, and other beautiful surrounding fantasies; and thus resolved, they were all engraved by Marcantonio causing all Rome to marvel.[8]

Vasari's phrasing leaves no doubt that Raphael's drawing of *Lucretia*, and that of *Paris* for that matter, were produced originally quite independently of their later conception as prints. The passage intimates that Marcantonio's initial success in engraving the design of such drawings (which were already made) was at the root of his later association with Raphael as engraver of some of the great master's drawings and, not surprisingly, the extant visual evidence seems to corroborate these points. Two engravings executed by Marcantonio resemble the design of *Lucretia* in the present drawing, *Dido* (B. 14.153.187) and *Lucretia* (B. 14.155.192), (fig. 2.1),[9] although they differ greatly in the details of facial features and landscape setting. Both engravings face in the same direction as the present drawing, whereas, it will be remembered, studies explicitly produced for prints are usually drawn in a reverse design orientation, given that the printing process reverses the image. Moreover, Marcantonio's two engravings inspired by Raphael are in a much smaller scale; in particular, the closely related print of *Lucretia* is in a scale of about 1:4 with respect to Raphael's drawing at the Metropolitan Museum of Art.[10] The engraving of *Lucretia* almost exactly follows Raphael's drawing in the pose and graceful arrangement of the chiton's folds over the gently

twisting curves of the matron's body, but differs entirely in the design of her head. This detail in Raphael's drawing is reflected in yet another engraving of *Lucretia*, by the Bolognese Jacopo Francia, from around 1510–1511,[11] when Francia's work exhibited its closest affinity with the Roman oeuvres of both Raphael and Marcantonio. The engraving of *Dido* is usually regarded as the earlier of the two designs by Marcantonio,[12] but the story of Dido was similar enough to have allowed Marcantonio to use Raphael's drawing as the basis for his print (Dido stabbed herself to death rather than marry Iarbus, the barbarian king of Libya, who had threatened her people with war if she rejected him).

Marcantonio's engraving of *Lucretia* enjoyed a wide adaptation in other media, including maiolica,[13] and further drawings (including a drawn partial copy in a chiaroscuro medium now in the Codex Resta[14]),while an oil-on-panel painting attributed to the school of Raphael closely reproduces Marcantonio's design (fig. 2.2), and its underdrawing reveals the firmly traced outlines of a cartoon-derived design.[15] This fact is especially interesting as the large scale of the present study of *Lucretia* is more commensurate with that of a painting, and the evidence of design-transfer on the sheet – the outlines of the recto being partly indented, and the verso being blackened with chalk or charcoal for a "*calco*," or "carbon paper" method of transfer[16] – suggests that it was a highly functional working drawing. The overall condition of the Metropolitan sheet is very good considering its strictly utilitarian purpose, and although the pen-and-ink drawing surface exhibits signs of light abrasion throughout, a considerable part of the energetic black-chalk underdrawing is well preserved. The losses of the original support along the right side and upper left corner of the sheet have been made up, and these replaced areas have been toned to harmonize them with the paper of the drawing.

A recent attempt to demote the attribution of the Metropolitan Museum sheet to the "School of Raphael" seems unpersuasive (the drawing style of Marcantonio Raimondi is sufficiently well-known to rule him out as author),[17] and much about the archaeological evidence in the drawing was overlooked. Affirming, rather than weakening the attribution to Raphael, and certainly discounting an attribution to Marcantonio, are the facts that the *Lucretia* drawing is in very large scale (four times larger than Marcantonio's *Lucretia* engraving[18]) and that it is in the same direction as the print, but displays substantial preliminary, black-chalk underdrawing. This underdrawing is bold – far from "now-indistinct" – as it has been described,[19] for the chalk strokes represent numerous reinforcement outlines, attesting to a creative exploratory process. The chalk strokes are now very rubbed, but this is a problem of condition, not of quality of execution. Although the underdrawing can be seen to cover the entire figure, it appears most prominently visible in the draperies, legs and feet. The use of stylus-indentation and black chalk, or charcoal, rubbed on the verso are quite explainable as part of Raphael's design process in developing preliminary drafts for compositions, many of these for paintings, and his frescoes exhibit the evidence of *incisioni indirette* from cartoon transfer.[20] Raphael drew the draperies precisely because they are likely based on an antique statue and, in his role as archaeologist-draftsman, the artist was interested in accurate recordings of drapery even when he freely altered the rest of his antique models.[21] This may also explain why Marcantonio bothered to copy this drapery so precisely in his prints of Dido and Lucretia, which present essentially the same design of drapery, but in mirror orientation with respect to each other. It may have been the antique model that carried the authority. Given that no examples of monumental drawings by Marcantonio exist (and certainly none of the scale of the Metropolitan *Lucretia*), it seems highly implausible that yet another copyist could copy Marcantonio's print from a small scale into a large imposing study, and create in the process a great deal of lively, exploratory underdrawing.

CARMEN C. BAMBACH

Fig. 2.1 Marcantonio Raimondi, after Raphael, *Lucretia*, 1511–1512, engraving, 21.4 × 13.4 cm. Museum of Fine Arts, Boston, Gift of Mrs. T. Jefferson Coolidge, 1921

Fig. 2.2 School of Raphael, *Lucretia*, oil on panel, 72.9 × 51.7 cm. The Samuel Courtauld Trust, The Courtauld Gallery, London

3

RAFFAELLO SANZIO, CALLED **RAPHAEL**
1483–1520

STUDY FOR ADAM IN THE DISPUTE
OF THE SACRAMENT *AND SKETCH FOR*
ARCHITECTURAL DECORATION c. 1509

Black chalk with white heightening
35.7 × 21 cm [maximum]
Gabinetto Disegni e Stampe degli
Uffizi, Florence

Fig. 3.1 Raphael, *Dispute of the Sacrament* (detail showing figure of *Adam*), c. 1509–1511, fresco. Stanza della Segnatura, Vatican Palace, Rome

The principal drawing on this sheet from the Uffizi is a preparatory study by Raphael for the figure of Adam in his fresco of the *Dispute of the Sacrament* in the Stanza della Segnatura (fig. 3.1), the first of the rooms to be decorated by the artist in the new apartments Julius II had chosen for himself in the Vatican Palace.¹ Raphael, who had come to Rome towards the end of 1508, found himself sharing the work on this room with Il Sodoma and the Netherlandish artist Johannes Ruysch. Vasari reports that Julius II, upon seeing the first examples of Raphael's efforts, decided to entrust him exclusively with the commission and dismissed the other artists.² The sequence of work in the Stanza della Segnatura remains, to this day, a matter of debate. The drawing in the lower-left corner of the sheet, showing the geometric division of a surface, supports the likelihood that while Raphael was finalizing the *Dispute of the Sacrament* he was also beginning to think about the

spatial organization of the decoration in the vault, which accordingly would have been realized only after the completion of the large fresco.³ The scenes depicted on the walls as well as in the vault document the moment of encounter between the humanistic ideal of universal harmony, which so fascinated Raphael, and the ecumenical conception of the Church promoted during the pontificate of Julius II, before the Protestant Reformation made clear that it would be impossible to stem the religious tensions that were eroding Rome's central authority.

Julius II took a personal interest in the decoration of the apartments and probably played an active role in the elaboration of the general iconographic program, which was intended to illustrate in concrete terms the spiritual and temporal mission of his pontificate.⁴ The *Dispute of the Sacrament*, in particular, appears to be an extremely learned work, presenting itself as a *summa* of the theological views of the time. Raphael thus had no choice but to follow the directions of the theologians of the papal court, though he did bring to the task an ability to impose order on a complex subject and actually contributed in his own way to the intellectual content of the project. It is to Raphael's credit that he knew how to communicate the intended theological message by involving the viewer on an emotional level, through the deeply moving sense of harmony that pervades the painted space and in the masterly representation of human feelings.⁵

The Uffizi sheet belongs to a late phase in the preparation of the fresco, when Raphael was working out compositional problems and analyzing individual figures through studies of live models.⁶ The three-quarters view from below and the positioning of the legs and right arm are carried through in the corresponding figure in the *Dispute*. In contrast to the treatment in the painting, however, the back here seems slightly more bent, there is a more pronounced torsion in the neck, and the head is inclined at a different angle. The facial features are only summarily sketched, while the muscular mass in the rest of the body is carefully and delicately worked up with dense hatchings and cross-hatchings to create depth. As well, the delineation of the contours is remarkably effective in shaping the figure and defining details. The style of draftsmanship shows how the artist, at this very early stage in his Roman period, had already acquainted himself with Michelangelo's new creations in the Sistine Chapel, just steps away from where he was working. Comparison with a nude study by Michelangelo from the Albertina (fig. 3.2) reveals that even if Raphael had not yet seen the frescoes completed

up to that point in the vault, he must nonetheless have been familiar with some of the preparatory studies. Michelangelo's drawing is strikingly similar in its graphic approach, its rendering of musculature, and its scarcely detailed definition of the face.[7]

Pursuing this comparison further, we may observe in both the figure of Adam and the nude study in the Albertina a reaching out towards a dialogue with the antique – a subject fraught with significance in the Rome of Julius II – in acknowledgement of the historical and moral continuity of the past. Beyond the particular reference in the Adam to the famous Spinario statue, this ambition is declared in the programmatic choice of representing the naked body and in the idealized rendering of the face, on the model of Greek and Roman sculpture. Following the principles originally formulated by Leon Battista Alberti, both artists use the antique in order to filter nature's givens and transpose them onto an ideal plane. But whereas in Michelangelo's drawing there is a prevailing sense of monumental drama, Raphael's figure of Adam, the first human to become aware of the complexity of his own nature, expresses a softer, more meditative attitude, as if resigned to his own incompleteness. The introspectiveness that gives form to the disposition of the limbs, in keeping with Alberti, is not meant to indicate the endless inner conflict to which humankind is born, but rather derives from a less rigid conception that looks to Fra Bartolomeo's manner of representing the emotions and to Leonardo da Vinci's views on the "motions of the mind" as submerged in the flow of nature.[8] We know the extent to which Raphael was influenced by Leonardo's work during his time in Florence, and the impact of that experience was still fresh in his memory when he was working on the frescoes in the Stanza della Segnatura.[9]

In the figure of Adam, the chiaroscuro softly envelops the body without creating strong contrasts, so that even under the right thigh, where the shading darkens near the meshed hands, light filters in and the hatchings establish a fluid relationship with the surrounding space, much in the spirit of Leonardo. We may consider further how the sense of inner awareness and meditation suggested by the

Fig. 3.2 Michelangleo, *Seated Figure and Arm Studies*, 1510–1511, red chalk with white heightening over traces of graphite, 27.2 × 19.2 cm. Albertina, Vienna

pose calls to mind the Leonardesque figure type in the *Saint John the Baptist* in the Louvre, which Raphael may have known through a drawing or cartoon in Florence.[10] That he might have drawn his inspiration for his Adam from this source is perhaps confirmed in the final version of the figure in the fresco, which, apart from changes made for compositional reasons, has lost something of the drawing's idealization. It is noteworthy, too, that the more pronounced features of the face in the end seem to derive from Leonardo rather than from antique statuary.

The sheet in the Uffizi thus shows how in preparing to execute the fresco Raphael fitted his style to the purpose at hand, favouring Michelangelo's method in the study of an isolated figure, in order to measure himself against the ideal of the antique. At the same time, the drawing reveals how profoundly he assimilated the teachings of Leonardo, by virtue of which he was able to achieve a harmonious integration of all the figures in his composition through the use of chiaroscuro and the rendering of emotional states. Thus the goal of "reviving the statues of antiquity" which, as Ortolani observed,[11] epitomized the Roman art of this period, was for Raphael, at the outset of his sojourn in the papal city, intimately tied to his preoccupation with Leonardo's theory of the motions of the mind.

RAIMONDO SASSI

4

RAFFAELLO SANZIO, CALLED RAPHAEL

1483–1520

STUDIES FOR THE DISPUTA (RECTO AND VERSO)

C. 1509–1511

Pen and brown ink over black chalk
31.1 × 20.8 cm
The J. Paul Getty Museum,
Los Angeles

This is one of a brilliant series of surviving studies for Raphael's fresco of the *Dispute of the Sacrament* in the Stanza della Segnatura in the Vatican.[1] Conveying immense drama and expression, the sheet takes us to the heart of the artistic challenge in this complex composition, with its myriad figures. At the same time that Raphael was searching for meaningful poses for each of the individual characters, he also needed to be certain that the poses would make sense in relation to the immediately neighbouring figures as well as in relation to the greater whole of the composition. This was a complicated dance, which the artist choreographed in drawings.

The principal sketch on the recto of the sheet and the two larger studies on the verso are for a prominent figure to the left of the altar who in the final painted composition has his back turned to the viewer (fig. 4.1). In the sketches Raphael struggles to give the figure, presumably a philosopher, a gesture of animated surprise with his right hand, and also seeks an appropriate position for the left hand. Placing the left hand out to the front would obscure part of the seated figure of Saint Gregory, who is indicated in a shorthand sketch at the right of the recto. The artist therefore places the hand as if to hold up folds of drapery, but is still not satisfied with this solution. In the fresco, by turning the figure's back to the viewer, Raphael not only solves the problem of the hands (only the right hand is visible, the left hand remaining behind the body), but also creates a useful punctuation in the line of people facing the centrally placed sacrament.

The recto drawing is remarkable for the assured manner with which the principal figure is set in space and also for the skilful foreshortening of the right arm. Economic hatching and cross-hatching are used for areas of shadow, and the profile of the face is deceptively simple and effective. In the upper study on the verso, Raphael squashes the face somewhat to give it more of a sense of bursting curiosity, but he abandons this in the lower sketch.

Fig. 4.1 Raphael, *Dispute of the Sacrament* (detail), c. 1509–1511, fresco. Stanza della Segnatura, Vatican Palace, Rome

The two ecclesiastics in animated conversation in the background of the drawing become mere onlookers in the finished fresco, compensated however by the addition of mitres. A small sketch at the centre right of the verso summarily explores a youth who points down with his right arm. This figure appears on the left of the earliest of Raphael's compositional sketches, although there gesturing upward, and goes through a number of mutations before ending up as the pointing youth seen full length by a balustrade on the left of the fresco.[2] At the top right of the verso a few lines indicate a youth leaning forward, and this seems to be an early idea for the philosopher leaning in front of the two onlooking ecclesiastics. The two circles sketched lightly at about his chest level are rough indications of the heads of two further kneeling onlookers, who appear in front of him.

In other commentaries on this drawing it has gone unnoticed that there is black chalk sketching in places beneath the pen and ink work. This is most visible in the right knee of the principal figure on the recto, but can be detected in various areas of both the recto and verso. A copy of the Getty sheet by a pupil is in the Louvre.[3]

JULIAN BROOKS

4 (recto)

4 (verso)

5
RAFFAELLO SANZIO, CALLED **RAPHAEL**
1483–1520
STUDY FOR THE FIGURE OF MELPOMENE
(RECTO); *STUDY FOR THE FIGURE OF VIRGIL*
(VERSO) C. 1509–1510

Pen and brown ink [recto]
Pen and brown ink over traces of
leadpoint [verso]
33 × 21.9 cm
Ashmolean Museum, Oxford

5 (recto)

5 (verso)

Fig. 5.1 Raphael, *Parnassus*, c. 1509–1511, fresco. Stanza della Segnatura, Vatican Palace, Rome

Raphael's highly developed vision of grace and decorum shines out in his exquisite study for the Muse of Tragedy, Melpomene, who appears in the *Parnassus* fresco on the north wall of the Stanza della Segnatura in the Vatican (fig. 5.1). A deeply recessed window on this relatively dark wall influenced the size and design of the painting, which was to explore the theme of Poetry. The other great fields of Renaissance humanist culture, Theology, Philosophy, and Law, were represented on the other three walls in a wonderfully orchestrated celebration of learning and civilization. With characteristic inventiveness, Raphael turned the conditions of the darker north wall to his advantage, placing the main elements of his composition above the window. He depicted a verdant, luminous landscape with a steep hillside upon which Apollo and the nine Muses harmoniously preside, surrounded by famous poets and writers.

Parnassus, a Greek mountain sacred to Apollo and the Muses, sheltered Delphi on its southern slopes, where Apollo was worshipped and an oracle spoke in his name. The protector of music and poetry, Apollo was the leader of the Muses, who were associated with the various arts. Melpomene, holding the traditional mask worn by actors in Greek tragedy, appears on the left of the group, with the epic poet Virgil nearby (on the verso of this sheet is a study for Virgil's pose and drapery).

As divine and inspirational figures in the classical imagination, the Muses were often portrayed in ancient art, especially in relief sculptures on sarcophagi. Raphael appropriately envisaged the figure of Melpomene in terms of antique sculpture, and endowed her with a remote, statuesque beauty. Similarly, her nearest companion, the seated Calliope, is based on a famous and much copied statue known as the *Ariadne*.[1] The purity and rigour of Raphael's line drawing is remarkable: his pen traces the contours of the figure and the folds of the drapery in fluid, continuous strokes and a strong, even pressure, with few revisions. His concept of Melpomene was to be modified in the final painting, but here she is a sister of the elegant figures of winged Victories seen on Roman triumphal arches. Her turning head, flattened profile, and rhythmic, floating shape recall figures in relief

sculpture, and her pose is partly defined by the curved, semi-circular line against which she seems to rest, which evokes the shape of an arch. Raphael certainly studied this type of Roman sculpture, as attested by a careful pen and ink drawing of the Victory on the right-hand spandrel of the east side of the Arch of Titus in Rome.[2] This type of study must have been his starting point, and he may have made some initial sketches in pen or chalk before refining his ideas in this lucid, considered pen drawing – only the rapid, almost scribbled lines that deepen the shadows and suggest greater volume and movement in the lower part of the drawing give any sense of impetuosity or creative re-thinking.

Raphael's delight in the expressive qualities of the pen is evident in the crisp, clear delineation of the form and the curving, sensuous folds of drapery. With great panache and sensitivity, he captured the classical essence of this Muse, who is a stylized yet commandingly beautiful figure. Not surprisingly, Nicolas Poussin admired Raphael's empathy with the culture and art of the antique world, and he apparently praised this figure of Melpomene, as we learn from an early source.[3] Nevertheless, the wildly fluttering though heavy draperies and the way in which Melpomene stands on tiptoe are elements that recall the sophisticated mythological paintings of Botticelli rather than classical sources. Although Raphael modified the figure in the fresco, mainly altering her head so that she looks inwards in a three-quarters view, he retained these decorative and engaging qualities.

A copy of a lost compositional study, in which typically Raphael studied the entire group of figures unclothed so as to establish fully their positions and gestures, shows the artist already clarifying his thoughts, and here Melpomene's head is no longer in profile, so that we see more of her face (fig. 5.2).[4] Perhaps, as K.T. Parker suggested, Raphael realized that the backward turn of her head would too closely echo that of Virgil (especially as he studied the figure of Virgil on the reverse of this sheet). Indeed, another male poet, usually identified as Anacreon, appearing at the lower left of the fresco, also looks back over his shoulder. In an engraving by Marcantonio Raimondi, which is often thought to record another lost compositional drawing from an earlier stage in Raphael's thinking, Melpomene still looks back over her shoulder. However, there are good reasons for supposing that Raimondi's print derives from various sources, including lost drawings and the fresco itself, and acts as a variation or re-interpretation of the *Parnassus*, made in collaboration with Raphael, rather than as a record of a particular phase of development.[5]

Fig. 5.2 Copy after Raphael, *Compositional Study for* Parnassus *fresco*, pen and brown ink over black chalk, 29.2 × 45.8 cm. Ashmolean Museum, Oxford

In studying the figure of the great Roman epic poet Virgil on the verso, Raphael focussed mainly on the rhetoric of his gesture and stance, exploring the density and weight of the folds of drapery and the effect of the robust pointing arm. He first made a rapid sketch with a leadpoint stylus to place the figure, before developing his study in pen and ink. The idea of the heavy book balanced on the thigh recalls the figure of Aristotle in the *School of Athens* fresco. In the end, Raphael gave this motif to another poet placed at the lower left of the *Parnassus*. Ironically, it is the joyful whirl of Melpomene's animated drapery that was to obscure Virgil's volume. In the fresco, Virgil and Dante flank the powerful figure of the blind Homer, whose grandeur is expressed both in his frontal pose and in his striking head, deriving from one of the most admired of classical statues, the *Laocoön*, which had been excavated only recently, in 1506. Although Virgil's pointing hand directs our attention towards the group of Apollo and the Muses, in his stance he looks backwards, reminding us of his role as companion and mentor to Dante, whom he guides through the underworld in the *Divine Comedy*. The expressiveness and lucidity of this drapery study is also found in other pen and ink drawings for the *Parnassus*, such as the preparatory study for the figure of Dante in the Royal Collection at Windsor.[6]

CATHERINE WHISTLER

6
RAFFAELLO SANZIO, CALLED RAPHAEL
1483–1520
ALLEGORICAL FIGURE OF POETRY
C. 1509–1510

Black chalk over stylus underdrawing, squared in black chalk
35.9 × 22.7 cm
The Royal Collection

Highly characteristic of his early Roman period, this sheet from Windsor Castle is undoubtedly one of the most monumental of all Raphael's drawings. In 1508 the young artist had been called to the work site in Julius II's Vatican Palace, initially to contribute to a cycle of frescoes decorating the room that would come to be known as the Stanza della Segnatura, a project whose enormously successful outcome was to have a decisive impact on his future career.

The drawing is a study for the seated figure in the allegory of *Poetry* (fig. 6.1), one of the frescoes in the Stanza della Segnatura's complex ceiling divided into panels and medallions illustrating Theology, Philosophy, Jurisprudence, and the poetic arts – themes presumably chosen in connection with the room's likely original use as Julius II's personal library.

Four years after being elected to the papacy, the della Rovere pope decided to take up quarters in a new suite of apartments on the third storey of the thirteenth-century wing of the Vatican Palace. According to contemporary sources, the reason was to escape the "horrible and villainous" memory of his loathed predecessor, Alexander VI Borgia, whose occupancy of the private apartments on the floor below had left too many visible traces. It may well be that the renovations were also prompted by the new pope's recollections of the splendid pontifical residence at the court of Avignon, where he had been sent as a papal legate in the decade prior to his own election – a site that featured attractive settings for public ceremonies and a private library adjoining the pope's chambers. Julius II must therefore have taken a special interest in the decoration of the new apartments. When Raphael arrived in Rome, his former teacher Perugino was already at work painting the ceiling of one of the other rooms, the Stanza dell'Incendio, and Il Sodoma, assisted by the Netherlandish artist Johannes Ruysch, was decorating the "camera bibliothecae," a room that Paul III would later assign to the supreme tribunal of the Roman curia, the "Signatura Gratiae" (remarked on by Vasari, who thus played a role in its eventual designation).

In his thorough investigation into the history of the Vatican rooms, Shearman was able to demonstrate how their decoration programs related to their original intended functions.[1] In support of the hypothesis that the Stanza della Segnatura was used in the past as a library, he pointed to such things as the absence of a fireplace, the *opus sectile* floor, and the wooden intarsia wainscot made by Fra Giovanni da Verona (subsequently removed in the time of Paul III).

The ceiling's decorative panels and medallions serve to reinforce the themes that were to be developed in the frescoes on the walls, where the concepts of theological truth, rational truth, beauty, and goodness are expanded upon. Work on the room presumably began, in the usual way, with the ceiling, which was subdivided by Il Sodoma into seventeen compartments, all framed with patterns of grotesques and structured around a central octagon that we now know, from conservation analysis, was originally a circle. The overlapping onto Raphael's frescoes of some portions of the *giornate* attributed to Il Sodoma makes one suppose – despite Vasari's rather confused account of the various execution times for the ceiling – that at least for a while the artists worked together on the decoration, and only later was Raphael given greater responsibility in the main frescoes, once he had demonstrated his skill in decorating the ceiling.[2] The internal chronology of the paintings executed in the Stanza della Segnatura is still a thorny matter of debate. The supposed disparity in stylistic maturity between sheets like the present one and those preparatory to the wall frescoes has also been used as an argument in favour of a later dating for the ceiling tondi, which partially replaced the original decorations by Il Sodoma.[3] A sheet in the Uffizi (cat. 4) featuring a study for the figure of Adam in *Dispute of the Sacrament* includes in one corner a rough sketch of the still unfinished ceiling divisions, suggesting that they were probably completed by Raphael only after he had done all his work on the walls.[4]

The Latin words "Numine Afflatur" in the fresco, inscribed on tablets held by the two putti, allude to the notion of divine inspiration. They are a contraction of a line in Virgil: "Nec mortale sonans, adflata est numine" (*Aeneid* 6.50). Vasari, in his *Life* of Raphael, first interpreted the figure as Polyhymnia, the Muse of sacred poetry, tuning the lyre she holds in her left hand, but in his *Life* of Marcantonio Raimondi, he refers to her as Calliope, the Muse of epic poetry. The correspondence between the painted version and the Windsor study is quite close in the pose and in the drapery over the lower half of the figure. The artist first

6

Fig. 6.1 Raphael, *Poetry*, c. 1509–1511, fresco. Stanza della Segnatura, Vatican Palace, Rome

drew a sketch of the nude model to articulate the proportions of the body and the position of the legs under the drapery, employing a stylus that left only an incised line in the surface of the unprepared paper – an apparently innovative technique that recurs frequently in Raphael's Roman drawings, allowing him to use his chalks more freely for the finished drawing without the risk of interference from the underdrawing. Although the squaring might lead one to assume that this figure was enlarged directly to its final dimensions in a cartoon, there exists an engraving by Marcantonio Raimondi that seems to document a slightly different later drawing by Raphael, now lost, that would have been even closer to the fresco version.[5]

The soft modelling achieved with a delicate *sfumato* helps give a timeless dimension to this allegorical figure, whose classical prototype remains unidentified, and whose simple and neutral expression allowed the artist to reuse her at least twice: in the roughly contemporary *Saint Catherine of Alexandria* (National Gallery, London) and in the *Triumph of Galatea* of 1511 (Villa Farnesina, Rome).

By about 1810, almost all of Raphael's drawings in the Royal Collection were bound in a volume entitled "Raffaello d'Urbino e Scuola," which suggests an Italian provenance, even if many drawings were inherited by George III rather than acquired by him. Along with another sheet by Raphael, *The Miraculous Draft of Fishes*, this drawing was probably part of an album described as being in Kensington Palace in 1727.[6]

GIORGIO MARINI

MARCANTONIO RAIMONDI
c. 1480–before 1534
A SATYRESS BEFORE A TERMINUS
c. 1509–1510

Pen and brown ink with traces of
red chalk
19.9 × 17.5 cm
National Gallery of Canada,
Ottawa

Fig. 7.1 Marcantonio Raimondi, *Bacchanal*, engraving, 14.3 × 50.7 cm. Bibliothèque nationale de France, Paris

This sheet by Marcantonio Raimondi, the most famous of Cinquecento Italian engravers, was probably intended to be made into a print, though no trace of one remains. The drawing was produced at the end of the first decade of the sixteenth century, when the artist had only recently left his native Bologna. The cultural baggage he set out with combined a taste for mythological allegory and a passion for antiquity that were frequently reflected in the subject matter of his previous graphic work. The journey, perhaps not his first to Rome, turned into a long stay that might have been a permanent one, had it not been rudely interrupted in 1527 when the city was sacked.

After the Bentivoglios were driven out of Bologna by papal troops, in November of 1506 Marcantonio went to the Rome of Julius II to seek his fortune and established a profitable relationship with Raphael's workshop. But in prints prior to his constant activity engraving Raphael's designs, he continued developing the interest in antiquity he had shown while still in Bologna.

The revival of antiquity found fertile soil in Bologna's richly diverse cultural life, fostered not only by its prestigious university and the theology schools that flourished in the monasteries of the various orders, but also by the intellectuals and scholars attached to the court of Giovanni II Bentivoglio.[1] Evidence of this vitality is provided by Angelo Poliziano, who in June 1491, along with Giovanni Pico della Mirandola, had the opportunity to admire the city's well-stocked libraries and many ancient stone inscriptions and also came in contact with numismatists. An impressive list of Bologna's antiquarians was later recorded in the *Descrittione di tutta Italia* (1550) by Leandro Alberti, a major contributor to the extension of Flavio Biondo's research into ancient Roman geography. Among those named was Giovanni Achillini, called Filotèo, whose collection featured marble statues as well as the more usual gold, silver, and bronze medals with portraits of Roman emperors, consuls, captains, and other famous men of ancient times. As well, there were collectors of inscriptions and gems among the scholars in Giovanni II's circle, including the jurist Tommaso Sclarici dal Gambaro, the jeweller Jacopo dal Giglio, and the notary Cesare Nappi, all three of whom compiled catalogues of antiquities and epigraphs that circulated in the city in the late fifteenth and early sixteenth century.

The subject of the Ottawa drawing derives from a sarcophagus originally in Rome and now in the Museo Archeologico Nazionale, Naples, that depicts a nocturnal bacchanalian festival in honour of Priapus.[2] Its theme was especially attractive to the many Bolognese artists who took an interest in antiquities and liked to travel to Rome (with a stop in Florence) to see classical remains, be they Greek and Roman originals or Roman copies of Greek prototypes. Although their curiosity was wide-ranging, the Bolognese were particularly interested in sarcophagi, which displayed a great variety of treatments. They turned to them often, sometimes recording full views of the front or the ends, and sometimes isolating a single figure. Even before Amico Aspertini and Marcantonio,[3] themes related to Bacchus were among their favourites – from the Discovery of Ariadne on a sarcophagus (now at Blenheim Palace, Oxfordshire)[4] known to Jacopo Francia possibly as early as about 1506 when he used it for a *Bacchus and His Retinue* (H. V, 232, 7) to the Triumphal Procession of Bacchus and Ariadne on a sarcophagus formerly in Santa Maria Maggiore (now in the British Museum)[5] that provided a source for a drawing of a *Bacchanal with Silenus* in the Hermitage by the venerable *caposcuola* Francesco Francia.[6]

The aforementioned sarcophagus in Naples was among those that exerted an especially strong and continuing fascination. Aspertini, the most prolific of Bologna's devotees of antiquity, sketched it at the very beginning of the sixteenth century, when it was in the garden of the Palazzo Venezia,[7] and returned to it in a later sketchbook that he completed around 1535.[8]

Indirectly influenced, it would seem, by Aspertini, here Marcantonio focused on the left edge of the front of the sarcophagus, where a satyress calls out to the herm of a satyr. He illustrated one of the sarcophagus' ends in a print from the early 1510s, *Two Fauns Carrying a Putto in a Basket*, and later depicted the entire front in two different engravings – both titled *Bacchanal* – the second being in reverse to the sarcophagus (B. 16.202.249, here fig. 7.1).

In Bologna, Marcantonio had regularly alternated engravings of his own invention with prints derived from other artists. In Rome, in his full maturity, he likewise elaborated his own subjects alongside those based on Raphael's designs. The present drawing, made just after his arrival in Rome, is of his own design, the choice of subject reflecting his antiquarian background. His post-Mantegna debt is evident in the linear stroke of his pen, and it is hardly surprising that the sheet was long attributed to the

Paduan School. Also worthy of note is the use of typically central Italian cross-hatching, which Marcantonio adopted to give the image a more convincing relief effect.

Characterized from the start by exchanges with the learned circles of Padua and Verona, in the realm of visual art Bologna's antiquarian culture was marked by the models of Mantegna and artists from Ferrara, by way of the stylistic synthesis achieved by Marco Zoppo. Indeed, one must look back to the 1460s, to Zoppo's temporary return to Bologna from 1460 to 1468, in order to understand the stylistic origins of antiquarian artists like Marcantonio and his senior, Aspertini, both of whom were initially influenced by the linear style of Mantegna through Zoppo's huge corpus of drawings.

It fell to Zoppo, possibly acquainted with Francesco del Cossa and certainly a friend of Andrea Mantegna and Giovanni Bellini, to play a strategic role in spreading not only visual ideas. Among his antiquarian friends was the renowned calligrapher Felice Feliciano, who is not only credited with the survival of the epigraphic survey of Ciriaco d'Ancona, but was himself the author of a Latin account (*Jubilatio*) of the famous archaeological expedition carried out in 1464 in the company of Mantegna and others.[9] Feliciano stayed in Bologna for some time as a guest in the home and scriptorium of Giovanni Marcanova, whose erudite and antiquarian interests are reflected in the celebrated compendium *Quaedam antiquitatum fragmenta*,[10] to which Zoppo evidently contributed.[11]

A decidedly erotic variation on the same sarcophagus in Naples occurs in a subsequent engraving that Marcantonio made on his own by about 1510–1512, a *Female Figure in the Act of Self-Arousal*, which survives in just a single impression, in the Nationalmuseum in Stockholm (fig. 7.2).[12] Here, the pose and attitude of the young woman engaged in giving herself pleasure with a phallus-shaped instrument derive from a free interpretation of the satyress who is about to grasp the genitals of the herm of Pan on the front of the sarcophagus, at the far left. At the same time, the standing female nude harks back to Marcantonio's customary typologies from his early Bologna days, for example the *Venus by the Seashore* (B. 16.234.312), dated 11 September 1506. The figure also relates to his journey to Venice around 1507–1508, exemplified by the presumably allegorical *Grammar* (B.16.292.383), and reaches as far as his first meeting with Raphael, which led to the *Lucretia* engraving (B.16.155.192), in which the influence of Lucas van Leyden's technical style and a fondness for silver tones are clearly visible.

From the quite faithful rendering of the Naples sarcophagus seen in the present drawing and in subsequent prints inspired by the same subject, Marcantonio went on to emphasize the priapic element, as in the *Female Figure in the Act of Self-Arousal*, perhaps also prompted by the ceremony in honour of Priapus depicted in a woodcut in the *Hypnerotomachia Poliphili* (1499), dominated at the centre by the "rude figure of the garden keeper."[13]

More than ten years after the execution of the present drawing, in an artistic environment altered by the death of Raphael, Marcantonio engraved the lively erotic fantasy *I modi*, based on Giulio Romano's designs. Here he returned to the sarcophagus with the nocturnal bacchanal that he had studied in his early Roman days; the poses of the Priapic herm and female satyr, presented in fig. 1, provided the compositional springboard for the pair of lovers in *Position no. 7* of the *I modi* series and perhaps also the pose of the woman in *Position no. 11*, echoing the slumbering maenad on the left.[14]

MARZIA FAIETTI

89

Fig. 7.2 Marcantonio Raimondi, *Female Figure in the Act of Self-Arousal*, c. 1510–1512, engraving, 14.1 × 7.0 cm. Nationalmuseum, Stockholm

LORENZO LOTTO 1480–c. 1556
SAINT JEROME c. 1509

Tempera with oil glaze on panel
80.3 × 60.3 cm
Inscriptions: *L. LOTUS*
Museo Nazionale di Castel
Sant'Angelo, Rome

Fig. 8.1 Lorenzo Lotto, *Saint Jerome* (detail), 1509. Museo Nazionale di Castel Sant'Angelo, Rome

Past the fence, beneath luminous clouds, along the bottom of the valley and into the far distance runs the Tiber River, under the Ponte Sisto and then curving to embrace the Leonine City with its encircling fortified walls commissioned by Pope Leo IV to serve along with the massive Castel Sant'Angelo in defence of the Vatican basilica.[1]

The artistic re-creation of Rome that Lorenzo Lotto included in the background of this painting (fig. 8.1) corresponds to the panorama of the city that could be seen at the time from the church of Sant'Onofrio on the Janiculum Hill, where Enrico Bruni[2] – the archbishop of Taranto, a man of letters long attached to the Roman Curia – had a chapel dedicated to Saint Jerome, for which this devotional panel representing the hermit saint and Doctor of the Church could have been commissioned.[3]

Datable to 1509, and signed "L. LOTUS" at the bottom centre, the painting is emblematic of the artist's Roman period, as it signals the fascinating and innovative encounter between his own visual culture (formed by the late fifteenth-century Venetians while permeated with Northern and Düreresque touches) and the classicism of Raphael as expressed in the Stanza della Segnatura, especially *The School of Athens*.

A painter of repute who had until then worked only in the provinces, Lotto reached Rome at the end of 1508 from Recanati, where he had painted a polyptych for the church of San Domenico and had managed to establish relations with representatives of the Curia, including Teseo De Cuppis, the new bishop of the dioceses of Recanati and Macerata, and his brother Bernardino, who served in the Papal Chancellery and the Apostolic Camera.[4] It was through Bernardino that Lotto made contact with Enrico Bruni, whom Pope Julius II had appointed as the Church's treasurer general in 1505.

Lotto was the first Venetian to join the multi-regional workforce that Donato Bramante had invited to the Vatican Palace to decorate the rooms of the new papal apartments. However, it was under Bruni's administrative control as treasurer, and perhaps actually under his personal protection, that Lotto was paid 100 ducats on 8 March 1509 and a further 50 ducats on 18 September to execute frescoes – carried out some years later, and now gradually being rediscovered – in the Stanza della Segnatura and the Stanza di Eliodoro respectively.[5] The Milanese jeweller Gian Piero Crivelli acted as guarantor for the painter in this project. Lotto's portrait of Crivelli (J. Paul Getty Museum, Los Angeles) and this *Saint Jerome* panel comprise the artist's entire production of paintings, other than frescoes, during his first stay in Rome. No other payments followed those of March and September 1509, for a variety of possible reasons, whether related to Lotto's insufficient familiarity with fresco (which was never as congenial a medium to him as oil), or his bristling at being placed in a subordinate role by the "divine" Raphael, or, perhaps not least, to the death of his protector, Bruni, in October of that year.

Lotto was particularly fond of the subject of Saint Jerome, the prototype of the Christian humanist. He had painted the saint a few years earlier (1506; Louvre, Paris) and returned to him repeatedly in the course of his career. Because of Jerome's quest for spiritual renewal and detachment from worldly things, the painting in Rome in a way foreshadows Lotto's destiny.

After having painted *Trebonian Presenting the Pandects to the Emperor Justinian* alongside Raphael in the Stanza della Segnatura in the second half of 1511, Lotto went back to working in the Marches – and this despite the fact that Bernardo de' Rossi, bishop of Treviso and Lotto's former patron and protector there, had arrived in Rome. He painted a *Transfiguration* in Recanati and a *Deposition* in Jesi, and then in May 1513 moved on to Bergamo, where he was employed on major new undertakings.[6] He returned

to Rome only to paint the ceiling of the Stanza di Eliodoro from drawings by Raphael, setting off again immediately afterward for Bergamo in the summer of 1514, leaving behind the reassuring ecumenical classicism of Raphael, the magnificent Rome of Leo X, the world of the Curia, and the city of indulgences.

It is dawn. On the white paving stones, nobly posed like a river god or Greek philosopher in his robe, detached from the things of this world and immersed in his books of Holy Scripture, the hermit contemplates as he recalls a disquieting night spent atop the rocky mountain, where he knelt penitently before a crucifix and beat his breast in struggle against the temptations of the shadowy female forms that seemed to emerge from the roots of those dry trees that now, as the workday begins, a woodcutter is chopping down, while in the valley a wayfarer drives his donkey and two shepherds tend their flock.

The keen attention that Lotto pays to his own inner life and that of his figures is directly linked to the very personal vision with which he presents them to us and which is manifest in the finished work. Here, for example, a recent laboratory analysis has revealed traces of an underdrawing, no pentimenti, and a very limited palette (reconstituted during a 2007 restoration) which was applied in extremely thin oil glazes everywhere except for the red drapery.

In 1916, four centuries after this *Saint Jerome* was painted, it was purchased by Mario Menotti, who donated it to the newly established Castel Sant'Angelo museum to be hung in Paul III Farnese's bedroom, now designated the "Cupid and Psyche Room."

FIORA BELLINI

9
MICHELANGELO BUONARROTI,
CALLED **MICHELANGELO** 1475–1564
STUDY FOR THE NUDE YOUTH OVER
THE PROPHET DANIEL ON THE SISTINE
CEILING (RECTO); *FIGURE STUDIES FOR*
THE SISTINE CEILING (VERSO) C. 1510–1511

Black and red chalk [recto];
red chalk with white heightening
[verso]
34.3 × 24.3 cm
Annotations: *55; V. /.* [verso]
The Cleveland Museum of Art

The recto of this drawing is preparatory for the *ignudo* above the prophet Daniel (fig. 9.1) in the penultimate bay before the altar wall on the Sistine Chapel ceiling. Michelangelo frescoed the vault starting in 1508 in two distinct campaigns moving from the entrance to the altar, so this drawing would belong to the second phase of work, and was probably executed in a period extending from the summer of 1510 to the summer of 1511 during a hiatus in the execution. The entire work was unveiled on 31 October 1512.

Functionally, these *ignudi* or nude males support the simulated bronze shields with long straps, as in this case, or hold bundles of acorns – an allusion to Pope Julius II's family name: della Rovere. In purely formal terms, these figures with elaborate, athletic poses and youthful features, produced on an unusually monumental scale by any standard, are artistic creations of the highest order. Beyond their decorative function, and their placement on the top of the piers travelling up the vault (one of the few concessions to illusionism Michelangelo introduced), their status within the complex subject matter of the Sistine ceiling is open to debate. Michelangelo idealized their bodies as he did Adam at the moment of creation and so at least expressed their divine nature.

The first *ignudi* executed recall the nudes in the Battle of Cascina cartoon in Florence. These examples seem more related to his sculpture and are defined against the picture plane as in a relief. By the time he painted the work represented in the Cleveland drawing, from the second campaign of painting, Michelangelo altered the mood of constraint to something more energetic, massive – even agitated – as if to make the figures more legible from the distant floor. Some of the last *ignudi* to be frescoed are even more extravagantly poised and frankly sensual than this one. Just considering this part of the decoration, in the space of about five years Michelangelo created twenty isolated nudes in a variety of poses that would have taken him decades to carve, as the tragedy of the tomb of Pope Julius II attests, and in this way also accelerated his stylistic development. It is little wonder that several popes insisted on forcing the artist to paint rather than return to his preferred sculpture.

Several extant drawings by Michelangelo for the Sistine *ignudi* (see cat. 10) reveal a shared approach with the Cleveland sheet. Michelangelo preferred red chalk for the nude studies for the Sistine Chapel *ignudi* as it clearly suited the naturalistic treatment of the anatomy. The present sheet retains the feeling of a drawing made from a young assistant posed in the workshop, but the artist has by now abstracted the nude away from life. The treatment of musculature, for example, is less physically descriptive than arranged into an attractive pattern, yet it still suggests extreme monumentality and constrained force. It is possible Michelangelo turned to the Belvedere torso, or to one of his own sculptural models after it, to further idealize this pose.[1] The face is only lightly indicated as the artist concentrated on the balletic effect of the body in its springy pose.

The verso contains several studies of the leading left foot, and one of a foot turned in the opposite direction. It also features two studies of a head and shoulders in different positions, presumably all from the life, apparently early ideas for other figures from the latter part of the ceiling either rejected or modified beyond recognition.

Both the drawings on the recto and verso have, in fact, not always been accepted as by the hand of Michelangelo, although it is true that controversy has surrounded the attribution of virtually every drawing by the artist at some point. Most recently, Goldner rejected the Cleveland sheet, describing it as a copy after a lost Michelangelo drawing by a sixteenth-century artist, pointing to the general weaknesses in the treatment of anatomy, and suggesting that it appears to have been executed first entirely in black chalk adhering to a method of transfer from another complete drawing the artist is not otherwise known to have used.[2] This opinion merits considerable respect. However, while it is true that the Cleveland drawing does not possess the same explosive quality as comparable studies in the Metropolitan Museum and the Teylers Museum in Haarlem, its powerful stylistic characteristics uphold the attribution to Michelangelo.

DAVID FRANKLIN

9 (recto)

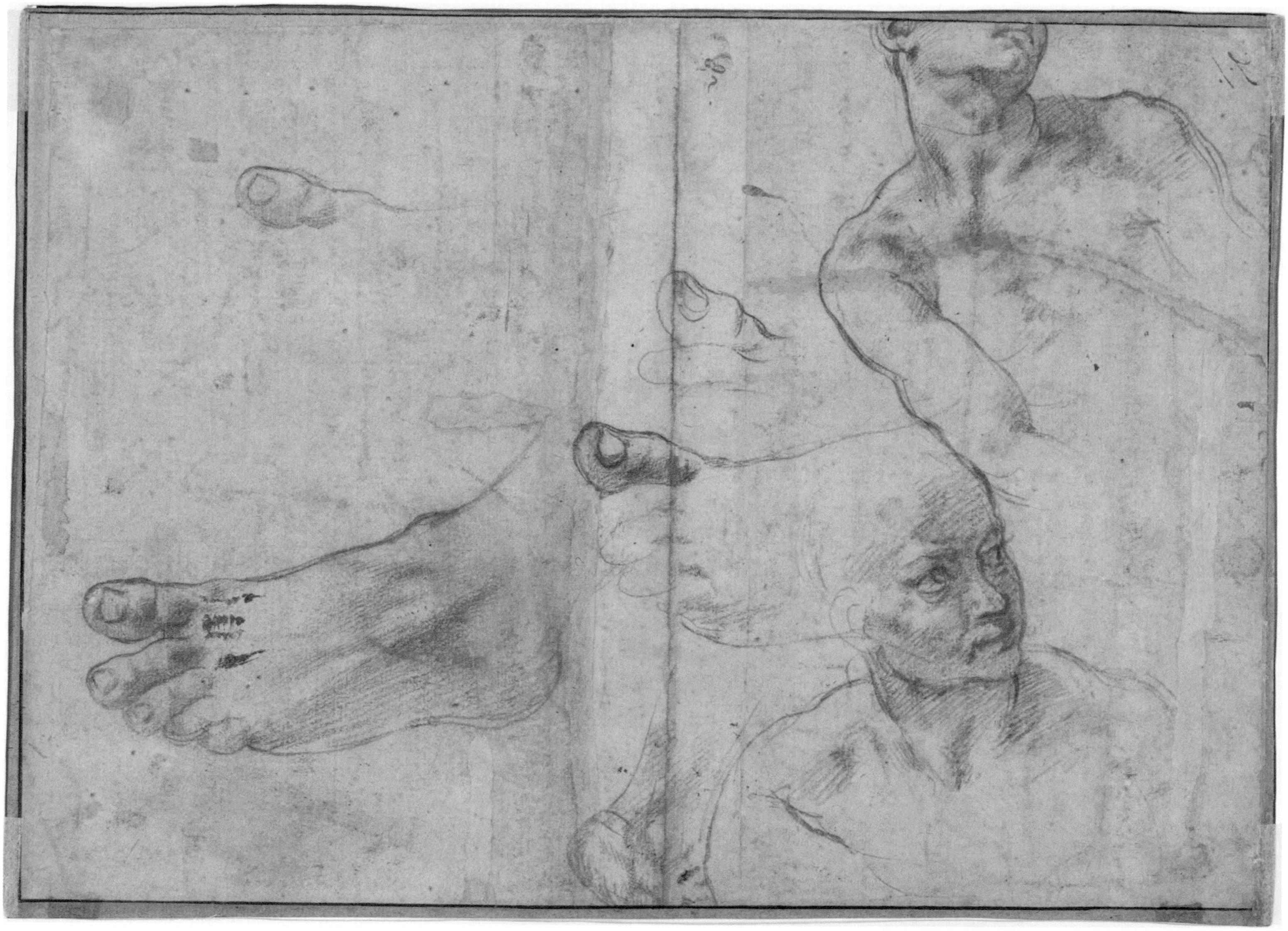

9 (verso)

Fig. 9.1 Michelangelo, *Nude Figure*, c. 1510–1512, fresco. Sistine Chapel ceiling, Vatican Palace, Rome

10

MICHELANGELO BUONARROTI,
CALLED **MICHELANGELO** 1475–1564
STUDIES FOR THE LIBYAN SIBYL (RECTO);
*STUDIES FOR THE LIBYAN SIBYL AND A
SMALL SKETCH FOR A SEATED FIGURE*
(VERSO) c. 1511 (recto), c. 1510–1511 (verso)

Red chalk with white heightening
[recto]; black chalk or charcoal
[verso]
28.9 × 21.4 cm
Annotations: *di Michel Angelo
bona Roti; 58; nº. zi.* [verso]
The Metropolitan Museum of Art,
New York

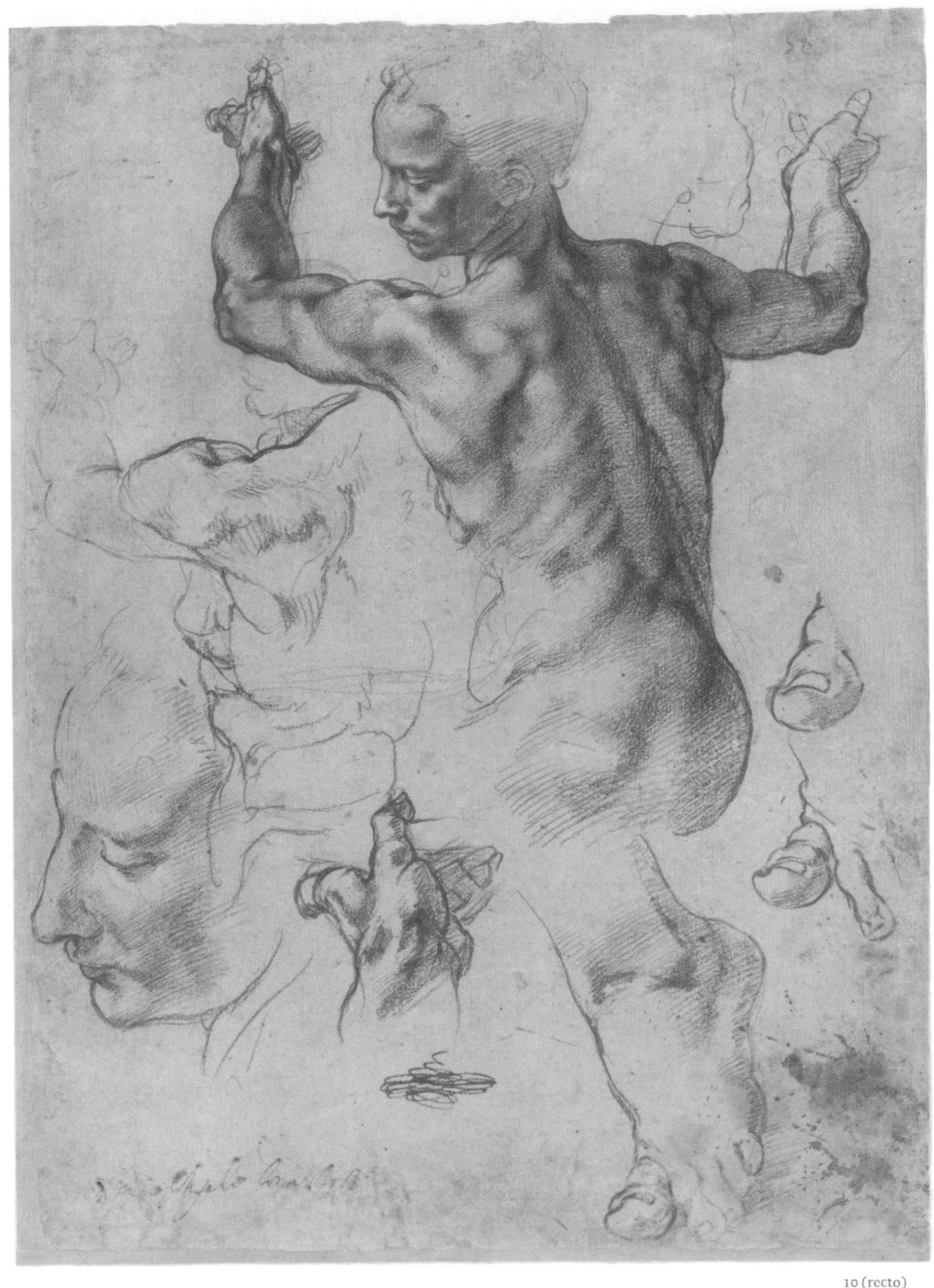

10 (verso)

This double-sided sheet of closely observed life studies is the most magnificent drawing by Michelangelo in North-America. The life studies on the famous recto side of the Metropolitan sheet were clearly done from a young male assistant posing in the artist's studio, being preparatory for the design of the *Libyan Sibyl*, the monumental enthroned female figure painted in fresco on the north-east end of the Sistine Chapel ceiling (Fig. 10.1). The *Libyan Sibyl* was the last of the seers to be frescoed on the north part of the vault, executed in a scale that is about three times life-size (this part in the fresco measures 4.54 m × 3.8 m);[1] she is clothed except for her powerful shoulders and arms, and wears an elaborately braided coiffure. Her complex pose in the fresco, evidently requiring study in numerous drawings, plays on the arrested motion of her stepping down from the throne, while holding an enormous open book of prophecy which she is about to close. Sketched in soft black chalk, the verso of the double-sided Metropolitan sheet was possibly drawn before the better-known recto

side with its meditated red chalk studies; many of Michelangelo's drawings for the early parts of the Sistine ceiling are in a similarly soft black-chalk technique,[2] while a preponderance of sheets done for the later parts of the frescoes are in red chalk. The verso of the present sheet portrays at centre, the large nude seated figure of the sibyl in profile (here, the softer anatomical forms may be feminine, rather than masculine as they evidently are in the studies on the recto), at upper right a summary design of a much smaller figure in three-quarter view facing left (its style resembling the motifs in the "Oxford Sketchbook"[3]), and at lower right the detail study of the sibyl's right knee. The main study on the recto portrays the seated youth with head in profile, bent arms and upper body turned in an elegant contrapposto stance, displaying the formidable musculature of his back in a rear view. Michelangelo gave special consideration to the position of the shoulders turning into the depth of space, and indicated the prominence of the *supraspinatus* muscles with two small circles (the

Fig. 10.1 Michelangelo, *Libyan Sibyl*, c. 1510–1512, fresco. Sistine Chapel ceiling, Vatican Palace, Rome

Fig. 10.2 Michelangelo, *Studies for the Sistine Ceiling and the Tomb of Pope Julius II*, c. 1510–1511, red chalk, pen and brown ink, 28.6 × 19.4 cm. Ashmolean Museum, Oxford

white chalk highlights on the left shoulder are likely a later retouching, and create a most intense highlight). The sequence of execution of the surrounding motifs on the recto is less clear, but it is likely that the reprise of the head in profile and the rough sketch of the torso and head at left were drawn before the main study (given that parts of their outlines seem to lie underneath the main study), while the highly rendered motifs of the left hand at lower centre and the three reprises of the left foot and toes at right probably followed the main study on the sheet. The manner of the weight-bearing on the toes of the sibyl's left foot was crucial for the overall design of the figure's contrapposto pose, and explains the multiple studies of this detail on the Metropolitan sheet. The facial features on the large head at lower left in the recto seem closer to those of the *Libyan Sibyl* in the final fresco, than the face of the youth in the main study. The recto of a sheet in the Ashmolean Museum (fig. 10.2), Oxford, dedicated to studies for the Sistine ceiling and sketches for the Tomb of Pope Julius II, represents at centre the attendant young boy *genius* who is seen to the immediate left of the frescoed *Libyan Sibyl*, as well as at lower left the sibyl's right hand, both motifs executed in red chalk.[4] While the overall dimensions of the Oxford sheet (28.6 × 19.4 cm) are similar to those of the Metropolitan sheet, the hue of the red chalk seems brighter and slightly orange. Nevertheless, it is clear that the Oxford and New York sheets are close companions – probably from the same sketchbook – without their necessarily being (in the present author's opinion) halves of the same sheet, as an earlier generation of scholars suggested.[5]

The scientific findings that emerged during the cleaning of Michelangelo's Sistine frescoes[6] provide a precise, though often overlooked, context in which to consider the dating and function of the Metropolitan Museum studies. Given that the great artist painted the enormous vault of the chapel from the west to east end – that is, from above the entrance to above the site of the altar – in two campaigns demarcated by the erection of scaffolding, as is suggested by both documents and a variety of recently emerged physical data,[7] the monumental Libyan Sibyl belongs to the latter phase of work on the project. At this point, Michelangelo's technical virtuosity as a fresco painter was at its height, having made a rough and inexperienced beginning in 1508 when the first scene of the vault he frescoed, *The Deluge*, grew mould because of incorrectly prepared *intonaco*.[8] Fresco is possibly the most difficult painting technique as it requires both speed of execution onto the wet plaster before it sets and great self-confidence. Writers of art treatises from the fourteenth to the eighteenth centuries judged the medium to be supreme, precisely because of the technical virtuosity it demanded.[9] Michelangelo would himself later complain to his biographer Vasari: "Fresco painting is not an art for old men."[10] Although the chronology of the Sistine ceiling is debated, the first phase of work, or *pontata*, was done between late summer – perhaps late July – of 1508 (the contract for the Sistine frescoes dates to May 10, 1508[11]) and late August 1510, ending with the painting of the *Creation of Eve*; the second *pontata* and final phase of work probably began after January 1511 (the winter months are not good for fresco-painting), and concluded on 31 October 1512 with the unveiling of the Chapel.[12] The recto of the Metropolitan

Museum study can be dated with great probability to the winter of 1511, when Michelangelo could draw rather than paint in fresco (he returned to Rome, from Bologna, by 11 January 1511[13]), and would have been prepared at the beginning of the second *pontata*. The gigantic figure of the Libyan Sibyl, together with her throne and attendants, was frescoed onto the large concave surface of the vault in twenty days' work (the fresco comprises 20 *giornate*, or patches of fine surface plaster), and the complex design was transferred by the laborious technique of *spolvero*.[14]

The recto study is done with a red chalk of slightly purplish hue sharpened to a point for the fine contours of the figure and some of the interior hatching, but it was also at times applied with the side of a stick; the red chalk medium was especially suited for the particularized, highly naturalistic study of anatomical detail. Although Michelangelo had begun to use red chalk in the early 1490s,[15] his greatest accomplishments with this medium connect with the later parts of the Sistine Ceiling. Yet the group of red chalk studies for the Sistine has also been among the most greatly contested of Michelangelo's drawings in terms of attributions.[16] The closest companions in style and technique to the Metropolitan *Sibyl* are studies on a sheet at the Ashmolean Museum, as well as three others at the Teylers Museum, Haarlem.[17] The red chalk used in two of the Haarlem sheets has a purplish hue similar to that employed for the present sheet. Clearly autograph, the sketches on the better preserved verso of the Metropolitan sheet are not ever mentioned by the scholars rejecting the attribution of the recto studies to Michelangelo.[18] This verso exhibits the similarly loose, impressionistic hatching and contours as most of the soft black-chalk studies for the early parts of the Sistine Ceiling.[19] The late sixteenth-century copy in red chalk after the Metropolitan *Libyan Sibyl* at the Uffizi, Florence,[20] is nearly the same size, but of remarkably inferior quality of execution, omitting also the two anatomical notations of circles on the shoulders and the tiny white chalk accents. Moreover, the drawn copy rearranges the positioning of the individual motifs, introduces the right foot of the sibyl (absent in the recto of the Metropolitan sheet), and records the abrupt terminus of outlines in the study of the toe. As the Uffizi copy emulates defects of condition in the original Metropolitan sheet (especially the outlines of the hole in the original paper support), it can be deduced that it derives directly from the Metropolitan sheet.

The verso sketches on the present sheet have always rightly been recognized as by Michelangelo, and the "n°. 2i." inscribed at lower centre adds further proof, as it fits precisely into a numerical sequence found on many other drawings by the great artist that have an early Buonarroti family provenance.[21] The annotation at lower left on the recto regarding the artist's surname, here spelled in the form of "bona Roti" is also significant in view of the corpus of drawings by Michelangelo and his school which bear this annotation by the so-called "Bona Roti collector," as Joannides has baptized him.[22] In any case, important groups of drawings inherited by the Buonarroti family appear to have been dispersed between c. 1684 and 1799, probably by the *senatore* Filippo Buonarroti.[23] The paraph in pen and dark brown ink inscribed at lower centre on the recto of the Metropolitan sheet is often mistaken as a mark of ownership by the collector Everhard Jabach (1618–1695), of Cologne and Paris;[24] rather, it closely resembles the paraphs scribbled on sheets of drawings in the Real Academia de San Fernando, Madrid, which were part of a large group of drawings acquired in 1775 from the widow of the painter Andrea Procaccini (1671–1734), who had died at La Granja de San Ildefonso and who had in turn inherited them from his master, Carlo Maratti (1625–1713).[25] Although the overall condition of this double-sided sheet is very good, it varies for each face of the paper: the original off-white hue is still nearly intact on the verso, but is considerably darkened on the recto. This is apparently due to prolonged exposure to light, and, as noted in 1925 by Burroughs, the red chalk studies on the recto were "fixed" with a solution of shellac in alcohol, which has intensified the differences of light and shade.[26] The recto also exhibits stains of brown wash at lower right; the triangular loss on the original support toward the centre of the right border is the result of very early damage, being made up and toned in restoration after 1951.

CARMEN C. BAMBACH

11

RAFFAELLO SANZIO, CALLED RAPHAEL
1483–1520

BINDO ALTOVITI c. 1512

Oil on panel
59.5 × 43.8 cm
National Gallery of Art,
Washington

This alluring portrait of a handsome young man, turning to look out at the viewer, depicts a banker, not an artist or poet, as one might expect. In his *Lives of the Artists* (1550, 1568) Giorgio Vasari relates how "for Bindo Altoviti, he [Raphael] made his portrait when he was young, which is considered most stupendous."[1] Vasari's statement has long been linked with the painting in the National Gallery of Art, Washington, which can be traced back to Altoviti's descendants. The sitter's features, moreover, resemble those in Cellini's bronze bust of Bindo as a bearded old man, in the Isabella Stewart Gardner Museum, Boston, as well as those in the work by Jacopino del Conte (cat. 61). Also in accord with Vasari, the author of the painting is now widely believed to be Raphael himself, rather than his favourite pupil Giulio Romano. And it has recently been dated earlier than was previously thought, to c. 1512, not 1518–20.[2] The earlier dating better agrees with the apparent age of the sitter and the circumstances of his life: in 1511, the twenty-year-old Bindo married Fiammetta Soderini, a likely occasion to commission a portrait (a slightly later female portrait from Raphael's studio, in Strasbourg, might be a pendant).[3] The ring worn by the sitter perhaps alludes to his newlywed status. Stylistically, too, the Washington portrait, with its dynamic pose and deep chiaroscuro, recalls similarly expressive figures in Raphael's fresco of the *Expulsion of Heliodorus* in the Vatican Stanze, of the same date.

Bindo Altoviti (1491–1556) inherited the family fortune upon his father's death in 1508. Dividing his activities between Florence and Rome, where he served as papal banker, Bindo used his vast wealth not only to support Republican exiles in their struggle against the Medici but also to patronize a number of major artists, including Michelangelo, Francesco Salviati, and Jacopo Sansovino, as well as the above mentioned Cellini and Vasari, who decorated Palazzo Altoviti in Rome.[4] From Raphael Bindo also commissioned the so-called *Madonna dell'Impannata*, later confiscated by Cosimo de' Medici and today in Palazzo Pitti, Florence.

The sitter's gaze, fixed on the beholder, suggests that Bindo is depicted at the moment when he falls in love with his beloved, a courtly convention found in such contemporary writings as Castiglione's *The Courtier* and Bembo's *Gli Asolani*, which describe the glance as the first step toward falling in love.[5] Whatever its origins, Bindo's pose and glance proved decisive for the later history of the painting, in which a succession of viewers – from Fiammetta to the present day – engaged passionately with the sitter's portrayal. A turning point came when Giovanni Bottari, the Vatican librarian, in a footnote to his 1759 edition of the *Lives*, misinterpreted Vasari's phrase *il ritratto suo* – "his portrait" – to refer not to Bindo, but to a self-portrait Raphael would have painted for Altoviti. Bottari's footnote, together with his substitution of a likeness based on Bindo for the woodcut portraying Raphael in Vasari's original edition, had fateful consequences for the Washington picture, catapulting it to instant fame. It was as a compelling image of the Prince of Painters that the portrait was acquired from the Altoviti family in Florence in 1808 for Prince Ludwig of Bavaria. Ludwig adored the painting, and numerous nineteenth-century artists, notably Ingres, used it as a model for their own self-portraits. But with the former family treasure now prominently displayed in a public museum (next to Dürer's *Self-Portrait* in Munich), doubts began to surface, first about the painting's sitter and then about its authorship. The sitter, in fact, does not resemble authentic Raphael self-portraits. The heated dispute reached a climax around the turn of the last century when connoisseurs such as Morelli and Berenson demoted the panel as part of a general re-evaluation of Raphael's work. The Munich museum catalogues followed suit until in 1938 the picture was deaccessioned in exchange for a putative Grünewald and two other works. Berenson had in the meantime reversed his opinion, however, and English dealers capitalized on the change to obtain the picture for American collector Samuel Kress, who donated it, as Raphael's portrait of Bindo Altoviti, to the National Gallery.

The fact remains, however, that this beguiling portrayal is unusual among Raphael's independent portraits, and its somewhat exceptional character needs explanation. The Washington portrait belongs, in fact, to a specific moment in Raphael's career when he was deeply impressed by contemporary Venetian painting. In August 1511 Sebastiano del Piombo, as perhaps the best available painter in Venice, accompanied the Sienese banker Agostino Chigi to Rome, where the artist embarked on a new career. Vasari claimed that it was the Giorgionesque character of Sebastiano's paintings that impressed the Romans.[6] Indeed, the novelty of Sebastiano's demonstration of Giorgione's manner in Rome had considerable effect, not least on Raphael, who was working alongside the Venetian in the fresco decoration of Chigi's villa – later called the Farnesina – in 1511–1512.

An echo of the new Giorgionesque type of pastoral landscape has been detected in Raphael's *Madonna of Foligno*, in the Vatican Pinacoteca, of 1512. And another of Giorgione's inventions, the romantic or lyrical type of portrait, was also introduced to the Roman art world by Sebastiano.[7] As seen, for example, in Sebastiano's *Warrior* in the Wadsworth Atheneum, Hartford, with its boldly expressive subject seen against a green background, the new type transcended physiognomical accuracy to convey a sense of the sitter's inner life.[8] Suffused with emotion, he was typically shown in an animated pose, turning to engage the viewer. Raphael thus seems to have been experimenting with the new Venetian mode of portraiture in *Bindo Altoviti*, resulting in an image that, for many, seemed to embody his own creative spirit.

DAVID ALAN BROWN

BALDASSARRE PERUZZI 1481–1536
RIVER GOD TIBER 1512–1520

Pen and brown ink and brown
wash, with white heightening,
on brown prepared paper
23.4 × 34.8 cm
The British Museum, London

Formerly ascribed to Giulio Romano on account of its vigorous drawing style,[1] this sheet entered the British Museum collection in 1946 with an attribution to Niccolò dell'Abate, which Pouncey soon corrected to Baldassarre Peruzzi.[2] In the varied and still incomplete graphic catalogue of this multi-faceted Sienese architect and painter who was also interested in sculpture, Pouncey and Gere identified a number of technically finished drawings that are useful as boundaries for comparison, such as the group of preparatory sheets for the ceiling frescoes of the loggia of the Villa Madama in Rome, which includes the outstanding study for *Daedalus Making the Wooden Cow* in the Uffizi.[3] The latter's attribution to Peruzzi has been debated: at one time, it too was attributed to Giulio Romano, and recently it was tentatively assigned to Giovanni Francesco Penni.[4] Yet, it shares with the London sheet the particular luministic technique of thin strokes, with delicate, regular touches of white that, besides articulating the rendering of the light, also construct the volume of the figures. In addition, the use of brown prepared paper for both drawings emphasizes a strongly chromatic rendering, which makes one wonder about the purpose of the present sheet, clearly arising out of a visual culture that brings together a specific interest in antique sculpture and in the plastic sense of form with a decidedly pictorial quality that may reflect the artist's Sienese training.

The drawing represents a colossal Imperial Roman statue that was unearthed in January 1512 during excavations undertaken for construction purposes by the Dominicans of Santa Maria della Minerva in Rome near their monastery, in an area of the Campus Martius that extended southward toward Santo Stefano del Cacco, on the site of an ancient temple dedicated to Isis and Serapis.[5]

Immediately recognized as a representation of the Tiber River because of the wolf, the twins Romulus and Remus, and the attributes of the cornucopia (symbolizing fertility) and the oar (symbolizing travel by water), the statue was acquired by Pope Julius II on 2 February. By August 1513, it had already been brought to the centre of the Cortile delle Statue in the Vatican Belvedere. There, no later than 1523, it was turned into a fountain, with a pendant River God Nile that had been discovered in the same excavation at Santa Maria della Minerva in 1513, in the first months of the pontificate of Leo X. Unlike the Nile statue, the Tiber instantly became famous and was frequently depicted in drawings and engravings throughout the sixteenth and seventeenth centuries.[6] From the analytically rigorous and graphically rendered drawing made by Enea Vico around 1540 (fig. 12.1) to the engraving by Nicolas Beatrizet for Lafrery's *Speculum Romanae magnificentiae* of 1555, and from its repeated echoes in Emilian culture, as seen in sheets by Amico Aspertini and Girolamo da Carpi, to the view of it in its original setting that Goltzius drew in 1591 (fig. 12.2), numerous illustrations attest to the sculpture's visual renown, which was almost on a level with other famous statues that had been installed in the new Cortile del Belvedere a few years earlier, such as the Laocoön, the Apollo, and the Cleopatra (turned into a fountain).

A specific program of rearrangement at the Vatican, requested by Julius II to highlight these masterpieces of classical sculpture, assembled them in a symbolic "Virgilian" reading, a celebration of the *Aeneid*'s account of the *gens Iulia*, whom Pope Julius wished to claim as his spiritual ancestors. The colossal river statues became an integral part of this arrangement. A drawing in the British Museum attributed to Maerten van Heemskerck,[7] even shows how, raised on a large plinth that clearly bore Leo X's Medici coat of arms, they served as the visual fulcrum of the entire Cortile delle Statue for the viewer.

Transferred to a room that was named for it in the eighteenth-century Pio-Clementino Museum at the Vatican, the Tiber statue was ceded to France following the Napoleonic occupation of the Papal States and transported to the Musée Napoléon in Paris in 1803, there to be exhibited in the Salle des Fleuves along with the Nile statue. But unlike the latter, the Tiber was not returned to Rome after Napoleon's downfall and remains in the Louvre today.

According to the detailed account of the statue's discovery written by Grossino, in his letters from Rome to the Gonzaga court, the Tiber was found slightly damaged: there were gaps in the wolf's snout and in the twins' heads, the main figure was without a nose, and almost the entire oar was broken away. Although the drawing restores all the missing parts except for the oar, the hypothesis that it could have been executed in connection with an early restoration of the statue around 1524–1525, by which time the fountain had already been set up in the Vatican Belvedere, seems at variance with the oblique viewpoint, in line with and at the same height as the bent knee of the right leg. The foreshortened view deviates from the careful frontal rendering of the best-known graphic representations and does not place the figure in any relationship to the surrounding space. It has been noted that the statue's pose is related to figures Peruzzi painted in the lunettes of the ceiling of the Loggia della Galatea in the Villa Farnesina about 1510–1511,[8] which would reinforce Pouncey and Gere's proposed dating of the sheet between 1512 and 1520. Their quite plausible hypothesis is that the drawing could have been a study for one of the river god figures frescoed in monochrome by Peruzzi (according to Armenini) on the facade of a house that Vasari says belonged to Francesco Buzio, near Piazza Altieri, not far from where the two statues would have been recovered. This would also explain the style of the drawing, which, with its extensive use of diluted ink and strongly rendered light, looks more like a study for a painting than a purely visual document carefully copied from the antique.

GIORGIO MARINI

Fig. 12.1 Enea Vico, *River-God after the Antique*, c. 1540–1542, pen and brown ink over black chalk, 17.9 × 30.9 cm. Morgan Library and Museum, New York

Fig. 12.2 Hendrik Goltzius, *The Tiber*, 1590–1591, black and white chalk, 32.5 × 53.7 cm. Teylers Museum, Haarlem

GIOVANNI DE' MEDICI

LEO X 1513–1521

13

RAFFAELLO SANZIO, CALLED RAPHAEL

1483–1520

SAINT PAUL PREACHING IN ATHENS

c. 1514–1516

Red chalk with traces of stylus
27.8 × 41.8 cm [maximum]
Inscriptions: *Raffaello*; *198*;
Rafaello da / urbino; *52*
Gabinetto Disegni e Stampe degli
Uffizi, Florence

Fig. 13.1 Raphael and studio, cartoon for the tapestry of *Saint Paul Preaching in Athens*, 1514–1516, bodycolour on paper mounted onto canvas, 304 × 404 cm. Victoria and Albert Museum, London

This is one of few surviving drawings by Raphael's own hand for the cartoons for the ten tapestries known as the *Acts of the Apostles*, commissioned by Pope Leo X to decorate the lower walls of the Sistine Chapel. The original tapestries, now in the Pinacoteca Vaticana, were woven in the famous workshop of Pieter van Aelst in Brussels. The execution of most of the cartoons, completed with the assistance of Raphael's young pupils, can plausibly be dated between 1514 and 1516.[1] The commission itself probably dates to late 1514, when Giovanni de' Medici, Lorenzo the Magnificent's sophisticated humanist son who was elected to the papacy as Leo X, was particularly intent on building and spreading the image of his power and fame, in keeping with a new political direction during the first years of his pontificate.

Raphael, then at the height of his career and simultaneously committed to various other projects for the pope,[2] rose wonderfully to the challenge of this demanding and prestigious commission, which would bring to completion the decoration of the Sistine Chapel. In this he had to compete with the splendid existing works created at the bidding of the two della Rovere popes – the scenes from the life of Christ and of Moses frescoed in the middle register by the most famous artists from the time of Sixtus IV, and the imposing ceiling frescoes recently completed by Michelangelo for Julius II, Leo X's predecessor, himself a great patron of Raphael. Following an iconographic program aimed at representing in images of dogmatic import the "allegorization" of the pontificate of Leo X, presented as Christendom's *pastor bonus*,[3] Raphael devised a sumptuously eloquent decorative series that had an immediate impact on the public, winning universal acclaim for its masterful execution and splendid weaving. A coherent reading of the original sequence of scenes was astutely worked out by Shearman, who was able to show how the series tells the history of the rise of the Church of Rome and enunciates its principles through the personalities of Paul, as theologian, and Peter, as pastor, with likely connections as well to the stories of Christ and Moses depicted in the fresco cycles.

The first known payment relating to the commission is dated 15 June 1515, when the artist was given 300 ducats for some cartoons. On 20 December of the following year, he received 134 ducats, probably as final payment.[4] On 26 December 1519, marking the Feast of Saint Stephen, seven tapestries that had arrived from Flanders were exhibited in the Sistine Chapel. Of the ten cartoons that were made, seven survive and are in the Victoria and Albert Museum in London, including the one for *Saint Paul Preaching in Athens* (fig. 13.1).[5] They are vividly and luminously coloured, meticulously detailed, and equal in size to the tapestries, reversed for the purpose of weaving.

Although it bore an attribution to Raphael upon entering the collection of Cardinal Leopoldo de' Medici,[6] the present sheet was long held to be a product of the artist's workshop. Raphael's authorship of the drawing was at one point accepted by Pasquale Nerino Ferri, who initially catalogued it as by Raphael but later had his doubts and proposed that it was a copy by Andrea del Sarto.[7] It was subsequently catalogued as School of Raphael,[8] and then at some later point reattributed to the artist himself. The consensus among recent scholars is that it is by Raphael's hand.

Fig. 13.2 Giovanni Francesco Penni (?), copy of the modello for *Saint Paul Preaching in Athens*, pen and brown ink, brown wash, black chalk, grid and white heightening, 27 × 40 cm. Musée du Louvre, Paris

This is the only known drawing for *Saint Paul Preaching in Athens*, apart from a *modello* in the Louvre (fig. 13.2) that some regard as the work of a pupil, Giovanni Francesco Penni,[9] and which Oberhuber judges to be a copy of the lost original *modello* by Raphael,[10] like the copy in the Uffizi that is ascribed to the workshop.[11] The present sheet contains studies of Saint Paul and five of the listeners around him expressing various reactions to his preaching. Numerous other figures and an architectural setting would eventually be added. Anticipating the fluid animation of the figures, the drawing clearly modulates the fall of light on their bodies, studied from life, and their broad but well-calibrated gestures and implicit energy effectively define the surrounding space.[12] Covering the traces of the preliminary stylus sketch, a diffuse and very delicate network of markings in red chalk defines the composition, faintly illuminating the surfaces of the compactly monumental figures while reinforcing some of the outlines as well as the shadowed folds of the drapery.

Like the corresponding cartoon, the study is reversed in relation to the tapestry, in keeping with the complex and exacting method used by the artist for the entire series: each of the scenes was conceived and drawn in reverse, by means of tracing or with a mirror.[13] There are only a small number of perceptible differences between the figures in this study and in the final version – in the proportions, the slight shifts in the placement of some of the hands, and the additional beards. The fall of the drapery is almost completely defined. Compared with the final spatial arrangement in the cartoon, and consequently in the tapestry, the figures here are set closer together. Standing on a stepped podium that is already discernible in this sheet, though barely sketched in, the main figure rises hierarchically above the onlookers.[14] The particular framing of the scene and the elaborate stage setting (found also in the contemporary fresco of the *Fire in the Borgo*), dominated by Paul's emphatic gesture with upraised arms, derive from two woodcuts by Dürer,[15] indicating Raphael's interest in the great German engraver, with whom he had come in contact during these years.

Saint Paul Preaching in Athens is one of three scenes from the tapestry cycle that were engraved by Marcantonio Raimondi and mentioned as such by Vasari.[16] However, the engraving is based on a different study, now lost.[17]

CRISTIANA GAROFALO

14
PIERO BUONACCORSI,
CALLED **PERINO DEL VAGA** 1501–1547
VIRGIN AND CHILD WITH SAINTS,
CROWNED BY ANGELS AND ADORED
BY LEO X c. 1515–1518

Red chalk, squared
45.8 × 37.8 cm
Annnotations: *Fra Sebastiano dal /*
Piombo / Ecole Vénitienne;
Ste Famille à la Sanguine [verso];
Lugt stamp: *1886*
Musée du Louvre, Paris

Long having been an unattributed work in the collection of the Louvre, this large drawing was assigned to Perino del Vaga by Pouncey some time before 1952.[1] That attribution gained universal acceptance when it was published by Davidson in 1966.[2] Davidson pointed out that although this composition resembling a Florentine *Sacre Conversazione* is squared, no doubt for enlargement to a cartoon or transfer to another medium, the drawing does not correspond to any of the artist's surviving paintings, nor does its subject – the Virgin crowned by angels as she holds the Child Jesus, who turns to face a pope kneeling in prayer, presented by Saint Peter – relate to any descriptions known to us of Perino's lost works. A thorough explication of the drawing also eludes us, as it is difficult to identify the figures on the right – a bearded saint interceding on behalf of a young man kneeling and, towards the edge of the sheet, another saint (possibly female).

If we accept Davidson's highly plausible supposition that the kneeling pope is Leo X, then the kneeling figure opposite him may perhaps be, as Parma claims,[3] not a saint or a sovereign (which is what Davidson had assumed) but rather a member of the pontifical family. The arguments adduced by Parma in favour of this proposal are interesting but not at all conclusive. On the evidence of a letter sent from Brussels on 21 July 1521,[4] it appears that Tommaso Vincidor, a former collaborator of Raphael's who had stayed in contact with other artists from his studio, was supposed to incorporate portraits of Cardinal Innocenzo Cybo and Cardinal Giulio de' Medici, a nephew of Leo X, in what he called a *"storie del leto"* – no doubt the tapestries adorning the throne in the consistory at the Vatican Palace). The figure, who looks youthful and whose silhouette bears some resemblance to that of Joseph receiving a golden necklace from Pharaoh in one of Andrea del Sarto's paintings for the Camera Borgherini (1515),[5] does not seem to be wearing priestly garb. Parma, going a step further, suggests that Perino's drawing may perhaps have been a sketch for the hangings in the consistory hall. However, the documentary and visual evidence relating to the tapestries, collected by Campbell,[6] does not bear out such a hypothesis, as we cannot find any work by Perino del Vaga nor any piece – sketch, cartoon, or tapestry – that relates to the subject in the present drawing.

It should be admitted, then, that we do not really know what Perino's purpose was when he made this drawing, or whether he or anyone assigned by him ever produced a work from it. The only painting that makes use of the entire composition is one by Domenico Alfani,[7] a Perugian artist who often painted works from compositions designed by others, including Signorelli, Raphael, Pontormo, and Rosso Fiorentino. Alfani's painting was commissioned on 18 December 1522 by Severo di Paride Petrini as the altar-piece for the Cappella del Buio in the church of Sant'Agostino in Perugia, and it was completed in 1524 (fig. 14.1).[8] Unlike in the drawing, the figures in the painting are set against an architectural background. A cherub has been added between the two crowning angels, and while Saint Peter has hardly been modified, the pope has been replaced by Saint Nicholas of Bari (who never wore a headpiece), the bearded saint to the right is clearly seen to be Saint Paul, and the figure kneeling in front of him is identifiable as Saint Lucy. The figure at the far right in the drawing was not used in the painting; the Virgin does not resemble Perino's in the slightest; and the Child is taken from a drawing by Raphael, though turned in the opposite direction.[9] By 1524, Perino's angels had become a recurring feature in Alfani's repertoire: the artist used them in a *Holy Conversation* in the church of San Francesco in Città della Pieve and in an altarpiece for the Collegio Gregoriano in Perugia, commissioned in 1517 and signed and dated 1518.[10] This last work provides a *terminus ante quem* for Perino's drawing, which until now has been dated very broadly between 1513, the year that Leo X's pontificate began (when Perino was twelve years old), and December 1521, when Leo X died,[11] though perhaps most likely after Perino's arrival in Rome, around 1516–1517 (when he was about sixteen).[12] Leo X's solemn entry into Florence on 30 November 1515, on which occasion Perino worked with Toto del Nunziata to produce a triumphal arch on the Piazza Santa Trinita,[13] may also have offered him an opportunity to design this sketch of the Virgin and Child with saints crowned by angels; his master, Ridolfo del Ghirlandaio, had been commissioned to decorate part of the interior of the Duomo and the pope's chapel in the convent in Santa Maria Novella.[14] It is worth noting that Ridolfo del Ghirlandaio was also charged with painting a *Coronation of the Virgin* for that chapel (a work still in situ), but formally and iconographically it has nothing to do with the present drawing.[15]

Fig. 14.1 Domenico Alfani, *Virgin and Child with Angels and Saints*, 1524, oil on panel, 305 × 211 cm. Galleria Nazionale dell'Umbria, Perugia

The drawing shows a strong Florentine influence.[16] The composition represents a synthesis, as well as a simplification, of Raphael's *Madonna of the Baldaquin*, painted in Florence in 1507–1508,[17] and Fra Bartolommeo's *Mystic Marriage of Saint Catherine*, painted in 1511.[18] The young Virgin holding the already large Child between her legs takes up an idea that Michelangelo had introduced in his *Madonna of Bruges* (1503, transported to Bruges in 1506).[19] The saint turning towards us on the right is drawn loosely, somewhat in the manner of Andrea del Sarto and Giovanni Antonio Sogliani,[20] and in a pose similar to that of Saint James in Pontormo's Pucci altarpiece of 1518.[21]

DOMINIQUE CORDELLIER

14

BALDASSARE PERUZZI 1481–1536

NATIVITY c. 1515

Oil on panel
100.6 × 76.4 cm
Private collection, Europe

Formerly ascribed to one of Raphael's closest followers, Giovanni Francesco Penni, the attribution of the painting to the Sienese artist Baldassare Peruzzi is due to Pouncey, who was also its previous owner.[1] That the work was in the collection of one of the greatest connoisseurs of Italian drawings adds to its overall significance today. An apparently related picture by Peruzzi of the *Coronation of the Virgin,* also dispersed from the Sebright collection in England, was last recorded in a private collection in Norway, but is not currently traceable.[2] The composition shares elements with the fresco of the *Adoration of the Magi* by Peruzzi in the vault of the Ponzetti Chapel in the church of Santa Maria della Pace in Rome, dated 1516, but the order of execution of the paintings is open to debate and it is quite possible that the Pouncey picture takes precedence. Certainly, it is the more forceful of the two paintings, while also being in much better state of preservation.

This painting – a rare work on panel by Peruzzi and little known – is a distinctive and original example of Roman art of the High Renaissance period, produced not long after the completion of Michelangelo's Sistine Chapel ceiling and while Raphael was active in the Vatican Stanze. Its purpose and patronage remain uncertain, but it should be recalled that Peruzzi had dedicated patrons as wealthy and distinguished as the Sienese banker Agostino Chigi, Cardinal Raffaele Riario and at least two Popes, Julius II and later, Paul III. Difficult to classify, Peruzzi was a highly versatile and pragmatic master – like so many artists of the period. As well as a painter and draughtsman, he was also an accomplished architect, theatre designer, and student of ancient art. Although Raphael and Bramante now eclipse Peruzzi's reputation, he was highly esteemed by his contemporaries and could be an artist of comparable originality. The relationship to Raphael is one key to analyzing this image, produced when the master from Urbino was the dominant painter in Rome, despite the attempts of

Michelangelo to rival him through the agency of the Venetian painter Sebastiano del Piombo. The figure of Joseph, who supports himself with his staff and whose partly hidden face bears an uneasy expression, is a reworking of a spectator in Raphael's *Saint Paul Preaching at Athens* tapestry cartoon (see fig. 13.1) prepared very close in time to Peruzzi's painting. The sculptural solidity of the figures and the crisp, metallic draperies, with the clinging *all'antica* folds, recall more generally Raphael's painting in Rome of the mid-1510s. It is notable in this context that Peruzzi was honoured with burial in a tomb adjacent to Raphael's in the Pantheon.

The relief-like composition with the figures massed outwards also reveals Peruzzi's keen awareness of the ancient art found in Rome and its seemingly limitless potential as a source and inspiration for modern painting. This is yet more obvious in the background, which contains a prominent inclusion of a ruined building resembling the Colosseum – an allusion to the fall of the ancient order with the birth of Christ. The night setting for this domestic subject – reinforced by the angel appearing in a nimbus in the sky to alert the shepherds watching their flocks to the Saviour's birth, as told in Luke's Gospel, is another artistic trope of this period. Increasingly, night scenes were attempted in Rome during the 1510s, as in Michelangelo's *Judith and Holofernes* lunette on the Sistine Chapel ceiling and Raphael's *Saint Peter liberated from prison* in the Stanza dell'Eliodoro, two major precedents in fresco. More generally, the dark tonalities combined with the hard, raking light entering from the side anticipate the paintings of such artists as Parmigianino and Rosso Fiorentino who followed in the decade to come and who also used these techniques as a way to focus action in the foreground and bind together strong patterns of figures. Certainly, Peruzzi's *Nativity* places the artist at the forefront of innovation in Roman painting around the mid-1510s.

DAVID FRANKLIN

16

RAFFAELLO SANZIO, CALLED **RAPHAEL**

1483–1520

COPY AFTER A HORSE ON THE QUIRINAL HILL (RECTO); *COPIES AFTER ANTIQUITY* (VERSO) C. 1515

Red chalk and pen and brown ink, with stylus underdrawing and traces of leadpoint; pen and brown ink [verso]
21.9 × 27.4 cm
Annotations: numerical notations overall. *desegno fato a Roma. D-1-.*
Perino 2 8. [verso]
National Gallery of Art, Washington

In his biography of Raphael written in the 1520s, Paolo Giovio praised the artist's efforts to measure the ancient architecture surviving in Rome in order to reconstruct the legendary city.[1] Raphael's interest extended even more passionately to sculpture as this unique drawing, a copy of one of the colossal stone horses from the "Horse-Tamers" monument on the Quirinal Hill, attests. If we accept that the measurements written in pen and ink over the red chalk on this sheet are in Raphael's own hand, or more likely by an artist from his workshop entrusted with this mechanical task, this would be the first known measured drawing after an ancient sculpture of the Renaissance.[2] It studies the sculpture not from the position of a viewer on the ground looking up but, for greater accuracy, more directly level with the work. A temporary scaffold must have been allotted to Raphael to raise him into a more satisfactory position for this explicit purpose. The drawing even carefully indicates where the original stone had cracked and was repaired, as between the neck and torso, and the broken off left leg is noted. It is not a reconstruction, but an obsessively accurate record. This dispassionate approach was unusual as artists of the period were not so scholarly in their approach, nor were they generally awed by the ancient works; rather, in competitive spirit, they instead aimed to surpass them. Nonetheless, only an artist of Raphael's sensitivity could enliven the animal with such immediacy, alertness and even emotion. And the handling is visually attractive, distinguished by its control and emphatic finish.

This sculpture, along with its pendant was a touchstone for artists of the Renaissance period and earlier for a representation of an active horse, not least because it was one of the few monumental ancient sculptures in Rome visible throughout the Middle Ages and in its original location. The statue copied by Raphael was inscribed as by Praxiteles and, given the legendary fame of that ancient Greek sculptor, this undoubtedly fueled its appeal for him. Furthermore, Raphael had numerous opportunities to depict rearing horses in the frescoes in the Vatican Stanze and he would also have been attracted to this sculpture not least as source material for his own work.

Pope Leo X appointed Raphael superintendent of antiquities in 1515, requiring the artist to inspect and report on the remains of antique art in Rome and within a ten mile radius of the city, in part as a means to preserve antiquity that had, traditionally, been rather casually treated by the modern local residents. This drawing may well have been made in that context, along with the weaker ones on the verso which includes a sketch after an ancient sculpture with some measurements by the same hand that has been attributed to artists in Raphael's workshop such as Perino del Vaga or Giovanni da Udine. As the Pope gave Raphael the authority to purchase antiquities, the obvious intention was to enlarge the papal collections wherever possible as recovered works could be permanently housed for safekeeping. Raphael inspired a formidable passion for ancient art among his pupils, especially the young Polidoro da Caravaggio.

DAVID FRANKLIN

16 (recto)

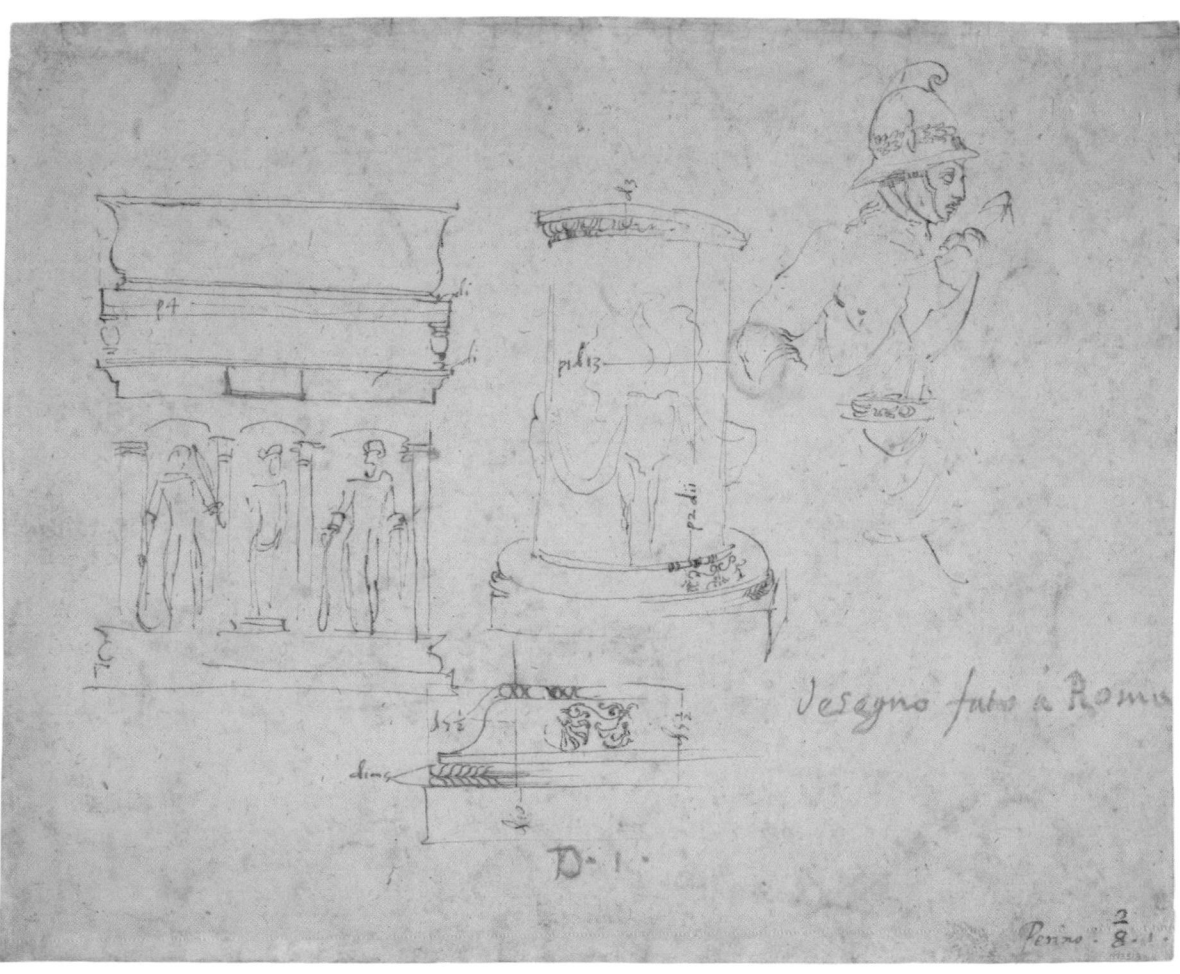

16 (verso)

17
RAFFAELLO SANZIO, CALLED RAPHAEL
1483–1520
STUDY FOR APOSTLES FOR THE MONTELUCE CORONATION OF THE VIRGIN c. 1516

Black chalk with white heightening on faded blue paper
26.9 × 22.1 cm
Staatliche Museen zu Berlin, Kupferstichkabinett

This drawing is a study for three apostles at the lower left of the Monteluce altarpiece (fig. 17.1), now in the Pinacoteca Vaticana. This massive painting depicting the *Dormition and Coronation of the Virgin* has an unusually protracted history.[1] The original commission dated back to as early as 1503 when Raphael was asked by the Franciscan nuns of the Monteluce convent, near Perugia, to paint an altarpiece of the same size and composition as one by Domenico Ghirlandaio in another Franciscan church at Narni in Umbria. A new contract was eventually negotiated with Raphael in 1516, who appears to have then made more preparatory drawings such as this one, but the work was only completed following his death in 1520 by his closest followers Giulio Romano and Giovanni Francesco Penni. In fact, the division of labour in this work, finally delivered in 1525, is perfectly clear as Giulio painted the upper part and Penni the lower part on two different horizontal panels that were wed together, the joins being easily visible. Typically for drawings related to late Raphael, the attribution has fluctuated. Gere has attributed this work to Penni, while Oberhuber considered it Raphael with a question mark. The quality of the drawing is high enough, however, to warrant a positive attribution to the master, as promoted by Joannides.

The Berlin drawing is a significant example of the mature Raphael's handling of black chalk, which develops the complex shadows from which these figures are constructed, ranging from the fleeting and almost velvety, to the more granular and absorbent. The introduction of white heightening reminds us of the sheer power of the contrast between light and dark the artist was seeking in what proved to be one of his final commissions. The only

sharp lines are those used to indicate the contours. Otherwise, the drawing is entirely about broad patterns of shadow rather than detail; even the drapery folds are kept to a minimum. The faces are not characterized, but could almost be of the same youthful studio model familiar from other drawings of this period taking each dramatic pose in sequence. The additive, staccato quality of the design and spectral aspect of the figures betray the origins of the drawing in the artist's studio. It was not uncommon for Raphael to isolate a group of three or four figures from a larger design for independent study.

Raphael frequently employed this accomplished, liberated technique of drawing in designing his compositions of the later 1510s. It was one presumably out of the technical reach of even his most talented assistants, hence the master's need to supply this particular type of study for a painting he may never have intended to touch himself. This is a graphic style less well known than the more polished, monumental figure drawings in red and black chalk for the bystanders in, for example, the *Transfiguration of Christ,* but just as critical to him in the design process as he studied the stark, hard shadows he came increasingly to prefer in his painting. This study must have been preceded by others as the poses are already reasonably close to the finished painting. This evocative, atmospheric style of drawing was ultimately informed by the works of Leonardo da Vinci, which Raphael had studied in Florence a decade earlier, as well as his later familiarity with Sebastiano del Piombo's drawings. The heightened emotional dramatic quality and powerful foreshortening of these figures, disposed as in a sculptural relief, are similar to those in the better-known altarpiece of the *Transfiguration*, also now in the Vatican.

DAVID FRANKLIN

Fig. 17.1 Giulio Romano and Giovanni Francesco Penni, *Coronation of the Virgin (Madonna of Monteluce)*, 1505–1525, oil on panel, 354 × 232 cm. Pinacoteca Vaticana, Rome

18
SCHOOL OF RAPHAEL

DAVID AND BATHSHEBA c. 1516–1517

Pen and ink with brown wash and
white heightening over indications
in black chalk; squared in black
chalk at 2.3 cm
37.9 × 26 cm
The British Museum, London

Fig. 18.1 School of Raphael, *David and Bathsheba*, 1516–1519, fresco. Logge, Vatican Palace, Rome

The thirteen-bay Loggia of Leo X designed by Raphael and executed by a team of assistants and specialists between 1516 and 1519 was an innovatory scheme of great richness that had an incalculable influence on many different areas of later art. It combines a pseudo-antique setting of decorative frescoes and stuccoes, much inspired by the Golden House of Nero, with an extensive biblical cycle. Its vaults contain fifty-two small frescoes comprising forty-eight scenes from the Old Testament and four from the New. A further twelve scenes – eleven from the Old Testament and one from the New – in fictive *bronzaille* relief were included in the *basamento* although little of these remains. Many of the narratives of the vault frescoes are rare and Raphael exploited both early Christian mosaics and classical sarcophagus reliefs, among other sources, enlivening them with his own – and no doubt his advisors' – reading of the texts. Concision of storytelling and clarity of design were necessary for small scenes that were planned to be seen from a distance, and the results are, for the most part, triumphantly successful. Their formulations permeate later Bible illustration and they were a major stylistic source for the "baroque classicism" practiced by Poussin and his followers.

The execution of the vault frescoes, probably datable 1516–1517, is by a number of different young artists. They are listed by Vasari, but, according to him, all worked under Giulio's control to Raphael's designs. However, the visual evidence suggests that the supervisor was not Giulio but Raphael's other major pupil, Giovanni Francesco Penni. The precise process of creation, communication and quality control has been much disputed but to this writer the most likely scenario is that Raphael made initial sketches in pen or chalk and that these were developed by Penni into *modelli* to be given to the executing artists. Only one preparatory sketch, universally agreed to be by Raphael, survives: this, in the Albertina, shows three figures for the scene of *David and Goliath*, taken from models posed in the studio. In the fresco, these three were supplemented by many others. This may exemplify the general pattern, with Raphael contributing the anchor figures upon whom his pupils expanded. Unfortunately, however, no *modello* survives for the *David and Goliath*.

From the *modello* stage survive twenty original drawings, plus several copies of lost ones. Of these, sixteen are, like the present drawing, in brush, wash and white body colour over black chalk, while four others are in pen. Nineteen of the twenty are squared for enlargement. The pen drawing representing the *Baptism of Christ* was probably also a *modello* that remained unsquared. Although some pen *modelli* have been attributed to other hands, it is likely that they too are by Penni, who was responsible for all but one of the multimedia *modelli*. The single exception is the dynamic *Moses Receiving the Tablets of the Law* (Paris, Louvre) which displays significant pentimenti, and is widely – and in the compiler's view, correctly – attributed to Raphael himself.

In the eighteenth century, most of the *modelli* were regarded as autograph Raphaels, but doubts arising in the nineteenth century led to a long period of uncertainty. Sir Karl Parker pioneered their allocation to Penni, but the case for Penni's authorship was most cogently argued by Pouncey and Gere. In 1999 Oberhuber and Gnann[1] attempted to return the whole group to Raphael but their views are rejected by most scholars and are unacceptable to this writer. An alternative hypothesis, that the black chalk lay-ins are by Raphael, was not comforted by the exposure of the underlying chalk lines of the *Expulsion*

18

from Eden in the Royal Collection. Other attempts have
been made to break up the group; some scholars give the
present *modello* to Perino del Vaga, reasonably, given that
Perino is named by Vasari as the executant of the fresco of
David and Bathsheba (fig. 18.1) – in the eleventh arcade –
and worked closely with Giovanni Francesco whose sister
he married. However, the compiler sees no good reason to
subtract this *modello* from Penni.

Whereas most treatments of David and Bathsheba
show only the aged monarch unexpectedly ravished by his
vision of the beautiful young woman at her toilet, this
drawing develops the story more fully, departing somewhat from the text of Samuel II, 11. King David, reviewing
troops from a loggia, is smitten by Bathsheba on the bal-
cony of her palace, washing her hair (a transposition of
Venus Anadyomene). His soldiers are marching to war,
and battle's imminence allows David to arrange the death
of Bathsheba's husband, his loyal captain Uriah the Hittite,
by abandoning him in the front rank of combat. The King's
sudden passion and its cruel consequence are economically
established. In its selective compression and its evocation
of the public dimension of a private passion, such a staging
can have been devised only by a master storyteller.

Although the execution of the David and Bathsheba
modello is uneasy in its spatial organization – never one of
Penni's strengths – and lack of precision, it effectively tran-
scribes – and no doubt amplifies – a sketch that Raphael

likely made in pen. The tripartite division of labour –
sketches by Raphael, developed *modelli* by Penni, frescoing by a young assistant – allowed subsidiary design input
at the second stage by Penni, whose very limitations stimulated the ambitious young executants to sharpen empha-
ses and expand detail. Running his team with a loose rein,
Raphael kept its members happy and obtained their most
imaginative efforts. Vasari speaks of Raphael's unique success in organizing his associates harmoniously; consequently, Raphael's school was supremely successful in
developing the individual talents of its members: the roll-
call of the Loggia's executants number some of the most
illustrious names of the next generation.

PAUL JOANNIDES

19
RAFFAELLO SANZIO, CALLED RAPHAEL
1483–1520
*NUDE STUDIES FOR SAINT ANDREW
AND ANOTHER APOSTLE FOR* THE
TRANSFIGURATION c. 1517

Red chalk, incised
32.8 × 23.2 cm
Devonshire Collection, Chatsworth

Fig. 19.1 Raphael, *The Transfiguration*, c. 1516–1520, oil on panel,
410 × 279 cm. Pinacoteca Vaticana,
Rome

For *The Transfiguration* (fig. 19.1), his last and most ambitious altarpiece, Raphael produced a large number of drawings, among them this exquisite nude study for the two apostles at the lower-left corner of the composition.[1] Executed in red chalk with stylus indentations, it is considered one of Raphael's most beautiful drawings, and its autograph status has rarely been in doubt.[2] The older figure in the foreground has traditionally been identified as Saint Andrew, while the younger apostle, pointing to the upper part of the composition, remains unidentified.[3] The monumental painting, now in the Pinacoteca Vaticana, represents the culmination of Raphael's exploration of the relationship between the earthly and the divine, a leitmotiv that can be traced throughout his career, as he varied his solutions to the challenge of making the miraculous, the visionary, visible.

The Transfiguration was intended for the cathedral of Narbonne in southwestern France. Its patron, Cardinal Giulio de' Medici (Pope Leo X's first cousin, who would become Pope Clement VII), was appointed archbishop of Narbonne in February 1515. The cardinal evidently commissioned Raphael in late 1516, and soon after commissioned his rival Sebastiano Veneziano (later called "del Piombo") to paint a second altarpiece for Narbonne, representing the Raising of Lazarus (now in the National Gallery, London).[4] The pictures were painted in a spirit of artistic competitiveness, intensified by the fact that Michelangelo supplied Sebastiano, who represented, as it were, the Venetian colouristic tradition, with drawings.[5] Both altarpieces are deeply indebted to the art of Leonardo da Vinci, where one finds paradigms for the investigation of intense emotion, the compositional structure, and the use of what has been called a *maniera oscura*, or dark manner.[6] Thus, in a single commission, the *paragone* between painting and sculpture

was, in effect, being put to the test – as were the relative merits of Venetian and Central Italian pictorial practice.

Raphael's *Transfiguration* and Sebastiano's *Raising of Lazarus* are narrative altarpieces representing scenes from the life of Christ commonly juxtaposed in medieval and Renaissance narrative cycles; both are prefigurations of the Passion and Resurrection of Christ. In Raphael's altarpiece, two separate though simultaneously occurring biblical events are combined in a single pictorial space. The miracle of the Transfiguration and the story of the apostles' failure to heal the demon-possessed boy are recounted by three of the four evangelists – Matthew (17:1–21), Mark (9:2–29), and Luke (9:28–44) – as well as by Saint Peter, one of the eyewitnesses to the event (II Peter 1:16–18). In Raphael's altarpiece, Christ of the Transfiguration appears in the upper half of the composition to three chosen apostles, Peter, James, and John, who have been called to Mount Tabor. He is flanked by the Old Testament prophets Moses and Elias (Elijah). To the left of the apostles are two figures plausibly identifiable as Justus and Pastor, the patron saints of the cathedral of Narbonne.

In the lower half of the composition, Raphael moves from the visionary to the dramatic. At the right a man and woman, followed by a crowd, bring a demon-possessed boy to the nine apostles who remained behind. The figures at the right and most of those at the left seem unaware of the miraculous event taking place above them. It has, however, recently been proposed by Kleinbub that the apostles who seem unaware of the events are to be understood as experiencing the miraculous vision above them internally.[7] While Christ was miraculously transformed into a divine presence on Mount Tabor, the apostles below were unable to heal the boy. Only after Christ had returned could the demon be cast out, and only Christ could perform the

Fig. 19.2 Raphael, *Figure of Saint Andrew (Study for* The Transfiguration), c. 1517, red chalk, incised, 12.6 × 14.5 cm. Albertina, Vienna

cure.[8] Upon his return, Christ would chide his followers for their lack of faith, which was one of the lessons of the Raising of Lazarus. The Transfiguration on Mount Tabor alone appears in the earliest compositional drawing for the altarpiece, now in the Albertina in Vienna.[9] Whether the decision to include the episode of the failure to heal the boy was made by the artist or by the patron is unclear and is debated among scholars.[10]

Once the decision had been made to include both the Transfiguration on Mount Tabor and the apostles with the demon-possessed boy, Raphael and his workshop produced numerous drawings that served different functions in the creative process. This was his practice for large-scale decorative projects such as the Stanza della Segnatura or the Sala di Costantino, and the intensity of preparation here demonstrates the singular importance of the commission for Cardinal Giulio's altarpiece intended for Narbonne. The surviving drawings include nude and clothed compositional sketches, studies of individual figures and figural groups, drapery studies, and a group of highly finished drawings of heads (and sometimes hands) in black chalk over pouncing that were characterized by Fischel in 1937 as "auxiliary cartoons."[11]

The Chatsworth sheet exhibited here belongs to a group of nude figural studies in red chalk for the lower half of the composition. Raphael first explored the apostle with a book alone in a more loosely sketched study in the Albertina (fig. 19.2).[12] In the present drawing, the middle-aged saint is juxtaposed with the more youthful apostle behind him and the poses of the two figures mirror each other; in the altarpiece they serve to frame the lower-left corner of the composition. The right leg and left arm of the older apostle are strongly foreshortened, and the younger saint's gesture creates a powerful diagonal move-

ment, which, in the painting, leads the viewers' eyes to the miracle on Mount Tabor. In the present drawing, Raphael varies the handling of the red chalk to suggest the intensely dramatic lighting of the realized altarpiece. The detailed modelling – particularly of the musculature – demonstrates Raphael's concern with the underlying structure of the figures, which are clothed in the painting. That Raphael was, in effect, competing against Michelangelo, must have spurred the younger artist to produce in this group of drawings some of his most accomplished and expressive visualizations of the nude male form.

Raphael died on 6 April 1520, at the age of thirty-seven. Days after his death, Sebastiano's *Raising of Lazarus* was displayed alongside his rival's *Transfiguration* in the Vatican Palace. Sebastiano's altarpiece was sent to Narbonne, where it stood in the cathedral until the early eighteenth century. Cardinal Giulio decided not to send Raphael's "last will and testament" to France, and in 1523 he donated it to the Roman church of San Pietro in Montorio. The painting stood there as the high altarpiece until 1797, when Napoleon appropriated it and had it sent to Paris. Ever since its return to Rome and installation in the Pinacoteca Vaticana in 1816, Raphael's *Transfiguration* has been one of the greatest treasures of the papal collections.

SHERYL E. REISS

GIULIO PIPPI, CALLED **GIULIO ROMANO**
1499?–1546
*THE HOLY FAMILY WITH THE INFANT
SAINT JOHN THE BAPTIST AND A YOUNG
WOMAN CARRYING TWO BIRDS IN A
BASKET* (KNOWN AS THE *SPINOLA HOLY FAMILY*) C. 1518

Oil [possibly mixed with tempera]
on panel
77.8 × 61.9 cm
The J. Paul Getty Museum,
Los Angeles

This *Holy Family* portrays the encounter of the infant Jesus and Saint John the Baptist in the presence of the Virgin, Saint Joseph, and a young woman carrying two birds in a basket.[1] It is known as the *Spinola Holy Family* due to the fact that Andrew Wilson, a Scottish businessman who brought it to England from Italy in 1803, had acquired it from an unidentified member of the Spinola family of Genoa. In the nineteenth century it was listed as among the best works by Giulio Romano,[2] but it subsequently fell into obscurity. Russell, followed by Joannides, rediscovered it in 1982 and firmly reinstated it in the catalogue of Giulio's paintings from his Roman period.[3]

Ferino Pagden was the first to compare the compactly proportioned figures in the *Spinola Holy Family* with those in the frescoes in the Vatican loggias commissioned by Leo X from Raphael and his studio, of which Giulio Romano was then a member.[4] Among these frescoes, painted in 1518–1519, the *Discovery of Moses*, explicitly attributed to Giulio by Vasari,[5] presents some suggestive points of comparison, notwithstanding the inherent differences between frescoes and oil paintings.

Ferino Pagden's implicit dating of the *Spinola Holy Family* to about 1518 is likely accurate. At that time, the young Giulio Romano was one of a group of assistants involved in the execution of several major projects directed by Raphael, including the decoration of the loggias, begun in the spring of 1518. Guilio was an important contributor to these projects, and his work was so deeply imbued with the master's techniques and figurative vocabulary, and so closely tied in to the complex, collaborative working methods of the studio, that it could often have passed for Raphael's own or been indistinguishable from the ensemble of works executed in Raphael's name.[6] Occasionally, however, even during Raphael's lifetime, a contributor's work emerged from the shadows in which it had matured: the *Spinola Holy Family* is one of the earliest and most valuable testimonies to this phenomenon.

The Raphaelesque lineage of the *Spinola Holy Family* is beyond question: the figures derive from motifs previously developed by Raphael in works such as the *Madonna of Divine Love* and the *Visitation*.[7] Ferino Pagden even suggested that Raphael may have laid out the "rapid sketch" and then handed it over to his assistants.[8] Yet Giulio Romano's hand is clearly recognizable here, in the tightly accentuated plasticity of the figures, the thick highlights that key up its surface, the acidic colours set off by abrupt contrasts, the skilful and calligraphic sinuousness of the brushwork (seen mainly in the drapery and Saint John's banner) – in short, through a whole array of characteristics usually associated with the work of this artist in his youth.

A glance at the *Little Holy Family* in the Louvre (fig. 20.1), painted around the same time, and similarly attributable to Giulio Romano though the details of its invention are altogether Raphael's,[9] brings out, by way of contrast, the particular inflections that distinguish the composition of the *Spinola Holy Family*. In the former, the confluence of the figures arises spontaneously out of their interaction and is supply ordered and focused toward the centre of the painting. In the latter, the grouping is more additive, divided, and uncentred[10] – the gestural cohesiveness seems to result not from the figures themselves but rather from the artist's ingenuity. The elegant young woman with the basket, suspended in space between the foreground and background like some priestess out of an ancient bas-relief, reinforces this impression. Saint John the Baptist, whose head and torso are arranged in the same manner as in the Louvre painting, here calls, from an anatomical perspective, for a naturally positioned profile, but instead turns partly outward in his attentive genuflection.[11] We can assume, as well, that the arcade in the background at the right, proposed in an earlier phase and then covered over (see fig. 20.2), would have added a refined ambiguity to the relative proportions of the painting.[12]

Fig. 20.1 Giulio Romano, after Raphael, *The Holy Family* (called the *Little Holy Family*), c. 1518, oil on panel, 38.6 × 29.5 cm. Musée du Louvre, Paris

Fig. 20.2 Giulio Romano, X-ray image of *The Holy Family* (p. 127). The J. Paul Getty Museum, Los Angeles

The young Giulio Romano did not work on his own in Raphael's studio, but functioned in a symbiotic relationship with other assistants. As a result of the "union" that the assistants maintained,[13] a painting of this period attributable, in its final form, to Giulio Romano might in fact have been prepared communally. Joannides thus suggests that the preparatory sketch at Windsor Castle of the young woman with the basket was drawn by one of Giulio's studio co-workers, Giovanni Francesco Penni.[14] A study of a head in the lower portion of a sheet in the Teylers Museum attributable to a member of Raphael's studio other than Giulio may also be associated with this figure.[15]

The remarkable underdrawing in the Spinola *Holy Family*, which has become visible to the naked eye due to the increasing transparency of the painted layer, reveals the final composition immediately before the picture was executed. Considering its style, we can be sure that Penni did not have any role in this last phase of preparation. From another point of view, its technique attests so well to the strongly Raphaelesque training of its creator,

Giulio Romano, that Oberhuber and Gnann in 1999 thought that they recognized in it Raphael's own hand.[16] However, the technical similarities that might have proved these experts right[17] seem to be refuted by the compositional logic inherent in the final sketch: it is as if Giulio's graphic skill was firmly under Raphael's sway, but his imaginative powers less so.

As a kind of by-product of the studio, the Spinola *Holy Family* capitalizes on the "approximately imitable"[18] nature of the later Raphael while assimilating it in an intelligent manner. Many engravings hold a similar place in the range of works from the master's school. As Oberhuber has remarked, some of them even share a comparable atmosphere.[19] The composition of the Spinola *Holy Family*, for its part, must have been quite popular. In addition to the derivations already noted is a medallion painted on enamel, produced in Limoges, in the sixteenth century and preserved at the Musée des Beaux-Arts de Troyes in France.[20]

SIMON LEGRAND

21

RAFFAELLO SANZIO, CALLED **RAPHAEL**
1483–1520

OR **GIULIO PIPPI,** CALLED **GIULIO ROMANO**
1499–1546

HEAD OF POPE LEO X c. 1520

Black chalk with white heightening, incised
33.7 × 26.8 cm
Annotations: *Ritratto de Leon "X" / Michelangelo Buonaroti*; and *KK 39*
Devonshire Collection, Chatsworth

The attribution of this extraordinarily vivid and powerful likeness of Pope Leo X has been controversial and still remains a matter of debate among specialists. Executed in black chalk with extensive white heightening, the drawing is annotated on the mount with the sitter's name and is attributed to Michelangelo in the hand of one of its early owners.[1] In 1899 Wickhoff assigned the drawing to Sebastiano del Piombo, an attribution used by Berenson in 1903 and followed in 1949 by Gere, who later revised it to "Raphael (?)."[2] Passavant, in his *Tour of a German Artist in England* of 1836, was the first to associate the Chatsworth portrait of Leo with Raphael, an attribution followed by a number of scholars, among them Berenson (in 1938), Shearman, Joannides, and Rosand.[3] The attribution to Giulio Romano, first proposed by Fischel in 1935, has been accepted by Hartt, Hess, Oberhuber, Jaffé, Ferino, and others.[4]

The attribution of the late drawings of Raphael and the early ones of Giulio Romano has been one of the thorniest problems in the study of the artists' oeuvres, and this work is among the most problematic. In 1987 Gere noted:

> The drawing thus poses a nice problem in connoisseurship. The technical arguments in favor of Giulio are difficult to gainsay. On the other hand, the draughtsman was clearly a most gifted portraitist, and it would be difficult to point to another portrait by Giulio that has anything of the power and psychological insight of this head.[5]

While the overall hardness of the draughtsmanship suggests Giulio, the extraordinary degree of psychological penetration suggests Raphael, leaving the authorship an open question.[6] Because of the sheer forcefulness of the characterization of the sitter, the present writer leans towards an attribution to Raphael.

The debates over attribution notwithstanding, most scholars do agree that the powerful evocation of the first Medici pope seen in this drawing suggests a study after the life. Leo's distinctive and corpulent features are best known from Raphael's group portrait of the pontiff with two cardinals in the Uffizi (see cat. 46, fig. 46.1 for illustration), where the sitter is more idealized than in the Chatsworth drawing. In contrast, here the artist has rendered the sagging flesh, and every wrinkle on the sitter's face with meticulous attention to detail.

The Chatsworth sheet, which has incised contours, has often been described as a cartoon for the head of the figure of Pope Clement I, shown enthroned between allegorical personifications of *Moderatio* (moderation) and *Comitas* (comity, or social harmony), on the east wall of the Sala di Costantino in the Vatican Palace (fig. 21.1).[7] This group forms part of a series of early pontiffs accompanied by figures of Virtues that decorate the corners of the great papal reception hall designed by Raphael and completed after his death by members of his workshop.[8] The dimensions of the head in the fresco and in the Chatsworth drawing do not correspond exactly.[9] In 1972 Shearman argued that the drawing originally served as the model for Domenico Aimo's colossal statue of Leo X commissioned by the Conservatori of Rome, now in the church of Santa Maria in Aracoeli, and that it was then re-used for the fresco.[10] This idea, however, has not generally been accepted.

As discussed in the entry on *Pope Sylvester I in a Sedia Gestatoria* (cat. 22), shortly after Raphael's untimely death Sebastiano del Piombo told Michelangelo that Raphael's *garzoni* wanted to paint the Sala di Costantino in oils, and in a subsequent letter he reported that Raphael's heirs had drawings for the room.[11] It has recently been suggested that for the figure of *Comitas* that flanks the representation of Leo X as Clement I, Raphael's *garzoni* used a cartoon by the master upon which they painted in oils.[12] While this hypothesis is intriguing, there is currently no scientific confirmation of it.[13]

SHERYL E. REISS

Fig. 21.1 Giulio Romano, *Pope Clement I with Moderatio and Comitas*, c. 1521, fresco. Sala di Costantino. Vatican Palace, Rome

Ritratto di Leon.° x°

5.

RAFFAELLO SANZIO, CALLED **RAPHAEL**
1483–1520
POPE SYLVESTER I IN A SEDIA GESTATORIA
C. 1520

Black, white, yellow, and red
chalks and brown wash, squared in
black chalk
39.8 × 40.4 cm
Isabella Stewart Gardner Museum,
Boston

This beautiful and unusual Raphael drawing shows a beardless, mitred pope carried in a *sedia gestatoria* (a portable throne used exclusively for popes), accompanied by his retinue. Although in the past occasionally attributed to members of the Raphael workshop, it is now generally accepted as by the master himself.[1] The Boston sheet is of great interest on a number of levels, including its technique, its iconography, and its place in the history of monumental wall painting during the pontificates of Leo X and Clement VII. It employs several colours of chalk, along with brown wash, and it features two systems of squaring.[2] Raphael used multiple coloured chalks (a technique practiced by artists in the Leonardo circle in Lombardy, and also by Umbrian artists such as Luca Signorelli and Timoteo Viti) for only one other surviving drawing, a head study of a cardinal in Wilton House.[3]

Associated in the nineteenth century with Raphael's *Expulsion of Heliodorus* fresco in the Stanza d'Eliodoro in the Vatican Palace, this drawing is now generally held to be an early idea for the north wall of the Sala di Costantino.[4] The north wall, with two large windows looking out over the Belvedere Courtyard, was frescoed with a representation of the Donation of Constantine in the first year of Clement VII's pontificate. The subject of the fresco was based on a forged document, probably of the eighth century, that was defended by the papacy well into the sixteenth century.[5] The largest and last of the suite of rooms in the papal palace to be decorated by Raphael and his followers, the Sala di Costantino (named after its frescoes dedicated to the first Christian emperor, Constantine) was an audience hall used in the sixteenth century for events such as banquets, weddings, and the ceremonial reception of foreign dignitaries; under Adrian VI and Clement VII, it was also used for consistories.[6] Scaffolding for painters was erected in the hall by October 1519, some six months before Raphael's untimely death in April 1520.[7]

Within days of Raphael's passing, his great rival in Rome, Sebastiano Veneziano (later called "del Piombo") undertook an ultimately unsuccessful campaign to obtain the Sala di Costantino commission for himself. In a letter of 12 April 1520, Sebastiano told Michelangelo that the late master's *garzoni* were bragging that they wanted to paint the "salla de' Pontifici" (one of several names used for the room in this period) in oils.[8] Although the commission was allocated to Raphael's heirs Giulio Romano and Giovanni Francesco Penni by early May 1520, Sebastiano still hoped to wrest it from them, and in a letter of 6 September 1520 he told Michelangelo that the pope, who

had offered him part of the job, said that Raphael's *garzoni* "have drawings by Raphael's hand" for the room.[9] In the same letter, Sebastiano describes what he knows of the subjects for the *istorie* (narrative paintings) in the great hall. According to Sebastiano (claiming to have been told by the pope himself) they were to be: (1) the appearance of the cross under which Constantine would be victorious, (2) a battle scene (the Battle of the Milvian Bridge), (3) the presentation of prisoners to the emperor, and (4) the preparation of a bath of blood taken from little children (to heal the emperor's leprosy). Sebastiano makes no mention of the two scenes eventually painted under Clement VII: Constantine's baptism by Pope Sylvester I (r. 314–335) and the Donation of Constantine.

Raphael's heirs worked in the room until their progress was stopped by the unexpected death of Pope Leo X in December 1521. Shortly thereafter, the room was described as more than half finished, and it was reported that Raphael's young followers wanted to finish it.[10] Nothing was done during the pontificate of Adrian VI, but work began again soon after Clement VII's elevation to the papal throne in November 1523 and was apparently complete by September 1524.[11] The frescoes carried out in the Clementine campaign focus on the relationship of Constantine to Pope Sylvester, and they emphasize imperial deference to papal authority.

The Boston sheet is related to a rapidly drawn pen and ink sketch by Giulio Romano in the Louvre (fig. 22.1a)[12] that shows a mitred pope, in this instance bearded, carried in a *sedia gestatoria*.[13] The mace bearer and the figure carrying a staff (for a processional cross) have been taken from Raphael's design, but the ecclesiastics in the pope's retinue have been replaced by members of the Swiss Guard, and a cardinal is shown in the background, riding a mule. The scene in the Louvre sheet takes place before a grand architectural setting. The Paris drawing has been identified as half of a compositional sketch by Giulio, the other half of which is in the Nationalmuseum, Stockholm (fig. 22.1b).[14] The Stockholm sheet, which might be based on a lost composition by Raphael, shows a kneeling figure dressed in *all'antica* armour, accompanied by attendants leading a riderless horse. A female figure is seen descending stairs in the left middle ground before a faintly sketched architectural background.

In 1917 Sirén was the first to associate the Stockholm and Paris fragments (without any mention of the Boston sheet).[15] He also referred to a highly finished *modello* generally given to Giulio Romano and now in the Rijksmuseum,

Fig. 22.1a Giulio Romano, *Pope Sylvester I in a* Sedia Gestatoria, c. 1521?, pen and ink, 42 × 28.8 cm. Musée du Louvre, Paris

Fig. 22.1b Giulio Romano, *Emperor Constantine with a Horse Kneeling before Pope Sylvester I*, c. 1521?, pen and ink, 42 × 28.8 cm. Nationalmuseum, Stockholm

Fig. 22.2 Giulio Romano, *Emperor Constantine before Pope Sylvester I*, 1521, pen and ink and brown wash with white heightening, 39.5 × 54.9 cm. Rijksmuseum, Amsterdam

Amsterdam (fig. 22.2), that shows a bearded pope carried in the *sedia gestatoria*, here wearing the papal tiara, meeting a kneeling, cuirassed figure.[16] As in the Boston and Louvre sheets, the pope's right hand is raised in benediction.[17] The setting in the *modello* has been identified as a piazza before the Lateran Palace in Rome, in which the Emperor Constantine lived with his second wife, Fausta.[18] In *The Donation of Constantine*, the first Christian emperor gives the Lateran palace – along with various insignia, privileges, and lands – to Sylvester I, in gratitude for curing him of leprosy.

In 1939 Hartt related the Paris-Stockholm composition to the Sala di Costantino.[19] Although Hartt did not identify the scene in the Paris and Stockholm fragments as the Donation of Constantine, several subsequent scholars have done so.[20] While this remains a controversial point, the identification of the figures as Pope Sylvester and Constantine in both the fragments and the Amsterdam *modello* seems plausible.[21] This is of critical importance for interpreting the Boston drawing, because if it was indeed for half of a composition similar to the Paris-Stockholm fragments and the *modello*, we may infer that it too represents a scene from the Sylvester-Constantine story (if not the spurious Donation per se). This, in turn, would suggest that the relationship of the emperor to the papacy – and particularly the issue of papal primacy – was already under consideration during Raphael's lifetime and was not a Clementine alteration of the program. It is also entirely possible that Sebastiano was misinformed about the intended iconography, or that various subjects were being considered simultaneously.[22]

The relationship of the papacy to the Holy Roman Empire was a timely matter when the decorations of the Sala di Costantino were conceived. In June 1519 a new emperor, Charles V of the House of Habsburg, was elected, and this was a moment when deference of the emperor to papal authority was a critical concern to the papacy. Moreover, at this time, the Germanic lands were torn apart by Martin Luther's assaults on the papacy, and the Donation of Constantine was condemned by the anti-papal humanist knight Ulrich von Hutten, who had published Lorenzo Valla's fifteenth-century refutation of the Donation.[23]

Hutten's text, which was dedicated to Leo X, came to Luther's attention, and he denounced the papacy's claims to temporal authority, writing in a letter of 24 February 1520, "I am in such a passion that I scarcely doubt that the Pope is the Antichrist expected by the world."[24] Significantly, just as work commenced on the Sala di Costantino, a series of curial commissions examined Luther's errors.[25] That Constantine's submission to Sylvester and his bestowing of privileges and lands upon the papacy may already have been planned during Raphael's lifetime, just as the Lutheran controversy came to a head, suggests that the artist was responding to pressing political and theological concerns during Leo X's pontificate. Thus, if the drawing exhibited here is Raphael's invention for part of a composition depicting Constantine kneeling before Pope Sylvester I, it suggests that the themes of papal primacy and imperial submission painted in the Clementine period were already in play in the early stages of the project.

SHERYL E. REISS

23

GIULIO PIPPI, CALLED **GIULIO ROMANO**
c. 1499–1546 and
GIOVANNI FRANCESCO PENNI,
CALLED **IL FATTORE**   c. 1496–c. 1528
FLAGELLATION OF CHRIST   c. 1520

Oil on panel
164 × 145 cm
Sacristy, Santa Prassede, Rome
Not in exhibition

Fig. 23.1 Giulio Romano, *Allegory of Dovitia* (so called *Ceres*), c. 1518, oil on panel, 38.4 × 31.3 cm. Musée du Louvre, Paris

In his life of Giulio Romano, Vasari describes only in passing a *Flagellation* for the Roman church of Santa Prassede: "*In un altro quadro grande fece un Cristo battuto alla colonna, che fu posto sopra l'altare della chiesa di Santa Prassede in Roma.*" According to Benigno Davanzati's 1725 *Notizie al Pellegrino della Basilica di Santa Prassede*, the painting was commissioned by Bernardo Dovizi da Bibbiena and donated to the church for display next to the venerated relic of the column of the flagellation.[1] The cardinal died in 1520, which would provide a convenient *terminus ante quem* for the commission. Although Vasari's account could suggest that the *Flagellation* was placed initially on the high altar, its iconography and Davanzati's account clearly indicate that it was from the outset intended to decorate the Zeno chapel, which is situated in the right aisle of the church and houses the holy column. Totti, in 1638, and Titi, in 1674, both describe the painting in this location. Some time before 1725, because of the humidity in the chapel, it was transferred to the sacristy, where Davanzati, as well as a 1726 inventory of Santa Prassede and the 1763 edition of Titi's guide book mention it.[2]

In 1954, noting Carlo D'Arco's description in his *Istoria della vita e delle opere di Giulio Pippi Romano*, which differs considerably from the *Flagellation* housed today in Santa Prassede, Calvesi argued that the original painting was replaced, possibly around 1585–1590, with the present one, which he attributed to the Lombard artist Simone Peterzano.[3] But D'Arco's 1838 description of the Roman painting is based, as Toesca has convincingly shown, on a 1588 print by Pietro Fachetti, which represents indeed another, now lost painting by Giulio Romano. Calvesi's provocative proposal to attribute the painting to Peterzano and to date it to the later 1580s has been accepted by some scholars,[4] but rests on stylistic grounds alone. There is indeed no positive evidence that the *Flagellation* mentioned by Vasari was ever replaced, and the painting itself seems to fit rather nicely the years around 1520 and the circle of the late Raphael, somewhere between Giulio Romano and Giovanni Francesco Penni. An attribution to both Penni and Romano or a collaboration between the two have been proposed.[5] More recently Dacos has argued instead for an attribution to the Netherlandish painter Peter de Kempeneer, imitating Raphaelesque models during his Italian sojourn in 1527–1537. The reconstruction of Kempeneer's Italian period remains highly hypothetical and it seems unlikely that a young foreigner would be awarded such a prestigious altarpiece commission. Based on Vasari's testimony, on the possible patronage of Cardinal

Bibbiena and the stylistic evidence of the painting in Santa Prassede, an attribution to Raphael's circle around 1520 still seems the most convincing. The roles of Penni and Romano in Raphael's workshop, their participation in his late works and the development of their individual styles have been more clearly defined in recent years but still remain somewhat difficult to pin down, especially in Penni's case.

The *Flagellation* in Santa Prassede is an imposing picture, in its monumental, carefully balanced composition and the foregrounding of vigorously modelled male nudes. Christ is tied to the centrally positioned black and white marble column, with his body turned slightly to the right and arms crossed in front of his chest. Two flagellators, one seen frontally, the other from the rear, threaten him with their birches. But the biblical drama seems suspended, the actors immobilized on stage and frozen in time. The athletic nudes are turned into classical sculptures posing for the viewer. The three figures are positioned in front of a barely indicated architectural setting, adorned with slender pilasters and a central niche behind

the column. The floor is covered with highly polished ancient marble, reflecting the brilliant light and even mirroring the feet of the protagonists. Veins and patterns of the costly coloured marble are described in naturalistic detail and seem to compete with the beauty and artifice of the twisted bodies and their undulating contour lines. Raphael employed such ancient marble for the decoration of the Chigi Chapel in Santa Maria del Popolo, and Giulio Romano inserted very similar painted marble panels in his *Allegory of Dovitia* (fig. 23.1), painted for Cardinal Bibbiena and now in the Louvre, and the *Madonna della Gatta* in Naples.[6] As Toesca has observed, there are marked differences between the figure types of the two flagellators and the execution of the draperies and nudes, which could well point to a collaborative execution by the Raphael's two most important pupils, identifying Penni's hand in the flagellator on the left and in the Christ figure, and Romano's hand in the flagellator on the right. The Santa Prassede altarpiece is obviously related to Sebastiano del Piombo's famous *Flagellation* for the Borgherini Chapel in San Pietro in Montorio (see fig. 5, p. 21), for which Michelangelo himself had provided a compositional sketch as early as 1516. It would seem that both paintings enter into a programmatic competition, confronting Raphael's and Michelangelo's artistic ideals, that is similar to that between the large altarpieces commissioned by Giulio de' Medici for the Cathedral of Narbonne, Sebastiano's *Resurrection of Lazarus* (London, National Gallery) and Raphael's *Transfiguration* (Rome, Pinacoteca Vaticana).

SEBASTIAN SCHÜTZE

ANDREA CONFUCCI,
CALLED **ANDREA SANSOVINO** C. 1467/70–1529
DESIGN FOR THE TOMB OF POPE LEO X
C. 1521?

Pen and brown ink and brown
wash
40 × 24.2 cm
Annotations: *GIOV. DOSIO*
Victoria and Albert Museum,
London

This sheet, along with two others by Andrea Sansovino and his shop, belonged in the eighteenth century to the British antiquarian and collector John Talman.[1] First published in 1934 by Middeldorf, the drawing has almost universally been identified as a tomb project for Pope Leo X, perhaps carried out during his lifetime or possibly afterwards, during the pontificate of his first cousin Pope Clement VII.[2] For reasons to be considered below, however, this understanding of the drawing's function is problematic. The drawing is annotated in the lower left corner, "GIOV. DOSIO," probably in Talman's hand.[3] Middeldorf attributed the sheet to the Tuscan sculptor and architect Andrea Sansovino, who designed a number of tombs in Tuscany and Rome in the later fifteenth and early sixteenth centuries and who worked at the church of Santa Maria in Domnica in Rome for Leo, and for both Medici popes at the Santa Casa in Loreto.[4]

The ambitious, multi-storey tomb drawn here – seemingly influenced by Michelangelo's early design for the tomb of Pope Julius II – consists of a high base, or *predella*, surmounted by a pedestal with fluted Doric pilasters and a Doric frieze with triglyphs and metopes.[5] The metopes carry alternating *bucrania* (ox-skulls) and *paterae* (shallow libation bowls). A recessed panel reserved for an inscription displays the first nine letters of the alphabet followed by "Leo / X." Beneath the inscribed panel are two *stemmi* (heraldic escutcheons) with cardinal's hats (the flat, brimmed *galero*) and *cordoni* (cords with tassels). The *stemmi* do not carry family signifiers that would help to identify either the deceased or the patron of the tomb. Above the pedestal is a stepped platform surmounted by a base supporting a classicizing claw-footed sarcophagus. This type of sarcophagus was popular in Renaissance tomb sculpture, with examples found in both Florence and Rome.[6] Above the sarcophagus is a recumbent effigy of the deceased, shown asleep, his head resting on his left arm. This is a motif introduced into Italian tomb sculpture by Andrea Sansovino himself, the origins and meaning of which have been debated.[7] Its first use was in Sansovino's own paired tombs of Cardinal Ascanio Sforza and Cardinal Girolamo Basso della Rovere in the Roman church of Santa Maria del Popolo, which were patronized by Julius II (fig. 24.1).[8] As in those tombs, the effigy in the London drawing wears a mitre and dalmatic and displays no papal insignia.

Standing on the *predella* here are female allegorical figures of Faith (with cross and chalice) and Fortitude (with column), and seated on the base of the stepped platform are Charity (shown with a flaming heart, but not with children, as was typical) and Hope. These figures are strongly *all'antica* in appearance and resemble some of the Virtues seen on the Sforza and Della Rovere tombs as well as in the preparatory drawings for them. In contrast to those tombs, the one delineated here does not use the triumphal arch format and tondo with the Madonna and Child found frequently in fifteenth-century tomb sculpture.[9] Its style, unlike that of the Santa Maria del Popolo tombs and the drawings associated with them, is decidedly characteristic of High Renaissance Rome, evoking the simple grandeur of the architecture of the Bramante-Raphael circle.

The identification of the tomb proposed in this drawing as Leo X's has rarely been questioned.[10] Closer examination, however, suggests otherwise. It would seem, in fact, that the only association with Leo is the presence of his name in the curious inscription. The effigy wears a mitre rather than the papal tiara, and while popes are indeed the bishops of Rome, papal effigies in Renaissance tombs were nearly always shown wearing the *triregnum* as a signifier of their exalted office.[11] Mitres, on the other hand, were generally worn by effigies representing either bishops (including archbishops) or cardinals. Furthermore, the escutcheons seen on the pedestal are clearly those of a cardinal, not a pontiff. While on rare occasions cardinals' *stemmi* could indicate a cardinal's patronage of a papal tomb (the tombs of popes Sixtus IV in Saint Peter's and Adrian VI in Santa Maria dell'Anima come to mind), the vast majority of Roman tombs with such heraldic devices were for deceased members of the Sacred College.[12] Such is the case with Sansovino's own Sforza and Basso della Rovere tombs in Santa Maria del Popolo (and drawings associated with them, such as fig. 24.2), where the cardinals' escutcheons indicate the station of those buried in the tombs and the papal *stemmi* of Julius II indicate the patronage of the monuments. Thus the present drawing, as noted by Blunt, was probably not intended to have been a tomb project for Leo X, despite the long tradition associating it with him.[13] It is more likely that the present design was for the tomb of a cardinal who had been prominent in the Leonine Curia. It is, in fact, possible that the drawing reflects Leo's own commission for a tomb to commemorate such a cardinal who died during his pontificate.[14] A more remote possibility is that this was a cardinal's commission for Leo's tomb, with the *stemmi* identifying the patron – the cardinal in question probably being Giulio de' Medici, the future Pope Clement VII. Yet this scenario still seems unlikely, given the lack of papal insignia.

The eventual burial of the Medici popes Leo X and Clement VII in the choir of the Dominican church of Santa Maria sopra Minerva in Rome in 1542 was the final step in a long process that involved many artists and architects (among them Michelangelo, Antonio da Sangallo (see cat. 41), Baccio Bandinelli (see cat. 42), Raffaello da Montelupo, and Nanni di Baccio Bigio) and several possible locations, including Santa Maria Maggiore in Rome, the choir and the New Sacristy of San Lorenzo in Florence, and, eventually, the Minerva.[15]

SHERYL E. REISS

Fig. 24.1 Andrea Sansovino, *Tomb of Cardinal Ascanio Sforza*, c. 1505– 1507?, marble. Santa Maria del Popolo, Rome

Fig. 24.2 Andrea Sansovino, *Design for a Cardinal's Tomb*, c. 1505, pen and ink with wash, 37.1 × 25.1 cm. Victoria and Albert Museum, London

25

PIERO BUONACCORSI,
CALLED **PERINO DEL VAGA** 1501–1547
STUDY FOR A WALL DECORATION C. 1522

Pen and brown ink, brush with
brown wash over underdrawing
in black chalk
40.9 × 26.8 cm
The J. Paul Getty Museum,
Los Angeles

This sheet is a design for the left-hand wall of the Cappella della Passione, Santa Maria della Pietà in Campo Santo Teutonico, a small church within Vatican City. With its complete articulation of the architecture and relatively high level of detail in the description of the scenes, it was likely intended for the consideration of the work's patron, Kaspar Roïst, a commander of the Pontifical Swiss Guard. Roïst's coat of arms was featured in a large roundel above the principal scene of the Crucifixion in the finished fresco, which also included a full-length portrait of him standing to the right of the cross. The chapel's use was allocated to the Swiss Guard in a contract dated 14 May 1520.[1] In the drawing, three papal coats of arms are included in the window embrasure: those of Leo X (left), Julius II (right), and Adrian VI (centre). These seem to have been repeated in the fresco, and it is likely that the chapel was decorated during the brief pontificate of Adrian VI, following the design in the drawing. Over time, the frescoes were badly damaged by damp. In 1912 they were removed (with the exception of the lunette scenes), transferred to canvas, and hung on the wall as paintings.

Although the frescoes were painted in accord with the arrangement in this drawing, many of the individual scenes were modified, which proves that it is not a copy of the frescoes. When it was in the Gathorne-Hardy collection, the drawing had a surprising attribution to Dosso Dossi, but Philip Pouncey established the link with the Vatican frescoes and recognized the sheet as the work of Perino del Vaga, an attribution that is now universally accepted. The design of the wall is carefully conceived, with the figures in the lunette Adoration – high up and less easily visible against the light of the window – considerably larger than the others. This composition is also inventively handled, in contrast to the scenes of the Passion, which broadly follow prototypes found in Dürer prints. The two arriving Magi on the left side of the lunette, conversing animatedly next to a rearing horse, provide a link across the window space to the Magus kneeling in front of the Holy Family. At the base of the wall design, black chalk has been used to project unidentifiable scenes in the bas-relief area.

While the drawing has been convincingly attributed to Perino, the identity of the painter of the frescoes remains a matter of conjecture.[2] Their poor condition makes an attribution difficult to ascertain, but it appears that the quality of execution is not high. It has generally been surmised that Perino designed the wall decorations, but that since he left Rome for Florence as the result of a plague in the spring of 1522, he could not have worked much, if at all, on the actual frescoes. Another name that has often been associated with these works is that of Polidoro da Caravaggio, although it has been pointed out that the earliest reference to his authorship (by Giulio Mancini, in the early 1600s) was in fact a refutation of it.[3] Recent scholarship has tended to see Polidoro's hand in the scenes of the Agony in the Garden and of Christ before Pilate, and perhaps also others.[4] Polidoro himself evidently fled from the plague to Naples well before March 1524, when he was recorded as having been in that city for some time. His involvement, or that of his studio, seems likely from a number of Polidoresque elements in the compositions, but the extremely lifeless handling of the Crucifixion speaks against his participation there. It should also be noted that the exciting composition of the Adoration of the Magi seen in the Getty drawing is toned down greatly in the fresco; the dramatic rearing horse in the lunette, for example, becomes a horse simply walking away from the viewer.

Kaspar Roïst, the patron of the frescoes, did not meet a happy end. In a dispute over the provision of the Guard in January 1527, he and some of his fellow soldiers were ordered to return home to Switzerland. Roïst refused, pledging to honour unto death his oath of service to the pope. Only months later, in May, Rome was sacked by the troops of the Emperor Charles V. Roïst valiantly defended Clement VII, who escaped to the Castel Sant'Angelo, but the captain was wounded, taken by troops in front of his wife, and executed.

JULIAN BROOKS

PIERO BUONACCORSI,
CALLED **PERINO DEL VAGA** 1501–1547
THE JUDGMENT OF ZALEUCUS c. 1520–1522

Detached fresco, transferred to canvas
148 × 197 cm
Galleria degli Uffizi, Florence

The sixteenth-century humanist and poet Pietro Bembo praised the Palazzo Baldassini as "the most beautiful and best made in all Rome."[1] Designed by Antonio da Sangallo the Younger, it was built for Melchiorre Baldassini (c. 1470–1525), a distinguished lawyer and professor of civil law at the Sapienza, and consistorial advocate during the pontificates of Leo X and Adrian VI. Its interior decoration, undocumented but almost certainly executed between 1520 and 1522,[2] was carried out by three former *garzoni* of Raphael – Perino del Vaga, Giovanni da Udine, and Polidoro da Caravaggio,[3] although only the most important frescoes, those in the main *salone*, by Perino (which survive in a diminished and fragmentary state), are expressly mentioned by Vasari.[4] His failure to note the existence of painted decoration in other parts of the palace's interior – the *all'antica* grotesque vault on the *piano terreno*, which most scholars assign to Giovanni da Udine, and the *stufetta* and a contiguous room with a decorative frieze on the *piano nobile* – or to mention with any specificity Polidoro da Caravaggio's narratives in the room adjoining the *salone* (see cat. 27), suggests that those private rooms, unlike the semi-public *salone*, were not accessible in the mid-sixteenth century. Writing in the late Cinquecento, the painter and theorist Giovanni Battista Armenini likewise discusses only Perino's frescoes in the *salone*.[5]

Both Vasari and Armenini recorded the existence in the *salone* of a historiated frieze illustrating scenes of ancient Roman history from Romulus to Numa Pompilius, a component of the once-splendid decorative program that is no longer visible. Two of Perino's narratives from the frieze (neither expressly cited in the inexact descriptions of the subject matter offered by Vasari and Armenini), this *Judgment of Zaleucus* and another of *Tarquinius Priscus and the Augur Attius Navius*, were removed in the nineteenth century, while remaining fragments are preserved *in situ* in what is now a mezzanine-level apartment.[6] Livy's *Ab urbe condita* provided the literary source for at least three of these scenes (Romulus, Numa, Tarquinius Priscus), but the *storia* of Zaleucus of Locri Epizephyrii, author of

the first written law code of the Greeks, is taken from the influential *Factorum et dictorum memorabilium*, by the first-century Roman historian and rhetorician Valerius Maximus. (Zaleucus is also mentioned in the historian Plutarch's *Moralia*, and in his life of Numa Pompilius.)

The code of Zaleucus prescribed blinding as punishment for the crime of adultery. When his own son was convicted of that transgression, Zaleucus ordered that only one of the offender's eyes be put out and one of his own. By upholding the law while still leaving the perpetrator with partial sight, he achieved a praiseworthy balance of justice and mercy. (Encoded in this narrative, that theme was symbolically illustrated in the pair of caryatids holding a rose and sword in one of the overdoors.)[7] The grisly subject of Perino's fresco – cited by Valerius Maximus as a notable "exemplum justitiae"[8] – was earlier portrayed by Raphael's workshop in one of the window embrasures of the Justice wall in the Stanza della Segnatura as a paradigm of the fair and just application of the law, the meaning it undoubtedly also communicated in the *salone* of the jurist Melchiorre Baldassini.[9]

In his account of the Palazzo Baldassini *salone* frescoes, Vasari remarks that the patron wished to determine who was the best of the young artists in Rome before awarding the commission to embellish the interior of his newly erected palace.[10] After much deliberation, he chose Perino del Vaga, who would go on to become the preeminent mural painter in the city in the 1520s. The Palazzo Baldassini frescoes, which were among his first independent works, reveal Perino's debt to the example of Raphael.[11] The *Acts of the Apostles* tapestry cartoons, particularly the *Blinding of Elymus*, appear to have been foremost in his mind when composing the *Judgment of Zaleucus*: the composition essentially reprises that model in reverse, and individual figures such as the muscular agent who blinds Zaleucus's son and the kneeling man at the lower left who gestures rhetorically toward this brutal act of retribution recall similarly posed and placed (if reversed) figures in the tapestry design.

LINDA WOLK-SIMON

27
POLIDORO CALDARA,
CALLED **POLIDORO DA CARAVAGGIO**
C. 1499–1543
A DEATHBED SCENE (RECTO);
SEATED WOMAN (VERSO) C. 1521–1522

Red chalk
21 × 29 cm
The National Gallery of Art,
Washington

27 (recto)

27 (verso)

Vasari's *Life* of Polidoro da Caravaggio offers a laconic mention of "graffiti e storie" by the artist and his shadowy collaborator and companion, Maturino da Firenze, in the Palazzo Baldassini in Rome.[1] Designed by Antonio da Sangallo the Younger and completed around 1519 or 1520, this handsome palace on the Via delle Coppelle was built for Melchiorre Baldassini, a professor of civil law and a prominent lawyer attached to the Roman Curia during the pontificates of Leo X and his short-lived successor, Adrian VI. The grand *salone* was embellished with frescoes (now in ruinous condition) by Perino del Vaga illustrating the sacral origins of Roman law[2] (see cat. 26), while the diminutive narrative scenes in a frieze in an adjacent room, probably the patron's *studiolo*, are presumably to be identified with the *storie* by Polidoro mentioned by Vasari. His authorship of these undocumented and otherwise unrecorded frescoes has long been posited on stylistic grounds, and is corroborated by this engaging red chalk study by him for one of the compositions (fig. 27.1), which displays the broad hatching and angular contours characteristic of his early graphic style. Recorded in the first half of the nineteenth century in the celebrated collections of Sir Thomas Lawrence and Samuel Woodburn, the drawing disappeared for roughly a century, resurfacing at auction in 1963.

The obscure subject matter of Polidoro's Palazzo Baldassini narratives has not been identified, but they appear to represent scenes from ancient history relating to the origins and implementation of Roman law, beginning with the bringing of the Code of Solon from Greece – a task entrusted to a committee of three *decemviri* – its introduction to Rome, and the compilation of the Twelve Tables, the law code of the Republic.[3] This course of events is described by the Roman historian Livy in the *Ab urbe condita*, the same literary source culled for parts of Perino del Vaga's decoration in the adjoining *salone*.[4] Other subjects include an orator (perhaps the jurist and rhetorician Cato); a trial; students studying law outside a basilica (scene of juridical proceedings in ancient Rome); and the deathbed scene depicted in the present drawing.

The suggestion that this enigmatic tableau may represent the death of Socrates is uncompelling, given the absence in both the drawing and the corresponding fresco of the telltale hemlock, not to mention the irrelevance of that subject to a decorative program that takes up as its theme justice and the law (obvious allusions to the profession of the patron). Another interpretation – that the fresco depicts Alexander the Great and his physician – may be refuted on similar grounds.[5] An alternative conjecture advanced here is that the scene represents the Testament of Eudamidas. This antique tale of friendship and moral virtue is told by the second-century satirical author and rhetorician Lucian (who enjoyed a heightened popularity following the publication of some of his works in Florence in 1499) in his *Toxaris: A Dialogue of Friendship*. Though rare, the subject was represented by Poussin in the seventeenth century and by Mengs in the eighteenth century.[6] In Poussin's treatment of the theme, which includes grieving family members and a loyal friend (perhaps the same cast of onlookers present here), singular prominence is accorded the notary or lawyer who dutifully sits at the bedside of the dying Eudamidas and records his last wishes; conceivably, this is the man with the writing tablet at the right of Polidoro's drawing (although the corresponding figure in the fresco lacks this implement). Such a subject would surely have appealed to Melchiorre Baldassini, both as an exemplum of moral rectitude and as a classical model or antetype for the practice of his profession.

The seated woman holding a cloth on the verso of the sheet has not been connected with a known painting or commission, but figures of this type frequently appear as maidservants or female attendants in representations of the birth of the Virgin, warming or drying a swaddling cloth before a fire. Polidoro's early drawings – most executed, like this sheet, in red chalk – reflect his proclivity for genre subjects and humble scenes from everyday life.[7] While the verso may be an idea for a painting or fresco, it is equally possible that, like his depictions of card players and school mistresses, this charming study is a record of his abiding interest in quotidian subjects, executed as an independent exercise.

LINDA WOLK-SIMON

ATTRIBUTED TO PERINO DEL VAGA 1501–1547
ST. JULIAN HOSPITALLER (?) C. 1520–1525

Tempera grassa on panel
127 × 80 cm
Inscriptions: *M Iacomo . F. F*
Galleria Colonna, Rome
The restoration of this painting
was made possible with the gener-
ous support of Alenia North
America, a Finmeccanica Company

This little known and puzzling work is thought to represent
Saint Julian Hospitaller. It was first attributed to Perino del
Vaga, with some reservations, by Federico Zeri. The problematic nature of that attribution is reflected in the fact
that the principal comparison adduced to support it, an
image of the *Redeemer* in the parish church of Rocca di
Papa, outside Rome, is not accepted as the work of Perino.
Further complicating the question of the panel's authorship
is its condition: a vertical split runs down the centre, where
part of the face has been repainted, and there are areas of
loss and of repainting in the standing saint's right foot and
right hand. Much of the inscription has also been repainted.
Other passages, however, are better preserved, notably the
strikingly naturalistic falcon, who sports a red ribbon
around his claws, and the saint's right thumb. A *pentimento*
reveals that the tip of the sword was originally painted
further to the left.

Interpreting the inscription on the *cartellino* at the
saint's feet as a reference to the patron rather than a signature of the unidentified artist (improbably identified by
Corti, on the basis of the same inscription, as the unknown
Pier Francesco di Sandro), Safarik conjectured that the
panel may have been commissioned by a "Maestro Iacomo,"
whom he proposed to identify with Jacopo da Carpi, physician to the powerful Cardinal Pompeo Colonna.[1] (After
recovering from an illness as a result of his ministrations,
the grateful cardinal gave Jacopo da Carpi a painting of
Saint John the Baptist in a Landscape by Raphael's workshop.[2]) While this hypothesis has a certain appeal, insofar
as it might account for the presence of the painting in the
Colonna collection by establishing a connection with the
purported original patron, it is highly speculative.

Although the figure represented here has long been
regarded as Saint Julian (San Giuliano), a subject treated
earlier, most notably, by Andrea del Castagno and Piero
della Francesca,[3] that interpretation, like much else that has
been posited about this enigmatic work, cannot be accepted
uncritically. While a sword is Saint Julian's conventional
attribute – it was with this weapon that he inadvertently
murdered his parents – he is seldom represented with a fal-

con. If this prominent detail cautions against the identification of the figure as Saint Julian, it is a clue to a possible alternative: the single saint whose attributes are invariably both a sword and a falcon is Bavo (also known as Allowin, his baptismal name, and as Bavon, or Bavone in Italian), who was venerated in parts of the Netherlands, particularly Ghent and Haarlem. Perhaps this is the saint represented in the Colonna panel. Although the subject is rare in Italian art, it is not difficult to imagine that such an image could have been commissioned by one of the many Northerners resident in Rome during the papacy of the Dutch pontiff Adrian VI.

If its subject has perhaps been clarified, the date and attribution of this enigmatic panel remain open to debate. The facial type and the gentle contrapposto of the figure's pose recall the standing Virtues in the Sala Paolina in the Castel Sant'Angelo, designed by Perino del Vaga and executed by his assistants between 1545 and 1547 (see cat. 50), but the comparatively more wooden and hieratic conception and the nondescript, airless setting invest the image with an archaizing character that those graceful inventions lack. Rather than being contemporary with the Sala Paolina frescoes, this conservative and conventional depiction of a hagiographic subject is in fact more likely to have been painted two or three decades earlier, in the late 1510s or the 1520s, thus making it roughly contemporary with Perino's frescoes in the Pucci Chapel, the Palazzo Baldassini (see cat. 26), and Santo Stefano del Cacco. The ruinous condition of most of those works inhibits meaningful stylistic comparisons, but there do exist certain morphological similarities to the seated Virtues in the Faith and Hope lunette in the Pucci Chapel, which hark back to the manner of Perino's Florentine master, Ridolfo Ghirlandaio.[4] The analogy is admittedly tenuous, however. At present, an attribution to Perino del Vaga can be advanced only tentatively and with caution.

LINDA WOLK-SIMON

GIOVANNI FRANCESCO PENNI,
CALLED IL FATTORE c. 1496–c. 1528
PORTRAIT OF A YOUNG MAN c. 1520–1527

Oil on panel
52 × 41 cm
Inscriptions : *G. Franc./Penni*
National Gallery of Ireland, Dublin

Curiously, few portraits painted by Raphael's students between the premature death of their master, on 6 April 1520, and the Sack of Rome, in 1527, have survived. No evidence remains of portraits painted by Giulio Romano in Rome after Raphael's death, even though Giulio excelled in this genre, as evidence by his *Portrait of Margherita Paleologo,* executed in Mantua in 1531 (English Royal Collection). The only artist from Raphael's studio who left portraits made during this period is the Florentine Giovanni Francesco Penni, known as "il Fattore." Two portraits bear his signature: the painting at the National Gallery of Dublin, and a lost portrait that was once in the gallery of Lucien Bonaparte (fig. 29.1).[1] Both works, though influenced by Raphael's prototypes, had a distinctly Florentine flavour. Because they resemble portraits painted in the same period by Ridolfo del Ghirlandaio, Franciabigio, Domenico Puligo, and the young Pontormo, the Dublin portrait has been regarded as being related to this school.[2] Little is known about Penni's pictorial style after Raphael's death and so other hypotheses of attribution may be suggested for the Dublin portrait, which has led to the suggestion that the inscription gives the name of the person portrayed rather than that of the painting's maker.[3] Nevertheless, a comparison with Giulio Romano's drawing (London, The British Museum)[4] of Giovanni Francesco Penni reveals that it cannot be the same person: the likeness of the subject's robust face is in clear contrast to the fine features of the model in the Dublin portrait. Furthermore, the large, legible writing on the sheet of paper looks more like a signature than a salutation, which suggests that the work is by Penni's hand. This seems to be confirmed by a stylistic comparison between this portrait and the only documented work by Penni dating from this period: the lower part of the Monteluce altarpiece (Vatican City, Pinacoteca Vaticana), made on a drawing by Raphael (cat. 17) after the master's death.

The model for the Dublin portrait has also been identified, erroneously, as Andrea Turini, physician to Pope Leo X.[5] Although Turini's physical features are not known, the young man portrayed cannot be a member of this family from Pescia as the crests on his ring do not bear any resemblance to the assurgent greyhound, the family's emblem, that can be seen on the funerary monument of his brother, Baldassarre Turini, in the cathedral in Pescia. The small book by Petrarch associated with the gold chain that the model is wearing – a mark of pontifical recognition often granted to humanists, men of letters, and artists – suggests that the person portrayed belonged to Pope

Fig. 29.1 Testa in the style of Giovanni Francesco Penni, *Portrait of a Man,* etching. In *Choix de gravures à l'eau forte...* (London, 1812)

Fig. 29.2 Giovanni Francesco Penni
(attrib.), *Portrait of an Artist,*
oil on wood, 57.8 × 44.4 cm. Kress
Collection, Hunter College,
New York

Clement VII's cultivated entourage. The painting was likely executed before Penni left Rome, around 1527.[6] This is the only known work signed by Giovanni Francesco Penni, and remains, in this author's opinion, the only basis for any attribution of portraits to this painter.

It is interesting to bring up in this regard the case of the *Portrait of an Artist* at Hunter College in New York (fig. 29.2), a work that has not drawn much critical attention, attributed in the past to Franciabigio.[7] Despite general wear of the pictorial layer and overpaintings (on the background, in particular), the work presents certain stylistic characteristics similar to those in the Dublin portrait, for example, in the modelling of the face, the drawing of the eyes, and the way the collar and cuffs of the shirt are painted. Of course, it cannot be a portrait of Giovanni Francesco Penni; the portrait of him executed by Giulio Romano does not present the aquiline nose that characterizes the face of the young man in the New York painting. In the years preceding the Sack of Rome, Penni spent time with his Florentine compatriots, as noted in a passage in Cellini's autobiography, in which the goldsmith recalls that he had eaten with Rosso, Penni, and other artists one Saint John's Day,[8] and Penni may have portrayed one of them in the painting. It seems to be the first portrait of an artist that Penni painted in Italy in which the model is clearly represented with his working tools. Although the identification of the artist of and model for this portrait remain problematic, it was definitely produced within the Roman milieu that precedes the sack of the city in 1527.

These portraits have the refinement that characterizes the works executed during the early reign of Pope Clement VII. They do not, however, have a place in the evolution of the genre in the service of the courts, in which the models, following the example of the *Portrait of Isabel de Requesens* painted by Raphael and Giulio Romano (Paris, Musée du Louvre), are presented in a palace setting. This mode of portrayal, which enabled "Clementine" artists to better render the licentious and elegant atmosphere that prevailed in Rome before the city was sacked, was taken up by Giulio Romano, of course (*Lady at the Mirror* – portrait or allegory? – Moscow, Pushkin Museum), as well as by Rosso Fiorentino (*Portrait of a Young Man*, Naples, Museo Nazionale di Capodimonte) and Parmigianino (*Portrait of a Young Man*, The Royal Collection, Hampton Court). The models for the paintings in Dublin and New York did not belong to the Roman aristocracy and could not be portrayed as such; thus, the artist opted for a more austere presentation that was more appropriate for a figure from the bourgeoisie. They nevertheless reflect the relationships maintained between artists and intellectuals in the Rome of the Medici popes.

PHILIPPE COSTAMAGNA

GIULIO DE' MEDICI

CLEMENT VII 1523–1534

30
POLIDORO CALDARA,
CALLED **POLIDORO DA CARAVAGGIO**

c. 1499–c. 1543
*PRISONER BROUGHT BEFORE A JUDGE
(CONDEMNATION OF PERILLUS?)* early 1520s

Pen and brown ink, brown wash,
heightened with white gouache,
over black chalk, on light brown
paper
16.5 × 23.2 cm
Inscriptions: *Polidoro da Caravaggio*;
*Crozat, De Tessin, Queen of Sweden
(Ulrica), Count de Steenbock, Count
de Barck*.
Morgan Library & Museum,
New York

Fig. 30.1a After Polidoro da
Caravaggio, *Death of Perillus*,
1516–1556, pen and brown ink,
29.4 × 19.6 cm. The British
Museum, London

Fig. 30.1b After Polidoro da
Caravaggio, *Prisoner before a
Judge*, 1516–1556, pen and brown
ink, 29.4 × 19.6 cm. The British
Museum, London

In the years before the Sack of Rome in 1527, Polidoro was one of the city's most prolific facade decorators. Most common were grisaille frescoes with scenes and heroes from antiquity, friezes of putti or vegetal motifs, and details, in imitation of antique reliefs. Nearly all such work, including Polidoro's efforts, has been lost, worn over time by the elements.

One of the few works that may be associated with a facade decoration, the Morgan study is thought to relate to a facade on the via dei Coronari, Rome, that once depicted the story of Perillus.[1] According to Ovid, the inventor Perillus devised for his master Phalaris, tyrant of Sicily, an instrument of torture consisting of a hollow, life-size bronze bull, large enough to contain a person, who would then bellow like an animal in distress when the metal was heated red hot. In a surprising and especially cruel turn of events, Phalaris commanded that Perillus should be its first victim.[2]

The critical scene showing Perillus being forced to enter the bronze bull is preserved in two engravings[3] and a partial drawn copy in the British Museum attributed to a follower of Girolamo da Carpi (fig. 30.1a),[4] all thought to have been made after the completed fresco. Vasari's brief description of the facade suggests that there may have been a second image to the programme, that of the tyrant Phalaris commanding the death of Perillus:

> In the road that leads to the Imagine di Ponte, there is a most beautiful façade with the story of Perillus, showing him being placed in the bronze bull that he had made; wherein great effort may be seen in those who are thrusting him into that bull, and terror in those who are waiting to behold a death so unexampled, besides which there is the seated figure of Phalaris (so I believe), ordaining an imperious air of great beauty the punishment of the inhuman spirit that had invented a device so novel and so cruel in order to put men to death with greater suffering.[5]

And indeed, when turned over, the British Museum sheet reveals a prisoner before an enthroned potentate (fig. 30.1b), a detail corresponding exactly to the left third of the Morgan drawing, thereby strongly suggesting that both scenes – the *Death of Perillus* and *Prisoner Before a Judge* – once belonged to the identical via dei Coronari facade. If indeed linked with the programme, as seems highly likely, the Morgan scene surely represents *The Condemnation of Perillus*.

A relationship of the Morgan drawing to an extant chiaroscuro fresco by Polidoro, formerly on the facade of a house on Piazza Madama and now in Palazzo Barberini, has also been postulated.[6] The fresco shows a similar composition with barbarian prisoners brought before a seated ruler, who, however, sits in profile to the left, instead of almost frontally as in the present example. The Morgan study includes a single prisoner, in similar "barbarian" dress as his captors, whereas the fresco makes a clear distinction between the Roman soldiers – in armour – and their captives, who wear leggings and Phrygian caps typical of how

barbarians (in effect all non-Romans) were represented during Roman times and the Renaissance. In short, the subject is unlikely to be that of the Morgan composition.

The Morgan sheet has been dated to 1522–1523 on stylistic grounds.[7] The shallow pictorial space and dense packing of the figures clearly reveal the artist's familiarity with antique reliefs such as appear on the Arch of Constantine, Polidoro's scene, however, possesses greater drama than many of its antique predecessors.

RHODA EITEL-PORTER

31
POLIDORO CALDARA,
CALLED **POLIDORO DA CARAVAGGIO**

c. 1499–c. 1543
A CAVALRY BATTLE c. 1524–1526

Red chalk
20.2 × 28.4 cm
Inscriptions: *d'mà Propria d'Raffaiel.*
d' Vr^no / C. 3. [verso]
Agnes Etherington Art Centre,
Queen's University, Kingston

Although this drawing bears an old attribution on the verso to Raphael, it is a good example of the red-chalk drawings by his pupil Polidoro da Caravaggio, as Noël Annesley was the first to point out.[1]

Born in Lombardy south of Bergamo in Northern Italy, Polidoro moved to Rome about 1515 and entered Raphael's workshop. There, he joined Giulio Romano and Perino del Vaga, both about his age, and the older Giovanni da Udine, in the decoration of the Vatican Logge. Pope Leo X had awarded the commission for the Logge to Raphael, who directed the overall operation while members of his workshop executed individual frescoes, the grotesques and stuccoes. For Polidoro, the way that antique grotesques had influenced the Logge's decoration must have been highly revealing, because he would himself go on to use Roman antiquity – especially Roman relief sculpture – as a major inspiration for his own paintings of the 1520s.

Polidoro adopted red chalk as his preferred medium, and although he also employed pen and wash with striking originality, he extended the use of red chalk to the delineation of an astonishing variety of subjects. Raphael had regularly employed red chalk in his later years, also with unprecedented vigour and suppleness, and Polidoro clearly observed and then assimilated the widespread practices of his master. No doubt, such drawings as Raphael's red-chalk figure studies for *Christ's Charge to Peter* (1515–1516) for the Sistine Chapel tapestries would have appealed enormously to Polidoro.[2] It should also be admitted, at least hypothetically, that Polidoro may have been predisposed to the medium from having already seen Lombard red-chalk drawings, such as those by Romanino.

The actual cavalry engagement shown in the Kingston drawing is difficult to identify, given the lack of specific detail. Clashes of rearing horses, with snarling riders and infantry trodden underfoot, appeared frequently in early sixteenth-century art, and Polidoro would have known many of them well. In Florence, the pre-eminent example was Leonardo da Vinci's uncompleted *Battle of Anghiari,* whereas in Rome numerous ancient reliefs provided classical precedents for contemporary commissions. Raphael's workshop had depicted battles in the Vatican Logge – in such a scene as *Joshua Stopping the Sun* – and more conspicuously in the Sala di Costantino, where Giulio Romano and Giovanni Francesco Penni painted the *Battle of the Milvian Bridge* between 1520 and 1524. The subject remained popular among Raphael's pupils and numerous variations on the theme exist, including a drawing in Weimar by Perino del Vaga (fig. 31.1).[3] Gere has also noted the similarities with an engraving by Marco da Ravenna of a Cavalry Skirmish after Raphael.[4]

Polidoro's pre-eminent contribution to Roman painting was the many frescoes he painted on the external facades of buildings throughout the city. These frescoes usually showed episodes from ancient Roman history or classical mythology, and were painted monochromatically to simulate classical sculpture. Because they were entirely accessible – and because they teemed with imaginative detail – they were copied incessantly. Prey to the elements, however, they have almost entirely perished. The Kingston drawing, which has been dated to about 1524 to 1526 by Pierluigi Leone de Castris,[5] could well have been intended for one of these facade decorations, but no specific site has ever been identified.

In light of the subject of this drawing, it is revealing that Gian Paolo Lomazzo – the sixteenth-century Lombard artist and writer who associated the major Renaissance artists with the rule of classical deities – placed Polidoro with Mars, the god of war.[6]

DAVID MCTAVISH

Fig. 31.1 Perino del Vaga, *A Cavalry Battle*, c. 1520, pen and brown ink and brown wash, with white heightening, on paper (attached to another sheet at top), 35.6 × 27.9 cm. Goethe-Nationalmuseum, Weimar

32
POLIDORO CALDARA,
CALLED **POLIDORO DA CARAVAGGIO**
c. 1499–c. 1543
BETRAYAL OF CHRIST c. 1524–1525

Pen and brown ink, brown and
grey washes, with white heightening on blue prepared paper
21.2 × 26.3 cm
Annotations: *Benevenuto Garofalo*
The Royal Collection

The Windsor drawing presumably served as the *modello* – the final sketch made in preparation for the glass, as it so finished and complete. Drawings of this elaborate type on blue prepared paper often did serve as demonstration pieces. Not surprisingly, however, given the inherent intricacy of carving on crystal, the finished work is more simplified and restrained in style. Formerly attributed to the Ferrarese artist Garofalo, and once owned by the accomplished British watercolourist Paul Sandby, who even allowed it to be turned into a print, Antal's inspired attribution to Polidoro in 1949 can be easily defended on stylistic grounds, though it has not always been accepted. Yet it is an example of Polidoro's richest and most elaborate graphic technique.

The vivacious, rather suffocating and staccato design peopled with aggressive, muscular figures is entirely typical of the artist. The closed-off background and use of a ledge for the figures can be paralleled with numerous examples of Polidoro's facade frescoes in Rome. For dramatic intent typical of his sensibility, the artist placed the figure of Christ, who blesses his betrayer Judas, just off the central axis. The handling of the white gouache in thin, ragged lines is distinctive of the artist, as are the rather stumpy figures with dishevelled hair and triangular faces. Notable also are the internal light sources indicating that it is a night scene and also help account for the reliance on a darkly prepared paper. A predilection for night scenes became increasingly prevalent among Polidoro's contemporaries in Rome in this period – it was a virtual artistic topos at the time – and this example specifically recalls Raphael's experiments in parts of the Vatican Stanze, such as the *Liberation of Saint Peter*. The youthful figure looking out of the design towards the viewer at the far right edge could also be a quotation from Raphael. Given that this was a papal commission, the dependence in places on Raphael, an artist who worked so successfully in the Vatican, may have served a symbolic purpose pleasing to the patron, as much as an artistic need.

DAVID FRANKLIN

161

Fig. 32.1 Valerio Belli, *Betrayal of Christ*, 1524–1525, carved crystal gilt with silver, 11.5 × 12.5 cm (oval). Museo Sacro, Biblioteca Apostolica Vaticana, Rome

Polidoro da Caravaggio was among the most talented, if unorthodox followers of Raphael, for his uncompromisingly severe, dramatic style rooted deeply in ancient art. His best-known works were the many external facade frescoes he produced in Rome in collaboration with an enigmatic Florentine painter known simply as Maturino, now mostly destroyed but recorded in numerous copies. Polidoro, prior to the Sack of 1527 that precipitated his departure from Rome for the south of Italy, appears to have provided designs of the Passion of Christ for three ovals executed in crystal (and signed) by the specialist glass engraver Valerio Belli from Vicenza. Belli's works survive in the collections of the Vatican (fig. 32.1). It has been reasonably assumed that these engraved crystal intaglios were executed as part of the base of a separate glass crucifix ordered by Pope Clement VII, and described by Vasari as a "croce di cristallo divina."[1] Records of payments to Belli survive for this object from 1524–1525, and so the date of the drawing is secure.[2] The crystal ovals also served as models for bronze replicas. Only this preparatory sketch by Polidoro – representing the entire composition of the Betrayal and Arrest of Christ – survives for the commission, but it is one of the most spectacular drawings he ever made.

Red chalk
31.5 × 17.8 cm
Annotations: *Chechino Salviati*
National Gallery of Scotland,
Edinburgh

Formerly ascribed to Francesco Salviati to judge by the annotation on the recto, the correct attribution of this red chalk drawing to Rosso was first made by Hirst, prior to its acquisition by the National Gallery of Scotland in 1962. Hirst, who first published the work in 1964, also noted the drawing's relation to the seated figure of Eve in the *Fall of Man* lunette in the chapel of Angelo Cesi in Santa Maria della Pace, Rome, and pointed out that this remains the only surviving autograph Rosso drawing – not only for this project, but for any fresco, Italian or French.[1] This was the first and only public commission Rosso received in Rome and it ended in failure as the project, which had only been subcontracted to him, was rescinded following the completion of this lunette.[2]

Because of the poor condition of the surviving fresco (fig. 33.1), which is inscribed 1524, the study presents a better idea of the original appearance of Rosso's figure than does the painting itself. At this stage in the design process, Rosso was not especially interested in describing the surface anatomy. Indeed, the drawing was certainly not made from a life model. More important to him were the description of active contour lines and the dramatic effect of the raking light on the angled body. Typically, for a Florentine draughtsman, the contours are more firmly drawn than any of the hatching lines, with only the slightest of pentimenti in the left leg and right arm that bring greater amplitude to the form. The rather tremulous contour effectively transmits, as much as the facial expression, the agitated, disquieted emotion of this nude stretching upwards.

The Edinburgh study is also unique among Rosso's surviving drawings as it shows the artist evolving a pose at a stage when the basic composition was established. The main figure is drawn over a lightly indicated red chalk sketch of the profile of the upper right torso and arm with the hand turned inwards on the left part of the sheet. Rosso settled on the more relatively relaxed of the two poses in the final fresco – that is, the figure in the more finished sketch. The drawing in the bottom corner appears to be a study for the right hand of Adam. The thumb is not fully drawn because it was to be hidden in the fresco by the branch of the tree of Original Sin grasped by Adam who seems almost to attempt to prevent Eve from grasping the apple offered by the serpent in the Cesi fresco.

Given Rosso's apparent antagonism to the styles of both Raphael and Michelangelo, it is safe to say that the Edinburgh nude represents his own statement about what he could contribute to art in Rome in this period following the election of the Medici Pope Clement VII. The drawing was made in what was an exceedingly hopeful period for many artists, who dreamed of a return to the glories of the papacy of Leo X – a dream destined to remain unfulfilled amidst the constant economic and military problems that doomed this papacy.

DAVID FRANKLIN

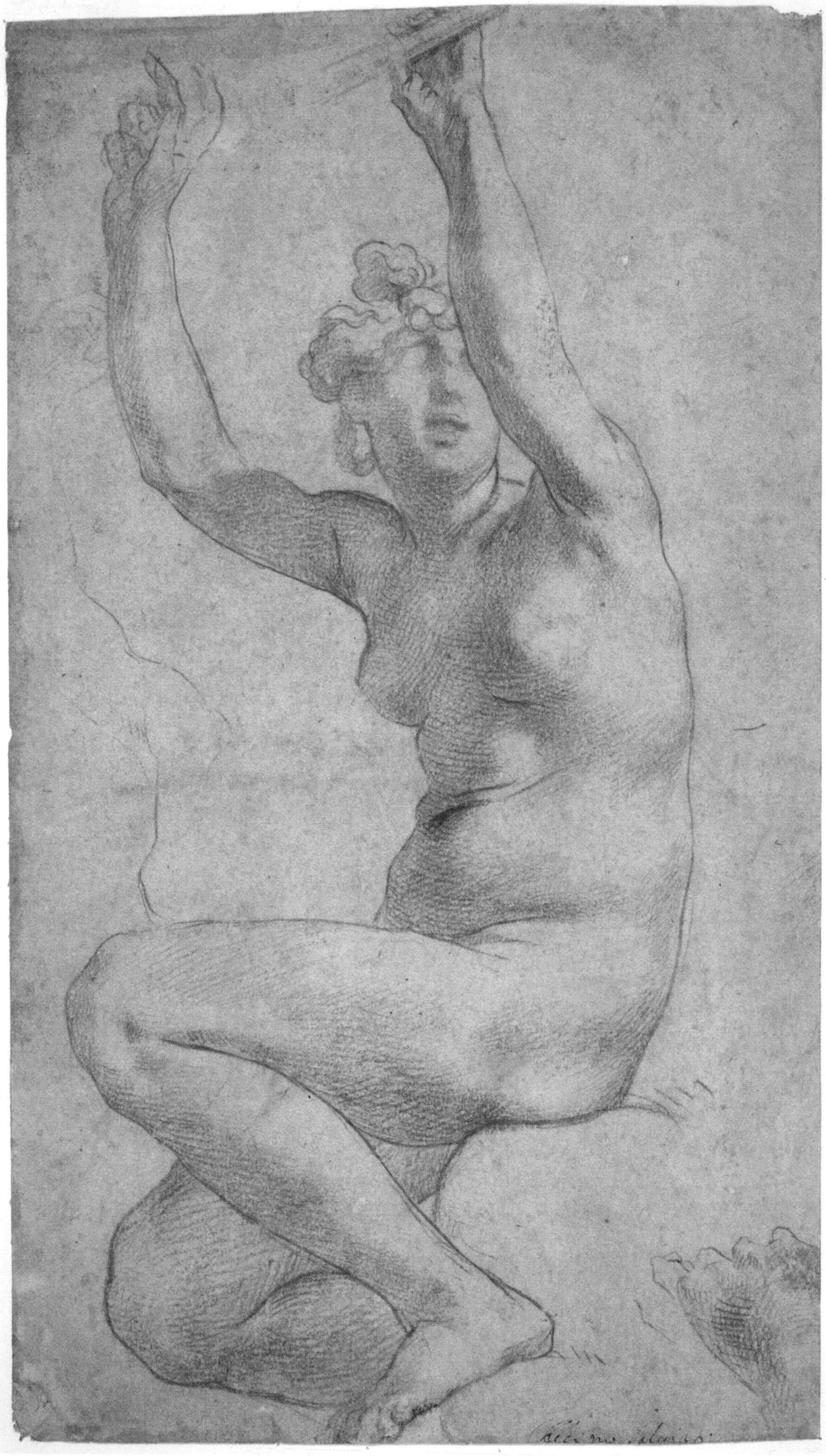

Fig. 33.1 Rosso Fiorentino, *Fall of Man*, 1524, fresco. Santa Maria della Pace, Rome

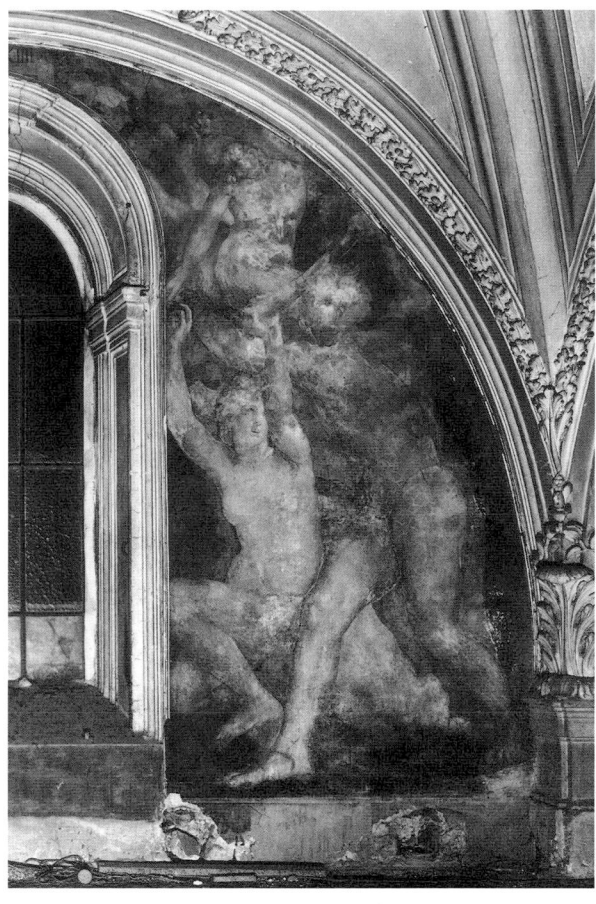

34
PIERO BUONACCORSI,
CALLED **PERINO DEL VAGA** 1501–1547
*SKETCH FOR A WALL DECORATION WITH
THE COAT OF ARMS OF A MEDICI POPE*
C. 1521–1527

Pen and brown ink
45.3 × 29.8 cm
Christ Church Picture Gallery,
Oxford

Following the untimely death of Raphael in 1520 and the partial dissolution of his workshop, Perino del Vaga emerged as the preeminent mural painter in Rome, a status he enjoyed until 1527, when the city was sacked by rampaging troops loyal to the emperor Charles V.[1] (That catastrophe effectively extinguished cultural life there for roughly a decade and forced most of the resident artists, Perino among them, to flee.) Surprisingly, given his prominence and stature in the 1520s, Perino does not appear to have received a single commission from Pope Clement VII from the time of his elevation to the papacy in 1523 until the Sack. Although much of Clement's energy and resources as a patron were directed to his native Florence, that pontiff did turn to Raphael's former *garzoni* when endeavouring to have work done in Rome, entrusting Giulio Romano and Gianfranceso Penni with the completion of the Sala di Costantino in the Vatican Palace, and Giovanni da Udine with more small-scale decorative projects such as the *stufetta* in the Castel Sant'Angelo. But as far as can be ascertained from surviving works, as well as documents and early written sources, Perino was never summoned to the pope's service. This design for an unidentified and apparently unrealized project featuring the coat of arms of a Medici pope, with two alternative ideas for framing figures, seemingly datable on stylistic grounds to the mid-1520s – that is, to the pontificate of Clement rather than his cousin Leo X (r. 1513–1521) – thus calls for some explanation.

One possibility is that the intended work was not ordered by Clement VII, but was commissioned as a tribute to him. Pursuing that scenario, the suggestion has been made that Perino's patron in this instance may have been Baldassare Turini da Pescia, papal datary to Leo X and apostolic secretary under Clement VII, whose heraldic devices included a dog – the animal possibly represented here, reclining beneath the papal escutcheon.[2] The design does not correspond to any of the surviving decorations in the Villa Lante on the Janiculum, the sole monument to Turini's activity as a patron in Rome. Moreover, Vasari, whose *Life* of Perino is lengthy and accurate, and who does describe another papal coat of arms that the artist painted for Cardinal Cesarini[3] – does not mention any such work for Baldassare Turini. Absent any supporting evidence, this inference remains tenuous. Another possibility to be considered is that this is a design for a facade painting of the type in which Polidoro da Caravaggio specialized in Rome in the 1520s. As such designs commissioned by papal favourites and familiars typically incorporated not just the

stemma (coat of arms) of the reigning pontiff but also that of the patron's own family[4] – an auxiliary detail absent here – this hypothesis, too, is uncompelling.

That the sole heraldic reference in the Christ Church drawing is to a Medici pope reinforces the likelihood that Perino's design does, in fact, record a papal commission. For what, precisely, has never been determined, but possibilities include an ephemeral structure such as a triumphal arch; a stucco relief or fresco; or a tapestry panel or other wall hanging. Both the format and composition call to mind a similar design by Giulio Romano showing a triumphal archlike structure with a papal escutcheon surrounded by winged victories and putti – probably a study for a temporary apparatus erected on the occasion Pope Paul III's visit to Parma in 1538.[5] That drawing is for a freestanding structure, while Perino's design, with its lack of spatial projection and its summarily sketched *basamento*, appears to be for the flat surface of a wall. The probability, then, is that this is a design for either a wall hanging or, more likely, a fresco.

If the question of the date of this sheet is reconsidered, a hitherto unconsidered possibility for its function arises. In the 1976 catalogue of drawings at Christ Church, Byam Shaw suggested that Perino executed this study during his early Roman period – the putti holding the papal tiara, for example, are typical of his draftsmanship of the early 1520s – and later reworked those passages bearing evidence of darker ink and redrawn contours. If this supposition is correct, the original design could be dated about 1520–1521, that is, during the pontificate of the Medici Pope Leo X (r. 1513–1521) rather than Clement VII. In or around 1520, Leo commissioned from Perino del Vaga and Giovanni da Udine the decorations of the Sala dei Pontefici in the Vatican, one floor below the Sala di Costantino, where Raphael's other *garzoni* Giulio Romano and Gianfrancesco Penni were then at work. When Leo died, in December 1521, only the ceiling (a complex astrological cycle abounding with symbolic references to the Medici pope that also illustrates his natal sky) was completed;[6] what was intended for the walls remains a mystery. Conceivably, the Christ Church drawing – whose pictorial vocabulary appropriates archaeologizing motifs from the lexicon of Raphael's late manner (the Egyptian *telamones* recall similar figures in the Stanza dell'Incendio, and the Diana of Ephesus had recently appeared in the *Logge* of Leo X, where both Perino and Giovanni had worked immediately before undertaking the Sala dei Pontefici[7]) – is a study for a wall in the Sala dei Pontefici.[8]

Several other factors bolster this conjecture. Perino's design is stylistically and iconographically consistent with that decoration, where putti supporting Medici papal emblems, poised before swagged draperies, occur in the four corner panels of the ceiling. In addition, the architectural elements articulated in the drawing conform to the existing physical space of the Sala dei Pontefici, which includes an architrave with projecting stone capitals identical to the one represented at the right above the *telamon*, and presumably, in its original configuration, also had a real or fictive *basamento*. An imposing room, the Sala dei Pontefici (also referred to in contemporary documents as the "Sala dei Papi" and "aula inferiorum") functioned as a papal audience chamber and as a setting for papal consistories and official ceremonies. Its erudite decorative program announced to all assembled within its walls that Leo's pontificate was ordained in the stars and that pontifical authority over temporal rule was divinely sanctioned and inviolable. Were it indeed envisioned for the Sala dei Pontefici, Perino's heraldic tableau may have been designed as a backdrop to the papal throne, the symbolic focal point of the space. The corresponding work was in all likelihood a fresco, perhaps interspersed with stucco elements analogous to the overdoors of the contemporaneous Sala di Costantino, but the possibility that the drawing records an idea for a woven throne canopy similar to one made for Clement VII in the mid-1520s cannot be entirely ruled out.[9] In any event, if the proposed connection with Leo X and the Sala dei Pontefici is correct, the ambiguous animal beneath the Medici stemma is probably not a dog but rather a hastily sketched lion or lioness, Leo's favourite heraldic and onomastic beast and a pictorial motif repeated throughout the ceiling.[10] And if there is any truth to Vasari's vague intimations that Clement VII contemplated a resumption of work in the Sala dei Pontefici,[11] which had been interrupted by the death of Leo X, perhaps Perino undertook the posited reworking of the drawing in the mid-1520s as part of an unsuccessful effort to recover that lost commission for himself.

LINDA WOLK-SIMON

GIROLAMO FRANCESCO MARIA MAZZOLA, CALLED PARMIGIANINO
1503–1540
THE HOLY FAMILY WITH SAINT ELIZABETH AND THE BABY JOHN THE BAPTIST
C. 1524–1527

Pen and brown ink and wash, with white heightening, over black chalk, on greenish prepared paper
16.2 × 11.9 cm
Agnes Etherington Art Centre, Queen's University, Kingston

Parmigianino came quickly to artistic maturity in his native Parma in Northern Italy, and was determined at an early age to visit Rome, and to be introduced to the papal court of the newly elected Clement VII. He arrived in Rome in mid-1524 and stayed until the Sack forced his retreat to Bologna and ultimately Parma. Although he failed to undertake any major papal commission, Vasari claims that Parmigianino was contracted to fresco the walls of the Sala dei Pontefici in the Vatican.[1] Vasari also remarks that Parmigianino endeavoured to imitate Raphael in everything, and that people said the spirit of Raphael had passed into his body.[2]

A mainstay of Renaissance art, images of the Virgin and Child or of the Holy Family and related figures, engaged almost every artist of the period. Parmigianino created innovative depictions of the subject – both as public altarpieces and as works for private devotions and aesthetic delectation – in every phase of his career. In a surprising number of these works he was commissioned, or chose himself, to include Saint John the Baptist, the forerunner and cousin of Jesus, and the present drawing is no exception.[3]

Parmigianino undertook drawings in a wide variety of media, but his use of paper prepared in colour, such as the greenish tonality here, was relatively limited. Another example is the well-known drawing, *The Adoration of the Shepherds*, of c. 1526 in the Uffizi, Florence.[4]

This drawing, which appears to date from Parmigianino's Roman period (1524–1527), does not connect with any known finished work by the artist.[5] Mary holds the Christ Child at the left, and a figure that must be Joseph (looking like a shepherd) stands in a doorway at the rear. In front of them, Saint John the Baptist, supported on what appears to be a cradle, turns to embrace the Christ Child. The most prominent figure, the old woman with craggy features seated at the right, places her right hand on the forehead of a somewhat apprehensive Christ Child. She is probably Saint Elizabeth,[6] who has brought her baby son, Saint John the Baptist, to visit their cousins in their home and to acknowledge the divinity of the Christ Child.

As a group, the figures fit neatly into a triangle, though one that is truncated at the left. This asymmetry may have been deliberate on Parmigianino's part, or it may be the result of mutilation at an early date. Triangular compositions for groups of the Virgin and Child and related figures had fascinated both Leonardo and Raphael, and here Parmigianino seems to be engaged in extending the tradition. In *The Canigiani Holy Family* in the Alte Pinakothek, Munich, Raphael arranged the same participants in an isosceles triangle in a landscape, with Joseph leaning on a staff at the apex. Parmigianino's composition is reminiscent of Raphael's, but with the difference that the four foreground figures are placed indoors and Joseph is moved back in space to the doorway. *The Canigiani Holy Family* dates to Raphael's Florentine period (before 1509), but later in Rome he and his workshop took up the theme again.[7] The last painting in a series on the subject, Giulio Romano's *Madonna della Gatta*, c. 1520–1522 (fig. 35.1), may well have been Parmigianino's starting point, because it too includes a cradle in the foreground, a bed with hangings in the background, and, perhaps most significant of all, Saint Joseph standing with a staff in the doorway.[8]

In addition, this drawing appears to betray a debt to Michelangelo. In 1985 the present writer noted the similarity between the drawing's spiralling pose of St. John the Baptist and that of the Christ Child in Michelangelo's *Medici Madonna*, begun in Florence during the 1520s (fig. 35.2).[9] Gould then adduced a connection with the same sculpture in Parmigianino's *Vision of St Jerome* of 1526–1527, now in The National Gallery, London, and concluded that Parmigianino must have seen Michelangelo's *Madonna* in Florence on his way from Parma to Rome in 1524.[10]

There is an old copy, once owned by Sir Thomas Lawrence, of this drawing in the De Pass Collection at the Royal Cornwall Museum, Truro. Presumably, it is the same drawing that belonged to Ercole Gallo, Bologna, and of which a facsimile was made in the eighteenth century.[11]

DAVID MCTAVISH

Fig. 35.1 Giulio Romano, *Madonna della Gatta*, c. 1520–1522, oil on panel, 171 × 143 cm. Museo Nazionale di Capodimonte, Naples

Fig. 35.2 Michelangelo, *Madonna and Child* (called the *Medici Madonna*), 1521–1534, marble, height 226 cm. Medici Chapels (New Sacristy), San Lorenzo, Florence

36

SEBASTIANO DEL PIOMBO 1485–1547
PORTRAIT OF ANTON FRANCESCO DEGLI ALBIZZI c. 1525

Oil on canvas, transferred from panel
134.6 × 87.7 cm
The Museum of Fine Arts, Houston

This painting was already attributed to Sebastiano del Piombo when it was first published in 1824, though the sitter was erroneously identified as Lorenzo de' Medici.[1] However, one early owner, Thomas Lister Parker, judged it optimistically instead to be by Michelangelo, while Benjamin West ascribed it, rather more astutely, to Bronzino. In fact, it was another painter, Henry Fuseli who returned it to Sebastiano by comparison to the *Raising of Lazarus*, now in the National Gallery, London. Yet this attribution still raised doubt in the late nineteenth century, apparently on the grounds of the surprising modernity of the image. Credit goes to Pallucchini in 1944 for suggesting, plausibly enough, that this was the very portrait of Anton Francesco degli Albizzi by Sebastiano praised by Vasari in his *Life* of the artist for its visual power and vivid depiction of the clothing.[2]

Venetian-born, Sebastiano spent his maturity working in Rome. Michelangelo, his friend and collaborator, mentioned this portrait of Albizzi in a letter written in Florence and sent to Sebastiano in Rome in 1525. He referred to the impatience with which his admirers were waiting to see the picture.[3] As it is relatively rare for a portrait to be so specifically documented – in comparison to a public commission – this citation adds to the importance of the work in question. Michelangelo's exaggerated stress on his friend's fame in Florence may well have been inspired by the fact that the sculptor was hoping to promote Sebastiano's style for personal gain, as he had designed some of the latter's Roman paintings. A date of about 1525 for the portrait indicated by the correspondence between the two artists places it just after the conclusion of Sebastiano's Borgherini Chapel frescoes in the church of San Pietro in Montorio of 1524 – the period of Michelangelo's collaboration with the Venetian painter. Given his explicit interest in the Albizzi portrait (sharing also the sitter's republican political sympathies) it cannot be ruled out that Michelangelo discussed the composition of the work with Sebastiano, as Fuseli first speculated; it is possible he even provided a drawing for the pose, which is unusually sculptural and geometric for the painter at this date, as well as the powerful disposition of the arm, recalling gestures on the Sistine chapel ceiling.

Anton Francesco degli Albizzi (1486–1537) was memorably characterized by the Florentine historian Benedetto Varchi as a fiery, proud and restless man.[4] While he found favour early in life through his allegiances with the

Medici – Pope Leo X made him governor of Narni in Umbria for example – he later turned dramatically against the family. Albizzi was among the leaders of the ill-fated Florentine Republic against the Medici of 1527–1530, after which he was exiled from his native city again to Rome. In 1537 he was captured by troops loyal to Duke Cosimo de' Medici following the Battle of Montemurlo and executed for treason in the Bargello.

Sebastiano's portrait was painted while Albizzi was temporarily resident in Rome and dispatched back to Florence. It escaped confiscation by the Medici for their collection following Albizzi's execution as it remained in his family's possession until the seventeenth century, when it was transferred to a relation in the Falconieri family in Rome.[5] Assuming a date of 1525, the sitter would have been thirty-eight years old at the time. Albizzi's distinctive short cropped hair and sideburns suggest an inspiration from ancient portrait busts easily available in Rome, either in life or in art. The classicizing quality of the image is also carried in the oratorial gesture, the remote gaze, and decorous removal of the hat to expose the head. The life-size portrait has a strongly formal and public aspect, as opposed to private intimacy. Albizzi even appears to be wearing some form of official dress with fur collar, but this aspect of the work has yet to be elucidated. It is curious that Albizzi did not commission a Florentine painter in Rome to produce his portrait. Perhaps he selected Sebastiano to please the Medici Pope, or on the explicit advice of Michelangelo, but it reveals how far Rosso Fiorentino's fortunes had fallen in the papal city after the loss of the Cesi Chapel commission, for he was an accomplished portrait painter. Ironically perhaps, the composition of the painting had an immediate and decisive impact on the conventions of Florentine portraiture, as in Pontormo's *Alessandro de' Medici*, now at Lucca, as is frequently noted.

The optimism felt by artists with the election of Pope Clement VII halted with the Sack of Rome of 1527, but this painting was produced prior to that terrible event, during the time of greatest optimism for this papacy. Sebastiano's loyalty to Clement VII during these difficult later years – for which the painter received the lucrative post of *piombatore* (keeper of the papal seals) – provided the context for a period of greater introspection and glacial severity to his style, whereas this work is among the most vivacious and robust of all his portraits.

DAVID FRANKLIN

37
BALDASSARE PERUZZI 1481–1536
AN ALLEGORY OF FORTUNE c. 1527

Pen and brown ink over black
chalk, pricked for transfer
27.3 × 20.4 cm
Annotations: *Baldassar da Siena*
Christ Church Picture Gallery,
Oxford

37

This drawing, pricked for transfer in most areas, bears an old attribution to "Baldassar da Siena" on the backing and was catalogued by Bell in 1914 as by Baldassare Peruzzi.[1] In 1926 Von Hadeln ascribed it to the Ferrarese school, specifically to Dosso Dossi, and this attribution was accepted by the Tietzes in 1937 and by Eisler in 1947. Two decades later, Frommel reaffirmed the old attribution to Peruzzi and was followed by Byam Shaw in 1976. The attribution to Peruzzi is now generally accepted.[2]

Von Hadeln was the first to recognize that the Christ Church sheet provided the design (with some changes) for the woodcut frontispiece to Sigismondo Fanti's *Triompho di Fortuna* (fig. 37.1), a fortune-telling book published in Venice in January 1527 by Agostino de Zani da Portese at the instance of the Florentine financier-publisher Giacomo Giunta.[3] Fanti was a Ferrarese mathematician, astrologer, and military engineer who, in 1514, had published a treatise on calligraphy.[4] In the Renaissance, Fortune was seen as a powerful force pitted against human endeavour, or *virtù*, and *libri di sorti* (books of lots) were popular, particularly in the sixteenth century.[5] A tablet at the lower-right corner of the frontispiece displays the intitials "I.M." (or possibly "T.M."), presumably referring to the form-cutter rather than the designer.[6] The colophon to the first edition is dated 1526, reflecting Venetian usage, wherein the year begins in March; for the second printing the date was changed to 1527.[7]

The volume is dedicated on the verso of the frontispiece to Pope Clement VII (Giulio de' Medici) and also includes a poem and explanatory preface addressed to the pontiff, whose patronage Fanti sought.[8] Fortune, astrology, and prognostication were the subjects of several works dedicated to Giulio de' Medici both as cardinal and as pope.[9] On *carta* Ir of the numbered pages, titled *Rota del Liofante* (fig. 37.2), the beardless, seated pontiff seen at the lower left is labeled "CLEMENTE SETTIMO."[10]

Peruzzi's complex allegorical composition shows a beardless pope, wearing the *triregnum* (papal tiara), seated precariously on a globe encircled by the Zodiac. The globe is held on the shoulders of giant who resembles Atlas, one of the Titans.[11] A winged, horned demon at the left and an angel-like female figure at the right (likely Malus Genius and Bona Fortuna of classical astrological theory) turn a great shaft running through the globe in opposite directions.[12] Two female personifications flank the praying pontiff, the one on the right pointing above, the other downwards. In the woodcut frontispiece, which reverses the composition, the scroll that carries the title of the work displays the words "VIRTUS" and "VOLUPTAS," suggesting a cosmic conflict between good and evil.[13] At the lower right of the drawing, a young male nude raises a die, and an aging astrologer holds an astrolabe aloft in one hand and a compass in the other.[14] The setting includes a battle-mented clock-tower that rises above a river with figures in a small boat.[15] In the frontispiece, but not in the drawing, a building that resembles the Pantheon suggests that the locus is to be understood as Rome.[16] As dedicatee of the book, Clement VII is presumably the pope depicted, and the aged figure in the foreground is likely the author, Sigismondo Fanti, who in the dedication styles himself "great mathematician."[17] In the frontispiece, thick clouds of smoke fill the background, and the instability of the pope, who seems to sit atop Fortune's wheel, suggests the situation of Clement himself, the helpless victim of Fortune's whim. By the time Fanti's *Triompho* was published in Venice early in 1527, Fortuna had indeed abandoned the second Medici pope. On 20 September 1526, Pompeo Colonna, long Clement's enemy, had attacked Rome and plundered the Vatican – a prelude to the far greater destruction soon to befall the Eternal City during the Sack of Rome, in May 1527.[18] Writing after the Sack, Clement VII's contemporary Francesco Vettori observed that the pope had been spurned by Fortune and had gone from being "a great and renowned cardinal" to "a small and despised pope."[19]

SHERYL E. REISS

Fig. 37.1 Frontispiece to Sigismondo Fanti's *Triompho di Fortuna* (Venice, 1527), woodcut, 34 × 24 cm. British Library, London

Fig. 37.2 From Sigismondo Fanti's *Triompho di Fortuna* (Venice, 1527), *Rota del Liofante* (Wheel of the Elephant), c. Ir, woodcut, 34 × 24 cm. British Library, London

38

SEBASTIANO DEL PIOMBO 1485–1547
PORTRAIT OF CARDINAL GIOVANNI
SALVIATI AND GIOVANNI DA CEPPERELLO
C. 1531

Oil on panel
105 × 99 cm
The John and Mable Ringling
Museum of Art, Sarasota, Florida

Fig. 38.1 Michelangelo, *Tomb of Giuliano de'Medici*, 1519–1534. Medici Chapels (New Sacristy), San Lorenzo, Florence

Giovanni Salviati was in both political and cultural terms a major figure in the first half of the sixteenth century.[1] His father, Jacopo Salviati, was one of the great Florentine bankers of the period; his mother, Lucrezia de'Medici, was the daughter of Lorenzo the Magnificent and the sister of Giovanni de'Medici, Pope Leo X.[2] Following a rigorous humanist education in Florence, he was made a cardinal in Rome on 26 June 1517 along with several of his cousins. A brilliant diplomatic career followed. He quitted Rome to serve as a papal legate, first to the Holy Roman Emperor Charles V in 1525, and then in 1526 to Francis I, King of France. He was instrumental in freeing Francis from imprisonment by the Spanish after the Battle of Pavia in 1525 and played an important role in the Treaty of Cambrai which ended the wars between Francis and Charles in 1529. He first reappeared in Italy in 1530 in connection with the coronation of Charles V at Bologna, and then returned to Rome. Salviati was an avid patron of the arts. The musician Jacques du Pont was in Salviati's service from 1527 until the Cardinal's death, and the painter Francesco de'Rossi Salviati

takes his name from the Cardinal, who was his patron.[3] Moreover, he collected numerous works of art including silver, porcelain, antiquities, medals, sculpture, and paintings, and transformed a room in his palace into a veritable *Wunderkammer*, the contents of which included bird cages, Portuguese vases, an assortment of objects made from precious and semi-precious materials, astrolabes, clocks, and a fountain fashioned from coral.[4]

On 1 July 1531 Cardinal Salviati wrote from Rome to Michelangelo, in Florence, gratefully acknowledging the artist's offer to make him a painting. The painting mentioned in this letter can be identified with the present portrait.[5] Michelangelo wanted to thank Salviati for his help in arranging a new contract for the tomb of Julius II.[6] He also wished to pay tribute to the Cardinal's politics – namely his allegiance to and leadership of the *fuoriscriti*, Florentine republican exiles who stood in opposition to the autocratic Duke Cosimo de'Medici. As it were, Michelangelo himself produced no painted portraits, but he often turned to Sebastiano to paint such works in his stead. These chiefly depict republican Florentines to whom Michelangelo had close ties, and important examples include the portrait of *Anton Francesco degli Albizzi* (1525, Museum of Fine Arts, Houston) and the *Portrait of Baccio Valori* (c. 1531–1532, Galleria Palatina, Florence).[7] In these pictures, Sebastiano deliberately quoted conspicuous works by the sculptor who had initiated, and to whom he owed, the commissions. In the Sarasota portrait, the Cardinal's pose echoes Michelangelo's figure of Giuliano de'Medici (fig. 38.1) in the Sagrestia Nuova of San Lorenzo in Florence. It is unlikely that Sebastiano would have seen the sculpture, but rather depended upon Michelangelo's drawings of the figure for the concept.

Prior to Gilbert, Salviati was identified as Cardinal Enckenvoert, a close companion of Pope Adrian VI, and was dated to 1522.[8] This association was made on the basis of a note in the 1922 sale catalogue stating that the painting was originally in the church of Santa Maria dell'Anima in Rome, where Enckenvoert commissioned Sebastiano to paint a fresco cycle depicting scenes from the life of St. Barbara. However, as Vasari recorded, Sebastiano procrastinated and was replaced by Michael Van Coxie who painted the cycle as well as a portrait of the cardinal, which is recorded in the church in 1721; perhaps the advisor of David Erksine (who owned the painting in the early twentieth century), one M. Colombo according to Gustav Waagen, confused the two pictures.

Fig. 38.2 Francesco Salviati,
Visitation (detail, portraits of
Battista da Sangallo and Giovanni
da Cepperello), 1538, fresco.
San Giovanni a Decollato, Rome

The portrait's design with a main figure and a second-
ary figure or figures was a compositional device favoured
by Sebastiano, as is exemplified by such works as *Cardinal
Ferry Carondelet and his Secretaries* (1510–1512, Museo
Thyssen-Bornemisza, Madrid), *Cardinal Bandinello Sauli,
His Secretary, and Two Geographers* (1516, National Gallery
of Art, Washington), and the unfinished *Portrait of Pope
Clement VII with a Companion* (Galleria Nazionale, Parma).
The secondary figure in the present painting was, however, only uncovered during a cleaning treatment of the
painting in Sarasota in 1960; no trace of this figure had
been visible in earlier photographs.[9] Hirst identified this
figure with Benvenuto della Volpaia, a close friend of both
the patron and the painter and a skilled maker of maps,
clocks, and other devices such as the astrolabes in the
Cardinal's collection.[10] More recently Costamagna made the
intriguing suggestion that this figure represents another
intimate of the Cardinal, Giovanni da Cepperello, citing
the similarity, particularly with regard to the unusual
shape of the nose, with a known portrait of Cepperello in a
fresco by Francesco Salviati in the oratory of San Giovanni
Decollato in Rome (fig. 38.2).[11] The nose was a family trait,
discernable also in tomb effigies of other members of the
Cepperello family.[12]

VIRGINIA BRILLIANT

39
GIULIANO BUGIARDINI 1475–1554
PORTRAIT OF POPE CLEMENT VII c. 1532

Oil on panel
91.2 × 74.2 cm
Deutsches Historisches Museum,
Berlin

This portrait of Pope Clement VII by the Florentine painter Giuliano Bugiardini was probably executed in 1532, in response to the demand for likenesses of the second Medici pontiff following the re-establishment of the Medici regime in Florence in 1530.[1] Given to Sebastiano del Piombo by Waagen in 1854, the painting was first tentatively reassigned to Bugiardini by Crowe and Cavalcaselle in 1871.

Correspondence between Michelangelo and Sebastiano from April through October 1531 suggests that Michelangelo, in Florence, wanted a portrait of the pope by his Venetian friend then residing in Rome.[2] By late July, Sebastiano had finished a "testa del papa" (head of the pope) on canvas, taken from the life, but Clement wanted another, on stone, for himself.[3] Sebastiano told Michelangelo that he would send a version to Florence as soon as he had done a copy.[4] By early October, Sebastiano had finished a portrait of the pope with which he was pleased, but he asked Michelangelo to be patient because the Duke of Albany (the Scottish-born John Stuart, who served as the French ambassador to Rome in the early 1530s) had seen it and desired it, and Clement had made the painter give it to the duke.[5] In addition, Bartolomeo (Baccio) Valori, who had until recently been the governor of Florence after the restoration of the Medici (and who had spared Michelangelo's life after he sided with the anti-Medicean rebels), wanted a portrait of the pope as well, and Sebastiano was asked to accommodate him.[6] As a result, Sebastiano promised yet another painting for Michelangelo and "el vostro amico pictore" (your painter friend), presumably Bugiardini.[7] In the spring of 1532, after additional delays, Sebastiano finished another portrait of Clement that was sent to Florence only in April.[8]

Vasari recounts the history of the "testa del papa" requested by Michelangelo in his *Lives* of Sebastiano del Piombo and Giuliano Bugiardini. In his *Life* of Sebastiano, Vasari says that Bugiardini himself wanted to paint for Baccio Valori a portrait of Clement with Valori, along with a second portrait, for Ottaviano de' Medici, of Clement

with Nikolaus Schomberg, Archbishop of Capua and Valori's successor.[9] According to Vasari, Clement's features were based on a very beautiful head supplied by Sebastiano del Piombo, presumably the one sent to Florence in the spring of 1532. Vasari also says that when Bugiardini was finished with the model sent by Sebastiano, Michelangelo presented it to Ottaviano de' Medici.[10] In his *Life* of Bugiardini, Vasari describes the two dual portraits in greater detail. In one, Clement was depicted seated, with Baccio Valori kneeling and speaking to him.[11] In the other, the pontiff was shown seated, with Nikolaus Schomberg standing; a later copy of this painting, in Florence (fig. 39.1), provides an idea of its appearance.[12] Both portraits are significant in the history of papal portraiture for adding narrative elements and for showing the interaction of the sitters rather than portraying them statically.

It has been suggested by Pagnotta that the Bugiardini portrait of Clement exhibited here is, in fact, a fragment of the double portrait with Baccio Valori described by Vasari.[13] If this proposal is correct, the figure of the kneeling Valori would have been cut from the panel prior to the 1850s, when it was seen in the collection of the Duke of Hamilton near Glasgow.[14] The picture then would have been cut once more at some point after it was sold at auction in 1938, when it showed the seated Clement at full length.[15]

In its present state, the knee-length portrait shows Clement, who had let his beard grow after the Sack of Rome as a sign of mourning, seated before a green drape.[16] Pierio Valeriano explained and defended Clement's growth of a beard in his *Pro sacerdotum barbis* of 1531, and in April of that year Sebastiano del Piombo wrote to Michelangelo that Clement's beardless likeness from before the Sack of Rome was no longer suitable.[17] Thus the group of portraits showing the bearded Clement can be seen as part of a process to disseminate a new and distinctive image of the pope in the post-Sack and post-Medici restoration era.

Fig. 39.1 Anonymous copy
after Giuliano Bugiardini, *Pope
Clement VII with Nikolaus
Schomberg*, 17th century, oil on
canvas, 160.5 × 122 cm. On deposit
at the Galleria degli Uffizi, Florence

Fig. 39.2 Sebastiano del Piombo,
Portrait of Pope Clement VII,
c. 1526, oil on canvas, 145 × 100 cm.
Museo Nazionale di Capodimonte,
Naples

The pontiff is dressed in relatively informal attire rather than in full pontificals, with a *camauro* (skullcap) and a *mozzetta* (cape) over a pleated white *rocchetto* (rochet).[18] The *camauro* and *mozzetta* appear to be of silk, rather than of ermine-trimmed velvet, suggesting lighter summer dress.[19] The pope's raised right hand can perhaps be understood as a conversational gesture or a gesture of acknowledgment if, as has been suggested, the pontiff was once accompanied by the kneeling figure of Baccio Valori. In his left hand Clement holds a white cloth, and he wears rings on two fingers and his left thumb.[20] As in the case of Raphael's *Pope Leo X with Cardinals Giulio de' Medici and Luigi de' Rossi* in the Uffizi (fig. 46.1, p. 199), the spherical finials of the pontiff's chair allude to the *palle* (balls) on the Medici coat of arms.[21] Bugiardini himself painted a copy of Raphael's celebrated group portrait, which had been in Florence since September 1518.[22] In the Bugiardini variant, Cardinal Luigi Rossi is replaced with the likeness of the patron, Cardinal Innocenzo Cybo.[23]

The sober and restrained image of the second Medici pope seen here is remarkably different from Sebastiano del Piombo's dramatic – indeed, even arrogant – characterization of only a few years before (fig. 39.2), now in Naples.[24] While this Bugiardini portrait shows how greatly Clement had aged after the Sack of Rome and a nearly fatal illness in 1529, it also consciously evokes the highly influential model of Raphael's *Portrait of Julius II* of 1512, now in the National Gallery, London (fig. 1, p. 19).[25] By returning to this authoritative example of how to represent papal majesty despite the effects of age and tribulations, Sebastiano and Bugiardini created a dignified and introspective image of Pope Clement VII that proclaimed his survival and triumph over adversity, along with the restoration of his status both as Medici and as pope.

SHERYL E. REISS

40

MICHELANGELO BUONARROTI 1475–1564
STUDIES FOR THE LAST JUDGMENT
(RECTO AND VERSO) C. 1534–1536

Black chalk
27.7 × 41.9 cm
Annotations: *di Bona Roti* [verso]
The Royal Collection

40 (recto)

40 (verso)

Michelangelo's fresco of the *Last Judgment* (fig. 40.1a) on the altar wall of the Sistine Chapel was his most important painting commission following the completion of the Sistine vault.[1] Originally ordered by Pope Clement VII near the end of his life, the project was confirmed by newly elected Pope Paul III, against the wishes of Michelangelo who would have preferred to make sculptures for the protracted execution of tomb of Pope Julius II. Work on the painting, which is over seventeen metres high, begun in 1536 and was completed by 1541. Reflecting literally the spirit of growing reformist tendencies in Catholic officialdom, this commission, covering virtually the entire wall surface, involved the destruction of even some of Michelangelo's own earlier frescoes in the vault, so great was the desire for new and more powerful imagery.

This double-sided drawing in black chalk features a bewildering variety of small, highly concentrated and particularized studies of individual figures and groups for the centre and left of the lower part of the fresco. As Hirst pointed out, the artist must have resolved one plan for an overall composition by this stage in the design process and was here restudying some previous ideas in more depth with the hope of finalizing them for what was the final part of the fresco to be executed.[2] A number of these relatively tiny, vigorous inventions survived on the monumental scale of the finished fresco, though many more drawings – not to mention the final *modello* for the entire work – would have been produced following this sheet. The reworking of pairs of figures in violent interaction, here in aerial combat and with some upside-down as the angels and demons wrestle for the bodies awakened by the trumpet call (fig. 40.1b), was a common, indeed obsessive approach of Michelangelo's. In fact, it was a method traditional to Florentine art

practice, but only Leonardo da Vinci rivalled the spontaneous energy and intense creativity of Michelangelo in making this type of drawing.

The verso features figures on a more monumental scale, not all of which are easily relatable to the *Last Judgment*.[3] The anatomical studies are especially notable for what they reveal about Michelangelo's practice as he developed the muscular nudes with an accurate understanding of the underlying structures of the human body, as well as for their sheer power and for his ability to create volume without dependence on external contour lines.

Michelangelo's *Last Judgment* fresco is an overpowering, frenzied vision. There is nothing joyous about the event, just an awesome inevitability as some souls struggle with and others resign to their fates. It is not symmetrical in its arrangement like the main prototypes, such as Luca Signorelli in Orvieto Cathedral, but approached more as a constellation of isolated and inherently dramatic incidents. There is not much spatial depth either and, with the exception of powerful foreshortenings of individual bodies, few concessions to illusionism in the fresco. For Michelangelo, the design is created solely by figures. The composition is, however, denser around the judging Christ and more open towards the lower part of the wall – the area for which these studies were made – where the main subject is the resurrection of the dead and the division of the elect and the damned. The fresco reveals Michelangelo's typical singularity as a painter with an almost exclusive concentration on the muscular male nudes in complex, aggressive poses. Compared with the nervous poise of the figures on the ceiling, while equally colossal and imposing, the bodies in the *Last Judgment* are heavier in proportion, but with smaller heads, and more abrupt in their contortions.

DAVID FRANKLIN

Fig. 40.1a-b Michelangelo, *The Last Judgment* (full view and detail), 1536–1541, fresco. Sistine Chapel, Vatican Palace, Rome

41

ANTONIO DA SANGALLO THE YOUNGER
1484–1546
DESIGN FOR A FREESTANDING TOMB SEEN IN ELEVATION AND PLAN c. 1534–1536

Pen and brown ink, brush and brown wash, over extensive compass-incised and stylus-ruled construction with pin-pricked measurements; the elevation drawing is inscribed by the artist with measurements
40.1 × 18.8 cm
The Metropolitan Museum of Art, New York

41

This drawing was rediscovered and sold at auction in 1998, together with three other tomb designs, all four sheets dating to the 1530s; their attribution and subject matter were confirmed by Frommel in the sale's catalogue.[1] The intended final projects with which the three other sheets were connected are less securely known than is true of the present sheet,[2] which renders the intended project with great clarity of design and in a relatively finished conception. The present drawing depicts the effigy of a bearded pope and the lower part of the podium includes the papal tiara with crossed keys over the Medici family's coat of arms – the six balls, or *palle* – which readily identifies the funerary monument as that of Clement VII de' Medici This detailed *modello*, or demonstration drawing, may be compared with Michelangelo's *Tomb of Pope Julius II* (cat. 1) as emanating from the same general tradition of clearly expository designs probably intended for the patron. Here, Sangallo rendered the freestanding tomb to be carved in marble in a consistent, precisely calibrated projection of the elevation with respect to the plan. This distinctive technique of drafting the dimensions of the plan and side views of a form in exact relationship to each other was still quite new in architectural drawings of the time. The Metropolitan Museum sheet by Sangallo is executed in pen and ink with wash over an extremely precise construction of direct stylus-incisions ("*incisioni dirette*"), done with compass and ruler, and with measurements carefully pricked with calipers; the grids of stylus-ruled lines coincide from plan to elevation above. While the overall condition of this working drawing is good, it exhibits small, scattered discolorations of the paper, slight soiling from handling, some minute worm holes, and foxing toward the upper border of sheet. The sarcophagus in the elevation (upper) part of the drawing was inscribed by the artist with several measurements; the cushion supporting the papal effigy apparently indicates "14" (probably *14 palmi*, or 3.12 metres); while the upper rim of the sarcophagus notes "20–10" (probably *20 palmi, 10 once*, about 4.6 metres); and the lion's head "4–12" (probably *4 palmi, 12 once*, or about 1.17 metres).[3] Both the bold, freehand manner of briefly sketching the figures and the precise, stylus-constructed drafting of the architecture are characteristic of the hand of Antonio da Sangallo the Younger.[4]

The exact historical origin and context of Sangallo's design, however, remain nebulous. As early as May 1524, Michelangelo had been requested by letter to produce designs for the marble double tombs of the Medici popes, Leo X and Clement VII, which were to be placed in the New Sacristy of San Lorenzo, Florence, but this selected location was abandoned after 6 June 1526 for lack of space.[5] According to Vasari, Clement, on his return from Rome, awarded Baccio Bandinelli the commission for the papal tombs to be erected at Santa Maria sopra Minerva.[6] In any case, the project was to receive serious attention again only after Clement's death in 1534,[7] when numerous sculptors and architects competed for the commission to design the sumptuous tombs. In March 1536, Clement's executors[8] selected Baccio Bandinelli to carry out what would be the most prestigious sculptural commission of early sixteenth-century Rome after Michelangelo's *Julius Tomb*. Two extant large drawings by Bandinelli detail his ideas for the double tombs of the Medici popes at a relatively advanced stage.[9] Completed in 1541, the tombs were finally installed facing each other in the choir of Santa Maria sopra Minerva.

In all likelihood the present drawing offers a detailed early idea by Antonio da Sangallo for the tomb of Clement VII, around 1534–1536, when the plan was still to produce separate tombs for the Medici popes, but it seems to be a carefully constructed *modello* summarizing preliminary thoughts explored in another drawing.[10] This first project by Sangallo seems to have evolved from a design concept previously explored by him in designs for a funerary monument to Piero de' Medici at Montecassino, c. 1531.[11] As was the case at Montecassino, Sangallo's ideas for the funerary project at Santa Maria sopra Minerva appear to have arisen from his involvement in the extensive architectural remodelling of the church's choir, in which his primary role was as architect, not sculptor.[12] In conception, the present drawing is totally unlike the highly developed later solution for a three-bay wall tomb for Clement VII, as drawn to scale in *palmi romani* on a sheet now at the Graphische Sammlung Albertina, Vienna (fig. 41.1), which may be attributed to the Sangallo workshop, but which exhibits notes by the Bandinelli family.[13] The Albertina sheet by the Sangallo workshop (a presentation drawing for the executors of Pope Clement's will) portrays the animated statue of the pope blessing from his throne within the design of a triumphal arch, in a solution closer to Bandinelli's ideas of the late 1530s. In contrast to the later Albertina design by the Sangallo workshop, the effigy of the dead pope in the present drawing rests flatly on a tall sarcophagus, which is supported by Egyptian-style sphinxes, while statues of seated male holy figures (likely prophets and evangelists[14]) holding books or tablets accent the engaged pilasters of the tall base in a rhythm of decoration that strongly evokes Michelangelo's *Tomb of Pope Julius II*, both in the preliminary drawings and in the final design of the monument as erected in 1545 at San Pietro in Vincoli, Rome.

Until the discovery in 1998 of this drawing, the design by Antonio da Sangallo the Younger for the Medici papal tomb had been known from a number of autograph summary sketches in pen and brown ink,[15] as well as from a "*disegno-ricordo*" – or studio "clean copy" without wash, or

183

stylus construction – attributed to Antonio's brother, Giovanni Battista da Sangallo "Il Gobbo."[16] Younger than Antonio by three years, Il Gobbo is documented as his assistant from 1521 onward and frequently performed as his brother's amanuensis even as he was an accomplished draftsman in his own right.[17] Antonio's drawing for the *Tomb of Clement VII* occupies a significant place in the history of Renaissance tomb design, as funerary monuments conceived of in the round were still relatively rare by the 1530s, although ambitious precedents existed in the bronze *Tomb of Pope Sixtus IV* by Antonio del Pollaiuolo, signed and dated 1493,[18] and in the preliminary drawings by Michelangelo for the *Tomb of Pope Julius II*, as explored in the early project of c. 1505–1506, and in the mature projects dating after 1513. In this history, the tomb of 1574 for Pope Paul III at Saint Peter's Basilica ranks among the first built freestanding funerary designs of the sixteenth century.[19] Sangallo's tomb design, with its elegantly unified massing and tidy oval plan, may have constituted a pointed reaction to Michelangelo's reworking of the *Julius Tomb* after 1513 as a gigantic mausoleum of innumerable figures. In this respect, it is noteworthy that Sangallo's and Michelangelo's personal differences over aesthetic vocabulary caused them to become hated rivals in the field of architecture during the late 1530s, and 1540s, in particular regarding the design of Saint Peter's Basilica.[20]

CARMEN C. BAMBACH

VINCENZO DE' ROSSI 1525–1587
PURPORTED DESIGN FOR THE TOMB OF
POPE CLEMENT VII after 1560

Pen and brown ink over traces of
black chalk and more extensive
underdrawing with stylus,
straightedge and compass
35.4 × 21.3 cm
Museum of Art, Rhode Island
School of Design, Providence

Fig. 42.1 Vincenzo de'Rossi, *The Labours of Hercules*, c. 1563, pen and brown ink with light touches of wash, 43.5 × 29 cm. Musée du Louvre, Paris

This is one of the best known of the drawings attributed to the Florentine sculptor Baccio Bandinelli. Closely tied to the Medici throughout his life, Bandinelli worked extensively in Rome and Florence for both the Medici popes, Leo X and Clement VII. After Clement's death in 1534, his heirs commissioned Bandinelli to create a pair of elaborate tombs, replete with statuary and reliefs, for both the popes in the Roman church of Santa Maria sopra Minerva. That project dragged on until the early 1540s, when Bandinelli definitively abandoned Rome to enter the service of the young Duke of Florence, Cosimo de' Medici.

The fame of this drawing rests partly on account of its imaginative and almost Baroque conception of the scenographic possibilities of group sculpture. Many of its figures float almost free of their backgrounds in a way that no sculptor would manage to realize in three dimensions before Bernini. Its notoriety owes still more to its peculiar and unprecedented iconography. Within a large architectural niche, two torch-bearing youths either unveil or cover the body of the dead pope (whose features identify him as Clement and whose pose alludes to the famous antique relief known as the *Bed of Polykleitus*), as he lies upon a bier recalling Antonio Pollaiuolo's tomb of Pope Sixtus IV in Saint Peter's (1484–1493). At the same time we see his soul, symbolized by a tiny, ideal nude figure framed within an oval *mandorla*, or nimbus, being carried

heavenward by angelic putti. In the semidome above, separated by an architectural moulding, Christ and the Virgin, seated amidst unidentified holy figures, make gestures of supplication to God the Father, as the dove of the Holy Spirit hovers overhead. The depiction of the soul as an ideal body has been interpreted by Goldberg in the light of theological debates among Catholic writers about its immortality, which had continued from the time of Dante until the sixteenth century.[1]

Stylistic examination of the Providence drawing suggests that, in spite of the traditional attribution to Bandinelli, it is in fact the work of one of his most important assistants, Vincenzo de' Rossi.[2] During the 1540s and 1550s Vincenzo worked sporadically for Bandinelli in Florence, but the younger artist spent the majority of those decades in Rome, ignoring his master's frequent pleas to return. In Rome Rossi carried out such major commissions as the *Young Christ with Saint Joseph* statue for the Accademia di San Luca (Pantheon) and the sculptures of the Cesi Chapel (Santa Maria della Pace). But immediately after Bandinelli's death in 1560, Vincenzo returned to Florence, where he hoped Duke Cosimo would allow him to complete Bandinelli's major unfinished sculptural ensembles. Instead, he received the commission for a monumental fountain adorned with statues of the twelve labours of Hercules (never finished; the extant sculptures are in the Palazzo Vecchio and at Poggio Imperiale); he continued to work for the Florentine court until his death.

Scholars have only begun the work of separating the autograph drawings of Bandinelli from those of Rossi and his many other students.[3] The point of departure for what we know of Vincenzo's style as a draftsman is a handful of drawings related to the *Hercules Fountain*, including a study now in the Louvre for a relief on the base of the fountain which is inscribed on the verso with a note in the artist's own hand (fig. 42.1). Rossi's style is clearly based in the formal repertory of his teacher, as we see in such works as Bandinelli's studies for the reliefs of Florence Cathedral. Rossi tended to exaggerate muscular proportions of Bandinelli's heroic figure types, and his works can often be spotted by a peculiar shorthand he devised: hair that consists of billowy tufts; eyes like dark, shadowed caverns, and drapery that resembles a two-dimensional, clingy film criss-crossed by monotonous rope-like folds. Vincenzo's outlines tend to be less confidently drawn and calligraphic; his hatching is frequently sloppy and usually incoherent in its failure to convey a consistent illusion of modelling and

Fig. 42.2 Baccio Bandinelli, *Adam and Eve Condemned by God* (study for the Choir of Santa Maria del Fiore), c. 1546–1547, pen and brown ink, 43.5 × 29 cm. École des Beaux-Arts, Paris

illumination. There are also considerable variations in quality and degree of finish in Rossi's drawings, at times refined and at other times gross and ham-fisted.

If one compares the Providence drawing with a group of Bandinelli's finished *modelli* or approval drawings that seem most reliably attributed to him – the project drawings for the reliefs that were to decorate the choir of Florence cathedral (c. 1546–1547) – it becomes evident that in reality the present drawing is not by Bandinelli, as generally maintained, but by his pupil and imitator Rossi. The Bandinelli choir relief drawings can be considered touchstones of his work, in part because Vasari mentions them in his life of Bandinelli, and in part because of their superlative virtuosity. Setting the Providence drawing alongside one of Bandinelli's works (fig. 42.2) reveals how Bandinelli's greater command of anatomy renders his figures more organic than the flatly shaded, disjointed or schematic bodies in the Providence sheet. Bandinelli's swiftly sketched draperies possess a three-dimensionality and a consistency of illumination that makes the niggling, flat draperies of the *Clement VII* drawing look pedestrian and belaboured.

Why, then, would Vincenzo de' Rossi have made a preparatory design for the tomb of Clement VII, a project that had been underway since he was ten years old? The plot thickens, since on the basis of stylistic comparison the present author has identified a group of drawings that were made, ostensibly, as studies for Bandinelli's works, but should in fact be seen as "restitutions" by Rossi's hand. These include other "studies" for the papal tombs,[4] and for the base of the *Doria Monument*,[5] the reliefs of the choir of Santa Maria del Fiore,[6] and the sculptural decoration of Castel Sant'Angelo,[7] as well as a *Lamentation* in which Duke Cosimo is depicted beardless (as he appeared only until around 1540).[8] It is not difficult to imagine that Rossi made these pastiches to feed the demand for Bandinelli's drawings after the master's death. In February 1564, after Don Vincenzo Borghini, one of Duke Cosimo's most trusted artistic advisors, had spent at least eleven months writing letters on Rossi's behalf in order to help him obtain commissions from the Medici duke, Borghini wrote to his friend Vasari: "Now will be the right time for Vincenzo to press his request... He had promised me some drawings by Bandinelli, I don't know which..."[9] Vincenzo de' Rossi's activity as a forger of ersatz "Bandinelli" drawings sheds a new light on his career, on his relation to his master, and on the history of art forgery during the Italian Renaissance.

LOUIS A. WALDMAN

ALESSANDRO FARNESE

PAUL III 1534–1549

43
FRANCESCO DE' ROSSI,
CALLED **FRANCESCO SALVIATI** 1510–1563
VIRGIN AND CHILD WITH AN ANGEL
c. 1535–1540

Oil on panel
112.3 × 83 cm
National Gallery of Canada,
Ottawa

Fig. 43.1 Francesco Salviati, *Visitation*, 1538, fresco. San Giovanni a Decollato, Rome

Although unsigned, the attribution of this painting to Francesco Salviati has by now received widespread support, beginning with Hirst (verbal communication). Purchased in 2005 by the museum, it was published for the first time by Costamagna.[1]

The painting features a seated, three-quarter length Virgin who firmly holds the sleeping Christ Child on her lap. She appears to look remotely out of the picture somewhere past the viewer's right. While the Madonna's mood might be described as benign and contented, the presence of an attendant angel who reverently contemplates a transparent veil, as well as the sleeping child himself, evokes the future Passion of Christ.

In formal terms, the sheer monumentality, weight and power of the figures that appear to be spread across the panel's surface deliberately recalls precedents Salviati knew from Michelangelo's Sistine Chapel ceiling. In particular, the Virgin's cross-legged pose references the Erythaean sibyl. The treatment of the Virgin contains other notably secular, rather noble touches including her elongated neck, her elaborate headdress, and the daring placement of the shawl falling off her neck to reveal part of the shoulder. The scalloped draperies and creamy, polished surface seems to emulate marble sculpture in a manner that also evokes, as if in rivalry as much as emulation, Michelangelo.

The compositional placement of the divine figures in what appears to be a grotto with a distant landscape opened up behind them, recalls too the paintings of Andrea del Sarto, who had been Salviati's teacher in Florence. The decorative objects in fictive gold on the Virgin's belt and on the angel's strap bring to mind the artist's training as a goldsmith. In making specific reference, however, to pagan imagery these ornaments add meaning, as does the landscape featuring fantastical ancient ruins, in the context of the triumph of the new religious order over the godless past.

Establishing Salviati's chronological development on stylistic grounds is difficult, but the panel likely dates to the second half of the 1530s when the painter, still in his twenties, was active in Rome, by comparison with such works as the San Francesco a Ripa *Annunciation* of c. 1535 and the *Visitation* in San Giovanni a Decollato, dated 1538 (fig. 43.1). Vasari in his relatively thorough *Life of Salviati* published in 1568, specifically mentions a painting of the Virgin and Child executed for Raffaello Acciaiuoli during his Roman period of the later 1530s, prior to the artist's sojourn in the north of Italy, which has never been linked to a surviving picture, yet this would be an excellent candidate.[2] Acciauioli had also been a patron of Vasari, who produced five pictures with subjects from the Passion of Christ in the 1540s and is known to have resided in Naples by around 1550. The concentration on the Passion in Vasari's work is intriguing given the treatment of the subject matter in the Ottawa painting, with its explicit references to Christ's suffering. The Acciaiuoli, an ancient Florentine family, were linked to the Certosa di Galluzzo, the Carthusian monastery outside of Florence, where Pontormo had earlier frescoed a cycle also on the theme of the Passion.

The composition of the Salviati panel now in Ottawa was known previously through a painting in the Royal Collection (fig. 43.2), formerly attributed to the artist with some reservation and usually dated a later stage in the artist's career.[3] The Royal Collection picture entirely lacks the rich landscape that is such a dominant and resolved feature of this painting. Technical examination reveals that the two supports were made by the same carpenter, and further, that both were painted simultaneously. While this seems to be unusual within Salviati's oeuvre, it is certainly part of contemporary practice. Sarto, for instance, made simultaneous versions of compositions with their own variations and adaptations, and Salviati would have likely had first-hand experience of this.

Fig. 43.2 Francesco Salviati, *Virgin and Child with an Angel*, c. 1535–1540, oil on panel, 112.3 × 84.5 cm. The Royal Collection

The starting point for the composition was a rather schematic cartoon, which appears to have been little more than an initial setting down of the location of forms. This cartoon was transferred to the prepared surface of the panel now in the Royal Collection by pressing with a stylus against a second piece of paper rubbed with charcoal. The design was then accented in freehand to a point where painting could begin. At a certain moment however, and logically at this stage, a tracing of this design was taken from the panel surface, possibly re-using the initial cartoon, to create the cartoon for the panel of identical size now in Ottawa.

The Ottawa painting deviates from the initial design in three significant areas: the inclusion of the distant landscape, the formation of a more complex sleeve for the Madonna, and a significant proportional correction to Christ's legs. The first two modifications occured while the cartoon was being transferred; the third was made freehand, after initial transfer. This clearly indicates that from the outset, the Ottawa painting was to be different and not simply a second version. The initial formation of the composition was certainly made on the surface of the Royal Collection panel, and the painting of this was in the early stages while the drawing on the Ottawa panel was still being refined. Some of these refinements then made their way to the work in the Royal Collection. Attempting to label either painting as the "prime" version misses an important element of contemporary practice; the paintings were instead worked on synergistically.

If this occurrence of variants is not unique in Salviati's practice, it is at least unusual, and we should consider this. An intriguing area of speculation, that also explains the visual differences between the two paintings, is that they are bear differences in technique and in condition. The Royal Collection painting has a distinctly coloured underpainting which contributes to its hotter coloration; the surface is wrought and brush-tracked, with areas of hatching reminiscent of Rosso. In contrast, the Ottawa painting has a more chromatically neutral underpainting, and the hatched modelling has been judiciously smoothed to produce the controlled and polished surface we tend to associate with Salviati's mature paintings. It may be that the two paintings represent a technical watershed for the artist in his development of different styles.

DAVID FRANKLIN AND STEPHEN GRITT

ATTRIBUTED TO FRANCESCO DE' ROSSI,
CALLED FRANCESCO SALVIATI 1510–1563
THE COUNCIL OF THE GODS c. 1530s

Red chalk
22 × 44.2 cm
The Phillips Family Collection

To ensure that the family business would continue to thrive, the Siennese banker Agostino Chigi (1465–1520) moved to Rome, where he became the senior financier for the papal state, around 1487. As a consequence, he was able to forge close ties and lucrative agreements with the popes in power, as evidenced by the presence of the coat of arms of Pope Jules II in his residence built by Baldassare Peruzzi in 1505, today known as Villa Farnesina. Probably the only figure with the stature to offer patronage rivalling that of the popes, Chigi employed the most sought-after artists, including Raphael, whom he asked to decorate his sumptuous residence between 1517 and 1519. Raphael took inspiration from the story of Cupid and Psyche as related in Apuleius's *The Golden Ass* (also titled *The Metamorphosis*); he was likely familiar with the myth through the text by Niccolò da Correggio as well as the annotated version by Filippo Beroaldo the Elder, both in circulation at the time.[1]

The present drawing replicates the right-hand side of the ceiling fresco depicting the *Council of the Gods*, in which Venus asks her father, Jupiter, to condemn the secret liaison between her son Cupid and the mortal Psyche (fig. 44.1). The left-hand side of the fresco, which does not figure in this drawing, portrays Psyche's victory: Mercury extends to her the cup of immortality that will grant her access to the world of the gods and, thus, marriage to Cupid. Although the composition of the drawn work corresponds to that of the painted work, a few details differ: in the drawing, the gods are beardless and wear voluminous headdresses; Neptune, beside Jupiter, has been stripped of his pointed ears and trident, his usual attributes; and Mars tilts his head toward the goddess Venus.

The Lugt collection in Paris retains a sheet illustrating a fraction of the drawing under study here – almost a carbon copy – with a few subtle variations such as the trace of pentimento forming Cupid's left wing (fig. 44.2). Although the state of conservation of the Lugt drawing shows some wear over the entire surface, which makes it less legible, the technique is nevertheless similar to that of the New York drawing. For example, in both drawings, the areas of saturation of sanguine are found in almost the same places (on Cupid's right wing and in the folds of the drapery) and similar hatching is used to portray the hair of the divinities. While the drawing in the private collection shows some awkwardness in the rendering of the modelling and the hands (those of Cupid holding his bow and of Neptune), the one in the Lugt collection reveals freer lines and a more supple treatment of the drapery, giving this work a superior quality.

Attribution of the Lugt drawing, as brilliantly argued by Byam Shaw, has alternated between Raphael and one of his most faithful collaborators, Giulio Romano. In fact, attribution of numerous drawings connected with the Farnesina project, listed by Shearman[2] and more recently by both Oberhuber and Harprath, inevitably raises controversy among art historians, who hesitate between the labels "Raphael," "workshop," "school," "circle of," and "copy." This drawing is no exception; Monbeig Goguel calls it a copy executed by Francesco Salviati. Her argument is based on a formal similarity with some of Salviati's earlier drawings and his highly finished red chalks (*Nude Man*, Louvre [inv. 2992] and *Meeting between Leo I and Attila*, Brunswick, Anton Ulrich Museum [inv. Z1787]).[3] Monbeig Goguel buttresses her hypothesis by stating that Salviati had access to Raphael's drawings through Perino del Vaga, a prolific artist who emerged from the master's studio, with whom Salviati worked in the Vatican for Pope Paul III. Del Vaga, who died in 1547, probably owned works by Raphael; the Mantuan merchant Giacomo Strada purchased from his widow "two crates" of drawings by del Vaga and his master in the mid-sixteenth century.[4] That said, the drawing under consideration here was either a preparatory drawing for the fresco or a copy of a lost drawing by Raphael. If we presume that it was a preparatory exercise, we must accept that Raphael trusted that his students, the young Giulio Romano and Giovanni Francesco Penni, were talented enough to take on a task linked to such a prestigious commission. This seems improbable, given the meticulousness with which Raphael orchestrated the decorative work at Farnesina.[5] If we subscribe to the hypothesis of a copy, the attribution to Penni seems very plausible, since, according to Vasari, he became adept at imitating Raphael's style faithfully.[6] However, his graphic corpus is still not well known, and so it remains difficult to discern its stylistic properties. This observation impedes our comprehension of Raphael's body of work, as Penni's exact role within the studio has yet to be defined.[7] A last possibility is that the drawing was used for an engraving by Jacopo Caraglio (c. 1505–1565). In fact, these two works do seem to have some similarities.[8] The print, however, showcases Caraglio's artistic licence, as he integrates, on two different planes, the present drawing and that of *Mercury Offering the Cup of Immortality to Psyche*, today in Munich.

The drawing in the Phillips collection is a fine example of the infatuation with Raphael's oeuvre among both his contemporaries and those who followed, both artists and collectors, as its provenance shows. This enthusiasm was directed not solely toward the finished work but also included preliminary studies, all of which feed into continued debates and reinterpretations.

NELDA DAMIANO

45
HERMAN POSTHUMUS c. 1500–after 1542
LANDSCAPE WITH ANTIQUE RUINS 1536

Oil on canvas
96 × 141 cm
Liechtenstein Museum, Vienna
Sammlungen des Fürsten
von und zu Liechtenstein,
Vaduz-Wien

TEMPVS EDAX RE
RVM TVQVE INVI
DIOSA VETVSTAS
OĨA DESTRVITIS

In his brief of 28 November 1534 appointing Latino Giovenale Manetti as papal commissioner of antiquities, Paul III called attention to the peril in which Rome's ancient monuments stood;[1] like Raphael before him (see cat. 16), Manetti's mandate was to preserve the remains of Roman antiquity, in part by studying and recording them. This unusual painting, by the little-known Dutch painter Herman Posthumus, is an archaeological fantasy that reflects the passionate antiquarianism that prevailed in Rome during the reign of Paul III.

In the foreground of Posthumus's painting, resting on a half-buried sarcophagus, a damaged marble tablet proclaims in the words of Ovid's *Metamorphoses* (15.234–235): "TEMPVS EDAX RERVM TVQVE INVIDIOSA VETVSTAS O[MN]IA DESTRVITIS ..." ("Ravenous Time and envious Age destroy everything..."). Scattered all around, in the shadow of ruined buildings and fountains, lie a plethora of ancient sculptures, many of which can be identified today with works the artist saw in various sixteenth-century collections.[2] But the human figures in the painting seem intent on resisting the corrosive effects of time described by the poet. Below the inscription we see the prominent figure of a draftsman with a drawing board (a self-portrait of Posthumus?) who intently measures an ancient column base with a compass. To the left a group of men with torches is about to explore a grotto, whose form recalls the ruins of the Golden House of Nero, or Domus Aurea. And in the middle ground another artist draws a statue of one of the reclining river gods, while his companion climbs on top of the other one to measure its arm.

In 1536, the year this work was painted, it appears that Posthumus was employed in Rome on the decorations for the triumphal entry into the city of the Emperor Charles V. The artist (mentioned by the documents as "maestro Ermanno") was paid for his work on the embellishment of the Porta San Sebastiano, the gate through which the emperor arrived in the city, for an arch erected near the Palazzo Venezia, and for other work in the papal palace.[3] Posthumus's presence in Rome seems to be documented by the fact that we can still see his name, "HER[MAN] POSTMA" [*sic*], scratched into the plaster of the vaults of the Domus Aurea (fig. 45.1), alongside those of fellow Dutchmen

Martin van Heemskerck and Lambert Sustris.[4] Stylistic evidence of this and other works by Posthumus suggests that, like his companions, the artist had been trained in the workshop of the Utrecht painter Jan van Scorel.

Prior to the emergence of this painting and its acquisition for the Liechtenstein collection in 1983, all that was known of Posthumus's career came from payment records of Duke Wilhelm IV of Bavaria, which indicate that during 1540–1542 he was the second-highest-paid painter employed on the decoration of the new Italianate wing of the *Residenz*, the duke's palace at Landshut some forty miles northeast of Munich. Those decorations are modelled directly upon those of the Palazzo Tè in Mantua, designed by Giulio Romano for Federico II Gonzaga (c. 1525–1535), which suggests that Posthumus spent time at the Mantuan court before 1540.[5]

Insight into Posthumus's own studies of Roman antiquity comes from his identification as the anonymous draftsman, previously known only as "Anonymous A," to whom Hülsen and Egger had attributed fifty-six folios in the second of the two famous albums in Berlin (Kupferstich-kabinett, Staatliche Museen), which also contain drawings of Roman antiquities by Heemskerck.[6] Some of these drawings depict ancient Roman remains, while others appear to have been made in and around Mantua. Taken together, the drawings in the Berlin albums represent one of our most important sources for understanding the history of ancient Roman art and its survival during the Renaissance.

On the basis of comparison with the Berlin albums, Dacos also identified Posthumus as the author of a sheet of studies, in a private collection in Rome, depicting a group of fanciful saltcellars and ewers (fig. 45.2), which is inscribed with an apparently eighteenth-century attribution to "Bacio Bandinelli [crossed out] après l'antique par Hemscherck."[7] In reality, the Rome studies are quite different in technique and handling from the drawings in the Berlin albums that Dacos attributes to Posthumus.[8] They should instead be attributed to Vincenzo de' Rossi, a pupil of Bandinelli active in Rome during the 1540s and 1550s, and whose graphic oeuvre is just now being untangled from that of his teacher Bandinelli (compare cat. 41).

LOUIS A. WALDMAN

Fig. 45.1 Graffiti with Dutch names, including HER POSTMA (Herman Posthumus?), HEMSKERC (Martin van Heemskerck), and LAM AMSTE (Lambert Sustris), c. 1536. Volta nera, Domus Aurea, Rome

Fig. 45.2 Here attributed to Vincenzo de'Rossi, *Studies for Ewers and Saltcellars*, c. 1560–70, pen and brown ink, 26.1 × 26.1 cm. Private collection, Rome

46

GIORGIO VASARI 1511–1574
POPE LEO X WITH THE CARDINALS
GIULIO DE' MEDICI AND LUIGI DE' ROSSI
(COPY AFTER RAPHAEL) 1537

Oil on panel
157.5 × 117 cm
Viscount Coke and Trustees of
Holkham Estate, Norfolk

Among all the portraits made of Leo X (Giovanni de' Medici), Raphael's portrait of this pope together with the two cardinals (fig. 46.1), now at the Uffizi in Florence, most vividly captures his features. Although it is the largest portrait from Raphael's brush, it is not an official state portrait, but a private family portrait of the pontiff between his two cousins Giulio de' Medici and Luigi de' Rossi. It was likely commissioned on the occasion the festive entry into Florence on 8 September 1528 of Lorenzo de' Medici, the Duke of Urbino and his wife Maddalena de la Tour d'Auvergne, a relative of the French King François I. The painting had been shipped from Rome to Florence only a few days earlier to represent the three highest dignitaries of the family of the bridegroom, to whom his uncle on the Holy See had granted not only Roman citizenship but also whom he had elevated in 1516 to the rank of Captain General of the Church. Lorenzo established, through his marriage, the secular power of the Medici. By representing the Pope during a symbolic ceremony at the bridegroom's place of office, Raphael's portrait became a diplomatic icon. If Vasari, in his biography of Raphael, describes the velvet, the damask, the leather, the gold, the silk, and the parchment as well as the bell and the pommel on the chair as if they were real, the entire work appears as a virtual reality, a role it would indeed play.

As they were posing for a family portrait, the three ecclesiastic cousins are depicted not in ceremonial liturgical regalia but in their traditional habits. The scene is set in a small, perhaps vaulted room, in an intimate study setting. The entire painting comprises majestic red hues and brilliant white. At centre sits Pope Leo X on a red upholstered armchair, at a table draped in red, both items placed at an angle. Over a white damask frock and a magnificent ermine-lined damask coat, he dons the *mozzetta*; he wears the *camaura* on his head. Both articles are made of red velvet and lined with ermine. Both cardinals also wear the *mozzetta* – their's made of red silk – over a white cassock. They are bare-headed; their tonsures are visible. Having set down his reading glass, Leo gazes up from a richly illuminated codex (preserved in the Hamilton Bible at the Kupferstichkabinett, Berlin) (cat. 23), opened to page 400v, the beginning of the Gospel of Saint John. Although not his patron saint (Giovanni de' Medici's patron saint was Saint John the Baptist), this was the apostle "sent by God" who bore the same name. An intricately crafted bell with the papal coat of arms and the Medici family emblem, the diamond ring, complete the still life on the table. The naturalistic details are an expression of Leo's

Fig. 46.1 Raphael, *Pope Leo X with Cardinals Giulio de'Medici and Luigi de'Rossi*, 1518, oil on panel, 155.5 × 119.5 cm. Galleria degli Uffizi, Florence

interest in the arts; the painting was to be an impressive token of his patronship. This portrait is, in every respect, a unique manifestation of the cultural refinement of this Pope which time and again shaped his challenging politics. Typical of Leo, his delicate hands bear no rings, in contrast to his predecessor, Julius II who had himself portrayed by Raphael boasting half a dozen rings, three on each hand.

Cardinal Giulio stands to the left of the Pope and, like him, looks out of picture to the opposite side. Only Cardinal Luigi behind Leo's chair and the golden ball that adorns the backrest, looks directly at the observer. Raphael's mastery reaches a high point in this picture not only through the naturalism of the materials and objects, but through the vitality of the portraits: although all three men are clean-shaven, the dark shading of facial hair, differentiated according to the heaviness of each individual's beard growth is visible. Raphael was familiar with the people represented here through his constant association with them. For a time he met with Leo X himself daily for personal discussions. The technical evidence – and the position of Cardinal Giulio – suggests that he had studied the three portrait subjects individually, then formed the composition in this picture.

Vasari had written one of the earliest, most enthusiastic descriptions of Raphael's virtuosity in his biography of the artist. He knew the panel well, having seen it frequently at the Medici's in Florence and through hours of his own careful study. In 1524 he was a pupil of Andrea del Sarto when the latter copied it; in 1537 Vasari himself received the difficult commission from Ottaviano de' Medici to produce another replica for the Florentine patrician family. Passavant identified this copy as that in the possession of the Earl of Leicester in Holkham Hall in England. While it is inferior in quality to the original, it reproduces even the smallest detail, with the exception of the buttons on the *mozzetta* worn by Cardinal Giulio. As its provenance can be traced back only to William Roscoe, the biographer of Leo X, the attribution of the picture, which has not yet been examined by the Vasari scholars research and which in general has received a positive evaluation from the Raphael scholars, is for now supported only by stylistic arguments. Vasari's posthumous portrait of Clement VII as Saint Donatus in the altar of the church of Saints Donatus and Hilarion in the Monastery of Camaldoli dated 1539, and his *Saint Gregory at Supper* in Bologna,[1] which references the chair from the Leo portrait,

reveal a painting technique also found on the head of Cardinal Guilio at Holkham Hall. The latter even seems somewhat aged compared to Raphael's Florentine original, which could be explained by his familiarity with the later portraits of the subject. Vasari's two portraits of Lorenzo the Magnificent, Leo's father[2] and of Duke Alessandro de' Medici,[3] commissioned only three years before the present portrait, are quite similar. The broad, flat lighting, the light point on the tip of the nose, the contrasting dark zones, the shadows and the beard growth seem to be related in terms of paint application. Furthermore, there are the similarly stark light reflections on Leo's damask cloak and Alessandro's armour. The height of the Holkham Hall panel deviates from that commissioned from Vasari, which measures 2.5 × 2 *braccia* (147 × 117 cm). Since the difference is slight and the height and width of the Holkham replica are almost identical to the original, which measures 155.2 × 118.9 cm, this does not argue against an identification with the replica by the Aretine artist. If it was not planned for a specific place, it would have been normal for the copyist to also take over the original measurements. Ottaviano de' Medici's requirements for the commission could have been approximate in this case. The marked, yellowed varnish makes an evaluation of the painting difficult.

ARNOLD NESSELRATH

47

PIERO BUONACCORSI,
CALLED **PERINO DEL VAGA** 1501–1547
*DESIGN FOR THE DECORATION OF A
CHAPEL WALL* (RECTO); *THE FEAST OF
HEROD* (VERSO) C. 1537

Black chalk, pen and brown ink,
with brown and grey washes
41.9 × 29 cm
Inscriptions: *paganazo / di viterbo
libre 15 / nero di fuma libre 2 / leone
batista alberti / le stampe d'alberto*
[verso]
Szépmüvészeti Múzeum, Budapest

47 (recto)

47 (verso)

One of Perino del Vaga's first commissions upon his return to Rome following a decade-long absence after the Sack was for the decoration of the Massimi Chapel in the church of Trinità dei Monti, which he embellished with frescoed narratives illustrating the miracles of Christ – a large scene in the centre of the wall flanked by a smaller *storia* on each side – surrounded by elaborate stucco reliefs and richly painted decorative fields. (That same formula was employed to great effect throughout the Palazzo Doria in Genoa, where Perino had worked in the late 1520s and 1530s as court artist to Admiral-Prince Andrea Doria, and would be reprised in the vault of the Sala Paolina in the Castel Sant'Angelo.) Perino's patron, Angelo Massimi, was ceded *jus patronatus* on 3 October 1537 – the *terminus post quem* for his activity in the chapel.[1] A letter of 29 July 1539 from the gem engraver Giovanni Bernardi to Cardinal Alessandro Farnese, grandson of Pope Paul III, referring to rock crystals based on Perino's compositions establishes the frescoes' *terminus ante quem*.[2]

Erected in the second decade of the sixteenth century, the chapel in question was endowed, according to Vasari, by a famous courtesan and dedicated to Mary Magdalene. Giulio Romano and Giovanni Francesco Penni were commissioned to paint scenes from the life of the Magdalene in the lunettes, the four Evangelists in the vault, and an altarpiece representing *Noli me tangere*.[3] Those elements of the decorative program remained after Angelo Massimi acquired the patronage rights to the chapel (even though its dedication evidently changed); Perino's campaign of the late 1530s was thus limited to the lateral walls. The Cinquecento decorations of the Massimi Chapel were destroyed in the mid-nineteenth century. Two detached frescoes entered British public collections: Perino's *Raising of Lazarus* is in the Victoria and Albert Museum, and a fragment of Giulio and Penni's *Assumption of the Magdalene* from one of the lunettes is in the National Gallery.[4] No other parts of the frescoed decoration are known to survive, but Perino's designs for Bernardi's rock crystals commissioned by Cardinal Farnese, which reiterated in condensed form his *storie* in the Massimi Chapel, provide a valuable record of those lost inventions.

At least four drawings by Perino for the Massimi Chapel decorations are known,[5] of which the most elaborate and finished is this beautiful sheet showing the entire elevation of one of the walls (the lunette, then filled with one of Giulio and Penni's Mary Magdalene frescoes, was here left blank) and, at the left, the pilaster and *sott'arco* of the entrance arch with a loosely sketched acanthus *rinceau*. The *all'antica* character of the now-vanished decoration is evident in the articulation of the wall surface as a series of geometric fields embellished with a rich array of classicizing motifs that included dancing putti, swans, trophies, and *grotteschi*. A large central panel with an image of Christ healing is flanked by two smaller scenes that appear to represent an ancient sacrifice on the left and a scene of judgment on the right. Between winged victories in the *basamento* is another square compartment with a seated female figure gesturing toward or writing on a tablet supported by two putti, possibly a sibyl whose prophesies announced the coming of Christ. Its polished and refined character and the absence of any changes or revisions suggest that the Budapest sheet may have been a presentation drawing submitted for the patron's approval. Although the design essentially conforms to Vasari's description of the chapel walls, this was not the final scheme: the secondary narratives seen here are not the New Testament scenes mentioned by the biographer, but rather are pagan subjects, and the central image clearly is neither the Pool of Bethesda nor the Raising of Lazarus, the two primary subjects he expressly mentions. (It may depict Christ Healing the Lame Man.)

On the verso is a rapid pen sketch of a banquet scene that has been identified as the Feast of Herod.[6] If that interpretation is correct, the design cannot relate to the Massimi Chapel: no scene from the life of John the Baptist is mentioned by Vasari or included among Bernardi's rock crystal derivations, and such a subject would in any case be iconographically incongruous with the other narratives which, as already noted, were devoted to Christ's ministry and miracles. As no painting of this subject by Perino nor any image based on this design is known, the purpose of this study remains a mystery.

One suggestion is that it relates to the frescoed decoration of the oratory of San Giovanni Decollato, which illustrates scenes from the life of Saint John the Baptist.[7] Executed over a protracted period in the middle of the sixteenth century by a group of artists, among them Francesco Salviati, Jacopino del Conte, and Battista Franco, that campaign was inaugurated at precisely the time Perino was engaged in the Massimi Chapel commission. At least one of the frescoes, Jacopino del Conte's *Preaching of the Baptist*, is evidently based on a drawing by Perino, whose participation in some facet of this project – expected because of the status he enjoyed upon his return to Rome and because, like the members of the *compagnia* of the Decollato, he was a Florentine – has long been speculated about by scholars, even if no documents exist to support such a hypothesis and none of the frescoes is by his hand. Surprisingly, the Feast of Herod is not among the principal narratives in the Decollato, appearing only as a background vignette in Pirro Ligorio's *Dance of Salome*; Perino's drawing may, then, represent an idea for an abandoned scene – one that was replaced in the final scheme by a composition combining two sequential moments from the life of the Baptist. (One detail from Perino's sketch that recurs in Ligorio's fresco is the Serlian arch delineated above the banquet table, seen in the upper tier of the painted architectural background, although such a detail is too minor and generic to establish a direct connection between the two.) The inscription in Perino's hand at the lower right refers to some books and prints, including works by Alberti and Dürer, that the artist presumably owned.[8]

An alternative interpretation of the study on the verso is worth considering. Conceivably, the banquet scene is not the Feast of Herod but rather the Marriage at Cana (John 2:1–12). This first miracle of Jesus' ministry was, like the Adoration of the Magi and the Baptism, an epiphany – a revelation of his divinity. It is a subject that is consonant with the other narratives of the Massimi Chapel, with their emphasis on Christ's miraculous healing and ministering powers – manifestations of the divine nature that is fully revealed in the Transfiguration, the subject of one of Perino's lost frescoes. (In the Gospel account, that epiphany follows and is contrasted with an episode concerning the disciples' failure to heal – a symbolic juxtaposition portrayed in Raphael's *Transfiguration*.) If this identification is correct, the assembled guests include Christ, his mother, and a servant bringing water jugs to the table; the crowned figure is the bride or groom, in keeping with established pictorial conventions for portraying this subject; and the participants and spectators marvel at and react to the miracle they witness. Like the scene of Christ Healing on the recto, the composition is delineated in a square field and occupies roughly the same position in the centre of the sheet, as though the artist were experimenting with an alternative for the principal narrative. Compositionally and thematically integral to the program of the Massimi Chapel, this drawing may well relate to that commission.

The ever-informative Vasari reports that Perino, after many unsuccessful months in Rome, despaired of winning the patronage of the powerful Cardinal Alessandro Farnese or his grandfather, the pope. Those worries were assuaged when, on account of his work in the Massimi Chapel, which he greatly admired, the cardinal "began to give him work and used his services for many things,"[9] thereby establishing the tie between Perino and the Farnese that would endure until the artist's death.

LINDA WOLK-SIMON

48

PIERO BUONACCORSI,
CALLED **PERINO DEL VAGA** 1501–1547
JUNO VISITING AEOLUS AND NEPTUNE CALMING THE TEMPEST 1540

Pen and grey ink, grey wash, with
white heightening, over traces of
black chalk
22 × 21.5 cm [at maximum]
Inscriptions: *QVOS EGO*
The Royal Collection

In a letter of 4 February 1540 to the Roman medallist Alessandro Cesati, the humanist and poet Annibale Caro, future secretary to Cardinal Alessandro Farnese, offered a lengthy and detailed description of a design he wished to have realized for the reverse of a portrait medal of Giovanni Guidiccioni, Bishop of Fossombrone.[1] Its subject, taken from Virgil's *Aeneid*, was Neptune calming the tempest that Aeolus, king of the winds, had summoned at the behest of Juno in order to defeat the Trojans. A design had already been presented by the gem engraver and medallist Giovanni Bernardi, but Caro confessed that he judged that submission so deficient as to be an embarrassment. For that reason he implored Cesati to furnish a sketch himself or to procure one from Perino del Vaga.

Perino evidently obliged with the present drawing, the subject and composition of which conform precisely to Caro's medallic tableau, brilliantly incorporating every element of his overly ambitious conceit. At the right, Juno – sporting the requisite diadem and "sober clothes" and deploying a suitably "imperious gesture" while clutching a lightning bolt and a tambourine – visits Aeolus, who dispatches the winds, represented by the cherub heads with "puffed-out faces." (The four winds were personified in the same manner in the *Grotesques* tapestries Perino had designed for his Genoese patron, Andrea Doria, a few years earlier.[2]) To the left, flanked by Tritons, is Neptune wielding his trident astride a conch-shell chariot. Looking heavenward at the cloud-borne Venus, mother of Aeneas, who helps to calm the tempest, the god of the sea threatens the rebellious winds with an expression of warning, "Quos ego" (*Aeneid*, Book 1, line 135), the words inscribed on the banderole.

Perino's muscular Neptune with windswept hair and upraised trident, the god's straining seahorses, and the storm-tossed sea with the hapless ships of Aeneas in the background all recall the same elements in Marcantonio Raimondi's celebrated *Quos Ego* engraving of c. 1515–1516[3] – a source the artist had mined in his earlier, monumental treatment of the theme on the ceiling of the east *salone* of the Palazzo Doria in Genoa. In that decoration, which depicted the *Quos Ego* together with the Shipwreck of Aeneas, (now lost, but known through a preparatory study by Perino in the Louvre and an engraving by Bonasone[4]), Perino reversed Marcantonio's Neptune and his marine quadriga, while copying virtually verbatim the Triton and swimming figure at the lower left and right. In the Windsor drawing, in contrast, Neptune is in the same direction as the Marcantonio model, but the swimming Triton holding a trident quoted in the *modello* for the ceiling has been reversed and shifted to a position behind the god's back.

Caro's letter to Cesati dates from roughly the moment that Perino entered the service of the Farnese following his return to Rome, working first for "il Gran Cardinale," Alessandro Farnese, and soon after for his grandfather, Pope Paul III (see the discussion under cat. 47). Within a few years, Caro himself would follow that path, eventually becoming secretary to Cardinal Alessandro. Whether this collaboration of 1540 helped pave the way for his introduction to the Farnese household is unknown. What is certain is that Caro's choice of the *Quos Ego*, and his detailed description of its every aspect, stemmed from his singular and profound familiarity with Virgil's *Aeneid*. (His Italian translation, first published in 1581, was Caro's most important and enduring literary achievement.) Unlike his sour reaction to Bernardi's design, Caro's appraisal of Cesati's portrayal of the *Quos Ego* is unrecorded, but it is difficult to imagine that he would have judged the murky and illegible distillation of Perino's splendid and complex evocation of Virgil's epic verses as anything other than a disappointing failure.

LINDA WOLK-SIMON

48

49

PIERO BUONACCORSI,
CALLED **PERINO DEL VAGA** 1501–1547
*SAINT PAUL LOWERED FROM THE WALLS
OF DAMASCUS IN A BASKET: STUDY FOR
THE COPE OF POPE PAUL III* c. 1542–1545

Pen and brown ink with brown
wash, with white heightening
25.4 × 15.2 cm
Devonshire Collection, Chatsworth

In the closing passages of his *Life* of Perino del Vaga, Vasari mentions that a number of the artist's drawings were engraved after his death. Among them were "eight scenes from the life of Saint Peter taken from the Acts of the Apostles," produced as embroidery designs for a cope for Pope Paul III.[1] No such papal vestment survives, but a stylistically and compositionally cohesive group of drawings by Perino and reproductive prints based on his designs illustrating scenes from the lives of Saints Peter and Paul in oval or *bombé* fields, some finely pricked in a manner suggesting that they were employed as cartoons for embroidery, have long been associated with this obliquely cited papal commission. Surveying this graphic corpus, Davidson in 1990 reasoned that the extant compositions were too numerous to be accommodated on a single vestment, proposing that Perino had designed not one but two copes for his papal patron, one embellished with Petrine imagery, the other showing Pauline subjects. That conjecture finds validation in a 1547 inventory of the contents of the papal sacristy, which lists two splendid brocaded pluvials embroidered with pearls, one with the "miracles of Saint Paul ... made for Paul III," and the other showing "the story of Saint Peter with the arms of the above [i.e., Pope Paul III Farnese]."[2] This pairing of Peter and Paul – allusions, respectively, to the pope's role as heir to Saint Peter and vicar of Christ on earth, and to his pontifical name – reprised the twinned subject matter of Raphael's *Acts of the Apostles* tapestries for the Sistine Chapel and Michelangelo's frescoes in the Pauline Chapel, the latter commissioned, like Perino's designs, by Paul III. The pope, in a magnificent display of papal majesty and liturgical *Gesamtkunstwerk*, may well have donned the copes in each of those sacred settings.

Four drawings by Perino for the Saint Paul cope, the compositions all set in oval fields, are known. (A fifth is recorded in a copy.)[3] The subject of this engaging sheet is Paul's escape from Damascus after his life has been threatened by the city's Jews (Acts 9:20–23). Two muscular companions orchestrate his nocturnal flight, straining as they carefully lower him down the city walls in a basket. That this is a night scene is brilliantly conveyed by the dramatic chiaroscuro. Opaque passages of wash describe the murky darkness of the enveloping sky, glimpsed beyond the walls, and the saint's penumbral shadow, which obscures the brickwork of the fortified gate like a smoky haze. Highlighted with white heightening applied in wiry lines, Paul's billowing cloak and right arm emerge from the shadow as though silhouetted in the moonlight. In the corresponding embroidery, those passages may have been picked out with silver thread.[4]

No contract or record of payment that would serve to confirm the date of the commission for the papal copes survives. The above-cited inventory drawn up for Paul III establishes that both existed by 1547 (the year of Perino's death). Such costly and elaborate vestments were the product of a painstaking technique and must have required many months to produce. Perino's drawings therefore could not have been executed later than 1544 or 1545, a period of intense activity for the artist, when his talents and energies were directed to myriad projects, of both monumental and miniature scale, for his papal patron.

LINDA WOLK-SIMON

50
PIERO BUONACCORSI,
CALLED **PERINO DEL VAGA** 1501–1547
ALEXANDER THE GREAT CUTTING THE
GORDIAN KNOT c. 1545

Pen and brown ink, grey wash,
with white heightening, squared
in black chalk
19 × 11.22 cm
The Metropolitan Museum of Art,
New York

Emulating the practice of his early master, Raphael, Perino del Vaga oversaw a large and industrious workshop in Rome in the 1540s, when he was engaged as court artist to Pope Paul III Farnese. Populating its ranks were a number of talented assistants who would come to embark on their own successful, independent careers, among them Daniele da Volterra, Guglielmo della Porta, Girolamo Siciolante da Sermoneta, and Marco Pino. To these painters, sculptors, and *stuccatori* (and to the goldsmiths, weavers, embroiderers, woodworkers, and rock crystal carvers who translated his ideas in a variety of media), the prolific and gifted Perino supplied figure studies, *modelli*, and cartoons. The consummate draftsman, ever absorbed in the process of *invenzione*, he was content to abstain from the labour of execution – a task he delegated to others.

One of the most important commissions of Perino's late career was the decoration of the papal apartments in the Castel Sant'Angelo. (Originally the mausoleum of the Roman emperor Hadrian, this lithic circular structure, which is proximate to the Vatican, had been converted into a papal fortress in the Middle Ages and dedicated to Saint Michael.) Its principal room is the monumental Sala Paolina, a grand gallery richly embellished with frescoes, gilded stucco, and feigned architectural elements that served as the pope's official reception hall. Records of payment to Perino and his assistants establish that most of the work was carried out between 1545 and 1547, the year of the artist's death. On the walls, Virtues in niches, framed by Ionic columns, alternate with monumental scenes from the life of Alexander the Great, the latter executed in gold monochrome in emulation of bronze reliefs. Painted tondi illustrating episodes from the life of Saint Paul, each framed by a pair of seated female personifications and winged putti, fill the overdoors. The protagonists of the bipartite narrative scheme were selected as obvious references to the baptismal and pontifical names of Perino's patron, Alessandro Farnese, who assumed the name Paul III upon ascending to the papacy in 1534. In this particular choice of a pagan ruler who conquered much of the known world and a Prince of the Church who spread the word of Christ to the gentiles, contemporaries were also meant to recognize an assertion of papal authority and dominion over the temporal and spiritual realms, pronounced with ever-increasing urgency at a time when the Protestant revolt in the north and the Turkish threat from the east gravely challenged those claims.

A number of preparatory drawings by Perino for the Sala Paolina survive. Among the most important is this study, executed in the appealing loose and fluid technique that characterizes his late graphic style, for the fresco representing *Alexander the Great Cutting the Gordian Knot*. Gordius, the king of Phrygia, had secured his chariot with a massive, seemingly intractable knot made of tree bark. An oracle prophesied that whoever succeeded in untying it would rule all Asia, a challenge Alexander ingeniously met by cutting it, the act represented here. The arrangement of the figures and the fall of light emanating from an unseen source at the left are fully delineated. Squared for transfer and corresponding in essential details to the finished fresco (except for the addition there of the standing soldier in profile at the left, who was introduced in order to adapt the design to a wider pictorial field), the drawing was produced as a *modello* to be used by the workshop assistant entrusted with executing this Alexander scene. Minor changes include the omission of the low platform on which Alexander rests his left foot in the drawing, and the altered position of the plumed helmet resting on the ground, seen frontally in the fresco rather than in profile. Indulging his love of fanciful decorative display, Perino lavished particular attention on this detail, which is one of the most prominent and articulated elements of the design; the helmets of Alexander and of the companion who supports the chariot harness in the fresco both appear to be based on the helmet in this drawing.

LINDA WOLK-SIMON

PIERO BUONACCORSI,
CALLED **PERINO DEL VAGA** 1501–1547
VARIOUS STUDIES AFTER THE ANTIQUE
1538–1540

Pen and brown and grey ink on
blue paper
23.7 × 39.8 cm
Inscriptions: *G . IV LIVS . L . F .
CAESAR / STRABO / AED CVR . O . TR .
MIL . BIS . X . VIR / ARGDAND . AD
TR . IVD . PONTIF*, and *a porta
Apostolo*
Agnes Etherington Art Centre,
Queen's University, Kingston

Throughout his career, Perino del Vaga demonstrated an exceptional versatility, willingly turning his hand to a variety of pursuits. For him, as for his near contemporary Parmigianino, drawing was both an investigative device and liberating exercise, and he explored a wide range of subject matter. From the time he entered Raphael's workshop and became engaged on the fresco and stucco decoration of the Vatican Logge, Perino involved himself in the recreation of antique Roman decoration. And in his narrative paintings, he frequently deployed the figures as if in a narrow frieze, again emulating a classical Roman trait.

Both sides of this drawing are devoted to copies after works from ancient Rome. In the seventeenth century, this drawing was part of the Museo Cartaceo, the "Paper Museum" put together in Rome by the noted collector and antiquarian, Cassiano dal Pozzo. To date, however, it has been little studied. The proposal that this drawing is by Perino del Vaga is based principally on the expressive and wiry pen line, and on certain idiosyncratic abbreviations such as the blank round eyes, which are typical of this artist's drawings, especially those done about the time of his return to Rome in 1537–1538.[1] Soon afterwards, Perino became the favourite artist, after Michelangelo, of Pope Paul III. In addition, the drawing reveals a connection with the taste for conspicuous collecting and display of antique works of Pope Julius II.

On the recto the drawing features an eagle with its wings outspread through an oak wreath that is tied at the bottom with a fluttering ribbon, and an informative inscription: *a porta Apostolo*. The subject is a famous Trajanic relief (fig. 51.1) that Cardinal Giuliano della Rovere (the future Pope Julius II) had installed in the portico of the Roman church of Santi Apostoli. Together with San Pietro in Vincoli, Santi Apostoli was the Cardinal's titular church,

and in about 1473 Giuliano della Rovere initiated its major restoration, including a complete rebuilding of its portico. Immediately below the relief, Giuliano della Rovere had an inscription installed that says he saved the eagle from so many ruins (TOT. RVINIS. SERVATAM. IVL. CAR. SIXTI. IIII. PONT. NFPOS. HIC. STATVIT).[2] This antique relief held obvious appeal for Cardinal Giuliano, and for his uncle, who at the time was the reigning pope (Sixtus IV). Their family name (Rovere) means "oak" in Italian; Giuliano had taken an oak tree as his personal device. The relief, however, enjoyed renown even before its association with the Rovere family and some time between 1447 and 1449, the fifteenth-century Florentine artist Benozzo Gozzoli copied it in a drawing that was subsequently owned by Giorgio Vasari (fig. 51.2).[3]

On the other half of the recto there are studies of a tripod and a composite capital, and a Latin inscription that appears to refer to Gaius Julius Caesar Strabo Vopiscus (c. 130 BC – 87 BC).[4]

Across the entire top of the verso there is a hasty copy after a sarcophagus with the Moon Goddess Diana in the middle stepping down from her chariot to admire the sleeping shepherd Endymion, who reclines with one arm over his head. The identification of the exact source of this copy is more difficult because several variants of this popular subject for Roman sarcophagi were known in the sixteenth century.[5] In addition, the drawing is so abbreviated that some of the figures are almost illegible. Elsewhere on the verso there are copies after a sphinx, a griffin and tripod candelabra. This spirited and sensitive sheet exemplifies the hypnotic allure of Roman antiquities throughout the entire sixteenth century, and likewise appears to express Perino del Vaga's personal fascination with them on his return to Rome after an absence of almost a decade.

DAVID MCTAVISH

51

52
FOLLOWER OF **PERINO DEL VAGA**
*DESIGN FOR A MANTLE PIECE FOR POPE
PAUL III* c. 1543–1548

Pen and brown ink, brown and
grey wash, over black chalk
26.4 × 21.8 cm
Inscriptions: *PAVLVS III PONT M*
Agnes Etherington Art Centre,
Queen's University, Kingston

Fig. 52.1 Luzio Romano, *The Arms
of Pope Paul III between Personifications of the Church and Rome,*
c. 1545, pen and brown ink with
grey-brown wash, squared for
transfer, 16.7 × 35.3 cm. The British
Museum, London

This little-known drawing for a fireplace and the wall
decoration above it represents a project of Pope Paul III,
whose involvement is clearly indicated in both verbal and
visual form. The prominent inscription on the mantle
piece – PAVLUS III PONT[IFEX] M[AXIMUS] – leaves no doubt
about the person honoured, and also provides a probable
date for the project: the years of Paul III's pontificate from
1534 until 1549. Paul III's papal office, together with his
ancestral family, the Farnese, is further adduced by the
visual symbols in the decoration above the fireplace.
There, the crossed papal keys of Saint Peter appear in the
central oval, framed in a rudimentary guilloche, above an
escutcheon where space has been left for the insertion no
doubt of the pope's own arms. Even more personal, the
heraldic unicorn at the left has been included as a device
commonly used by the Farnese family.

Of Paul III's various artistic enterprises, the Kingston
drawing is most likely to relate to his renovation of the
Castel Sant'Angelo, even though no definitive connection
has yet been discovered. For centuries the ancient fortress
had played a critical role in the city's defences, which were
being rebuilt after the Sack of Rome by the architect
Antonio da Sangallo the Younger. Paul III seized this opportunity to amplify the construction and hired Raffaello da
Montelupo to renovate the interior of the Castel's central
rectangular tower – transforming it into a sumptuous suite
of papal apartments. The fresco decorations were entrusted
to Girolamo Siciolante da Sermoneta, Luzio Romano, and
Perino del Vaga, each working with a team of assistants.
Execution of the frescoes had started by at least the end of
1543 and continued until April 1548.[1]

The most revealing connections with the Kingston
drawing are found in the Sala della Biblioteca, an imposing
room decorated entirely in fresco and stucco, and located
at the other end of the same floor as the better known Sala
Paolina (see cat. 50) A broad mantle piece at one end of the
Sala della Biblioteca is inscribed identically to the Kingston
drawing, and the wall fresco immediately above it shows
the Pope's arms in an oval between female personifications of the Church and Rome. A squared drawing of the
papal arms of Paul III, again in a guilloche-framed oval,
and flanked by the same allegorical figures (fig. 52.1) is in
the British Museum, but it is clearly not by the same hand
as that of the Kingston drawing.[2] In all the payments for
the decoration of the Sala della Biblioteca the only artist
named is "Lutio da Todi" or Luzio Romano, and the British
Museum drawing has also been generally assigned to him
in recent years.[3] Formerly an assistant to Perino del Vaga
in the Palazzo Doria in Genoa, Luzio Romano was active
(from 1528? to 1575) as a painter and stuccoist in Rome,
but otherwise is little known.

Since Romano worked with a team of unnamed assistants in the Sala della Biblioteca, it is possible that the
Kingston drawing was done by one of them; perhaps it is
even a discarded design for the same fireplace.[4] It is also
possible that the drawing was intended for one of Paul III's
domestic projects outside Rome, as yet unidentified. Since
Perino del Vaga appears to have been the predominant artistic force in all of these papal commissions, it is no coinci-
dence that such features as the large-breasted female figure
(mermaid?) and the leering male mask of the Kingston drawing relate closely to similar figures in Perino's designs for the
contemporaneous Sala Regia in the Vatican (fig. 52.2).[5] In
short, the drawing epitomizes Paul III's exuberant spirit in
relentlessly promoting his church as well as his own family.

DAVID MCTAVISH

Fig. 52.2 Perino del Vaga, *Winged Caryatid*, c. 1542–1545, pen and grey and brown ink and wash over black chalk and charcoal, with white heightening, 37.8 × 24.8 cm. Gabinetto Disegni e Stampe Uffizi, Florence

PAVLVS III PONT M

PELLEGRINO TIBALDI 1527–1596
PRUDENCE c. 1545–1550

Black chalk, brown wash (added by
a later hand)
31.7 × 25.7 cm
Inscriptions: *Pelegrino da Bologna*
Staatliche Museen zu Berlin,
Kupferstichkabinett

Attributed by a seventeenth-century hand to Pellegrino da Bologna, as Tibaldi was known in earlier times, this drawing was identified by Hermann Voss in 1913 as a study for the figure of Prudence painted on the facade of a house in Rome. That figure was part of a larger decoration, then already lost but known to Voss by a reproductive print made in the nineteenth century by Enrico Maccari (fig. 53.1).[1] In his *Life of Primaticcio*, Vasari mentions the decoration briefly among other Roman works by Tibaldi: "In the house of Francesco Formento, between the via del Pellegrino and via del Parione [off today's Corso Vittorio Emanuele II, east of the Chiesa Nuova], he painted in a courtyard a facade and two other figures."[2] Formento was a rich textile merchant from Como, dealing in Dutch and Flemish cloth and tapestries, who seems to have also been a collector of paintings.[3] Maccari's print shows our figure in the lower register to the left of the patron's coat of arms. Her right arm, cut off in the Berlin drawing, holds up a snake, her traditional attribute. In the print, her left hand is empty (though this area may have become illegible by Maccari's time), while in the drawing she holds what Voss interpreted as a mirror – another traditional attribute – that appears to be conceived as a polished slab of stone. On the other side of the coat of arms, clearly identifiable by the sword and scales, is the figure of Justice. This central group is flanked by satyr herms. Above, on the left, is Ceres on her chariot drawn by dragons, and on the right, a young man mounting a chariot drawn by horses (difficult to identify, but possibly Phaeton). The reclining figures on either side surrounded by armour are in the tradition of personifications of conquered provinces. On top is a frieze with griffins and armour as war trophies. This facade decoration is an important example of the continuation of *all'antica* facades such as those painted by Polidoro da Caravaggio in Rome in the 1520s, which Tibaldi would have studied extensively.

A Lombard by birth, Tibaldi moved to Bologna early in life. In his brief description of Tibaldi's life Vasari states that the young artist had spent his formative years copying the latter's paintings of 1539–1540 in the refectory of San Michele in Bosco, Bologna, before moving to Rome in 1547. It seems more likely, however, that Tibaldi came to Rome much earlier, perhaps as early as 1543, entering the workshop of Perino del Vaga to assist in the decoration of the Sala Regia and then of the Castel Sant' Angelo. In any event, unlike his older fellow Bolognese painter in Rome,

Prospero Fontana (see cat. 65), Tibaldi remained entirely unaffected by Vasari's *maniera*. Under Perino he worked alongside numerous other artists, including Girolamo Siciolante da Sermoneta, Marco Pino, Domenico Zaga, and Fontana. He quickly emerged as the most talented of Perino's assistants, and his role went beyond executing his master's cartoons to contributing original designs. His superior talent was already noted by Vasari, who pointed out that Tibaldi proved himself better than many of his more senior colleagues as far as *fierezza, grazia, colorito,* and *disegno* were concerned.[4]

Tibaldi's drawing style in the 1540s owes much to Perino, most obviously in the pen and ink drawings, which often emulate the latter's ease and fluidity, but even the handling of his red chalk and black chalk figure studies, such as this one, is fairly close to his master's. The figures themselves, however, are more directly modelled on Michelangelo, espousing a similar taste for monumental and masculine forms. This is evident in the present drawing, whose lower part, particularly the right leg, seems directly inspired by Michelangelo's *Libyan Sibyl* from the Sistine Chapel ceiling (see fig. 10.1, p. 98). Though it cannot be dated precisely, the drawing is identical in style and technique to Tibaldi's drawing of a *Sibyl* in the British Museum, which served as a study for his 1549 painting of the *Adoration of the Magi* (Galleria Borghese, Rome), which could be considered the pinnacle of his Michelangelesque manner.[5] Tibaldi's chalk technique is also indebted to that of Daniele da Volterra, Michelangelo's friend and follower (with whom our artist worked in the della Rovere Chapel in the church of the Trinità dei Monti, from 1548), though it is generally less dry and smooth. But despite these close affinities, Tibaldi's figures, in torsion and exaggerated pose, go well beyond those of Michelangelo and Daniele. And as we know from Vasari,[6] it was precisely the originality and audacity of his figures that caught the attention of Cardinal Giovanni Poggi, who was to become the artist's most important patron, first in Rome and then, from the early 1550s, in Bologna. There, removed from immediate contact with the works of Michelangelo and his circle, that influence somewhat eased, and Tibaldi quickly emerged with a highly personal synthesis of his Roman experience, as can be seen in perhaps his most famous work, the frescoes of the story of Ulysses in the Palazzo Poggi.

FLORIAN HÄRB

Fig. 53.1 Enrico Maccari, *Graffiti e chiaroscuri, esistenti nell'esterno delle case riprodotti in rame*, Rome

54
MICHELANGELO BUONARROTI,
CALLED **MICHELANGELO** 1475–1564
ANNUNCIATION TO THE VIRGIN C. 1547–1550

Black chalk, outlines indented
38.3 × 29.7 cm
Inscriptions: *From Mr. Lawrence-*
Woodburn colln / sale catalogue
no. 103 / J.C. Robinson
Morgan Library & Museum,
New York

This magnificent drawing represents Michelangelo's design for an altarpiece commissioned around 1547 for the Cesi family chapel in Santa Maria della Pace, Rome. Roused from her reading by the sudden appearance of a large angel, who announces that she is to conceive and bear a son, the Virgin turns to look over her shoulder and raises a protective hand. The figures are evoked by a dense layering of delicate, black chalk strokes whereas the accoutrements of the domestic setting – a cabinet supporting a statue of Moses and containing a basket, book and pitcher, are only lightly outlined. The painting was removed from its original location in the mid-seventeenth century and has since been lost.[1] It is, however, recorded in three smaller replicas, now in the Galleria Nazionale Palazzo Corsini, Rome;[2] the Pinacoteca Manfrediniana, Venice;[3] and the Rijksmuseum, Amsterdam,[4] of which the Corsini version slightly extends the composition on all four sides.[5]

From Vasari's *Lives,* we learn that as a favour to his young friend Tommaso dei Cavalieri, Michelangelo agreed to provide Cardinal Federico Cesi (1500–1565) with a drawing for an altarpiece depicting the *Annunciation to the Virgin.* The painting was to be executed by the master's protege Marcello Venusti.[6] In fact, one may infer a more direct request than Vasari implies, for Michelangelo himself certainly knew the Cardinal: he had received a gift, apparently of food, from Federico Cesi as early as 1543, and was also acquainted with the Cardinal's brother.[7]

The Morgan drawing served as a small cartoon, a "cartonetto," for Venusti to use as a model while painting the altarpiece. The two artists likely first met around 1542, when both commenced work on the decoration of the Cappella Paolina in the Vatican. During the last decades of his life, the celebrated Michelangelo was besieged with numerous commissions and demands on his time, which may help explain why he collaborated with Venusti, a competent painter and meticulous copyist. The Cesi *Annunciation* was only one of several paintings by Venusti after Michelangelo, the most notable being the *Last Judgment* now in the Museo di Capodimonte, Naples.[8]

The Morgan drawing was likely created during the summer of 1547 or soon thereafter. An undisputed study by Michelangelo, in pen and ink, for the Virgin's right hand holding a prayer book that exists in a manuscript in the Vatican Library,[9] carries on its verso the draft of a letter Michelangelo had written at some point between April and July 1547, thereby implying a similar date for the Cesi commission.

Besides the outstanding quality of the drawing, the faint indication of an arched top at upper left is further evidence that the Morgan sheet is Michelangelo's original preparatory study for the altarpiece rather than a copy by Venusti. (The extant painted replicas, all thought to be by Venusti, are rectangular). Due to a late nineteenth-century taste for the rapid sketch, many of Michelangelo's more deliberate and highly finished drawings, including the present one, were nevertheless rejected on the grounds that they were inconsistent with the artist's supposed spontaneous handling and *terribilità.* Thus, although the collector and dealer Charles Fairfax Murray bought the drawing at auction as by Michelangelo, it was classified as by Venusti by the time it appeared in the catalogue of his collection only ten years later. In 1959 Johannes Wilde rehabilitated the drawing as an autograph work by Michelangelo, a reappraisal that has been generally accepted.

RHODA EITEL-PORTER

54

55
GIULIO CLOVIO 1498–1578
PIETÀ c. 1546–1553

Black chalk
34.8 × 25.7 cm
Victoria and Albert Museum,
London

Fig. 55.1 Diana Scultori, *Pietà*,
c. 1575, engraving, 35.2 × 25.8 cm.
Victoria and Albert Museum,
London

Already attributed to Giulio Clovio at the time of its bequest to the Victoria and Albert Museum in the nineteenth century, this drawing reveals the artist's profound obsession with the art of Michelangelo. This image was engraved (fig. 55.1), in reverse, by the Mantuan printmaker Diana Scultori, around 1575, but with the invention identified as Michelangelo's.[1] The credit to Michelangelo was not misinformed as Clovio's sketch probably reproduces a now lost drawing by the master – a version of the composition best known from the highly finished study of the *Pietà* made for Vittoria Colonna, now in the Isabella Stewart Gardner Museum, Boston. A print by Giulio Bonasone of 1546 establishes a date for Michelangelo's invention and indirectly, for the drawing by Clovio, who was a friend of the Florentine master. Clovio produced a painted version of this image, now in the Uffizi; the dimensions are virtually the same, yet variations include the addition of the

Cross, for Duke Cosimo de' Medici in Florence, where the artist had gone in the company of Cardinal Alessandro Farnese for reasons of political caution following the election of Pope Julius III.[2] He likely completed the work by 1553 – the date on a stylistically related painting by Clovio of the *Crucifixion*, also in the Uffizi. Vasari claimed to have owned the drawing for the *Pietà*, but it is not known if this was the same sheet now in the Victoria and Albert Museum.[3] It is not certain either whether Clovio made the drawing now in London in direct preparation for the painting for Duke Cosimo or for another purpose. The drawing is not incised for transfer, however, and it was not the cartoon for the later engraving by Scultori.

Born in Croatia, Giulio Clovio trained in Venice and became the most important manuscript illuminator of the sixteenth century – the "Michelangelo of small works" in Vasari's memorable phrase.[4] Clovio trained with Giulio Romano and so was also strongly influenced by the style of Raphael and his followers. In 1540 he joined the entourage of Cardinal Alessandro Farnese, grandson of Pope Paul III, for whom he executed his finest object, the so-called "Farnese Hours," now in the Morgan Library & Museum. Clovio recognized the talent of the young El Greco and through his intervention the latter was given lodgings by the Farnese. In formal stylistic terms, this drawing is a typical example of Clovio's graphic work for its almost magical reduction of monumental forms onto a small scale and for the smooth, immaculate handling leaving a surface resembling ivory. This particularly exquisite and refined technique in black chalk requiring close viewing was inspired by Michelangelo's own "Presentation" drawings.[5]

As with the work of Marcello Venusti, the London drawing provides a significant example of the Michelangelo copy industry around the mid-sixteenth century. The coherent design with the clear disposition of figures and rather rhetorical expression of emotion betray the new taste of the Counter-Reformation as it pushed art towards simplification and unmistakable narrative intent. The three additional figures around the Virgin and Christ – namely, John the Evangelist, Joseph of Arimathea, and Mary Magdalene – provide the keys in their poses and gestures to appropriate spiritual reactions in the viewer. The simplified costumes would appear to be an attempt to revive early Christian values – another interest of the Counter-Reformation against the excesses of art of the previous generation.

DAVID FRANKLIN

GIOVANNI MARIA CIOCCHI DEL MONTE

JULIUS III 1550–1555

56
TADDEO ZUCCARO 1529–1566
SCENE FROM ROMAN HISTORY c. 1550

Pen and brown ink over black chalk,
brush with brown wash, with
white heightening, on blue paper
25.7 × 28 cm
Private collection, New York

Many of the narrow streets of Renaissance Rome were once dominated by palaces and houses featuring painted facades of historical and mythical subjects. In a world where images were relatively sparse, their impact would have been tremendous. Today, few signs of this abundance survive. Most of the paintings have been weathered away, and our best knowledge of them comes from drawings such as this one by Taddeo Zuccaro. Taddeo had moved to Rome at the age of fourteen, and had suffered through several unproductive apprenticeships before achieving fame in the field of facade decoration. In 1548, when he was only eighteen, he won the prestigious commission to decorate the facade of the Palazzo Mattei.[1]

This drawing from a private collection in New York is similar in format, style, and technique to those that survive from the Mattei commission, and it likely dates from about the same time. While the Roman military subject matter is characteristic of the genre, the drawing cannot be related to any particular lost facade.[2] Typically, the action is seen from a low viewpoint, as the artist took into account that the composition would be placed high up on the wall. The figures are arranged across the space as in a shallow sculptural relief, a reminder that these facades were indeed intended to imitate the facade-mounted sarcophagi of ancient Rome. The composition is anchored by standing figures at left and right.

Most facades of the period were painted in a chiaroscuro technique of either brown or grey, thus faithfully mimicking stone and – perhaps more to the point – avoiding the need to use expensive coloured pigments over such a large area. In a relatively highly finished drawing such as this, possibly a modello for the work, Taddeo has anticipated the desired effect by using blue paper and by working up the surface – darkening it with brown wash – and

creating sculptural moulding through the use of abundant white highlights applied with the brush. As in many of Taddeo's facade episodes, the light seems to be falling strongly from the upper left and from slightly in front, thereby accentuating the relief-like properties of the scene. It is a considered and confident drawing, with hardly a trace of the turbulent penwork characteristic of many of Taddeo's preparatory studies.

Most unusually (in fact, uniquely, as far as we know), this facade drawing by Taddeo can be linked with a figure study, a beautiful red chalk drawing in the Metropolitan Museum for the principal striding soldier.[3] In it, particular attention is given to the soldier's musculature and the torsion of his spine; the area around the middle of the figure is left unstudied, since Taddeo knows that it will be covered by a tunic. Evidence that the drawing was made especially for this composition can be seen in the inclusion of a few lines for the reins extending from the figure's left hand. Taddeo is likely to have retained the figure study for use in other facade frescoes, since such striding poses were common. However, no facades are recorded in which this precise pose reappears.[4] The Metropolitan drawing demonstrates the care with which the artist prepared these scenes, studying the principal figures in detail, and most likely from life. Taddeo's exact working process for his facade frescoes is unknown, and his drawings are the only evidence of it that remains.

Tellingly, the private collection drawing was attributed in the 1800s to the greatest exponent of facade painting, Polidoro da Caravaggio, whose works Taddeo himself greatly admired. Polidoro's name became almost synonymous with the genre, and many drawings of this type were automatically ascribed to him.

JULIAN BROOKS

56

57
GIORGIO VASARI 1511–1574
DESIGN FOR THE CAPPELLA DEL MONTE IN SAN PIETRO IN MONTORIO, ROME c. 1550

Black chalk, brown wash, partially drawn with a ruler and a pair of compasses; the *Pietà* drawing executed on a separate sheet of paper in pen and brown ink, brown wash, over black chalk, with pen and brown ink framing lines
51.1 × 31.4 cm
Inscriptions: *IVLIVS III P. M* [below the altarpiece]
Gabinetto Disegni e Stampe degli Uffizi, Florence

This splendid drawing is a study for the decoration of the Cappella del Monte in San Pietro in Montorio, Rome, designed and executed by Vasari in 1550–1552 (fig. 57.1).[1] Probably in February 1550, right after his election as Pope Julius III, Giovanni Maria Ciocchi del Monte decided to lavishly decorate a chapel in San Pietro in Montorio, where his uncle, Antonio del Monte, formerly titular cardinal of San Prassede, was buried. In his testament, Antonio had requested a marble tomb, for which he also provided the funds. Julius III, however, had more ambitious plans. He envisaged a monumental funerary chapel that would contain, as a pendant to his uncle's tomb, the cenotaph of his grandfather Fabiano del Monte, who was buried in Monte San Savino.

Vasari may have received the commission as early as March 1550.[2] All matters of design had to be approved by Michelangelo, whose advice was indispensable to the pope. According to the *Ricordanze*, Vasari's account book of his own commissions, he made a wooden model of the chapel, on the basis of which a contract was drawn up on 3 June 1550. The contract stipulated that the chapel be made entirely of new Carrara marble and that it be completed within thirty months, by December 1552.[3] (Painting began probably in early 1551, and in a letter of 22 October 1552, Vincenzio Borghini, Vasari's friend and adviser, referred to the chapel as finished.[4]) The vault was to contain frescoes with scenes from the life of Saint Paul, adorned with stucco ornaments; the top of the chapel's arch would show the del Monte coat of arms, with the four evangelists placed in pairs on either side, embellished with festoons and putti. On the travertine pilasters on either side of the chapel, Vasari was to paint in oil the four Latin Fathers of the Church (only three of whom are still visible). The altarpiece would show Ananias Restoring Paul's Sight. Vasari's *ricordo* does not mention the smaller frescoes of Faith, Hope, Charity, and Fortitude, located between the frescoes of Saint Paul in the vault, nor the three smaller horizontal ones depicting sibyls and prophets. The chapel would further contain the marble tombs of the pope's uncle and grandfather and statues of Religion and Justice, which, after some arguments between Vasari and Michelangelo, were commissioned from Bartolomeo Ammannati.[5]

The project as described in the contract, however, was in fact a compromise, resulting from several months of disagreements between the artist and his patron. Vasari initially had planned an exuberant decoration of coloured marble and plaster carvings (*qualche cosa d'intaglio straordinaria*), which he wanted to assign to the sculptor Simone Mosca. He had submitted numerous designs to the pope, as he remarked in his *Life of Mosca*.[6] Yet these designs – and the present one may well have been among them – were rejected because Michelangelo was reluctant to use *intagli* in the chapel's decoration, fearing that they would weaken the impact of the sculptures. Instead, as Vasari further noted, Michelangelo suggested adding paintings, which he believed would better support the sculptures. Vasari subsequently inserted in the vault several smaller paintings, which are not represented in the surviving drawings, including the present one. Coloured marble was also abandoned in favour of a cooler overall effect dominated by Ammannati's white marble sculptures set within a classical, Michelangelesque architecture. And while Vasari clearly worked hard to please the pope, the latter proved a difficult patron. In his *Life of Garofalo* Vasari expressed his frustration at the pope's fickleness: he could "never be satisfied in such matters, and to make things worse, he understood very little of design, and disliked in the evening what had pleased him in the morning."[7]

The present drawing dates from this early phase in the design process, as do two further sheets in the Louvre, one of which, Vasari's only known drawing with watercolour, gives a particularly good idea of the colourful decoration initially intended.[8] The Uffizi drawing, unfinished in the upper left, is a vigorous design, drawn with a sharp black chalk and no pen work but with some additional brown wash.[9] While the overall design is similar to the final work, there are considerable differences in the decoration and the iconography. Below the altar, the drawing shows another sarcophagus, presumably that of Julius III, whose name is inscribed above it. This third tomb was later abandoned and the size of the altarpiece significantly increased. The two lateral tombs, with the reclining figures of Antonio and Fabiano del Monte, and the two figures in the niches correspond broadly with the decoration as executed, except that the segmented pediments above the niches were later replaced by triangular ones. Above the arch, to the right of the del Monte coat of arms where Vasari later depicted the evangelists, the drawing shows a female figure, presumably a virtue. Below this figure, putti are holding another del Monte coat of arms, surmounted by a cardinal's hat (above Antonio's tomb), a design that was eventually abandoned. The drawing further shows that the pilasters were to be decorated with grotesques *all'antica*, which were later replaced by more sombre representations of the four Latin Fathers.

For the vault, Vasari planned a rich stucco decoration with large winged figures and *amoretti* holding three ovals containing scenes from the life of Saint Paul. While the central oval shows the Assumption of Saint Paul, the two lateral compositions are more difficult to identify. The one on the right may be Paul at Malta (a subject not depicted in the end), if the serpent-like chalk stroke in the centre can be read as a viper. It does not appear to represent Paul before Agrippa, the subject that was eventually chosen. The left oval probably shows Paul Preaching at Athens. Vasari later adopted a trapezoid format for these frescoes. Above the altar, the Uffizi drawing projected a splendid broken pediment with grotesque heads, ultimately replaced by a much less extravagant arched pediment.

The drawing of the Pietà in the centre, though clearly by Vasari's hand and drawn on a separate piece of paper, was certainly not the original design for the altarpiece, as Charles Davis has correctly observed. Its subject would have been inappropriate in the context of a papal funerary chapel. The drawing is not directly related to any known project by the artist and was probably inserted later, to give the whole sheet a more finished appearance, possibly with an eye to including it in his *Libro de' Disegni*. Vasari may have reused an existing drawing, or even made one specifically for this purpose, and it cannot be ruled out that the drawing was added by someone else, perhaps a later owner of the sheet.

The Cappella del Monte is arguably Vasari's most successful chapel decoration, in spite of – or perhaps because of – its more restrained appearance, due largely to Michelangelo's intervention. Yet, as his disagreements with Michelangelo and the exuberance of his early designs demonstrate, Vasari, though often unjustly accused of being too close a follower of the great master, had in fact rather different aesthetic ideas. His preference for colour and for rich carvings clashed with Michelangelo's wish for a restrained decoration dominated by an unadulterated architecture and the main sculptures. The surviving pre-liminary drawings such as the present one are therefore of particular interest, for they give an idea of what such a chapel decoration made at the height of the *maniera* might have looked like had Vasari been given a freer hand.

FLORIAN HÄRB

57

Fig. 57.1 Del Monte chapel,
San Pietro in Montorio, Rome

58
DANIELE DA VOLTERRA c. 1509–1566
A BEARDED MAN LEANING AGAINST A WALL c. 1548–c. early 1550s

Black chalk on pale grey paper
37.1 × 22.7 cm
The British Museum, London

Fig. 58.1 Daniele da Volterra, *Assumption of the Virgin*, c. 1550s, fresco. Church of the Trinità dei Monti, Rome

This drawing is a study for an Apostle in Daniele da Volterra's fresco of the *Assumption of the Virgin* on the altar wall of the della Rovere chapel in the church of the Trinità dei Monti (fig. 58.1), the main church of the recently founded order of Minims, or Frati Minimi of San Francesco. The Minims, founded by St. Francesco di Paola, were an influential force in Catholic reform, calling for a return to the penitence, poverty and abstinence that had inspired St. Francis of Assisi in the foundation of the Franciscan order in the thirteenth century. Julius II approved the Rule of the Minims in 1506, fending off attempts by the Franciscan order to absorb them; he also supported the Church of the Trinità dei Monti with plenary indulgences to the faithful who visited on key feast days, and he began the canonization process for Francesco di Paola after the founder's death in 1507.

The chapel's patron, Lucrezia della Rovere (1485–1552), had family ties to the Church of the Trinità dei Monti as the daughter of the pope's sister Luchina. Julius had made a marriage for her to the Roman condottiere Marcantonio Colonna (1478–1522), Duke of Paliano and head of one of Rome's most important aristocratic families, who received the lordship of Frascati from his father-in-law the pope as a wedding gift.[1] Lucrezia's marriage, like that of the pope's illegitimate daughter Felice della Rovere to Gian Giordano Orsini, formed part of Julius II's program of matrimonial politics aimed at securing his own power and reconciling the feuding Roman aristocratic families, the Colonna and Orsini.[2] Lucrezia della Rovere's choice of Daniele da Volterra may have been influenced by the fact that he had been commissioned to decorate the Orsini chapel directly opposite in the same church (c. 1542–1548), belonging to her powerful relative Elena Orsini, Baroness of Filacciano (only Daniele's detached fresco of the *Deposition* survives.[3] It is likely that Lucrezia herself joined the Minim Third Order, which di Paola had established to permit aristocratic women to share in the penitential devotion of the Minims while continuing to live in the world. Membership in the Third Order brought the privilege of burial inside a Minim church; upon her death Lucrezia was interred in front of the altar of her chapel.[4]

The *Assumption* above the altar forms the central focus of the decorative cycle of the life of the Virgin on the della Rovere chapel's walls and vault. Our main contemporary source for the chapel, the 1568 edition of Vasari, states that Daniele's designs were executed mainly by a group of assistants (Marco da Siena, Pellegrino da Bologna, Bizzera *spagnuolo*, and Giovan Paulo Rossetti da Volterra), with the master himself painting only the frescoed *Assumption* altarpiece and the *Presentation of the Virgin*.[5]

The chronology of the chapel's decoration is not precisely understood. Della Rovere received the patronage rights to the third chapel on the right in the church from the Minims, or Padri Minimi of San Francesco di Paola, on 18 August 1548.[6] The decoration was still incomplete at the time of Lucrezia's death in 1552, as we know from an estimate of the work done to date that was drawn up on behalf of her heirs in January 1553.[7] Vasari claims the painter worked there for fourteen years, while the latter claim may be somewhat exaggerated, it is likely that work on the chapel dragged on through most of the 1550s.

Fig. 58.2 Anonymous engraver after Daniele da Volterra, *Assumption of the Virgin*, c. 1691–1729, engraving, 32 × 23.2 cm. Musei Civici del Castello Sfozesco Raccolta delle Stampe Achille Bertarelli, Milan

The figure in the British Museum drawing appears to the left of the altar in Daniele's fresco of the *Assumption*. In the painting as we see it today, the foreground figures have been truncated at the bottom, so that only the upper half of the figure represented in the drawing can still be seen there. Early engravings of the *Assumption* fresco before it was mutilated (fig. 58.2) confirm that the composition originally extended down to the floor on either side of the altar, with the figure shown in the British Museum drawing appearing at full length. Vasari explains the innovative composition thus:

> because the space was not sufficient to hold such figures, and Daniele desired to invent something new there, he pretended that the altar of the chapel was the tomb, and around it he placed the Apostles, having them place their feet at the floor level of the chapel, where the altar begins: some liked this way of doing things, while others, who made up the larger and better part, did not like it at all.[8]

Despite Vasari's reservations, Daniele's decision to let the figures in the fresco expand into the spectator's space must have created a powerful illusion of the interweaving of real and fictive space, analogous to the Sacri Monti that proliferated during the Counter-Reformation. The immediacy with which the Apostles in Daniele's *Assumption* spill out into the spectator's space around the altar can also be compared to the vivid and dramatic style with which the miracle was evoked in Counter-Reformation sermons of the type Lucrezia della Rovere would have heard regularly at Trinità.[9] Daniele's innovative employment of a real altar as a "tomb" in his composition is usually discussed in isolation, but in fact it is very likely that he drew inspiration from an earlier decorative scheme: Pontormo's *Pietà* (or *Lamentation*) in the Capponi Chapel at Santa Felicita in Florence (fig. 58.3). Although Pontormo's altarpiece is contained within the wooden panel on which it is painted, as argued by Shearman the composition implies that Christ's body is about to be moved in the direction of the chapel altar, traditionally a symbol of the tomb where the Christ is resurrected during the celebration of the Eucharist.[10] The influence of Pontormo on Daniele is generally overlooked, but it is remarkable that in the lunette immediately above his della Rovere *Assumption* Daniele apparently copied another motif from the Capponi Chapel that fuses real and fictive worlds – the *Annunciation* divided by a window, with the real light from the window replacing the rays of painted light traditionally shown in such scenes.[11]

Daniele undoubtedly had opportunities to study Pontormo's work in Florence at various points during his career. He must have passed through in Florence when he migrated from his native Volterra to Rome c. 1534–1535, and he could not have failed to take note of the innovative integration of real and fictive space in the Capponi Chapel, which had been completed only a few years earlier. At least one other, rather lengthy stay in Florence during the spring and summer of 1557 was apparently an intermission in the later stages of work on the della Rovere Chapel.[12] In a draft of a letter to Eleonora di Toledo (undated but evidently written after late 1556) the Florentine sculptor Baccio Bandinelli mentions a recent visit from Daniele, who had offered to paint the Salone dei Cinquecento in the Palazzo Vecchio:

> ... seeing that one cannot have a Leonardo da Vinci nor a Raphael of Urbino nor Buonarroti, I have had a visit from Daniele da Volterra, whom Buonarroti celebrates above all other painters, and he has told me he will serve Your Excellencies in painting this hall if you wish, and I beg this of you, since I know for certain that he will not make his paintings so unrestrained and full of errors, of broken legs and arms and upside-down hands and feet [as Giorgio Vasari would].[13]

LOUIS A. WALDMAN

Fig. 58.3 Jacopo Pontormo, *Pietà* (or *Lamentation*), above the altar of the Capponi chapel, and *Annunciation* at right, flanking the window, c. 1525–1528. Santa Felicita, Florence

MARCELLO VENUSTI c. 1512/15–1579
THE PURIFICATION OF THE TEMPLE
after 1550

Oil on panel
60 × 38 cm
The National Gallery, London

Marcello Venusti's painted representation of Christ driving the money-changers and livestock vendors from the Temple in Jerusalem adheres faithfully to the biblical narrative as presented in the gospels of Matthew (21:12–13), Mark (11:15–18), Luke (19:45–46), and John (2:13–16). The detail of the "scourge of small cords" held by Jesus in his right hand is found only in John. Though not widely treated in religious iconography, this episode from the life of Christ gained prominence in the Counter-Reformation period, as it symbolized the purification of the Catholic Church.

The earliest recorded mention of the painting is in the Palazzo Borghese inventory (dated by Paola della Pergola to about 1787–1795),[1] where it is listed as "discacciamento dei venditori dal tempio [driving of the vendors from the Temple], Marcello Venusti."

The painting is directly related to a group of three sheets in the British Museum in London, featuring a number of compositional sketches by Michelangelo.[2] The most completely realized sketch (fig. 59.1) is the one that clearly served as the model for Venusti's painting. According to Tolnay, Michelangelo made the drawings for a fresco that was to have been executed in the Pauline Chapel, which would date them to about 1550. Venusti, who specialized in small-format painted copies of the Tuscan master's drawings, has imbued the scene with a feeling of spirituality and a sense of respect for the institutional religiosity of the period that is typical of all his Michelangelesque works. The figures in the painting are clothed to play down the extreme muscularity that Michelangelo typically emphasized and they are placed in a solemn architectural setting that does not appear in the drawings. As Tolnay has noted, the twisted columns in the background are reminiscent of the Solomonic columns in Saint Peter's Basilica (which, according to a long-standing tradition, had been taken from the Temple in Jerusalem).

The date of the painting remains somewhat uncertain. Its vibrant chromatic range suggests an affinity with Venusti's celebrated copy of the *Last Judgment*, painted in 1549, now in the Museo di Capodimonte in Naples. The personages in the London painting, arranged in a semicircle, are animated by a strong sense of movement that radiates outward from the figure of Christ. The dramatic expressions in some of the male faces call to mind the Apostles in the lower half of Raphael's *Transfiguration* (1516–1520, Pinacoteca Vaticana). The composition as a whole, however, is marred by a certain imbalance, owing to the disproportion between the building's architecture and the reduced scale of the figures.

SIMONA CAPELLI

Fig. 59.1 Michelangelo, *Christ Purifying the Temple*, c. 1555–1560, black chalk, 17.8 × 37.2 cm. The British Museum, London

FRANCESCO DE' ROSSI,
CALLED **FRANCESCO SALVIATI** 1510–1563
PORTRAIT OF ANNIBALE CARO C. 1550

Oil on marble
Diameter approx. 10 cm
Collection of
Mr. and Mrs. Marco Grassi

60

This painting is remarkable for the sensitive execution and the mottled marble surface that enhances its elegance. Recently attributed to Salviati by Philippe Costamagna, the work was published for the first time in the exhibition catalogue devoted to the artist in 1998.[1] From a formal perspective, it is plausible to see Salviati's hand in the work. Indeed, the delicate rendering of details – the garment's collar and the hair, for example – and the intensity of the brushwork are characteristic of his style. The play of shapes also adds an appealing dimension to the reading of the work: the superimposition of two circles and the shift of the portrait to the upper part of the area give the marble a unique energy and configuration. The diagonal vein on the right-hand side takes nothing from the quality of the work.

Although Vasari has reported abundantly on Salviati's work as a portraitist and various inventories attest to his prolific production, it is difficult to make a conclusive chronology, or even a repertory, of the portraits that he produced.[2] The limited number of portraits that have survived, and the lack of preparatory drawings and source documents (contracts, correspondence) that could serve as precise temporal references, only exacerbate this difficulty. That said, we know that Salviati depicted members of the Salviati family, his benefactors, and the scholars toward whom he gravitated, including Pietro Aretino. Costamagna hypothesized that the model for the present portrait could have been Annibale Caro (1507–66).

A native of Civitanova, in the Marche region, Annibale Caro began a quick ascent through the ranks of the intellectual elite in Florence in 1525, under the protection of Giovanni de' Gaddi, whom he was to follow to Rome. He worked for Pier Luigi Farnese, and, briefly, for Cardinal Ranuccio, before establishing himself, in 1548, as secretary and then artistic advisor[3] in the court of Cardinal Farnese, nephew of Pope Paul III. Although in his letters Caro mentioned that his portrait was executed by Bronzino, Salviati, Jacopino del Conte, and an anonymous artist working for the Academicians of Bologna (Accademia Bocchi), to date none of these portraits has been positively identified.[4] Unfortunately, we do not know the current location of the painting, formerly in the Schäfer collection in Berlin, possibly portraying Caro and already associated with the one attributed to Salviati (fig. 60.1).[5] If we posit

that the subject of the Berlin canvas was Caro, we may confirm, simply by looking at a reproduction, that the man whose portrait is in the Grassi collection is physically similar, though older. In fact, the only accepted likenesses that could serve as a point of comparison are two posthumous sculpted portraits: a bust by Giovanni Antonio Dosio in San Lorenzo in Damaso and one by Antonio Calcagni conserved in London (fig. 60.2).[6] In comparing those with the painted marble portrait under consideration, we recognize common facial features such as the beard and moustache, the frowning eyebrow arch, and pronounced furrows in the cheeks. It is, however, chancy to establish identification on the basis of comparison with a portrait executed in a different medium. This is also true for a pen-and-ink drawing at the Fine Arts Academy of Venice, with the inscription "Comendatore Anibal Caro," which does not offer much help with elucidating the identity of the figure under study here.[7]

According to Vasari, the relationship between Salviati and Caro went back to at least 1541, when the artist executed the portrait of his friend, then 34 years old.[8] While the model for the Berlin portrait could be this age, the one in the New York portrait is definitely older. But since the relationship between the men intensified through the 1540s, it is possible that Salviati undertook a second portrait. After a five-year stay in Florence, during which he worked for the Medici on the decoration of the Palazzo Vecchio, Salviati returned to Rome in 1548. There, he regularly spent time with Caro, who was responsible for formulating the iconographic program for the Pallio chapel at the Palazzo della Cancelleria, a commission that Salviati obtained thanks to his friend's warm recommendation to the cardinal.[9] In fact, it was not unusual for Caro to praise Salviati's talent or to go to his assistance, as he did in 1544, keeping him out of prison during his dispute with Pier Luigi Farnese, Duke of Castro and son of the sovereign pontiff Paul III.[10]

The commission to decorate the altar of the Farnese chapel, portraying an *Adoration of the Shepherds,* offered an opportunity for Salviati to experiment with different techniques, including painting on stone; in this regard, he was likely encouraged by the acclaim garnered by Sebastiano del Piombo, who had used the method during the 1530s, notably for the Ghigi chapel at Santa Maria del Popolo.[11] With the death of both Sebastiano and Perino del Vaga in 1547, the path was open to Salviati to establish his reputation in the highly competitive climate of Rome at the time.

In summary, the argument in favour of Caro as the model for the work under consideration here is based on the technique used during the second half of the 1540s and on Salviati's gesture of recognition of one of his most ardent defenders. With his tireless support, Caro had procured for Salviati a major commission with a distinguished patron, Cardinal Farnese. A painted portrait would have enabled the artist to pay the most elementary compliment to his friend. In addition, the modest size of the piece of marble corroborates the idea that the work was a testimony to friendship, as its weight enabled its owner to take the object when he travelled or to keep it with him. The lasting quality of the material would ensure that this token of affection would not be forgotten.

NELDA DAMIANO

Fig. 60.1 Attributed to Francesco Salviati, *Portrait of a Man,* c. 1541, oil on canvas, 70 × 55 cm. Whereabouts unknown

Fig. 60.2 Antonio Calcagni, *Annibale Caro,* c. 1569, bronze and marble, Victoria and Albert Museum, London

JACOPINO DEL CONTE 1510–1598
PORTRAIT OF BINDO ALTOVITI early 1550s

Oil on panel (transferred)
128.5 × 103 cm
The Montreal Museum of Fine Arts

Jacopino del Conte trained in Florence with Andrea del Sarto. He moved to Rome in the early 1530s, where his style was influenced by exposure to the mannerism of Francesco Salviati and Daniele da Volterra. Indeed, by the early 1540s in Rome, he had evolved a *manierà* more advanced, complex, and developed than any other artist in the city, including Salviati. His *Deposition* of 1552 and other earlier paintings for the Oratorio di San Giovanni Decollato (the Florentine church in Rome) are among his most distinguished accomplishments, but the artist was also, according to Vasari, renowned for his portraiture,[1] which included as subjects such notables as the Pope, Michelangelo, and the leading clerical and social figures of Rome.

Certainly one of the most distinguished – and wealthiest – among these was the banker Bindo Altoviti. Born in 1491 to Dianora, daughter of Clarenza Cybo, the sister of Pope Innocent VIII, and to Antonio Altoviti, Bindo took over the Roman family bank on his father's death in 1507, and, despite his youth, met with great success. When the Chigi bank closed in 1528, the Altoviti bank became the most powerful bank in Rome. Managing accounts for the Vatican, it also lent to Henry II of France and even to Duke Cosimo I de Medici, despite Bindo's own pro-Republican, increasingly anti-Medici sentiments. Indeed, Altoviti had funded the escape of the assassinator (a Medici nephew of Bindo's own wife) of the repressive Duke Alessandro de' Medici in 1537. Nonetheless, he maintained a working relation with Pope Clement VII de' Medici, as he had earlier with Leo X de' Medici. In 1531 and 1550 he was appointed Florentine Consul in Rome, and in 1546 (nominated by Duke Cosimo himself) a Senator of Florence. In 1552, Bindo imprudently recruited forces and funded Siena in its attempt to overthrow Medici rule, openly allying himself with Florentine exiles. Declared a traitor in 1554, his Florentine property and that of his wife were confiscated, and Cosimo was reputed to have sent agents to assassinate him in 1555. He died of natural causes in January 1556.

Despite these intrigues, Cosimo de' Medici permitted Cellini, his court sculptor, to go to Rome and execute his celebrated bronze bust of Bindo (Isabella Stewart Gardner Museum, Boston, c. 1550) [cat. 11]. Earlier, as a handsome, leonine youth with long blond hair, he had been portrayed by Raphael (National Gallery of Art, Washington, c. 1515). An active patron, Bindo ordered, besides several versions of his own portrait,[2] the *Madonna dell'impannata* from Raphael (Pitti), and he also owned or commissioned works by Bugiardini, Michelangelo, Salviati, Sansovino, and Vasari, who executed an altarpiece of the *Immaculate Conception* for the Altoviti family chapel in Santi Apostoli in Florence, a small replica of the same, an *Allegory of Justice*, and a *Pietà* for his Roman residence, and also decorated the latter in 1554.[3]

In Jacopino's portraiture – notably in this image of Altoviti – the influences of the monumental gravitas of Sebastiano del Piombo, the pre-eminent portraitist in the city during the previous two decades, conjoined with those of Salviati, Parmigianino, and even Titian, are evident. The statue towards which Bindo points is a figure of Fortitude or Constancy, isolated on a rock in the midst of a windy tempest and entwined around a pillar (a symbol of strength) above a roiling sea, a device that appears with minor differences and reversed on the verso of a surviving contemporary portrait medal of Bindo, its design variously attributed to Cellini or his circle.[4] In the background of the painting, the off-coast storm may have further allegorical significance. When considered together with Bindo's appearance (approximately the same age as his depiction in the Cellini bust of 1550) and the personal and financial situation he was facing in the 1550s, a dating around 1554 seems reasonable.

In 1940, when still in the possession of the Altoviti family, the portrait was given to Ridolfo del Ghirlandaio (a common, generic Florentine portrait attribution of the period). The picture was confirmed in its attribution to Jacopino by Zeri in 1973.[5] The same year, the attribution was changed to Jacopino by Wildenstein Gallery, the owner since 1965, when the painting was exhibited in Paris. Zeri subsequently published his attribution in an article on the artist in 1978. Natale also accepted that attribution (1978).[6] After initially suggesting the possibility of Vasari (1988), Costamagna also has accepted the authorship of Jacopino (2002).[7]

Comparisons with other male portraits by Jacopino including one in the Johnson Collection at The Philadelphia Museum of Art, the portrait of *Giannettino Doria* at the Doria Gallery, and of *Francesco de Pisis* at the Fitzwilliam, are stylistically compelling. Jacopino's work, distinctive from those of Bronzino and Vasari, with whom his portraits are sometimes confused, is characterized by a softer modelling of the flesh; creamier skin tones; more subtle transitions and atmospheric lighting that tend to round forms, reflecting his Roman experience; an emphasis on expressively posed and highlighted hands; and, a more painterly rendering of the beard and hair, distinctive from the sharper, more abstracting contours of his contemporary Florentine colleagues. The painting also shares quite distinctive mannerisms of Jacopino found in a significant number of portraits securely attributed to him, including the Borghese portrait of *Cardinal Cervini*, the ex-Watney Collection *Portrait of a Lady*, and the Philadelphia portrait, notably an archly cocked eyebrow to energize the gaze of the subject.[8]

HILLIARD T. GOLDFARB

62
GIROLAMO SELLARI,
CALLED GIROLAMO DA CARPI 1501–c. 1556
PORTRAIT OF A MAN c. 1550

Oil on canvas
109.2 × 82.6 cm
Seattle Art Museum

There is now no longer any doubt that this portrait is by Girolamo da Carpi. Stylistically, it is comparable to the *Descent of the Holy Spirit* in the church of San Francesco in Rovigo, painted around 1549, notably in the modelling of the flesh, the treatment of the brocades, and the way the light is held in the folds of the drapery. It is probably this stylistic connection that encouraged historians to consider the portrait to be a work painted in Ferrara, although Pattanaro has brought forth a number of elements that situate its execution between 1550 and 1553, when Girolamo was in Rome following Hippolytus II, Cardinal of Este. Pattanaro rightly notes the influence of Francesco Salviati's style on the Seattle portrait, as well as its close relationship to the *Portrait of Pietro Aretino*, painted by Titian (Florence, Galleria Palatina), sent to Duke Cosimo I de Medici in Florence in 1545.

The pose of the model, who holds his coattails in his left hand, is a literal reprise of the *Portrait of Pietro Aretino* and may indicate that Girolamo had had a viewing of Titian's painting. Although the duke's majordomo, Pier Francesco Riccio, hid the portrait from Cosimo during his reception in Florence in order to show it only to artists in the service of the court, it was no doubt easily accessible after 1548, when Riccio stepped down from power for health reasons.[1] In 1549 on his way to Rome Girolamo probably passed through Florence, where he studied the major works on view in the city. Thus, the Seattle portrait must have been executed after he arrived in Rome. In this regard, it is interesting to compare it with another portrait Girolamo painted during his stay in Rome, the *Portrait of Bindo Altoviti*, a Florentine banker, which sold recently at Sotheby's in London (New York, private collection, fig. 62.1).[2] This portrait is notable for the magnificent, surprisingly realistic brocade in the background, which finds its genesis in part in the marble support. Girolamo copied numerous ancient works in Rome, including those at the banker's property, Hadrian's Villa in Tivoli[3] – near the residence being constructed by the cardinal – from where the marble used as the support may have come. The fact that the portrait of the banker was made by the official painter of Hippolytus of Este is based on the close connections formed between the Florentine *fuorusciti* and the French party, of which the cardinal was the main representative in Rome. Despite the absence of any plausible attempt at identification,[4] the gentleman portrayed in the Seattle painting likely belonged, as did Bindo Altoviti, to the diplomatic and financial circle of papal Rome. In 1550, just after the conclave that brought victory to the French party by the elevation to the pontificate of Cardinal Giammaria Ciocchi del Monte as Jules III, Hippolytus of Este showed his gratitude for Altoviti's financial support by offering him his portrait painted by his own artist. For similar diplomatic reasons, the Cardinal of Este obtained for Girolamo da Carpi the responsibility for supervising the restructuring of the Vatican Belvedere. Girolamo's trade of architecture, which would become his principal occupation until the end of his career, is evident in the emphasis on the chimney in the Seattle portrait. This feature occupies the entire background of the painting, like a theatre set, in a subtle play between the marble, the gold-leafed decorative elements and the black-bordered green brocade.

In both the Seattle portrait and the portrait of Bindo Altoviti, Girolamo da Carpi presented his models with a particularly well-developed sense of theatricality. The fashion of situating the character in a luxurious setting corresponded to the expectations of members of the Roman priesthood who sought to emphasize their social rank. It belonged to a tradition inaugurated by Raphael and his studio and developed by the Clementine artists, particularly Il Parmigianino. The reference to this artist – evident in the two portraits by Girolamo that undoubtedly evoke the *Portrait of a Man Known as "Malatesta Baglione"* in Vienna (Kunsthistorisches Museum, Gemäldegalerie), painted in Bologna just after 1527 – is certainly not gratuitous. Like Il Parmigianino, who, when he arrived in Rome in 1524, tried to make an impression on the Roman scene as a portraitist, Girolamo, in 1550, with his Emilian tradition behind him, could legitimately hope to become the principal portraitist of the priesthood and claim the place that Francesco Salviati left vacant after the defeat of his protector, Cardinal Giovanni Salviati, in the conclave of 1549–1550.

PHILIPPE COSTAMAGNA

Fig. 62.1 Giolamo da Carpi, *Portrait of Bindo Altoviti*, c. 1549–1550, oil on marble, 88 × 73 cm. Private collection, New York

63
GIROLAMO SELLARI,
CALLED GIROLAMO DA CARPI 1501–C. 1556
SHEET OF STUDIES (RECTO AND VERSO) 1553

Pen and brown ink
25.8 × 20.6 cm
Inscriptions: *lai 12 hotobre di 1553*
in roma
Szépmüvészeti Múzeum, Budapest

63 (recto)

63 (verso)

The Ferrarese painter, architect, and designer Girolamo da Carpi is today most highly regarded for his numerous and varied drawings. Most of these come from the time of his sojourn in Rome, between August 1549 and November 1553, when he was in the service of his Ferrarese patron, Cardinal Ippolito d'Este, as antiquarian, archeologist, and keeper of the cardinal's collection of antique sculpture. Girolamo's drawings include depictions of a large array of works from antiquity as well as from his own era.

In 1976, Canedy published the artist's "Roman Sketchbook," representing 180 sheets preserved in three separate collections: the Royal Library in Turin, the Rosenbach Museum and Library in Philadelphia, and the British Museum in London.[1] According to Canedy, Girolamo did not actually make drawings of original sculptures, reliefs, or frescoes, but rather copied other mid-sixteenth-century drawings, mainly by renowned artists working in the all'antica style, such as Michelangelo, Raphael, Perino del Vaga, Polidoro da Caravaggio, and Giulio Romano.[2] It is known that he began sketching examples of these motifs well before 1549, during his travels to Florence, Mantua, and Parma in the 1530s.[3] Nonetheless, most of the drawings in the "Roman Sketchbook" are of subjects Girolamo found in Rome, and the only dated sheet in it is inscribed "ali 24 daprille 1553 in Roma" (on 24 April 1553 in Rome).[4]

The sheet of sketches preserved in the Szépmüvészeti Múzeum in Budapest is inscribed "lai 12 hotobre di 1553 in roma" (on 12 October 1553 in Rome). Although the Budapest sheet, with its different format, is not directly linked to the "Roman Sketchbook," the similarity in subject matter, drawing style, handwriting, and date would strongly suggest that it comes from the same period in Rome. Unfortunately, some important evidence may have been lost when the Budapest sheet was trimmed slightly: parts of the drawings have been cut away, and no stitch holes are visible. Nevertheless, the linear handling of pen and ink, the filling up of all the available space, and the fact that both the recto and verso have been used all suggest that this sheet may have come from a sketchbook not unlike the "Roman" one.

The Budapest sheet is known to have been in the collection of the sixteenth-century Nuremberg merchant Paulus Praun, where it was considered the work of Giuseppe Salviati. In 1804, along with many other drawings auctioned from the Praun collection, it was acquired by the Hungarian collector Prince Miklós Esterházy, in whose inventory it was listed as by Giulio Romano. With the purchase of the Esterházy collection by the Hungarian state in 1870, the sheet went to the Országos Képtár (the forerunner of today's museum), where it was catalogued as an anonymous sixteenth-century Italian drawing. Antal,

in an annotation on the mat, suggested the name of Battista Franco. Davidson, in a subsequent annotation, convincingly associated the drawing with Girolamo da Carpi, a conclusion that has been widely accepted, notably by Pouncey, and was supported most recently by Zentai in an extensive discussion of the Budapest sheet.[5]

Like the drawings in the "Roman Sketchbook," the Budapest sheet is replete with motifs after ancient and mid-sixteenth-century models in the all'antica style. The arcade with semicircular arches supported by half-columns, drawn in a slightly different ink, is an architectural motif that was known at the time mainly from the Theatre of Marcellus and the Colosseum, as well as from the facades of several fifteenth- and sixteenth-century Roman buildings, and appears again in another drawing by Girolamo (Uffizi, Florence, 230A).[6] The figure of Marsyas, on the left, recalls a Roman marble statue (after a Greek original) that was in the famous collection of Cardinal Andrea della Valle in Rome[7] and may have been known to Girolamo through a 1553 engraving by Hieronymus Cock after a drawing from the 1530s by Maarten van Heemskerck.[8] Like many of the artist's motifs, the marble statue (in its unrestored state) was one that he drew repeatedly: it is also seen on two sheets in the "Roman Sketchbook."[9]

The original source of the drawing of Pan with a nymph and Eros has not yet been identified. The slightly stiff arrangement and poses of the figures are suggestive of an antique relief. A print by Giulio Bonasone, *Pomona and Pan*, engraved before 1561, closely resembles the principal group shown here, and Parma has proposed that the composition of the print may have been borrowed directly either from the Budapest sheet or from the nearly identical variant of it that surfaced on the art market in 1985.[10] But if Canedy is right that Girolamo himself invariably worked from drawings, then it is just as likely that Bonasone's print and Girolamo's two drawings were based on a similar model circulating in the Roman workshops.

The verso of the Budapest sheet is in a somewhat different style. The Perinesque origin of the two draped females is clearly reflected in the penwork, which successfully and intelligently imitates the fluid and scribbly sketches of Perino del Vaga tempered by the grace of his mature drawing style. As Zentai has observed, the four grotesque lion heads could be compared with a sheet of studies in the Metropolitan Museum of Art, New York, attributed (with some reservations) to one of Perino's assistants, Pellegrino Tibaldi.[11] The New York drawing is markedly different in style and details, but like the Budapest sheet, it illustrates the keen interest of the Mannerists in the *grotteschi* frequently occurring on all'antica decorations.

ZOLTÁN KÁRPÁTI

ATTRIBUTED TO **ERCOLE SETTI** 1530–1617
CARDINAL GIOVANNI DE'MEDICI'S
TRIUMPHAL RE-ENTRY INTO FLORENCE
IN 1512 (AFTER RAPHAEL) c. 1550s

Pen and brown ink and wash
12.6 × 28.3 cm
Private collection, Toronto

This carefully executed drawing is a precise copy after the lower border of one of the tapestries designed by Raphael in 1515–1516 to hang on the lower walls of the Sistine Chapel. In contrast to the full range of colour in the principal scenes, these borders are meant to look as if they were bronze bas-reliefs.[1] The subjects are taken from the life of the patron of the tapestries, Pope Leo X, who was the son of Lorenzo de'Medici (il Magnifico) and was made a cardinal in 1492. The incident represented in this drawing is one of two related events, separated by a pair of lions, in the border below the *Death of Ananias*. This tapestry belongs to the series with subjects from the life of Saint Peter, and was intended to hang on the right wall of the chapel, as the furthest of three tapestries from the altar. The scene in the left half of the border has been interpreted as a communal meeting (*parlamento*) of Florentines, gathered in their central piazza to approve the return of the Medici family to its native city in 1512, after eighteen years of exile.[2] The scene on the right half of the border is the subject of the present drawing, and represents the specific return of Cardinal Giovanni de'Medici, the future Pope Leo X, to Florence on 14 September 1512. The sheet has evidently been cut at the right and so eliminates some of the followers of the cardinal, but otherwise the drawing closely repeats the relief-like composition originally designed by Raphael.

In the drawing, the cardinal, at the extreme right, rides forward triumphantly on horseback with his right hand extended. The direction of his movement in fact is the same as that of a visitor to the chapel who is moving towards the altar. The cardinal is welcomed by the men of Florence, who advance from the opposite direction, their arms outstretched.[3] With an even more commanding gesture, the allegorical figure of Florence (*Florentia*) bends forward at the far left. Her enveloping drapery blows out in an arc to the left, and both her arms stretch out to the right, as if to embrace the newly returned cleric across the very breadth of the composition. Below her, the lion of Florence, the emblematic Marzocco, looks on with evident self-satisfaction. Even the river god at the lower left, which must represent the Arno River, directs his gaze across the Florentine citizens to the cardinal's entry. Obviously, the composition sought to proclaim the message that Florence had collectively welcomed Cardinal Giovanni back to his homeland in the warmest fashion imaginable.

The drawing was acquired by the present owner as a work by Girolamo da Carpi, but it has more recently been attributed to Ercole Setti, a little-known painter from Modena.[4] Typical of Setti's draftsmanship is the neat use of pen and ink, especially to delineate such details as profile heads, hands and feet. It is not known, however, how the artist knew Raphael's design as manifest in the border of the Sistine Chapel tapestry.

DAVID MCTAVISH

64

65
PROSPERO FONTANA 1512–1597
BACCHANALIAN FEAST c. 1553–1555

Pen and brown ink, brown wash,
over black chalk, with white
heightening, on blue paper, squared
for transfer in pen and brown ink
36.8 × 47 cm
Musée du Louvre, Paris

Fig. 65.1 Prospero Fontana,
Bacchanalian Feast, mid-1550s,
fresco. North Room, Villa Giulia,
Rome

66

PROSPERO FONTANA 1512–1597
THE MARRIAGE BANQUET OF PELEUS AND
THETIS c. 1553–1555

Pen and brown ink, brown wash,
over black chalk, with white
heightening (partly oxidized), on
blue paper, squared for transfer
35.4 × 54.2 cm
Inscriptions: *prospero*
The British Museum, London

Fig. 66.1 Prospero Fontana, *Feast
of the Gods*, mid-1550s, fresco.
North Room, Villa Giulia, Rome

Fig. 66.2 Prospero Fontana, *A
display of tableware with servants
and an infant satyr on the back of
a tiger* (left section of Fontana
drawing, cat. 66), c. 1553–1555, pen
and brown ink with brown wash,
heightened with white, over black
chalk, 30.9 × 21.6 cm. The British
Museum, London

In a pioneering article in 1965, Gere noted that the large and finished drawing from the Louvre, *Bacchanalian Feast*, traditionally attributed to Giovanni Francesco Penni and later to Giorgio Vasari, relates to a ceiling fresco in the North Room on the ground floor of the Villa Giulia, Pope Julius III's suburban retreat (fig. 65.1). Located on the slopes of Monte Parioli, the villa was built in 1551–1553 by Giacomo da Vignola, who, according to Vasari's *Lives*, owed this commission to the latter's mediation with the pope.[1] The villa, surrounded by vineyards, contained a nymphaeum in the centre, which housed a fountain that drew its water from the Aqua Virgo, an ancient Roman aqueduct that the pope had restored. The fresco decoration included also the South Room, as well as several rooms on the floor above. At the time, the frescoes were generally attributed to the young Taddeo Zuccaro, but Gere knew from a passage in Vasari's life of Taddeo that one "Messer Prospero painted many things there [in the Villa Giulia] … and Taddeo was employed in many ways, which was to be of great benefit for him."[2] In fact, payments to Fontana were recorded for April and May 1553 and from then on regularly until the pope's death in March 1555. Based on these clues, and recognizing that the style of the Louvre drawing was inconsistent with Taddeo's, Gere convincingly attributed both the drawing and the fresco to Fontana. Subsequent scholarship confirmed Fontana as the leading master responsible for the overall design and much of the execution of the existing fresco decoration of the villa, with Taddeo as his talented assistant.[3] The Louvre *Bacchanalian Feast* is thus an important document of Fontana's drawing style around 1550 and forms the basis for other attributions to the master, whose oeuvre of securely attributed drawings is relatively small.[4]

After training with Innocenza da Imola at Bologna, Fontana seems to have worked with Perino del Vaga, first at Genoa, and then in Rome on the decoration of the Castel Sant'Angelo. In the mid-1540s his somewhat chameleonic style matured, amalgamating Giulio Romano's decorative arrangements and occasionally heavy figures with the more elegant and lighter style of Perino and the fashionable second-generation Tuscan Mannerists. Only one year his junior, Fontana closely modeled his style on Vasari's, which he had first encountered during the latter's sojourn in 1539–1540 in Bologna, where Vasari had made several paintings and frescoes for the refectory of San Michele in Bosco. The two became friends, and Fontana later occasionally assisted Vasari, though generally in a minor role. From the 1540s on, for about thirty years, Fontana often

based his own works directly on drawings by Vasari; in fact, Vasari provided Fontana with drawings, and very likely even made some specifically for several of the latter's projects.[5]

The Villa Giulia brought the two artists together once more, for the pope had asked Vasari, in the spring of 1553, to supervise its decoration. And it may well have been Vasari who recommended Fontana or in some other way helped his less well established friend to secure this prestigious commission. According to his autobiography, in addition to this supervisory work Vasari was also commissioned to produce frescoes for the villa's loggia (designed by Bartolommeo Ammanati), overlooking the nymphaeum.[6] By June 1553 he was already working on the cartoons,[7] and while it remains unclear whether these frescoes were ever executed, several preparatory studies survive.[8] These, in turn, are based on an iconographic *invenzione* for the loggia decoration written by Vasari's friend the poet Annibale Caro and dated 1550.[9] Going by Caro's text, the decoration included three main frescoes reflecting the villa's function as a country house with its associated themes of wine and husbandry: the *Fontanalia* in the middle (a reference to the fountain in the nymphaeum), flanked by the *Baccanalia* on the left and the *Cerealia* on the right.

Fontana's Louvre *Bacchanalian Feast* along with its related fresco, and Vasari's *Baccanalia*, whose likely appearance we know from drawings in the Louvre, the Uffizi, and a private collection,[10] are closely related thematically, if not compositionally. Both painters surely knew of each other's projects, and Fontana may even have known Caro's text, as many of its elements can also be found in his drawing. Fontana set his *Baccanalian Feast* in a wood. Bacchus is seated at the far end of the table, drinking from a flask, in the company of satyrs and merrily feasting bacchants. At the left, Pan rests one arm on the table, while behind him the drunken Silenus is supported by his companions. In the fresco Fontana introduced several changes, most notably in the foreground: at the right he replaced the old satyr being served wine by a bacchant with a younger one, and at the left he added a satyr pouring wine into a large goblet from which two others drink.

On the opposite side of the ceiling in the North Room, Fontana painted, in the same format as his *Bacchanalian Feast*, a fresco of the *Feast of the Gods* (fig. 66.1). Though not identical, its composition, as Gere pointed out, bears a general resemblance – particularly in the angle of the table and the way the figures are arranged around it – to a large drawing from the British Museum. Acquired in 1875 with an attribution to Perino, and later given to Taddeo, the drawing was correctly attributed to Fontana by Gere, who noted its close ties, in style and figure repertory, to the Louvre *Bacchanalian Feast*. In addition, it bears a six-teenth-century inscription at the lower right, *prospero*, which clearly points to Fontana as its maker. The subject of the drawing, however, could not be fully explained, so it was merely described as "gods disturbed at a banquet by the oversetting of a side-table." It was not then known that the drawing was but the central part of a larger compos-ition that at some point had been trimmed on both sides. Recently, a fragment that had surfaced on the New York art market in 2002 was identified by Hugo Chapman as the left-hand part of that composition and was subsequently acquired by the British Museum (fig. 66.2).[11] Drawn on a separate sheet of paper, upon which the left edge of the larger drawing was originally pasted, it shows the continu-ation of the procession of servants and a large sideboard with extravagant tableware. In the foreground a young satyr is straddling a tiger, whose head, half cut off, con-tinues in the lower-left corner of the larger drawing. There can be little doubt that the composition of the larger draw-ing originally extended on the right as well, and that the missing part would have shown the object that the atten-tion of the main figures seems to be directed at.

It has recently been suggested, quite convincingly, that the subject of the entire composition is that of the Marriage Banquet of Peleus and Thetis, at the moment in which the festivities are interrupted by Eris, the Greek goddess of discord and rivalry war.[12] Outraged at not hav-ing been invited, Eris tossed into the party a golden apple with the inscription: "to the fairest one." Juno, Minerva, and Venus all claimed the prize, and Jupiter asked Paris to decide. Falling for Venus's promises – the love of Helen of Sparta, the world's most beautiful woman – Paris chose beauty rather than wealth (Juno) or wisdom (Minerva), and thus caused the Trojan war. The main protagonists, except for Jupiter and Paris, are all assembled at the table. Near the middle on the left sits the crowned bridegroom, Peleus, next to his bride, Thetis, rising and with her arms outstretched, ready to catch the prize. To his left sits Minerva in armor, and to Thetis's right is Venus, being served by Ganymede while pointing with her left arm at the intruder. Opposite Venus at the table is Juno, seen from the back, her head turned, and accompanied by her peacock, with Bacchus seated to her right. There can be

little doubt that the still missing part of the composition would have shown Eris about to throw the "apple of dis-cord" into the crowd.

Perhaps more than the Louvre *Bacchanalian Feast*, the two British Museum drawings reveal Fontana's eclectic attitude. Several motifs are taken from Giulio Romano's fresco on the west wall of the Sala di Psiche in the Palazzo Te, Mantua (1527–1530), either directly copied (the child satyr straddling a tiger), or borrowed with some differen-ces (the three-stepped sideboard with tableware, which sits at the centre of Giulio's composition).[13] The figures in the British Museum drawings, particularly those in the background, as well as the handling of the pen, are close to Vasari's. The servants bringing food from the left and those making music on the right seem directly inspired, in fact, by Vasari's large *Wedding of Esther and Ahasuerus*, painted only a few years earlier, in 1548–1549, for the refectory of the Badia of Saints Flora e Lucilla, Arezzo, and now in the Museo Statale d'Arte Medievale e Moderna of that city. In that painting one also finds the large side-board (for Vasari, too, was a great admirer of Giulio), the columns, and the staircase in the background.[14]

Despite the close connection between the British Museum *Marriage Banquet* and the Villa Giulia decoration in general – in style, composition, and subject matter – one cannot be absolutely certain that the drawing was made for that project. Its elongated horizontal format, rounded off by a semicircle (as its left part suggests), concurs with neither the frescoes in the North Room nor those in the South Room of the villa. Fontana did use elements from the larger British Museum drawing in the fresco decora-tion, such as the seated figure of Juno, which appears in the *Bacchanalian Feast*, while other figures, such as Bacchus and Ganymede, are similarly employed in the *Feast of the Gods* fresco. One must not read too much into these recurrences, however, for artists such as Fontana and Vasari usually worked with a stock of readily available figures that could be employed in different compositions, even over an extended period of time. Nonetheless, the British Museum drawings may well belong to an earlier phase in the design process, when perhaps only one central ceiling fresco was planned. In fact, a few years later, in the second half of the 1550s, when he worked without Vasari at Città di Castello, Fontana actually produced a similar *Feast of the Gods* as a single ceiling painting in a room of the Palazzo Vitelli a Sant' Egidio.[15]

FLORIAN HÄRB

67
FRANCESCO DE' ROSSI,
CALLED **FRANCESCO SALVIATI** 1510–1563
VICTORY C. 1550–1555

Black chalk, with white
heightening, on blue paper
29.5 × 25 cm
Annotations: *286* and *Salviati*
National Gallery of Canada,
Ottawa

67

The attribution of this hitherto unpublished drawing to Francesco Salviati made by Monbeig Goguel (private communication) is supported by an old annotation ("Salviati") on the recto. The same annotation appears on a drawing by Salviati in Amsterdam.[1] There seems no reason to question either attribution.

The drawing appears to represent a seated allegorical female figure of Victory, as indicated by the classicising drapery, the sensual exposure of the underlying body, and the military references including a trophy of arms and a shield. Especially striking for its elaborative conception is the massive throne, decorated with a lion's head evoking the Old Testament throne of Solomon. In terms of style, the slow rhythms and ethereal, decorative quality of the drawing are characteristic of Salviati's later work. The sheet can be dated on stylistic grounds to the period around 1550 to 1555 in Rome based on parallels with figures in the Palazzo Sacchetti and Palazzo Farnese decorations. If it were not for the additional attributes present, it would be tempting to believe the sketch was preparatory, in reverse, for the seated female guest in the foreground of the *Feast at Cana* fresco in San Salvatore in Lauro – another major project of Salviati's Roman period of the 1550s. The Ottawa study was presumably intended for a monumental framing figure to be executed in fresco in relation to a narrative scene, likely for a Roman palace commission.

The drawing is best classified as a drapery study – the face and one of the arms are not even represented. The circulating quality of the fabric, which appears almost alive, is typical of Salviati's highly ornamental late style. The black chalk itself, applied mostly in close parallel lines, suggests the smoothness of a marble surface and betrays the artist's obsession with recreating (and rivalling) in his paintings the extreme polish and suppleness of Michelangelo's sculptures. An awareness of Michelangelo is further revealed by the scissor-like pose of the legs that evokes the sculptures of the New Sacristy in San Lorenzo in Florence. The Ottawa drawing, one of three by Salviati in the collection of the National Gallery, is a major addition to the artist's corpus.

DAVID FRANKLIN

GIAN PIETRO CARAFA

PAUL IV 1555–1559

68

JAN VAN DER STRAET, CALLED STRADANUS
1523–1605

SAINT PETER, AFTER SEBASTIANO DEL PIOMBO c. 1550–1560

Pen and brown ink and brown wash, with white heightening, over black chalk, on blue paper
33.9 × 15.7 cm
Annotations: *Bast. Del Piomb.*; *Sebastiano del Piombo (Sebastiano Luciano.) 1485–1547; Collection P. Lely peintre de Charles Ier.*
National Gallery of Canada, Ottawa

Fig. 68.1 Sebastiano del Piombo, *Saint Peter,* c. 1520, fresco. San Pietro in Montorio, Rome

The attribution of this drawing to Giovanni Stradanus was made on stylistic grounds by Baroni Vannucci, who first published it in 2006.[1] The artist's distinctly adept handling of a mixed graphic technique with vivid, fluent lines, sagging drapery folds and soft treatment of contours, can be seen in any number of Stradanus drawings, many of which survive, fortunately, for comparison.

The drawing is not an original composition but a complete copy after the *Saint Peter* frescoed by Sebastiano del Piombo in the Borgherini chapel in San Pietro in Montorio on the Janiculum hill in Rome, c. 1520 (fig. 68.1).[2] The principal painting in this chapel was the *Flagellation of Christ* executed by Sebastiano from Michelangelo's drawn designs – one of the most celebrated and influential new works produced in Rome during the first part of the sixteenth century – and it is not surprising that Stradanus, like so many artists, was attracted to the site.[3] Stradanus copied one of the massive saints from the lower part of the chapel, accentuating the audacious figure-eight pose and the active, circulatory folds of drapery. It is not clear if the inscription on the drawing itself identifying the source is in the copyist's own hand, but it is certainly old.

Stradanus, who was Flemish-born, but spent most of his career in Florence, is known to have visited in Rome as a young artist around 1550 and again a decade later. Presumably, he made this drawing as a relative youth on one of those occasions, although precise dates for copies are generally difficult to settle. In addition to the evidence that it provides for his source material, the copy is significant in helping to reconstruct Sebastiano's original, especially in the now-damaged areas of the fresco. In creating this work, Sebastiano experimented – much to the displeasure of Michelangelo, who was always an advocate of pure fresco – with a hybrid technique blending fresco and oil in an attempt to slow the drying process and also to introduce darker tonalities into the final work, such that the original is now in a poor state of preservation. The drawing also assists in the particular appreciation of the strong diagonal of the saint's key at his feet making a dramatic *trompe l'oeil* effect in the original. One assumes that such a relatively resolved drawing was not made directly from the original fresco but in the artist's workshop from more spontaneous studies, although it does still contain numerous spontaneous pentimenti. Unusually, the black chalk serves not just as an underdrawing, but it is also introduced on top of the wash suggesting a longer and more mediated drawing session in the studio.

DAVID FRANKLIN

Basti del Domb

69
DANIELE DA VOLTERRA c. 1509–1566
DAVID AND GOLIATH c. 1555

Black chalk
33.8 × 40.8 cm
Biblioteca Apostolica Vaticana,
Vatican City

69

This highly finished black chalk drawing is related closely to one of the two views of the struggling group of *David and Goliath* in Daniele da Volterra's remarkable double-sided painting on slate in the Louvre in Paris (fig. 69.1a-b). Now restored and returned to public view, this masterpiece can once more be admired as an unusual attempt to equal in painting the three-dimensional presence and, given its stone support, the durability of sculpture.[1] As Giorgio Vasari stated in 1568, Daniele's painting is a *cosa capricciosa* (capricious thing). It can also be seen as the artist's tribute to his friend and artistic mentor Michelangelo Buonarroti, recalling Michelangelo's own treatment of this subject on the Sistine Chapel ceiling (c. 1509), and evoking, stylistically and conceptually, the struggling groups of angels and damned souls in the fresco of the *Last Judgment*. Daniele's complex double design might also be said – in the spirit of Renaissance artistic rivalry – to improve on Raphael's version of the victory of David over Goliath frescoed in the Vatican loggia (c. 1516), and widely disseminated in a print by Marcantonio Raimondi.[2]

According to Vasari, the *David and Goliath* was commissioned by Giovanni della Casa, the poet and author of the famous dialogue on manners *Il Galateo* (1551–1555). Apparently, the Florentine writer intended to produce a treatise on painting, and "wanting to clarify for himself some minutiae and particulars from men of the profession," he ordered from Daniele both a clay model of David and a corresponding painting to be made with all possible diligence.[3] Given Daniele's closeness to Michelangelo, it may be that della Casa hoped to gain some insight into Michelangelo's working practices and to better understand his well-known opinion that sculpture was the "lantern of painting."[4] The *David and Goliath* was part of a group of five paintings commissioned by della Casa from Daniele at the same time, and for which Michelangelo provided his friend with designs. The likely date for this group of works is from between June 1555, when della Casa settled in Rome, and November 1556 when he died (probably leaving his treatise on painting unwritten). Recent scholarly work on the dating of the drawings that Michelangelo provided

for Daniele supports this conclusion.[5] When Vasari wrote his life of Daniele, the double-sided painting was in the possession of Annibale Rucellai. It remained in Rome, possibly in the Montalto collection, until 1715 when it was presented to King Louis XIV of France by the Spanish Ambassador, the Prince of Cellemare.[6]

Surviving drawings in the Uffizi (inv. 14965F) and the Louvre (inv. 1512) show Daniele evolving the design for the view of the group of *David and Goliath* in the Vatican drawing exhibited here. His starting point for this view was a group of four small, vigorous *pensieri* drawings by Michelangelo, now in the Pierpont Morgan Library in New York, that provide variations on the theme of two combatants where a smaller figure strikes a larger recumbent foe. In the Uffizi drawing by Daniele, Goliath's right leg is not yet extended diagonally backwards, helping to define the foreshortened recession of the figure into the picture plane, and David's sword-bearing right arm is held out in an awkwardly straight manner. The Louvre drawing shows Goliath gripping David's left arm at the elbow and not, as here and in the final painting, by the wrist. Two further drawings, in the British Museum and the Louvre (inv. 1513), respectively, demonstrate Daniele exploring the group of interlocked combatants from the opposite side. The Louvre drawing of this view of the group was made under the same artificial light conditions as in the Louvre study discussed above (inv. 1512), with Daniele carefully recording cast shadows in both views. Michelangelo had not provided Daniele with drawings for this view of the group and the artist was able to realize it through the use of a three dimensional model in clay. In the context of Della Casa's commission, Daniele's development of two pictorial views from a sculptural model could be said to address both the so-called *paragone* question – namely whether painting or sculpture was the better art form – and the argument, deriving from Leon Battista Alberti and advanced by Leonardo da Vinci, that the many potential points of view of a statue could be reduced to a front and back view in painting.[7] There was, however, nothing out of the ordinary about Daniele's employment of sculptural models as tools for designing pictorial compositions. The method of refining a figural design by translating it into three dimensions, or studying foreshortened or complex poses through the use of models, was a routine practice employed extensively by Daniele in such public projects as the frescoes in the Della Rovere chapel in the Roman church of SS Trinità dei Monti (1548–c. 1556).

The attribution to Daniele da Volterra of the drawing exhibited here was advanced in 1990 by Giovanni Morello, who in support of this claim pointed to the drawing's Roman provenance (it entered the Vatican library with papers from the Rospigliosi family), the evidence of watermarks on the paper dating to the second half of the sixteenth century, and also the presence of *spolveri* ("pounce marks") by which the design had been transferred to the paper.[8] Although this attribution was accepted by Laura Corti and the present writer, the drawing has been described by Joannides as "a copy, probably by a member of Daniele's studio."[9] The difficulty of distinguishing between authentic drawings made by Daniele after sculptural models and copies has been noted by Hirst.[10] In this case the minor differences between the finished work and the Vatican drawing (David's slingshot and Goliath's sword are absent from the drawing), together with the evidence of *spolveri* suggest that the drawing was probably made towards the end of Daniele's exacting design process, and that he is therefore the likely author of the drawing.

BEN THOMAS

Fig. 69.1a-b Daniele da Volterra, *David and Goliath*, c. 1555, double-sided painting on slate, 133 × 172 cm. Musée du Louvre, Paris

70

TADDEO ZUCCARO 1529–1566
A MALE FIGURE ON CRUTCHES AND
A RIGHT ARM (recto); *A MAN BENDING*
FORWARD (verso) c. 1556–1559

Black chalk, with white heightening, on blue paper (both sides)
24.5 × 34.8 cm
Inscriptions: [Ta]*ddeo Zuccaro*
[verso]
Private collection

This unusually well preserved double-sided study is a major – and until now unpublished – addition to the graphic corpus of Taddeo Zuccaro, unquestionably one of the most gifted of the younger generation of Roman artists that came to maturity in the mid sixteenth century.[1] Like the majority of artists working in the papal city, Taddeo was not a native Roman. The son of a minor painter from Sant'Angelo in Vado, a small town in the Duchy of Urbino in the Marches on the eastern side of Italy, his background was profoundly provincial. In the early 1540s the young Taddeo, still in his early teens, left for Rome where his precarious struggle to maintain himself while studying and copying the city's artistic treasures over the subsequent six or seven years was mythologized in his younger brother Federico's series of pen-and-wash drawings, now in the J. Paul Getty Museum, Malibu. This decade was a stimulating time for a young artist to be in Rome. The titanic figure of Michelangelo was still at work in the Pauline chapel in the Vatican, while nearby in the Castel Sant'Angelo, Raphael's most gifted pupil, Perino del Vaga, was directing the decoration of the papal apartments. Michelangelo's work remained a touchstone for Taddeo, as it did for most artists of his generation in Rome, the two Sistine chapel frescoes providing a rich quarry of figurative ideas to quote and adapt. Perino was no less important to Taddeo's development, although in a less direct fashion. The eclecticism of the Castel Sant'Angelo frescoes heralded a new phase in Roman painting, one that confidently married the opulent decorative language of Imperial Rome with the modern idiom of Michelangelo and Perino's long-dead master Raphael. A comparable synthesis of artistic sources is present in the work that made Taddeo's reputation – the Mattei chapel in Santa Maria della Consolazione completed after four year's work in 1556.

The present drawing is related to Taddeo's decoration of the Frangipani chapel in the Roman church of San Marcello with scenes from the life of Saint Paul. The exact date of the commission from Mario Frangipani is not known, but it must have been between 1556 and 1558, soon after Taddeo's completion of the Mattei chapel. Unlike in the earlier project where Taddeo is said by Vasari to have painted only when he felt inspired, the Frangipani commission suffered from Taddeo's meteoric success that meant that his services were much in demand. Consequently, work on the chapel had not been concluded by the time Taddeo died in 1566 and it was left to Federico, his younger and less talented sibling, to do so. The stuttering progress and Taddeo's need to delegate much of the execution of the frescoes to his assistants can be seen in the uneven quality of the chapel's decoration. The poor preservation of the works, exacerbated in some cases by later repainting, has further diminished their appeal.

A sense of what Taddeo might have achieved for the Frangipani, had he been able to devote himself to it without interruption, can be gained from his preparatory studies for the commission, which rank among his finest graphic creations. The present example focuses on figures in two scenes on the altar side of the chapel. The main study on the recto is a study for the stricken figure on the left in the *Healing of the Lame Man at Lystra* (Acts 14:8-10) on the right-hand wall of the chapel (fig. 70.1). The right arm does not correspond to anything in the finished work, but it is most likely a rejected idea for the gesture of Saint Paul commanding the lame man to stand. The drawing on the verso is related to the fresco compartment immediately above on the barrel-vaulted roof, the *Raising of Eutychus at Troas* (fig. 70.2), an episode described in Acts 20:10. The figure studied on the sheet is one of the youths supporting the fallen body of Eutychus, his lower arms and hands obscured behind the corpse.

Fig. 70.1 Taddeo Zuccaro and studio, *Healing of the Lame Man at Lystra*, c. 1556/58–c. 1567, fresco. Frangipani chapel, San Marcello al Corso, Rome

70 (recto)

Fig. 70.2 Taddeo Zuccaro and
studio, *Raising of Eutychus at Troas*,
1556/58–c. 1567, fresco. Frangipani
chapel, San Marcello al Corso, Rome

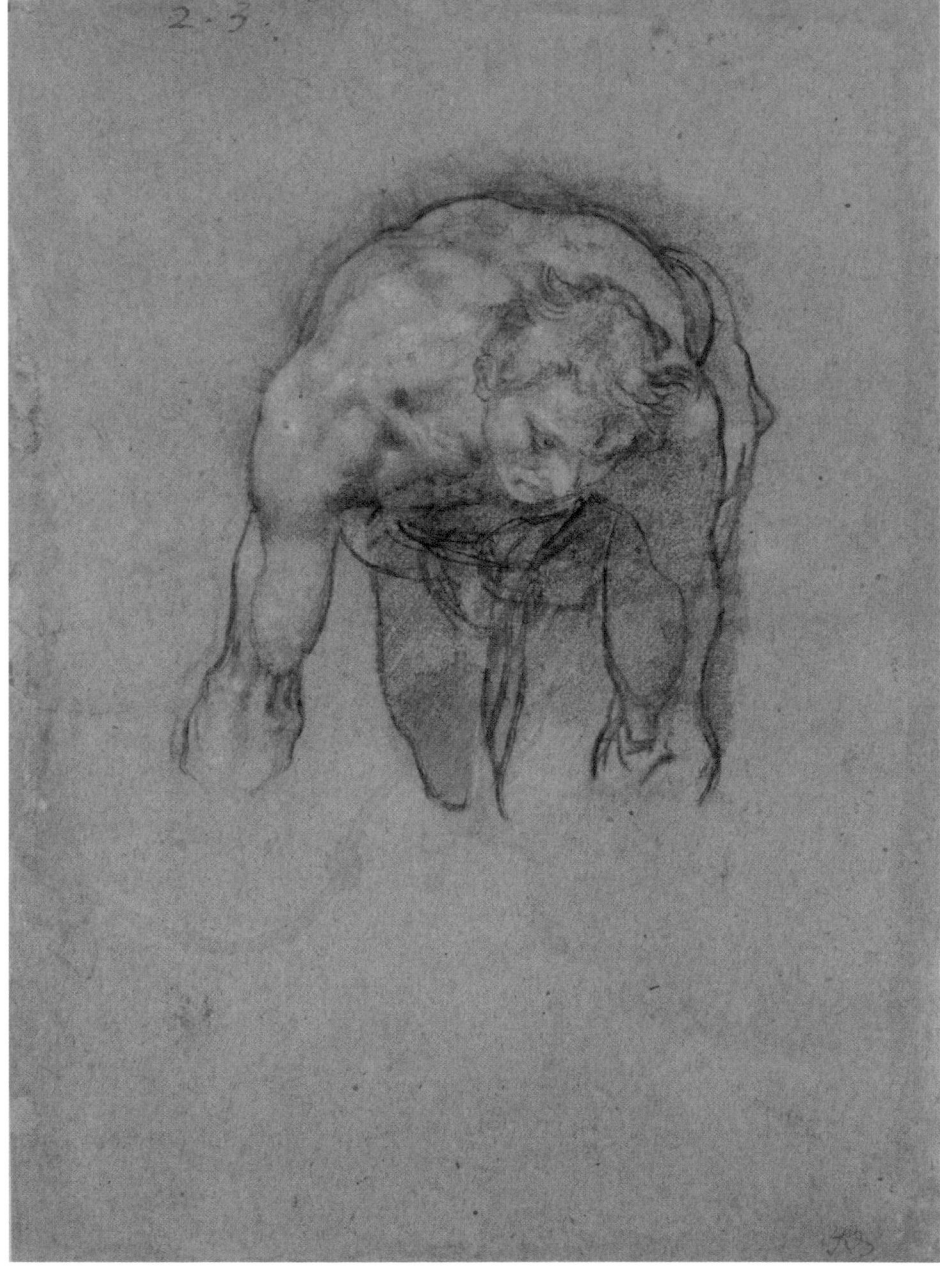

70 (verso)

It is clear from the truncation of the forearms of the figure studied on the verso that the sheet must date from the final stage of Taddeo's preparatory process, post-dating a now lost compositional study for the *Raising of Eutychus* that fixed the positions of the protagonists. The minimal changes of the contours of both figures indicate that the purpose of the drawing was not to explore the poses; rather it was to study closely the illumination. The figures are lit from the top left in accordance with the actual lighting of the chapel from above the altarpiece. The choice of black chalk and white heightening on blue paper, a combination introduced to Rome by Michelangelo's Venetian ally Sebastiano del Piombo in the second decade of the century, was ideally adapted to analysing the tonal gradations of light and shade. Lighting was a key element in the composition because strong chiaroscuro helped to make the figures visible in the discretely lit chapel. On both sides, the artist's focus is fixed firmly on the upper half of the bodies, the figure's wasted legs eloquently described in a few bold strokes of the chalk. From Taddeo's profoundly tactile rendering of the musculature of the two figures it seems likely that he worked from posed models in chiaroscuro lighting. The delicacy of naturalistic observation is matched in the drawing by the empathetic description of the subject, his intense gaze directed at Paul who is on the point of curing him. The figure's expression was changed to a less ambiguous show of open-mouthed amazement in a surviving fragment of the cartoon for the figure in the Ashmolean Museum, Oxford (a work that deserves to be more celebrated despite its darkened condition) and in the fresco that followed it.[2]

HUGO CHAPMAN

71

FEDERICO ZUCCARO c. 1542/43–1609
VISION OF SAINT EUSTACE c. 1558

Brush with brown, grey, green,
yellow and red washes, with white
heightening, pen and brown ink,
over traces of red and black chalk,
squared in black chalk
34.1 × 20.2 cm
The Metropolitan Museum of Art,
New York

While nearly all of the famous Renaissance frescoes painted on the facades of Roman palaces have been worn away by the ravages of weather and time, one of the most significant early works in Federico Zuccaro's career can still be seen today, and this colourful drawing is the modello for it. The commission came in 1559, when Federico was only about eighteen years old, from Tizio Chermandio da Spoleto, master of household to the powerful Cardinal Alessandro Farnese. Federico had been studying and working in Rome with his older brother Taddeo since the age of about ten, having been left there by his parents during a visit from the Marches for the 1550 Jubilee.[1] Chermandio's commission, which came to Federico via Taddeo, who was then busy with his own projects, involved the decoration of scenes from the life of Saint Eustace on the facades of the patron's corner house on Piazza della Dogana (now Piazza Sant'Eustachio) [fig. 71.1].[2] Judging from this *modello* and the remnants that survive today, one of the most remarkable aspects is the bright colouring used by Federico, in contrast to the monochrome brown or grey decorative schemes of Taddeo, who followed the chiaroscuro tradition of Polidoro. Federico in effect treated the facade walls as if they were an interior surface, employing bright reds, blues, and greens.[3]

Lightly squared in black chalk for transfer, the colourful modello must have served as a useful anticipation of the finished fresco. It shows the Roman general in the forest as he comes across a white stag with an apparition of the crucified Christ between its antlers – a vision that would prompt him to convert to Christianity. The composition is a dramatic and successful one: Eustace's point of view within the scene is shared by the viewer, and a strong V shape creates a distance between the soldier and the stag. It should be noted that the quality of Federico's draftsmanship, even at this young age, was superb. Eustace's dramatic pose perhaps derives from one studied by Taddeo in a famous drawing now in Chicago.[4] It contrasts with a kneeling, forward-leaning pose used in Federico's initial

study for the composition, an interesting working drawing in the Uffizi.[5] In fact, the specific moments represented in the Metropolitan Museum's *modello* and in the Uffizi drawing are quite different.[6] In the Uffizi sheet Eustace is shown resting and calmly regarding the vision, with his cap on the ground and the dogs at ease. In the *modello*, on the other hand, he is caught in a moment of surprise, as if he has just come across the stag. That Federico did not fully resolve his new solution is apparent in the contrast between the two dogs: one springs excitedly forward while the other, in the foreground, unmodified from the earlier drawing, looks as if it has been resting for some time.

In the *Lives*, Vasari tells a revealing story about the two brothers and this commission.

> Taddeo, who reflected that the work was in a public place, and that it was of great consequence to Federico's reputation ... at times insisted on retouching and improving some part. Federico, having had patience for some time, finally seized a mason's hammer and smashed to the ground some of what Taddeo had painted, and in his anger stayed several days without returning home. [Eventually] the two were reconciled, on the understanding that Taddeo should be able to set his hand on the drawings and cartoons of Federico as much as he pleased but never on works in fresco, oil, or any other medium.[7]

The veracity of this account is proved by Federico's few modifications to it in the annotations he made in his personal copy of the *Lives*, which survives in the Bibliothèque Nationale in Paris.[8] Taddeo's brotherly concern and his desire to uphold the standards of the Zuccaro studio are certainly understandable.[9] The incident seems to have been a rare exception in an otherwise harmonious working relationship.

The composition influenced Girolamo Muziano's design of the same subject, a drawing for an engraving by Cornelis Cort, dated 1573.[10] The print was one of a series of seven known as "The Penitent Saints in Vast Landscapes."

JULIAN BROOKS

Fig. 71.1 Federico Zuccaro, Facade of the Palazzetto Chermandio, c. 1559. Piazza Sant'Eustachio, Rome

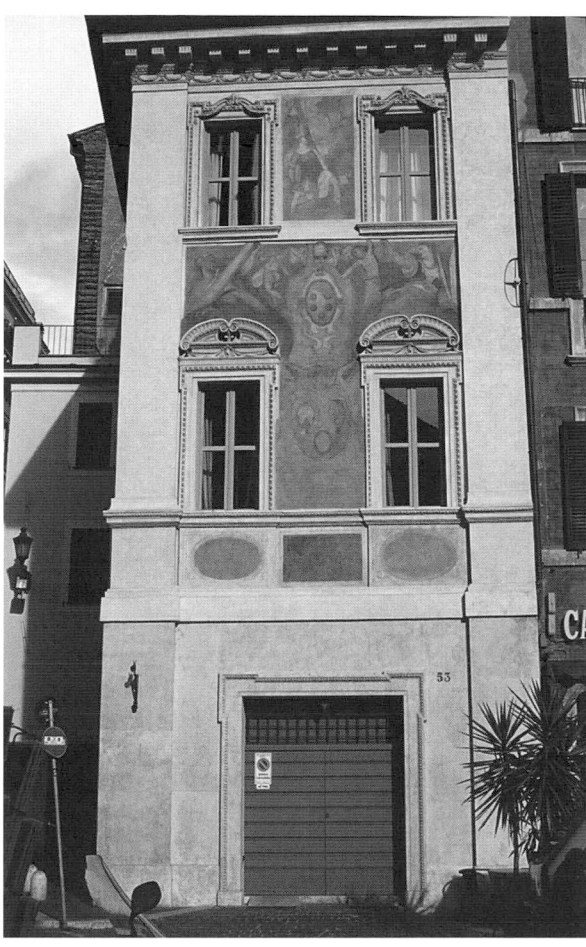

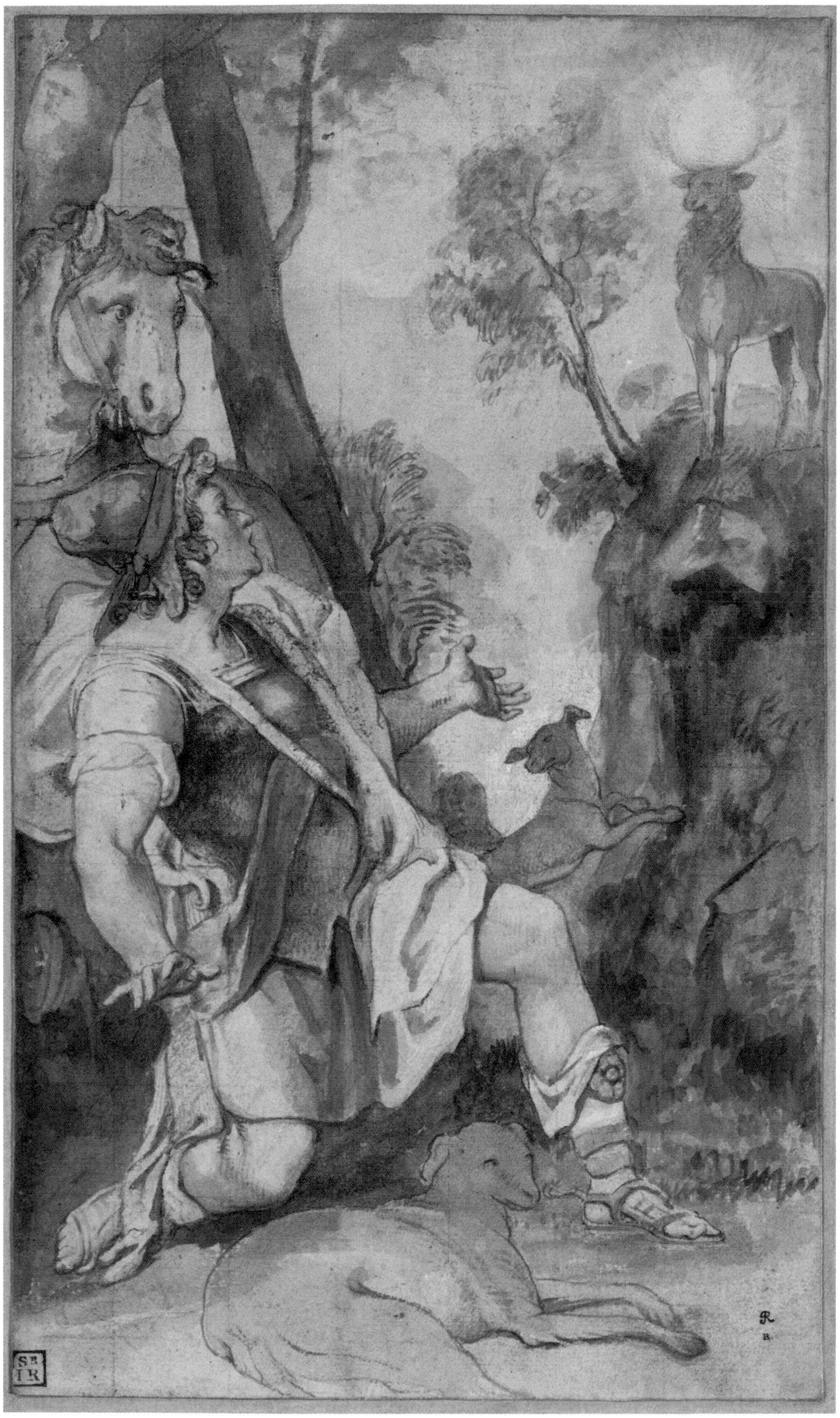

72
FRANCESCO DE' ROSSI,
CALLED **FRANCESCO SALVIATI** 1510–1563
THE SIEGE OF PARMA:
DESIGN FOR A WALL DECORATION
FLANKED BY PILASTERS 1557–1558

Pen and brown ink and brush and
brown wash, heightened with
white gouache (oxidized in places)
15.2 × 11.3 cm
Inscriptions: *parma piano*
Private collection, Chicago

72

These two quickly studied battle scenes were both prep-aratory for the northwest wall of the Salotto Dipinto (Sala dei Fasti Farnesiana), the principal room on the piano nobile of the Palazzo Farnese. The commission was argu-ably the artist's most important decorative project and the most significant in Rome between Michelangelo's Sistine Chapel and Annibale Carracci's Farnese Ceiling.

Reuniting the two drawings here presents a rare opportunity to compare alternative *primi pensieri*, reveal-ing the thought process of the artist as he searched for his composition. The two drawings are similar in style, media, and size. Both are vertical-format battle scenes that use the same light source emanating from the right. Both are composed as panoramas framed by an imaginary *trompe l'oeil* architecture of Corinthian piers. They represent not only two different compositional proposals, but two dif-ferent iconographic ideas for the Siege of Parma. Executed during the earliest stages of planning, they probably date from about 1557–1558.

In 1551–1552 Ottavio Farnese, aided by French forces, successfully defended his illegitimately obtained family duchy of Parma (created by Pope Paul III) against papal and imperial troops. This celebrated event in Farnese his-tory then became the subject of one of the major frescoes recording the great accomplishments of the family. Ottavio's younger brother, Cardinal Ranuccio Farnese, commissioned the project, consisting of five vertical sec-tions on each wall, with an alternation of allegorical and historical subjects. It was for one of the historical panels that both these sheets were studied. The *concetto* of the program glorifies the Farnese family by depicting their military feats on one wall and their role in the service of the Church on the other.

The idea for the battle scene belongs to an early phase in the planning of the iconographic program, which must have undergone several modifications due to the quickly changing political landscape in Rome in the early 1550s. With the death of the Farnese pope, Paul III, in 1549, the family suffered a reversal of fortune. The new pope, Julius III del Monte, sought to reclaim the duchy of Parma and Piacenza for the papal state. In the ensuing battle, in 1551–1552, Ottavio Farnese, supported by French Imperial troops, successfully defended the territory. His brother, Orazio, protected the town of Mirandola. Peace was nego-tiated in 1552. Work on the frescoes resumed probably around 1555, only to be interrupted again by Salviati's trip to France in 1556.[1] Painting continued upon his return.

73
FRANCESCO DE' ROSSI,
CALLED FRANCESCO SALVIATI 1510–1563
THE SIEGE OF PARMA:
DESIGN FOR A WALL DECORATION
FLANKED BY PILASTERS 1557–1558

Pen and brown ink and brown
wash over black chalk
15.2 × 11.5 cm
National Gallery of Canada,
Ottawa

David McTavish was the first to suggest that the private collection drawing, inscribed "parma" in the upper left, represents the papal siege of that city and that the Ottawa sheet is perhaps an alternative design.[2]

The private collection drawing is probably the earlier of the two. It provides convincing evidence, with the inscription "parma," for the subject of the original idea for the northwest wall. This *primo pensiero* documents an iconography significantly different from the one illustrated in the Ottawa sheet. Whereas the earlier idea focuses on the battle itself, the later version emphasizes the successful siege. It introduces Ottavio Farnese, in armour, on horseback in the foreground. Above him swirls the banner with the Farnese lilies surmounted by a crown, indicating the triumph. These references, with their imperial trappings, were probably suggested by members of the family, intent on displaying their power and prestige in this important room.

While the private collection version depicts the actual battle, and locates it geographically, the Ottawa version celebrates the victory. By leaving no doubt as to the outcome, this subtle shift to certainty and success would have been far more attractive to the family. The iconography changes from feats of valor in the first thought to victory in the second drawing.

The imagery in the second drawing belongs to a long tradition of scenes of triumph in palace decoration. Rulers appropriated it from Roman monuments as a means of conveying the mythology of the princely family in their role as generals. By establishing their territorial claims, no matter how specious, it validated their rule. With this intention, the Gonzaga of Mantua commissioned from Mantegna nine panels illustrating the triumphs of Julius Caesar to display in the ducal palace. The imperial connotations subtly refer to the family. The Farnese followed this example not only in the Sala Dipinto but also at their villa at Caprarola. Contemporaneously, Vasari was frescoing the Sala del Cinquecento in the Palazzo Vecchio for Cosimo de' Medici with battles, victories, and triumphs.

The iconographic change recorded in the two *primi pensieri* necessitated a shift in composition. The private collection drawing opens as a window, seen through an imaginary architecture of entablature and columns, onto a vast panorama of a battlefield where troops are engaged in combat in the far distance. A group of soldiers on the right lead us into the battle. The rhythmic repetition of their drawn-sword postures is a characteristic *maniera*

73

device favoured by Salviati. The landscape elements are particularly beautiful, with the foliage in the trees more detailed than the sketchy figures.

To emphasize the Farnese triumph, the composition in the Ottawa sheet is anchored by a group of men on horseback before a fortress. Now shifted to the left, and including the Farnese leader, this foreground group serves a function similar to that of the soldiers on the right in the private collection drawing, leading us into the scene. The figures make eye contact with the spectator while gesturing toward the landscape, where the design opens up to a wide view of the ground below the horizon line with rows of battling soldiers. The group in the immediate foreground at the right is engaged in combat on top of the body of a fallen horse.

At some point, it was deemed politically unwise to prominently display a Farnese victory against papal forces in a reception room where the guests frequently might include cardinals and other leading members of the Church. Accordingly, the scene was replaced by the more neutral subject of Pope Eugenius IV appointing Ranuccio Farnese commander of the papal army. Tactfully, a Farnese military triumph is replaced by a Farnese achievement on behalf of the Church. Another Farnese, Ranuccio, now leads papal troops rather than his own.

After Salviati's death in 1563, responsibility for the decoration passed first to Taddeo Zuccaro and, on his death in 1566, to his brother Federico. By then Cardinal Ranuccio had also died (1565), and so his older brother, Cardinal Alessandro Farnese, supervised the completion of the frescoes.

JEAN GOLDMAN

GIAN ANGELO DE' MEDICI

PIUS IV 1559-1565

Pen and brown ink over black chalk;
boars' heads in red chalk [verso]
28 × 44 cm
Edinburgh, National Gallery of
Scotland

74
GIOVANNI BATTISTA NALDINI 1537–1591
VIEW OF THE COLOSSEUM (RECTO); *THE RAPE OF THE DAUGHTERS OF LEUCIPPUS, TWO BOARS' HEADS* (VERSO) 1560–1561

Fig. 74.1 View of the Colosseum and Arch of Constantine, Rome

Fig. 74.2 Hadrianic sarcophagus depicting the *Rape of the Daughters of Leucippus*, 2nd c. A.D. Galleria degli Uffizi, Florence

The present sheet comes from Battista Naldini's Roman sketchbook, documenting his first visit to the Eternal City. The twenty-three-year-old artist left Florence for Rome in late September 1560 and remained there until the spring of 1561.[1] During this time he drew intensely, making numerous copies of antique sculpture, as well views of the city and its architectural monuments.

The drawing at Edinburgh offers a good example of the variety of modes in which Naldini typically drew, in response to different kinds of subject matter. On the recto he drew a topographically detailed panorama of the Colosseum (AD 70–76) and the surrounding area (fig. 74.1), even labelling the individual monuments, as it would appear, in his own hand. The text at lower right contains his annotations indicating the Colosseum (labelled with the letter A) and, to the left, the crumbling mass of the Meta Sudans. This was the ruin of an ancient fountain which marked the meeting point of four of the fourteen regions into which Rome had been divided by Augustus. It was later demolished to allow for widening of the street. A third note in the same handwriting, at the extreme lower right, indicates the way *a l'arco di Costa[n]tino* ("to the Arch of Constantine"). Naldini studied the details of the Colosseum with careful attention to its construction and its urban setting, rendering the whole scene with very delicate strokes of the pen.

By contrast, the artist sketched the scene on the verso, copied from a Roman sarcophagus depicting the rape of the daughters of Leucippus (or Leucippids) with the coarse, heavily reinforced outlines, and intense, jagged hatching that he often employed in drawings of figure groups or compositional studies. The sarcophagus copied by Naldini is of a type dating from the period of Hadrian. Just to right of centre an unidentified female figure calls for help while, on either side of her, the Dioscuri, Castor and Pollux carry off the writhing daughters. To the left two men are locked in frantic combat, while beside them stands the winged figure of Victory who originally held a gorgon in her hands. In the Renaissance the subject of this sarcophagus type was generally believed to be the Rape of the Sabines; it was only in the eighteenth century that the German archaeologist and art historian Johann Joachim Winckelmann (1717–1768) was able to arrive at the correct interpretation.

Thiem has identified Naldini's specific model with a sarcophagus that survives today in the Uffizi Gallery in Florence (fig. 74.2).[2] That work was in the collection of Cardinal Andrea della Valle, who installed it under the loggia of his Roman palace as the basin of a fountain. The della Valle sarcophagus was acquired in the mid-sixteenth century, by Cardinal (later Grand Duke) Ferdinando de' Medici, who installed it in the Villa Medici on the Pincian Hill, before it eventually found its way to Florence.

LOUIS A. WALDMAN

74 (recto)

74 (verso)

75
GIROLAMO MUZIANO 1532–1592
CHRIST WASHING THE FEET OF THE APOSTLES 1560–1561

Pen and brown ink with brown
wash, with white heightening
36 × 49 cm
Private collection

Fig. 75.1 Louis Desplaces after
Girolamo Muziano, *Christ
Washing the Feet of the Apostles*,
1697–1739, etching, 45.7 × 64.2 cm.
The British Museum, London

Born in Lombardy and trained in the Veneto, Muziano arrived in Rome in 1549. He spent several more years as a student, occasionally assisting other artists or taking on minor commissions, before he achieved a level of fame with the unveiling in 1555 of his *Resurrection of Lazarus* (Pinacoteca, Vatican). On the heels of that success, he was invited to Orvieto to supervise the pictorial decoration of the ten chapels along the side walls of the great cathedral.[1] Muziano spent the next three years there, but after painting only two of the chapels (the altarpieces are today in the Museo dell'Opera del Duomo, Orvieto) he left the city, partly to escape the jealousy of local painters. He moved to Foligno to paint an altarpiece of *Saint Elizabeth of Hungary* (lost, but recorded in an engraving by Beatrizet), and by 1560 was back in Rome, where he received offers of work from the two leading Roman patrons of his day, the cardinals Alessandro Farnese and Ippolito d'Este. Accepting the latter offer, Muziano became the principal painter at Este's Quirinal Palace and Monte Giordano (Palazzo Orsini-Gambara) in Rome and at the Villa d'Este in Tivoli.[2]

Unfortunately, almost nothing survives of Muziano's work for the cardinal between 1560 and 1566. Documents record payments for painted panels for carriages, cupboards, beds, and ceilings, painted leather hangings, cartoons for a set of tapestries, an altarpiece of the *Annunciation*, miscellaneous paintings, and decorative frescoes, especially landscapes, at the Quirinal and Monte Giordano palaces at Rome and at the Villa d'Este in Tivoli.[3] The Quirinal and Monte Giordano frescoes were lost in the later rebuilding of the palaces; the surviving landscapes at the Villa d'Este are much repainted. One of Muziano's first major projects for the cardinal was a canvas depicting *Christ Washing the Feet of the Apostles* for the church of San Salvatore in Lauro. Recorded and praised by Muziano's anonymous biographer and by Borghini, the painting probably perished in a fire that damaged the church in 1591.[4] While the contract for the painting does not survive, documents in the Este archive record payments to Muziano's workshop for the production of a replica that was sent to Este in France.[5] Este went to France in April 1561 as the papal legate, and the payment to Muziano's workshop was made in November of that year; presumably, the commission for the San Salvatore in Lauro painting was given by the cardinal in late 1560 or early 1561 before his departure. The painting sent to France was later in the cathedral at Reims, and after 1803 in the church of Saint Jacques

in Reims, where it was destroyed by fire in 1914. The composition is recorded in an etching by Louis Desplaces (fig. 75.1) and also in a painted copy in the Spada-Portensiani collection in Rome.

The San Salvatore canvas was enormous, measuring 18 by 24 *palmi*, roughly 400 by 525 centimetres, and Este must have considered it an important work, as attested by the fact that he requested a replica. It is of little surprise, then, that Muziano produced an elaborate preparatory drawing like the present sheet. It probably served as a *modello* to be shown to the patron for approval, and it matches the finished composition (as recorded by the Desplaces etching and the Spada-Portensiani copy). It is an impressive work, more finished than nearly any other preparatory drawing by the artist; the carefully delineated style and the layering of wash seen here were techniques that Muziano generally used only in the 1550s and 1560s.[6] When he was better established as an artist, Muziano probably no longer needed to produce *modelli* of this type and adopted different methods of drawing, although there is a similar example from later in his career (albeit still less carefully finished than this sheet), the large *Pentecost* in the Louvre (cat. 107), which may have been required of him because it was his first project for another important patron, Gregory XIII.

Muziano had by this time arrived at the sombre, slow-moving figure canon that would characterize his works for the rest of his career, but the composition still calls to mind the works of the artists who had been his early models. Before moving to Rome in 1549, Muziano had spent time in Venice, and his *Christ Washing the Feet of the Apostles* recalls two important Venetian examples: Giuseppe Porta's painting of that subject in the church of San Polo, and Tintoretto's in the Prado. Muziano's early work has many

75

points of comparison with Porta's Venetian canvases, and it is clear that the two artists were associated during Muziano's time in Venice.[7] In contrast, Muziano's art usually has relatively little to do with Tintoretto's dramatic style, but it is hard to ignore the similarity of the off-centre vanishing point used for the tile floor or the foreground motif of an apostle removing a sandal, both of which seem to derive directly from Tintoretto's example.[8] Although Christ kneels and washes the feet of a seated apostle in Muziano's finished drawing (and in the lost painting), a preparatory study in the Uffizi (fig. 75.2), drawn with the blunt red chalk that Muziano often used for his *primi pensieri*, shows Christ kneeling before a standing apostle, again close to Tintoretto's example.[9] (The photograph shown here of the Uffizi drawing requires a word of explanation, for it is actually a composite. The top half, Uffizi 18261, has always been attributed to Muziano, as the old annotation on it indicates. The lower half is the verso of Uffizi 12900, a *Deposition* wrongly attributed to Titian and kept with his drawings at the Uffizi. The *Deposition* is actually another of Muziano's preparatory drawings from the 1560s, and its verso is the lower half of the compositional fragment 18261.)

Apart from the etching by Desplaces and the copy in the Spada-Portensiani collection, there are a number of further copies of the composition, including a drawing in the Louvre[10] that is apparently after this *modello* and not after the painting. Another drawn copy is in the J.F. Willumsen Museum, Denmark.[11] Borghini notes that the important Florentine collector Niccolò Gaddi owned a "quadro di chiaro oscuro" of the same composition, but this work has not been traced.[12] Although Muziano is not known to have produced another large painting of the subject, there were also three further versions recorded in the posthumous inventory of his studio.[13]

JOHN J. MARCIARI

NICCOLÒ TROMETTA c. 1540–1611
DESIGN FOR A CEILING WITH THE COAT
OF ARMS OF POPE PIUS IV c. 1559–1565

Pen and brown ink and brown wash
over black chalk, with white heightening on blue paper
55.9 × 36.9 cm
Staatliche Museen zu Berlin,
Kupferstichkabinett

Formerly ascribed to Santi di Tito, this drawing was attributed to Niccolò Martinelli, known as Niccolò da Pesaro or
Niccolò Trometta, by Gere, who also published it for the first
time in 1971.[1] Born in the town of Pesaro, Trometta to seems
to have come to Rome as a young artist to enter directly into
the workshop of the Zuccari brothers, who were also native
to the Marche region. This complex study for a ceiling contains the arms of Pope Pius IV in two places, as well as an
inscription with his name, Hence it can be dated without
controversy to his reign of 1559–1565. Gere connected it specifically to the decorations Trometta apparently collaborated
on with the Zuccari in the Casino of Pius IV in the gardens
of the Vatican, which would allow for a more specific dating
of c. 1561–1563, although this is unconfirmed as it does not
correspond to anything produced there.

Certainly this intricate design for a vault with spandrels containing stucco as well as fresco (and *grotteschi*) is
characteristic of the type found at the Casino. Yet it seems
inherently unlikely that Trometta would have been at lib-
erty to design such an elaborate decoration in a location
where more senior artists were in charge. The subject matter – such as it is decipherable – might indicate a different
destination in any case, as there is a figure of Ganymede
appearing in the oval in the lower part and mythology was
not a prevalent subject matter for the painted decoration
there, unlike the sculpture by Pirro Ligorio. Perhaps the
design was executed following the completion of the Casino
for Pope Pius IV, but in a more exclusively secular location,
such as a palace or villa. Clearly this aspect of the work
requires further research.

The Berlin drawing is an earlier work by Trometta, for
whom only about forty sheets survive. This example is typical of his extant drawings for its fluid draftsmanship in
pen and brown ink and wash with abundant white heightening on blue paper. His figure style is elegant but with an
unmistakable ponderousness. Yet his ability to conceive
and delineate such a dense, elaborate decorative scheme
reveals an artist of great innovation. Trometta here introduced a convincing illusionism that anticipates artists such
as the Alberti at end of the century.

DAVID FRANKLIN

77
FEDERICO BAROCCI c. 1528–1612
TEMPERANCE c. 1561–1563

Pen and brown ink with brown
wash, with white heightening on
blue paper
22.5 × 10.1 cm
Annotations: *Baroci*
**National Gallery of Canada,
Ottawa**

Fig. 77.1 Federico Barocci,
Temperance, c. 1561–1563, fresco.
Casino of Pius IV, Vatican

Fig. 77.2 Federico Barocci, *Study
for a Wall Decoration*, c. 1561–1563,
pen and brown ink with brown
wash, heightened with white, over
black chalk, 24.1 × 21.8 cm. The
Detroit Institute of Arts, Founders
Society Purchase, William H.
Murphy Fund

Around the year 1550, the nature of artistic education in Rome began to change. Traditionally, young artists arriving in the city would join the large workshops responsible for the decorative fresco campaigns in the Vatican and elsewhere. After Perino del Vaga's death in 1547, however, his entourage at the Castel Sant'Angelo began to fall apart, and with the death of Pope Paul III in 1549, work on the Sala Regia came to a halt. Although Salviati, Vasari, and other artists of a slightly older generation would intermittently work on Roman projects in the late 1540s and into the 1550s, they tended to use assistants brought from Florence and did not maintain the sort of workshop that younger artists might join; Michelangelo, likewise, is famous for his general reluctance to use assistants or to train pupils. The generation of young artists born around 1530 and arriving in Rome around 1550 were thus left largely to their own devices. They tended to spend time together, sketching the most famous works in the city: ancient sculptures, paintings by Raphael and Michelangelo, and the facade decorations of Polidoro da Caravaggio. One consequence of this shift in artistic training, in which artists drew side by side and often copied each other, is that their styles sometimes merged, such that some early drawings by Muziano, Zuccaro, or Barocci can be difficult to tell apart. A further consequence was that when work ultimately resumed in the Vatican, following the election of Pius IV, fresco projects tended to be collaborative affairs, with numerous artists of more or less equal status working together. In the earlier projects directed by Vasari or Salviati, all the artists of a large workshop would paint in the style of the single supervising artist, but in the later Roman system, multiple styles can be seen side-by-side even in one room. The new collaborative organization in fact probably encouraged greater differentiation, for the "collaboration" seems instead to have fomented competition.[1]

The present drawing clearly attests to these new developments in Roman art. Traditionally ascribed to Barocci, on the basis of the old annotation at the lower left, the drawing was reattributed to Taddeo Zuccaro by Popham.[2] Smith recognized the link between the drawing and the figure representing Temperance in one of the corners of the vault in the upper room of the Casino of Pius IV in the Vatican gardens (fig. 77.1).[3] Although the figure is reversed and the pose somewhat modified, there are so many common motifs (Smith noted the "bared breast" and "bird-like profile," the bunching of sleeve drapery, and "the precious way in which she crooks her fore-finger over the handle of the pitcher") that the connection between the drawing and the painting is now universally accepted. Taddeo, however, is not among the many artists documented on that project, which was principally the work of Barocci, Federico Zuccaro, Santi di Tito, and Orazio Sammacchini.[4] Smith suggested that Taddeo could have made the drawing to assist his brother, Federico, who would then have painted the corresponding figure. This is a documented working practice for the two brothers.[5] Yet,

the attribution of the sheet is complicated not only because the collaborative organization of the work could mean that a figure might be designed by one artist but executed by another, but also because of the similarity of Barocci's and Taddeo's drawing styles in these years.

In arguing for the attribution to Taddeo, Popham compared the sheet particularly to a study (The British Museum, London, pp.2–127) for a sibyl above the altar of the Mattei chapel in Santa Maria in Consolazione, Rome. Despite the general stylistic similarities, however, the *Temperance* drawing does not fit perfectly among Taddeo's works. In 1978 Pillsbury argued in favour of returning the drawing to Barocci, noting that Taddeo's drawings "are built up systematically in different media to enhance the plastic effect," whereas Barocci's drawings "are conceived in terms of light and dark; the wash and the whites play a role in refining the design as well as putting the forms into relief."[6] The drawing has since become one of the most disputed from mid-century Rome, with the attribution continually alternating between Barocci and Taddeo.[7] Most compelling to the present author is Pillsbury's comparison of the Ottawa sheet with the *Study for a Wall Decoration* in Detroit (fig. 77.2) and the *Adoration of the Magi* from the Regteren Altena collection (now Rijksmuseum, Amsterdam).[8] To Pillsbury's arguments might be added the observation that the mature Taddeo's drawings in this combination of media (pen, wash, and white heightening on blue paper) tend to be relatively clean and finished *modelli*, while Barocci used these same media (on blue or brown paper) not only in *modelli* but also often in free, much-revised, sketchier studies comparable to the *Temperance* and *Study for a Wall Decoration*.

The Ottawa and Detroit sheets, moreover, are part of a larger set of studies that seem to affirm the significance of Barocci's role in the decoration of the Casino.[9] The paintings in the room have been attributed variously to Santi di Tito, Sammacchini, Federico Zuccaro, and Barocci, and, as noted above, these artists probably worked as equal associates on the project. The frescoes vary in quality, but those that Barocci executed, especially the *Holy Family* at the centre of the vault, stand out remarkably from the surrounding works, with a sense of energy and a rich colour scheme that break from the cool, mannered reserve more common in Roman art of the time and unmistakably presage Barocci's later work. It must already have been clear at the Casino that Barocci would be the greatest painter of his generation, though this revelation apparently led to treacherous action. Barocci's seventeenth-century biographer Giovanni Pietro Bellori relates that the artist's jealous rivals invited him to a meal and fed him a poisoned salad.[10] Whether or not the story is true, a gravely ill Barocci went home to Urbino in 1565 and never returned to Rome. He would nonetheless go on to create paintings for cities across Italy and beyond, an extraordinary body of work that in great measure pointed the way to the Carracci reform of painting at the end of the century.

JOHN J. MARCIARI

78

ORLANDO PARENTINI active c. 1560–1590
*STUDY FOR THE APARTMENT OF POPE
PIUS IV IN THE VATICAN* c. 1559–1565

Pen and brown ink and brown wash
16 × 27.6 cm
Annotations: *Sc[uola]. di Lelio da
Novellara*; *S.R. no. 108* [verso]
National Gallery of Canada,
Ottawa

This drawing is preparatory for frescoes in the apartments of Pope Pius IV in the Belvedere apartments in the Vatican – what is today the Etruscan Museum. Formerly attributed to the workshop of Lelio Orsi, this is, in fact, the only drawing that has been ascribed with certainty to this obscure artist, Orlando Parentini, and so is of extreme interest to scholars of the period. It will become the touchstone for any future attributions to the painter.

Orlando Parentini is cited in various archival sources as active in Rome with his brother Dante from about the 1550s to the 1590s. Orlando and Dante, who appears to have worked more as a sculptor and stuccoist, participated on decorations in the Vatican ordered by Pius IV during his relatively short pontificate (1559–1565). The two artists are documented as having decorated a number of rooms in Vatican apartments, including, it would appear, this one in 1563, according to Ackerman. They are also credited with also another room with stucco ornaments designed specifically designed by Dante, as well as the Cosmographical Loggia in the Belvedere.[1] By June 1564 they had also completed no less important a commission than the last three bays of the so-called Raphael's Loggia in the Vatican, also for Pius IV.[2]

The decoration of Pius IV's apartment (known as the Sala del Buon Governo) features as its main scenes some relatively obscure subjects, including *Atlas, Saul at Samuel's Banquet* and the *Banquet of Tieste*.[3] The principal subjects are flanked by various caryatids, putti, *ignudi* (male nudes), allegorical figures representing the Virtues and cartouches containing the coat-of-arms of Pius IV. This drawing is preparatory for the ornamentation and allegorical figure of Concord (*Concordia*) to the right on the wall featuring *Atlas* (fig. 78.1), who was clearly modelled on the ancient sculpture then found in the Casino del Bufalo. Although the general composition had been established by this stage, there are a few differences compared with the fresco. The most significant is the description of the chair formed by two intertwined cornucopias that was covered by drapery in the fresco: the figure as painted holds a sliced pomegranate (symbolizing the Catholic Church) as an attribute. In addition to Concord, the figure of Humanity is seated to the left of the central scene of *Atlas* on this wall in the finished work. Whatever the complexities of this program, it is clear that the overall message was to relate the subject matter to the self-image of Pius IV as a powerful and unifying Christian ruler.

In respect of style, an unavoidable rapport with Michelangelo's Sistine Chapel ceiling is apparent in certain poses, but also with the more recent work of such artists as Francesco Salviati and Perino del Vaga for the general decorative scheme. It is also now possible to appreciate Parentini's agile and liberated handling of the pen and ink, closest, not surprisingly, to the style of the Zuccari, who were among the dominant painters in Rome just after the middle of the sixteenth century. It should be stressed, however, that we know nothing about the training of this artist, who Vasari never mentioned in the *Lives*.

DAVID FRANKLIN

Fig. 78.1 Orlando Parentini,
Detail of the decoration of the
Sala del Buon Governo of Pius IV,
c. 1559–1565, fresco. Museo
Gregoriano Etrusco, Vatican

TIBERIO CALCAGNI 1532–1565
*PROJECT FOR A STATUE COURT IN
FARNESE PALACE* c. 1564

Pen and brown ink and wash
32 × 25 cm
Gabinetto Disegni e Stampe degli
Uffizi, Florence

This drawing, which once belonged to Vasari, has long been attributed to the sculptor and architect Tiberio Calcagni, who, as a minor pupil of Michelangelo, worked on the *Brutus* and the finish of the *Florentine Pietà*.[1] Having moved to Rome, he became interested in architecture, assisting Michelangelo with the plans for the church of the Florentines, San Giovanni dei Fiorentini, and for the Sforza Chapel in Santa Maria Maggiore around 1559–1560, though neither of these plans came to fruition.[2]

The drawing shows an elevation of a wall with two bays containing basins for fountains and much classical statuary. That this is a commission of a Cardinal of the powerful Farnese family, descended from Pope Paul III (1534–1549) is clear from the cartouche between the bays, which contains the Farnese arms of six lilies surmounted by a Cardinal's hat. There were two Farnese cardinals in the 1560s – both grandsons of Paul III: Alessandro (1520–1589) and his younger brother Ranuccio (1530–1565). It is likely that Ranuccio commissioned this project. Other Farnese emblems are represented above the cornice in the three-fold bunches of lilies, which had been an emblem of Paul III, and the single armorial lily above. At the centre is a sculptural group of a virgin with a unicorn, symbol of purity, which was also a family emblem.[3] In the left-hand bay above the fountain basin, which is supported by marine deities with fishy tails, putti unveil a sculptural group representing *Pan and a Youth*, who is variously identified. The group is known to have been in the Farnese collection, since it was described by Ulisse Aldrovandi in 1556, and is now in the Museo Nazionale at Naples.[4] Above in a triangular pedimented niche is a draped female figure, which was presumably also part of the Farnese collection. On the right, in a similar arrangement, there is a kneeling female nude, which resembles an antique *Crouching Venus*, of which there are two versions from the Farnese collection now in Naples.[5] In the niche above is a male prisoner or slave, again of a type that is documented in the Farnese collection.[6] Between the two bays a draped female figure stands on a pedestal.

The architecture shown in the drawing corresponds in many respects with that of a small cortile on the mezzanine of Palazzo Farnese, just off the main staircase, although what is now there differs in a number of respects (fig. 79.1). Cardinal Ranuccio has been documented as having work done there, as part of a building campaign to bring water to the fountains at the family palace in April 1564. Indeed one payment refers to the placing of the slave in the cortile.[7] While fountains were often decorated with antique sculpture at this period, the inclusion of celebrated pieces from the family collection conforms very well with Michelangelo's plan to convert the huge group known as the *Farnese Bull* into the central fountain in the garden behind the palace, as well as a scheme for another fountain adorned with a group of the *Horatii and Curiatii*.[8]

It is not known how Cardinal Ranuccio Farnese, the chief inhabitant of the family palace at this time, might have come to employ Calcagni. Michelangelo had been involved in the palace's design many years previously, and Ranuccio apparently tried to revive Michelangelo's ambitious plans for the completion of the rear of the palace.[9] Although at this time Vignola was Ranuccio's principal architect, it may have seemed appropriate to employ one of Michelangelo's pupils. Moreover, Cardinal Guid'Ascanio Sforza, patron of the Sforza chapel, was Ranuccio's cousin. Calcagni's project was presumably not realized because of Ranuccio's death, after which there was a hiatus in building work on the palace for almost a decade. The cortile in its present form seems to have been realized somewhat later.

CLARE ROBERTSON

Fig. 79.1 Courtyard, mezzanine of Palazzo Farnese, Rome

80

GIUSEPPE PORTA,
CALLED GIUSEPPE SALVIATI c. 1520–1575
THE SEVEN KINGS PAYING HOMAGE TO A POPE c. 1565

Pen and brown ink and brown
wash, over black chalk, with white
heightening on blue paper, squared
in black chalk
39 × 50 cm
Inscriptions: *PIVS.IIII/PONT.MA*
Devonshire Collection, Chatsworth

Like the drawing by Girolamo Siciolante da Sermoneta (cat. 81), this large sheet was identified by Pouncey as a fully worked up study for one of the frescoes in the Vatican's Sala Regia that were commissioned during the pontificate of Pius IV. Unlike the fresco by Siciolante, however, *The Seven Kings* by Giuseppe Salviati no longer exists.

Giuseppe Porta was a pupil of Francesco Salviati in Rome during the second half of the 1530s. In 1539 the two artists visited Venice, where Giuseppe Porta, who later adopted his master's surname, decided to take up permanent residence. His only documented return trip to Rome lasted from 1562 until late 1565 or early 1566. During that time he worked on two large frescoes in the Sala Regia, the first showing *Pope Alexander III Reconciling with Emperor Frederick I Barbarossa in Venice in 1177* (fig. 80.1), and the second *The Story of the Seven Kings*. For the '*historia delli sette Re*,' he received the considerable sum of 300 *scudi* between 20 July and 23 November 1565,[1] but after the death of Pope Pius IV on 9 December of that year work in the Sala Regia came to a halt, and it was not resumed by his successor, Pope Pius V. In the 1568 edition of his *Vite* Giorgio Vasari infers that at the time of the pope's death Giuseppe Salviati had just started *The Seven Kings*.[2] Shortly afterwards, in 1572–1573, Vasari himself was involved in the destruction of the fresco of the Seven Kings – as part of his campaign to bring the protracted pictorial decoration of the Sala Regia to a quick conclusion. During this undertaking, Vasari replaced Giuseppe Salviati's *Seven Kings* with his own fresco of *The Return of Pope Gregory XI to Rome from Avignon in 1376* (cat. 96)

No overall program for the pictorial decoration of the Sala Regia is known, and in any event the subject matter evolved over the course of several pontificates. A Latin *titulus* located above or below most of the extant frescoes helps define their individual meanings, but no contemporary explanation of *The Seven Kings* has ever been found. Like the other scenes, it clearly represents the submission of the agents of temporal power to papal authority – as is fitting for a room in which kings and emperors were received by the pope – but the specific identity of the Seven Kings remains a mystery.[3]

This drawing shows seven crowned figures, each accompanied by a retainer holding a small trophy. The last of the group has yet to dismount from his horse at the left, while the kings before him mount a broad flight of stairs and fall on their knees before a seated pontiff at the upper right. The architectural setting is similar to that found in depictions of *The Presentation of the Virgin in the Temple* – such as Peruzzi's in Santa Maria della Pace in Rome or Titian's in the Scuola della Carità in Venice, both of which Giuseppe Salviati would have known – but the Roman connection is emphasized by the presence of colossal yet life-like statues of Saints Peter and Paul flanking the lower part of the staircase. In addition, the particular pope responsible for the commission is emphasized by the inscription "PIVS IIII PONT[IFEX] MA[XIMUS]" on the pedestal beneath Saint Paul. The principal architectural setting recalls Pope Pius II's renovations of 1460–1462 to the approach to the Vatican, including the broad flight of steps flanked by colossal statues of Peter and Paul by Paolo Romano (also located on the same sides) and the Loggia of Benediction, finished at a later date.[4] Although Giuseppe Salviati is not otherwise known to have taken an interest in representing civic settings for his narrative paintings, in his first fresco for the Sala Regia he included an accurate view of the Piazza San Marco in Venice, and here he appears to have attempted a contrasting view of Rome, with elements both antique and Renaissance.

It is often said that *The Seven Kings* was never painted,[5] but this is belied by the sum of 300 *scudi* paid to Giuseppe Salviati, as well as by the visual evidence of an anonymous drawing in the Kunstsammlung, Basel.[6] (fig. 80.2) The drawing includes copies after various frescoes in the Sala Regia, and must have been done by a young or inexperienced artist working in the room itself, either at the end of the pontificate of Pius IV or during that of his successor Pius V, and certainly before the changes made by Vasari under Gregory XIII. Since the copy after *The Seven Kings* shows a number of changes in the positions of the figures approaching the pontiff – and also suggests that, flanking him, there may have been portraits of other ecclesiastical officials – it cannot be a copy after the Chatsworth drawing. The drawing in Basel confirms the Giuseppe Salviati had completed the climactic section of the fresco with the foremost kings paying obeisance to the seated pope, but in the absence of further details it suggests that the lower part was not yet completed. If it had been finished, *The Seven Kings* would have been one of Giuseppe Salviati's most impressive compositions.

DAVID MCTAVISH

80

GIROLAMO SICIOLANTE DA SERMONETA
1521–1575
PEPIN THE SHORT TAKING CAPTIVE AISTULF, KING OF THE LOMBARDS, AND RETURNING THE EXARCHATE OF RAVENNA TO THE CHURCH c. 1565

Black chalk and pen and brown ink, with brown wash and white heightening on yellow prepared paper, squared in black chalk
Inscriptions: *1, 2, 3, ... 9*
Annotations: *324; trois cent vingt quatre*
45.5 × 42.8 cm
Musée du Louvre, Paris

Attributed in the seventeenth century, when it was in the Jabach collection, to Santi di Tito, an artist of the Florentine School active in the second half of the sixteenth century, this drawing was credited to Girolamo Siciolante da Sermoneta by Pouncey, who recognized it as the presentation drawing for a fresco executed by the artist in the Sala Regia in the Vatican Palace (fig. 81.1).[1] Commissioned by Pope Pius IV, who reigned from 1559 to 1565, and whose coat of arms can be seen on the standard unfurled at the upper left, the work depicts the king of the Franks, Pepin the Short (714–768), conqueror of the Lombards, taking captive their king, Aistulf, and restoring the territories of the former exarchate of Ravenna to the Church. Certain liberties have been taken with the historical sources, which situate the episode in the year 756, so as to allow for an allegorical treatment of the subject,[2] in keeping with the iconographic program of the Sala Regia. This program, as revised toward the end of the pontificate of Pius IV, in 1563–1565, and directed by Cardinal Marco Antonio Amulio and Baldo Ferratini, Bishop of Forlì, was meant to celebrate various kings from the Middle Ages whose deeds had served the temporal designs of the Holy See.[3] The other subjects above the doors were painted by Livio Agresti, Taddeo Zuccari, Giovanni Battista Fiorini, and Zamaria Zoppelli, and were quite closely related to Siciolante's work.[4] Siciolante, for his part, was entrusted with the execution of two frescoes:[5] a larger one, *Authority Conferred by the Holy See on the Electors of the Empire*, and a smaller one, placed over the doorway leading to the Sistine Chapel, *Pepin the Short Taking Captive Aistulf, King of the Lombards, and Returning the Exarchate of Ravenna to the Church*. Only the latter composition, which took the form of a fictive tapestry, following a Raphaelesque prototype, was completed before Pius IV's death on 9 December 1565.[6] The former probably never went beyond the cartoon stage, and in 1572 a replacement fresco would be provided by Vasari,[7] who was additionally commissioned, under Pius V and then Gregory XIII, to complete the entire decoration of the Sala Regia. Payment for Siciolante's two works was spread out between 9 February 1565 and 4 December 1568.[8]

Vasari, in his 1568 edition of the *Lives*, states that he had in his *Libro de' disegni* "the drawing by the very hand of Girolamo" containing the "much-praised depiction of the story" in which "Pepin, king of the Franks, donates Ravenna to the Church of Rome and takes captive Aistulf, king of the Lombards."[9] It was probably the same drawing that ended up in the possession of Everhard Jabach, a collector from Cologne living in Paris, and that was then purchased for Louis XIV's Royal Collection, whence it finally entered the Louvre.[10] In this very finished drawing, already squared off for transfer presumably to the cartoon, the overall composition is virtually the same as that of the fresco. Yet there are some noticeable differences in the number of figures and their precise disposition, and also in certain architectural and perspectival details.[11] Iconographically, the most important changes in the fresco are, first, the addition of a small statue of a woman (carried by the young man preceding the captive Lombard king) that personifies Ravenna[12] and, second, the greater prominence given to the round temple in the distant urban perspective, recalling, in its shape, Bramante's Tempietto in Rome, erected on the site of the martyrdom of Saint Peter, reinforcing the idea that the temporal actions of the popes are part of a long history.[13] In both the drawing and the fresco, Pepin the Short, who is presented as the civilized and positive "double" of Aistulf, appears – unrealistically, but following an iconographic convention adopted earlier by Raphael and Giulio Romano,[14] and then in 1541 by Francesco Salviati[15] in his paintings along the lower part of the wall in the Stanza dell'Incendio di Borgo in the Vatican Palace[16] – dressed as an ancient Roman general,[17] though wearing an obviously more modern crown. He is surrounded by cardinals whose features, varying slightly between the drawing and the painting, are quite individualized. They are evidently prelates in Pius IV's curia, but their specific identities remain to be established. Although we can number among the possible candidates those who were proclaimed cardinals during the consistories of 30 January 1560, 26 February 1561, and 6 January 1563, we must discount, simply on chronological grounds, those who were raised to this dignity during the consistory of 12 March 1565. It is quite possible that Cardinal Ranuccio Farnese, bishop of Ravenna from 1549 to 1564, is represented here immediately beside Pepin, with Cardinal Alessandro Farnese next in the row. Alessandro Farnese shared in the responsibilities for the Sala Regia, together with Marco Antonio Amulio and Baldo Ferratini.

81

Fig. 81.1 Girolamo Siciolante, *Pepin Restores Ravenna to the Church and Takes Aistulf to Prison,* c. 1563–1565, fresco. Sala Regia, Vatican Palace, Rome

Siciolante apparently sought to match his artistic ambition to the prestige of the site and of the commissioning authorities. His very rigorous drawing – deeply serious, even a bit stiff and cold,[18] technically akin to some of his *modelli*[19] and comparable in style to his studies for the *Saint Agatha* at Santa Maria sopra Minerva and for the Fugger chapel at Santa Maria dell'Anima in Rome[20] – contains elements of the great Roman decorations from before 1520: the series of steps in the foreground, the palace in perspective, the man holding onto a column, and the classical figure of the captive on foot in the foreground are all variations on motifs that can be seen, for example, in Raphael's frescoes in the Vatican Stanze[21] or Baldassare Peruzzi's *Presentation in the Temple* in the church of Santa Maria della Pace.[22] Similarly, the urban perspective conforms to principles underlying some of the most sophisticated stage design of the period by masters like Peruzzi or Serlio.[23] However, in contrast to artists of the High Renaissance, Siciolante, like many of his generation, allows for much less breathing space in his composition, preferring instead to accentuate the dense texture of the narrative.

DOMINIQUE CORDELLIER

CIRCLE OF **GUGLIELMO DELLA PORTA**
active 1532–1577
PROJECT FOR THE TOMB OF PIUS IV MEDICI
c. 1565?

Pen and ink and wash
38.7 × 21.2 cm
Victoria and Albert Museum,
London

This drawing shows the plan and foreshortened elevation of a papal tomb, which has been connected with Pope Pius IV through the coat of arms on the main relief's pediment. However, there is no further evidence beyond this drawing that there were ever plans for such a lavish, free-standing monument for Pius IV (whose body was first humbly buried in Saint Peter's Basilica, and later transferred to Santa Maria degli Angeli, where Alessandro Cioli had carved a simple wall monument in his memory in 1582–1583). Still, despite the coat of arms' small measurements and the likelihood that the tiny circles could easily stand for some other heraldic element (similar to the letters in the rectangular field for the inscription, which are substituted with X marks), their oval arrangement makes it clear that they indeed stand for the six Medici *palle* and not, for instance, the six *fleurs-de-lys* of the Farnese, which would have been arranged in three rows according to a 3-2-1 scheme.

As a free-standing structure incorporating a mortuary chapel, the sepulchre represented in this drawing is derived from projects related to the early planning phase of Guglielmo della Porta's tomb of Paul III (cat. 116). Since it is also quite similar to Guglielmo's drawing style, Ward-Jackson has tentatively attributed the sheet to the sculptor

himself. Ward-Jackson also points out that the figure of the enthroned, blessing pope crowned by two angels at the top of the tomb recalls a page in Guiglielmo della Porta's second Düsseldorf sketchbook with two preparatory drawings for a tomb of pope Paul IV Carafa. This confirms that the present drawing, if not by Guiglielmo himself, can only have originated in della Porta's closest circle.

The coronation of the pope with the tiara is the drawn tomb's central theme, appearing twice: the large relief on its front depicts the pope's coronation in the church of Saint Peter's in his present life; his coronation by two angels hovering above the throne in the three-dimensional group on top represents the pope's eternal coronation. While we do not know whether della Porta's project for the tomb of Paul IV reflects an earlier idea he had for the tomb of Paul III, this hypothesis is extremely attractive as it helps to explain an iconographical anomaly of his bronze statue of the pope. In fact, Paul III is shown in full ceremonial papal garments, but bareheaded. A group of angels holding the tiara above his head – which might have been initially foreseen by the sculptor – would have completed the figure, as it has come down to us, to perfection.

EIKE D. SCHMIDT

ANTONIO (MICHELE) GHISLIERI

PIUS V 1566–1572

BARTOLOMEO PASSAROTTI
AND WORKSHOP 1529–1592
PORTRAIT OF POPE PIUS V c. 1566

Oil on canvas
129 × 94.5 cm
Inscriptions: *PIUS V GHISLERIUS.*
P.[ontifex] M.[AXIMUS] CRE.[ATUS]:
ID[IBIS]: FEB[RUARIS]: MDLXVI.
OB[IIT].K[ALENDIIS].MAII[S] MDLXXII
VIX[IT]: AN[NOS]: LXVII.M[ENSES].
III.D[IES]. XIV
The Walters Art Museum,
Baltimore, Maryland

The portraits of Pope Pius V by the Bolognese Bartolomeo Passarotti (and by other artists derived from ones by Passarotti) contribute significantly to the developing iconography of the papal portrait and more generally to portraiture reflecting the spirituality of the Catholic reform movement in which this pope was so prominent. The Walters' painting appears to be a replica of the initial "official" portrait, now lost.[1]

The work is inscribed in white letters on a strip of canvas later added across the bottom.[2] Shown in a three-quarter view facing to our left, the pope is seated in his red velvet-covered throne adorned with finial(s) in the shape of a cartouche with the arms of the pope's family, the Ghislieri, surmounted by the papal crossed keys and tiara. The green velvet draped behind him, suggestive of a chamber for receiving visitors, is drawn up slightly at the lower left, revealing a fringed edge. The pope is dressed formally, as for an audience, as is Julius II in the famous portrait by Raphael (London, National Gallery) that initiated the modern type of papal portrait. His costume includes the white pleated rochet, crimson shoulder cape (*mozzetta*) and cap covering the ears (*camauro*), the winter version lined with white ermine. Turning slightly to look up toward his visitor, the viewer, Pius raises his right hand in blessing and holds a small thick book – with gilded edges and a handsome, jewelled, sixteenth-century binding – in his left hand, marking his place with one finger. The book is probably a breviary.[3] At least by the eighteenth century, the painting was in the collection of the Hercolani palace in Bologna, where it was admired there in 1780 by the poet J. Calvi who wrote "... this portrait reveals how good Passarotti was in this kind of painting; ... there are many, many portraits of that Pope, but none, in my opinion, portrays him better than this one."[4] The portrait of Pius V by Passarotti, which the Bolognese writer Raffaello Borghini, the artist's first biographer, noted in 1584 as "marvellously

like" its subject, may be the Baltimore version as well,[5] but he was more likely referring to the version formerly in the Sacchetti collection in Rome.[6]

Pius V (1504–1572) was born Antonio Ghislieri into a modest family in the duchy of Milan. In the portrait he wears the white of the Dominican order he had entered as a youth (taking the name Michele). Until his death he maintained their austere lifestyle, combating lax discipline and heresy throughout his rise within the church. Appointed cardinal in 1557, after the death of Pius IV, he was elected pope on 7 January 1566 and crowned as Pius V ten days later. Central to his reign was the implementation of the reforms decreed by the Council of Trent (1545–63), among which was the unfinished work of revising the liturgy, involving a reassertion of tradition with the elimination of unnecessary accretions and errors. For this discussion, the most significant result was his promulgation of a new Roman breviary – the "Pian Breviary" – in 1568, and missal in 1570. He was canonized in 1712.

The new pope probably sat for Passarotti in Rome shortly after his coronation.[7] The artist moved between his native Bologna and Rome throughout his career, at times working with Taddeo Zuccaro.[8] According to Borghini, Passarotti painted the portrait of Pius V in Rome after he moved out of the quarters he shared with Taddeo when the latter's brother Federico arrived in the city from Florence in January 1566. Passarotti returned to Bologna at some point that year. While Passarotti produced many altarpieces, he is best known today for his vigorously modelled portraits and vignettes of peasant life. His earliest datable work, an altarpiece for the church of San Iacomo Maggiore in Bologna (1564–65),[9] includes vivid portraits of the donor and her husband. Passarotti's portrait of Pius V is acknowledged as the artist's earliest known datable independent portrait.[10]

PIUS·V·GHISLERIUS·P·M·CRE·ID·FEB·*MDLXVI* OB·K·MAII *MDLXXII* VIX·AN·LXVII·M·III·D·XIV

Fig. 83.1 Bartolomeo Passarotti,
Bust-length Portrait of Pope Pius V,
probably 1566, oil on canvas,
56 × 42 cm. Private collection, Rome

There are numerous portraits of the pope by Passarotti and his shop as well as by other contemporary hands extant today that all appear to be ultimately derived from Passarotti's 1566 portrait model.[11] Besides variations on the formal, seated composition, he made simple bust-length portraits. It is impossible to say if the sensitive, recently published example of the latter in a private collection in Rome (fig. 83.1)[12] is the initial study from life (later completed to create a finished work) or a subsequent, more casual, intimate piece, perhaps meant for family. As Petrucci (2005) noted, the brushwork and transitions in modelling are subtle and the beard is carefully delineated.[13] In comparison, the harder surfaces of the Baltimore painting confirm the suspicion that it is a replica: the face is alarmingly gaunt, the mouth harder, and the brows beetling.[14]

In the more formal, distanced composition of the seated pope, the artist has evidently used the same basic model but lowered the eyelids to give the impression that the pope is looking slightly up at a standing visitor. The more open eyes in the bust portrait look nearly directly across at the viewer (thus at a seated artist). While earlier Renaissance portraits of popes had introduced the blessing gesture[15] – looking back to medieval images of Saint Peter and ultimately to the frontal Salvator Mundi – the pose here gives this right hand gesture special prominence, visually isolated against the curtain. The inclusion of the breviary in active use makes this the first of the modern papal portraits to explicitly suggest the pope's personal spirituality.[16] That at the onset of his reign, he should choose to represent himself combining the traditional role of high priest with that of humble communicant, symbolized by the breviary, could be construed as a forceful statement of the experiential value and significance of the traditional liturgy, just at the moment he has committed himself to its re-examination.

JOANEATH SPICER

TADDEO ZUCCARO 1529–1566
MARINE DEITIES IN A CARTOUCHE c. 1566

Pen and brown ink, brown wash,
over black chalk
11.9 × 24.7 cm
National Gallery of Canada,
Ottawa

84

Lachenmann first suggested that Taddeo Zuccaro made this study for one of two cartouches featuring marine deities, executed soon after the artist's death in 1566 by his younger brother Federico Zuccaro and Giovanni Antinoro (a specialist in *grotteschi*) in the vault of the Salone del Corpo delle Guardie in the Palazzo Farnese at Caprarola. The relationship to either field is not exact, but the suggestion that this idea is from an earlier yet still evolved stage in the development of the design is entirely plausible, given the cognate subject matter. As Gere pointed out in first publishing the sheet in 1995, the artist must have altered the shape from an oval in the sketch to a quadrilobate in the final fresco – painted, not incidentally given the classical theme, in monochrome – as studied in a further double-sided drawing by Taddeo in a private collection.[1]

While Taddeo's art in general is distinguished by its blend of stylistic elements derived from both Raphael and Michelangelo, this drawing shows him engaged directly with ancient art. Several different sarcophagi were known by the Renaissance period that provided a model for this type of image such featuring marine deities as nereids, sea centaurs, tritons and amoretti, often moving excitedly in procession or in combat.[2] Taddeo's representation appears to show an awareness of one sarcophagus then in the

church of San Francesco a Ripa in Trastevere in Rome, though not surprisingly, given the artist's level of creativity, none of the correspondences are very precise. In developing the subject matter, artists such as Taddeo ignored the funerary implications of the sarcophagi and instead heightened the vigorous action and abandoned eroticism of the naked human and half-human creatures found on the sculptures. His virtuoso creation here – made not long before his premature death at age thirty-seven – of an intricately entwined figures in complex motion represents the artist at the peak of his creativity. Completed by the architect Jacopo Vignola around 1555–1556, the Villa Farnese was located about thirty miles northwest of Rome at Caprarola. Taddeo was commissioned in 1561 by Cardinal Alessandro Farnese (the grandson of Pope Paul III), after Girolamo Muziano declined, to make designs for the painting and stucco decorations in Rome; assistants were to execute the work at the villa itself under the artist's occasional supervision.[3] This manner of working, not uncommon in the Renaissance period for large and elaborate decorative projects involving fresco, underscores the importance of the original drawings for this secular commission, which was among the most significant and influential of the sixteenth century in Italy.

DAVID FRANKLIN

FEDERICO ZUCCARO c. 1542/43–1609
SAINT JOHN THE BAPTIST c. 1566–1567

Pen and brown ink and brown
wash over traces of black chalk on
light brown paper; repair at lower
left
23.1 × 17.5 cm
Annotations: *.gb.* [by "Pseudo-
Resta"]
Private Collection

Fig. 85.1 Federico Zuccaro, *Saint
John the Baptist*, 1566–1567, fresco.
Villa Farnese, Caprarola

Fig. 85.2 Federico Zuccaro, *Christ,
John the Baptist and Paul Preaching
in the Wilderness*, pen and ink and
brown wash, 17.1 × 23.5 cm.
Gabinetto Disegni e Stampe degli
Uffizi, Florence

This drawing has been published on several occasions in recent years as a work by Federico Zuccaro from reasonably early in his career. The descriptive pen line with varied densities of ink and the subtly modulated washes reflect the influence of his older brother, Taddeo Zuccaro, who died unexpectedly in September 1566. With time and as an independent artist, Federico adopted a more uniform and simplified manner of drawing. Here, the artist has represented Saint John the Baptist as the intense and sparsely clad ascetic who grew up in the desert. The subject is clothed solely in the camel skin mentioned in the Gospel of Saint Mark (1:6) and a billowing sash tied at his shoulder. He holds the usual reed cross – in this case encircled by a banderole – and points with his right hand to the coming of Christ. At the lower left, the lamb, which refers to John the Baptist's own description of Christ as the Lamb of God (*Agnus Dei*) (John 1:36), reclines on a book. A male and female figure evidently listen to John's preaching the baptism of repentance for the remission of sins.

Partridge proposed that this drawing is a study for the fresco of John the Baptist in the chapel of the Farnese villa at Caprarola, undertaken immediately after Taddeo's death in September 1566 and probably finished by early 1567.[1] (fig. 85.1) There are no exact correspondences between the drawing and fresco, but a number of similarities exist, and James Mundy has concluded that the sheet could be at least an early idea for the Caprarola painting.[2] The fresco of Saint John is located at the mid-point on the right wall of the small round chapel designed by the architect Giacomo Vignola. In the fresco, which is arched, Saint John appears full length, the onlookers are omitted and the lamb is placed on the ground at the lower left. John points with his right arm outstretched horizontally, a gesture clearly designed to link him with the altar, where Federico's fresco of the dead Christ supported by Nicodemus and four angels is located. If the pose of the protagonist in the present drawing had been used in the fresco, the tie between the two images would not have occurred, but on

85

the other hand John's focused gaze to the right in the drawing was perhaps meant to engage a worshiper when first entering the chapel. In the fresco, the latter connection is impossible, since John turns his head more in the direction of his pointing hand. It might be noted that on the ceiling of the Sala della Solitudine in the same villa, Taddeo Zuccaro had the year before depicted John the Baptist with his head turned sharply towards the left but with his right arm pointing horizontally in the opposite direction to Christ. That Federico knew the composition intimately is proven by a drawing in the Uffizi that is clearly by his hand and shows not only John the Baptist but also the entire composition of the ceiling fresco in the Sala della Solitudine (fig. 85.2).[3]

Mundy has noted that there are also drawings by Federico Zuccaro of Saint John the Baptist in Berlin and Stockholm, both showing the saint with his right arm raised, as in the drawing exhibited here but unlike the fresco in the chapel at Caprarola.[4] There is also a drawing in the Uffizi that shows John the Baptist standing, again pointing upward and holding a staff with a scroll and the lamb located on the ground at his feet, but the saint is now located in front of an ample landscape including a coastline at the right.[5] However, no study that comes closer to the final painting has yet been found.

DAVID MCTAVISH

ATTRIBUTED TO FEDERICO ZUCCARO
c. 1542/43–1609
CONVERSION OF SAINT PAUL c. 1566

Oil on canvas
68 × 47 cm
Galleria Doria Pamphili, Rome
Not in exhibition

In 1556 Taddeo Zuccaro completed the decoration of the Cappella Mattei in Santa Maria della Consolazione, receiving immediately thereafter the commission for another important Roman family chapel: the Frangipane Chapel in San Marcello al Corso. The fourth chapel on the left, recently analyzed in detail by Acidini Luchinat and Balass, was endowed by Mario Frangipane in the main church of the Servite Order and dedicated to the apostle Paul. The decoration includes a monumental altarpiece on slate with the *Conversion of Saint Paul* (fig. 86.1) as well as frescoed scenes from the life of the apostle on the vault and side walls. The decoration was begun in 1559, but was still incomplete at the time of Taddeo's sudden death in 1566, and finished by his younger brother Federico. The altarpiece was executed, according to Vasari, by Taddeo while Federico travelled to Venice – likely some time in 1564. The small canvas in the Galleria Doria Pamphili has been described by Sestieri as a *bozzetto* for the altarpiece, and more recently as a copy thereafter. It corresponds exactly to the altarpiece, and its detailed rendering points rather to a small-scale version executed possibly by Federico after his return from Venice in 1566 as a kind of *ricordo*.

The conversion of Saint Paul is described three times in the Acts of the Apostles (9:1–19; 22:6–16; 26:12–18), and is also mentioned by Paul himself in his letters. The Jewish Saul, the later apostle of the Gentiles, was at first a fierce persecutor of the Christians, and had asked the high priests in Jerusalem for permission to continue his task in Damascus. The most impressive account of his conversion is offered in book 12:

On that journey as I drew near to Damascus, about noon a great light from the sky suddenly shone around me. I fell to the ground and heard a voice saying to me, "Saul, Saul, why are you persecuting me?" I replied, "Who are you, sir?" And he said to me, "I am Jesus the Nazorean whom you are persecuting." My companions saw the light but did not hear the voice of the one who spoke to me. I asked, "What shall I do, sir?" The Lord answered me, "Get up and go into Damascus, and there you will be told about everything appointed for you to do." Since I could see nothing because of the brightness of that light, I was led by hand by my companions and entered Damascus. A certain Ananias, a devout observer of the law, and highly spoken of by all the Jews who lived there, came to me and stood there and said, "Saul, my brother, regain your sight." And at that very moment I regained my sight and saw him. Then he said, "The God of our ancestors designated you to know his will, to see the Righteous One, and to hear the sound of his voice; for you will be his witness before all to what you have seen and heard. Now, why delay? Get up and have yourself baptized and your sins washed away, calling upon his name."

Taddeo's composition illustrates the most dramatic moment of the biblical narrative. Saul, struck by the "great light" from heaven has fallen off his horse. With closed eyes and wide open arms he lies backwards on the ground surrounded by his confused and terrorized fellow soldiers trying to protect themselves from the light. In the upper register Christ appears in a swirling drapery pointing toward Saul with a powerful gesture of his right arm. Zuccaro's dynamic altarpiece is based on the most illustrious artistic representations of the conversion of Saint Paul in sixteenth-century Rome: Raphael's tapestry cartoon for the Sistine Chapel, Michelangelo's fresco for the Pauline Chapel, Francesco Salviati's invention engraved by Enea Vico and his fresco in the Pallio Chapel in the Palazzo della Cancelleria. On the other hand Zuccaro's altarpiece for San Marcello will become the most important point of reference for Caravaggio's two versions of the *Conversion of Saint Paul* executed in 1602 for the Cerasi Chapel in Santa Maria del Popolo.

SEBASTIAN SCHÜTZE

Fig. 86.1 Taddeo Zuccaro,
Conversion of Saint Paul, prob. 1564,
altarpiece. Frangipane chapel,
San Marcello al Corso, Rome

GIOVANNI ANTONIO DOSIO 1533–1609
DESIGN FOR THE TOMB OF PAUL IV 1566

Pen and brown wash with under-
drawing in leadpoint
34.9 × 33.5 cm
Inscriptions: *Jul: Romano*
GIOVANANTONIO DOSIO
DA SANGIMIGNANO SCVLTOR
FIORENTINO
The British Museum, London

87

Compared with his namesake Paul III Farnese or his successor Pius IV Medici, Paul IV Carafa managed to carry out
relatively little architectural patronage. Though Paul was
interested in art and architecture, his brief papacy was
harried by financial woes, and his great unpopularity –
accruing from his war against Spain and the scandalous
behaviour of his nephews – drew other obstacles into his
path. What he did achieve was centred chiefly on the Vatican
complex: expanding and redecorating the papal apartments
(though later transformations have obscured his efforts
there) and the inception of the small villa in the Vatican

Gardens (now known as the Casino di Pio IV), whose design
Paul entrusted to his court architect Pirro Ligorio, but which
was completed by Pius IV after Paul's death.

With the help of the architect Guglielmo della Porta,
in 1558 Paul IV developed his most ambitious, though
never-realized, artistic project: the rebuilding of the
Quirinal Hill. Originally the pope had attempted to recruit
Michelangelo for the project, which in many ways reflected
the great artist's earlier renovation of the Capitoline under
Paul III. As there, Paul IV planned for the Quirinal to be
approached via a series of monumental stairways, while

Fig. 87.1 Guglielmo della Porta, *Design for the Tomb of Paul IV*, c. 1558. Kunstmuseum, Düsseldorf

Fig. 87.2 Pirro Ligorio and collaborators, *Tomb of Paul IV*, 1566. Carafa Chapel, Santa Maria sopra Minerva, Rome

dominating the summit was to have been the church of San Silvestro al Quirinale, which Paul had hoped to rebuild on a grandiose scale.

Ever a champion of church reform, decades before his election Paul IV had co-founded the Theatines (1524), and in 1555 he had invited the order to establish its Roman headquarters in the modest church of San Silvestro. What we know about the pontiff's project for the rebuilding of San Silvestro comes largely from a drawing by della Porta and his assistant, Giovanni Antonio Dosio, now in the Ashmolean Museum.[1] A drawing in della Porta's Dusseldorf sketchbook (fig. 87.1) records a project for the pontiff's tomb that is probably contemporary with the 1558 project for the rebuilding of San Silvestro. But such was Paul's unpopularity that after his death, his remains were deposited unceremoniously in the Crypt at Saint Peter's.

Only seven years later, in 1566, the newly elected pope, Pius V, announced plans to erect a tomb for the pope in the chapel of his relative, Cardinal Oliviero Carafa, at Santa Maria sopra Minerva (fig. 87.2). Though he ultimately awarded the commission to Ligorio, Pius V had solicited designs from other artists, including Giacomo del Duca, and it is likely that the drawing by Dosio shown here represents another competing proposal. The inscription in capital letters along the plinth of the tomb, attributing the drawing to Dosio, appears to have been added by Giorgio Vasari, a contemporary of the artist who probably owned the drawing (while the inscription attributing the sheet to "Jul:[io] Romano" was added by an unknown collector in the seventeenth century).

The pope in Dosio's drawing can be identified as Paul IV thanks to the Carafa arms over his head. The statues (the pontiff, flanked by a figure labelled *forteza* or fortitude, on the left, and justice on the right) and the panels of

relief are framed by a classical three-bay structure clearly inspired by Baccio Bandinelli's twin monuments to the Medici popes, Leo X and Clement VII (see cat. 42), located nearby in the choir of the Minerva. On the two sides of the drawing Dosio has presented alternative solutions for the decoration of the architecture: in the attic storey a decorative panel with a carved festoon alternates with a relief with a figure on horseback (possibly Saint George); at left on the basement level he quickly sketched a pair of Michelangelesque captives and scrawled a note indicating the use panels of variegated stone (*mistio*). Other iconographic possibilities are suggested on either side of the candelabra, where the draftsman wrote [rel]igione (religion) and *pietà* (piety).

LOUIS A. WALDMAN

TIZIANO VECCELLIO, CALLED TITIAN

c. 1488/90–1576

ST. MARY MAGDALENE IN PENITENCE 1567

Oil on canvas
128 × 103 cm
Inscriptions: *TITIANUS P.*
Museo Nazionale di Capodimonte,
Naples

Renaissance viewers believed that Saint Mary Magdalene was a prostitute, who converted and became a devoted follower of Christ. According to apocryphal accounts, she later went to France, where she lived as a hermit in penitence, naked in the wilderness, clothed only by her miraculously long hair.[1] Titian made this painting of the penitent Magdalene and sent it to Cardinal Alessandro Farnese in 1567.[2]

Cardinal Farnese had previously commissioned from Titian a painting of Danae. Titian delivered this work during his only trip to Rome, in 1545–1546. The Danae is frankly sensuous, lolling back on cushions with her legs open. In a letter addressed to the Cardinal, writer Giovanni della Casa described the painting as so erotic, that it made Titian's *Venus of Urbino* look like a nun, and offered to have Titian paint the face of Danae as the cardinal's mistress Camilla.[3] Twenty years later the atmosphere in Rome had changed as the result of Protestant criticism of Catholic corruption. Giovanni della Casa (d. 1556), who had been known for burlesque poetry, had become in his later years an inquisitor and oversaw the first Venetian Index of Prohibited books.[4] It makes sense that in this new climate, Titian would paint a pious image for the cardinal, of Mary Magdalene in penitence.

The cult of the Magdalene, the model for penance, was promoted by Catholics in this period, partially in an attempt to curb Protestant critiques of penitential rites.[5] This image of the weeping sinner seems antithetical to the Danae, except that Titian did not envision the Magdalene as a wasted hermit but rather as a beauty, much like Danae, with rounded flesh, richly curled golden hair and drapery slipping off her shoulder, clinging closely enough to her breast to reveal her nipple. When the writer Valori visited Titian's house a few years earlier, the elderly Titian showed him a painting of "a very pleasant Magdalene." When Valori told the painter that the Magdalene was "too fresh and dewy in her penance," Titian "responded, smirking, that it was a portrait of the first day of her penitence before she began to fast ..."[6] This anecdote, which evokes a vivid image of the leering Titian, suggests the problems inherent in such a sensual image of saintliness. The story may be a fabrication, however, and we know that Titian's paintings of the Magdalene must have been taken seriously by some of their owners, who included the pious poetess Vittoria Colonna and the strict Counter-Reformation prelate Federico Borromeo.[7]

This composition is one of several variants on Titian's earlier image of Mary Magdalene in penitence, now in the Pitti Gallery, which was painted in the 1530s.[8] Evoking the Magdalene as a lusciously sensual beauty with spectacular golden hair cascading over her body, cropped by the frame so that she is brought into intimate range of the viewer, but with her eyes cast heavenward, was Titian's invention. Previous artists showed the Magdalene fully clothed. Depicted as a hermit, she was thin, even horrifyingly gaunt.[9] One poet of the period described Titian's unusually luscious image of the Magdalene as having "a lascivious chastity or a chaste lasciviousness."[10] This arresting portrayal of the sinner who was forgiven because she loved so much was well received and Titian and his shop made several variants of the composition for the most important patrons of the day, including Cardinal Farnese and King Philip II of Spain. In many later versions of the composition, including this one, Titian partially veiled the Magdalene's body with drapery, added the skull and book, and made her eyes more obviously red from weeping, surely in response to the changing mood, though she always remains ravishingly beautiful according to the standards of the time.[11] Titian's paintings of the penitent Magdalene are all small, intimate works meant for private devotion or delectation. In the following century, Baroque painters based their many small and large images of the penitent Magdalene on this sensuous type.[12]

The handling of this painting is more precise than Titian's more loosely painted works of the period, which suggests that it was done by assistants. Titian, who had a large shop by this period, is unlikely to have invested much time in painting a replica. He would, however, have ensured the quality of a work for the powerful Alessandro Farnese, and his small works of the period, which were meant to be seen close up, display a more polished level of finish. Surely his assistants copied the composition from earlier versions, then the master added final touches to animate the flesh, tear-filled eyes, and silken hair.[13]

Gentili offers an eccentric and deliciously unsubstantiated reading of these images as a part of his theory that Titian was a heretic who hid secret messages in his paintings.[14] He sees the clear glass ointment pot (Mary Magdalene's attribute) in other variants of the scene as a "risky" reference to the Virgin Mary – an implication that the Magdalene and the Virgin are somehow equivalent. In this interpretation, the opaque ointment pot in this painting, made for the orthodox Cardinal Alessandro Farnese, suggests that it does not contain any such heretical message. Gentili's only evidence for his view is that Titian knew heretics, which could be said of anyone who mingled with writers or artists in the period. The atmosphere changed rapidly and many writers who were considered completely orthodox in Titian's youth fell under investigation in his later years.[15] While it is tempting to search for secret messages in paintings, such interpretations imply that Titian's sophisticated patrons were pathetic dupes and belie the passionate immediacy of these works.

UNA ROMAN D'ELIA

Oil on panel
60 × 43.5 cm
Bob Jones University Museum
and Gallery, Greenville, South
Carolina

This painting is one of several Vasarian replicas that belonged to Vincenzo Borghini, the Benedictine Prior of the Foundling Hospital in Florence.[1] The surviving replicas, representing works by Vasari from the 1540s to the 1570s, share a high standard of finish, an attention to detail and a lucid colouring that renders them jewel-like. However, this *Conversion of Saint Paul* is unusual in two respects. First, because it is not so much a replica, as a variation of Vasari's altarpiece of the early 1550s for the Del Monte Chapel in San Pietro in Montorio, Rome; second, because it was not executed by Vasari, but by a studio member whose identity has been something of a mystery.

Borghini died on 15 August 1580. An inventory of his possessions compiled nine days later described this painting, still on display in his rooms, as: "uno quadro grande con cornice dorata della conversione di San Paolo" (a large painting in a gilded frame of the conversion of Saint Paul).[2] The *Conversion* remained within the walls of the Ospedale until 1833, when it was sold to the Marchese Panciatichi. The inventory of sale identified the subject as Paul before Ananias, as did the catalogue of the Panciatichi auction of 1902.[3] Some sixty years later the subject of the Greenville painting was reinterpreted as *Abraham and Melchisedek*.[4] In part, this later reading was a consequence of Vasari's attempt in his Roman altarpiece to express the Pauline subject in an entirely original way. He certainly knew how to represent *Abraham and Melchisedek*, as evidenced by his panel of 1545–1546 for the sacristy of San Giovanni a Carbonara in Naples.[5] This also shows a figure, armed *all'antica*, in an attitude of deference before an elder, but here that elder is portrayed in the headgear and vestments of an Old-Testament high priest.[6] Though the disposition of figures in the Greenville painting is broadly analagous, this is where the similarities end.

The iconography of Vasari's Roman altarpiece was unusual for the time. He explained how he had sought to vary his rendering of the subject from Michelangelo's *Conversion* in the Pauline Chapel. Instead of showing his blinding, Vasari depicted Ananias's laying-on of hands – "imposizione delle mani" – to restore his sight.[7] Both altarpiece and replica adhere faithfully to the biblical account, showing the blinded Saul in Damascus with his armed attendants. The younger centurion steadies his weight as Saul lurches forward sightlessly. Before him Ananias, in the plain robes of a disciple, restores Saul's sight and fills him with the Holy Spirit, which descends onto the scene.[8] With Saul's sight restored, Ananias baptized him.

The replica incorporates numerous changes, doubtless on Borghini's instigation. In accordance with the Acts of the Apostles, the scene is set before a house rather than the grand colonnaded edifice in Vasari's altarpiece.[9] Also, in keeping with tradition, Paul is shown bearded, as Michelangelo had represented him, and greater emphasis is given to the pitcher and dish at the lower left, emphasizing Paul's imminent baptism. More strikingly, the interplay of hands is different. Where in the altarpiece the older centurion holds Saul's left hand, in Borghini's version he supports his brow, preventing his head from tilting. Saul's hand is held instead by Ananias's youthful attendant. By establishing physical contact between the disciples and their former persecutor, Borghini's composition places greater emphasis on the transformation of their relationship after Ananias's intervention, with Paul as God's "chosen instrument."[10]

Borghini's painting departs from its Roman model in several other respects. Figures carrying food descend the staircase.[11] Below, on the corner of a table draped with a white cloth – reminiscent of an altar – is a loaf of bread on a folded napkin. These motifs, which are entirely absent from the Del Monte altarpiece, were derived from an earlier Vasarian composition: *Christ in the House of Martha*, with its steep staircase, food-bearing servants and laid dining table.[12] The bread is of course is an overt reference to the Eucharist, which, as Paul wrote, unites the disparate many into a single body of believers.[13] Significantly, it is depicted directly beneath the clasped hands of Paul and Ananias's disciple. Finally, where the Del Monte altarpiece shows a centurion restraining Paul's rearing horse, Borghini's version shows a woman bearing a child on her shoulder. In Vasari's altarpiece she climbs the monumental stairway at the upper right. Relocated to the foreground of Borghini's composition, it would be appropriate to identify her as Carità. Not only is this personification particularly apposite to the social role of the Ospedale degli Innocenti, within whose walls the painting hung, but it also makes direct reference to Charity as the founding principle of Pauline theology.[14]

The question of how the artist responsible for Borghini's painting replicated so many details of Vasari's altarpiece is easily resolved. Another inventory compiled after Borghini's death, listing the works of art he bequeathed to a certain "Livo," confirms that he owned Vasari's large preparatory chiaroscuro drawing for the Del Monte altarpiece. It has since been lost, but its height corresponded almost exactly to that of the Greenville painting. It could therefore have served as the model for Borghini's picture.[15]

The Greenville painting is patently by a comparatively inexperienced hand. In the past it has been attributed to Morandini, but this has since been contested.[16] It may represent the earliest known work attributable to another of Borghini's protégés, Ventura di Vincenzio Ulivieri. He was a foundling who grew up at the Ospedale, a likeable and capricious character who endeared himself to Borghini, who affectionately called him "Livo" or "Ulivo."[17] By 1565 Livo was working for Vasari and later began assisting Morandini, before ultimately assuming responsibility for the tapestry workshop at the Ospedale.[18] The *Conversion* probably dates from 1567 or shortly after, when Livo executed the predella for Morandini's *Adoration of the Shepherds* at Colle Val d'Elsa.[19] The predella is lost, but there are distinct points of contact in handling, morphologies and facial types between the Greenville painting and the few works attributed to Livo.[20] Indeed, his close connection with Morandini would explain his artistic development and the latter's palpable influence on the style of the Greenville painting. But a preparatory drawing for the left-hand corner of the painting provides further evidence that the *Conversion* is by someone other than Morandini (fig. 89.1).[21] Though the technique is inspired by Vasari, the drawing is obviously by another hand. It is certainly not by Morandini or Naldini. This leaves Livo, the proposed author of the Greenville painting, as the most likely candidate.

As Vasari's first papal commission, the Del Monte chapel was especially significant.[22] The altarpiece was a great success, so much so that Taddeo Zuccaro would later incorporate Vasari's configuration of Paul and Ananias into his own version of the subject (fig. 89.2).[23] Little wonder, therefore, that Borghini should have wanted a replica of his friend's early *capolavoro*. However, there was a more fundamental reason for Borghini's fascination with this image. As a Benedictine monk of the Congregation of Santa Giustina, Borghini was particularly devoted to St. Paul whose theology, as interpreted by the Church Fathers of Antioch, had been central to his education.[24] The theme of the Greenville painting and Vasari's altarpiece, which inspired it, was therefore tailor-made for him. Moreover, it includes a representation of the man who was perhaps his closest friend. According to Baglione, the Del Monte altarpiece contained Vasari's self-portrait, and indeed, he looks out towards the spectator from the extreme left.[25] In Borghini's version his friend is shown much older, with grey hair, looking up towards Paul, his hands joined in prayer.

RICK SCORZA

Fig. 89.1 Here attributed to Ventura di Vincenzio Ulivieri, *Kneeling Youth (Study for the Conversion of Saint Paul)*, c. 1567, black chalk, pen and brown ink, incised, 24.7 × 18.9 cm. Whereabouts unknown

Fig. 89.2 Taddeo Zuccaro, *Study for the Conversion of Saint Paul*, 1563–1565, pen and brown ink, brown wash and white heightening, 27.2 × 20 cm. Gabinetto Disegni e Stampe Uffizi, Florence

90
JACOPO ZANGUIDI, CALLED BERTOIA
1544–C. 1572/74
THE ENTRY OF CHRIST INTO JERUSALEM
C. 1568

Oil on canvas
49 × 38.5 cm
Galleria Nazionale di Parma

This small but very significant canvas was painted by Bertoia in a masterful *bozzettismo* style at the age of about twenty-four, as he was preparing to leave Parma for Rome, summoned by Cardinal Alessandro Farnese to devise the decorative scheme for the oratory of Santa Lucia del Gonfalone and contribute to the fresco painting in it. The theme is the Entry of Christ into Jerusalem, an episode perennially attractive to artists, narrated, with minor variations, in the Gospels of Matthew (21:1–11), Mark (11:1–11), Luke (19:28–44), and John (12:12–19). In it, a triumphant Christ astride a donkey enters the city with great solemnity, while the throng of onlookers lay their cloaks on the ground and strew his path with palm branches. Even on this small scale, Bertoia manages to adhere faithfully to the details of the story. The figures stand out animatedly and in vibrant colour against a nocturnal backdrop, resulting in an appropriately dignified tone that was characteristic of the artist's work.

Bertoia went on to do a series of preparatory sketches for the large fresco that he would execute between spring 1568 and summer 1569 on the right wall of the first space of the Oratorio del Gonfalone, as part of a Passion cycle. The Parma sketch anticipates, with just a few differences, the fresco version, which is set between elegant fictive twisted columns surmounted by elaborately detailed Corinthian capitals. The changes are mostly in the background – the fresco reveals a large section of the city, and daylight suffuses the scene. The small Parma canvas may have been the presentation sketch shown to the commissioners of the project, the brotherhood of the Compagnia del Gonfalone, for whom the artist had worked before moving to Caprarola.

Bertoia's career developed almost entirely under the patronage of the Farnese family, from Duke Ottavio Farnese, who engaged him alongside Girolamo Mirola, the remarkably imaginative interpreter of literary sources, in Parma's Palazzo del Giardino, to his great sponsor, Cardinal Alessandro Farnese, who in the end favoured him over Federico Zuccari for his richly varied designs and the enthrallingly sinuous contours of his painted frescoes. Bertoia, in fact, though principally schooled in the Emilian manner, was seduced by the atmosphere in Rome, thus bringing the style of Parmigianino (his foremost inspiration) to the more fanciful mode that would blossom as Mannerism and go on to influence the figurative language of artists in the Netherlands, in Prague, and at Fontainbleau.

LUCIA FORNARI SCHIANCHI

FEDERICO ZUCCARO c. 1542/43–1609
CALUMNY OF APELLES c. 1569

Oil on canvas
144 × 237 cm
Inscriptions: *INPAVIDUM FERIENT*
(originally *IMPAVIDUM FERIENT*)
The Royal Collection

91

Fig. 91.1 Federico Zuccaro,
Calumny of Apelles, c. 1569, pen
and brown ink and wash, over
traces of graphite, 40 × 53 cm.
Hamburger Kunsthalle, Hamburg

While large numbers of antique sculptures were rediscovered during the Renaissance and Baroque periods, virtually none of the paintings of the ancients came to light. Artists, antiquarians and patrons had to turn to literary descriptions by Pliny, Lucian or Achilles Tatius to learn about the works of Apelles, Zeuxis, Timanthes, Aristeides of Thebes and their likes. Apelles in particular, the court painter of Alexander the Great, offered a compelling model for the artistic and social ambitions of early modern artists.

In his famous essay on *Slander,* Lucian of Samosata recounts the story of the Calumny of Apelles. Out of envy, Antiphilus traduced his fellow painter Apelles of being part of a conspiracy against King Ptolemy of Egypt. The king accepted these denunciations without verifying the facts, and Apelles would have paid for them with his life if not for an eye witness that declared his innocence. The disgraced king compensated the artist with a gift of 100 talents and gave him Antiphilus as a slave, but Apelles was truly shaken by this frightful experience and decided to represent it in a painting, which Lucian describes in detail:

> On the right of it sits a man with very large ears, almost like those of Midas, extending his hand to Slander while she is still at some distance from him. Near him, on one side, stand two women – Ignorance, I think and Suspicion. On the other side, Slander is coming up, a woman beautiful beyond measure, but full of passion and excitement, evincing as she does fury and wrath by carrying in her left hand a blazing torch and with the other dragging by the hair a young man who stretches out his hand to heaven and calls the gods to witness his innocence. She is conducted by a pale ugly man who has a piercing eye and looks as if he had wasted away in long illness; he may be supposed to be Envy. Besides, there are two women in attendance on Slander, egging her on, tiring her and tricking her out. According to the interpretation of them given me by the guide to the picture, one was Treachery and the other Deceit. They were followed by a woman dressed in deep mourning, with black clothes all in tatters – Repentance, I think her name was. At all events, she was turning back with tears in her eyes and casting a stealthy glance, full of shame, at Truth, who was approaching.[1]

This famous example prompted Federico Zuccaro, following in the footsteps of Andrea Mantegna, Sandro Botticelli and other Renaissance masters, to transform his own bitter experiences with Cardinal Alessandro Farnese into a painted allegory of the *Calumny of Apelles*. After the sudden death of his brother Taddeo Zuccaro in 1566, the artist had continued to work on the decoration of the Palazzo Farnese in Caprarola, but soon frictions with his powerful patron arose and in 1569 he was supplanted by Jacopo Bertoja. Zuccaro's *Calumny of Apelles* is known in a detailed drawing in the Hamburger Kunsthalle (fig. 91.1), in a 1572 engraving by Cornelis Cort, and two painted versions in the Royal Collection in London and the Palazzo Caetani in Rome, respectively. The London canvas, which corresponds closely to both the drawing and the engraving, was later followed by the monumental version now in the Palazzo Caetani (335 × 490 cm) which, at the time of Federico's death, was still in his house on the Pincio. The London painting might be identical with a *Calumny of Apelles* by Zuccaro described in 1599 and 1609 in the Ducal Palace in Urbino.[2] It is first recorded at Kensington Palace in 1818, and was transferred to Hampton Court in 1835.

The complex iconography of Federico's invention is described by his son Ottaviano Zuccaro in his 1628 *Parallelo tra la Calumnia d'Apelle e del Cavalier Federico Zuccaro*, and has been analyzed in detail by Shearman and Acidini Luchinat. Compared with Lucian's description and earlier representations of the scene, Federico offers a more optimistic perspective. Ptolemy, seated on his throne to the left, is surrounded by female allegorical figures of Insidiousness, Envy and Calumny as well as by a series of symbolic animals representing Cruelty (fox), Malice (wolf), Avarice (paddock), Fraudulent Betrayal (feline creature) and Gluttony (harpy). The king is about to liberate the bound figure of Blind Anger in the foreground, but the wise Minerva standing behind his throne is holding his right arm back. The artist, crowned with a laurel wreath, has been liberated from the chains and the yoke which are lying on the ground and taken away by Mercury and the allegorical figure of Innocence, while the serpent-like figure of Fraud at centre is still trying to hold him back. Smaller allegorical scenes add to the central narrative. On the back wall a painting illustrates a group of peasants that assist helpless at a tempest destroying their harvest, alluding to the hard work of the artist unjustly deprived of his success. The highly elaborate painted frame contains further allusions to the final victory of the virtuous hero: at left Aeneas holds the golden branches of destiny, below a young hero ascends the mountain of virtue; on the right a more mature hero stands triumphant over vicious animals, while on top Juno rides her chariot over a calm sea symbolizing peace. Four nude figures executed in grisaille present the club of Hercules, a lion and an eagle, a bull, and a broken yoke, symbolizing virtue, spirit, hard work and liberation from servitude. The central cartouche contains a Latin inscription, "IMPAVIDUM FERIENT," taken from the third book of Horace's *Odes* (III, 3, 8) underlining that the "man of just and firm intentions" (III, 3, 1) faces events, however grave, unafraid. In the London picture the virtuous artist saved by Mercury and Innocence clearly bears the physiognomy of Federico Zuccaro, and the strongly autobiographical dimension is further strengthened by his coat of arms with the sugar loaf inserted into the painted frame. Later Zuccaro would continue to express similar personal experiences in allegorical representations such as the *Lament of Painting* and the *Porta Virtutis*.

SEBASTIAN SCHÜTZE

301

ALESSANDRO ALLORI 1535–1607
LAOCOÖN c. 1570

Oil on panel
73.7 × 57.2 cm
Private collection, United States

Fig. 92.1 Alessandro Allori, *Abduction of Proserpine*, 1570, oil on panel, 228.6 × 348 cm. The J. Paul Getty Museum, Los Angeles

Almost from the moment of its discovery on 14 January 1506 on the Esquiline Hill, near the Roman church of Santa Maria Maggiore, the ancient marble *Laocoön* (see fig. 30, p. 41) received universal acclaim. Michelangelo, who immediately recognized the subject of the work from a description in Pliny's first-century *Natural History*, venerated the remarkable sculpture. The life-size marble that he and other Renaissance artists admired was, in fact, an excellent, first-century Roman copy of the Hellenistic Greek original, which was said by Pliny to have been the creation of the sculptors Hagesandros, Polydorus, and Athenodorus of Rhodes. The sculpture dynamically represents the death of the mythological priest Laocoön, who, having displeased the gods, was set upon by two monstrous snakes, which killed his sons as well. Virgil, in the *Aeneid* (II, 203*ff*), gives the most famous account of the episode.

Alessandro Allori no doubt examined the *Laocoön* (now Vatican, Belvedere) when he first visited Rome in 1554–1556 to study antique sculpture, and again during his residence there in 1558–1559. His enthusiasm for the piece must have grown during brief, intermittent trips to Rome throughout the 1560s and 1570s; several paintings produced by Allori in the early 1570s, including the present work, demonstrate his lingering fascination with the sculpture. The sublime struggle and contortions of Laocoön and his sons are echoed in the tortured poses of the crucified thieves in Allori's *Deposition* (c. 1570–1575) in the Prado

as well as in the figure at the upper right of his *Deposition* (finished 1571) in the Florentine church of Santa Croce.[1]

Allori's beautiful painting of the *Laocoön* – more a coloured facsimile of the sculpture than a narrative recasting – likely dates to this same period, when he was also occupied with his paintings for the Studiolo of Francesco I de' Medici (c. 1570–1571). Having largely extricated himself from the manner of his master Agnolo Bronzino, Allori, at this moment, had achieved his signature mature style. In the Michelangelesque musculature of the figures and delicate handling of landscape elements, Allori's *Laocoön* relates to his Studiolo depiction of *Pearl Gatherers*; the physiognomies correspond to those in his Studiolo *Banquet of Cleopatra*.[2] Yet, as George Goldner has (verbally) pointed out, in style, touch and detail the *Laocoön* most closely approximates Allori's rich, panoramic painting of the *Abduction of Proserpine* (signed and dated 1570) in the J. Paul Getty Museum, Los Angeles (fig. 92.1). Indeed, the figures' cant and diagonal sweep of movement in the two pictures are cognate, if reversed. It seems likely that the *Laocoön* dates to the same year as the *Proserpine*.

Following the antique sculpture as faithfully as he does, even including the base, Allori creates a certain ambiguity as to whether we are intended to perceive the Laocoön group as a polychrome sculpture placed on a loggia or as fleshly figures. Such aesthetic tension recalls earlier paintings by the artist Daniele da Volterra, particularly his *David and Goliath* (c. 1555–1556) now in the Louvre, which were intended to evoke the issue of the *Paragone*, the debate about the comparative merits of painting and sculpture. In any event, Allori's Roman archaeological tendencies and overt Michelangelism ran counter to the more prevalent trend in Florentine painting at that time, which, led by Mirabello Cavalori, Maso da San Friano, Santi di Tito, and other Studiolo masters, looked primarily to earlier sixteenth-century Florentine art for inspiration, notably the works of Andrea del Sarto and Jacopo Pontormo.

LARRY J. FEINBERG

DOMENIKOS THEOTOKOPOULOS,
KNOWN AS **EL GRECO** 1541–1614
*A BOY BLOWING ON AN EMBER TO LIGHT
A CANDLE ('EL SOPLÓN')* c. 1570–1572

Oil on canvas
60.5 × 50.5 cm
Museo Nazionale di Capodimonte,
Naples

Although El Greco was born in Crete, then a Venetian colony, and spent the latter part of his life in Spain; he resided in Rome for about six years in the 1570s. There, he enjoyed ties with prominent members of the papal court, though he is not known to have worked for the papacy itself. El Greco is first mentioned in Rome in a letter of introduction dated 16 November 1570 from Giulio Clovio to Cardinal Alessandro Farnese.[1] Clovio relates that El Greco was a follower of Titian and had done a self-portrait that astonished all the painters in Rome. Clovio solicited the cardinal's protection of the newly arrived artist and provision of temporary accommodation in the Palazzo Farnese. El Greco in fact resided in the palace until 1572 and established close ties with Fulvio Orsini, the resident librarian and classical scholar, who became one of his first significant patrons. Perhaps at this time El Greco also met Federico Zuccaro, whose annotated 1568 edition of Giorgio Vasari's *Vite* he later owned and further annotated.[2] In 1572 El Greco was reported to have been working at the Villa Farnese at Caprarola, though there is no evidence of that today, and probably in 1575 he painted the full-length portrait of Vincenzo Anastagi, the recently appointed *sergente maggiore* of the Castel Sant'Angelo, now in The Frick Collection, New York.

The first owner of El Greco's *Boy Blowing on an Ember to light a Candle* is not known, although it could well have been Cardinal Alessandro Farnese. Certainly, the canvas was amongst the family's possessions, being first mentioned (in 1644) in an inventory of the *Stanza dei quadri* (picture gallery) in the Palazzo Farnese, Rome. The Farnese connection also plays some part in the usual dating of the painting to the early 1570s, when the artist was in closest contact with the family. For its time, the subject of a boy blowing on an ember was innovative, especially as an autonomous composition. And technically, the rendering of the dramatic effects of a single source of light on different surfaces is a visual *tour de force*, exploiting as it does the Venetian use of oil paint variously applied to canvas.[3] At the same time, the painting is part of a growing fascination with the depiction of nocturnes. In Venice,

immediately before moving to Rome, El Greco had himself represented *The Adoration of the Shepherds* (fig. 93.1) as a night scene, closely following the Gospel text (Luke, 2:8).[4] In that painting, the night is pierced by divine illumination, but the artistic challenges involved in depicting such an effect are not so different from those involved in creating the naturalistic appearance of a glowing ember in the midst of darkness.

Although *The Boy Blowing on an Ember* seems to represent an everyday event with an ordinary boy as protagonist, the artist may have been prompted to depict the subject by an antique literary source – as Jan Bialostocki was the first to observe.[5] In his *Natural History* Pliny the Elder thus tells how the Greek painter Antiphilus was praised for depicting a "*Boy blowing a fire [] and the light thrown on the boy's face.*"[6] The humanist circle around Fulvio Orsini would have provided the perfect setting for re-creating such an image, reinforced by El Greco's own Greek heritage. That Pliny's text was indeed being discussed at about the same time is proven by a letter of 1564 from Vincenzo Borghini to Giorgio Vasari: not only is the same passage cited but also it reminds the writer of Vasari's *Adoration of the Shepherds* at Camaldoli, which is shown as a night scene.[7] Venetian paintings that include a subsidiary detail of a boy blowing on an ember by such artists as Titian and members of the Bassano family have also been suggested as providing inspiration for El Greco.[8]

El Greco's interest in *El Soplón* (the Blower) – as the subject is called in early Spanish inventories – went well beyond the canvas at Capodimonte. A closely related version of almost the same dimensions and bearing a partial signature, formerly belonging to the Payson family in the United States and now in the Colomer collection in Madrid, is generally thought to have slightly preceded the present painting.[9] El Greco also extended the composition laterally, by adding an ape at the left and a "fool" to the right, in several variations of an allegory (*Fábula*) he painted in Spain.[10] In the seventeenth century, such Dutch artists as Jan Lievens and Gerrit von Honthorst, continued the tradition.[11]

DAVID MCTAVISH

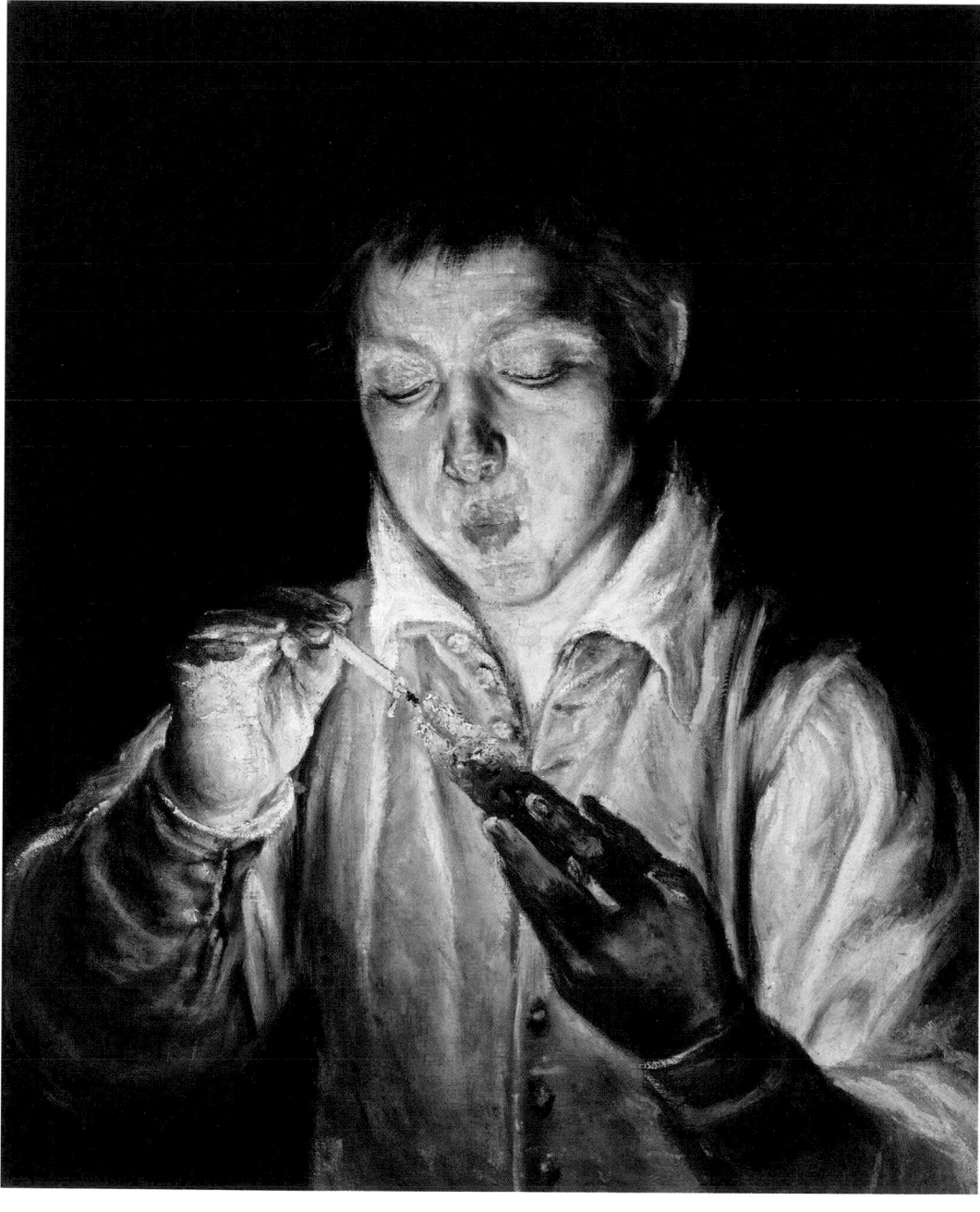

Fig. 93.1 El Greco, *Adoration of the Shepherds*, c. 1567, oil on panel, 23.8 × 19.1 cm. Agnes Etherington Art Centre, Queen's University, Kingston, Gift of Isabel and Alfred Bader 1991

94

GIORGIO VASARI 1511–1574
*SAINT PETER MARTYR STAVING OFF
THE DEVIL ON THE PIAZZA DEL MERCATO
VECCHIO, FLORENCE* c. 1570–1571

Pen and brown ink, brown wash,
over black chalk, partially drawn
with a ruler and a pair of compasses; the drawing of the main
composition mounted on a larger
sheet containing the architectural
frame and the figure of Christ in a
lunette
45.4 × 35.2 cm
Private collection, New York

GIORGIO VASARI 1511–1574
*SAINT PETER MARTYR STAVING OFF
THE DEVIL ON THE PIAZZA DEL MERCATO
VECCHIO, FLORENCE* c. 1570–1571

Executed at the height of his career, the decoration of the three chapels in the Torre Pia of the Vatican was Vasari's third project for Pope Pius V Ghislieri. He had previously painted two altarpieces for the church of Boscomarengo, the pope's birthplace: an *Adoration of the Magi* in 1566–1567, and two years later its main altarpiece, *The Last Judgment*, his largest ever. In a letter of 5 December 1569, Monsignor Guglielmo Sangalletti informed Vasari in Florence of the pope's desire to commission from him the decoration of one of the three chapels in the Torre Pia, located one above the other on three levels: the chapel of Saint Michael on top, that of Saint Peter Martyr below it, and that of Saint Stephen on the ground floor. Sangalletti's letter specifically mentions the chapel of Saint Peter Martyr, which was on the same floor as the pope's private chambers.[1] Vasari immediately prepared an offer, and a model of the chapel with precise measurements was sent from Rome to Florence. Two weeks later, the pope decided to decorate the other two chapels as well.

Vasari and his friend and iconographic adviser Vincenzio Borghini together devised the chapels' iconographic programs, which had to be adapted to the pope's changing ideas more than once. Work in the chapels began officially on 2 December 1570, by which time many of the drawings and some full-scale cartoons had already been prepared. By 11 May 1571 the Saint Peter Martyr chapel was finished (the ceiling had already been completed by 17 February).[2] While the chapels of Saint Peter Martyr and Saint Stephen have essentially retained their original decoration (only their altarpieces were removed and are now in the Kunsthistorisches Museum, Vienna, and the Pinacoteca Vaticana respectively), that of Saint Michael suffered a more invasive later restructuring.

Fig. 94.1 Giorgio Vasari, *The Preaching of Saint Peter Martyr*, c. 1570–1571, fresco. Chapel of St. Peter Martyr, Vatican

The central design in this large drawing is a finished study for one of four frescoes depicting events in the life of Saint Peter Martyr (fig. 94.1).[3] More specifically, it shows a miracle performed by him in Florence. While the saint was preaching on the Piazza del Mercato Vecchio, the devil appeared in the guise of a black horse, scaring the people away with a deafening noise. Making the sign of the cross, Saint Peter struck the horse like a lightning bolt and thus caused it to disappear. Borghini's idea for this scene survives in a letter addressed to Vasari, written between 9 and 13 December 1570.[4] According to a letter of 1 January 1571 from Vasari to Principe Francesco de' Medici, at that point all the preparatory drawings had been executed – to the pope's evidently great satisfaction – which suggests a date for the present drawing in the second half of December 1570.[5]

The drawing's composition corresponds closely with that of the fresco, apart from a notable difference in the treatment of the monumental column in the background, the fifteenth-century Colonna della Dovizia, so called because it was surmounted for nearly 300 years by Donatello's statue of *Dovizia* (Abundance). In the fresco, the statue is intact, as indeed it still was in Vasari's day (over time its condition worsened, and it collapsed in 1571). In the drawing, however, the sculpture is broken, with only its lower part visible. It seems that in this detail Borghini and Vasari originally meant to allude to Roman times. In antiquity, according to tradition, there was a similar column on the same spot, also surmounted by a statue. That statue was long gone by the time the new column was erected, but Vasari and Borghini would have known of it through local traditions. Considering that Donatello's *Dovizia* was

itself a tribute to its Classical precursor, and given that Borghini and Vasari had a strong interest in the early history of Florence, this hint at antiquity would have seemed to them quite appropriate. Such an allusion, however, might not have been easily understood by their contemporaries, which is presumably why in the end, when the fresco was painted, the statue was left intact.

The separate drawing of Saint Peter's miracle in the centre is laid onto a large sheet of paper that shows a simple altar within a receding architecture. That it was Vasari himself, or else an assistant under his supervision, who arranged these drawings in this way is supported by the fact that the figure of Christ blessing, added in the lunette above the Saint Peter scene, is undoubtedly by Vasari's hand. His hand is less discernible, however, in the architectural drawing, which may have been executed by an assistant, as Fairbairn has suggested.[6] It does not correspond with the chapel's architecture, and furthermore Vasari and Borghini would hardly have chosen the scene of Saint Peter Martyr preaching for the altarpiece, in which case the much more important scene of the saint's martyrdom would have been relegated to one of the sidewalls. There is no evidence for this to be found either in Vasari's correspondence or in Borghini's above-mentioned letter. Rather, it seems quite conceivable that the architectural drawing was made for an entirely different purpose: to serve as a frame for Vasari's drawing of Saint Peter. In adding such an elaborate frame to his drawing, and then completing the new composition with the figure of Christ in the lunette, Vasari may well have been creating a new page for his *Libro de' Disegni*, his drawings collection bound in several large volumes.

FLORIAN HÄRB

95
PIRRO LIGORIO c. 1513/14–1583
SHEET OF STUDIES WITH MYTHOLOGICAL
SUBJECTS ("EFFECTS OF DRUNKENNESS")
c. 1570

Red chalk
37.2 × 24.3 cm
Inscriptions: *P 80; 11, 13*; *Giulio
Romano* [verso]
Szépmüvészeti Múzeum, Budapest

It is in the lower half of this sheet that the principal subject is seen: several putti are trying, with little success, to
heave a drunken, aged Silenus onto a donkey while he
holds up a heavy wine vessel in his right hand. The beast
of burden, for its part, has already collapsed to the ground,
exhausted and apparently unable to move. The bucolic
theme is echoed in several additional sketches filling the
upper half of the sheet: a youth flanked by two putti is
straining under the weight of a vessel on one shoulder and
has in his hand a large cluster of grapes; next to him, three
carefree putti are playing with a goat; and at the very top,
a seated Venus holds a putto in her protective embrace.
The landscape background is a fantasy-like mingling of
ancient and contemporary architectural elements.

In its subject matter and physical appearance, the
Budapest sheet relates to a group of similar drawings by
the artist, most of which are to be found in his "Libro dei
disegni" in Turin.[1] Others are in the British Museum's
Prints and Drawings collection, the Louvre, and Christ
Church Picture Gallery at Oxford.[2] In all of these, the figures are drawn in red chalk in a rather painterly manner,
with the muscles softly modelled and the background
architecture fading out in a *sfumato* technique. But what
essentially unites this group of drawings is their common
theme. Putti at play, the drunken Silenus, a variety of trappings of a theatrical sort – vases, balustrades, goats, architectural devices – in addition to stylized elephants, panthers,
and dogs all combine to form an allegorical representation
of "the effects of drunkenness." A comparable treatment
of the same theme can be found in a drawing in the Uffizi
attributed to Giulio Romano (fig. 95.1).

Probably dating from the period of Ligorio's work at the actively humanist court of the Duke of Ferrara, Alfonso II d'Este, these drawings definitely have two parallel objectives: *prodesse* and *dilectare*. The warnings against amorous excesses and moral lapses stemming from drunkenness are expressed in sensuous and joyful depictions of nudity – an area in which pagan mythology provided free range for artistic creativity.[3]

Whereas the drawings in Turin appear to be mostly unified and complete – each consists of one or two scenes filling the entire space, incorporating architectural and landscape elements (see fig. 95.2) – the Budapest sheet seems more like a conglomeration of various scenes that do not come together. As opposed to the Turin drawings, whose manner of execution indicates that they may have been intended as designs for works in stucco, the drawing in Budapest seems to be made up of an assortment of *primi pensieri*.

In subject matter and style, all of these drawings are clearly unlike the ones that Ligorio made as part of his extensive written studies of Roman antiquities. Born in Naples, Ligorio settled in Rome in 1534, where he established himself as an architect and painter. Upon his death, he left behind over forty handwritten volumes summarizing his knowledge of epigraphical, topographical, numismatic, and iconographic aspects of the ancient world, richly illustrated with an assortment of ink drawings of reliefs, coins, inscriptions, and architectural elements. Though he had received numerous painting commissions in Rome, had risen to the level of papal architect (succeeding Michelangelo), and had won acclaim for his garden designs at the Villa d'Este in Tivoli for Cardinal Ippolito d'Este, he appears to have found true fulfilment only as an antiquarian in the service of Alfonso II in Ferrara, where he spent his latter years, from 1568. It would seem that he had acquired the skill of drawing for no other reason than to be able to set down his record of the ancient world as masterfully as possible.[4] The body of material that he assembled for the Duke of Ferrara provided him with the means to produce, in effect, an encyclopedia of antiquity.[5]

Unlike other draftsmen of his time, Ligorio chose not to depict ancient works in their fragmentary state but rather as reconstructed objects. For example, from the surviving portion of a statue consisting only of the feet and the base, he managed to recreate an image of Diana, goddess of the hunt, with her arrows and bow.[6] He came to be widely criticized for this approach, primarily by specialists in archeology, beginning late in the nineteenth century.[7] Although his method sometimes resulted in sheer fantasy, Ligorio nevertheless deserves credit as one of the forerunners of the science of archaeology. In his painstaking explorations of the vestiges of antiquity, which he incorporated into his reconstructions, he liberated the study of classical civilization from the straitjacket of philology, which focussed exclusively on the written record.[8]

Although the scene with the drunken Silenus on the Budapest sheet is reminiscent of an ancient relief fragment that can be observed in one of Ligorio's manuscript volumes,[9] this sheet is altogether quite different from his antiquarian drawings. It is much freer in its treatment of the figures, even if they still evoke classical precedents and are clearly not based on any observation of human models.[10] Deriving from his antiquarian reconstructions, these Bacchanalian scenes testify to Ligorio's delight in pictorial representation along with his passionate devotion to the recovery of the splendours of antiquity.

ANNA SCHREURS

UGO BONCOMPAGNI

GREGORY XIII   1572–1585

96
GIORGIO VASARI 1511–1574
POPE GREGORY XI RETURNING FROM AVIGNON c. 1572–1573

Pen and brown ink, brown wash,
over black chalk, squared in black
chalk
37.3 × 48.3 cm
Musée du Louvre, Paris

On 7 October 1571 the Holy League of Rome, Spain, and Venice defeated the Turks in the naval battle of Lepanto. News of the victory reached Florence on the 23rd of that month, and almost immediately thereafter Vasari, in a now lost letter addressed to Monsignor Guglielmo Sangalletti in Rome, proposed to paint this event. On 10 November, Cardinal Pier Donato Cesi informed Vasari of Pope Pius V's decision to commemorate the battle of Lepanto in the Sala Regia.[1] This marked the beginning of Vasari's work in the Sala Regia, the great reception room begun under Pope Paul III and still unfinished nearly forty years on. Two further frescoes of the Holy League's campaign against the Turks were subsequently planned, though work on neither had begun by the time of Pius's unexpected death on 1 May 1572. On 14 June 1572, the new pope, Gregory XIII Boncompagni, asked Vasari to proceed with the execution of these two scenes, but only one, the *Preparation of the Battle of Lepanto*, was painted.[2] The other, *Pope Pius V Appointing Don Juan of Austria Commander of the Holy League*, was later replaced by the subject of the present drawing. This is a highly finished study for one of altogether five frescoes that Gregory commissioned from Vasari for the Sala Regia in 1572. Three of these were dedicated to the massacre of the Huguenots during the night of Saint Bartholomew, which had taken place on 23 August 1572, and two were to show important events in the life of two earlier popes named Gregory.

In a letter dated 11 December 1572 to Vincenzo Borghini, his friend and iconographic adviser, Vasari suggested as subjects for the latter two frescoes Pope Gregory XI Returning from Avignon and Gregory IX Excommunicating Emperor Frederick II.[3] In his reply, written probably in January 1573, Borghini approved of the Return of Gregory XI, a subject that he considered most appropriate – in contrast to that of the Huguenot massacre, which he thought too low and unworthy of the Sala Regia.[4] He also corrected a slight iconographic error on Vasari's part, stating that it was not Saint Bridget of Sweden but Saint Catherine of Siena who had prompted the pope's return to Rome on 13 January 1377. Borghini also suggested including the saint in the composition, provided it could be done with a certain gravitas, to avoid any ridicule.[5] Following this proposal and ignoring the council of Trent's recent call for verisimilitude, Vasari set the scene in front of Saint Peter's as it looked in his own time. Led by Saint Catherine of

Siena, the pope is carried by Prudence, Charity, and Faith. On the left he is received by the personification of Roma, flanked by the Church and Justice, and the people of Rome.[6] The figure of Roma, wearing a helmet *all'antica* and holding a sphere and sceptre, appears to be inspired by one of the so-called Marcus Aurelius reliefs, *Rome Welcoming an Emperor*, which Vasari certainly knew, as it was built into the wall of a Roman house before being moved to the Palazzo dei Conservatori in 1573, where it remains.[7]

The Louvre drawing matches the fresco (fig. 96.1) in most details. Its composition is based largely on Vasari's earlier fresco of the *Entry of Leo X in Florence* (c. 1556–1558) in the Palazzo Vecchio, Florence. As Hermann Egger first pointed out, the pope's features in the fresco are those of Gregory XIII, and Prudence's small snake no doubt alludes to the dragon in the Boncompagni coat of arms.[8] We know from several letters that the pope had sat to Vasari for the purpose of using his likeness in the fresco.[9] Egger tentatively identified the three cardinals behind the pope as Pier Donato Cesi, Filippo Buoncompagni, and Tolomeo Galli, three men with whom Vasari dealt extensively during his various papal projects. Saints Peter and Paul hovering above are a quotation from Raphael's fresco of the *Meeting of Leo the Great and Attila* in the Stanza di Eliodoro, an easily recognizable reference and an indication of Vasari's great admiration for his famous predecessor.

The completion of the Sala Regia marked the climax of Vasari's work in the Vatican. Fully aware of his own achievement, particularly the speedy execution of seven large-scale frescoes, he sought to commemorate this feat. In a letter of 23 April 1573, informing Borghini of the imminent conclusion of the frescoes, Vasari revealed his plan for an inscription that would memorialize his contribution to the Sala Regia, by means of a play on the number 13: "The decoration of the Sala Regia was begun under Pope Paul III thirty-nine [3 × 13] years ago," wrote Vasari. "Six popes and twelve artists failed to complete it, before the thirteenth pope of the name of Gregory, and the thirteenth painter, Vasari, finished it in only thirteen months" [roughly May 1572 to May 1573].[10] No inscription of this kind was ever put up in the Sala Regia, but Vasari, evidently pleased with the thought, repeated it in a letter to Francesco de' Medici on 15 May 1573.[11] The frescoes were unveiled to great acclaim on 21 May 1573, as the painter proudly reported to Borghini the following day.[12]

FLORIAN HÄRB

96

Fig. 96.1 Giorgio Vasari, *Return of Gregory XI from Avignon*, c. 1572–1573, fresco. Sala Regia, Vatican Palace, Rome

97
SCIPIONE PULZONE c. 1550–1598
PORTRAIT OF JACOPO BONCOMPAGNI 1574

Oil on canvas
121 × 98.8 cm
Inscriptions: *Scipio. Caietano
faciebat. 1574; Ill.mo et Ecc.s.mo
S.or Jaco.*
Private collection, Washington

Jacopo Boncompagni was the natural son of the Bolognese cleric Ugo Boncompagni, later Pope Gregory XIII and Maddalena da Carpi. Legitimized early on, Jacopo moved to Rome when his father was elected to the papacy in 1572. He was nominated castellan of Castel Sant'Angelo and shortly thereafter commander general of the papal troops. His prominent role in the Rome of Gregory XIII is given expression in Jacopo Zucchi's grand altarpiece with the *Mass of Saint Gregory the Great* for the church of the Santissima Trinità dei Pellegrini (fig. 97.1). Executed for the Holy Year 1575, the painting includes numerous contemporary portraits arranged strategically around the celebrating Pope, who bears the features of Gregory XIII. Some of the most powerful cardinals, including Ferdinando de' Medici, Antonio Carafa, Marcus Sitticus Altemps and Girolamo Morone, dominate the foreground while the two cardinal nephews, Filippo Boncompagni and Filippo Guastavilla, kneel in the middle ground behind the pope.[1] From his place between the two nephews, Jacopo Boncompagni gazes directly at the viewer. His likeness has also been identified with the figure in profile at left kneeling next to the altar, but this identification appears less convincing.[2] In 1576 the pope arranged for his son an appropriate marriage with Costanza Sforza di Santa Fiora, and in 1577, 1579 and 1583, respectively, assured him the fiefdoms of Vignola, Sora and Aquino. Just a few years after the Council of Trent and the severe, reform-minded pontificates of Pius IV and Pius V, Jacopo Boncompagni's career marked the most definite return of papal nepotism.

Pulzone's exquisite half-length portrait, signed and dated 1574, is a perfect expression of Boncompagni's wide-ranging ambitions. It first appeared on the London art market in 1899 and again in New York in 1910. Briefly mentioned by Venturi, it resurfaced only in 1990 and was first published by Vannugli. The commander of the papal troops wears a parade armour of the latest fashion. Executed with meticulous detail, its rich decorative apparatus represents allegorical figures and military trophies, a bound Turk as well as Mars and Saint Michael, and designates Boncompagni as heroic defender of the Christian faith. Holding a letter in his right and a commander baton in his left hand, he stands in a slightly diagonal position in front of a dark background, while in the upper right a dark blue drapery with a golden trim balances the composition. His helmet and glove are arranged on the shiny red velvet-covered table to his right. With this portrait Pulzone has achieved a penetrating characterization of his sitter – then about twenty-five or twenty-six years of age – who gazes with utmost confidence and determination at the viewer.

Pulzone's *Portrait of Jacopo Boncompagni* builds on a rich tradition of portraits in armour that includes Titian's *Philip II* in the Prado in Madrid and Siciolante da Sermoneta's *Francesco II Colonna* in the Palazzo Barberini in Rome (fig. 97.2). The painter quickly established himself as the leading portraitist of his generation, and his sitters included such powerful patrons as Marcantonio Colonna and Francesco de' Medici, as well as Cardinals Ferdinando de' Medici, Alessandro Bonelli, Alessandro Farnese, and Antoine Perrenot de Granvelle. The *Portrait of Jacopo Boncompagni* emblematically illustrates also how Pulzone through portraiture, strategically built a wide-ranging network of clients and patrons; in the very same year 1574, he named his first-born son Giacomo, and Jacopo Boncompagni acted as his godfather.[3]

SEBASTIAN SCHÜTZE

The *Saint Jerome* in the Vatican Pinacoteca has since the late seventeenth century been attributed largely without question to Girolamo Muziano. The saint's Michelangelesque anatomy recalls Muziano's work, and the figure type compares to such paintings as the *Saint Andrew* of the mid-1570s (Galleria Regionale, Palermo). Stylistically, however, this attribution presents some difficulties. The saint's boldly twisting body is not in keeping with Muziano's usually more stolid figures. Even more problematic is the crisp manner of execution – noticeable in the treatment of the saint's face, the chisel-sharp depiction of the fingers, and especially the careful delineation of the beard and hair – which is inconsistent with Muziano's more painterly technique, as seen in the *Saint Francis*, the *Resurrection of Lazarus*, and the *Hermit Saint*, all by Muziano, in the same room of the Vatican museum. Even the original wood support of the *Saint Jerome* is extremely uncommon in Muziano's oeuvre.[1]

The documentary evidence for the attribution likewise proves troubling upon closer examination. The picture is absent from the generally complete lists of works in Muziano's early biographies.[2] Gaspare Celio and Giovanni Baglione, the two earliest writers to mention the panel, attributed it to Daniele da Volterra,[3] probably on the basis of an engraving of the composition by Diana Scultori (fig. 98.1) that bears the inscription "DANIEL VOLATER INVENT DIANA ROMAE INCIDEBAT."[4] Muziano was first mentioned in connection with the work only in the late seventeenth century, by Gasparo Alvieri, who wrote that the painting was "thought to be by Muziano, although others say that it was after a design by Daniele da Volterra." Alvieri's ascription of the painting to Muziano was soon after repeated by Filippo Titi and was then echoed by virtually all subsequent writers.[5]

The painting comes from the small church of Santa Marta in Vaticano, which stood until its destruction in 1930 behind Saint Peter's, beside Santo Stefano degli Abissini. Little is known about the decoration of the church prior to a renovation campaign in the late sixteenth and early seventeenth centuries, during the papacies of Sixtus V, Clement VIII, and Paul V.[6] The *Saint Jerome* ultimately hung in a chapel decorated under the patronage of Ludovico Canossi (c. 1560–1628), and inscriptions suggest that this patronage came at the end of Canossi's life.[7] To judge by its style, the *Saint Jerome* cannot be as late as the 1620s, so it must have belonged to one of the earlier, undocumented decorative campaigns.

The only basis upon which to date the painting, apart from its style, is the engraving by Diana Scultori. As noted by Benedetta Moreschini, the print must have been made in 1575, for Scultori had only arrived in Rome around the beginning of that year and the print is one of the works mentioned in a papal brief of 5 June 1575.[8] By that time, Daniele da Volterra had been dead for almost a decade, and Scultori's decision to record so prominently his invention of the composition was perhaps an attempt to bolster the reputation of her Volterran husband, the architect Francesco Capriani (more commonly known as "Francesco da Volterra"). While this alone would not rule out the possibility that Muziano had painted the picture following a design by Daniele, there is no parallel case of Muziano working after another artist's design. Moreover, Francesco da Volterra had by 1575 worked with Muziano on the Goldi chapel in San Bartolomeo degli Bergamaschi, and if the print were made after a painting by Muziano, one of the leading artists in Rome at the time, Scultori presumably would have credited him. To these objections must also be added the above-mentioned stylistic differences between the painted *Saint Jerome* and Muziano's own works. Tosini, noting the difficulty of reconciling the picture with Muziano's mature style, placed it in the first years of his career.[9] Even here, however, the picture sits uneasily, for there is little of the anatomical awkwardness seen in Muziano's early frescoes at Santa Maria sopra Minerva and Santa Caterina della Rota. Moreover, if the Santa Marta painting is by Muziano and earlier than the 1575 print, we should expect to find it included in the virtually complete list of works in the biography written by Muziano's confessor in the early 1580s, and it is not.[10]

Looking beyond Muziano, however, there is another artist to whom the Vatican painting can more plausibly be attributed: Giulio Mazzoni. Born in Piacenza in the 1520s, Mazzoni received his first training as a painter from Vasari. He travelled with Vasari to Naples, but after their return to Rome in 1546 he moved over to the studio of Daniele da Volterra, from whom he also learned the art of stucco.[11] By 1550 Mazzoni was engaged in his most famous project, providing stuccowork and frescoes for the palace of Cardinal Girolamo Capodiferro – now known as the Palazzo Spada – and throughout the 1550s and 1560s he also worked on projects in the Vatican, often at Daniele's side.[12] He learned the lessons of *michelangelismo* from Daniele, and the massive figure of the Vatican *Saint Jerome* finds many parallels in Mazzoni's work, even in the still-mannerist compositions of the Palazzo Spada frescoes.

Fig. 98.1 Diana Scultori, after
Daniele da Volterra, *Saint Jerome*,
1575, engraving, 29 × 22 cm.
Gabinetto Disegni e Stampe,
Uffizi, Florence

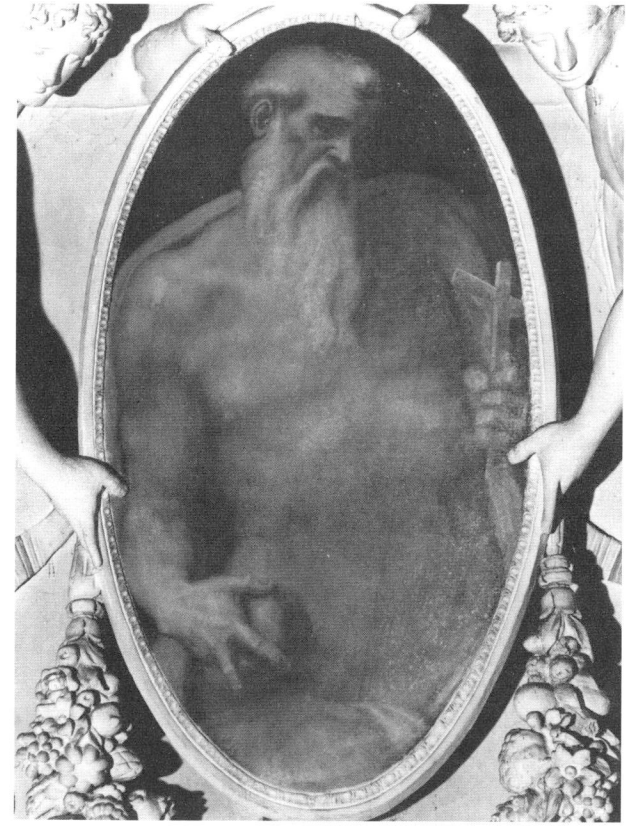

Mazzoni's little-studied later works include the Theodoli chapel, adjacent to the Cerasi chapel in Santa Maria del Popolo. The Theodoli family acquired the chapel in 1569, and decoration began soon after.[13] The central marble statue of *Saint Catherine* is signed by Mazzoni, and to those familiar with the Palazzo Spada the stucco and painting of the vault is even more recognizable as his work. The painted *Saint John the Baptist* and even more so the *Saint Jerome* in the chapel (fig. 98.2) offer some parallels to the Vatican *Saint Jerome*. There are similarities in the delineation of the muscles and in details such as the hard, bony hands, and both the Theodoli and Santa Marta paintings have the touch of mannerism – clearly inherited from Vasari – that is absent in Muziano's work. Likewise, despite the hints of a landscape at the right of the Vatican panel, both the Theodoli *Saint Jerome* and the Santa Marta *Saint Jerome* contrast the pure, bright red of the saint's robes with an almost-black background, and thus depart from Muziano's brighter landscape settings and tendency to eschew pure primary colours.[14] One imagines that the Vatican *Saint Jerome* belongs to the same phase of Mazzoni's career as the Theodoli chapel, around 1570 or else shortly thereafter. The literature on Mazzoni includes very few paintings dated between 1570 and his departure from Rome in 1576. If the painting was made in this period, however, we can better understand Scultori's motivation for engraving a composition by the long-dead Daniele. Conversely, no Roman artist at that time besides Mazzoni was likely to use one of Daniele's designs.[15] The attribution of the painting to Mazzoni thus not only helps clarify his artistic personality, and particularly the evolution of his work in the later part of his career, but also removes one of many problematic paintings that have hitherto confused our understanding of Muziano's work.

JOHN J. MARCIARI

Fig. 98.2 Giulio Mazzoni, *Saint Jerome*, c. 1570. Theodoli chapel, Santa Maria del Popolo, Rome

99

FOLLOWER OF GIROLAMO MUZIANO 1532–1592
LANDSCAPE WITH SAINT ONUPHRIUS
after 1574

Oil on copper
39.7 × 28.6 cm
National Gallery of Canada,
Ottawa

In the first half of the 1570s, Girolamo Muziano produced a series of remarkable drawings depicting Penitent Saints in landscapes. These were far from being his first essays in landscape art: when he had arrived in Rome around 1550 he was known as *il giovane de' paesi*, "the youth of the landscapes."[1] Yet, Muziano's drawings of Penitent Saints, six of which were engraved by Cornelis Cort, marked a significant new development in the rise of landscape art in Italy. Landscapes *all'antica* had long been a mainstay of villa decoration – Muziano himself painted them at the Villa d'Este in Tivoli – but Polidoro da Caravaggio's Fetti chapel in San Silvestro al Quirinale, painted in the 1520s, was the only notable earlier Roman example of what might be called "sacred landscapes," with small-scale religious figures set in a broad panorama. Muziano's Penitent Saints had a great and lasting impact on Roman art. They lie behind the subsequent rapid proliferation of landscape painting in the projects carried out, often under Muziano's supervision, during the papacy of Gregory XIII, of which the Gallery of Maps and rooms in the Tower of the Winds in the Vatican are the most notable. Still more schemes of this type would be commissioned during the next decade, including Paul Bril's "contemplative corridor" at Santa Cecilia, with scenes of hermit saints in landscapes covering the walls and vault, and the frescoed depiction of martyrdoms in landscapes painted at San Vitale by Tarquinio Ligustri and Giovanni Battista Fiammeri. Muziano's designs inspired the very much larger suites of saints in landscapes engraved by Jan and Raphael Sadeler at the end of the century. The contemporaneous development in Rome of landscape easel painting, by Matthijs and Paul Bril, Jan Breughel, and many others, must likewise be considered a related phenomenon. It should be noted, too, that Muziano's role in the evolution of the sacred landscape genre was not limited

to the Penitent Saints prints, but extended to some of the most important paintings in the city. His massive *Saint Jerome* altarpiece for the Gregorian chapel in Saint Peter's, for example, was, until its transfer in the mid-eighteenth century to the church of Santa Maria degli Angeli, perhaps the most prominent example of landscape painting in the city. One need only think of Titian's *Saint Peter Martyr* altarpiece to realize that the association of landscape and sacred imagery can hardly be considered Muziano's invention, but the Venetian-trained Muziano was the bridge between the artistic innovations of Giorgione and Titian and the religious and intellectual climate of Counter-Reformation Rome.[2]

For the Penitent Saints suite, Cort engraved six of Muziano's designs, and an unidentified engraver made one additional print. Several other extant drawings, in the same pen and ink technique and of the same size (roughly 50 × 38 cm), were never printed.[3] Muziano and Cort had worked together on a Life of Christ series in the 1560s, but for that series Muziano provided the engraver with red chalk drawings that allowed for the easy reversal of the design by counterproofing, so that the prints would come out in the same direction as the original scheme. Chalk drawings also afforded the engraver some interpretive latitude: Cort translated the chalk shading into his distinctive patterns of cross-hatching and swelling lines. Whereas the Life of Christ series seems to have been a project conceived by Cort (Muziano was one of several artists to contribute designs), the Penitent Saints series was essentially Muziano's endeavour,[4] and he provided Cort with pen drawings that he apparently expected the engraver to copy line for line, albeit with the result that the final prints are reversed with respect to the drawings.

Fig. 99.1 Cornelis Cort, after Girolamo Muziano, *St. Onuphrius*, 1574, engraving, 53.4 × 38.8 cm. Rijksmuseum, Amsterdam

Fig. 99.2 Girolamo Muziano, *St. Onuphrius*, c. 1574, pen and brown ink over black chalk, 52.1 × 38.6 cm. Institut Néerlandais, Lugt Collection

The National Gallery of Canada's *Saint Onuphrius* painting relates to one of the prints in Cort's series (fig. 99.1). Muziano's preparatory drawing for it is in the Frits Lugt Collection at the Institut Néerlandais, Paris (fig. 99.2). Painted in brilliant colour on a copper support, the Ottawa picture is in the same direction as Muziano's drawing and derives from it, and not from Cort's print.[5] Although Muziano was one of the earlier Roman artists to experiment with copper panels – some of the paintings for his Ruiz chapel (c. 1570) in Santa Caterina dei Funari are on copper – the precision of detail and the small scale of this painting seem alien to Muziano. The *Saint Francis* altarpiece in Santa Maria della Concezione and the *Saint Jerome* altarpiece now in the Pinacoteca Nazionale, Bologna, both relate to engravings by Cort, but those paintings favour instead a broader, if no less evocative, treatment of the setting. Even in relatively small works such as the *Hermit Saint* in the Vatican Pinacoteca, the landscape details are in a wholly different, more painterly mode, quite unlike that of the Ottawa painting.

If not by Muziano, the *Saint Onuphrius* may nonetheless have been executed by an artist in his immediate orbit, for, as noted above, the painting derives from Muziano's drawing – not only is it in the same direction, but it lacks certain details that were added to the print by Cort, such as the rock in the lowest part of the stream, and corresponds more closely to the drawing. The painting is not, however, a slavish copy. The format of the composition is slightly different, making the saint a bit larger in relation to the setting. The grove of trees in the middle ground has been reworked, and to rather beautiful effect, with long shadows emphasizing the crepuscular light. The practice of painting on copper would become a particular specialty of Northern artists working in Rome. It is tempting to suggest that the painting might be by Matthijs Bril, who worked among Muziano's entourage in the Vatican, but a definitive attribution remains elusive for now.

JOHN J. MARCIARI

100

RAFFAELLINO MOTTA, CALLED
RAFFAELLINO DA REGGIO 1550?–1578
TOBIAS AND THE ANGEL after 1575

Oil on panel
107 × 69 cm
Galleria Borghese, Rome

The painting is first recorded in 1616 by Raffaellino's biographer Bonifacio Fantini,[1] among the works the artist executed "for Countess S. Fiore" (Santafiora) of Sala, in Parmigiano. Faldi[2] identified the painting mentioned by Fantini with one owned by the Borgheses, based on information from Manilli,[3] who documented it with the correct attribution in 1650. According to della Pergola,[4] this identification would seem to be confirmed by the fact that other paintings passed from the Santafiora collection to Scipione Borghese, including the *Saint Catherine* of Correggio that is now at the Louvre.

Except for the mention by Fantini (a fairly reliable source, as other particulars he gives of the painter's life are verifiable), nothing is yet known about the commission of the painting by Santafiora, nor are any specific studies on art patronage by this family known. However, the Sforzas of Santafiora are recorded among the illustrious houses of Parma,[5] a minor branch of the Sforza family of Milan granted various *signorie* in the duchies of Parma and Piacenza (Castellarquato, Varsi) and near Rome (Genzano) in the course of the fifteenth century. In the sixteenth century, they allied themselves with the Farnese family through marriage, having the support of Pope Paul III.

Fantini describes *Tobias and the Angel* as a "work so rare, that it was then made into prints, because of the movement it has in showing the wonder of the young Tobias, and the majesty of the Angel."[6] The biographer was not exaggerating his judgement, as was common at the time, for the work – the only panel painting indisputably attributed to Raffaellino da Reggio – was highly acclaimed in its day. Two very similar preparatory drawings have been known for some time. One (fig. 100.1) was noted by Venturi "in the corridors of the Uffizi Gallery" in 1893.[7] The other, in a private collection in Reggio Emilia,[8] was first presented by Winkelmann, who in 1977 pointed out the relevance of both drawings to different stages in the planning of the painting, as well as such variants as the absence of the dog and the disappearance of Tobias's hat. Several engravings were also made of Raffaellino's painting.[9] Those by Agostino Carracci (1581) and Matthias Greuter (1581) and an anonymous chiaroscuro woodcut printed from two blocks are missing the same elements as the drawings. This led Beretta to suggest that the three engravings derive from the Uffizi's preparatory drawing rather than from the Borghese painting.[10] In addition, the Louvre has an older copy of Raffaellino's *Tobias and the Angel*.[11]

Fig. 100.1 Raffaellino da Reggio,
Tobias and the Angel, pen and
bistre, 36.5 × 27.5 cm. Gabinetto
Disegni e Stampe degli Uffizi,
Florence

In 1983, Gere and Pouncey compared a *Study of a Young Man* now in Rennes to the painting, relating it to the figure of Tobias.[12] They make passing mention of a red chalk *Figure Study* at the Uffizi (fig. 100.2), so far unpublished, that exhibits a convincing similarity to the young Tobias.

It should be emphasized that although the choice of subject matter – which Raffaellino also used in a fresco in the Sala degli Angeli in Caprarola – cannot be called rare, it is certainly somewhat unusual in Italian painting of the second half of the sixteenth century. The iconography derives from the Book of Tobit, a familiar popular story of edifying spiritual intent that constitutes a kind of code of family virtue. Raffaellino (perhaps not coincidentally, a nickname for Raphael) has represented a moment in Tobias' journey to Ecbatana, in Media, aided by the angel Raphael: "So the boy left with the angel, and the dog followed behind" (Tobit 6:2). In Ecbatana, Tobias married his cousin Sarah, who was possessed by a demon. Her first seven husbands had died on their wedding nights. But with Raphael's help, Tobias finds a cure: when placed on the embers of the incense in the bridal chamber, as instructed by the angel, the heart and liver of the fish Tobias caught in the Tigris River emits an odour that would free any human being from the vexations of a demon. Thus, Sarah is exorcised and they begin a long and happy life together.

In the traditional iconography, Tobias is generally portrayed as quite young, almost a child, in accordance with the Scriptures (hence Tobiolo or "little Tobias," in the Italian title of the work). Curiously, however – and unlike the fresco at Caprarola – in Raffaellino's painting, Tobias appears older, at least an adolescent.

While the attribution to Raffaellino has never been questioned, the chronology of the painting is still controversial, vacillating between the end of the painter's career (he died in 1578) and the period of the fresco at the Oratorio del Gonfalone in Rome (1573–1575). Huys[13] has related the painting to Raffaellino's activity at Caprarola and the Vatican and to the fresco of *The Angel Appearing to Saint Joseph* in the church of San Silvestro al Quirinale in Rome, and thus proposes a date between 1574–1575 and 1576. Sricchia Santoro[14] also favours a date previous to the artist's last period and proposes the time of Raffaellino's contact with Bertoja at the Oratorio del Gonfalone and Caprarola "because of the pronounced Parmesan inflections" and above all because of the influence he exerted on Netherlandish painters, as seen in Spranger's *Saint Dominic* (engraved by Cort in 1573) and Speckaert's drawing *Abraham and Isaac*.

On the other hand, in 1938 Collobi[15] included the painting among the artist's last works and thus close to the frescoes at San Silvestro al Quirinale. De Grazia[16] subsequently concurred, specifying a date of 1575–1576. More recently, Bernardini[17] returned to the question, seeking to establish an overall chronology for Raffaellino's oeuvre. He places the frescoes in the Gonfalone and the San Silvestro oratory of the church of the Santi Quattro Coronati in the artist's early Roman period, between 1573 and 1574, and *Tobias and the Angel* in parallel with the frescoes at the church of San Silvestro al Quirinale, about 1577.

Clearly, the problem in dating the work is closely related to the difficulty of placing Raffaellino's Roman works in a precise sequence as a result of the near-total lack of contemporary documentation. Only an in-depth examination of the documents and a work of ample scope on the artist will provide more reliable dates and chronologies.

Yet, if, as we believe, the fresco of *Raphael and Tobit* at Caprarola was done by Raffaellino around 1574–1575, the Galleria Borghese painting should come later, because it conveys a different complexity and richness of cultural references. Drawing upon Wollesen Wisch's analysis,[18] one might say that in the Caprarola fresco, Raffaellino still shows the effects of "muscular vitality," characteristic of the works from his early years in Rome.

Comparison with a sheet attributed to Pellegrino Tibaldi at the Uffizi representing Tobias and the Angel seems intriguing.[19] In the fresco at Caprarola, the angel's powerful muscles and monumental bearing, and the sense of movement suggest that Raffaellino was well acquainted with similar works by Tibaldi, although he revisited them in a more elegant, slender form. In the following years, the artist's exposure to Perino and Tibaldi and the wealth of cultural experience connected with his Emilian training – Lelio Orsi, Parmigianino and Correggio, as well as Bertoja and Mirola – were enriched, refined and distilled through direct contact with the highly coloured enamelled painting of the Netherlandish artists in Rome, and above all, as has been emphasized, with the work of Spranger, Speckaert and Soens. The result, highlighted in the Borghese *Tobias and the Angel*, is a more international, less Roman style of painting, characterized by a bright, luminous palette but with strong contrasts of light and shadow, elongated, tapered proportions that open to distant horizons. Even the faces are more modern and the feminine angel at Caprarola develops unexpectedly northern physical traits.

Fig. 100.2 Raffaellino da Reggio, *Study for the figure of Tobias*, c. 1572–1582, red chalk, 42 × 21 cm. Gabinetto Disegni e Stampe degli Uffizi, Florence

The glimpse of landscape at the right (where a miniature Tobias and Raphael perhaps appear) and the large tree in the left foreground are clearly indebted to the ample landscapes of the Netherlandish painters Soens and Van Winghe. These elements also suggest the artist's new capacity to "create unity between elements that express a descriptive truthfulness and – unlike the Netherlandish artists – an extreme freedom of draftsmanship."[20] There is a different, vital relationship between the figures and nature, which still references the lasting link between the Raffaellino's later works and his Emilian training, which looked to Parmigianino, Orsi and Correggio.

GIULIO ZAVATTA AND ALESSANDRA BIGI IOTTI

101

ATTRIBUTED TO **CESARE NEBBIA** c. 1536–1614
THE EMPEROR CHARLEMAGNE c. 1572–1582

Pen and brown ink and brown
wash, with white heightening,
traces of black chalk, squared with
black chalk on prepared blue
washed paper
30.6 × 16 cm
National Gallery of Canada,
Ottawa

Although this drawing has long been attributed to Girolamo Muziano, its technique, featuring a broad use of fluid brown wash and white heightening, is not one typically found among the artist's works. The sheet might usefully be compared, however, to drawings by Muziano's primary pupil and assistant, Cesare Nebbia. Nebbia's drawing for a figure of *Solomon*, a study for the frescoes in the Cappella Sistina at Santa Maria Maggiore, Rome, provides an interesting case in point, and his large *modelli* for the renovation of the tribune in the Duomo of his native Orvieto offer further analogies.[1]

Although not by Muziano himself, the drawing nonetheless seems to relate to a project for which Muziano was responsible. Some time in the 1570s, Muziano was commissioned to paint an Assumption of the Virgin, along with flanking images of Charlemagne and Saint Louis, for the choir of San Luigi dei Francesi, Rome. In his 1584 *Il riposo*, Borghini writes that the patron for that work was "Mattio Contarini Datario,"[2] but this would appear to be a slightly mistaken identification: Matteo Contarelli served as papal datary from 1572 to 1583, and the high altar was adjacent to the Contarelli chapel, originally also commissioned from Muziano but later decorated by Giuseppe Cesari and Caravaggio. Borghini describes the *Assumption* as being on the high altar, but Muziano never received any money for the painting from Contarelli or, following Contarelli's death in November 1585, from his heirs. Eventually, in January 1592 (two years after Francesco Bassano's replacement high altarpiece was installed at San Luigi), Muziano sold his picture for 500 scudi to the monastery of San Paolo fuori le Mura, where it remained until it was destroyed by fire in 1823.[3]

When the *Assumption* was sold, the frescoed *Saint Louis* and *Charlemagne* remained behind in the choir of San Luigi, but they too have since vanished, presumably in the eighteenth-century rebuilding of the east end of the church. Most of the early sources attributed them to Muziano, but Gaspare Celio, who was closest to the various artists involved, gives them instead to Nebbia.[4] As with other projects from the 1570s, the work was probably a collaborative endeavour of the two artists. Other visual evidence bears this out, for in addition to the Ottawa *Charlemagne*, another drawing of a standing king, in the Louvre (fig. 101.1), is unquestionably in Muziano's own hand and surely relates to this same project. Muziano, throughout his career, seems to have avoided working in fresco whenever possible, favouring instead the technique of oil on canvas, but Nebbia was a proficient fresco painter, and Muziano on more than one occasion handed over fresco projects to the younger artist. For the Altoviti chapel in the basilica at Loreto, for example, also executed in the mid- to late-1570s, Muziano painted canvases to decorate the pilasters, altarpiece, and side walls, but for the frescoed vault he merely made drawings and sent Nebbia to carry out the frescoes themselves. It is likely that when commissioned to paint both the high altarpiece (on canvas) and flanking frescoes at San Luigi, a similar division of work ensued. Muziano's Louvre drawing would have served as an initial reference, but – as has been documented for other joint projects by the artists[5] – Nebbia would also have made preparatory sketches. The final products often included aspects of both artists' designs. In this instance, unfortunately, there is no surviving image of the completed fresco that would allow us to understand how the two ideas were merged in the final work.

JOHN J. MARCIARI

Fig. 101.1 Girolamo Muziano, *Study of a Standing King*, c. 1572–1582, black and white chalks, 40.2 × 23.4 cm. Musée du Louvre, Paris

102
LIVIO AGRESTI c. 1530/31–1579
CHRIST HEALING THE PARALYTIC
c. 1573–1575

Pen and ink, wash, white lead,
traces of black chalk, squaring off
with natural black stone on very
faded blue paper
42.9 × 29.2 cm
Gabinetto Disegni e Stampe degli
Uffizi, Florence

LIVIO AGRESTI c. 1530/31–1579
CHRIST HEALING THE PARALYTIC
c. 1573–1575

The drawing under examination is a preparatory sketch by Livio Agresti for the fresco in oil, *Christ Healing the Paralytic,* executed in the chapel of the Holy Trinity in the church of Santo Spirito in Sassia in Rome, which the Forlì-born artist – according to the documents – decorated between 1573 and 1575.[1] The high quality of the finish and accurate squaring off suggest that the sheet might have been conceived as a model for the cartoon. However, the addition of a patch of paper (still visible today) to redesign the upper part of the figure of the paralytic reflects some dissatisfaction on the part of the artist with his initial effort. A comparison of the Uffizi sketch and the painting (fig. 102.1) indicates that the artist made further revisions in the final work. The two main figures in the foreground are presented differently; the temple in the background has been replaced with a large obelisk. Clearly the different versions refer to two successive moments in the story: in the drawing, Christ orders the stricken figure to rise, whereas in the painting the miracle has already occurred as Christ is gesturing towards the paralytic's empty bed. Likewise, while the exchange of glances between Christ and the lame man who has been touched by divine grace serves as a dramatic device in the Uffizi design, the final work favours the immediacy of the great miracle that has just taken place and more explicitly references to the text of the Gospel according to John.

The clear sharp contours and the use of chiaroscuro in the Uffizi sketch, indicates an interpretation of the Florentine, or more specifically the Vasarian, tradition. Certainly the background, which features ancient monuments studied with philological precision, and a throng of spectators, evokes the work of Giorgio Vasari. However, the figures of Christ and the half-naked paralytic as well as the style of the drapery suggest a Michelangelesque

influence, filtered by a sensitivity typical of the Muziano school. The compositional structure derives from the Orvieto frescoes of Girolamo Muziano himself, and of Federico Zuccari, portraying respectively the *Resurrection of Lazarus* and the *Resurrection of the Son of the Widow of Naim* – works that the artist likely had the opportunity to admire during his stay in Umbria in the late 1560s.[7]

While the years marking his birth and the outset of Agresti's artistic career remain the subject of debate,[3] art historians agree that his success is linked inextricably to his decorative assignments for the chapels of the church of Santo Spirito in Sassia. The chapel of the Holy Trinity was the second he painted in the Roman church. Between 1554 and 1557, Agresti had already worked on the chapel of Saint Stephen for Alfonso Gonzaga; this was also the artist's first important documented project in Rome.[4] To these two, a third might have been added had the chapel of the Assumption not remained unfinished at the time of his death in 1579. According to Vasari, Agresti's successful completion of his assignment at the church of Santo Spirito led to an invitation to take part in the decoration of the Sala Regia at the Vatican between 1561 and 1564 during the papacy of Pius IV.[5]

In the decoration of the Chapel of the Holy Trinity, initiated soon after the papacy of Gregory XIII, a rigorous interpreter of Counter-Reformation trends, there is a noticeable effort on the part of Agresti to adapt his vocabulary to the new iconographic guidance of the Church. This is particularly evident in comparison to the highly ornamental chapel at Saint Stephen's, executed twenty years earlier, where the richness and complexity of its decoration deeply impressed his contemporaries. By contrast, in the execution of the decoration of the Chapel of the Holy Trinity there is a manifest effort achieve formal simplification, which encompasses the entire work, from the stuccos to the spatial composition of the scenes. And, as demonstrated by the drawing under study here, the artist's interest in a daring perspective gives way to a more immediate legibility of content and a faithful adherence to the sacred text.

RAIMONDO SASSI

Fig. 102.1 Livio Agresti, *Christ Healing the Paralytic,* c. 1573–1575, fresco in oil. Chapel of Santissima Trinità, Santo Spirito in Sassia, Rome

103

RAFFAELLINO MOTTA, CALLED
RAFFAELLINO DA REGGIO 1550?–1578
DESIGN FOR THE DECORATION OF A
CHAPEL mid-1570s

Pen and brown ink and wash over
black chalk, laid down
26.6 × 17.8 cm
Annotations: *Zuccaro*
National Gallery of Scotland,
Edinburgh

104

JACOPO ZUCCHI c. 1541–c. 1589/90
DESIGN FOR THE DECORATION OF A CHAPEL mid-1570s

Pen and brown ink and brown
wash over black chalk
36 × 27.7 cm
Annotations: *Boscolie f.*
Christ Church Picture Gallery,
Oxford

These two drawings are here catalogued together because, despite their significant differences, they were almost certainly made as alternative – presumably rival – designs for the decoration of the same chapel.[1] As the old inscriptions attest, each was traditionally misattributed to another artist, and in both cases it was the great connoisseur of Italian drawings Pouncey who first recognized their true authors (the Raffaellino in 1950, the Zucchi in 1967).[2] Both designs conform to a basic arrangement widely adopted for the decoration of small chapels in later sixteenth-century Rome.

The scheme devised by the younger artist, Raffaellino, is the simpler of the two. A concave niche with a half-dome above is framed by an arch flanked by tall pilasters. Into this apse-like space is inserted a rectilinear altar with an altarpiece of the Adoration of the Magi. The segmental pediment above is broken by a cartouche surmounted by a crown. In niches to either side appear statues, the one on the right identifiable as the Evangelist Matthew, who is inspired by an angel while writing his gospel. A glory of angels on clouds was to be painted in the vault, while the Annunciation appears in the spandrels on the nave wall above. Grotesque decoration is sketched on the inner pilasters.

Jacopo Zucchi's design, "a *tour de force* among the artist's finished *modelli*,"[3] is altogether denser, with every available space, bar the altar, filled with narrative scenes or encrusted with sculpture and ornament – a *horror vacui* that is a consistent feature of Zucchi's art as a whole.[4] A much higher proportion of his project than Raffaellino's must have been intended for realization in the round, in marble or stucco, which would have been a much more expensive option. The extensive annotations on Zucchi's drawing establish that the planned decorations had a typological program, paralleling scenes from the conception and infancy of Christ with prefigurations and prophecies from the Old Testament relating to the coming of the Messiah.[5] This theme is introduced by the quotation from the book of Isaiah (7:14) inscribed in the frieze above the chapel: "Behold, a young woman shall conceive and bear a son, and shall call his name Immanuel," which is juxtaposed with the Annunciation in the spandrels directly below. Zucchi's design enables us to identify the left-hand statue in Raffaellino's drawing, whose only attribute is a crown, as King David, who was regarded both as a prefiguration and a direct ancestor of Christ (Matthew 1:1–17). In Zucchi's project the vault is occupied by the tablet-bearing figures of Saint John the Evangelist and the prophet Hosea, flanked by blank fields destined to portray the Nativity and the Flight into Egypt. The star that appears at the centre of the vault in both drawings no doubt represents the brilliant star of Bethlehem that guided the wise men to the newborn Jesus; the relevant verses from Matthew's gospel are inscribed in the central cartouche in Zucchi's drawing. The concave profile of the altarpiece in Zucchi's drawing implies that it was intended to be painted in fresco directly onto the wall of the chapel, whereas Raffeallino's rectilinear altarpiece would presumably have been on panel or canvas.

There is no surviving or documented chapel decoration by either artist that corresponds closely to the arrangement in either drawing, but the designs have been linked with the much-altered second chapel on the left (originally the third) in San Silvestro al Quirinale (fig. 104.1).[6] The vault of this chapel was indeed decorated by Raffaellino. His frescoes of the *Holy Ghost with Angels*,[7] the *Dream of Saint Joseph*[8] and the *Massacre of the Innocents*,[9] with small figures of *David* and *Isaiah* on the arch soffit, bear little obvious connection with the Edinburgh design, although the location of the narrative scenes does echo the blank fields in Zucchi's project. And an *Annunciation* did originally appear in the spandrels above the arch, as it does in both designs.[10] Zucchi, for his part, contributed two frescoes of the *Adoration of the Magi* and the *Circumcision* on the lateral walls below, in place of the statues in niches featured in the two drawings. His *Adoration of the Magi* resembles in significant respects the central sketch in the Christ Church project. In the event, the altarpiece of the *Adoration of the Shepherds*, which remains *in situ*, was commissioned from a third, much older painter, Marcello Venusti, who is best known for his small-scale paintings based on designs by Michelangelo.[11]

This chapel, which has a dedication to the Nativity of Christ, is usually referred to in the literature as the Ghislieri chapel, although the physician Giuseppe Ghislieri assumed responsibility for it only in 1641.[12] It has recently been established that its patron from the 1570s until her death in 1626 was in fact the Roman noblewoman Francesca Baglioni Orsini, one of the most remarkable female patrons of late sixteenth- and early seventeenth-century Rome.[13] She dedicated much of her life and all of her wealth to acts of charity and pious devotion, founding the Dominican church and convent of Santa Maria dell'Umiltà around 1600, and taking responsibility for several chapels in other Roman churches. It was she who paid for the decoration of the chapel in San Silvestro under discussion here, selling a valuable pearl necklace in order to raise the necessary funds.

335

Fig. 104.1 Chapel of the Nativity,
San Silvestro al Quirinale, Rome

For the connection between the two designs exhibited here and Francesca Baglioni Orsini's chapel in San Silvestro al Quirinale to be tenable, one would have to argue that they belong to an early phase in what was a more ambitious renovation of the whole church that took place around this time.[14] To judge from the fundamental difference in the height of the arch in the two drawings, the standard proportions of the nave chapels had not yet been fixed (pentimenti in the black chalk underdrawing indicate that Raffaellino was initially contemplating an even higher arch), nor had the chapel recesses, which in both designs are concave, but which in the church as built are rectangular in plan. But on balance, iconographic considerations, combined with the fact that both Zucchi and Raffaellino did actually contribute to the decoration of this chapel, argue in favour of the connection. The complex typological program put forward in Zucchi's design was rejected in favour of a more straightforward one, which was nevertheless equally appropriate to the chapel's dedication to the Nativity. Both the preference for relative simplicity and the devotion to the mysteries of the birth and infancy of Christ are features of Francesca's broader patronage, as is the absence in the chapel of her coat of arms or any other personal reference.[15]

The documents recording Francesca's involvement with the chapel unfortunately shed no direct light on the date of the decorations or the division of labour, so some key questions remain. Was the commission awarded jointly to Zucchi and Raffaellino, who had both submitted attractive designs and who in the 1570s were among the rising stars of the Roman art scene? Or did Raffaellino alone emerge victorious from the competition but complete only the vault frescoes before his early death in 1578 prompted the recall of Zucchi to finish the project? And at what stage did Venusti become involved? Scholarly opinion is divided over these issues,[16] but the evidence for a date in the mid-1570s seems the most persuasive. Francesca Baglioni Orsini's virtue attracted the admiration of Pope Gregory XIII, and an inscription embedded in one of the exterior pilasters of the chapel records that he granted its altar privileged status in 1576, which is a credible date for the completion of the decoration.[17] It may be significant that Zucchi and Raffaellino almost certainly collaborated on another project around that time, the decoration of two small rooms in Palazzo Firenze for Cardinal Ferdinando de' Medici (another of Francesca's great admirers).[18] The combination of decorative elements in Zucchi's Christ Church design is strikingly similar to the painted vault of the Sala degli Elementi in Palazzo Firenze.[19] An alternative, less directly collaborative scenario is that Raffaellino began the decoration around 1575, painting the vault first (as was standard practice), but was prevented from completing it by the demands of more important commitments elsewhere, notably in the Vatican Palace; it would have been at that stage that Zucchi and Venusti were drafted in to finish the job.[20]

AIDAN WESTON-LEWIS

105

DURANTE ALBERTI 1538–1613
SCENE FROM ROMAN HISTORY (RECTO);
*STUDY OF SAINT MATTHEW AND
THE ANGEL, A STANDING BISHOP AND
OTHER STUDIES* (VERSO) C. 1575

Pen and grey and brown ink,
brown wash, over black chalk
[recto], pen and brown ink, red
wash, and black chalk [verso]
23.2 × 28.2 cm
Annotations: *Durante del Borgo*
[recto]; *Durante del Borgo* and
Consolo… [illegible words] [verso]
National Gallery of Canada,
Ottawa

105 (recto)

Hitherto unpublished, the drawing under consideration constitutes the most complete and by far the most important known drawing by the later sixteenth-century artist active in Rome – Durante Alberti. Given the rarity of his work and the relative obscurity of this figure, there seems no reason to doubt the old attributions found on both recto and verso. While other drawings by this artist certainly remain to be discovered, at the moment his total corpus constitutes no more than about half a dozen sheets.

Durante Alberti was from a different branch of the Sansepolcro family than his better-known cousins Cherubino and Giovanni Alberti. Like many members of this distinguished family of artists, Durante moved to Rome as a youth to seek his fortunes – by the early 1560s in his case. He would distinguish himself primarily as a painter of altarpieces for a several prominent churches in Rome, although the present drawing provides unique evidence of his secular work. He also dutifully entertained commissions from time to time back home in regional Sansepolcro. Durante was the father of Pier Francesco Alberti, who is celebrated in the history of art for his edition of Leonardo's *Trattato della Pittura* (published in 1651). Of note, two of Durante's daughters are also documented as painters.

The subject of this work remains to be identified, though the intent seems clear as a captured King is brought before a military commander to plead for clemency. For its frieze-like design with a dramatically posed central figure, the image betrays the influence of the frescoes executed by Polidoro da Caravaggio in the 1520s on so many palace facades in Rome, most often with violent scenes of Roman history. Durante was clearly a conscientious student of the art of post-Raphael Rome. For example, the bending figure of the child on the right hand side is a direct quotation from Pellegrino Tibaldi's fresco featuring a fictive doorway opened to reveal two servants in the Sala Paolina in the Castel Sant'Angelo, Rome. The purpose of the drawing is not entirely evident, however it is reasonable to assume it was for an external facade fresco on a Roman palace. The fluid style of drawing with its incisive, probing lines is clearly related to the graphic work of the other Alberti, especially Cherubino, and significantly expands the context for our understanding of these later sixteenth-century artists transplanted from Sansepolcro to Rome.

DAVID FRANKLIN

RAFFAELLINO MOTTA,
CALLED **RAFFAELLINO DA REGGIO** 1550?–1578
*THE APPARITION OF THE ANGEL TO
SAINT JOSEPH* c. 1575

Pen and brown ink and wash over
red chalk
38.1 × 28.2 cm
Inscriptions: *Zuchero.*
Morgan Library & Museum,
New York

This magnificent drawing is a late compositional study for the fresco *The Apparition of the Angel to Saint Joseph*, painted around 1575 on the vault of the Orsini (later Ghislieri) Chapel in the church of San Silvestro al Quirinale in Rome, still extant today (fig. 106.1).[1] Dedicated to the Nativity of Christ, the chapel was founded in 1575 by Francesca Orsini and decorated at her behest by Marcello Venusti, Raffaellino da Reggio, and Jacopo Zucchi; it was ceded to Giuseppe Ghislieri in about 1640.[2] Venusti's altarpiece depicts the *Adoration of the Shepherds*, the lateral paintings, by Zucchi, an *Adoration of the Magi* on the left, and a *Circumcision* on the right. The vault, decorated in fresco by Raffaellino, comprises a tondo of the *Holy Spirit with Angels* flanked by the *Massacre of the Innocents* on the left and the *Dream of Saint Joseph* on the right, with figures of the prophets *David* and *Isaiah* on the arch soffit (underside of the arch). The *Annunciation* mentioned by the sixteenth-century biographer Baglione as *in faccia* – in other words above the entrance arch – was lost in the course of a restoration in 1641.[3] The chapel decoration was presumably completed shortly before 7 April 1576, the date of the privilege to celebrate mass granted by Pope Gregory XIII and inscribed on the right-hand pilaster.[4] Originally the third on the left upon entering, the chapel of the Nativity became the second on the left when, in the nineteenth century, part of the church was demolished to make way for a wider road.

Raffaellino is said to have arrived in Rome during the pontificate of Gregory XIII, or possibly somewhat earlier, and spent the rest of his brief career there. By the time he received the San Silvestro commission, Raffaellino had worked as Giovanni de' Vecchi's assistant on the frescoes in the Villa Farnese at Caprarola (c. 1574) and was working independently on the Loggia of Pope Gregory XIII in the Vatican (1575–1577), the Oratorio del Gonfalone, and his only known oil painting, the *Tobias and the Angel* in the Galleria Borghese (cat. 100). Both Raffaellino's paintings and drawings reveal him to be a close follower of Taddeo Zuccaro, who had died before Raffaellino settled in Rome. Inspired by both Taddeo's and his brother Federico's calligraphic handling, Raffaellino developed a virtuoso style characterized by an elegant pen line, generous dark brown washes that modulate the design, dynamic compositions and elongated facial types.

The idea that the drawing might have been after the fresco rather than a study for it originated in an article of 1939 by Collobi, who had incorrectly assigned to Raffaellino the frescoes by Zucchi and therefore dated them too early, c. 1572–1573, but rightly understood that the *Apparition to St. Joseph* drawing was a later work, created closer to the end of the artist's career. Knowing the drawing only from its illustration in the 1937 publication by Borenius and Wittkower, Gere and Pouncey in 1983 adopted this idea, suggesting that the sheet could have been made by Raffaellino with the intention of executing a chiaroscuro woodcut. However, the differences between drawing and fresco would be unusual for a copy. In the painted version the angel's wings are lowered, whereas in the drawing they are upright. In addition, the secondary biblical episode of the Flight into Egypt has been moved further back in pictorial space; thus in the fresco the warning to Joseph to flee Herod, communicated by an angel appearing in a dream as recounted in the Gospel of Matthew (2:13), more emphatically dominates the composition. It seems reasonable to conclude, as have many other scholars since, that the Morgan sheet is a late preparatory study for the fresco.[5]

RHODA EITEL-PORTER

Fig. 106.1 Raffaellino da Reggio, *The Apparition of the Angel to Saint Joseph*, c. 1575, fresco. Orsini (later Ghislieri) Chapel, San Silvestro al Quirinale, Rome

107
GIROLAMO MUZIANO 1532–1592
PENTECOST c. 1576

Pen and brown ink and black chalk
28 × 54.5 cm
Musée du Louvre, Paris

Although he would eventually become superintendent of artistic projects under Gregory XIII, Muziano received no papal commissions from the time of Gregory's election in 1572 until late in 1576, when he began receiving payments for a large *Pentecost* for the ceiling of the Sala del Concistoro in the Vatican Palace (fig. 107.1).[1] Most of the new Bolognese pope's commissions in the first years after his election went to Emilian artists and not to artists like Muziano who had previously been established in Rome.[2] Muziano's earlier association with Cardinal Ippolito d'Este, among the primary proponents of French interests in Rome, may also have led to his initial exclusion from the circles of the strongly pro-Spanish Boncompagni pope. Whatever the reason for Muziano's absence from these first projects, the death in August 1576 of Lorenzo Sabatini, who had been the supervising artist at the Vatican, probably facilitated Muziano's entry into the Gregorian decorative endeavours.

The commission was the artist's first ceiling painting on this large scale, and although fresco was the common technique for such decorations, Muziano instead painted a large canvas to be set into the richly painted and gilded coffered wood ceiling. He made little attempt at an illusionistic depiction of space from the viewpoint below. Rather, treating the ceiling as a *quadro riportato*, Muziano's composition combined elements found in paintings from his entire career. The depiction of a large crowd displaying varied expressions in reaction to a miracle, ranging from expectant piety to anxiety, harks back to Muziano's first great success, the *Resurrection of Lazarus* of 1555 (Pinacoteca, Vatican), but also recalls some of his other paintings from the 1570s, including his lost *Assumption of the Virgin* (see discussion under cat. 99) and another *Resurrection of Lazarus* that was the high altarpiece of Santa Marta al Collegio Romano (now Birmingham City Art Gallery).[3]

The Louvre drawing is unquestionably a preparatory study for the Vatican ceiling. The general disposition of figures is the same, but there are enough changes between the drawing and painting to indicate without question that the former was not copied from the latter. In the final work, the crowd reaches higher up the sides of the composition, for example, and the figures adjacent to Saints Peter and John (who flank the Virgin, at the centre) have also been changed. The sheet is, nonetheless, somewhat atypical for a preparatory study by Muziano. It is both larger and more finished than most of his compositional drawings,[4] while it lacks the brilliantly detailed draftsmanship of his usual red chalk figure studies.[5] Presumably, the drawing was not part of the set that Muziano would have made for his own purposes, but was a *modello* meant to serve as a preview of the work for Gregory XIII and his advisors – needed perhaps because this was Muziano's first papal commission.

The *modello* may also have been required because the composition represented a departure from the common depiction of the Pentecost scene. Traditionally, the event was shown with the apostles, the Virgin Mary, and sometimes the "three Marys," but Muziano's canvas includes a "gran numero di figure," unusual enough for both Borghini and Baglione to have noted them.[6] The inclusion of this large number of figures is particularly unexpected when one considers the strong interest in textual accuracy that so often characterizes the art of Muziano's time. As Carolyn Valone has shown, however, the presence of a multitude had a particular theological significance, for "no Renaissance pope was more aware of the ideas inherent in the Pentecost than Gregory XIII. Elected pope on 13 May, 1572, he chose to receive the papal crown on 20 May, the feast of the Pentecost, a gesture which already announced his understanding of the new missionary imperative of the Catholic Church."[7] The many-figured Pentecost, Valone explains, is apparently a deliberate reflection of Gregory's ecumenical program. The motif was repeated several years later in Jacopo Zucchi's similarly thronged *Pentecost* in the apse of Santo Spirito in Sassia, painted in 1582 for Egnazio Dante, one of Gregory's foremost advisors on matters of art and science.[8]

The Louvre drawing is the only known study made specifically for Muziano's Vatican ceiling. Another of the artist's compositional studies for a Pentecost is in the Walker Art Gallery, Liverpool, but that seems to be related to an altarpiece executed by Cesare Nebbia in 1579.[9] It is likely, though, that Muziano reused his figure studies from other projects as he constructed the Vatican composition, such that a sheet like Farnesina F.C.127667,[10] initially drawn for the lost *Assumption of the Virgin*, can probably also be counted among the preparatory studies for this later work.

JOHN J. MARCIARI

107

Fig. 107.1 Girolamo Muziano, *Pentecost*, 1576, ceiling fresco. Sala del Concistoro, Vatican Palace, Rome

108
CESARE NEBBIA c. 1536–1614
NOLI ME TANGERE 1579

Pen and brown ink, brown wash,
with white heightening, over red
chalk
30 × 19.2 cm
Private collection, Toronto

A native of Orvieto, Nebbia trained with Girolamo Muziano and flourished in Rome during the papacies of Gregory XIII and Sixtus V. Large frescoes above the doors of Old Saint Peter's Basilica, commissioned by Pope Gregory XIII for the 1575 Jubilee (since destroyed), count among his earliest works in the city. Two frescoes featuring scenes from the Passion of Christ in the Oratory of the Gonfalone, executed between 1575 and 1576, mark his establishment as an independent artist. Soon thereafter he received important private commissions from the Roman nobility, as was the case in 1579 when Consalvo Alverio entrusted him with the decoration of his chapel in Santa Maria degli Angeli. As recognized by Pouncey and Gere in 1983, the present drawing is a late study for the altarpiece of the Alverio chapel, the first on the left, where despite extensive renovations to the chapel, the painting is still in situ today (fig. 108.1).

Alverio may have come to know Nebbia during the course of negotiations initiated around 1578 concerning the decoration of the Oratory belonging to the Arciconfraternità del Santissimo Crocifisso di San Marcello, of which Alverio was a member and for which Nebbia was to paint several frescoes.[1] The Alverio family, also called "degli Alberi" in Amayden's *La Storia delle Famiglie Romane,* originated in Spain, though Consalvo was already the third generation living in Rome.[2] The contract with Nebbia specified that the artist was to paint for a total of 350 *scudi* five histories in oils with scenes from the life of Mary Magdalene according to his own design, of which the altarpiece was to represent a *Noli me tangere.* Two of the scenes and the altarpiece were to be completed within six months, no later than the feast of the Magdalene, on 22 July 1579, the remainder by the same date the following year. The vault decoration was assigned to the painter Hendrick van den Broeck, a circumstance which caused the seventeenth-century art historian Giovanni Baglione and later writers to attribute also the altarpiece to van den Broeck.[3] It was not until 1966 that, on the occasion of the restoration of the painting, the original contract was examined and, in conjunction with stylistic considerations, the error was rectified.[4]

The choice of subject matter likely was predicated upon the fact that Alverio was born on the feast day of the Magdalene.[5] *Noli me tangere* ("touch me not") – according to the Gospel of St. John (20: 14–18) the words spoken by Christ to the Magalene after his resurrection – refers to the scene in which Christ appeared to the Magdalene as she visits the empty tomb. At first she mistook him for a gardener, but when recognized, he bade her not to touch him but to tell the disciples that he was risen.

Both Nebbia's drawing and painting are clearly indebted to the work of Muziano in the conception of the landscape setting and the figures.[6] Interestingly, these qualities were demanded in the contract, which specified "with a landscape as decoration" and that the painting should be of a quality comparable to Muziano's work.[7] The composition derives from that of a painting of the same subject in Santa Maria sopra Minerva, traditionally thought to have been made around 1575 by Marcello Venusti, but for which an attribution to Muziano (or Nebbia) might be considered, as recently suggested by John Marciari.[8] The major difference between the so-called Venusti and the later versions is Christ's gesture: in Venusti's painting Christ lowers his hand to ward off the Magdalene's advances, whereas in Nebbia's versions he almost touches her forehead. As noted by Émile Mâle, this new iconography, which first arose in the sixteenth century, probably originated in France.[9]

The present compositional study by Nebbia, one of the most fluid and evocative of his career, evolves out of generous sweeps of the brush that cast deep shadows across parts of the scene. Occasional touches of white gouache, thus on the forehead of the Magdalene, and her left hand, and directly below her right, represent the artist's corrections to his earlier draft. As in the Venusti altarpiece, Christ almost casually shoulders a hoe or spade, whereas in the final painted version, he stands it upright by his side. Similarly, in the drawing, as in Venusti's painting, Christ's mantel swings high to reveal his right thigh, whereas in Nebbia's painting it more decorously falls below the knee. For the painting, the half-figure portrait of the patron was added at lower left. A later study in the Uffizi, in red chalk and squared for transfer, is preparatory to the figure of Christ. This has traditionally been attributed to Muziano, but in my view is by Nebbia.[10]

RHODA EITEL-PORTER

343

Fig. 108.1 Cesare Nebbia, *Noli me tangere*, 1579, oil on canvas. Alverio chapel, Santa Maria degli Angeli, Rome

109
FEDERICO ZUCCARO c. 1542/43–1609
DESIGN FOR QUARANT' ORE DECORATION
c. 1580

Pen and brown ink with brown
wash with white heightening over
black chalk
38.9 × 28.5 cm
Inscriptions: *Federigo Zuccaro*
The Metropolitan Museum of Art,
New York

The present drawing, one of Federico Zuccaro's most elaborate architectural designs, once belonged to the famous collection of Sir Thomas Lawrence. After his death in 1830, it was acquired by the London art dealer Samuel Woodburn, who included it in an album of seventy-two drawings by or attributed to Taddeo and Federico Zuccaro. In 1990 the album was disassembled and the drawings were sold at auction in New York.

Gere first identified the highly finished sheet as design for a Forty Hours' Devotion, likely dating, as the heraldic Boncompagni dragons indicate, from the pontificate of Pope Gregory XIII.[1] For a period of forty hours, the consecrated host was presented for the adoration by the faithful, displayed within a highly elaborate ephemeral architecture erected in front of the altar and dramatically illuminated by hundreds or even thousands of candles and oil lamps. Increasingly popular from the late sixteenth century, the liturgical devotion reflected both the centrality of the Eucharist for the Counter-Reformation church and the theatricality of its cult. These ephemeral, staged settings increased steadily in grandeur and size and presented evermore elaborate iconographic programs. They offered important opportunities for innovative design and would decisively inform the later development of permanent church and altar solutions.[2]

Zuccaro's design corresponds to a triumphal arch over a central niche, framed on either side by two pilasters, each supporting an entablature with crowning balustrades. Each side presents slight variations, intended as options for his patron. Through an open curtain the viewer looks into a shrine, where the host sits on a sarcophagus atop a towering pedestal. Between the lateral pilasters, latticed windows allow further viewing access to the Holy Eucharist. The motifs of the curtain and the windows underscore the mystical revelation of divine truth through a process of disguise and disclosure. God the Father appears above the arch in a brightly illuminated glory of clouds and angels offering his blessing and holding a globe in his left hand. He sacrificed his son for the salvation of mankind – a sacrifice miraculously renewed during the celebration of mass through the trans-substantiation of Christ's body and blood. Statues of Moses and the Prophet Elijah stand on high pedestals in front of the arch. Both had witnessed Christ's transfiguration on Mount Tabor, "with his face shining like the sun, and with brilliant white clothes." The transfiguration revealed Christ's divinity and marked the transition from the old laws of Moses to the new law of Christ. According to the synoptic Gospels, Moses and Elijah appeared on either side of Christ and talked to him, when from a bright cloud overhead a voice proclaimed: "This is my son, the beloved. Listen to him." Zuccaro's design, referencing these scriptural sources, gives form to the complex theology of the Eucharist and transforms it into a spectacular sacred theatre. His Forty Hours' Devotion was probably intended for the Pauline Chapel in the Vatican and executed when Gregory XIII commissioned him in 1580–1584 to complete the fresco decoration of the chapel that Michelangelo had begun almost four decades earlier under Paul III. The detailed and highly refined execution of Zuccaro's drawing, with its subtle play of light and shadow, certainly underlines the importance of the project.

SEBASTIAN SCHÜTZE

110

FEDERICO ZUCCARO c. 1542/43–1609
PORTA VIRTUTIS (GATE OF VIRTUE) OR
*MINERVA TRIUMPHANT OVER IGNORANCE
AND CALUMNY* 1581

Pen and brown ink, brown wash,
with some corrections in white
gouache; squared for transfer in
red chalk
37.8 × 27.6 cm
Inscriptions: *fama, porta virtus;
fama; gloria; disegnio; colorito;
inventione; inteligentia; decoro;
faticha; diligenzia; studio;
inteligenzia; sic semper; spirito;
adulatione; ignioranzia crasa;
persuasione; presumptione;
inscitia; ministro de la invidia;
parto di maldicenzia; detratio;*

*prospetiva; architectura; invidia
comites; ingniorantia crassa;
rifugio di maligno; serva delli
dapochi.*
Christ Church Picture Gallery,
Oxford

Together with studies by Federico Zuccaro at the Morgan Library & Museum, New York (cat. 111) and in Frankfurt,[1] the present sheet relates to a large coloured cartoon of *Minerva Triumphant over Ignorance and Calumny* that was unveiled on the facade of the church of San Luca in Rome on 18 October 1581, the feast day of Saint Luke, patron saint of artists. Federico spent the morning explaining his satirical allegory to his painter colleagues who arrived for the traditional ceremony that took place in San Luca annually on that day. He had planned the prominent display in response to criticism by Bolognese artists, whom he felt were responsible for the rejection of his painting The Procession and Vision of Saint Gregory.[2] The altarpiece had been commissioned by Paolo Ghiselli, the steward (*scalco*) and confidant of Pope Gregory XIII Boncompagni, a fellow Bolgonese, for his family chapel in the church of Santa Maria del Baraccano in Bologna. Upon its arrival in Bologna, however, a coterie of Bolognese painters heavily criticized the work, causing Ghiselli to reject it and instead entrust the project to the lesser known Cesare Aretusi. In hindsight, the painting may have seemed indecorous because of the nude corpses in the foreground and other mannerist elements, although Federico's suspicion of professional envy on the part of his Bolognese competitors also rings true.

The *Porta Virtutis* or *Minerva Triumphant* cartoon was executed primarily by Federico's pupil Domenico Passignano and both artists thereupon stood trial for having slandered the Bolognese painters and Ghiselli. On 27 November 1581, Pope Gregory XIII personally intervened to have the pair banished permanently from Rome. This incident signified a complete reversal of fortune for Federico, who had previously been employed by the Pope on the decoration of the Pauline Chapel in the Vatican and had contributed to frescoes in the Casino del Belvedere and the Sala Regia for Gregory XIII's predecessor, Pius IV. Even though Federico was granted a pardon less than two years later through the vigorous intervention of the Duke of Urbino, he had to leave Rome within four days of the proclamation of the ban.

Although the cartoon (a large study for a painting or fresco, on a scale of one to one) that hung on the facade of San Luca is no longer extant, its satirical content illustrating the ultimate triumph of the virtuous artist over his ignorant critics is clear even today from the related drawings.[3] At centre of the Christ Church drawing stands Minerva, the traditional embodiment of Virtue, defending the portal that leads to the realm of artistic excellence. She rests her foot and a spear on the vanquished figure of Vice. Flanking her in niches on the arch are allegorical figures of Study and Intelligence and statues representing Labour and Diligence holding shields or roundels displaying Roman monuments. Seated on the cornice are the four cardinal virtues; beyond, holding aloft Federico's disputed altarpiece, cherubs representing Design, Colour, Invention, and Decorum. The three Graces at left, and an allegorical figure of Spirit, inhabit this exalted space. Seated before the arch at left, with the ears of an ass, is Crass Ignorance, variously interpreted as a reference to the ignorant patron (possibly Ghiselli) or asinine artist (possibly Federico's Bolognese adversaries), who is being fawned over and deviously advised by Adulation and Persuasion. In the foreground at centre, snakes entrap the recumbent figure of Envy, and at right, a satyr and two fauns, representing Satire, Slander, and Defamation rage against Minerva, who blocks their entrance to the path of honour.

For his large cartoon, Federico made use of passages from an earlier allegorical drawing, *The Garden of the Liberal and Fine Arts*, in the collection of the Morgan Library & Museum, where he represented a porta virtutis leading to the temples of honour and fame in the background.[4] The Christ Church drawing, replete with pentiments, probably served as the modello for the 1581 cartoon, whereas the Frankfurt and possibly also the Morgan sheets were most likely created by Federico during his trial or after his expulsion from Rome to defend his position in the affair.

RHODA EITEL-PORTER AND LAURA B. ZUKERMAN

111
FEDERICO ZUCCARO c. 1542/43–1609
PORTA VIRTUTIS (GATE OF VIRTUE) OR
*MINERVA TRIUMPHANT OVER IGNORANCE
AND CALUMNY* 1581–1582

Pen and brown ink, brown wash,
over black chalk
38.7 × 28.6 cm
Inscriptions: *porta vertutis; gloria;
disegnio; colorito; inventione;
decoro; prudenza; temperanza;
giustitia; fortezza; faticha; diligenza;
studio, intiligenza; gratie; spirito;
Adulatione; persuatione; ministro
della Invidia; parto di maladicenza;
destratio; prospetiva; pitura;
Ignorantia crasa; Refugio dei
magligni; serva da dapochi.*
Morgan Library & Museum,
New York

The drawing is one of three studies related to the "Porta Virtutis" scandal that caused Federico Zuccaro to be expelled from Rome in November 1581 on the orders of Pope Gregory XIII Boncompagni (see entry 110). The artist had painted a wall hanging, often referred to as a large cartoon, depicting Minerva beneath a triumphal arch guarding the realm of artistic virtue from Crass Ignorance and Envy. The cartoon had been prominently displayed on the facade of the church of San Luca in Rome on 18 October 1581, the feast day of Saint Luke, when painters traditionally gathered for a religious celebration. The image was interpreted – and probably originally intended – as a satire on the ignorance of Federico's former patron Paolo Ghiselli (who had rejected the artist's altarpiece commissioned for his chapel in Bologna), and the circle of Bolognese artists who had advised Ghiselli. In the wake of the Council of Trent and the precepts on art that it promulgated, the Bolognese altarpiece, which featured large nudes in the foreground, was probably considered unseemly. Nevertheless, the criticism from the Bolognese artists may indeed have been motivated by their desire to keep foreign artists out of their city rather than the actual appearance of the painting.

Whereas a drawing in Christ Church, Oxford, (cat. 110) probably served as the *modello* for the 1581 cartoon, the Morgan and Frankfurt versions of the composition were most likely created by Federico in his own defense during his trial or after his expulsion from Rome. In the Oxford drawing, for instance, Federico's disputed painting, *The Procession and Vision of Saint Gregory* can be seen carried heavenward in the distance beyond the triumphal arch, whereas the Morgan and Frankfurt compositions depict in its place a painting of an enthroned ruler with sceptre and attendants. Furthermore, at his trial Federico emphasized that the *Porta Virtutis* was to be interpreted in a general fashion and not seen as a specific reference to Ghiselli and the imbroglio. This argument was probably an attempt by Federico to mitigate the scandal and to disassociate the *Porta Virtutis* from the Bolognese affair. During his trial, Federico wrote to his patrons in Florence and Urbino to solicit their support and the Morgan sheet may be been created to accompany such a letter.[1]

Federico had already developed a similar allegorical subject in an earlier drawing, *The Garden of the Liberal and Fine Arts*, also in the Pierpont Morgan Library,[2] where a *porta virtutis* leading to the temples of honour and fame is represented in the background.

RHODA EITEL-PORTER AND LAURA B. ZUKERMAN

112
GIROLAMO MUZIANO 1532–1592
*SEATED DRAPED MALE FIGURE,
GESTURING TO THE RIGHT* C. 1582

Red chalk
31.3 × 23.6 cm
Inscriptions: *Mutiano.*
Morgan Library & Museum,
New York

This impressive figure study is characteristic of Muziano's finest draftsmanship of the early 1580s, when the artist was almost exclusively employed by Pope Gregory XIII. Inspired by the highly finished, late chalk drawings of Michelangelo (for which see cat. 54), Muziano, like Daniele da Volterra and others of his generation, precisely outlined the draperies, capturing the underlying musculature, and, with fine hatching, created rich tonal effects that impart a sense of weight and volume to his figures. The barefoot, bearded man in the present drawing is shown seated on an earthen mound or rocky ledge, fixing his gaze and attention on something beyond the paper's edge. He holds a handkerchief-like piece of cloth in his raised right hand.

The purpose of the drawing remains unknown. The figure resembles a saint or prophet, who, however – with the possible exception of the small piece of cloth – lacks attributes. A certain similarity of the figure and the handling of the medium to a red chalk study by Muziano in the Louvre, which is preparatory to a figure of Saint Jerome in a painting now in Santa Maria degli Angeli, has long been noted.[1] This similarity extends to three further drawings also preparatory to the same figure of Saint Jerome (in the Louvre[2] and at Windsor Castle),[3] as well as to a study in the Istituto Nazionale per la Grafica, Rome, for a second saint featured in the same painting.[4] Regarding the Morgan study, there is however no direct correspondence in pose or even folds of draperies with the figure of Saint Jerome in the painting (fig. 112.1) and its related studies, where furthermore the saint clearly points toward a crucifix at left. Nevertheless, even if not for the same commission, these drawings surely must date from the same moment in the artist's career.

An unusual subject, but one treated often by Muziano, the Santa Maria degli Angeli painting depicts hermits in the wilderness, more specifically Saint Jerome preaching to a group of five saints, the most prominent of which is a figure generally (but incorrectly) referred to as Saint Romuald.[5] It was one of two paintings commissioned in 1582 by Pope Gregory XIII for the Gregorian Chapel in Saint Peter's; both begun in 1584 and left incomplete at the time of the artist's death in 1592 – presumably Muziano had ceased working on them upon the death of the pope in 1585.[6] At the behest of the pope's nephew Giacomo Boncompagni, Muziano's erstwhile pupil Cesare Nebbia completed the paintings.[7] At the time of the renovation of the Gregorian Chapel in the eighteenth century,[8] the altarpiece of the *Preaching of Saint Jerome* was transferred to Santa Maria degli Angeli, where it remains today.[9] The other work, representing the *Mass of Saint Basil,* has been lost.[10]

Fig. 112.1 Girolamo Muziano, *The Preaching of Saint Jerome,* c. 1582–1592, oil on canvas. Santa Maria degli Angeli, Rome

A compositional chalk sketch by Muziano in the Uffizi, which includes a seated figure similar to the one in the Morgan drawing, may shed some light on the matter (fig. 112.2). There, enthralled by a heavenly vision, the saint is seated on rocks beneath a tree, accompanied by an additional male saint who rests against a pillar in the background, apparently reading an opened book.[11] The similarity tempts one to speculate whether the Morgan drawing could not have been a rejected study for the figure of Saint Jerome in such a composition. Muziano originally may have begun with the Uffizi composition, revised the figure so as to be interacting with his companion (i.e. the Morgan sheet), and then finally discarded this solution in favour of a more traditional representation of Saint Jerome with crucifix and lion.

Jerome was one of the major early Christian writers on the subject of repentance. He spent five years in the Syrian Desert giving himself over to prayer, penance and study. The most commonly cited paragraph of his well-known letter, the Epistle 22 to his friend Eustochium, reads: "And so, when all other help failed me, I used to fling myself at Jesus' feet; I watered them with my tears, I wiped them with my hair; and if my flesh still rebelled I subdued it by weeks of fasting." Though seldom represented, the saint also experienced a vision while in the desert, mentioned in a later passage in the same letter: "There, sometimes also – the Lord Himself is my witness – after many a tear and straining of my eyes to heaven, I felt myself in the presence of the angelic hosts."[12] The handkerchief might be understood as a reference to the wiping away of these tears.

The suggestion – made by John Marciari – that the Morgan drawing may instead have been a study for the mosaic of the prophet Isaiah in one of the lunettes of the Gregorian Chapel of Saint Peter's,[13] for which Muziano supplied the cartoons in 1578 (actual mosaics completed in 1580), is intriguing but possibly less convincing. The correspondence of the lower part of the body is indeed very close, but the figure in the Morgan drawing seems clearly engaged, as if addressing a companion or other counterpart, and thus appears to be a detail study for a larger composition rather than an individual figure. In addition, the prophet Isaiah is generally not shown in an outdoor setting, but is depicted with a book or scroll, or writing and turning to divine inspiration coming from above, as in the extant mosaic. Admittedly, the mosaics were restored in the eighteenth century, but it seems unlikely that such great liberties would have been taken.

RHODA EITEL-PORTER

353

Fig. 112.2 Girolamo Muziano, *Compositional study with two figures in a landscape*, red chalk, 20.3 × 13.5 cm. Gabinetto Disegni e Stampe degli Uffizi, Florence

113
GIOVANNI DE' VECCHI 1536–1615
PRESENTATION OF THE VIRGIN IN THE TEMPLE c. 1583

Oil on canvas
323 × 182 cm
Museo Civico Sansepolcro

Giovanni de' Vecchi was a painter from Sansepolcro who found success as a young artist in papal circles in Rome starting in the 1560s, possibly having been introduced by his compatriot Santi di Tito.[1] He also operated in the circle of Federico Zuccaro. Having spent the balance of his career in Rome, Giovanni's work for his native Sansepolcro forms only a small part of his corpus. Born slightly later than Santi di Tito, in 1536, Giovanni Liso de' Vecchi (sometimes referred to as Giovanni "dal Borgo") produced no fewer than four altarpieces for Sansepolcro. Three of these paintings survive, including this *Presentation of the Virgin in the Temple,* as well as the *Birth of the Virgin,* also in the Museo Civico, and the *Stigmatization of Saint Francis* still in the church of San Francesco. A fourth altarpiece of the *Annunciation* executed for the Cathedral is lost without a trace. Yet the latter work in this group is unique of the four in that unpublished documents survive to allow for an accurate dating to 1578 – the same year the artist was elected to the Congregazione dei Virtuosi at the Pantheon in Rome.[2] Just how frequently and for what duration Giovanni de' Vecchi returned to Sansepolcro is uncertain. There is evidence that two if not each of the four altarpieces, all executed on canvas, were dispatched from Rome, hence it is presumed that he never maintained a workshop in his hometown. Indeed, as he did not apparently produce anything for Sansepolcro until he approached his fortieth year, well after his reputation had been established in Rome.

The only other accurate date for Giovanni de' Vecchi's work in Sansepolcro is provided by the *Presentation of the Virgin in the Temple,* which was also definitely painted in Rome as an episcopal visitation of 1583 indicates that the dispatch of the completed object was eminent.[3] This altarpiece was painted for a chapel of the same dedication endowed in Santa Maria dei Servi in Sansepolcro by Filippo Farsetti who was the *curatore* of the church of Santa Maria dei Monticelli in Rome. Why he was ordering an altarpiece for Sansepolcro remains a mystery, as "Farsetti" is not a

common local name. By 1583 the new chapel had only then been constructed, its stone frame and furnishings complete, but the altarpiece had not yet arrived. This indirect evidence establishes that the altarpiece must date from after 1583, but perhaps not much later. Although definitely painted in Rome it is, ironically, in formal stylistic terms the most Venetian of the works Giovanni de' Vecchi supplied for Sansepolcro and in its general spaciousness, as well as aspects of the architecture the work evokes the designs of painters like Titian and Veronese. In respect of his production in Rome, this work comes closest to his decorations for the True Cross cycle in the Oratorio del Santissimo Crocifisso di San Marcello of c. 1578–1582 and whether it was deeply understood or not, it was the modern Roman tenor of the altarpiece that must have generally impressed the audience in Sansepolcro.[4] Notable is the placement of the Virgin ascending the steps to the temple in the central middle ground of the painting with larger figures anchoring the foreground. This complex and elegant "inversion" was a stylistic feature of much painting of this period in Rome and indicates, in artistic terms at least, a great distance from the reformist tendencies affecting art in other parts of Italy, which sought a more simplified and direct manner of painting. This popular subject from the early life of the Virgin is not mentioned in the Gospel, but derived from the apocryphal book of James.

Giovanni de' Vecchi died in Rome as late as 1615 and having made four altarpieces – including the work under discussion here – for Sansepolcro during a period lasting just over a decade, it appears that after a certain point around 1590 he was too much in demand to continue supplying work for his native city. In the same period Santi di Tito also produced altarpieces for Sansepolcro; hence, in terms of quality, this work characterizes a final golden age for painting in the Tiber Valley town towards the end of the Renaissance period.

DAVID FRANKLIN

113

114
FEDERICO BAROCCI c. 1528–1612
CARTONCINO FOR THE VISITATION
c. 1584–1586

Pen and brown ink, light and dark
brown wash, with white heightening, red chalk over black chalk,
incised, squared in pen and brown
ink, black chalk and red chalk on
blue paper
46.2 × 31.6 cm
National Gallery of Scotland,
Edinburgh

On 15 July 1575 Pope Gregory XIII assigned Philip Neri and his newly founded Congregation of the Oratory the church of Santa Maria in Vallicella in Rome. The old church was destroyed and a new building erected on a much grander scale. The side chapels were granted to private patrons, but the dedication of the altars and the decoration of the chapels had to follow a unifying program celebrating the mysteries of the Virgin devised by the Oratorians. The Chapel of the Visitation on the left side of the nave was assigned in 1582 to Francesco Pizzamiglio, and Federico Barocci, court painter of the Dukes of Urbino, was chosen to execute the altarpiece. The aging artist was highly esteemed but notoriously slow and hesitant to accept new commissions, and so the Oratorians sought immediately the support of Francesco Maria II, Duke of Urbino. Barocci accepted the commission in June 1584, and the altarpiece was probably unveiled on the feast day of the Visitation, on 2 July 1586.

A large number of preparatory drawings, ranging from compositional sketches and detailed figure studies to the final cartoon, document the complex planning process and Barocci's meticulous preparation.[1] The small cartoon in Edinburgh immediately precedes the execution of both the full-scale cartoon, partially preserved in the Uffizi in Florence, and the final altarpiece (fig. 114.1). The architectural background is carefully constructed in its perspective foreshortening. The figures are outlined in pen and modelled in black chalk and wash, as well as white and red chalk, achieving chromatic effects of rare delicacy. The whole sheet is squared for transfer. In the altarpiece Barocci has further clarified the spatial relation between the protagonists and the figures in the foreground. Elizabeth and the Virgin are now situated at a slightly greater distance from the viewer, and the figure of Saint Joseph is decisively reduced in size.

The encounter of Elizabeth and the Virgin is described in the gospel of Luke (I, 39–56). Following the Annunciation, the Virgin paid visit to her aging cousin Elizabeth, who was six months pregnant with the future Saint John the Baptist, in the city of Juda. Barocci stages their encounter on a stair leading up to a vaulted archway. Two monumental figures, classical *Repoussoirfiguren* standing on either side in the foreground, lead the viewer into the composition. Saint Joseph bends forward at the left and a beautiful young maid with a basket stands at the right. In the centre of the composition Elizabeth salutes and embraces the Virgin, while Zachary stands in his doorway to the upper right. According to the gospel, at the moment of their salute, Elizabeth felt the infant in her womb leap, and pronounced the prophetic words "Blessed art thou among women, and blessed is the fruit of thy womb" (I, 42), recognizing the Virgin as the "mother of my Lord." The grand simplicity of Barocci's composition underlines the solemn importance of the event, while expressing at the same time the beatitude and joy of the Virgin ("… my spirit hath rejoiced in God my Saviour" I, 47) through the sublime sensuality and softness of his brush and the extreme refinement and sweetness of his colours. Barocci's altarpiece won immediate acclaim in Rome and elsewhere, and was quickly reproduced in engravings and painted copies. The *Visitation* perfectly expresses the spirituality of Philip Neri and the Oratorians, and can be described as one of the most emblematic images of the Counter-Reformation. According to his first biographer, Pietro Giacomo Bacci, the *Visitation* became Philip Neri's preferred painting, and he was often found in a state of ecstasy in front of it.

SEBASTIAN SCHÜTZE

357

Fig. 114.1 Federico Barocci, *Visitation*, c. 1584–86, altarpiece. Santa Maria in Vallicella, Rome

JACOPO ZUCCHI c. 1541–c. 1589/90
ALLEGORY OF CREATION c. 1585

Oil on copper
50 × 40 cm
Inscriptions: *A / Ω; SAN[CTVS]*
SAN[CTVS] SAN[CTVS]; OMNIA IN
SAPIENTIA FECISTI / ET SVBIECISTI SVB
PEDIBVS EIVS
Galleria Borghese, Rome

The early attributions of this painting reflect the extent to which it embodied artistic trends prevalent in Rome towards the end of the *Cinquecento*, from Arpino's highly wrought cabinet paintings to Brueghel's small landscapes, with still-life elements executed in miniaturist detail.[1] The painting, however, also demonstrates the lessons Zucchi learnt in his native Florence where, under Vasari, he collaborated in the production of small-scale paintings for Francesco de' Medici. A project of 1567, which anticipated the *Studiolo*, saw the production of a series of cabinet pictures of uniform dimensions. Inspired by the work of Giulio Clovio, the master of the genre, they illustrated *invenzioni* by Vincenzo Borghini. These *Quadretti*, as Vasari and Borghini described them, represented the ideal vehicle for rendering intricate detail in miniature, and Borghini's programmes were correspondingly rich in imagery.[2] Inscriptions played an important role in their iconography, enhancing the narratives and embellishing the compositions, and the stamp of Borghini's approach can be seen in Zucchi's *Allegory of Creation*, executed some twenty years later in Rome.

Contemporary documentation of this painting has yet to emerge, but comparisons with Zucchi's Roman works strongly suggest it was executed around 1585.[3] The most likely patron was Cardinal Ferdinando de' Medici, Francesco's brother. Just as Borghini's *invenzioni* for Francesco were destined for a private context and comprised subjects eminently suitable for a young prince, so that of Zucchi's *Allegory* could not have been better suited to a cardinal's study or place of prayer.

Zucchi's God the Father, enthroned on clouds, raises his right hand in benediction. He wears the triangular nimbus, alluding to the Trinity, while Alpha and Omega, inscribed on the open book, denote his eternity and infinitude.[4] The scroll wrapped around the cloud is inscribed SAN[CTVS] SAN[CTVS] SAN[CTVS]. These words from the Book of Isaiah underpin the theme of the composition, uniting God with the world he has created, which unfolds in the landscape below. In this passage the Prophet describes his vision of God's throne, "high and exalted," and attendant seraphim calling to one another: "Holy, holy, holy Lord of Hosts: the whole earth is full of his glory."[5] The lips of the central seraph are, indeed, slightly parted, as though he were chanting. The chant would have been familiar to any churchgoer, since for centuries a slight variation on this passage had been part of the Mass. It is during the *Sanctus*, which precedes the eucharistic prayer, that worshippers symbolically join the choirs of angels in praising God's creation.[6]

The compositional structure draws the eye down the acute diagonal from God in the distant sky to the youth in the opposite corner. There the ox's horns echo the shape of the crescent moon in a conceit that is both visual and literary, since *cornua* in Latin – like *corna* in Italian – signifies both the horns of a beast and those of the new moon.[7] At the lower left, the inscription carved on the face of the all'antica altar combines two additional biblical quotations, this time from the Psalms: "OMNIA IN SAPIENTIA FECISTI / ET SVBIECISTI SVB PEDIBVS EIVS."[8] Together they build on the central theme of Zucchi's pictorial celebration of the "whole earth full of glory," which God created and put at mankind's disposal.

Psalm 104 in particular describes much of what Zucchi depicted.[9] His meticulous rendering of detail reflects the beauty of the biblical words and imagery, with its account of divine architecture harnessing primordial chaos into a world vibrant with life. This Psalm extols the Creator's wisdom and describes him exactly as he is depicted, with the clouds as his chariot "riding on the wings of the wind," like the flock of herons to his right.[10] There are "flames of fire" on the escarpment, and the landscape below is ordered into mountains, hills and valleys, the waters flowing "to the place appointed for them." Wild beasts, including deer, an elephant and a rhinoceros, drink from springs that "break out in the gullies." Left of centre an ass approaches "to quench its thirst." while birds – including swans, owls and ducks – "nest on the banks and sing among the leaves." There are trees, "green and leafy" for the birds, hills for mountain goats and rocks for badgers.[11] There is vegetation for cattle to eat and for men to cultivate. All of creation looks to God "to give them their food at the proper time; what thou givest they gather up"; hence the harvest of root vegetables and fruits of the land and sea in the foreground, including aubergines, red onions, crayfish and oysters. As night falls and the moon rises, "... all the beasts of the forest come forth; the young lions roar for prey"; nearby, a wolf and a wild dog also emerge from the undergrowth. With the rising sun, "man comes out to his work"; there are miners, fishermen, and women washing by the riverside.[12] And then, "the great immeasurable sea, in which move creatures beyond number. Here ships sail to and fro."[13] The Psalm concludes: "May the glory of the Lord stand forever and may he rejoice in his works!"[14] The broad, light palette, the diversity of textures and variety of objects – from flowers to foliage; from shells, coral and crustaceans to fish with silvery scales – enhance the jewel-like qualities of the painting. With such ravishing attention

to detail, Zucchi clearly strove to do the subject justice, no less than to delight his patron with a visual commentary on the abundance of creation as celebrated in this Psalm.

Appropriately enough, the youth's head is modelled on that of Adam in Michelangelo's *Creation of Man*.[15] But in the disposition of his legs, the arrangement of drapery and in his solitude, there is certainly an echo of Raphael's youthful *St John in the Wilderness*. The eighth Psalm places man at the centre of creation: "little less than a god," but master over the creatures roaming the earth, even the most ferocious. Against a sun-drenched background of relative calm, there are scenes of rapaciousness around the youth. Seemingly unaware of God's presence, his gaze is fixed on the ominous sight of an eagle on a scorched tree disembowelling a hare.[16] In this context, Zucchi's figure in the wilderness may stand for *Sapienza umana* – in all its fragility and with all its shortcomings – thereby counterpointing God's *Sapienza divina*, the first and most important Gift of the Holy Spirit. Thus, "rejoicing in his works," man makes his tribute to the Creator. Having placing objects alluding to the elements on the sacrificial altar, he rests the terrestrial sphere – showing the oceans and continents – on its corner, while holding aloft the armillary sphere.[17]

Armillary and terrestrial spheres were commonly the respective attributes of astronomers and of geographers; they were instruments of measurement, charting the heavens and earth. Sages contemplating armillary spheres frequently appeared not only on the title pages of tracts such as Giovanni da Sacrobosco's *Sphaera mundi* (fig. 115.1), but also on those of works associated with the art of divination, like Francesco Marcolini's *Sorti* (fig. 115.2).[18] There are several references to the physical heavens and earth in the aforementioned Psalms; notably that contemplating the heavens, "the work of thy fingers, the moon and the stars set in their place by thee, what is man that thou shouldst remember him."[19] In this context, the underlying message of Zucchi's painting is clear. *Sapienza umana* has creation at his feet, but, since man is "little less than a god," he lacks the divine wisdom necessary to predict the unpredictable and understand the unfathomable.

RICK SCORZA

FELICE PERETTI

SIXTUS V 1585-1590

116

CIRCLE OF GUGLIELMO DELLA PORTA
active 1532–1577
PROJECT FOR THE TOMB OF POPE PAUL III FARNESE c. 1585–1588

Pen and brown ink and wash
55.9 × 34.5 cm
Annotations: *Fra Gu(glie)lmo Porta brother of Giacomo d(itt)o / A Monument in St. Peter*
Victoria and Albert Museum, London

Guglielmo della Porta's Tomb of Pope Paul III was the second most important sculptural project in sixteenth century Rome after Michelangelo's Tomb of Pope Julius II (cat 1). Not only was its tormented history similar to that of its famous precedent, Michelangelo's tomb for Julius II (together with his Medici tombs in the New Sacristy of San Lorenzo, Florence) was also its main source of formal inspiration. Soon after Guglielmo della Porta was nominated *piombatore* by the aged pope Paul III in 1547, he began working on the model for the statue of the seated pope. Subsequently, the sepulchre was planned and erected in various configurations, as a free-standing structure and as a wall monument, until the epitome of its most central components was eventually installed as a counterpart for Bernini's Tomb of Urban VIII in the tribune of Saint Peter's Basilica in 1628 (where it is still *in situ* today).

The present drawing has been published frequently as evidence of the tomb's installation in the niche of the crossing's southeast pier, which was completed by 1588. However, while the sheet is undoubtedly related to this stage of the monument's history, it cannot be taken as a truthful testimony of its former state. It differs in many regards not only from the actual tomb (fig. 116.1), but also from a much more reliable drawn copy[1] and two later engravings (after lost drawings) by Martino Ferrabosco, which also show it in the pier's niche. Ward-Jackson, taking his cue from the deviations of the figures' poses, concluded that the drawing must have been made from memory. Conversely, Werner Gramberg, who pointed out the architectural differences of the statue's socle and especially of the cartouche for the inscription, interpreted the sheet as a preliminary study in preparation for the tomb's installation at the pier.

Since the personification of Justice in the lower left is shown nude, the drawing must have been made before 1593, when the artist's son, Teodoro della Porta, at the pope's behest, clothed the figure with the metal garment we still see today. The fact that in the drawing the spandrels beneath the pediment are filled with two symmetrical figures holding laurel crowns – which were never carried out – speaks very much in favour of Gramberg's hypothesis that the drawing was made before the tomb was actually set up in its new location. Therefore it was probably executed between 1585 and 1588.

But the drawing is not a to-scale rendering of the tomb's intended installation. As if under a magnifying glass, the statue of the enthroned pope in the niche and his coat of arms on the pediment are blown up to more than twice their correct size. It is therefore probable that the drawing was made to illustrate the reinstallation project to someone who took a specific interest in these two components – that is, most likely Paul III's grandson, the great art collector and patron, Cardinal Alessandro Farnese.

As the result of a mix-up with another drawing related to a papal tomb at the Victoria and Albert Museum (see cat. 82), Herbert Siebenhüner ascribed the present drawing to the Ligurian sculptor Leonardo Sormani. This attribution was adopted – sometimes with a question mark, sometimes without – by all authors cited in the references, with the exception of Ward-Jackson, who assigned it to an anonymous artist. In contrast to what is stated by Gramberg, no eighteenth-century attribution to Sormani can be found on the mount, but a nineteenth-century pencil inscription on the verso reads: *Fra Gu(glie)lmo Porta brother of Giacomo d(itt)o / A Monument in St. Peter.*

Clearly the drawing was carried out at two distinct moments in time, possibly by two different hands within the same workshop. A draughtsman whose style is close to that of Guglielmo della Porta (perhaps Teodoro?) was responsible for the outlines of the architectural setting, the statue of the pope, and the two female allegories of Justice and Prudence beneath him. At a later stage, an extension of 16.0 cm in height was glued on the back to the upper edge of the main sheet, which originally was only 40.2 cm high. In addition to the pediment with its personifications of Peace and Abundance, the two winged *all'antica* figures in the spandrels were added at that point. The difference of hands is not only evident stylistically, but also technically, as the author of the orginal drawing used a brown wash, whereas the wash of the additions has a greyish tone. As a final point in support of Gramberg's hypothesis, the drawing's execution in two stages very much appears to reflect the atmosphere of a work in progress during the planning process of the tomb's reinstallation, whereas it would seem difficult to justify for a drawn copy.

EIKE D. SCHMIDT

Fig. 116.1 Guglielmo della Porta, *Tomb of Pope Paul III*. Saint Peter's Basilica, Rome

117
FEDERICO ZUCCARO c. 1542/43–1609
*THE TIBURTINE SIBYL FORETELLING
THE BIRTH OF CHRIST TO THE EMPEROR
AUGUSTUS* c. 1586–1589

Pen and brown ink and wash,
squared in red chalk, on cream
paper
52.6 × 38.3 cm
Devonshire Collection, Chatsworth

Fig. 117.1 Federico Zuccaro,
Augustus and the Tiburtine Sibyl,
c. 1566–1589, fresco. Pucci chapel,
Trinità dei Monti, Rome

Gere was the first to publish this drawing as a work by
Federico Zuccaro.[1] As he pointed out, the drawing is
closely related to Federico's fresco of the same subject on
the upper right-hand wall of the Pucci Chapel in the north
transept of the Church of the Trinità dei Monti, Rome
(fig. 117.1). On 8 June 1563, Federico's brother, Taddeo, had
contracted to finish the frescoes in the chapel, the rights
to which had recently been acquired by Giacomo Cauco,
the Archbishop of Corfu. In the 1520s, Perino del Vaga had
done frescoes on the vault, the upper part of the altar wall,
and above the exterior arch for Cardinal Lorenzo Pucci,
but the patron had died in 1531 and his heirs gave up their
rights to the chapel in 1548. Taddeo's work in the chapel
proceeded slowly, at a time when he was burdened by many
commissions, and the frescoes were far from complete
at the time of his unexpected death in September 1566.
The project was then taken over by Federico, but it was
not finished until 1589.

According to Taddeo's contract with Archbishop Cauco,
the scenes from the life of the Virgin by Perino del Vaga in
the upper reaches of the Pucci Chapel were be to continued on the walls, with frescoes of the Dormition, the
Assumption and the Sibyl Showing a Vision of the Virgin
and Child to the Emperor Augustus.[2] The latter story is
included in the text for Christmas day in Jacobus de
Voragine's *Golden Legend* (*Legenda Aurea*). At noon, the
Sibyl of the Tibur showed the Emperor Augustus an apparition of a golden circle around the sun, in the middle of
which a most beautiful virgin was holding a baby at her
bosom. And a voice proclaimed, "This is the altar of
Heaven" (*Haec est ara coeli*), the words that are frequently
used to explain the foundation of the church of Santa
Maria in Ara Coeli on the Capitoline Hill in Rome.[3]

Drawings in the Uffizi and the Louvre show Taddeo
Zuccaro's initial ideas for the Sibyl and Augustus.[4] Focusing
on the protagonists, Taddeo drew the two figures with their
bodies directed to the left, and the standing Sibyl in the
middle. She points heavenward with her right arm, and
rotates her upper body to look down at Augustus, kneeling
with hands clasped at the lower right. As Gere observed,
Taddeo's interpretation owes much to Parmigianino's treatment of the subject known through a chiaroscuro woodcut.[5]
In Federico's composition, the protagonists assume stances
related to Taddeo's, but the intertwined relationship is simplified, and the two figures are separated and confront each
other across a central space. The Sibyl, now on the right but
still standing and pointing heavenward, faces the kneeling
Augustus, now at the left. The two figures thus anchor the
lower corners of an elongated triangle with the Virgin and
Child at the apex. Federico also pursued this arrangement
of the Sibyl and Augustus in a drawing that was formerly
on the London art market.[6]

It is probably impossible to know how interested
Federico was in the Pucci Chapel, and in particular in the
subject of the Sibyl and Augustus, when his brother was
awarded the commission in 1563. Later that year Federico
accepted the invitation of Giovanni Grimani, Patriarch of
Aquilea, to work in Venice, where he remained until 1565.
While there, Federico made a series of drawings after one
of the patriarch's most treasured possessions, the lavishly
illuminated Flemish manuscript (c.1510–1520) known as
the Grimani Breviary (Biblioteca Marciana, Venice).[7]
Today, seven drawings in red and black chalk by Federico
after illuminations in the Grimani Breviary are known,

117

Fig. 117.2 Federico Zuccaro,
Augustus and the Tiburtine Sibyl
(after the Grimani Breviary),
c. 1563–1565, red and black chalk,
22.6 × 16.5 cm. Musée du Louvre,
Paris

including a sheet (after folio 44r) that proves his fascination with the subject of Augustus and the Tiburtine Sibyl. (fig. 117.2)[8] In the copy, Augustus is again shown kneeling with his hands clasped before him, though in the central position, and again the Sibyl stands behind, pointing (discreetly) upward, but instead of the classical attire of the other Zuccari interpretations, here the figures are conspicuously clothed in contemporary Northern court dress. The architectural setting is also thoroughly Gothic. Naturally, when Federico came to design his own rendition, he ignored these typically Flemish embellishments of a classical Roman subject, and his finished fresco in a monastic Roman setting follows closely his drawing at Chatsworth, with only minor variations.

DAVID MCTAVISH

ANDREA LILIO, CALLED **LILLI** c. 1565–after 1635
SAINT JEROME WASHING THE FEET OF
PILGRIMS c. 1586

Pen and brown ink and brown wash
19.3 × 12.7 cm
Art Gallery of Ontario, Toronto

This lively and well-preserved drawing was one of the first purchases made by the Art Gallery of Ontario on the advice of Walter Vitzthum, but only recently has it been given a convincing explanation. When acquired, the drawing was said to be by Domenico Cresti, il Passignano, a Florentine artist who worked in his native city, Venice and Rome, but this attribution was rejected in favour of the more generic "anonymous Italian, c. 1600." Now, thanks to the research of Eitel-Porter, the drawing can be tied to a specific papal commission in Rome and assigned a probable date. The work can also be connected with two other preparatory sheets that have only recently been linked to the same project.

The drawing represents four distinct activities: the welcoming of pilgrims to a monastic institution at the lower right, the washing of their feet at the left, the serving of a meal to them in a refectory at the upper right, and the provision of rest and succor in a dormitory seen through an arch at the upper left. The same charitable acts appear in an arched fresco (fig. 118.1) on the right-hand wall of a small chapel to the left of the Cappella Sistina in the Church of Santa Maria Maggiore, Rome. The chapel as a whole takes its name from Pope Sixtus V, who instituted a wave of artistic projects in Rome during his short rule. Sixtus V had himself expressed a particular devotion to Saint Jerome, and it is to this fourth-century Church Father that the small chapel is dedicated. In the arched fresco, the act of washing the pilgrim's feet is given much greater prominence by being re-located to the right foreground, and it is Saint Jerome himself who administers this humble task. The entire scene takes place in the hospice and monastery built by Saint Jerome towards the end of his life, near the church of the Nativity in Bethlehem. The fresco is to be dated about 1586.[1]

Although the decoration of the Cappella Sistina in Santa Maria Maggiore was carried out under the general supervision of Cesare Nebbia and Giovanni Guerra, Giovanni Baglione, the seventeenth-century biographer of artists in Rome, says that Andrea Lilio painted the fresco of Saint Jerome.[2] Born in Ancona on the Adriatic Sea, Lilio came early to Rome and quickly secured employment in many of Sixtus V's projects, including the Cappella Sistina in Santa Maria Maggiore, the Scala Santa in the Lateran Palace and the Sistine Library in the Vatican. The exact date of his birth is unknown, but his ascendancy in Rome appears to have occurred when he was very young. His first known work is the fresco of Saint Jerome, evidently painted when he was not much more than a teenager.[3]

In style, the Toronto drawing is close to the quick pen-and-ink sketches of Nebbia. A second drawing of the same four acts of charity (Paris, Louvre) has likewise been connected by Eitel-Porter with the Saint Jerome fresco, though again there are substantial differences between every part of the composition and the final fresco as well as the Toronto drawing.[4] Eitel-Porter has attributed the drawing in the Louvre to Nebbia, but stylistically it is close to the Toronto drawing. In both drawings, the pen line is splintered and nervous and is augmented with a carefully adjusted, dappled wash. Especially similar is the handling of the backgrounds of the two drawings, with an angular treatment of the figures and their setting.

Shortly after Eitel-Porter published her discoveries, Viatte identified yet another drawing by Andrea Lilio for the fresco. (fig. 118.2)[5] Now in the Musée Bonnat in Bayonne, this drawing, like the sheet in Toronto, had previously been attributed to Domenico Passignano. Both the Toronto and Bayonne drawings exhibit a similar handling of pen, ink and wash, but the latter shows the foreground figures in positions much closer to the completed fresco, notably the significant relocation of Saint Jerome washing the feet of a newly arrived pilgrim to the front right corner. For that reason, the drawing in Bayonne is likely to be the latest of the three drawings only recently connected with the fresco of Saint Jerome in Santa Maria Maggiore, Rome.

DAVID MCTAVISH

Fig. 118.1 Andrea Lilio, *Saint Jerome Washing the Feet of a Pilgrim*, c. 1586, fresco. Cappella di San Girolamo, Santa Maria Maggiore, Rome

Fig. 118.2 Andrea Lilio, *Saint Jerome Washing the Feet of a Pilgrim*, c. 1586, pen and brown ink and brown wash, 14.9 × 9.6 cm. Musée Bonnat, Bayonne

119
FERRAÙ FENZONI 1562–1645
MOSES AND THE BRAZEN SERPENT c. 1587

Pen and brush and brown ink with
black chalk, with occasional
incising; ruled in pen and black
ink, right, left, and lower edges
38.8 × 27 cm
Annotations: *Ferrau Faensone*
Private collection, Chicago

Fig. 119.1 Cesare Nebbia, *Moses
and the Brazen Serpent*, c. 1587,
pen and brown ink and brown
wash, over red and black chalk,
35.5 × 26.5 cm. Private collection

Fig. 119.2 Francesco Villamena,
Moses and the Brazen Serpent,
1597, engraving, 51 × 38 cm. The
British Museum

This vigorously drafted, finished compositional study corresponds closely to the fresco Fenzoni executed in the Scala Santa, Rome, which he completed around 1587 (see fig. 120.1, p. 373).[1]

The Scala Santa was installed in its present location by order of Pope Sixtus V to preserve the sacred relic of the "Holy Stairway," the staircase that Christ is purported to have walked up on his way to trial in the palace of Pontius Pilate in Jerusalem. It comprises five parallel staircases flanked on each side by two double sets of staircases, all linked together at the top by a corridor. It is in the centre of this corridor that the fresco *Moses and the Brazen Serpent* is located.

The walls and ceilings of the three innermost staircases, as well as the corridor, are frescoed with scenes from the Old Testament and the Passion of Christ. Giovanni Guerra and Cesare Nebbia supervised the work, which involved the participation of nineteen different painters. The entire decoration was completed by October 1588.

Nebbia and Guerra were project coordinators for many papal commissions issued by Sixtus V. Nebbia was responsible for the design of the spaces to be decorated, providing drawings for the team of artists who were recruited. It was he who gave Fenzoni the idea for the *Moses and the Brazen Serpent*. Nebbia's compositional study for Fenzoni's fresco, executed in his characteristic graphic style, survives in a private collection (fig. 119.1). Comparing it to the present drawing, one can see that Nebbia did not exert strict control over his artists, but allowed them latitude to refine his ideas and to present some of their own.[2]

In his treatment of the scene, Fenzoni created a more forceful and dramatic narrative than Nebbia, emphasizing the contrast between the writhing, snake-entangled bodies of the Israelites in the foreground and the quiet authority of Moses, who points to the brazen serpent, the God-given cure to their suffering.[3] In the biblical story, the Israelites, wandering in the desert, complained against God and Moses for needlessly bringing them out of Egypt to die without bread and water. As punishment for their discontent, God sent a plague of "fiery serpents," causing many to die. As soon as they repented, God instructed Moses to make a "serpent of brass" and to place it upon a pole, so that "every one that is bitten, when he looketh upon it, shall live." The writhing, contorted figures in the lower part of the composition attest to the influence of Michelangelo's *Last Judgment*. As opposed to these anguished victims, Moses and the surrounding group of believers, now saved from peril, look on adoringly at the brazen serpent. This poignantly expressed contrast calls to mind Michelangelo's division of the damned and the saved in the *Last Judgment*.

The present drawing is one of a group of studies prepared by Fenzoni for frescoes in the Scala Santa. It is among his earliest and most powerful datable drawings to have survived. Part of the vigour derives from the strong underdrawing in black chalk and the heavy jagged pen lines that pick out the forms from it. The artist seems to have habitually executed *modelli* in which he eschewed the use of wash, preferring red or black chalk in combination with pen and brown ink.[4] This is the most complete study by Fenzoni for the composition and the only one drawn in pen and ink.[5]

The present drawing probably also served as the *modello* for an engraving of the subject by Francesco Villamena dated 1597, dedicated to Clemente Bartholo of Urbino (fig. 119.2).[6]

JEAN GOLDMAN

120
FERRAÙ FENZONI 1562–1645
STUDY OF A MALE NUDE ENTWINED BY A SERPENT 1587

Red and black chalk, some pen and
dark brown ink
40 × 27.5 cm
Inscriptions: *Anibbal Caracci*
Szépművészeti Múzeum, Budapest

According to Mancini's near-contemporary biography, Fenzoni learned his art in his native Faenza before moving to Rome during the papacy of Gregory XIII (reigned 1572 to 1585).[1] Nothing is known of Fenzoni's early years in Rome until his debut on the artistic scene in 1587, when he joined the team of artists working under the supervision of Cesare Nebbia and Giovanni Guerra on the extensive fresco cycles commissioned by Pope Sixtus V. It was the *Moses and the Brazen Serpent* in the Scala Santa, completed by 10 May 1587 (fig. 120.1),[2] that launched his career; his first dateable drawings were made in connection with this fresco and other Scala Santa compositions. Today Fenzoni's reputation largely rests on his extant corpus of about 160 drawings, which comprise bold and inventive compositional and figural studies executed with great technical virtuosity.[3]

The composition *Moses and the Brazen Serpent* in the Scala Santa clearly originated with a design by Cesare Nebbia, now in Florence (fig. 119.1), which itself ultimately derives from Michelangelo's treatment of the subject on the ceiling of the Sistine Chapel.[4] Nebbia executed his drawing as a general guide for the fresco, but then allowed Fenzoni to develop the composition according to his own more dynamic design, as is revealed by four preparatory studies. These include a compositional pen-and-ink drawing in the Uffizi and a later, more finished one, in the Goldman collection (cat. 119), as well as two figures studies in red chalk.[5] One of these, formerly in the Archibald Russell collection, but whose present location is unknown, represents a young man, doubled over and crying out in agony, struggling to rid himself of a serpent. The second is the Budapest sheet, one of Fenzoni's masterpieces, first published and related to the Scala Santa fresco by Hermann Voss.[6] It maps out the figure of the young man wrestling with a serpent near the right-hand edge of the fresco – clearly one of the artist's own inventions as a comparison with Nebbia's design reveals. The open mouth and

the head thrown back in despair recall the left-hand son of the Laocoön group in the Vatican, an obvious source of inspiration for such a subject.[7] The figure and the snake have been vigorously silhouetted in red chalk, with smooth continuous lines defining the pose and musculature before sharp flicks of the pen in dark brown ink were added to emphasize certain facial details. This masterful rendition of the male nude, which may have been drawn from life, demonstrates a perfect grasp of human anatomy. Such realism was unusual for Roman artists of the time but finds parallels in some studies after the model made only a few years later in the Carracci academy in Bologna, thus explaining the previous incorrect attribution of the drawing to Annibale Carracci recorded in the inscription. Nevertheless, the beauty of the line that defines the undulating silhouette also affirms the mannerist tendencies of Fenzoni's art.

The *Brazen Serpent* is one of three large frescoes that dominate the back wall of the corridor at the top of the Scala Santa staircases.[8] According to the Old Testament (Num. 21:4-9), God punished the Israelites in the desert for having spoken out against him and their leader Moses by sending a plague of poisonous snakes. When the Israelites repented, Moses was told to fashion out of brass an image of a snake (the brazen serpent) and to erect it on a pole so that whoever looked upon it would be cured. The Scala Santa, or Holy Staircase, usually refers to the entire building constructed by Sixtus V to house a relic of the flight of steps in the Palace of Pilate in Jerusalem which Christ is said to have ascended during his trial. It consists of five parallel staircases that lead to a corridor and two chapels. With the exception of the outermost flights of stairs, the walls and ceilings are frescoed with scenes from the Old Testament and the Passion of Christ. The decoration of the Scala Santa, which comprised seventy-four frescoes, was begun in 1587 and completed by October 1588.

RHODA EITEL-PORTER

121
JACOPO ZUCCHI c. 1541–c. 1589/90
DESIGN FOR AN ALTAR c. 1587–1588

Pen and brown ink and brown
wash, black and red chalks, and
some grey wash on two sheets of
overlapping paper
54.8 × 32.2 cm
Annotations: *G. Vasari*; on verso,
t.r.c., 2550; b.l.c., coll. 11050
National Gallery of Canada,
Ottawa

Fig. 121.1 Jacopo Zucchi, Decoration
of the della Tolfa chapel, Santo
Spirito in Sassia, Rome

Formerly given to Giorgio Vasari, the attribution of this hitherto unpublished drawing to another Florentine artist, Jacopo Zucchi, must be supported, initially, on stylistic grounds. The spirited and assured style of handling and rather extravagant treatment of the forms is entirely characteristic of Zucchi. Born in Florence, Zucchi settled in Rome in 1572, after already having worked there as Vasari's assistant in the Vatican, executing decorations for Pope Pius V. Zucchi became court artist to Cardinal Ferdinando de' Medici in Rome during the 1570s, and at the end of the 1580s he painted major frescoes in the Palazzo Ruspoli for the Rucellai, another aristocratic Florentine family.

The sheet is a fully resolved design for a substantial frame, including the predella, altar table, and surmounting elements featuring two angels holding palms of martyrdom. There is a slight trace of a figure drawn in black chalk in the horizontal field above the cornice, presumably of a God the Father receiving the martyred saint who would have been represented in the main field for the altarpiece.

According to Härb, the drawing might relate to a project commissioned by one of Zucchi's Roman patrons, Vittoria della Tolfa, a niece of Pope Paul IV and wife of Camillo Orsini. More specifically, it could be a study for one of the chapels Zucchi designed on behalf of Vittoria della Tolfa for the church of Santo Spirito in Sassia in Rome during the 1580s. The most relevant chapel, in this instance, is the first one to the right, firmly documented to 1587–1588, containing the *Pentecost* as the main altarpiece (fig. 121.1) with a *Saint John the Baptist* and the prophet *Joel* on either side.[1] The coat of arms of the Tolfa family included a tower placed on top of a mountain, as seen in the chapel itself. Although the chapel was decorated in a different manner, the presence of what appear to be the Tolfa arms in this drawing, the tower with two symbolic mountains on either side, suggests that this may have been an early idea for the decoration, later discarded for some as yet unknown reason. Alternatively, it could have been executed in the same period for a different Tolfa altar as yet unrecognized, possibly even in another church – an aspect requiring further research.[2] Certainly the presence of the martyr's palms needs to be accounted for if the subject of the main altarpiece was that of the Pentecost.

While it seems that the design was ultimately modified, this particular solution was regarded as resolved, judging by the blind stamp (possibly that of the notary who drafted the formal written contract) in the middle of the empty field. The drawing would thus appear to have had the status of an official legal document. Indeed, there is considerable evidence of some rough physical handling of the sheet, which could mean that it was used for its particular purpose, perhaps even delivered as a model to the sculptors of the frame. The drawing also shows indications of scale in the lower-left area and a profile of the columns, drawn in red chalk, in the upper left. There is also an unusual correction by the artist on a small flap of paper in the coat of arms in the cornice, as well as a sketch of a right hand in black chalk on the verso (not necessarily from the same period as the drawing on the recto). Whatever its original purpose, the quality and ambition of the drawing are not in question. It is a major example of a design for a frame, generally inspired by Michelangelo's architecture, for a Roman altarpiece from the second half of the sixteenth century.

DAVID FRANKLIN AND FLORIAN HÄRB

122

CESARE NEBBIA c. 1536–1614

SAINT JEROME WITH TWO PUTTI c. 1588

Pen and brown ink, brown wash,
over black chalk
26 × 21.2 cm
Inscriptions: *N.° 251. Muziani; 4(3);*
gl i (?) [verso]
Morgan Library & Museum,
New York

With intermittent visits to his native Orvieto, Nebbia resided in Rome from the late 1570s, occupied on private and papal commissions. When Felice Peretti, who was once aptly described as possessing a feverish "almost pathological" drive to rebuild the face of Rome,[1] ascended the papal throne in 1585 as Sixtus V, he appointed Nebbia and the Modenese artist Giovanni Guerra as superintendents for his decorative projects. Together, Nebbia and Guerra commanded a large team of artists who decorated the vast interiors of the newly erected buildings and renovated structures with expansive fresco cycles and occasional stucco framing elements. The new papal projects included the Cappella Sistina in Santa Maria Maggiore, a major new building for the Vatican Library (see cat. 124), the construction of the Scala Santa (cat. 119), the Lateran Palace, and the Benediction Loggia adjacent to San Giovanni in Laterano. The abundance of designs by Nebbia for Sistine projects suggests that from 1585 to 1590 the artist was working almost exclusively in the service of the pope.

The present drawing is a preparatory study for a spandrel fresco of the Benediction Loggia adjoining the church of San Giovanni in Laterano (fig. 122.1), decorated c. 1587 at the behest of Sixtus V.[2] Following the old inscription "Muziani" at lower left, it was long thought to be by Nebbia's much revered teacher, Girolamo Muziano, until the relationship to the fresco was noted and it became clear that Muziano was not involved in the design of the Sistine projects. Nebbia started the study with a light underdrawing in black chalk which he then worked up with pen and ink and wash. A few black chalk pentiments remain visible, including earlier drafts for the folds of Saint Jerome's

drapery and the position of the putto at upper left. The attributes borne aloft by the putti – an inkwell and a crucifix – indicate the dual nature of the saint as author/church father and penitent. For the fresco, his most common attribute, a lion, was added. The escutcheon outlined below the figure of the saint is empty, almost certainly because the decorative elements and allegories were the responsibility of Guerra, while the narrative compositions and figures generally fell to Nebbia. Beneath the saint, the painted version contains the six-pointed star and the three *monti* of the Peretti coat of arms.

Sixtus V ordered the demolition and rebuilding of the Lateran Patriarchium soon after his election and by June 1585 the work was already well underway. The new Lateran Palace was a massive cubic construction whose south side adjoins the church of San Giovanni, a clear manifestation of the power and majesty of the papacy. To the west, adjacent to the Lateran Palace and church and accessible from both, lies the Benediction Loggia, which was the first part of the complex to be completed.[3] It consists of a porticoed ground floor, decorated in 1588 with a series of standing apostles, prophets, and angels, and the loggia proper on the floor above decorated in 1587 with a series of five frescoes illustrating the life of Saint Peter and accompanied by frescoes of the church fathers in the spandrels. According to Baglione, the Lateran frescoes were executed by a team of artists including Paris Nogari, Ventura Salimbeni, Ferraù Fenzoni, Baldassare Croce, Giovanni Battista Pozzo, Giovanni Battista Ricci, Giacomo Stella, Andrea Lilio, and Prospero Orsi.[4] Baglione himself was probably also involved.[5] Baglione further notes that Giacomo Stella painted the fresco of Saint Jerome.[6] Besides the present study, several drawings by Nebbia and at least one by Giovanni Guerra (a female allegory)[7] for the Benediction Loggia are known.[8]

RHODA EITEL-PORTER

377

Fig. 122.1 Giacomo Stella, after a design by Cesare Nebbia, *Saint Jerome with Two Putti*, c. 1587, fresco. Benediction Loggia, San Giovanni in Laterano, Rome

CESARE NEBBIA c. 1536–1614
DANIEL SLAYS THE SERPENT OF BABYLON
(DANIEL 14:22–26) c. 1588

Pen and brown ink, grey-brown
wash
26.7 × 19.1 cm
Szépművészeti Múzeum, Budapest

Fig. 123.1 After Cesare Nebbia,
*Daniel Slays the Serpent of
Babylon*, c. 1588, fresco. Sala di
Daniele, Lateran Palace, Rome

Fig. 123.2 Cesare Nebbia, *Daniel
Slays the Serpent of Babylon*,
c. 1588, pen and brown ink and
wash over black chalk, with
touches of white heightening,
squared in red chalk, 23.2 × 20.3 cm.
With Sotheby's, London, 1989

In 1964, Philip Pouncey convincingly attributed to Nebbia the present drawing, which had previously been published as by Parmigianino and Bartolomeo Passarotti.[1] It was later identified by Zuccari as a study for a fresco of c. 1588 on the vault of the Room of Daniel in the Lateran Palace, Rome (fig.123.1),[2] for which there exists a second, more finished drawing by Nebbia (fig. 123.2).[3] The Budapest version shown here is a rare example of Nebbia's freely worked designs – most extant drawings by the artist are highly finished compositional studies.

The unusual subject, taken from a later addition to the Book of Daniel in the Old Testament, often considered apocryphal, tells of the destruction of the great serpent worshipped by the Babylonians (Daniel 14:22-26). Previously Daniel had destroyed the idol Bel after having exposed grievous deception on the part of the priests who had simulated that it was a living god. Thereupon Daniel was led by the Babylonian king to a serpent, challenged to admit that it was a live divinity, and asked to worship it. Daniel, however, requested, and was granted, permission to slay the serpent without club or sword to prove its

mortality and ungodliness. By melting together pitch, fat, and hair into cakes that he fed to the animal, he promptly killed it, thereby exposing, once again, the false belief of the Babylonians.

The two preparatory studies related to this episode show Daniel at upper left on the verge of hurling his missile at the dragon, which emerges from an underground chamber in the temple. Whereas in the drawing, the fire-spewing dragon is a fierce, threatening creature that spreads its wings and Daniel reaches back as if to throw a stone, in the fresco, the dragon cowers much like a snarling dog, with the young prophet gingerly reaching out to feed it. The changes reveal a closer adherence to the biblical narrative and possibly also a conscious attempt to make the animal, now with lowered wings, appear less heraldic.[4] Just above the dragon stands a pedestal with the remains of the idol Bel (two legs) and, at right, the statue's broken off torso. The prophet is accompanied by the king, identifiable by his crown and sceptre; the kneeling figure in the right foreground of the Budapest drawing represents a priest leaning over a prie-dieu, as is revealed by the

later drawing and fresco. It is not known who painted the fresco, though Paolo Guidotti,[5] the young Ventura Salimbeni,[6] and also Giorgio Picchi[7] have been suggested on stylistic grounds.

The Room of Daniel is situated between the Room of the Seasons and that of Elijah on the north side of the Lateran Palace.[8] Sixtus V had ordered the demolition and rebuilding of the Lateran Patriarchium soon after his election and by June 1585, work was already well underway. A clear manifestation of the power and importance of the papacy, the new Lateran Palace is a large building adjoining the Church of San Giovanni in Laterano and consisting of four wings surrounding an inner courtyard. A monumental staircase, accessed from the portico of the church, gently rises to the *piano nobile*. Starting with the Room of Constantine, two suites of large halls or rooms extend along the north and west sides of the palace, culminating in the Hall of the Popes. Consonant with the scene *Daniel Slays the Serpent of Babylon*, the Lateran frescoes present events and personalities from the Old Testament and early church history, selected to underscore the necessity of counteracting false beliefs and to celebrate defenders of the true Catholic faith. With the exception of the Room of the Popes, which also features frescoes on the walls, the decoration was limited to the ceiling vaults. Payment records suggest that the painting probably commenced with the north-western corner of the building in 1587 and was completed by August 1589.[9]

RHODA EITEL-PORTER

124

CESARE NEBBIA c. 1536–1614

EMPEROR AUGUSTUS IN THE PALATINE LIBRARY c. 1588

Pen and brown ink, brown wash over black chalk, with paper correction
26.4 × 20.4 cm
Inscriptions: *Augustus Cæs Palatina Biblioth. magnifice / ornata viros literatos fovet; Ces. Nebbia*
Private collection, Chicago

The drawing is a study for the wall fresco of c. 1588 in the Salone Sistino, Vatican Library, showing Emperor Augustus visiting the library he had founded in his palace in Rome (fig. 124.1). As the inscription on the drawing – which recurs identically in a cartouche beneath the fresco and translates as "Caesar Augustus cherished literary men at his magnificent Palatine Library" – might suggest, the emperor is depicted in the company of scholars and poets. A scribe sits in the foreground at lower left, while the emperor's favourite poets, Virgil and Horace, crowned with laurel, stand beside a lectern covered with an impressive array of books. Beyond this group at upper right, an allegorical representation of the river Tiber with the she-wolf and Romulus and Remus situates the scene in Rome.

To be precise, the sheet represents two studies for the fresco since at upper left is pasted a paper correction, which when lifted reveals that initially Augustus was to be shown seated with his learned companion looking down at the book and engaged in the act of writing. The version created by means of the added flap of paper gives more prominence to the central character by isolating Augustus while the foreground figure looks up at him in respectful attention; these changes were adopted and correspond to the fresco.

The Salone Sistino was the largest and most lavishly decorated space in Pope Sixtus V's new Vatican Library.[1] The old rooms located on the ground floor of the palace of Pope Nicholas V had become too small for the collection and too damp for the books and its users. The new building, which sliced through Bramante's only recently completed (in 1565) Cortile del Belvedere, was begun in May 1587.[2] Composed of a suite of rooms, the library is located on the second floor, with the Salone Sistino functioning as the reading room. Besides a painted ceiling, the Salone is decorated with a cycle of eight frescoes dedicated to famous libraries of antiquity, culminating in a representation of the papal library. Paired with this series is a suite of eight frescoes depicting scenes of ecumenical church councils in chronological order on the opposite wall. In addition, full-length representations of the historical personages known as inventors of alphabets decorate the row of pillars that bisects the hall.

A near-contemporary commentary on the project, Rocca's *Bibliotheca Apostolica Vaticana* of 1591,[3] provides information on the selection of this erudite subject matter. It cites cardinal librarian Federico Ranaldi as the programme's prime iconographer, a claim substantiated by Ranaldi's notes of 1587 preserved in the Vatican archive.[4] According to Rocca, Silvio Antoniano, the privy councillor of the cardinals and Pietro Galesino, the apostolic protonotary were also involved; together with Ranaldi they devised the inscriptions for the library and council scenes. Rocca also records that Giovanni Guerra and Cesare Nebbia were ultimately responsible for the frescoes, with Guerra designing the decorative elements and Nebbia the narrative scenes and figures associated with the alphabet – a division of labour between the two supervisors common to many of the Sistine projects.[5] Böck intereprets Rocca's statement to mean that Nebbia was responsible for the cartoons (the final designs on the same scale as the frescoes), but Rocca's phrase could equally well apply to other studies for the projects, as is borne out by the numerous compositional drawings for these cycles by Nebbia identified in recent years.[6]

Payment records indicate that the frescoes of the vault of the Salone Sistino were executed from 1588 to 1589; this project was followed by the walls, which were presumably completed by 20 May 1589 when Nebbia received compensation for the "painting from the cornice to the floor."[7] Only the supervisors, Nebbia and Guerra, are mentioned in the accounts; however, Baglione lists an additional fifteen painters including himself, Hendrick van den Broeck, Andrea Lilio, Paris Nogari, Giovanni Battista Pozzo and Giacomo Stella. Judging by the extant drawings, most of which are by Nebbia, few of the other artists were involved in the actual design of the frescoes. The frescoist of *The Emperor Augustus in the Palatine Library* is unknown, though Zuccari quite plausibly has proposed, on stylistic grounds, the little-known associate of Nebbia, Ferdinando Sermei.[8]

RHODA EITEL-PORTER

Fig. 124.1 Cesare Nebbia and
workshop, *Emperor Augustus in
the Palatine Library*, c. 1588, fresco.
Salone Sistino, Vatican Library,
Rome

125
PASQUALE CATI c. 1550–c. 1620
DEATH OF THE VIRGIN c. 1588–1590

Pen and brown ink and brown
wash over black chalk, squared for
transfer in red chalk
28.4 × 19.7 cm
Annotations: *Mutiani*; *Luccarno
Mutiani* [verso]
National Gallery of Canada,
Ottawa

Fig. 125.1 Altemps chapel vault,
Santa Maria in Trastevere, Rome
(fresco representing *Death of
the Virgin* appears at bottom right)

Formerly given to Girolamo Muziano, this hitherto unpublished drawing was first attributed to Pasquale Cati by Cristiana Romalli, who also connected it to the artist's most important work, the fresco in the chapel built by Cardinal Marco Sittico Altemps in Santa Maria in Trastevere in Rome (fig. 125.1).[1] A contract for the painted decoration was signed in 1588, and the date 1589 appears in the chapel, which was built according to the designs of Martino Longhi. Following standard procedure, Cati's work was assessed for final payment in 1590 by two painters – Tommaso Laureti and Muziano.

The side walls in the lower part of the ambitious chapel illustrate scenes from the 1562–1563 sessions of the Council of Trent, while more conventional narratives from the life of the Virgin appear in the vault. This compositional drawing is preparatory for the upper section of the space featuring the *Death of the Virgin*, a subject related only in apocryphal sources. Cati even drew the rather intrusive cuts in the upper corners of the irregular field on the entrance wall of the chapel. The drawing is close to the finished fresco and must have been produced near the very end of the design process. The major difference is in the treatment of the Virgin on the funeral bed: in the painting she is less upright and more successfully foreshortened, while in the sketch she almost seems to levitate. Other drawings for the vault frescoes for the Altemps chapel survive in Berlin and in the McCrindle Collection, but this is the only one known for this particular scene.[2] Drawings by Cati are extremely rare, and those that do survive tend to display the light, almost gliding touch and preference for broad areas of wash that characterize this drawing. His style tends also, as here, to be rather restrained and clear, but with some attempt at emotional vigour, at least in individual figures.

Born in Jesi in the Marche region of Italy, Pasquale Cati is first recorded in Rome in 1577, during the pontificate of Gregory XIII. He seems to have spent his entire career in Rome, and although little known today, he had the confidence of a succession of popes for whom he worked on major decorative projects.

DAVID FRANKLIN

126
GIOVANNI DE' VECCHI 1537–1615
VIRGIN AND CHILD WITH TWO SAINTS
c. 1589?

Pen and brown ink on laid paper
29.8 × 22.5 cm
Gabinetto Disegni e Stampe degli
Uffizi, Florence

Giovanni de' Vecchi, originally from Sansepolcro, was one of the leading late Mannerist artists working in Rome during the last quarter of the sixteenth century in a style that Zeri characterized as "timeless" (*senza tempo*).[1] This drawing is apparently a study for an altarpiece. The Virgin sits on a raised throne next to a standing Christ child, whose arms are raised in a gesture of benediction. Lilies adorn the arm-rests of the throne. These, together with the coat of arms at its base, indicate that the drawing must have been a commission from Cardinal Alessandro Farnese (1520–1589), known as "Il Gran Cardinale," the most lavish individual patron, apart from certain popes, in sixteenth-century Rome.[2] Seen from behind, two male saints wearing monastic habits kneel before the holy pair. Flames rise out of ornamental vases placed on each side of the throne. Swags of drapery frame the scene.

While the intention behind this drawing is not absolutely certain, its apparent date indicates that it may be an unrealized project for an altarpiece for the church of Santa Maria Scala Coeli at the Abbey of the Three Fountains on the outskirts of Rome. This was an ancient Cistercian monastery constructed at the traditional site of Saint Paul's beheading.[3] According to legend, his head bounced three times, creating a fountain on each spot, from which the abbey takes its name. Cardinal Alessandro was commendatory abbot from 1536 to 1544 and again from 1565 until his death in 1589. When lightning destroyed the original church at the site, Alessandro built a new octagonal church with three apses on the foundations, designed by his chief architect Giacomo della Porta between 1582 and 1584. Alessandro's death halted plans for the interior decoration of the church, despite appeals to his heirs to complete the work. He had commissioned de' Vecchi to design a mosaic for one of the apses, and likely intended to decorate the others in similar fashion. The use of mosaic in church interiors had recently become popular, as part of the early

Christian revival, which was a significant aspect of counter-reformatory thought in late Cinquecento Rome, but was also specifically intended to recall the decoration of the earlier church on the site.[4] The mosaic was only completed by Francesco Zucchi on de' Vecchi's cartoons, under Alessandro's successor, Cardinal Pietro Aldobrandini. The design must have been changed to incorporate not only Aldobrandini and his uncle Pope Clement VIII, but also Cardinal Alessandro in the guise of Saint Anastasius, one of the saints whose relics were held at the Tre Fontane.

De' Vecchi was at this stage among Alessandro's favourite artists, having worked for him on the fresco decoration of his sumptuous villa at Caprarola, and later on the decoration of the Gesù, the mother church of the Jesuits, which the Cardinal had built.[5] Alessandro must surely have had plans for the altarpieces for the three altars in the church's apses, and it seems quite likely that the present drawing should be a study for one of these. It is also stylistically consistent with the design for the mosaic. Indeed it is tempting to suggest that the two kneeling figures might represent saints Vincent and Anastasius, the saints to whom the adjoining church at the Three Fountains was dedicated. Given that both saints were represented in de' Vecchi's apse mosaic, it is possible that this project was intended for the altar immediately below.

De' Vecchi's evident success led to his continued employment by Cardinal Aldobrandini at the church, where he also executed an altarpiece showing the *Vision of Saint Bernard*. This event, in which the saint saw the souls for whom he was praying ascend a staircase into heaven, was the miracle that inspired the foundation of the church of the Scala Coeli. De' Vecchi would continue to enjoy success under the Aldobrandini, culminating with his designs for the mosaics for the pendentives of the crossing of the basilica of Saint Peter's.

CLARE ROBERTSON

126

127

GIUSEPPE CESARI,
IL CAVALIERE D'ARPINO 1568–1640
POPE SIXTUS V KNEELING IN PRAYER 1589

Black and red chalk on light tan
paper, frame lining in pencil, top
corners cut
38.6 × 23.5 cm
Inscription: *Aquino* [verso]
Teylers Museum, Haarlem

Pope Sixtus V, a Franciscan friar of humble origins, is well known for his piety and religious zeal, but also as a highly energetic patron of art and architecture. During his five-year reign, the dome of new Saint Peter's Basilica was finally completed and numerous grand-scale decorative programs were executed in the papal residences at the Vatican and the Lateran. Sixtus decisively changed the physiognomy of the holy city by cutting large new streets through its densely populated medieval fabric, marking the focal points of these visual axes with the erection of ancient obelisks. His most ambitious building project was the Cappella Sistina, attached to the north transept of the early Christian basilica of Santa Maria Maggiore. Designed by the papal architect Domenico Fontana, the chapel was conceived as a monumental shrine to house the highly venerated relic of the *Presepio* (a type of simulacrum of the grotto of the Nativity) and the tabernacle of the Holy Sacrament, as well as triumphal wall tombs for Sixtus and his predecessor Pius V.

The adolescent Giuseppe Cesari embarked on his Roman career as a prodigy already under Pope Gregory XIII, but was only marginally involved in the grand-scale decorative projects launched by Sixtus V and directed by his preferred artists Giovanni Guerra and Cesare Nebbia. The vigorous black and red chalk drawing of *Pope Sixtus V Kneeling in Prayer* closely resembles the statue for his tomb in the Cappella Sistina executed by Giovanni Antonio Paracca Il Valsoldo between 1588 and 1591 (fig. 127.1). Compared to the rather stiff marble figure, Cesari's representation has a stunning physical presence and liveliness. Sixtus has turned his head slightly more to the left, his liturgical garments are more voluminous and his facial features suggest greater portrait likeness. The drawing attests to the young artist's extraordinary talent as a draughtsman. The sharp contour lines, the modelling of the drapery and the vigorous cross-hatching can be compared with a number of preparatory drawings for Cesari's roughly contemporary but later destroyed fresco decorations in San Lorenzo in Damaso in Rome.[1]

389

Fig. 127.1 Giovanni Antonio Paracca (il Valsoldo), Statue of Sixtus V, 1588–1591. Cappella Sistina, Santa Maria Maggiore, Rome

The drawing in Haarlem shows the kneeling figure of Sixtus V isolated from its niche in the Cappella Sistina. It was executed in preparation of an etching, signed and dated by Prospero Scavezzi il Bresciano: *PROSPER DE SCAVEZZI BRIXIENSIS INVENTOR 1589*. The etching, in reverse, follows the drawing closely, while elaborating ornamental details of the stola and adding the papal tiara to the left. The contours in the drawing are traced for transfer. Prospero Scavezzi is most likely identical with the sculptor Prospero Antichi da Brescia. Van Tuyll has suggested that the drawing might reproduce a stucco model by Prospero Antichi which was transferred into marble by Valsoldo. Prospero did indeed prepare such stucco models for two other statues in the Cappella Sistina representing saints Peter and Paul, which Leonardo da Sarzana later executed in marble. The inscription of the engraving would thus identify Prospero Antichi as the creator of the model, while neither specifically indicating the draughtsman nor the printmaker. The drawing in Haarlem documents the collaboration between Prospero Antichi and the young Cesari, who, according to Mancini,[2] were on very friendly terms.

SEBASTIAN SCHÜTZE

128
CESARE NEBBIA c. 1536–1614
POPE PIUS V CROWNS COSIMO I DE'
MEDICI GRAND DUKE OF TUSCANY
late 1580s

Pen and brown ink, brown wash,
heightened with white gouache
over black chalk
60.7 × 52.9 cm
Inscriptions: *iLo*ᵗᵗ·; *Paolo Veronese*,
and *Ventura Salimbeni*
Museum of Art, Rhode Island
School of Design, Providence

This highly finished drawing – the largest of Nebbia's oeuvre – is one of three studies for a composition depicting Pope Pius V Crowning Cosimo I de' Medici as Grand Duke of Tuscany, an event that took place in 1570 in the Sistine Chapel in the Vatican in the presence of Cardinal Felice Peretti, the future Pope Sixtus V. The two other drawings consist of an early free sketch in the Staatliche Graphische Sammlung, Munich,[1] and a second finished design in the Albertina, Vienna.[2] The pope appears on a dais below a baldachin at left ceremoniously placing a crown on the ruler kneeling before him, while an assisting ecclesiastic supports the heavy cope. The ceremony is sectioned off by two low walls and protected from curious onlookers by two members of the Swiss guard. A large architrave bearing the pope's coat of arms (Ghislieri: diagonal striped bands) and that of the Medici frames the scene at top. Visible at upper right is a detail of Michelangelo's *Last Judgment*. The earlier Munich study, freely sketched in pen and brown ink, which according to a note on the mount was attributed to Nebbia by Alessandro Cecchi, shows the same event, but is in reverse to the other two designs. White gouache was used to eradicate the serpentine column that originally stood behind the Medici ruler but was transposed to frame the scene at right and left in the later designs.

The purpose of the drawings remains unknown. However, it seems likely that they were intended as studies for a tapestry or print, since the Ghislieri coat of arms is reversed in the two more finished versions,[3] and furthermore the artist himself experimented with the direction of the composition when he moved from the early Munich study to the larger ones in Vienna and Rhode Island. In particular the size, detail and high degree of finish of the present sheet – the latest in the series – suggests a major, important commission. Since there is no evidence that Nebbia ever worked for Pope Pius V or for a member of the Medici family, it probably was made at the behest of Sixtus V, as suggested by Morello.[4] Nevertheless, the subject was also an important one for the Medici dynasty, appearing for instance on Cosimo's catafalque in 1574 and in a painting of 1591 by Jacopo Ligozzi, prominently placed in the Salone dei Cinquecento of the Palazzo Vecchio, Florence.[5]

In the context of Sixtus V's patronage, the depiction of the crowning of Cosimo may be seen primarily as an act of homage to Felice Peretti's great benefactor Pius V. Sixtus V had much to be thankful for: Pius V had appointed him Vicar General of the Franciscan Conventuals and, in 1566, bishop of Sant'Agata de' Goti, elevating him in 1570 to the cardinalate.[6] Clear outward signs of Peretti's lifelong esteem for Pius include the Ghislieri coat of arms that were once painted in Peretti's villa and above the gate to his property,[7] the tomb erected opposite his own designated place of burial in Santa Maria Maggiore, and the *translatio* and exequies of Pius V held in the presence of twenty-four cardinals in Santa Maria Maggiore on 13 January 1588. Conceivably the tapestry or print was made on the occasion of these exequies.[8] The Medici too had been strong supporters of Peretti. Besides having purportedly assisted him financially when Pope Gregory XIII abolished the stipend that needy cardinals received, they were instrumental in his election to the papacy.[9] Cardinal Ferdinando de' Medici presented Pope Sixtus V with the generous gift of a painting by Alessandro Allori from 1583 depicting the Holy Family.[10] A tapestry or print after a design by the papal court painter Nebbia may well have been part of such reciprocal gift giving, at the same time subtly reinforcing the fact that the Medici had received their title by the grace of the papacy.

Less likely but also possible is that not Sixtus V but his great nephew, Cardinal Alessandro Peretti da Montalto, commissioned Nebbia's design. A series of drawings of c. 1593 by Ludovico Cardi, called il Cigoli, represent designs for a tapestry depicting Pope Sixtus V writing under divine inspiration a treatise (see cat. 130), possibly his revision of the Vulgata which became the "Editio Sixtina" (1589).[11] Cigoli's drawings, likely made for Cardinal Alessandro Peretti, and Nebbia's studies might have belonged to a projected set of wall hangings with scenes from the life of Sixtus V.

RHODA EITEL-PORTER

129
GIOVANNI BAGLIONE c. 1566–1643
STUDY FOR THE BABYLONIAN LIBRARY
c. 1588–1589

Black chalk on blue paper
36.7 × 29.2 cm
Teylers Museum, Haarlem

Fig. 129.1 Attributed to Giovanni
Baglione, *The Babylonian Library*,
1588–1589, fresco. Salone Sistino,
Vatican Library, Rome

This drawing is a preparatory study for the left part of the *Babylonian Library*,[1] the second of eight frescoes devoted to the great libraries of antiquity in the Sistine Salon of the Vatican Library (fig. 129.1). More specifically – as the caption below the painting indicates – it represents Daniel and his companions studying the language and learning of the Chaldeans. The extensive decoration, commissioned by Sixtus V for the new site of the pontifical library, was carried out between 1588 and 1589 under the supervision of Giovanni Guerra and Cesare Nebbia, the two artist-entrepreneurs who directed the majority of the Peretti pope's pictorial projects. Guerra designed the ornamental arrangement, provided drawings for the allegorical figures, and assigned the painters their individual tasks; Nebbia mainly made the drawings for the historical and narrative scenes and followed their execution in *buon fresco*. Artists of various statures and cultural backgrounds took part in the commission, among them Ferraù Fenzoni, Andrea Lilio, Giovanni Baglione, Giovan Battista Pozzo, Paris Nogari, Giovan Battista Ricci, Arrigo Fiammingo, and Paul Bril.[2]

The fresco representing the Library of Babylon is generally attributed to Giovanni Baglione, a capable and prolific painter often remembered only as a biographer of artists and the rival of Caravaggio. The attribution was proposed by Guglielmi, who recognized the same hand in the left part of the *Bibliotheca Romanorum*[3] and identified these contributions as Baglione's based on a comparison with *The Finding of Moses*, which the painter records having painted in the Sala Santa (now dated to 1587). She relied on other information from the autobiography as well "Cesare del Nebbia of Orvieto and Giovanni of Modena, Painters of the Pontiff Sixtus V, assigned him to work with his colours in the Library of the Vatican; and he put his brush to use in the ceiling. Then, they gave him two large histories with life-size figures to paint on the lower part of the wall, and he accomplished them with such confidence and beauty that Pope Sixtus, seeing that this work was done by a young man only fifteen years of age, was quite delighted with it."[4]

129

This invaluable information on the painter's public beginnings nonetheless harbours a chronological distortion. Baglione was actually about twenty-three when he made this painting, not fifteen: the walls of the Vatican Library were painted in 1589,[5] and Baglione's death certificate states he was seventy-seven in December 1643, which places his year of birth around 1566.[6] So it seems that to emphasize the precocious skill that had earned him the praise of Sixtus V, the artist exaggerated how young he was. Furthermore, his autobiography says little about his training and minimizes his apprenticeship with the Florentine painter Francesco Morelli, which he declares as inadequate to his talent. He fails to cite a prestigious youthful work completed outside Rome before the commissions from Sixtus – the frescoes at the Palazzo Santacroce in Oriolo Romano – though he mentions subsequent activity in Naples. Baglione likely could not claim authorship of the Oriolo cycle because he worked on it at his master's side. In addition, his *Lives* inexplicably contain no biography of Morelli, a painter still little known, who – based on documents located by Bon – worked for the Santacroce family on a number of occasions and was also in contact with Baglione near the time of his death.[7] Between the omissions and distortions, it seems clear that the painter-biographer was manipulating the facts to underscore his strengths. Leaving out his teacher also served the image he wished to convey of himself.

Such observations have led this author to believe that the two Vatican Library frescoes were not the work of Baglione alone, but the fruit of a collaboration between Morelli and his ambitious pupil.[8] Based on the observation that the study in Haarlem is freer and more refined than parts of the corresponding fresco (for example the young man in the foreground who is posed in an awkward turn), it has been suggested that either the drawings or some passages in the painting might be Morelli's work, and the more hesitant areas mainly Baglione's. This hypothesis has garnered interest.[9] Yet, in the absence of works securely attributed to Morelli, Morello and van Tuyll propose retaining the attribution of the drawing to Baglione for the time being. The suggestion is certainly welcome and, until further research brings new data to light, the question can only remain open. Strinati's recent proposal in this matter should be taken into account: agreeing with Morelli's attribution of the authorship of the frescoes at Oriolo and believing that the Florentine painter can probably be identified as the artist Zeri called the "Master of the Pietà of Stockholm," Strinati assigns a specific group of paintings to him.[10]

Of the eight drawings for the Vatican Library catalogued by this author so far, the Haarlem drawing is the exception: it is the only one related to the Library and Council Chambers executed by the same author of the corresponding fresco. Nebbia's graphic style is unmistakable in the other seven: five complete drawings (three of them squared for transfer), a small sketch, and a figure study (also squared), each of which can be related to paintings by Giacomo Stella, Arrigo Fiammingo, Giovan Battista Pozzo, Andrea Lilio, Vincenzo Conti, Antonio Viviani, and Ferraù Fenzoni.[11] This particularity is explained by the fact that Nebbia and Guerra sometimes entrusted the execution of preparatory drawings to the more gifted collaborators, as occurred with Fenzoni and Bril at the Scala Santa.[12] This does not mean that Baglione created the image on his own, but that he would have prepared it from a sketch supplied by Nebbia. This suggests the practice followed by Fenzoni at the Scala Santa. To paint *The Bronze Serpent*, he made at least four studies from an "initial idea" provided by Nebbia (cats. 119 and 120).[13] In any case, the Haarlem sheet demonstrates that Baglione (or whomever it was) was not considered a simple executer, but a mature professional. And the fluent style of the drawing – which reveals a Tuscan origin abreast of late Roman Mannerism – is not that of a beginner but the product of a skilled and elegant hand.

ALESSANDRO ZUCCARI

130

LUDOVICO CARDI, CALLED IL CIGOLI
1559–1613

THE DOVE OF THE HOLY GHOST
APPEARING TO POPE SIXTUS V,
SEATED AT A TABLE,
ASSISTED BY TWO ANGELS c. 1590–1593

Pen and black and brown ink and
watercolour, heightened with
touches of lead white over black
chalk, squared
26.6 × 22.8 cm
Private collection, Chicago

LUDOVICO CARDI, CALLED IL CIGOLI

This brightly coloured and finished drawing is preparatory
for a tapestry design commissioned from Cigoli by
Cardinal Alessandro Peretti Montalto shortly after 1590,
the year that the cardinal's great uncle, Pope Sixtus V, had
died. In his life of the artist, Cigoli's nephew, Giovanni
Battista Cardi, refers to the project, citing "many watercolour drawings as designs for panels of tapestry, which,
according to the terms of the commission, represented
religious subjects."[1] Evidence for the dating of the tapestry
project to the first half of the 1590s is provided by studies
on the verso of another drawing for this same composition
now in a private collection in New York. The verso studies
are connected with an altarpiece that Cigoli completed in
1593.[2] The New York private collection drawing is equally
important for the present sheet because it offers evidence
of what the complete composition must have looked like
(fig. 130.1). The tapestries themselves do not appear to
have been executed.

The use of colour in the present drawing distinguishes
it from the other known studies for the composition. With
its rich palette of yellows, blues, and purples, it conveys
the effect of an actual tapestry. The sheet is drawn in the
same direction as the finished tapestry would have been.
Its intended purpose is difficult to ascertain. It is possible
that it was meant for use by the weavers, who would have
needed it in colour.

The composition depicts Pope Sixtus V seated at a table,
working on his revised version of the Vulgate Bible.[3] As he
writes, the Dove of the Holy Ghost descends from the top
left corner to impart divine wisdom. Reinforcing the theme
of heavenly inspiration, two angels on either side of the
pope are given more prominence than his amanuensis, who
is glimpsed in the shadows at the extreme left.

As Turner has noted, comparison with other drawings
for the same tapestry indicate that the artist intended the
main compositional field to be rectangular, with the centre
of the rectangle marked at the top by the Dove of the Holy
Spirit. Turner further hypothesizes that the missing other
half of the present drawing would have depicted the doorway leading out of the pope's study, on the other side
of which would have been a table in front of a bookcase,
around which a group of Franciscans and other prelates
would have been seen discussing the finer points of biblical exegesis.[4]

One of the interesting aspects of the present drawing is
its presentation of an alternative idea for the allegorical figure on the pedestal at the right. Judging from her attributes, a lighted candle in one hand and Saint Peter's key to

the Church in the other, she evidently symbolizes the Catholic Faith. At her side, grasping a scroll, is the Angel of Saint Matthew, who assisted the evangelist in the writing of his Gospel. At her feet are symbols of the three other evangelists: the Eagle of Saint John, the Lion of Saint Mark, and the Ox of Saint Luke. The female statue is drawn on an overlaid flap covering a less articulated, taller variant of a similar figure, in profile, sketched in pen. In the rejected alternative, her attributes accord with a more conventional representation of Catholic Faith: she holds two large tablets, symbols of the Old and the New Testaments.

Cigoli has not only rethought the figure's attributes, but has refined her form. In the New York private collection drawing, she is not yet conceived. In a drawing in the Louvre (fig. 130.2), she holds different attributes and stands on a pedestal that is more restrained in its decoration. At its base is a child who in the present drawing peeks out from behind her. The Louvre sheet also introduces a similar allegorical figure on a pedestal at the left, balancing the one at the right. The introduction of a balancing element, together with the enlarged composition of the New York private collection variant, corroborates Turner's hypothesis that the present drawing represents only half of the composition.

The present drawing at one time had an additional flap, attached at the bottom, showing the Peretti lion restrained by a putto. That flap was cut away and stolen during an exhibition in London in 1991.[5]

The conception of the drama in the tapestry is similar to that of a composition sketched by Cigoli in a related drawing in the Louvre, known as *Saint Gregory the Great Receiving Divine Inspiration for His Writings*. The sainted pope Gregory the Great is traditionally depicted with a dove flying at his ear.[6] Chappell was the first to point out, from a comparison with other likenesses, that the pope represented in the Louvre drawing is Sixtus V rather than the clean-shaven Saint Gregory.[7] Chappell further pointed to the Louvre drawing's representation of Saint Francis Receiving the Stigmata in the over-door of the pope's study as proof that the subject could not be Saint Gregory, for Saint Gregory had died more than five centuries before the birth of Saint Francis. On the other hand, an image of the stigmatization of Saint Francis was entirely appropriate in connection with the Franciscan Sixtus V. Franciscans are represented in several of the preparatory drawings for this tapestry.

Other studies for the tapestry composition of the *Holy Ghost Appearing to Sixtus V* include two in the Uffizi. One is for the tapestry border, where the lateral elements consist of two statues, *Christian Faith* and *Catholic Faith*, to the left and right respectively. The other is a quickly sketched study for the central tapestry panel. Like the Louvre and New York private collection drawings, it is in reverse to the present drawing. It shows the entire rectangular field, with the pope seated at his table, accompanied by two angels on either side of his chair, two Franciscan brothers by the side of his table, and, in the far corner of the room, a table around which some assistants are gathered – all unaware of the profound vision the pope is experiencing in their presence.[8] Yet another compositional drawing for the *Holy Ghost Appearing to Sixtus V* is in the Gabinetto Nazionale delle Stampe, Rome.[9]

Chappell recently identified another drawing for a section of the tapestry border, in pen and brown wash, in a private collection.[10]

JEAN GOLDMAN

Fig. 130.2 Ludovico Cardi (called il Cigoli), *A Pope Writing with Divine Inspiration*, 1590–1593, pen and brown ink with blue and white wash, 26.5 × 46.5 cm. Musée du Louvre, Paris

131
HENDRICK GOLTZIUS 1558–1617
STUDY AFTER THE FLORA FARNESE 1591

Red chalk
41.8 × 22 cm
Teylers Museum, Haarlem

Hendrick Goltzius, the famous engraver and draughtsman, is one of the most influential personalities in Dutch art around 1600. In November 1590 he left Haarlem for an extended period in Italy studying the great works of antiquity and the masters of the Renaissance. He travelled to Venice, Bologna, Florence and Naples, but stayed most of the time in Rome. Throughout his Italian sojourn he met celebrated contemporary artists such as Girolamo Muziano, Giambologna, Giovanni Stradano, Giacomo Palma il Giovane and Pietro Francavilla, and recorded their likenesses in highly refined portrait drawings. In Rome, where he arrived on 10 January 1591 and stayed till 3 August 1591, Goltzius made drawings after such modern masters as Raphael and Polidoro da Caravaggio, but dedicated his time mainly to the study of famous antique statues.

The Teylers Museum preserves an entire album containing forty-three large-scale drawings representing twenty-seven antique statues and Michelangelo's *Moses* (often included among the ancient masterpieces). Goltzius documented the most-admired antique works in a very systematic fashion, including the *Apollo Belvedere*, the *Torso Belvedere* and the *Laocoön*, as well as the *Hercules Farnese*, the *Commodus Farnese*, the *Dioscuri,* and the *Pasquino*, and was planning likely from the outset to publish a set of engravings that would surpass the existing collections by Antonio Lafrery or Giovanni Battista de' Cavalieri. In the end the project was never realized and only three drawings

were actually engraved by Goltzius and published after his death in 1617. Probably around 1611–1612 the album with his studies after the antique was acquired by Emperor Rudolph II in Prague. Later it belonged to Queen Christina of Sweden and Prince Livio Odescalchi in Rome, from whose heirs it was acquired in 1790 for the Teylers' Stichting in Haarlem.

The *Flora Farnese* (fig. 131.1) was one of the most admired female statues in Rome. Today housed in the Museo Nazionale in Naples, it was once part of the famed Farnese collection. The large fragment of a female Roman statue was restored by Guglielmo della Porta in the late 1550s as *Flora* and displayed in the courtyard of the Palazzo Farnese. Goltzius would normally draw, on site, a sketch in black chalk on blue paper, and then later in his study execute a more detailed and refined drawing, mostly in red chalk on white paper, that could serve for an engraving. For the *Flora Farnese* both these drawings are preserved in Haarlem. The black chalk sketch roughly indicates the actual setting in the Farnese courtyard, while the final drawing concentrates on the detailed rendering of the thin and finely plaited drapery, which seems to delicately emphasize, rather than cover, the nude of the female body. Goltzius' Roman sojourn and his intense study of antique sculpture and Italian Renaissance art decisively changed his own artistic style, moving away from the late mannerist models of Bartholomäus Spranger towards a more classically oriented art.

SEBASTIAN SCHÜTZE

Fig. 131.1 *Flora Farnese*, 2nd–3rd century A.D., marble. Museo Archeologico Nazionale, Naples

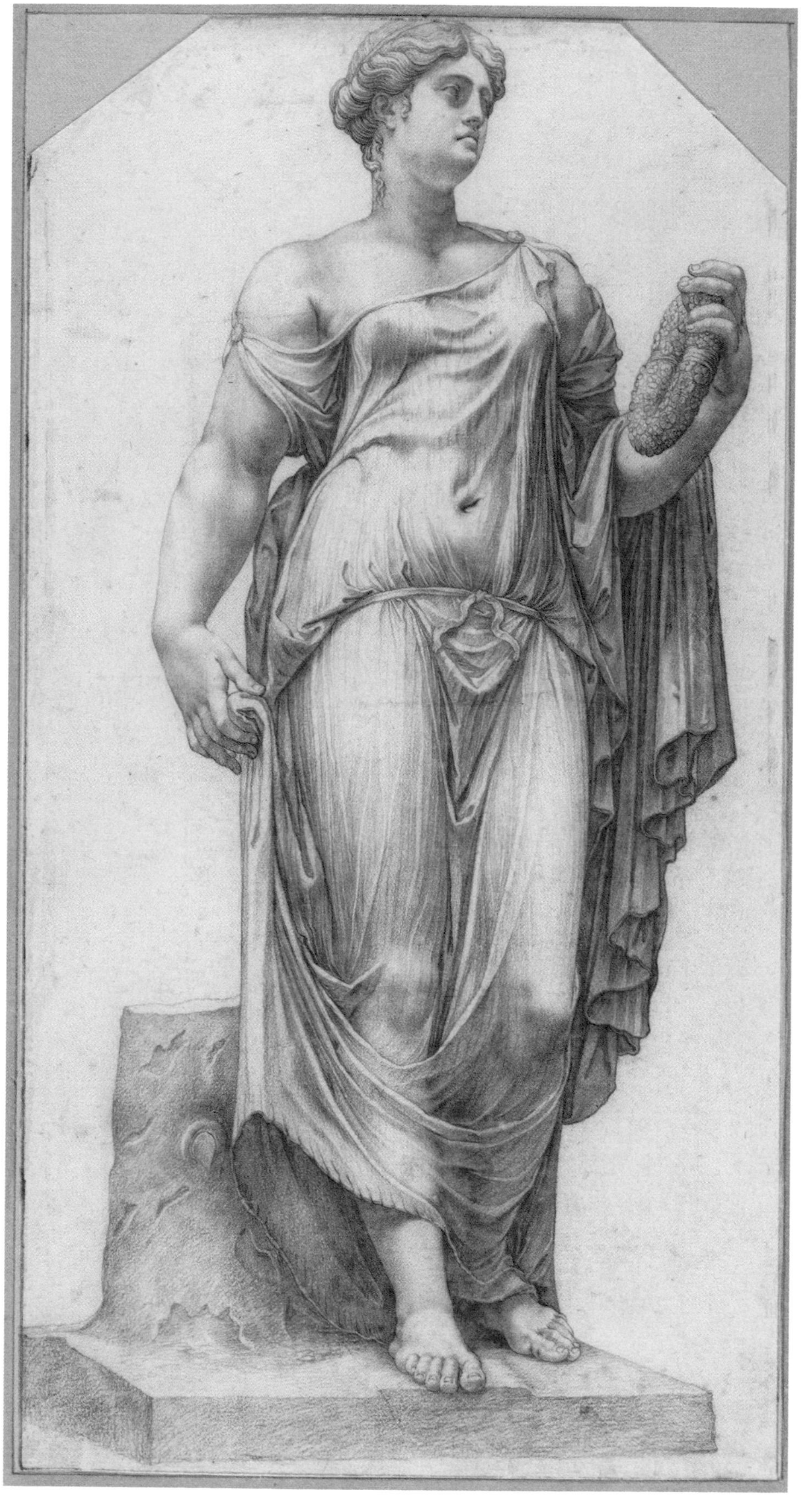

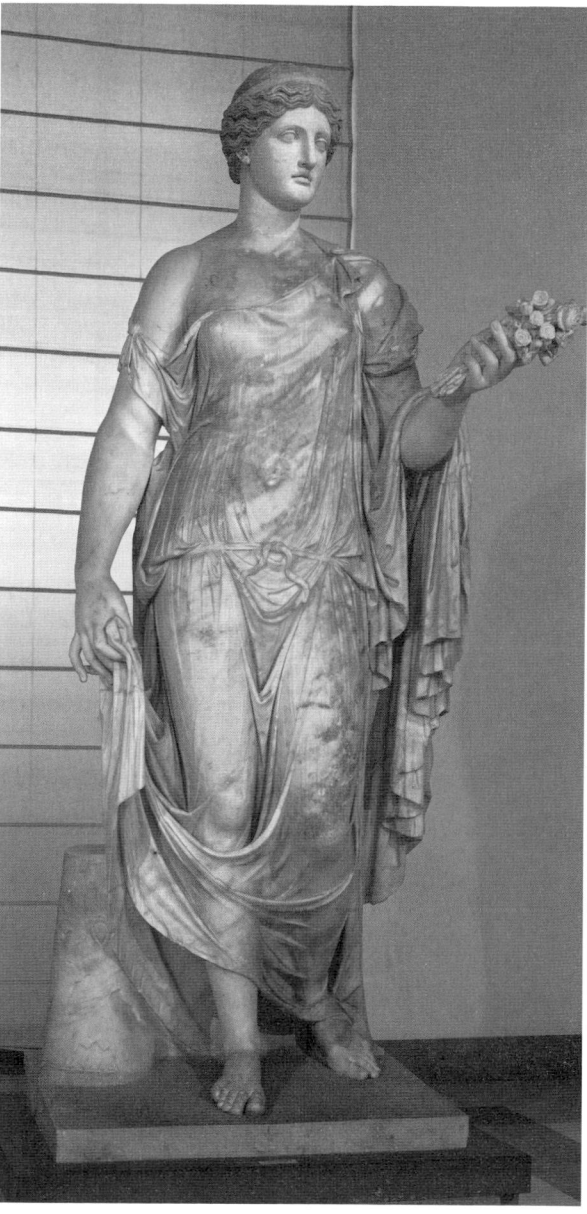

IPPOLITO ALDOBRANDINI

CLEMENT VIII 1592–1605

132

ANNIBALE CARRACCI 1560–1609
HERCULES RESTING c. 1596–1597 (1599?)

Black chalk, with white heightening on blue paper (faded to
brown-green), partly squared in
black chalk, laid down
35.5 × 52.4 cm
The Cleveland Museum of Art

In a letter dated 12 February 1595 Cardinal Odoardo Farnese informed his brother, Ranuccio Farnese Duke of Parma and Piacenza, of his decision to commission the Carracci to decorate the grand hall of their Roman family palace with the heroic deeds of their recently deceased father, Duke Alessandro Farnese. The three Carracci, Ludovico and his younger cousins Agostino and Annibale, had set up a highly successful workshop in Bologna, and from the earlier 1580s onwards started to accumulate important commissions in Bologna and other centres in Emilia. In the fall of 1594 Agostino and Annibale made a first trip to Rome, and after completing some of his pending Bolognese commissions, Annibale transferred permanently to the papal city in November 1595 and was assigned quarters in the Palazzo Farnese, the grandest of Roman Renaissance residences.

The decoration of the Camerino Farnese, a relatively small room on the *piano nobile* which probably served as the cardinal's study, has been traditionally dated to the beginning of Annibale's Roman sojourn about 1595–1597. Ginzburg has recently argued instead for an execution in 1599,[1] during an interruption of the works in the Galleria Farnese, and for a decisive participation of Agostino Carracci and Innocenzo Tacconi. The program is based in part on an exhortatory poem dedicated by Antonio Querenghi to the young Odoardo Farnese in 1586,[2] and was likely devised by Fulvio Orsini, the learned humanist and antiquarian in the service of the Farnese. Annibale designed a highly elaborate decorative scheme for the coved ceiling with gilded stucco bands framing frescoed scenes of the deeds of Hercules. In the centre of the ceiling a *quadro riportato* with the *Choice of Hercules,* executed in oil on canvas and today at Capodimonte, was inserted. The complex planning process is documented by a large number of preparatory drawings, including sketches for the decorative scheme, compositional studies for the narrative scenes, and nude studies for the main figures.[3]

The black chalk drawing in Cleveland is a relatively recent addition to this group, and is preparatory for Annibale's fresco of *Hercules Resting* (fig. 132.1), one of the two scenes framing the central *Choice of Hercules.* Annibale's composition is closely based on a famous ancient gem, at the time in the collection of Fulvio Orsini (fig. 132.2). The Cleveland drawing shows the pensive and exhausted Hercules resting in a barely indicated landscape setting after the accomplishment of his twelve labours. On the right side, the golden apples from the garden of the Hesperides and the Erymanthian boar indicate two of these labours. In the right background a sphinx seated on a block of stone is traced with a few lines. Based on the drawing Annibale prepared a cartoon, which is preserved in the Uffizi in Florence, but was never used. The actual fresco presents a reversed composition and differs in many details from both drawing and cartoon, attesting to a last minute change. Although the attribution of the Cleveland drawing has been questioned by Robertson, giving it to an anonymous follower of Annibale, it seems to fit stylistically rather nicely into the group of preparatory drawings for the Camerino, now attributed in part to Agostino by Ginzburg.[4] The move from Bologna to Rome provided Annibale with the opportunity to study, first-hand, the unsurpassed treasures of ancient sculpture, especially those housed in the Palazzo Farnese, as well as the High Renaissance masterpieces by Raphael and Michelangelo. Integrating the continuous study from nature – so essential to the reform program of the Carracci Academy – with those classical models became the principal challenge and main focus of Annibale's Roman art. The Cleveland drawing beautifully illustrates this complex process of adaptation and integration at an early stage of his Roman sojourn.[5] The vigorous study of the male nude is clearly based on a profound knowledge of the human body while trying, at the same time, to assimilate the artificial pose of ancient models such as the two river gods at the time in the Farnese collection.

SEBASTIAN SCHÜTZE

132

Fig. 132.1 Annibale Carracci, *Hercules Resting* (also called *Hercules and the Sphynx*), 1595–1597, fresco. Camerino Farnese, Palazzo Farnese, Rome

Fig. 132.2 *Hercules Resting*, engraving, after gem owned by Fulvio Orsini. From "La Cheau et Le Blond, Description des principales pierres gravées, …", 1780

ANNIBALE CARRACCI 1560–1609
FIGURE STUDY FOR A BACCHANTE c. 1598

Black chalk, pen and brown ink,
with white heightening on blue
paper
47.8 × 27.9 cm
Inscriptions: *h. m.*
Szépművészeti Múzeum, Budapest

Fig. 133.1 Annibale Carracci, *Triumph of Bacchus and Ariadne*, 1597–1601, fresco. Galleria Farnese, Palazzo Farnese, Rome

If Cardinal Odoardo Farnese had initially summoned the Carracci to Rome to decorate the grand hall of the Palazzo Farnese with the heroic deeds of his father Alessandro, plans changed quickly. In 1597 he instead commissioned Annibale to create the ceiling frescoes of the Galleria Farnese, likely with the idea to provide a spectacular stage for the wedding of Ranuccio Farnese and Margherita Aldobrandini. By the end of that year, Annibale was joined by his brother Agostino to assist him in this task. The Galleria, originally a loggia positioned on the garden side of the palace, was later closed and destined to house the most famous pieces of the Farnese antique collection. An artistic dialogue with the ancient sculptures or rather a competition (*paragone*) between ancient sculpture and modern painting was thus encouraged from the outset.

The Galleria is a long and rather narrow room covered by a steeply curved ceiling. A large number of preparatory drawings document the conceptual complexity of the project as well as the meticulous preparation Annibale applied to every detail. Dozens of drawings are preserved, from compositional sketches and single figure studies to parts of the final carton, while many more are certainly lost.[1] Initially Annibale was first and foremost concerned with devising an appropriate structure for the ceiling that would accommodate narrative scenes and decorative elements, while details of the iconographic program were addressed only at a later date.

The large central fresco shows in a frieze-like composition the *Triumph of Bacchus and Ariadne* (fig. 133.1). Annibale's composition is inspired by a drawing of the subject, which Perino del Vaga had provided decades earlier for the decoration of the famous Farnese Casket. The composition is dominated by two distinct groups, Bacchus and Ariadne on their chariot on the left, and Silenus with his companions to the right. Compared with an early compositional study in the Albertina, the two groups are more clearly separated in the fresco. At centre appears a dancing, tambourine-playing bacchante, which creates an important compositional link between the two groups. The Budapest drawing is a life study preparing this figure and is mainly concerned with its complex twisted movement. The bacchante appears almost identical, but now wrapped in a beautiful swirling drapery, in the right half of the cartoon in the Galleria Nazionale in Urbino and then in the final fresco. Annibale apparently prepared for all major figures in the Galleria Farnese such vigorous studies from nature, attesting to the continuous importance of life models during his Roman sojourn.

An *avviso* dated 2 June 1601 reports the inauguration of the Galleria Farnese. It won immediately universal acclaim and presents a grand synthesis of sixteenth-century Italian ceiling painting, from Michelangelo's Sistine Chapel and Correggio's spectacular domes in Parma to the most recent achievements of Pellegrino Tibaldi at Palazzo Poggi or the Cavaliere d'Arpino at the Cappella Olgiati. At the same time it decisively prepares the grounds for the glorious age of Roman Baroque ceiling painting, from Giovanni Lanfranco and Pietro da Cortona to Giovanni Battista Gauli and Andrea Pozzo.

SEBASTIAN SCHÜTZE

133

134
ANNIBALE CARRACCI 1560–1609
HOLY FAMILY WITH INFANT
SAINT JOHN THE BAPTIST
("THE MONTALTO MADONNA") c. 1597–1598

Oil on copper
35 × 27.5 cm
Inscriptions: *591 Annibale Carracci*
and *77* [verso]
The National Gallery, London

Apart from his grand-scale public commissions, Annibale continued to execute throughout his Roman sojourn smaller paintings for important private collectors. Especially valued were his exquisitely refined works on copper. Bellori, in his 1672 biography of the artist, describes in detail two such copper plates in the collection of Monsignor Lorenzo Salviati:

> … there are two other paintings on copper belonging to the most illustrious Monsignor Lorenzo Salviati; in one the Virgin is painted sitting with the Child on her lap blessing Saint Francis: the saint bends one knee on the ground and he is swooning with divine love, with his hands on his breast, accompanied by an angel with a hand on his shoulder. In the other painting on copper there is the Virgin seated on the cradle; and while she embraces Jesus on her lap, who holds an apple, the young Saint John gazes at him and tugs at the Virgin's mantle, and at the other side Saint Joseph pauses from reading a book, with his spectacles in his hand. Because for its beauty this little picture was copied continually while it was in the Villa Montalto, it was already then being worn away in the hands of copyists.[1]

The two paintings can be identified with the *Vision of Saint Francis*, now in the National Gallery in Ottawa (cat. 135) and the *Montalto Madonna* in the National Gallery in London. The latter picture is still mentioned by Fioravante Martinelli in the Villa Montalto in his *Roma ornata dall'architettura, pittura e scoltura* written in 1660–1663.

The Holy Family is placed in front of an architectural background with a fluted classical column, opening on the left into a hilly landscape. The Virgin, seated almost parallel to the picture plane, seems to turn around in this very moment to address the viewer, while the child, playfully balancing on her lap, looks over to Saint Joseph. The young Saint John nears, curious, from the left. The small jewel-like copper, datable to the early years of Annibale's Roman sojourn, is characterized by its highly refined execution and a colour scheme dominated by the brilliant reds and blues of the Virgin's dress. The composition reveals Annibale's interest in Raphael's late representations of the subject, such as the *Holy Family Under Oak Tree* (fig. 134.1) in the Prado in Madrid executed with the assistance of Giulio Romano, and is a perfect example of Annibale's classical Roman style.

The small copper was highly esteemed throughout the seventeenth and eighteenth centuries, as many painted copies as well as several engravings demonstrate.[2] According to Bellori, the continuous copying almost ruined the picture when it was still in the Villa Montalto. Known for a long time only through these copies, the original resurfaced in 2003 and was acquired in 2004 for the National Gallery in London, adding yet another painting to their spectacular group of copper paintings by Annibale. The early provenance of the *Montalto Madonna*, recently investigated by Costamagna and on the occasion of its London sale, still needs further clarification. But it is highly likely that it belonged originally to Cardinal Alessandro Peretti Montalto. The cardinal nephew of Pope Sixtus V continued to play an important role at the Roman curia after his uncle's death in 1590, and was an exceptional patron of art and architecture as well as music. For the Villa Montalto he commissioned in 1615–1616 a famous cycle of eleven oval paintings illustrating the deeds of Alexander the Great, including pictures by Annibale Carracci's most important pupils in Rome, Giovanni Lanfranco, Domenichino, Francesco Albani, Sisto Badalocchio, and Antonio Carracci. In 1622–1623 Giovanni Lorenzo Bernini executed his famous *Neptune and Triton*, today at the Victoria and Albert Museum in London, for a fountain in the same villa. The cardinal also patronized one of the most magnificent new church buildings in Rome, the Theatine church of Sant'Andrea della Valle, later decorated by Domenichino and Lanfranco.

SEBASTIAN SCHÜTZE

Fig. 134.1 Raphael and Giulio Romano, *Holy Family under Oak Tree*, c. 1518, oil on panel, 144 × 110 cm. Museo del Prado, Madrid

135
ANNIBALE CARRACCI 1560–1609
VISION OF SAINT FRANCIS c. 1597–1598

Oil on copper, two copper strips of
2.5 cm added on each side
46.8 × 37.2 cm
National Gallery of Canada,
Ottawa

ANNIBALE CARRACCI 1560–1609
VISION OF SAINT FRANCIS c. 1597–1598

The Vision of Saint Francis in Ottawa can be identified with a small copper painting described by Bellori in the possession of Monsignor Lorenzo Salviati in Rome: "... the Virgin is painted sitting with the child on her lap blessing Saint Francis: the saint bends one knee on the ground and he is swooning with divine love, with his hands on his breast, accompanied by an angel with a hand on his shoulder."[1] The earlier provenance of the painting remains to be established, but it might very well have been originally commissioned by Cardinal Antonio Maria Salviati for whom Annibale executed an altarpiece for the Salviati chapel in San Gregorio al Celio in Rome, the *Saint Gregory in Prayer,* which was later destroyed during World War II at Bridgewater House in London.[2] Unfortunately *The Vision of Saint Francis* is not mentioned in the cardinal's post-mortem inventories. A considerable number of contemporary copies, including those in the Art Institute in Detroit, in the Staatliche Kunstsammlungen in Kassel, in the Pinacoteca Capitolina in Rome, and the Academia de San Fernando in Madrid, attest to its fame and appreciation. The later provenance of the small copper can be traced from Nicolas de Launay and the Duc d'Orleans right up to the collection of the 5th Earl of Ellesmere and 6th Duke of Bridgewater at Bridgewater House.

The painting belongs stylistically to the very same moment as the *Montalto Madonna* (cat. 134) and the *Coronation of Saint Stephen* (private collection), and can be dated to around 1597–1598. The Virgin is seated on the left side on a slightly higher plane holding the blessing child on her lap. She holds a prayer book in her right hand, further underlining the devotional character of the image. The red and blue tones of her robe contrast with the grey-brown cowl of Saint Francis and dominate the small copper's delicate colour scheme. Both mother and child are bending forward toward Saint Francis, who kneels deeply moved in front of them, comforted by an angel. The ecstatic movement of his body, his eyes closed, his lips

slightly parted and his hands crossed on his chest, underlines the mystical character of his vision. A double archway in the background, placed parallel to the picture plane, frames the central protagonist. Its Doric order recalls the courtyard of the Palazzo Farnese in Rome. On the far right Saint Joseph stands with his donkey, alluding to the Holy Family on its journey to Egypt. Two preparatory drawings for the painting are known, one in Windsor Castle[3] and a slightly later one in the National Gallery in Ottawa (cat. 136). The rapid compositional sketch in Ottawa, in pen and brown ink with broad wash, traces only the central group. In the painting, Annibale has intensified the emotional expression and further clarified the compositional and narrative structure. Copper strips, about 2.5 cm each, were added on both sides of the original plate to enlarge the composition.

Saint Francis dedicated his whole spiritual life to the devotion and imitation of Christ. One night, when he was walking in a forest, the Madonna appeared to him and placed the infant in his arms. The scene is represented probably for the first time in 1584–1585 by Ludovico Carracci in his painting now in the Rijksmuseum in Amsterdam (fig. 135.1),[4] and became very popular especially in the Carracci circle. In Annibale's small copper painting Francis is simply kneeling in front of the Christ child, communicating with great emotional and spiritual intensity, his privileged mystical experience. His hands do not show the stigmata, as the vision here described occurred before his stigmatization on mount La Verna. In the later sixteenth and early seventeenth centuries Franciscan mysticism saw a strong revival, promoted in particular by the reform branches of the order, the Conventuals and the Capuchins. Almost contemporarily with Annibale's *Vision of Saint Francis* the young Caravaggio conceived his *Ecstasy of Saint Francis*, one of his first religious paintings and today at the Wadsworth Atheneum in Hartford, which conveys a similar sense of intense spiritual experience.

SEBASTIAN SCHÜTZE

Fig. 135.1 Ludovico Carracci, *Vision of Saint Francis*, 1584–1585, oil on canvas, 103 × 102 cm. Rijksmuseum, Amsterdam

ANNIBALE CARRACCI 1560–1609
VISION OF SAINT FRANCIS (RECTO);
*STUDY OF A DOOR OR TABERNACLE
FRAME* (VERSO) C. 1597–1598

Pen and brown ink with brown
wash; pen and brown ink and
black chalk [verso]
20.9 × 22.6 cm
National Gallery of Canada,
Ottawa

136 (recto)

136 (verso)

137
PAUL BRIL 1554–1626
*LANDSCAPE WITH ROMAN RUINS
OVERLOOKING A BAY* c. 1594

Pen and brown ink over black chalk
13.7 × 20.7 cm
Annotations: *27* (encircled) : *258870*
[verso]
Private Collection, Toronto

Fig. 137.1 Paul Bril, *Landscape with
Ruins and Hay Wagon*, 1595, pen
and brown ink and grey wash,
27.2 × 20.4 cm. Museum Boijmans
Van Beuningen, Rotterdam

The brothers Matthijs and Paul Bril came to Rome during the pontificate of Gregory XIII, who was known to favour the "oltramontani." As they were Northerners, it was assumed they were well trained in painting landscapes, and Matthijs, the first to arrive, was soon hired by Lorenzo Sabbatini to paint frescos throughout the Vatican. Although the exact date of Paul's arrival is not known, records indicate he had arrived in the Eternal City by 1582, and that he began to work closely with his brother on the many papal commissions in progress. Matthijs died the following year and Paul continued to be patronized by a succession of popes and cardinals until his death in Rome in 1626.

Landscape with Roman Ruins Overlooking a Bay was executed in the early 1590s, under the pontificate of Clement VIII. Clement commissioned Paul Bril for a number of significant landscape frescoes in the Vatican, in the Sala del Consistoro and, most impressively, the monumental *Seascape with Martyrdom of St. Clement* in the Sala Clementina of the Vatican. Bril worked on the Sala Clementina with the Alberti brothers, who turned down a commission for the Galleria Farnese in order to work for the Pope.[1] Bril also worked for Clement in 1599–1600 at San Giovanni in Laterano, where he painted landscape backgrounds for the main frescos in the transept as part of the team headed by Cavaliere d'Arpino.[2]

Not surprisingly, given its early date, this sheet displays many of the characteristics of the draughtsmanship of his brother Matthijs, such as the muscular hatching strokes and heavy striations in the rocks at the left. In fact, there is a strong similarity of the composition, though in reverse, to that of a fresco started by Matthijs and finished by Paul, in the second room of the mezzanine in the Torre dei Venti of the Palazzo Apostolico Vaticano. While the fantastical tower on the hill in the fresco is more typical of Matthijs, the lowered horizon line and outlined town in the background are more typical of Paul. The interest in light indicated by the sun streaming in from the left, the attention to spatial development, and the calm nature of the scene are also all hallmarks of Paul's style. It was during the time this drawing was executed (1592–1594) that Paul Bril and Jan Brueghel were developing their signature views of harbours that were to become so popular in the early part of the next century with such patrons as Federico Borromeo, Scipione Borghese and Carlo de Medici.

Although many drawings of Roman ruins have been attributed to Paul Bril over the years, autograph examples are somewhat rare. Ruins are more common in the frescos he executed with his brother or after his brother's designs, which explains why they appear more frequently in the drawings from Paul's earlier period, such as the drawing in Rotterdam dated 1595 (fig. 137.1). Neither Matthijs nor Paul depicted ruins in their natural settings, but rather as compositional elements, to create pleasing, if totally fictional, landscape views.

LOUISA WOOD RUBY

137

138
PAUL BRIL 1554–1626
FANTASTIC LANDSCAPE 1598

Oil on copper
21.3 × 29.2 cm
Inscriptions: *PA. BRIL. ROMAE. 1598.*
National Gallery of Scotland,
Edinburgh

The Flemish painter and draughtsman Paul Bril was apprenticed to his father and, according to Karel van Mander, to Damiaen Wortelmans in Antwerp.[1] Bril travelled to Lyon in 1574 or 1576 and then on to Italy where he joined his brother Matthijs in Rome before 1580. He is documented in the Vatican in 1582 and is first mentioned as a master painter in 1584, the year after the death of his brother. Bril apparently spent the rest of his life in the Eternal City in the service of popes Gregory XIII, Sixtus V, and Clement VIII as well as such important patrons as the cardinals Scipione Borghese, Federico Borromeo, and Francesco del Monte. He was a friend of Rubens and Elsheimer with whom he collaborated.[2] In 1620 he was elected the first Flemish "Principe" of the Accademia di San Luca, the Roman academy of painters.

Starting in Rome as a painter of landscape murals, Bril combined the Flemish tradition of Pieter Bruegel the Elder and Hieronymus Cock with the example of native Italian landscapists, especially the Brescian Girolamo Muziano, who was active in Rome. Bril began easel painting only in the early 1590s. His canvases and especially his small-scale works on copper were in high demand. Bril's compositions were widely disseminated in prints and became seminal for Baroque landscape painting throughout Europe.

The *Fantastic Landscape* is an exquisite example of Bril's elaborate coppers from around 1600. The last golden sunbeams flood this imaginary landscape. Framed by ruins on the left and a huge tree on the right, the prospect is seen from a high viewpoint. The river landscape, dominated by a rocky mountain at centre, unfolds like a stage set in brown, green, and deep blue. Two boats arrive at the riverbank that leads to the foreground. In the middle, a gypsy woman with her two children addresses a traveller;

at left in the shadow of the columns a blacksmith is still busy in his workshop. Both figures represent picturesque elements that Bril often placed in settings with ancient ruins. The ruins are only rarely actual sites but they are clearly modelled on buildings he knew. The Corinthian columns to the left resemble the ruins of the temples of Castor and Pollux or of Vespasian, both on the Roman Forum. The three-bayed vaulted ruin on the right shore just below the church is closely related to the substructure of the Temple of the Sibyl in Tivoli. Bril's knowledge of this place is demonstrated by drawings he made of the spectacular temple crowned rock and waterfall in Tivoli.[3] The massive cliff with the adjacent bridge in the centre of the Edinburgh painting is similar to this setting, albeit without the temple. The domed cubic building in the far background, the outer walls of which are adorned with columns, however reflects of the Dome of the Rock in Jerusalem. Bril probably was familiar with prints of this famous sanctuary.

An autograph repetition of the *Fantastic Landscape* (fig. 138.1) with minor deviations was in Dresden until World War II.[4] It had a companion picture, *View of the Roman Forum* (fig. 138.2), signed and dated 1600.[5] Bril included variations of the ruins of the Temple of Castor and Pollux (from a different angle) and of the Basilica of Maxentius; the dome of Saint Peter's is visible in the distance. The painting in Edinburgh may have had a pendant similar to this one now lost. However, Bril frequently produced autograph variants, sometimes even in pairs. For example, he produced a larger version on canvas of the painting still extant in Dresden with considerable changes and added a companion piece that does not resemble the *Fantastic Landscape* at all.[6]

CHRISTIAN TICO SEIFERT

138

Fig. 138.1 Paul Bril, *Fantastic Landscape*, c. 1600, oil on copper, 22 × 30 cm. Whereabouts unknown

Fig. 138.2 Paul Bril, *View of the Roman Forum*, 1600, oil on copper, 21.5 × 29.5 cm. Gemäldegalerie Alte Meister, Staatliche Kunstsammlungen Dresden

139
HANS ROTTENHAMMER 1564–1625
DIANA AND ACTAEON 1595

Black and red chalk
18.1 × 22.6 cm
Inscriptions: *HRottenhammer/1595*
Roma
Private collection

This drawing depicts a tale told by Ovid (Metamorphoses III, 138–252). The hunter Actaeon spies upon Diana and her nymphs as he discovers them bathing; the goddess transforms him into a stag, which is then torn apart by his hounds. The scene shown is the moment at which the hunter, spear in hand, enters a river clearing where the deity and her cohorts are disporting themselves unclothed.

Actaeon is however portrayed in the left background so diminutively and lightly executed in black chalk that he is not the centre of attention. The artist, Hans Rottenhammer, apparently felt it necessary to identify the subject, because he has inscribed the name "ACTEON" in red chalk above the hunter. The placement of the protagonist in the extreme background represents not only a typically "mannerist" inversion of the composition, but also, by shifting the focus to the nude female figures drawn in red chalk in the middle ground, diminishes the possibility of reading a moralizing or allegorical message into the theme. In contrast with this way of treating mythologies, Rottenhammer intensifies the erotic potential of the theme as it had been recast c. 1556–1559 by Titian in one of his famed *poesie* for Philip II of Spain (now at the National Gallery of Scotland, Edinburgh) (fig. 139.1), and subsequently developed by other artists active in Venice such as Paolo Veronese (painting c. 1560, Philadelphia Museum of Art, Johnson Collection).

While Rottenhammer's inspiration may ultimately be derived from art in Venice, where the Munich-born artist resided between 1591 and 1594 and probably executed his first version of the theme,[1] the inscription in black chalk in the lower right corner (*HRottenhammer/1595 Roma*) indicates that he drew it in Rome, where he sojourned during the years 1594 and 1595. There are numerous other Roman elements present in the drawing. The prominent river god drawn in red and black chalk in the left foreground, who is echoed in the sculpted fountain shown in the centre background, is an element taken from the antique that was revived in Roman Renaissance works, as by Michelangelo. The architectural setting in which the fountain is set also suggests a familiarity with ancient Roman buildings. The

pose of the seated female figure in the right middle ground with raised leg crossed recalls that of the famed ancient sculpture of a boy pulling a thorn from his foot, which is known as the Spinario (now in the Musei Capitolini, Rome). And the pose of Actaeon with spear in right hand and upraised left hand, placed before a sculptural coulisse, seems to be derived from a print of the subject from the circle of Marcantonio Raimondi.[2]

Rottenhammer's adoption of the combination of red and black chalk on a pale ground may also come from his experience in Rome. This technique may be related to the drawing practices employed by Federico Zuccaro and artists in the reformed Accademia di San Luca.[3] This technique had moreover previously been adopted by another northern artist who was probably a member of Rottenhammer's circle in Rome, the Swiss Joseph Heintz the Elder (1564–1609), court artist to Emperor Rudolf II.[4] Slightly after Rottenhammer began his engagement with the theme, Heintz also painted a much copied version of *Diana and Actaeon*, and he also drew studies of nymphs in a technique using two colours of chalks similar to that employed by Rottenhammer.[5]

No painted version of Rottenhammer's composition is known. The signature and date together with the high level of finish, seen especially in the foreground, suggest that it might not have been intended as a study for a painting, but as an independent work in itself. Nevertheless, many painted copies after it by other artists do exist, so it might be hypothesized that Rottenhammer did make a painting after this drawing. If such a painting did exist, and if it were executed on copper – as were many other mythologies and religious subjects by Rottenhammer – then it might have influenced subsequent coppers not only by Heintz but by such Roman painters as Giuseppe Cesari (Cavaliere d'Arpino) and Francesco Albani. In any case, this drawing is probably the second surviving version of the theme by Rottenhammer, which the artist depicted frequently thereafter. He thereby contributed mightily to the success of the subject in cabinet painting north and south of the Alps.[6]

THOMAS DACOSTA KAUFMANN

139

Fig. 139.1 Titian (Tiziano Vecellio), *Diana and Actaeon*, 1556–1559, oil on canvas, 184.5 × 202.2 cm. Duke of Sutherland Collection, on loan to the National Gallery of Scotland

140
FEDERICO ZUCCARO c. 1542/43–1609
AN ALLEGORY OF MEDICINE c. 1596–1597

Pen and brown ink and wash over
traces of black chalk
17.6 × 23.2 cm (oval)
Inscriptions: *APOLLINI / medicina /
SALVTARI*
Agnes Etherington Art Centre,
Queen's University, Kingston

Fig. 140.1 Federico Zuccaro, *Allegory of Medicine*, 1598, fresco. Sala del Disegno, Palazzo Zuccari (Bibliotheca Hertziana), Rome

In 1590 Federico Zuccaro acquired property on the Pincio, the Roman hill dominated by the church of Trinità dei Monti. His purpose was to build a grand house for his family, a studio for himself, and a meeting place for his pupils.[1] Construction began the following year, and fresco decoration of the major rooms continued thereafter. In his will of 1603 Federico bequeathed the Palazzo Zuccaro to the Accademia di San Luca, the artists' association that he had reorganized and of which he became president in 1593. Today the Palazzo Zuccaro houses the Bibliotheca Hertziana, the great art library.

The drawing in Kingston, done in Federico's late, scratchy style, is for part of the frescoed ceiling in a ground-floor room called the Sala del Disegno. The intended function of the room has been interpreted in various ways. Herrmann-Fiore suggested that it may have been used as a library or a study for the painter, and she calls its fresco decoration the most important in the house.[2] More recently, Demirsoy has argued that it was meant for the members of the academy and especially for drawing from life.[3] The Kingston drawing is dominated by the figure of Aesculapius – the Greek and Roman god of healing and son of Apollo – shown seated and semi-nude, with a large book propped open at his left hip and the caduceus clasped in his right hand. On the plinth supporting the god, Federico had initially written *medicina*, but he crossed this out and replaced it with *APOLLINI /SALVTARI*. To the left of the statue, a student studies diligently at a desk laden with books and anatomical models. To the right, two men are dissecting a corpse.

The drawing corresponds relatively closely to an oval medallion on the ceiling, where Aesculapius appears as a living statue on a pedestal surrounded by the medical treatises of Hippocrates, Galen and Avicenna (fig. 140.1). The activities behind him are similar to those in the drawing, but the fresco shows the physician at the left looking admiringly at Aesculapius from the far side of his desk. At right, the two surgeons performing the dissection appear much as they did in the drawing, but an instructor and his student have been added, observing the operation from behind the cadaver. Believing that it was important for artists to understand human anatomy, Federico is known to have organized dissections for the benefit of members of the Accademia di San Luca.[4]

On the other side of the ceiling, Aesculapius is paired with Julius Caesar, who is likewise contained in an oval and raised on a pedestal in front of activities that are relevant to his genius – military prowess. On one of the two narrow sides of the ceiling, an enthroned matron displaying texts in Greek, Latin and Hebrew personifies Science; on the other side Apollo, playing the viol, personifies Music. In the middle of the vault, a personification of Disegno, Jove-like and triple-crowned, reigns supreme, surrounded by his "daughters," who are feminine personifications of Painting, Sculpture and Architecture.[5] All four are seen from below – *di sotto in sù* – with their heads silhouetted against the empyrean. Vasari had also proclaimed the fundamental nature of *disegno* (drawing in its widest sense), but Federico added metaphysical overtones. On the ceiling of the Sala del Disegno, he put into visual terms what he had expounded upon in a lecture to the Accademia in 1594 and what appeared in print more than a decade later in his treatise *L'idea de' pittori scultori ed architetti* (Turin, 1607).

The fresco decoration of the Sala del Disegno has been dated to 1596–1597.[6]

DAVID MCTAVISH

APOLLINI
medicina
SALVTARI

141
CHERUBINO ALBERTI 1553–1615
STUDY OF A MALE NUDE AND LEG STUDIES c. 1596–1600

Red chalk and black chalk
26.3 × 19.7 cm
Annotations: *b.r.c.* and *41*
National Gallery of Canada, Ottawa

As Herrmann Fiore first pointed out, this drawing is a study for a framing figure near the allegory of *Benignancy* in the southwest corner of the Sala Clementina in the Vatican Palace.[1] The patron of this ambitious decorative project, contracted in 1596 and completed by 1600, was the Aldobrandini pope – Clement VIII, who preferred to support Tuscan artists such as those of the Alberti family, as opposed to the likes of Caravaggio or Annibale Carracci. Two stories high, this monumental room glorified, in a particularly ostentatious manner, both the Aldobrandini family and his choice of papal name. The illusion is of a room opened to the sky in which Saint Clement kneels before the Trinity. This was one of several highly visible projects initiated by Pope Clement VIII intended to demonstrate the power and the glory of the Catholic Church with approach of the Jubilee year of 1600.

Compared with the more robust style of his brother Giovanni Alberti (see cat. 142), Cherubino reveals here his more relaxed, elegant side in his approach to the figure. Both artists, however, had an equal competence in their ability to foreshorten figures to be viewed from the ground. This drawing contains alternate ideas for the dangling legs, drawn on a slightly larger scale than the main figure, which

Herrmann Fiore attributed to Giovanni Alberti because of the more intense treatment – a judgment that is not entirely convincing as the touch is consistent overall. In the fresco as completed, these alternatives were rejected for a solution closer to the main drawing here. A related drawing was formerly in the Bertini collection in Prato,[2] but certainly a great many drawings must have been produced to realize this highly complex papal commission.

The Alberti brothers belonged to a family of painters and woodworkers in Sansepolcro, located southeast of Florence, near Arezzo. Among them, Cherubino Alberti had the most natural talent, and was also a major printmaker who produced nearly two hundred engravings after the work of such artists as Raphael, Polidoro da Caravaggio, Rosso and Michelangelo, as well as ancient sculptures. While continuing to honour commissions in their native city, the family also established themselves as leading decorative artists in Rome by 1600, working on an influential group of papal commissions with illusionistic ceiling frescoes of which the Sala Clementina was the largest. There is considerable dispute about the attribution of drawings emitting from their workshop, not least because the brothers often worked in tandem.[3]

DAVID FRANKLIN

41

142
GIOVANNI ALBERTI 1558–1601
STUDY OF A MALE NUDE (RECTO);
STUDY OF A MALE NUDE (VERSO) c. 1596–1600

Black chalk and red chalk on laid
paper
25.2 × 12.3 cm
Annotations: *HL*
National Gallery of Canada,
Ottawa

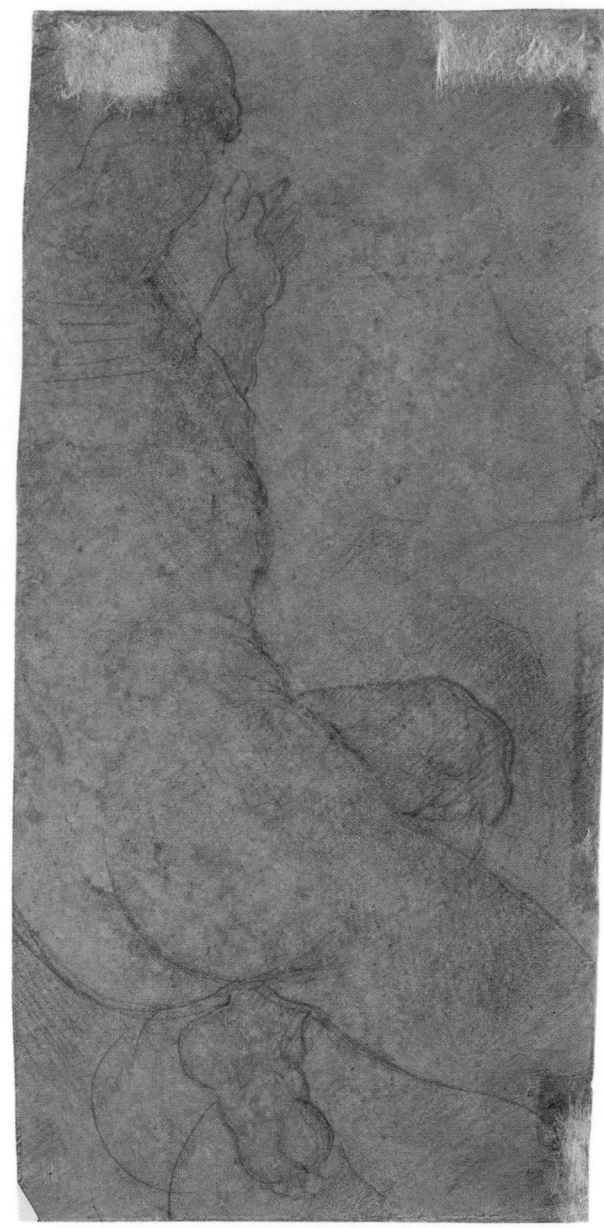

142 (recto)

142 (verso)

Formerly attributed to Pellegrino Tibaldi, this is, as first put forward by Herrmann Fiore, a study for the nude Atlas figure supporting the arms of the Aldobrandini pope Clement VIII depicted in the decoration in the northeast corner of the Sala Clementina in the Vatican Palace.[1] It is located close to the allegorical figure of Religion dominating this part of the vast room glorifying this pope and his family name. Given the influence the Bolognese artist Tibaldi had on both Giovanni and Cherubino Alberti, the earlier attribution is certainly comprehensible. The major influence in this instance, however, is that of Michelangelo. Indeed, this monumental, powerfully foreshortened nude owes much to both the *ignudi* on the ceiling and to the *Last Judgment* in the Sistine Chapel. It is important in this context to remember too that the Carracci were active frescoing comparable nudes in the Gallery in the Palazzo Farnese at the very same date, but in a style more rooted in life drawing. Giovanni's ability to paint complex illusionistic ceilings, as in the Sala Clementina, was, nonetheless, a major influence on Baroque artists with comparable interests.

Although for a particular figure, this study is a virtual demonstration piece by an artist with sophisticated theoretical interests in drawing and foreshortening. Giovanni Alberti was also especially praised by his contemporaries for his competence as a fresco painter of architecture rendered in accurate perspective, both linear and aerial.

The verso of the drawing contains a study of a male nude, hitherto unpublished, also very much in the style of Michelangelo's nudes in the Sistine *Last Judgment*. It cannot yet be connected to any known work.

DAVID FRANKLIN

143

CRISTOFORO RONCALLI,
CALLED **IL POMARANCIO** C. 1553–1626
DIANA KILLING THE CHILDREN OF NIOBE C. 1595–1610

Black chalk with white heightening
on blue paper
27.1 × 42 cm
Inscription: *67*
Teylers Museum, Haarlem

The story of Niobe, queen of Thebes, is told in detail in Ovid's *Metamorphosis* (VI, 146–312). It is a story of human hubris punished by the gods. Proud of her fourteen children, Niobe offended the goddess Latona who had only two children. Not tolerating the excessive pride of the mortals, Latona ordered her children, Diana and Apollo, to kill all of Niobe's daughters and sons. The dramatic event had been represented in a famous sculptural group executed by either Praxiteles or Scopas, which was later housed in the Temple of Apollo Medicus in Rome, according to Pliny's account in the *Historia Naturalis* (XXXVI, 28). In 1583 a spectacular antique group of Niobids, possibly based on the aforementioned Greek sculptures, was unearthed in the Villa Tommassoni in Rome. It was acquired the very same year for 800 *scudi* by Cardinal Ferdinando de' Medici for his villa on the Pincio and displayed in a theatrical, stage-like fashion in the gardens. This dramatic sculptural narrative offered a whole range of exemplary expressions or *affetti* and was studied intensely by contemporary artists. The story of Niobe became vastly popular in the following decades and was interpreted in numerous prints, drawings and paintings, including the large canvases by Abraham Bloemaert in the Statens Museum for Kunst in Copenhagen and by Andrea Camassei in the Palazzo Barberini in Rome.

The present drawing, traditionally given to Agostino Carracci, was attributed by van Tuyll on stylistic grounds to Roncalli. The clearly defined contours of the figures, the vigorous handling and intense use of cross-hatching are typical of his Roman drawings. Roncalli was trained in Volterra and Florence, but later went to Rome, like so many Tuscan artists at the time, and established himself as one of the leading painters in the papal city. His most important commissions include the altarpiece representing the punishment of Ananais and Sapphira for the Vatican Basilica (cat. 145) and the dome of the Santa Casa di Loreto. In Roncalli's Haarlem drawing Diana is entering the scene from the left pointing her bow toward a group of Niobe's daughters who, wracked with fear and gesturing wildly, try to escape divine punishment, while a beautifully foreshortened male is lying already dead on the ground. The composition was clearly inspired by Polidoro da Caravaggio's famous Niobe frieze on the facade of Palazzo Milesi in Rome (fig. 143.1).

SEBASTIAN SCHÜTZE

143

Fig. 143.1 After Polidoro da Caravaggio's *Niobe* frieze, pen and brown ink and wash. Albertina, Vienna

144
CRISTOFORO RONCALLI,
CALLED **IL POMARANCIO** c. 1553–1626
SAINT DOMITILLA BETWEEN SAINTS
NEREO AND ACHILLEO c. 1596–1597

Black chalk, squared in black chalk
41.4 × 26.2 cm
Inscriptions: *B.*
The Courtauld Gallery, London

Domitilla, the niece of Emperor Vespasian, adhered to the Christian faith and also converted her loyal servants Nereo and Achilleo. She was exiled to the island of Ponza and finally suffered her martyrdom in Terracina. Roncalli's squared drawing is highly finished and corresponds closely to the final altarpiece. Domitilla stands in the centre, her eyes raised heavenward and wearing a crown indicating her imperial lineage, while the two servants accompany her on either side. All three saints hold the palms of martyrdom, while flying putti offer them the martyr crowns. Compared with the drawing, the executed altarpiece shows only minor differences, namely the servant on the right seems to be turned slightly more inward and the central putto is more dramatically foreshortened and lifting the crown with both arms upwards. Roncalli's composition programmatically refers to early Christian and medieval imagery, in particular a representation of *Saint Gregory with His Parents* in the Monastery of San Gregorio Magno in Rome. The related fresco – still existing in the late sixteenth century – was annalized in detail in Angelo Rocca's 1597 treatise *S. Gregorii eiusdem parentum imagines* and reproduced on its title page. Baronio included the engraving in the eighth volume of his *Annales Ecclesiastici* in 1599. While the fresco, with its frontal presentation of three standing figures, clearly provides the model for the *Saint Domitilla with Saints Nereo and Achilleo*, the latter also recalls Raphael's famous 1514 *St. Cecilia* for San Giovanni in Monte in Bologna. Roncalli's historicizing altarpiece for Santi Nero e Achilleo itself would then inspire Rubens' 1606–1608 high altarpiece for the Chiesa Nuova in Rome.

SEBASTIAN SCHÜTZE

Fig. 144.1 Cristoforo Roncalli (called il Pomarancio), *Saint Domitilla with Saints Nereo and Achilleo*, 1596–1597, altarpiece. SS. Nereo e Achilleo, Rome

The Courtauld drawing was identified by Pouncey as preparatory for Roncalli's altarpiece for Santi Nereo e Achilleo in Rome (fig. 144.1), which was commissioned in 1596–1597 by Cardinal Cesare Baronio, the greatest historian of the Counter-Reformation church and famous author of the *Annales Ecclesiastici*. A fundamental aspect of the catholic reform was the preservation and recovery of early Christian traditions, which included a renewed interest in the writings of the church fathers and early liturgy and in early Christian churches and the burial sites of venerated martyrs. On becoming a cardinal in 1596 Baronio elected the small early Christian church of Santi Nereo e Achilleo on the Via Appia as his titular church and launched, in 1597–1602, a programmatic campaign of renovation and re-decoration. Roncalli's altarpiece was designed to fit this specific context, with its archaic composition programmatically interpreting the simplicity and truthfulness of early Christian imagery. In a similar historicizing fashion, Baronio also restored and decorated in the very same years the nearby church of San Cesareo a Via Appia and the three oratories dedicated to Saints Andrea, Barbara and Silvia at the convent of San Gregorio Magno on the Celio.

145
CRISTOFORO RONCALLI,
CALLED **IL POMARANCIO** C. 1553–1626
DEATH OF SAPPHIRA C. 1599–1603

Oil on canvas
124.5 × 85 cm
Inscriptions: *Pietro da Cortona; 578*
[verso]
National Gallery of Canada,
Ottawa

After studying in Florence and Siena, the Tuscan painter Cristoforo Roncalli had settled in Rome by 1582. His eclectic Florentine manner, as evidenced in numerous church decorations, was fashionable enough for Pope Clement VIII Aldobrandini (1592–1605) to grant him major commissions in 1597 for decorations in Saint Peter's and San Giovanni in Laterano, in preparation for the Holy Year of 1600.[1]

This large grisaille preparatory oil sketch, or *bozzetto,* is a study for Roncalli's most famous painting, the so-called *altare della bugia,* or Altar of the Lie, painted for the basilica of Saint Peter's in the Vatican Palace. It is so called because in the Bible story (Acts 5:1–11) the protagonist Ananias sells a piece of land and falsely claims to Peter that he has handed over all the profits to the church for redistribution to the poor. Because he holds back some of the money and thereby lies to God, Ananias is rebuked by Peter and drops dead on the spot. A short while later his wife Sapphira tells the same lie and is likewise struck dead. In Roncalli's image Peter stands at centre left with keys and a heavenward gesture, Sapphira's body lies at lower right, and in the distance two men carry off the body of Ananias. The men in the left and right foreground are presumably Apostles, and most of the figures generic bystanders.

This narrative was timely in 1599 when Roncalli was appointed by Clement VIII to supervise the Petrine cycle in Saint Peter's. At the same time, he was awarded the commission to decorate the newly constructed Cappella Clementina. In addition to designs for various mosaics, his contribution extended to the *Sapphira* altarpiece on the *pilone di S. Andrea* (one of the four piers supporting the cupola). The painting, almost eight metres high, was painted in situ on twenty-four pieces of slate. Admired in its time,[2] the colossal work was ruined by humidity and replaced by a mosaic. The original was removed in 1726 to the church of Santa Maria degli Angeli, where it remains (fig. 145.1).

The elaborate genesis of the painting is documented in numerous contracts, the present sketch, and no fewer than sixteen drawings – fifteen of them now in the Uffizi.[3] Roncalli received his first payment in October 1599, and the last in October 1606. A fairly recent innovation, oil sketches had become common practice by Roncalli's day.[4] Given the differences between this extensively wrought sketch, the ensuing drawings and the final product, it seems reasonable to assume that the *bozzetto* represents an early stage in the conception. The most striking difference between the *bozzetto* and the brightly coloured altarpiece is fact that the topless Sapphira becomes fully clothed in the final version – as one would expect given the location.

The most important precedent for this rare subject is Raphael's depiction of the *Death of Ananias* for a tapestry in the nearby Sistine Chapel. There the husband (not the wife) appears dramatically foreshortened in the lower corner. Given the similar palette, it is likely that Roncalli knew Ugo da Carpi's chiaroscuro woodcut after the same Raphael design, and the Apostle at right recalls the head in the same artist's chiaroscuro woodcut of Diogenes, after Parmigianino.[5] There are further homages in the conceit of the lunging man in the upper register, which harks back to other nudes-on-ledges including Michelangelo's Sistine *Ignudi* and the reaching boy in Pontormo's *Vertumnus and Pomona* fresco at Poggio a Caiano. The surrounding flurry of limbs and heads recalls – without representing – the outline of Giambologna's famous *Rape of the Sabine Women* sculpture (1574–1582) in the Loggia dei Lanzi in Florence.

This work exemplifies an important strain of Italian painting in its day. Giulio Mancini, commenting some dozen years after the altarpiece was completed, saw the late-Mannerist, proto-Baroque eclecticism of artists such as Roncalli as representative of one of four modern 'schools' of painting – the others being associated with the names of Caravaggio, the Carracci, and Cavaliere d'Arpino.[6] For all its timeliness, Roncalli's style is firmly rooted in an earlier Florentine tradition dating to the second and third decades of the previous century.

GRAHAM LARKIN

Fig. 145.1 Cristoforo Roncalli (called il Pomarancio), *Death of Sapphira*, c. 1599–1603, oil on slate. Santa Maria degli Angeli, Rome

146
GIUSEPPE CESARI,
CALLED IL CAVALIERE D'ARPINO 1568–1640
REST ON THE FLIGHT TO EGYPT c. 1596–1597

Oil on copper
43.2 × 31.7 cm
Inscription: *F 22*
Museum of Fine Arts, Boston

Fig. 146.1 Giuseppe Cesari (called il Cavaliere d'Arpino), *Flight into Egypt*, 1593–1595, oil on panel, 47 × 34 cm. Galleria Borghese, Rome

During the reign of pope Clement VIII Giuseppe Cesari established himself as the leading painter in Rome. On the occasion of the Holy Year 1600 he was responsible for the redecoration of the transept of San Giovanni in Laterano, executed by a multitude of painters under his guidance. In recognition of his achievements, the pope granted Cesari the title of Cavaliere dell'Abito di Cristo in 1600, and ever since he has been known as the Cavaliere d'Arpino. Apart from a growing number of prestigious public commissions, executed with the assistance of a well-organized and highly specialized workshop, the artist continued to paint smaller scale works for private patrons. The Boston *Flight into Egypt* belongs to a group of exquisitely rendered works in oil on copper. The perfectly even surface allowed a highly refined execution combined with a jewel-like luminosity and brilliance of colour. Such small copper paintings were highly appraised by connoisseur collectors. They were meant to be contemplated and enjoyed in the intimacy of the patrons study, and were often adorned with particularly precious frames.

The Boston painting was exhibited in 1922 at the famous *Mostra della pittura italiana del Sei e Settecento* in Florence with an attribution to the school of Carlo Maratti. In 1928, Longhi recognized the authorship of the Cavaliere d'Arpino. The painting reportedly comes from the Barberini collection, but its early provenance still needs to be established. While not mentioned in any of the seventeenth-century Barberini inventories, Röttgen has identified the painting with an anonymous entry in the 1738–1740 inventory of Cardinal Francesco Barberini Junior: "*Altro Rappresentante il Riposo d'Egitto con S. Giuseppe in atto di toglier dattole, Somarello e Paese dipinto in Roma.*"

The Holy Family is resting on their flight into Egypt in a wide luminous landscape clearly inspired by the work of such northern specialists as Paul Bril who had been working in the papal city since the 1570s. The Virgin holds the child in her lap, while Saint Joseph hands his family a few dates that he has picked from the palm tree. According to the Gospel of Pseudo-Matthew 20–21 at the request of the Christ child, a nearby palm tree miraculously bent down to allow Joseph to pick the dates for the Virgin, while in our representation it is rather Joseph himself who has pulled the palm branches down. The Boston picture is in

excellent condition, allowing us to perceive in every detail the refinement of d'Arpino's brush: from the minute execution of the leaves and the luminosity of the phantasmagoric landscape to the intimacy of expression and the brilliance of red, blue and yellow tones. Röttgen has dated the Boston *Flight into Egypt* convincingly to 1596–1597. Similar qualities can be observed in roughly contemporary small-scale paintings on copper, slate or panel such as the various versions of *Perseus and Andromeda* in Rhode Island, Berlin and London, the *Taking of Christ* in the Villa Borghese, or the *Agony in the Garden* formerly with Colnaghi's in London. A similarly delicate, slightly earlier representation of the *Flight into Egypt*, datable to 1593–1595, is preserved in the Villa Borghese in Rome (fig. 146.1).[1]

SEBASTIAN SCHÜTZE

147
GIUSEPPE CESARI,
CALLED IL CAVALIERE D'ARPINO 1568–1640
DAVID WITH THE HEAD OF GOLIATH 1598

Oil on canvas
100 × 76.5 cm
Inscriptions: *1598 IOSEF.A.*; *Di mano del Cavalier Giuseppe d'Arpino del no 255* [verso]
Koelliker Collection

Fig. 147.1 Michelangelo Merisi da Caravaggio, *Self-Portrait as Bacchus*, c. 1593, oil on canvas, 67 × 53 cm. Galleria Borghese, Rome

Being the favourite painter of pope Clement VIII, the Cavaliere d'Arpino was soon employed by the cardinal nephew Pietro Aldobrandini as well. The recently rediscovered *David with the Head of Goliath* is signed and dated 1598. It is first mentioned in the 1603 inventory of the cardinal's possessions at the Villa Aldobrandini on Monte Magnanapoli: *Un quadro con David con la testa del gigante Golia alto palmi quattro con cornice dorata di Gioseppe d'Arpino segnato n. 255.*[1] The inventory number is still inscribed on the back of the canvas. The painting might well be identified with one of those works, for which the painter received unspecified payments from the cardinal on 11 and 25 march 1599 (Terzaghi). The *David* remained in the Aldobrandini collection for the next generations, and is well documented in the inventory of Ippolito Aldobrandini in 1638, and in those of Olimpia Aldobrandini Junior in 1663 and 1682.[2] In 1787 it was still seen by Friedrich Wilhelm Basilius von Ramdohr in the Villa Aldobrandini a Magnanapoli, which during the Napoleonic occupation became the residence of the French Governor of Rome, General Sextus-Alexandre-Francois Miollis. Possibly during the years of the French occupation, the *David with Head of Goliath* entered the collection of Vincenzo Camuccini only to resurface a few years ago on the art market.

The story of David is told in the first book of Samuel (I, 17). The young shepherd, not yet old enough to partake in the war against the Philistines, brings provisions to his older brothers at the war camp. When he sees Goliath, who again ridicules and offends the Israelites, he fearlessly confronts the giant, killing him with a single stone's throw of his sling. With the giant's own sword David cuts off his victim's head to present to King Saul and his people. The Cavaliere d'Arpino portrays the young hero frontally in a three-quarter length composition of great immediacy. Standing in front of a dark blue drapery, David holds the sword in his right hand, while presenting Goliath's severed head with his raised left arm. He gazes directly at the viewer, his lips parted slightly, wavering between triumph and regret, as if he is just starting to realize the extreme consequences of his accomplishment. The beautifully painted young David, draped in delicate yellow and blue, with his curly blond hair contrasts sharply with the frightful, grey-haired Goliath, thus dramatically emphasizing the heroic quality of his action. The artist had just painted a very similar *David* for the sacristy of the Certosa di San Martino in Naples, but there the young hero seems to fulfill his daunting task with much more self confidence. The physical presence of the protagonist and his direct confrontation with the viewer stand out among d'Arpino's works, and it might very well be that he is responding here to the stunning naturalism of Caravaggio's first Roman works (fig. 147.1).[3] The young Lombard had, some years earlier, worked for a few months in d'Arpino's studio, and would soon challenge the Roman art scene with his first public works in the Contarelli Chapel in San Luigi dei Francesi.

SEBASTIAN SCHÜTZE

147

148
GIUSEPPE CESARI,
CALLED IL CAVALIERE D'ARPINO 1568–1640
AN ANGEL IN FLIGHT 1599–1600

Black and red chalk
38 × 35.7 cm
Inscriptions: *Joseppo d'Arpinas* and *16.10.*
Private collection, New York

Fig. 148.1 Giuseppe Cesari (called il Cavaliere d'Arpino), *Ascension of Christ*, c. 1599–1600, fresco. Cappella del Sacramento, San Giovanni in Laterano, Rome

Preparing Rome for the *anno santo*, the holy year of 1600, Pope Clement VIII launched a major artistic refurbishment of the city's two foremost basilicas, Saint Peter's in the Vatican, and Saint John Lateran, the cathedral of Rome. Both churches underwent significant architectural modifications and subsequent decoration by the leading painters and mosaicists of the time. While the pope entrusted Cristoforo Roncalli with the decoration of the small naves in Saint Peter's and also asked him to decorate the Cappella Clementina (see cat. 145), he put Giuseppe Cesari in charge of the refurbishment of Saint John Lateran. In addition to overseeing and managing numerous artists working under them, both painters also supplied major works themselves. For both, these projects marked the culmination of their careers to date.

The architectural restructuring of the Lateran church, carried out by Giacomo della Porta between 1597 and 1600, involved the raising of the transept, which was effectively turned into a nave of its own, and the introduction of large windows for better illumination. The altar of the Holy Sacrament was transferred from the right transept to the end of the left, and from then on was commonly called the Cappella del Sacramento. According to Baglione, Cesari's biographer, the artist abandoned his work at the Palazzo dei Conservatori on the Campidoglio to heed the pope's call and assume the *sopra intendenza di tutto il lavoro* (supervision of the entire work) in Saint John Lateran.[1] It

was the first project for which Cesari had sole responsibility, and he was also highly paid, receiving about 9,000 *scudi* in total: 8,000 for his own paintings and 1,000 for the supervisory work. Upon completion of the project he was made Cavaliere di Cristo. From then on he was known as the Cavaliere d'Arpino, perhaps that small town's most distinguished son after Cicero.[2]

Under Cesari's supervision, the walls of the transept were decorated with frescoes in two registers, the lower one comprising the fresco cycle dedicated to the life of Emperor Constantine, founder of the basilica circa 313–318 A.D., and the upper one to the apostles. These frescoes were executed between May 1599 and the end of that year or the beginning of the next by Bernardino Cesari, Giuseppe's brother, and by Cesare Nebbia, Giovanni Battista Ricci, Paris Nogari, Cristoforo Roncalli, Giovanni Baglione, and Orazio Gentileschi. The murals were conceived as painted tapestries, with elaborate borders and festoons flanking the Apostles. This decorative scheme was designed and partially executed by Cesari, certainly having in mind Raphael's famous tapestries made for the Sistine Chapel about eighty-five years earlier.

For his own painting contribution, the vast fresco of the *Ascension of Christ*, with its nearly twice-life-size figures (measuring about 14 by 8.5 metres; fig. 148.1), Cesari reserved the most prominent space in the left transept, the rectangular field above the main altar of the Holy Sacrament, built by Pietro Paolo Olivieri in 1600. It shows the figure of Christ flanked by two angels ascending above eleven apostles (Paul is absent, for he was not witness to this event). This fresco, too, was designed as a fake tapestry, an *arazzo finto*, with an extensive border featuring cherubs, stars, and the figures of Charity and Faith. According to Röttgen's comprehensive analysis of this work, it was executed in at least twenty *giornate* (individual plaster patches making up an entire fresco) from the end of 1599. It was unveiled on 10 August 1600 in the presence of the pope who "saw it and praised it."[3]

The frescoes, including Cesari's, follow the compositional rules of the Counter-Reformation laid out by humanists such as Giovanni Battista Armenini, and are characteristic of the style promoted by Clement: They observe the principles of symmetry, narrative clarity, and historical accuracy, while rejecting superfluous ornament that might divert the viewer's attention. Though of horizontal format and slightly different iconography, Cesari's fresco seems also inspired by Raphael's *Transfiguration of Christ* (1517–1520), then located on the high altar of the

Josepo d'Arpinas

148

church of San Pietro in Montorio and today in the Pinacoteca Vaticana, Rome. While avoiding direct quotations, Cesari borrowed from Raphael's painting the idea of the two figures hovering on either side of Christ (Elijah and Moses), which he replaced with the two magnificent angels in his own *Ascension*. The present drawing is a highly finished study for the angel on the left linking the realm of the apostles with that of Heaven above. The drawing is executed in a combination of black and red chalk, Cesari's preferred technique for such figure studies. In its clarity of line and classical conception of the nude, it is arguably one of his most successful emulations of Raphael's figures in Mannerist terms.

There are some differences between our figure and its painted counterpart, notably in the gesture of the right hand, which the artist eventually used for the angel on the right. In keeping with Counter-Reformation requirements, the nude figure in the fresco was draped in a sumptuous garment. Though Cesari must have produced finished drawings for all the figures in his fresco, in addition to composition and detail studies, only two other drawings related to this work are known. One, a relatively small study for the bust of Saint Andrew, was on the art market in 1998; the other, a fragment of the cartoon for the head of Christ, is in the Musée Granet, Aix-en-Provence.[4]

The drawing has been considered to be by Cavaliere d'Arpino's hand at least since its inclusion in de Bisschop's 1671 publication of etchings after original master drawings, *Paradigmata graphices variorum artificum*. This important publication contains more than a hundred reproductions of mostly Italian drawings to which the Dutch artist had direct access, from Michelangelo, Salviati, and Giulio Romano, to later masters such as the Carracci, Domenichino, and Cigoli. One of the choicest selections of Italian drawings ever assembled, it included three drawings by Cavaliere d'Arpino, the other two also being studies of nudes and today preserved at Chatsworth and in the Louvre.[5]

FLORIAN HÄRB

149
GIOVANNI BAGLIONE c. 1566–1643
SAINT PETER BAPTIZING SAINT PRISCA
c. 1599–1600

Pen and ink, brown wash,
red chalk with white heightening
on blue paper
37.7 × 26.6 cm
The British Museum, London

Fig. 149.1 Domenico Passignano,
Saint Peter Baptizing Saint Prisca,
c. 1600, altarpiece. Santa Prisca,
Rome

For the Holy Year 1600 Cardinal Benedetto Giustiniani (1556–1621) undertook an extensive renovation and re-decoration of his titular church of Santa Prisca on the Aventine, which included a frescoed cycle of *Saints* and *Angels with the Instruments of Passion* by Anastasio Fontebuoni in the nave and a high altarpiece with *Saint Peter Baptizing Saint Prisca* by Domenico Passignano (fig. 149.1). As Gere first observed, in those years Baglione was in close contact with both Benedetto and his brother Vincenzo Giustiniani, two of the most influential art patrons and collectors in Rome. His highly finished drawing in the British Museum was likely produced to compete for the new high altarpiece in Santa Prisca. Benedetto Giustiniani's 1621 post-mortem inventory lists five paintings by Baglione, including the two versions of his *Divine Love Conquering Profane Love*, today in Rome and Berlin.[1] A drawing for *Saint Prisca and Her Companion* in Chantilly and a rapid compositional sketch in the British Museum.[2] are also related to the same project. Another Baglione drawing in the collection of Federico Zeri, illustrating *Saint Peter Baptizing Saint Prisca* and *Saint Peter Preaching*, preserves on the verso a detailed *Memoria et schandaglio dele Pitture che vano a sa.ta Prisca per servizio Del. Ill.mo et Rev. mo Sig.re il Sig.re Cardinal Giustiniani.*[3] This detailed account shows that Baglione was hoping to receive from Cardinal Giustiniani the commission for large parts of the decoration of Santa Prisca.

Historical accounts of the life of Saint Prisca are somewhat contradictory and probably conflate the lives of three different personalities. Baptized by the Prince of the Apostles in Rome, she was, after terrifying martyrs, finally beheaded on the Via Ostiense at the age of thirteen under Emperor Claudius. Venerated as the first woman to suffer martyrdom in the West, in the fourth century the basilica on the Aventine was dedicated to her memory.

In Baglione's drawing, the baptism of Sant Prisca is situated in a vast church interior, characterized by two fluted Corinthian columns flanking the altar on the left and a high vaulted ceiling, which clearly alludes to the actual basilica on the Aventine. Peter is dressed in a long antique tunic and towers at the centre of the composition as he stands on a flight of stairs leading to the altar, which is adorned with a representation of the Crucifixion. At the bottom of the stairs Prisca kneels to the left with her arms crossed at her chest, while a young acolyte at right carries two small water carafes on a tray. Peter appears to read from a huge open missal held by a man on the right as he pours, with his right hand, water from a small baptismal cup over Prisca's head. A multitude of onlookers, strictly divided into women to the left and men to the right, assists with the baptism. The whole composition is characterized by solemn simplicity, inscribing the protagonists in a clear-cut triangle in the foreground. It is seen from a decisively low viewpoint, from *sotto in sù*, perfectly adapted for the supposed location on the high altar. The drawing once belonged to the famed collection of Pierre Crozat and was reproduced at the time in a facsimile engraving by P.P.A. Robert and N. le Sueur.

SEBASTIAN SCHÜTZE

150
CARLO SARACENI c. 1579–1620
MARS AND VENUS c. 1600

Oil on copper
39.5 × 55 cm
Carmen Thyssen-Bornemisza
Collection, on loan at the Thyssen-
Bornemisza Museum, Madrid

Around 1598 Saraceni moved from his native Venice to Rome, where he spent the rest of his career, returning to Venice only in 1619 shortly before his death. Baglione and Mancini enlist him among Caravaggio's followers, but it is only during the second decade of the seventeenth century that the young Venetian really adhered to the Caravaggesque model. During the first decade of his Roman sojourn he specialized in paintings of small format and was attracted by the work of northern masters such as Adam Elsheimer. The classical tone and refined execution of his small copper plates suggest the influence of Annibale Carracci, Francesco Albani, Domenichino, and the Cavaliere d'Arpino. The *Mars and Venus* in Madrid belongs to a group of early mythological paintings, like the *Andromeda* in Dijon or the *Bath of Mars and Venus* in Minneapolis, and can be dated to around 1600. It first appeared on the art market in 1979 and was acquired for the Thyssen-Bornemisza collection in 1982.

The love affair between Mars and Venus is described in great detail in Homer's *Odyssey* (VIII, 267–366) and in a more succinct fashion in Ovid's *Metamorphoses* (IV, 169–189). According to Homer, the famous bard Demodocus entertained Ulysses during a banquet at the court of the Phaeacians with the story. Venus' husband, Vulcan, learned about the affair from the sun and both jealous and infuriated, decided to trick the couple. With admirable artistry, he forged invisible yet unbreakable chains, woven thinly like a spider's net, and cocooned them around the nuptial bed. Thereafter he pretended to leave his home for a journey to Lemnos. Burning with passion Mars hurried to join the beautiful goddess of love, but when the two embraced each other on the nuptial bed they were trapped and immobilized by the invisible chains. Vulcan returned and in his fury, alerted the mighty gods to witness the shameful spectacle, exposing the lovers to the laughter of the immortals. Only after Neptune's intervention did Vulcan finally agree to liberate his prisoners.

Saraceni represents the culminating moment of the narrative. Mars and Venus embrace passionately on the sumptuously appointed nuptial bed. The sculptural, "ivory-like"[1] nudes bedded on the bright white linens already seem to be immobilized by Vulcan's invisible chains. The bed is arranged parallel to the picture plane in front of an *all'antica* architecture. An arch decorate richly with statues and reliefs rises directly behind the bed, while at left a long vaulted portico leads to Vulcan's forge. The lovers have strewn their vestments to the right, while Mars' armour lies scattered in the left foreground. Putti frolick with pieces of linen cloth and armour. The winged figure of Cupid gazes narcissistically at his imaged mirrored in Mars' shield. The compositional setting recalls, in reverse, Sodoma's famous *Marriage of Alexander and Roxane* (fig. 150.1), executed in 1518–1519 for the bedchamber of Agostino Chigi in the Villa Farnesina,[2] where the putti playing with Alexander's armour make direct reference to Aetion's famous painting of *Alexander and Roxane* described in Lucian's *Herodot*. Botticelli, in 1487–1488, had already paid hommage to this ancient ekphrasis in his *Mars and Venus,* today in the National Gallery in London.

Saraceni's *Mars and Venus* recreates the classical spirit that Raphael, Sebastiano Del Piombo, Peruzzi, and Sodoma had so successfully evoked in the Villa Farnesina. His copper plate is both extremely refined in its jewel-like execution and exceptionally well preserved. Conceptionally, it engages in a complex dialogue with Homer's text and Lucian's ekphrasis as well as with Sodoma's pictorial interpretation thereof, exploring representational synergies between text and image. Saraceni's virtuosity in imitating the beautiful nudes, the faint sculptures and reliefs, and the richly woven drapery behind the bed, which unfolds a hidden witness, all seem to compete with the supreme artifice and invention of Vulcan's chains, celebrated again and again in Homer's account. The artist's brushes – just like Vulcan's chains – trap the viewer, who, like Narcissus, the inventor of painting, remains petrified in admiration. The painting is a playful tour de force of disguise and disclosure, which represents the art of love as much as the art of painting.

SEBASTIAN SCHÜTZE

Fig. 150.1 Giovanni Antonio Bazzi
(known as Sodoma), *The Marriage
of Alexander the Great and Roxane*,
1518–1519, fresco. Villa Farnesina,
Rome

ADAM ELSHEIMER 1578–1610
THE FLIGHT INTO EGYPT c. 1604

Oil on silvered copper
9.8 × 7.6 cm (oval)
Kimbell Art Museum, Fort Worth,
Texas

The German-born artist Adam Elsheimer is known to have treated the theme of the Flight into Egypt at least twice during his short career. The second of these two paintings, from 1609, is his unquestioned masterpiece, the magical nocturne, on copper, in the Alte Pinakothek, Munich. Its chief sources of wonderment are the starry expanse, the wondrously detailed moon, and the great mushrooming trees that dwarf the Holy travellers in the foreground. The earlier of his two *Flights* is this exquisite copper in the Kimbell Art Museum, Fort Worth, showing the Holy Family bathed in cool light on a perilous mountain traverse. In this tiny oval, the surrounding landscape is much less dominant, although it is painted with the same eye for dramatic realism that made Elsheimer one of the most celebrated artists in Rome during Clement VIII's papacy.

Elsheimer came to Rome around 1600 after periods in his native Frankfurt, southern Germany, and Venice. As a German-trained artist, he was surrounded by great examples of miniaturist painting – including works by Albrecht Dürer – and it is not surprising that he chose to centre his production on small paintings on copper. His preference for this format was only reinforced during his time in Venice, where he became closely associated with the Munich-born painter Hans Rottenhamer I, who also favoured a delicate painting style and made frequent use of copper supports. Rottenhammer showed the younger artist how to assimilate the powerful figural styles of Titian, Tintoretto, and other Venetian masters of the late Renaissance. Elsheimer was quick to endow his art with a new monumentality, a change that is apparent in his impressive *Baptism of Christ* in the National Gallery, London.[1]

The Jubilee of 1600 was likely an important factor in Elsheimer's decision to move south after his short – perhaps year-long – sojourn in Venice. He was already installed in Rome by April of that year, joining the large community of international artists who had been gathering in the Eternal City for decades.[2] Blessed with the uncanny ability to absorb a great diversity of styles and forge them into one of singular power, Elsheimer was at home in Rome, culling from the art of antiquity, Caravaggio, and Netherlandish landscape specialists like Paul Bril. Bril had been in Rome for more than twenty years and was likely one of the first artists whom Elsheimer sought out, especially considering that Rottenhamer had previously collaborated with Bril and could have furnished an introduction.[3] By all accounts, Bril and Elsheimer bonded quickly. Not only were they close friends – Bril was a witness at Elsheimer's wedding in

1606 – but also they were great admirers of each other's art.[4] This last point is amply documented by the present *Flight into Egypt,* whose glorious landscape is inconceivable without Bril's example. In composing the *Flight into Egypt,* Elsheimer was particularly drawn to Bril's cool blue skies, high points-of-view, and distant recessions, traits that are apparent in Bril's *Fantastic Landscape* in the National Gallery of Scotland, Edinburgh (cat. 138). Bril's influence is also evident in the trees, which appear as shimmering confections of green and gold. The one major change to Bril's approach is that Elsheimer has suffused the most distant reaches of his alpine view with a greater haziness or atmospheric perspective.

The connection to Bril is one part of the argument that the *Flight into Egypt* likely dates from about 1604. Already by this time, Bril had lightened his landscape palette considerably, and Elsheimer, too, was starting to bathe his landscapes in a softer, more crepuscular light. Andrews originally advanced the idea that the *Flight into Egypt* was stylistically close to a series of saints and Old Testament figures painted by Elsheimer for a cabinet now at Petworth House.[5] Andrews claimed this series had to date before 1605 because its landscapes exerted a strong influence on Elsheimer's pupil David Teniers I, who is known to have returned to Antwerp by 1605.[6] To this writer's eyes, the similarities are not so precise as to allow Teniers to function as a reliable dating device for the series. Even if we accept this date as correct, we must still question how similar they are to the *Flight into Egypt*. A major difference concerns the brushwork. The *Flight into Egypt* is much more tightly painted, and also in consideration of its more intensely blue sky, there seems good reason to date it slightly prior to the Petworth series – perhaps around 1604, which would bring it closer to works like Elsheimer's *Stoning of Saint Stephen* in the National Gallery of Scotland, Edinburgh, a work owned by Bril in which the landscape is sometimes thought to have been painted by Bril.[7]

The enormous sensitivity that Elsheimer brought to his renderings of the landscape may reflect influences well beyond Bril. A tailor's son with little formal schooling, he kept company with a deeply intellectual crowd, some of whom – like Federico Cesi, founder of the Accademia dei Lincei – were among Europe's leading naturalists.[8] Plausible theories have been advanced that Elsheimer was conversant on topics such as optics, astronomy, and natural philosophy and that his landscapes, in the way they combine a poetic vision of nature with rigorous observation, reflect these discourses.[9]

Beyond Rome's scientific community, Elsheimer was thoroughly enmeshed in the city's artistic life and a constant source of inspiration for all types of painters, from Peter Paul Rubens to Carlo Saraceni. He appears to have been exceptionally open to sharing his works with his fellow artists, and we can be certain that the present painting was seen and admired. Three early copies of it are known (one with a variation on the landscape), and strong echoes are present in paintings by Pieter Lastman and Ludovico Cardi, "il Cigoli".[10]

C.D. DICKERSON III

151

4   D. Frapiccini, "Lorenzo Lotto tra frequentazioni curiali e strategie mercantili," in *Pittura Veneta nelle Marche*, ed. V. Curzi (Milan, 2000), pp. 149–173.
5   A. Nesselrath, "L. Lotto in the 'Stanza della Segnatura,'" *The Burlington Magazine* 142 (January 2000), pp. 4–12; A. Nesselrath, "Lotto as Raphael's Collaborator in the Stanza di Eliodoro," *The Burlington Magazine* 146 (November 2004), pp. 732–741.

9
MICHELANGELO BUONARROTI, CALLED MICHELANGELO
1475–1564
Study for the Nude Youth over the Prophet Daniel on the Sistine Ceiling (recto); *Figure Studies for the Sistine Ceiling* (verso)
c. 1510–1511
Black and red chalk (recto); red chalk with white heightening (verso)
34.3 × 24.3 cm
Annotations: 55; (verso) *V. /.*
The Cleveland Museum of Art (40.465.a–b)
Gift in memory of Henry G. Dalton by his nephews George S. Kendrick and Harry D. Kendrick, 1940

Provenance: Mariette (L. 1852); Alexander von Frey, Romania; Henry G. Dalton.

References: Miller 1990, pp. 146–174; De Grazia and Foster 2000, no. 6.

Notes
1   De Grazia and Foster 2000, p. 30.
2   G. Goldner, review of "Master Drawings from the Cleveland Museum of Art," in *Master Drawings* 40 (2002), p. 175.

10
MICHELANGELO BUONARROTI, CALLED MICHELANGELO
1475–1564
Studies for the Libyan Sibyl, c. 1511 (recto); *Studies for the* Libyan Sibyl *and a Small Sketch for a Seated Figure*, c. 1510–1511 (verso)
Red chalk with white heightening (recto); black chalk or charcoal (verso)
28.9 × 21.4 cm
Annotations: *di Michel Angelo bona Roti; 58; 58; nᵒ. 2i* ." (verso)
The Metropolitan Museum of Art, New York (24.197.2)
Purchase, Joseph Pulitzer Bequest, 1924

Provenance: Buonarroti family, Florence (?); Carlo Maratti, Rome (?); Andrea Procaccini, Rome and La Granja de San Ildefonso (?); Aureliano de Beruete, Madrid; by inheritance, his wife Isabel de Regoyos, Madrid; purchased by The Metropolitan Museum of Art, 1924.

References: Utrillo 1907, pp. 193–198, fig. 198; Thode 1908, vol. 1, pp. 167, 254, 378, fig. LVI; Frey 1909, vol. 1, pp. 2–4, vol. 3, pls. 4, 5; Brinckmann 1925, no. 32, p. 33, pl. 32; Burroughs 1925, pp. 6–14; Berenson 1938, vol. 2, no. 1544D, pp. 194–195, fig. 631; Popham and Wilde 1949, no. 486, p. 268; Wilde 1953, pp. 26, 101; Parker 1956, under no. 297, p. 141; Dussler 1959, pp. 183–184, no. 339, pls. 39, 174; Berenson 1961, vol. 2, p. 334, no. 1544D, figs. 564, 565; Bean and Stampfle 1965, no. 36, p. 34, pl. 36; Goldscheider 1966, p. 39, fig. 39; Tolnay 1969, vol. 2, pp. 61, 204, 209, pls. 80, 236; Hartt 1970, pp. 83–84, figs. 87–88, 100; Tolnay 1975–1980, vol. 1, pp. 116–117, no. 156; Perrig 1976, pp. 42, 61, 72–73, 76, pl. 54, fig. 21; Bean and Turçic 1982, p. 137, fig. 131; Hirst 1988a, p. 67; Hirst 1988b, no. 16, pp. 42–43; Perrig 1991, pp. 22, 26, 30, 50–51, 58, 132 (nn. 167–168), fig. 8 (recto); Kornell 1992, pp. 162–163, fig. 154; Bambach 1997, pp. 69–70; Wallace

1998, p. 168, fig. 168; Logan and Plomp 2005, pp. 66–69, no. 3; Chapman 2005, pp. 134–137; Joannides 2007, pp. 32, 36, 51, 120–122, 125–126, under no. 18; Zöllner et al. 2007, pp. 528, pl. 69 recto only ("after Michelangelo").

Notes
1   F. Mancinelli, "Rapporto sul restauro degli affreschi della volta," in *Michelangelo, La Cappella Sistina, Documentazione e Interpretazione*, 3 vols., ed. G. Colalucci et al. (Vatican City-Tokyo, 1994), II, pp. 124–126, fig. 52, and following unpaginated diagrams.
2   Examples of early Sistine studies in soft black chalk are British Museum inv. 1859-6-25-567, London; Teylers Museum inv. A 18 verso, Haarlem; Casa Buonarroti inv. nos. 64 F and 75 F, Florence; Musée du Louvre, Département des Arts Graphiques inv. 860, Paris; Biblioteca Reale inv. 15627 D.C., Turin.
3   See the sheets Ashmolean Museum nos. 1846.45 to 1846.52, Oxford.
4   Joannides 2007, pp. 120–126, no. 18, with previous bibliography.
5   Summary of discussion in Joannides 2007, p. 120.
6   Mancinelli, "Tavole: La volta restaurata" and "Rapporto sul restauro degli affreschi della volta," in *La Cappella Sistina*.
7   Mancinelli, "Rapporto sul restauro degli affreschi della volta," in *La Capella Sistina*, vol. II, pp. 16–22, essays by P. Silvan, F. Mancinelli, and A. Forcellino in ibid., vol. 3, pp. 37–59.
8   Compare esp. A. Condivi, *Vita di Michelangelo Buonarroti ...*, Rome, 1553, p. 24: *fatto il quadro del Diluuio, se gli cominciò l'opera a muffare che appena si scorgeuan le figure... Mandò il Papa il San Gallo, il quale cio vedendo, conobbe ch'egli haueua data la calcina troppo acquosa e per questo calando l'umore, faceua quell' effetto* (A. Condivi, *The Life of Michelangelo*, English trans. A.S. Wohl [Baton Rouge, 1976], p. 57).
9   C.C. Bambach, *Drawing and Painting in the Italian Renaissance Workshop: Theory and Practice, 1300–1600*, Cambridge, New York, Melbourne 1999, pp. 66–69.
10   Vasari-Milanesi 1878–1885, vol. 7, p. 216: *... la pittura passata una certa età, e massimamente il lavorare in fresco, non è arte da vecchi*.
11   L.B. Ciulich and P. Barocchi, *I Ricordi di Michelangelo* (Florence, 1970), pp. 2–3, no. 3.
12   The date of completion is marked by the entry in the diary of Paris de Grassis, papal master of ceremonies: *Vesperae in vigilia omnium sanctorum ... Hodie primum capella nostra, pingi finita, aperta est* (E. H. Ramsden, *The Letters of Michelangelo*, Stanford, 1963, vol. 1, p. 76). On the chronology, compare Creighton E. Gilbert, "On the Absolute Dates of the Parts of the Sistine Ceiling," *Michelangelo On and Off the Sistine Ceiling*, New York 1994, pp. 191–224 (reprint of essay, *Art History*, vol. 3, [1980], pp. 158–181); Mancinelli, *La Cappella Sistina*, pp. 16–22; K. Weil-Garris Brandt, "Atti del Convegno Internazionale di Studi, Roma, marzo 1990," in *La Cappella Sistina*, vol. 3, pp. iv–vii.
13   P. Barocchi and R.Ristori, *Il Carteggio di Michelangelo* (Florence, 1965), vol. 1, p. 112, no. 80.
14   Mancinelli, "Rapporto," in *La Cappella Sistina*, pp. 124–126, fig. 52, and following unpaginated diagrams; C.C. Bambach, "Problemi di tecnica nei cartoni di Michelangelo per la Cappella Sistina," in *La Cappella Sistina*, vol. 3 (Vatican City-Tokyo, 1994), pp. 83–102.
15   One of Michelangelo's earliest sheets using red chalk, dating to the early 1490s, is Staatliche Graphische Sammlung inv. 2191 recto, Munich.

16   For a variety of opinions regarding the attributions and rejected attributions of the red-chalk Sistine drawings associated with Michelangelo, compare Thode 1908; Frey 1909; Brinckmann 1925; Berenson 1938, vol. 2; Wilde 1953; Dussler 1959; Berenson 1961, vol. 2; Tolnay 1969, vol. 2; Tolnay 1975–1980, vol. 1; Perrig 1976; Hirst 1988a; Hirst 1988b; Perrig 1991; Bambach 1997, pp. 69–70; van Tuyll van Serooskerken 2000, pp. 100–108, nos. 48–50; Zöllner et al. 2007.
17   van Tuyll van Serooskerken 2000, pp. 100–108, nos. 48–50.
18   Compare Perrig 1976, pp. 42, 61, 72–73, 76, pl. 54, fig. 21; Perrig 1991, pp. 22, 26, 30, 50–51, 58, 138 (nn. 167–68); Zöllner et al. 2007, pp. 528, pl. 69 recto only ("after Michelangelo").
19   For example, the sheets British Museum inv. 1859-6-25-567, London; Teylers Museum inv. A 18 verso, Haarlem; Casa Buonarroti inv. nos. 64 F and 75 F, Florence; Musée du Louvre, Département des Arts Graphiques inv. 860, Paris.
20   The sheet Uffizi inv. 2318 F, Florence, in red chalk measures 28.9 × 21.6 cm.
21   As pointed out in Bambach 1997, "Michelangelo's Drawings," pp. 69–70. For example, see the sheet Casa Buonarroti 36 F verso, bearing a "nᵒ. 20."
22   On the "Bona Roti" collector, see now esp. Joannides 2007, pp. 30–32. Joannides has also noted that many of this group of sheets bears inscriptions by the "Irregular Numbering Collector."
23   Joannides 2007, pp. 22–23.
24   Tolnay 1975–1980, vol. 1, pp. 116–117, no. 156; Logan and Plomp 2005, p. 66, no. 3.
25   Manuela B. Mena Marqués, *La procedencia del dibujo de la Sibila Líbica de Miguel Angel en el Metropolitan Museum de Nueva York* (Madrid, 1982), pp. 90–94, fig. 1. The Real Academia of San Fernando did not buy all of the drawings in the possession of Procaccini's widow; a year later in 1776 another group with this provenance was offered for purchase to the Academy and was turned down.
26   Burroughs 1925, p. 7.

11
RAFFAELLO SANZIO, CALLED RAPHAEL
1483–1520
Bindo Altoviti
c. 1512
Oil on panel
59.5 × 43.8 cm
National Gallery of Art, Washington (1943.4.33)
Samuel H. Kress Collection

Provenance: Bindo Altoviti, 1550, and his descendants in Florence and Rome; Prince Ludwig of Bavaria, 1808; Alte Pinakotek, Munich; Agnew & Sons, London, 1938; Duveen, London; Samuel H. Kress, New York, 1940; donated by Kress to the National Gallery of Art, 1943.

Notes
1   Vasari–Milanesi, 1878–1885, vol. IV, p. 351: "A Bindo Altoviti fece il ritratto suo quando ere giovane che è tenuto stupendissimo." [author's translation].
2   D.A. Brown and J. Van Nimmen, *Raphael and the Beautiful Banker. The Story of the Bindo Altoviti Portrait* (New Haven and London, 2005), pp. 20–23.
3   Brown and Van Nimmen, *Raphael*, pp. 27–29.
4   For an exhaustive treatment of Bindo's activities as patron and collector see Chong et al. 2004.
5   Brown and Van Nimmen, *Raphael*, 2005, pp. 25–26.
6   Vasari–Milanesi 1878–1885, vol. V, p. 567

7   For the Giorgionesque portrait see most recently D.A. Brown, "Portraits of Men," in *Bellini, Giorgione, Titian, and the Renaissance of Venetian Painting*, exh. cat. (Washington, 2006), pp. 236–243; and M. Koos, *Bildnisse des Begehrens. Das lyrische Männerporträt in der Venezianischen Malerei des frühen Jahrhunderts, Giorgione, Tizian, und ihr Umkreis* (Berlin, 2006).
8   About Sebastiano's portrait see Brown in *Bellini*, 2006, cat. no. 51, pp. 258–261; and *Sebastiano del Piombo 1485–1547*, exh. cat. (Rome and Berlin, 2008), cat. no. 23, pp. 148–149.

12
BALDASSARRE PERUZZI
1481–1536
River God Tiber
1512–1520
Pen and brown ink and brown wash with white heightening on brown prepared paper
23.4 × 34.8 cm
The British Museum, London (1946-7-13-15)

Provenance: Samuel Woodburn; Phillipps-Fenwick.

References: Pouncey and Gere 1962, no. 244; Frommel 1968, no. 99; Bober and Rubenstein 1986, p. 103; A. Gnann in Vienna 1999, no. 59.

Notes
1   According to the inventories of the Woodburn and Phillipps-Fenwick? collections, the attribution to Giulio Romano was noted in pencil on the mount. This attribution was subsequently confirmed by A.E. Popham in his *Catalogue of Drawings in the Collection Formed by Sir Thomas Phillipps* (London, 1935), p. 61, no. 11.
2   Pouncey's attribution was made in June 1948; see N. Turner, *The Study of Italian Drawings: The Contribution of Philip Pouncey* (London, 1994), p. 113, no. 138.
3   Gabinetto Disegni e Stampe degli Uffizi (569E); see Petrioli Tofani 1986, p. 254, no. 569E.
4   The attribution to Peruzzi was similarly by Pouncey, followed by Hartt (handwritten notes on the inventory card and the mount). For the recent literature on this drawing see A. Gnann in Vienna 1999, no. 193.
5   For the history of the statue see F. Haskell and N. Penny, *Taste and the Antique: The Lure of Classical Sculpture, 1500–1900* (New Haven and London, 1981), pp. 310–311, no. 79; Bober and Rubinstein 1986, pp. 102–103, no. 66.
6   See, for example, H.H. Brummer, *The Statue Court in the Vatican Belvedere* (Stockholm, 1970), pp. 191–204; Bober and Rubinstein 1986, p. 103.
7   See M. Winner, "La collocazione degli fluviali nel Cortile delle Statue e il restauro del Laocoonte Montorsoli," in *Il Cortile delle Statue / Der Statuenhof des Belvedere im Vatikan*, ed. M. Winner, B. Andrete, and C. Pietrangeli (Mainz, 1998), pp. 118–119.
8   Brummer, *The Statue Court in the Vatican Belevedere*, pp. 191–192.
9   Gnann in Vienna 1999, no. 59.
10   G.B. Armenini, *De' veri precetti della pittura* (Ravenna, 1587), p. 203; Vasari 1966–1987, vol. 4, p. 596.

13
RAFFAELLO SANZIO, CALLED RAPHAEL
1483–1520
Saint Paul Preaching in Athens
c. 1514–1516
Red chalk with traces of stylus
27.8 × 41.8 cm [maximum]
Inscriptions: *Raffaello*; *198*; *Rafaello da / urbino*; *52*
Gabinetto Disegni e Stampe degli Uffizi, Florence (540 E)

Provenance: bought by Cardinal Leopoldo de' Medici, 1658.

References: Oberhuber 1972, p. 137, no. 451; Shearman 1972, pp. 105–106 n. 56, 124, fig. 39; Petrioli Tofani and De Vecchi 1982, pp. 13–20, no. 25; Ferino Pagden in Marmugi 1984, pp. 280, 304–305, no. 13 (with previous literature); Ames-Lewis 1986, pp. 134–136, fig. 145; Petrioli Tofani 1986, pp. 242–243; A. Gnann in Mantua 1999, p. 74, under no. 12; Shearman 2007, p. 90.

Notes

1 Fundamental to the study of Raphael's cartoons and tapestries is Shearman 1972, esp. pp. 1–20, p. 138ff. For an analysis of issues relating to the tapestries and cartoons see also J. White and J. Shearman, "Raphael's Tapestries and Their Cartoons," *The Art Bulletin* 40 (1958), pp. 193–221, 299–323; J. Pope-Hennessy, *Raffaello* (Turin, 1983), pp. 67–69. On the tapestries themselves see R. Harprath, "Raffaels Teppiche in der Sixtinischen Kapelle," in Oberhuber 1986, pp. 117–126.
2 The planning of the fresco decoration of the Stanza dell'Incendio del Borgo is among the projects that dates to this highly productive period in which the artist had many commissions; see K. Oberhuber, "Die Fresken der Stanza dell'Incendio in Werk Raffaels," *Jahrbuch der Kunsthistorischen Sammlungen in Wien* 12 (1962), pp. 23–72, and L. Dussler, *Raphael: A Critical Catalogue of His Pictures, Wall-Paintings and Tapestries* (London and New York, 1971), pp. 82–86. After the death of Bramante in 1514, Raphael was appointed architect of Saint Peter's, as well as curator of Roman antiquities; see R. Jones and N. Penny, *Raphael* (New Haven, 1983), pp. 199–205.
3 On the cycle's iconographic program see D. Ettlinger, *The Sistine Chapel before Michelangelo* (Oxford, 1965); D. Redig de Campos, "I Tituli degli affreschi del Quattrocento nella Cappella Sistina," *Rendiconti della Pontificia Accademia Romana di Archeologia* 42 (1970), pp. 299–314. See also J. Shearman, "La costruzione della Cappella e la prima decorazione al tempo di Sisto IV," in *La Cappella Sistina: I primi restauri. La scoperta del colore* (Novara, 1986), pp. 22–87.
4 On the payments see V. Golzio, *Raffaello nei documenti, nelle testimonianze dei contemporanei e nella letteratura del suo secolo* (Vatican City, 1936, rev. ed., Farnborough, 1971), pp. 38, 51; J. Shearman, *Raphael in Early Modern Sources (1483–1602)* (New Haven and London, 2003), vol. 1, pp. 205–206, no. 1515/6, pp. 271–272, no. 1516/31 (with bibliography). There is a tradition that states that Leo X had a second set of the tapestries (formerly in Berlin, and since destroyed) woven for presentation to Henry VIII of England; see Shearman 1972, pp. 43, 143 note 107; T. Campbell, "School of Raphael Tapestries in the Collection of Henry VIII," *The Burlington Magazine* 138:1115 (1996), pp. 69–78.
5 The cartoons passed through the workshop of Jan van Tieghen, where they remained until about 1540. In Genoa in 1623, they were purchased by Charles I of England, on the advice of Rubens. They were located at Hampton Court in 1698, which is apparently about when they were transferred to canvas. Recent cleaning and laboratory examination of the cartoons brought to light some contributions by assistants as well as a pentimento showing through Saint Paul's ear in the cartoon of *Saint Paul Preaching in Athens*; see S. Fermor and A. Derbyshire, "The Raphael Tapestry Cartoons Re-examined," *The Burlington Magazine* 140:1141 (1998), p. 244, fig. 22.
6 On the provenance of the drawing see Oberhuber 1972; A. Forlani Tempesti in *Omaggio a Leopoldo de' Medici: Parte I, Disegni*, exh. cat., ed. A. Forlani Tempesti and A. Petrioli Tofani (Florence, 1976), p. 77, no. 53; M. Fileti Mazza, ed., *Archivio del collezionismo mediceo: Il Cardinal Leopoldo. Volume II, Rapporti con il mercato emiliano* (Milan, 1993), vol. 2, p. 998. The three figures on the left were reproduced in prints by Stefano Mulinari in 1774 (no. 74) with the inscriptions *Raffaello inv: e del:* and *S. Mulinari inci:* (Gabinetto Disegni e Stampe degli Uffizi, inv. 403 st. vol.).
7 See the Uffizi inventory card; P.N. Ferri, *Catalogo dei disegni esposti al pubblico nel Corridoio del Ponte Vecchio nella R. Galleria degli Uffizi, con l'indice dei nomi degli Artefici* (Florence, 1881), p. 33; P.N. Ferri, *Catalogo riassuntivo della Raccolta di disegni antichi e moderni posseduta dalla R. Galleria degli Uffizi compilato ora per la prima volta dal conservatore Pasquale Nerino Ferri* (Rome, 1890), p. 204; P.N. Ferri, "Catalogo dei Disegni, Cartoni e Bozzetti esposti al pubblico nella R. Galleria degli Uffizi ed in altri Musei di Firenze compilato da Pasquale Nerino Ferri, ispettore preposto al Gabinetto dei disegni e delle stampe nella detta Galleria" (manuscript, 1895–1901, in the Gabinetto Disegni e Stampe degli Uffizi), p. 72v.
8 This reattribution was made by Giulia Sinibaldi (archival report and handwritten note on the Uffizi inventory card).
9 See Shearman 1972, pp. 106–107; Joannides 1983, p. 225, no. 366r; Ames-Lewis 1986, p. 136, fig. 146.
10 Oberhuber 1972, p. 139, no. 452. On the extant preparatory drawings for the Sistine Chapel tapestries and the role of the master's assistants see Ames-Lewis 1986, pp. 126–136 (with bibliography); Shearman, "L'organizzazione della bottega di Raffaello," in Shearman 2007, pp. 88–95.
11 Inv. 1217E; see Ferino Pagden in Marmugi 1984, p. 306, no. 14 (with bibliography). On the sheets in the Louvre and in Florence and the related attribution history see also Harprath, "Raffaels Teppiche," p. 125; Cordellier and Py 1992, p. 280, no. 413 (with bibliography); Gnann in Mantua 1999, p. 74, under no. 12; Shearman 2007, p. 90. There is a further copy of the Louvre's *modello* in the Metropolitan Museum in New York (Vanderbilt Gift 80-3-30); see Ferino Pagden in Marmugi 1984, p. 306. For a listing of other copies mentioned in the literature see Shearman 1972, p. 107, note 61.
12 For an analysis of the style employed by Raphael in his graphic work relating to the tapestries see Oberhuber, "Lo stile classico di Raffaello e la sua evoluzione a Roma fino al 1527," in Mantua 1999, pp. 17–18.
13 On Raphael's work method in planning the design see Shearman 1972, pp. 105–111; Ferino Pagden in Marmugi 1984, p. 304; Ames-Lewis 1986, pp. 134–136.
14 On the variants in the Uffizi drawing, the Louvre *modello*, the cartoon, and the tapestry see Shearman 1972, pp. 105–107; Ferino Pagden in Marmugi 1984, p. 305.
15 These are the prints *Christ before Pilate* from the "Small Passion" series (see Oberhuber 1972, no. 451; Shearman 1972, p. 124) and *The Presentation of the Virgin in the Temple* from the Life of the Virgin series (see R. Quednau, "Raphael und 'alcune stampe di maniera tedesca,'" in *Zeitschrift für Kunstgeschichte* 46 [1983], pp. 161–162).
16 Vasari-Milanesi 1878–1885, vol. 5, p. 413.
17 See H. Delaborde, *Marc-Antoine Raimondi* (Paris, 1888?), pp. 133–134, no. 84; P. Kristeller, "Marcantons Beziehungen zu Raffael," *Jahrbuch der Königlich Preussischen Kunstsammlungen*, vol. 28 (Berlin, 1907), pp. 206–207; Gnann in Mantua 1999, p. 74, no. 12 (with bibliography and an analysis of the print).

14
PIERO BUONACCORSI, CALLED PERINO DEL VAGA
1501–1547
Virgin and Child with Saints, Crowned by Angels and Adored by Leo X
c. 1515–1518
Red chalk, squared
45.8 × 37.8 cm
Annotations: *Fra Sebastiano dal / Piombo / Ecole Vénitienne; Ste Famille à la sanguine* (verso); Lugt stamp: *1886*
Musée du Louvre, Paris (10070)

Provenance: Ch.-P.-J.-B. de Bourgevin Vialart de Saint-Morys; confiscated as the property of emigrés, 1793; returned to the Museum, 1796–1797.

References: Davidson 1966, no. 2; Oberhuber 1966, p. 175; Bacou and Béguin 1983, no. 83; Cordellier in Paris 1992, no. 35; Parma 2001, no. 12.

Notes

1 P. Pouncey, handwritten note, cited by R. Bacou in *Nouvelles attributions: Dessins du XVIe au XVIIIe siècle* (Paris, 1978), no. 32.
2 Davidson 1966, no. 2.
3 Parma 2001, p. 106.
4 Published in N. Dacos, "Tommaso Vincidor, un élève de Raphaël aux Pays-Bas," in *Études d'histoire de l'art publiées par l'Institut historique belge de Rome, tome IV – Relations artistiques entre les Pays-Bas et l'Italie à la Renaissance* (Brussels and Rome, 1980), pp. 94–95.
5 Galleria Palatina, Florence (88).
6 T. Campbell, "Pope Leo X's Consitorial 'Letto de paramento' and the Boughton House Cartoons," *The Burlington Magazine* 138:1120 (July 1996), pp. 436–445.
7 P. Pouncey, handwritten note.
8 Galleria Nazionale dell'Umbria, Perugia, dated "M.D.XXIIII." F.F. Mancini and P. Scarpellini, eds., *Pittura in Umbria tra il 1480 e il 1540: Premesse e sviluppi nei tempi di Perugino e Raffaello*, [entry by Anna Alberti](Milan, 1983), p. 92.
9 Musée des Beaux-Arts, Lille (Pl. 458).
10 Respectively, in situ and in the Galleria Nazionale dell'Umbria, Perugia; see Mancini and Scarpellini, *Pittura in Umbria*, pp. 144, 92.
11 According to Davidson (1966), the pope's death may have interrupted the completion of Perino's work.
12 Cordellier in Paris 1992, p. 75.
13 Ciseri, cited by A. Cecchi in Parma 2001, p. 42.
14 Ciseri, ibid. Our dating of c. 1515–1518 implies a downgrading of the supposed importance in this work of Raphaelesque models from Rome, a view that has been repeated often in the literature since 1966.
15 Ciseri, ibid.
16 Davidson 1966, p. 12; Oberhuber 1966, p. 175; Oberhuber in Parma 2001, p. 53; Gere 1971, p. 12; Bacou and Béguin 1983, p. 75; Cordellier in Paris 1992, p. 75.
17 Galleria Palatina, Florence; see Cordellier in Paris 1992, p. 75.
18 Musée du Louvre, Paris; see Davidson 1966, p. 12.
19 Church of Our Lady, Bruges; see Davidson 1966, ibid.
20 Ibid.
21 Cordellier in Paris 1992, p. 75.

15
BALDASSARE PERUZZI
1481–1536
Nativity
c. 1515
Oil on panel
100.6 × 76.4 cm
Private collection, Europe

Provenance: Casa Vai, Prato. Sebright Collection, Beechwood, near Boxmoor, as Giovanni Francesco Penni. Pouncey Collection, London by 1965. On loan to the Fitzwilliam Museum, Cambridge. Private collection, Europe.

References: Frommel 1968, pp. 79–80, no. 40; Brugnoli 1973, pp. 115–116.

Notes

1 For the painting see esp. Frommel 1968, pp. 79–80, no. 40. The attribution has never been questioned, although P. De Castris has tentatively suggested that Polidoro da Caravaggio might have worked on it (in *Polidoro da Caravaggio*, Naples, 2001, p. 215, fig. 262).
2 According to the entry in *Between Renaissance and Baroque, European Art 1520–1600*, exh. cat., Manchester, 1965, no. 185.

16
RAFFAELLO SANZIO, CALLED RAPHAEL
1483–1520
Copy after a Horse on the Quirinal Hill (recto)
Copies after Antiquity (verso)
c. 1515
Red chalk and pen and brown ink, with stylus underdrawing and traces of leadpoint (recto); pen and brown ink (verso)
21.9 × 27.4 cm
Annotations: numerical notations overall. *desegno fato a Roma. D-1-. Perino 2 8.* (verso)
National Gallery of Art, Washington (1993.51.3.a)
Woodner Collection

Provenance: Unidentified Italian collection (armorial blind stamp like L. 2736a); P. Lely (L. 2092); presumably W. Cavendish, 2nd Duke of Devonshire (L. 718), by descent at Chatsworth; Sold Christie's, 6 July 1987, lot 10, purchased Colnaghi's; I. Woodner and family; donation to NGA, 1993.

References: Joannides 1983, p. 234, no. 398; Nesselrath in Frommel et al. 1984, p. 408, no. 3.2.10; Oberhuber in Grasselli 1995, no. 33.

Notes

1 P. Giovio in *Scritti d'Arte del Cinquecento*, ed. P. Barocchi, 3 vols. Milan and Naples, 1971, I, p. 13ff.
2 R. Jones and N. Penny, *Raphael* (New Haven and London, 1983), p. 205. A. Nesselrath, *The Burlington Magazine* 124 (1982), p. 357, proposed that the drawing may have been made specifically in preparation for a repair of the damaged sculpture.

17
RAFFAELLO SANZIO, CALLED RAPHAEL
1483–1520
Study for Apostles for the Monteluce Coronation of the Virgin
c. 1516
Black chalk with white heightening on faded blue paper
26.9 × 22.1 cm
Staatliche Museen zu Berlin, Kupferstichkabinett (5123)

Provenance: Von Beckerath (L. 2504). Acquired in 1902.

References: Dreyer 1979, no. 20. Joannides 1983, no. 391.

Notes
1 *Raffaello in Vaticano*, exh. cat. (Rome, 1984–1985), pp. 286–296, nos. 108–114.

18
SCHOOL OF RAPHAEL
David and Bathsheba
c. 1516–1517
Pen and ink with brown wash and white heightening over indications in black chalk; squared
37.9 × 26 cm
The British Museum, London (1900.611.2)

Provenance: J. Barnard? (what may be L 1419 has been crossed out in lower l.-hand corner); R. Willett; F.J. Duroveray (both according to Lawrence Gallery catalogue); Sir T. Lawrence (L. 2445); King of Holland (sale, The Hague, 1850, 12 Aug. lot 56, bt 'Woodburn, 60 florins'); S. Woodburn (sale, Christie, 1860, 7 June, lot 724, bt *Dr. Radford*, £18–18–0); Miss Kate Radford, by inheritance; acquired by the British Museum, 1900.

References: Parker 1956, p. 564; Pouncey and Gere 1962, no. 66; Oberhuber 1972, no. 469; Dacos 1977, pp. 197–179; Parma 2001, p. 17.

Notes
1 Mantua 1999.

19
RAFFAELLO SANZIO, CALLED RAPHAEL
1483–1520
Nude Studies for Saint Andrew and Another Apostle for The Transfiguration
c. 1517
Red chalk, incised
32.8 × 23.2 cm
Devonshire Collection, Chatsworth (51)

Provenance: Sir Peter Lely (L. 2092); William, 2nd Duke of Devonshire (L. 718)

References: Reveley 1820, pp. 7–8; Ruland 1876, p. 28, no. 61; Crowe and Cavalcaselle 1882–1885, vol. 2, p. 488; Fischel 1898, no. 336; Oberhuber 1962, pp. 132–134; Oberhuber 1982, pp. 54, 57; Gere and Turner 1983, pp. 217–218, no. 175; Joannides 1983, p. 126, pl. 47, no. 426; Knab et al. 1983a, no. 605 (as Saint Matthew); Ames-Lewis 1986, p. 141ff.; Jaffé 1987, p. 109, no. 62; Jaffé 1993, p. 111, no. 118; Jaffé 1994, no. 319; Jaffé 1995, no. 12; Meyer zur Capellen 2005, p. 204 (as Saint Matthew); Talvacchia 2007, p. 218.

Notes
1 The bibliography on Raphael's last altarpiece is vast. For recent summaries of the literature see Meyer zur Capellen 2005, p. 195; C.K. Kleinbub, "Raphael's *Transfiguration* as Visio-devotional Program," *The Art Bulletin* 90 (2008), p. 387, note 1. Noteworthy studies include H. von Einem, *Die 'Verlärung Christi' und die Heilung des Besessenen von Raffael* (Wiesbaden, 1966); K. Weil-Garris Posner, *Leonardo and Central Italian Art: 1515–1550* (New York, 1974), chapters 1–3; E. Gombrich, "The Ecclesiastical Significance of Raphael's Transfiguration," in *Ars auro prior* (Warsaw, 1981), pp. 241–243; F. Mancinelli, *A Masterpiece Close-up:* The Transfiguration *by Raphael* (Vatican City, n.d. [1981]); C. King, "The Liturgical and Commemorative Allusions in Raphael's *Transfiguration and Failure to Heal*," *Journal of the Warburg and Courtauld Institutes* 45 (1982), pp. 148–159; Oberhuber 1982; D.A. Brown, "Leonardo and Raphael's *Transfiguration*," in *Raffaello a Roma: Il convegno del 1983* (Rome, 1986), pp. 237–243; S. Ferino Pagden, "Iconographic Demands and Artistic Achievements: The Genesis of Three Works by Raphael," in Oberhuber 1986, pp. 24–26; C. Gardner von Teuffel, "Raffaels römische Altarbilder: Aufstellung und Bestimmung," *Zeitschrift für Kunstgeschichte* 50 (1987), pp. 33–41; R. Preimesberger, "Tragische Motive in Raffaels 'Transfiguration,'" *Zeitschrift für Kunstgeschichte* 50 (1987), pp. 89–115; K. Weil-Garris, "La morte di Raffaello e la 'Trasfigurazione,'" in *Raffaello e l'Europa*, ed. M. Fagiolo and M. L. Madonna (Rome, 1990), pp. 177–187; M.B. Hall, *Color and Meaning: Practice and Theory in Renaissance Painting* (Cambridge, U.K., and New York, 1992), p. 130ff.; M. van Eikema Hommes, "Discoloration or Chiaroscuro? An Interpretation of the Dark Areas in Raphael's *Transfiguration of Christ*," *Simiolus* 28 (2000/2001), pp. 4–43; L. Agoston, "Transfiguring Raphael: Identity, Authenticity and the Persona of Christ," in *Coming About...: A Festschrift for John Shearman*, ed. L.R. Jones and L.C. Matthew (Cambridge, Mass., 2001), pp. 115–122; R. Goffen, *Renaissance Rivals: Michelangelo, Leonardo, Raphael, Titian* (New Haven and London, 2002), pp. 246–255; J. Cranston, "Tropes of Revelation in Raphael's *Transfiguration*," *Renaissance Quarterly* 56 (2003), pp. 1–25; M.B. Hall, *Rome* (Cambridge, U.K., and New York), 2005, pp. 149–152; A. Henning, *Raffaels* Transfiguration *und der Wettstreit um die Farbe: Koloritgeschichtliche Untersuchung zur römischen Hochrenaissance* (Munich, 2005); Meyer zur Capellen 2005, pp. 195–209, no. 66; G. Bernhart-Königstein, *Raffaels Weltverklärung: Das berühmteste Gemälde der Welt* (Petersberg, 2007); Kleinbub, "Raphael's *Transfiguration*," pp. 367–393. See also S.E. Reiss, "Cardinal Giulio de' Medici as a Patron of Art, 1513–1523," Ph.D. diss., Princeton University, 1992, chap. 7; S.E. Reiss, "Pope Clement VII and the Decorum of Medieval Art," forthcoming in *Revisioning the High Renaissance*, ed. Jill Burke. On the drawings related to *The Transfiguration* see esp. Oberhuber 1962; Oberhuber 1982, p. 39ff.; Joannides 1983, pp. 27–28; Ames-Lewis 1986, pp. 136–149; C. Bambach, *Drawing and Painting in the Italian Renaissance Workshop: Theory and Practice, 1300–1600* (New York, 1999), p. 321ff.
2 Exceptions include Crowe and Cavalcaselle (1882–1885, vol. 2, p. 488), who characterized it as a replica by Penni of a drawing in the Albertina; Fischel (1898, nos. 335, 336); and Gere and Turner (1983, p. 218), who alone among modern scholars felt that it could perhaps be by Giulio Romano.
3 The older figure has also sometimes been identified as Saint Matthew (see, for example, Knab et al. 1983a, p. 645; Preimesberger, "Tragische Motive in Raffaels 'Transfiguration,'" pp. 99–100; Meyer zur Capellen 2005, p. 204, 208, note 345) or simply as an apostle with a book (Kleinbub, "Raphael's *Transfiguration*," p. 375). Some of those who identify the figure as Saint Matthew argue for the importance of his Gospel account of the Transfiguration for Raphael's interpretation. See also Cordellier and Py 1992, p. 532ff.
4 For recent bibliography on Sebastiano's painting see R. Contini in Strinati et al. 2008, pp. 178–180, no. 34. Important discussions include C. Gould, *The Raising of Lazarus by Sebastiano del Piombo* (London, 1967); Hirst 1981, chap. 5; C. Gardner von Teuffel, "Sebastiano del Piombo, Raphael and Narbonne: New Evidence," *The Burlington Magazine* 126 (1984), pp. 765–766; C. Gardner von Teuffel, "An Early Description of Sebastiano's *Raising of Lazarus* at Narbonne," *The Burlington Magazine* 129 (1987), pp. 185–186. See also Reiss, "Cardinal Giulio de' Medici as a Patron of Art," chap. 7, passim, and for a more recent discussion T. Carratù, *Sebastiano del Piombo a Roma 1511–1547* (Milan, 2008), pp. 50–53.
5 On the rivalry between Sebastiano and Raphael see Hirst 1981, chap. 5; Reiss, "Cardinal Giulio de' Medici as a Patron of Art," pp. 310–321; Goffen, *Renaissance Rivals*, p. 243ff.; C. Barbieri, "The Competition between Raphael and Michelangelo and Sebastiano's Role in It," in Hall 2005, pp. 141–164; Carratù, *Sebastiano del Piombo*, pp. 50–53. See also S.E. Reiss, "'*Per havere tutte le opere ... da monsignor reverendissimo*:' Artists Seeking the Favor of Cardinal Giulio de' Medici," in *Possessions: Renaissance Cardinals – Rights and Rituals*, ed. M. Hollingsworth and C.M. Richardson (University Park, Pa., 2009).
6 On Leonardo's influence and the *maniera oscura* in Cinquecento painting see esp. Weil-Garris Posner, *Leonardo and Central Italian Art*; Brown, "Leonardo and Raphael's *Transfiguration*."
7 Kleinbub, "Raphael's *Transfiguration*," pp. 367–393, with reference to the theology of vision. See also Oberhuber 1962, p. 142, for one of the apostle's inner sight.
8 The inclusion of the apostles' failure to heal the demon-possessed boy underscores the healing powers of Christ as Divine Physician, called in Latin *Christus medicus*, a name evoking that of the Medici patron. It is a theme that also alludes to the name of the painter, Raphael, which in Hebrew means *medicina dei*, or "God heals." On the use of the healing metaphor in art produced during the pontificate of Leo X see Shearman 1972, pp. 17, 50, 77–8, 80. See also Reiss, "Cardinal Giulio de' Medici as a Patron of Art," pp. 222–223, 229, 331–333, 564–566. On the *Christus medicus* theme in Raphael's *Transfiguration* see Weil-Garris Posner, *Leonardo and Central Italian Art*, pp. 45–46; Weil-Garris, "La morte di Raffaello," pp. 185–186. On analogous healing imagery in Sebastiano's *Raising of Lazarus* see Hirst 1981, p. 68. On the meaning of Raphael's name see L. Dussler, *Raphael: A Critical Catalogue of His Pictures, Wall-paintings and Tapestries*, trans. S. Cruft (London, 1971), p. 38; G. Benderesky, "Remarks on Raphael's Transfiguration." *Source* 14 (1995), pp. 20–23; P.D.G. Britton, "Raphael and the Bad Humours of Painters in Vasari's *Lives of the Artists*." *Renaissance Studies* 22 (2008), p. 189ff.
9 On this drawing, attributed variously to Giovanni Francesco Penni, or to Giulio Romano (sometimes with a question mark), or simply to the *bottega*, after Raphael, see Oberhuber 1962, p. 116ff.; Oberhuber 1982, p. 29ff., 39ff.; Mantua 1999, no. 171 (with bibliography).
10 The key issue is whether the inclusion of the subject matter in the lower half was due to aesthetic considerations, and thus the result of the artist's desire to make the scene more dramatic, or whether it was an iconographic choice of the patron's, intended to emphasize the Medicean healing theme or theological concerns. I tend to favour the latter explanation, but it is certainly possible that the change in iconography was the result of discussions between artist and patron that encompassed both the form and the content of the original proposal. For a summary of both points of view and an argument that the expanded iconography was the result of artistic concerns see Ferino Pagden, "Iconographic Demands and Artistic Achievements," pp. 24–26.
11 O. Fischel, "Raphael's Auxiliary Cartoons," *The Burlington Magazine* 71 (1937), pp. 167–168. In 1990 Bambach characterized Fischel's term as "extremely problematic" (review of Hirst 1988a, *The Art Bulletin* 72 [1990], p. 498, note 43) and has subsequently called for further research (Bambach, *Drawing and Painting in the Italian Renaissance Workshop*, p. 328).
12 For discussions of this drawing see Oberhuber 1962, p. 129; Oberhuber 1982, p. 53; Joannides 1983, no. 425; Knab et al. 1983a, no. 604; Ames-Lewis 1986, p. 143; A. Gnann in Mantua 1999, p. 247, no. 173a (with bibliography).

20
GIULIO PIPPI, CALLED GIULIO ROMANO
1499?–1546
The Holy Family with the Infant Saint John the Baptist and a Young Woman Carrying Two Birds in a Basket (known as the *Spinola Holy Family*)
c. 1518
Oil (possibly mixed with tempera) on panel
77.8 × 61.9 cm
The J. Paul Getty Museum, Los Angeles (95.PB.64)

Provenance: Vincenzo (?) Spinola, Genoa, 1803; sold to Andrew Wilson, who imported it to England, 12 October 1803; Admiral Sir William Waldergrace, 1st Baron Radstock; Radstock sale, Christie's, London, 13 May 1826, lot 47; George Byng, M.P., Wrotham Park, and estate sale, Christie's, London, 8 December 1994, lot 37; Simon Dickinson Inc., New York, who sold it to the J. Paul Getty Museum, Los Angeles, 1995.

References: Buchanan 1824, vol. 2, p. 196; Waagen 1857, p. 319; Redford 1888, vol. 1, p. 73 note c; Russell 1982a; Joannides 1982; Russell 1982b; Brigstocke 1982, pp. 422, 446, 454 note 3, 490; Joannides 1985, p. 36–38, fig. 27; Ferino Pagden in Gombrich et al. 1989, pp. 70–71, 93 note 47, 95, repr. p. 72; Cannatà and Giavarina Ghisetti 1991, p. 108; Cordellier and Py 1992, p. 390; Coccia in Massari 1993, p. 334, no. 330; Joannides and Young 1995, p. 728 note 12, 733 note 22, 733–734, fig. 14; Getty Museum 1996, p. 111; Ruiz Manero 1996; Jaffé in Getty Museum 1997, p. 24, no. 9; Jaffé 1997, p. 53, repr.; Gribbon 1997, p. 825, no. XI; Clayton 1999, p. 171, fig. 76; Mantua 1999, no. 181 (p. 256), pp. 31, 35, repr. pp. 16, 257; Oberhuber 1999, fig. 218; Joannides 2000, pp. 10–11, 31, 40 note 16, fig. 2–3; Gribbon 2001, p. 101.

Notes
1 The offering of birds evokes the Presentation to the Temple and may be a reference to Pseudo-Bonaventura's *Meditations of the Life of Christ* (see English edition by I. Ragusa and R.B. Green, Princeton Monographs in Art and Archeology, no. 35 [Princeton, 1961], p. 64), in which the Encounter follows the Presentation. This observation is

based on research conducted by the Getty Center in Los Angeles; I am grateful to Scott Schaefer for allowing me access to the painting's conservation dossier, which contains the results of this research.
2 Waagen 1857, p. 319. Peltro William Tomkins (1760–1840) made an engraving of it that was published in 1820; see Mantua 1993, no. 330.
3 Russell 1982a; Joannides 1982; Joannides 1985, pp. 36–38.
4 Gombrich et al. 1989, p. 71.
5 Vasari-Milanesi 1878–1885, vol. 5, p. 524. Reproduced in Oberhuber 1999, fig. 160.
6 For a summary of the thorny problems involved in the attribution of Raphael's works and those of the members of his studio, see, in particular, A. Weston-Lewis et al., *Raphael: The Pursuit of Perfection*, exh. cat. (Edinburgh, 1994), and, more recently, M. Natale, *Rafael: Retrato de un joven*, exh. cat. (Madrid, 2005).
7 Studio of Raphael (Giovanni Francesco Penni with Giulio Romano?, from a sketch by Raphael), *Madonna of Divine Love*, c. 1517–1518, Museo di Capodimonte, Naples (146); Studio of Raphael, *Visitation*, c. 1519, Museo del Prado, Madrid (300).
8 Gombrich et al. 1989, p. 70.
9 On the *Little Holy Family* see esp. J. Meyer zur Capellen 2005, pp. 258–261.
10 Russell (1982a) noted, for example, the rather low position of the main group.
11 From an anatomical point of view, compare the Saint John the Baptist in the 1506 *Madonna of Belvedere* (Kunsthistorisches Museum, Vienna [638]), where the identical positioning of the legs as in the *Spinola Holy Family* causes a dipping of the figure's torso and head to the right.
12 A landscape adorned with a monumental ruin is not unprecedented in Raphael's work, as seen in the *Madonna with the Blue Diadem* in the Louvre, probably from about 1512. But the inclination to move the ruin, in a more patently artificial way, closer in or farther back, as if it were a stage set may attest to the partially developed inventiveness of the young Giulio. Hartt 1958, vol. 1, p. 41, describes "the reduction from the colossal to the miniature" as one of the artist's favourite techniques.
13 To use an expression coined by Vasari. See Vasari-Milanesi 1878–1885, vol. 4, p. 384.
14 Royal Library, Windsor Castle (0804 v.); see Knab et al. 1983a, no. 544. Joannides (1982) was the first to describe the relationship between this sketch and the *Spinola Holy Family*. He also raised the possibility that the drapery of the corresponding painted figure could be credited as well to Penni (Joannides 1985, p. 36).
15 Teylers Museum, Haarlem (A66). Concerning this drawing see esp. C. van Tuyll van Serooskerken, *The Italian Drawings of the Fifteenth and Sixteenth Centuries in the Teyler Museum* (Gand and Doornspijk, 2000), no. 239, pp. 266–267, who compares the head study with a preparatory drawing (Louvre, 3862) of the Virgin in the *Holy Family of Francis I* in the Louvre, following, in this line of thought, Knab et al. 1983a, no. 556. The upper part of the sheet in the Teylers Museum presents two other head studies, no doubt pertaining to the decoration of the Villa Farnesina in Rome executed in 1518 by Raphael and his studio.
16 Mantua 1999, p. 256. For the infrared reflectogram of the *Spinola Holy Family*, which clearly reveals the underlying drawing, see Joannides 2000, figs. 2 and 3.
17 Joannides (2000, p. 11), in response to Mantua 1999, opined that the underlying drawing in the *Spinola Holy Family* was technically identical to that in the *Madonna of Apsley House* (see C.M. Kauffman, *Catalogue of Paintings in the Wellington Museum* [London, 1982], no. 145). On the attribution of the *Madonna of Apsley House* to Giulio Romano see his detailed article in Joannides and Young 1995.
18 S.J. Freedberg, *Painting of the High Renaissance in Rome and Florence* (Cambridge, 1961), p. 272.
19 See Mantua 1999, p. 256. This would apply to the *Madonna of the Palm Tree* (see G. Bernini Pezzini et al., *Raphael invenit: Stampe da Raffaello nelle collezioni dell'Istituto Nazionale per la Grafica*, exh. cat. [Rome, 1985], 34, p. 205, repr. p. 738) and the *Madonna with the Long Thigh* (ibid., 38, p. 207, repr. p. 744).
20 See M. Vasselin in *Raphaël et l'art français*, exh. cat., ed. J.-P. Cuzin (Paris, 1983), no. 380, repr. p. 256.

21

RAFFAELLO SANZIO, CALLED RAPHAEL (1483–1520) **OR GIULIO PIPPI, CALLED GIULIO ROMANO** (1499?–1546)
Head of Pope Leo X
c. 1520
Black chalk with white heightening, incised
33.7 × 26.8 cm
Annotations: *Ritratto de Leon °X° / Michelangelo Buonaroti*; and *KK 39*
Devonshire Collection, Chatsworth (38)

Provenance: J. Richardson sen.; William, 2nd Duke of Devonshire (L. 718)

References: Passavant 1836, vol. 2, p. 145; Wickhoff 1899, p. 208; Berenson 1903, no. 2477; Fischel 1935, pp. 484–486; Berenson 1938, no. 2477; Hartt 1944, p. 83, note 55; Gere 1949, p. 170; Hess 1947, p. 105; Hartt 1958, vol. 1, pp. 51, 289, no. 39; Oberhuber 1972, pp. 199–200, no. 482; Shearman 1972, p. 60, note 88, p. 61; Quednau 1979, pp. 110 and 595–596, no. 365; Gere and Turner 1983, pp. 226–229, no. 183; Knab et al. 1983a, p. 142; Joannides 1983, p. 27, no. 455; Gere 1987, pp. 160–163, no. 42; Rosand 1988, pp. 359–360; Ferino Pagden in Gombrich et al. 1989, p. 258; Jaffé 1993, p. 67, no. 70; Jaffé 1994, p. 86, no. 202; Jaffé 1995, no. 23; Altringer in Bonn 1999, p. 433, no. 25; Woods-Marsden in Hall 2005, p. 133.

Notes

1 According to Gere (1987, p. 160) the annotations are in the hand of Padre Sebastiano Resta (regarding whom see G. Warwick, *The Arts of Collecting: Padre Sebastiano Resta and the Market for Drawings in Early Modern Europe* [Cambridge, U.K., and New York, 2000]). Jaffé (1993, p. 67; 1994, p. 86; 1995, no. 23) attributes all of the annotations to J. Richardson, Sr.
2 For attributions to Sebastiano see Wickhoff 1899, p. 208; Berenson 1903, no. 2477; Gere 1949, p. 170. See also Gere 1987, pp. 160–163, for the revised opinion.
3 Passavant (1836, vol. 2, p. 145) wrote about the Chatsworth sheet: "here ascribed to Michelangelo, although from one of Raphael's own paintings." For attributions to Raphael see Berenson 1938, vol. 2, no. 2477 (revising his attribution in 1903 to Sebastiano); Shearman 1972, p. 60, note 88, p. 61; Joannides 1983, p. 27, no. 455; Gere 1987, pp. 160–163, no. 42; Rosand 1988, pp. 359–360. L. Wolk-Simon also attributes the Chatsworth head of Leo X to Raphael (personal communication); I am most grateful to her for sharing her opinion with me.
4 For attributions to Giulio see Fischel 1935; Hartt 1944, p. 83, note 55; Hess 1947, p. 105; Hartt 1958, vol. 1, pp. 51, 289, no. 39; Oberhuber 1972, pp. 199–200, no. 482; Knab et al. 1983a, p. 142; Rosand 1988, pp. 359–360; Ferino Pagden in Gombrich et al. 1989, p. 258; Jaffé 1993, p. 67, no. 70; Jaffé 1994, p. 86, no. 202; Jaffé 1995, no. 23; L. Altringer in Bonn 1999, p. 443; Woods-Marsden in Hall 2005, p. 133.
5 Gere 1987, p. 162. Gere further states (p. 163): "It is always possible – in theory at least – that Giulio was put on his mettle and inspired to an unusual pitch of creativity by the challenge of doing justice to Leo's alarmingly formidable personality." For recent discussion of the attribution problems in the study of Raphael's late drawings see L. Wolk-Simon, "Raphael Drawings, *Pro-Contra*," in Hall 2005, pp. 207–219.
6 For a nuanced discussion of the white heightening and arguments for Raphael's authorship see Rosand 1988, p. 360. Joannides (1983, p. 27) states that the Chatsworth sheet "is a study of brutal power, where fine subtleties of grading in the shadows are set against the most lavish and forceful application of white."
7 The head was first described as such in Fischel 1935. On the frescoed group of Pope Clement I with *Moderatio* and *Comitas*, see Quednau 1979, pp. 204–232.
8 Recent scholarship on the Sala di Costantino includes Quednau 1979; G. Cornini, A.M. De Strobel, and M.S. Crescenzi in G. Cornini et al., *Raphael in the Apartments of Julius II and Leo X* (Milan, 1993), pp. 167–201; P.P. Fehl, "Raphael as a Historian: Poetry and Historical Accuracy in the Sala di Costantino," *Artibus et historiae* 14 (1993), pp. 9–76; Rohlmann 1994; F. Fernetti, "Gli allievi di Raffaello e l'insolito utilizzo di un cartone del maestro nella Sala di Costantino," *Prospettiva* 87/88 (1997), pp. 133–136; B. Paul, "Issues of Political Iconography: Clement VII's Personal and Political Concerns in His Representation as Leo I in the Sala di Costantino," in *Coming About ...: A Festschrift for John Shearman*, ed. L.R. Jones and L.C. Matthew (Cambridge, Mass., 2001), pp. 267–274.; J. De Jong, "Universals and Particulars: History Painting in the 'Sala di Costantino' in the Vatican Palace," in *Recreating Ancient History: Episodes from the Greek and Roman Past in the Arts and Literature of the Early Modern Period*, ed. K. Enenkel et al. (Boston and Leiden, 2002), pp. 27–56. See also my discussion in cat. 22.
9 For discussion of the dimensions see Gere 1987, p. 163.
10 Shearman 1972, p. 60, note 88. Shearman (Ibid., p. 61) called the Chatsworth head "the most intensely realized (and the last) of all Raphael's portraits of Leo."
11 J. Shearman, *Raphael in Early Modern Sources (1483–1602)* (New Haven, 2003), vol. 1, pp. 587–588, doc. 1520/26, p. 615, doc. 1520/58.
12 Fernetti, "Gli allievi di Raffaello," p. 136.
13 Arnold Nesselrath (personal communication with David Franklin) has examined the figure and finds no visual evidence to confirm Fernetti's proposal, which can be validated only by technical analysis.

22

RAFFAELLO SANZIO, CALLED RAPHAEL
1483–1520
Pope Sylvester I in a Sedia Gestatoria
c. 1520
Black, white, yellow, and red chalks and brown wash, squared in black chalk
39.8 × 40.4 cm
Isabella Stewart Gardner Museum, Boston (1.1.r.12)

Provenance: William Russell (L. 2648), his sale, Christie's, London, 10–12 Dec. 1884, lot #457; Sir J.C. Robinson (L. 1433).

References: Waagen 1857, p. 187; Ruland 1876, p. 200, no. 29; Crowe and Cavalcaselle 1882–1885, vol. 2, p. 140; Pratt 1966; Hadley 1968, pp. 17–18, no. 8; Oberhuber 1972, pp. 205–207, no. 490; Quednau 1979, pp. 464, 469–470; Joannides 1983, no. 447 and commentary to pl. 45; Knab et al.1983a, no. 602; Gere 1987, pp. 154–160, no. 41; Ferino Pagden in Gombrich et al. 1989, p. 260; McGrath 1994, pp. 109–110; Rohlmann 1994, p. 165, note 22; Goldfarb 1995, p. 79; McGrath 1998, p. 4; A. Gnann in Mantua 1999, pp. 230–231, no. 159; Monbeig Gougel 1999, p. 498; Wolk-Simon and Bambach 1999, p. 171

Notes

1 For a summary of the attribution history see Mantua 1999, p. 230, no. 159. In correspondence with the Gardner Museum, Oskar Fischel (4 April 1937) and Philip Pouncey (March 1957) attributed the drawing to Giovanni Francesco Penni. I am grateful to Robert Colby of the Gardner Museum for sending me copies of this correspondence. I am particularly grateful to Dr. R. Mack for sharing with me her unpublished paper of August 1966 (under the name Rosamond E. Pratt) on the Boston drawing (for discussion of which see Hadley 1968, p. 18).
2 On Raphael's use of this unusual technique see Joannides 1983, p. 122; McGrath 1998, p. 4. Hadley (1968, pp. 18–19) and Monbeig-Gougel (1999, p. 498) wondered if the coloured chalks are later additions.
3 On the Wilton House head study see Gere and Turner 1983, pp. 172–173, no. 141; Joannides 1983, no. 459; Knab et al. 1983a, p. 641, no. 601; McGrath 1994, p. 111; McGrath 1998, p. 5.
4 In the nineteenth century both Waagen (1857, p. 187) and Ruland (1876, p. 200) associated the Boston drawing with the Stanza d'Eliodoro. Wolk-Simon has suggested that the related drawings discussed below may have been for the Sala dei Pontefici, directly below the Sala di Costantino. See L. Wolk, "Studies in Perino del Vaga's Early Career," Ph.D. diss., Ann Arbor, 1987, p. 125, no. 108; Wolk-Simon and Bambach 1999, p. 179, note 11. Quednau (1979, p. 463ff.) doubted the relationship of the Boston sheet and the other drawings discussed here to the Sala di Costantino.
5 See G.W. Bowersock's introduction to Valla's *On the Donation of Constantine* (Cambridge, Mass., 2007), an edition that appends the Latin text of the Donation along with an English translation, and J. Fried, *"Donation of Constantine" and "Constitutum Constantini"* (Berlin and New York, 2007), which argues for Frankish rather than curial authorship. On Lorenzo Valla's refutation of its authenticity in the fifteenth century see Bowersock's introduction to *On the Donation of Constantine*. On condemnations and papal defences of the Donation see Quednau 1979, p. 450ff.

6   On the functions of the Sala di Costantino see Quednau 1979, pp. 44–69. Recent scholarship on the room also includes G. Cornini, A.M. De Strobel, and M.S. Crescenzi in G. Cornini et al., *Raphael in the Apartments of Julius II and Leo X* (Milan, 1993), pp. 167–201, with many colour illustrations; P.P. Fehl, "Raphael as a Historian: Poetry and Historical Accuracy in the Sala di Costantino," *Artibus et historiae* 14 (1993), pp. 9–76; Rohlmann 1994; F. Fernetti, "Gli allievi di Raffaello e l'insolito utilizzo di un cartone del maestro nella Sala di Costantino," *Prospettiva* 87/88 (1997), pp. 133–136; B. Paul, "Issues of Political Iconography: Clement VII's Personal and Political Concerns in His Representation as Leo I in the Sala di Costantino," in *Coming About … : A Festschrift for John Shearman*, ed. L.R. Jones and L.C. Matthew (Cambridge, Mass., 2001), pp. 267–274.; J. De Jong, "Universals and Particulars: History Painting in the 'Sala di Costantino' in the Vatican Palace," in *Recreating Ancient History: Episodes from the Greek and Roman Past in the Arts and Literature of the Early Modern Period*, ed. K. Enenkel et al. (Boston and Leiden, 2002), pp. 27–56.
7   J. Shearman, *Raphael in Early Modern Sources (1483–1602)* (New Haven, 2003), vol. 1, pp. 484–485, doc. 1519/60.
8   Ibid., p. 587, doc. 1520/26.
9   Ibid., p. 615, doc. 1520/58.
10   Ibid., p. 707, doc. 1521/38
11   Ibid., p. 780, doc. 1524/8. An inscription in the *Baptism of Constantine* fresco reads "CLEMENS VII/PONT MAX/A LEONE X/COEPTVM/CONSVMMAVIT/MDXXIII." See also Quednau 1979, p. 859, doc. 61a; Shearman, *Raphael in Early Modern Sources*, vol. 1, p. 789, doc. 1524/17.
12   On the Louvre sheet see F. Hartt, "Drawings by Giulio Romano in the National Museum in Stockholm," *Nationalmusei årsbok* 9 (1939), pp. 39–40; Hartt 1958, vol. 1, p. 50, p. 288, no. 32; Bacou and Beguin 1983, no. 35; B. Magnusson, *Rafael: Teckningar en utställning inga°ende i Nationalmuseums 200-a°rsjubileum*, exh. cat. (Stockholm, 1992), p. 69, no. 44; Cordellier and Py 1992, no. 937; Wolk-Simon and Bambach 1999, p. 171; Gnann in Mantua 1999, p. 232, no. 160 (with bibliography).
13   The Boston and Paris sheets were first associated in Fischel's letter of 1937 mentioned in note 1 above. On the significance of papal beards see M.J. Zucker. "Raphael and the Beard of Pope Julius II," *The Art Bulletin* 59 (December 1977), pp. 524–533. See also my discussion under cat. no. 39. Hartt ("Drawings by Giulio Romano," p. 40) identified the bearded pontiff as Clement VII, who appears beardless in the realized frescoes of the Sala di Costantino.
14   On the Stockholm sheet see O. Sirén, *Italienska handteckningar från 1400-och 1500-talen i Nationalmuseum: Catalogue raisonné* (Stockhom, 1917), no. 316, pp. 82–83; Hartt, "Drawings by Giulio Romano," pp. 39–42; Hartt 1958, vol. 1, p. 50, p. 288, no. 33; Ferino Pagden in Gombrich et al. 1989, p. 260; Magnusson, *Rafael*, pp. 69–70, no. 45 (with bibliography); Wolk-Simon and Bambach 1999, p. 171.
15   Sirén, *Italienska handtecknin-gar*, no. 316, pp. 82–83.
16   On the Amsterdam *modello* (then in the Liechtenstein collection in Vienna) see Sirén, *Italienska handteckningar*, p. 83; Hartt 1958, vol. 1, p. 50, vol. 2, no. 369; Ferino Pagden in Gombrich et al. 1989, p. 260; Gnann in Mantua 1999, pp. 232–233, no. 161 (with bibliography).

17   On this open-handed gesture of blessing see Quednau 1979, pp. 182, 654–655, note 615; L.M. Giles, "A Drawing by Raphael for the Sala di Costantino," *Master Drawings* 37 (1999), p. 160.
18   On the Lateran setting see J. Traeger, *Der reitende Papst: Ein Beitrage zur Ikonographie des Papsttums* (Munich, 1970), p. 18; Quednau 1979, p. 469; Ferino Pagden in Gombrich et al. 1989, p. 206; Gnann in Mantua 1999, p. 232.
19   Hartt ("Drawings by Giulio Romano," p. 41) suggested that the subject was a meeting of the pope and the emperor before the Battle of the Milvian Bridge. Sirén (*Italienska handteckningar*, p. 83) had already tentatively brought the Sala di Costantino into his discussion of the Stockholm sheet, which he titled "Attila before the Walls of Rome."
20   See Quednau 1979, pp. 465–466, for opinions.
21   Significantly, other sources, such as Eusebius's *Life of Constantine* and the *Liber pontificalis*, also speak of Constantine's bestowing of treasures and properties on Pope Sylvester, and Gere (1987, p. 158) proposed a generic identification of the scene as a representation of Constantine submitting to papal authority, rather than the Donation itself.
22   As suggested in Oberhuber 1972, p. 207; Gere 1987, p. 159; Ferino Pagden in Gombrich et al. 1989, p. 260; Gnann in Mantua 1999, p. 230.
23   On the Donation and Valla's refutation see note 5 above. Concerning this period of upheaval see P.W. Kalkoff, *Forschungen zu Luthers römischen Prozess* (Rome, 1906); P.W. Kalkoff, *Ulrich von Hutten und die Reformation: Eine kritische geschichte seiner wichtigsten lebenszeit und der entscheidungsjahre der Reformation (1517–1523)* (Leipzig, 1920); L. von Pastor, *The History of the Popes from the Close of the Middle Ages, Drawn from the Secret Archives of the Vatican and Other Original Sources*, ed. F.I. Antrobus et al., 3rd. ed. (London, 1901–1933), vol. 7, chap. 8; H. Holborn, *Ulrich von Hutten and the German Reformation*, trans. R. Bainton (New Haven, London, and Oxford, 1937). Hutten's publication of Valla is dated 1517, but Kalkoff (*Ulrich von Hutten und die Reformation*, p. 66) argued that it actually dates to 1519. For the relation of these events to the decorations of the Sala di Costantino see Quednau 1979, p. 453ff.; De Jong, "Universals and Particulars," pp. 30–31.
24   Luther's letter to Georg Spalatin is translated in L. Partridge, *The Renaissance in Rome: 1400–1600* (London, 1996), p. 159. See also De Jong, "Universals and Particulars," p. 31.
25   Concerning which see Kalkoff, *Forschungen zu Luthers römischen Prozess*; Pastor, *History of the Popes*, vol. 7, passim. Some of these commissions were headed by Cardinal Giulio de' Medici, the future Pope Clement VII. The errors of Luther's writings were condemned in the Bull *Exsurge Domine*, promulgated in June 1520, and he was subsequently excommunicated in January 1521 in the Bull *Decet Romanum Pontificem*.

23
GIULIO PIPPI, CALLED GIULIO ROMANO (1499?–1546) AND GIOVANNI FRANCESCO PENNI, CALLED IL FATTORE (c. 1496–c. 1528)
Flagellation of Christ
c. 1520
Oil on panel
164 × 145 cm
Sacristy, Santa Prassede, Rome
Not in exhibition

References: Vasari 1568, V, S. 531–532; Totti 1638, p. 483; Titi 1674–1763, p. 134; Davanzati 1725, pp. 232, 242; Hartt 1944, p. 94; Calvesi 1954; Hartt 1958, pp. 274–275; Toesca 1966; Baccheschi and Calvesi 1978, S. 532, Nr. 16; Joannides 1985, pp. 20–23; Ferino Pagden in Gombrich et al. 1989, pp. 66–67; Calvesi 1990, pp. 45–47; Dacos 1993, pp. 153–156.

Notes
1   I would like to thank Margherita Fratarcangeli for her assistance in preparing this catalogue entry. Davanzati 1725, p. 242: *Nella medesima Sagrestia si conserva il famoso quadro di Giulio Romano, che rappresenta il nostro Redentore battuto alla Colonna da due Manigoldi, il quale fu fatto fare dal Cardinal Bibbiena, che lo donò alla chiesa di S. Prassede, acciò fosse collocato sopra alla Santa Colonna; giacchè così al vivo rappresenta la flagellazione del medesimo nostro Signore; opera veramente degna, e che va sulle storie, la quale benche abbia un poco patito per cagione dell'umidità, come si è detto di sopra, dove la sudetta S. Colonna, ad ogni modo gli due Signori Cavalieri Ghezzi, e Benedetto Luti, Pittori Eccellenti stimarono il quadro del valore di due mila scudi.*
2   Another inventory drawn up in 1823 mentions the painting again in the sacristy. For the 1726 and 1823 inventories see Toesca 1966.
3   C. D'Arco, *Istoria della vita e delle opere di Giulio Pippi Romano* (Mantua 1838), p. LI.
4   See for example Hartt 1958 and Baccheschi and Calvesi 1978.
5   For an attribution to Penni see Hartt 1944 and Ferino Pagden in Gombrich et al. 1989; Joannides 1985 has proposed an attribution to Giulio Romano, while Toesca is inclined to see a collaboration between the two.
6   Joannides 1985, pp. 20–23.

24
ANDREA CONTUCCI, CALLED ANDREA SANSOVINO
1467/70–1529
Design for the Tomb of Pope Leo X
c. 1521?
Pen and brown ink and brown wash
40 × 24.2 cm
Annotations: *GIOV. DOSIO*
Victoria and Albert Museum, London (2260)

Provenance: J. Talman (L. Suppl. 2886A, Talman's mark); Sir T. Lawrence (L. 2445); S. Woodburn; sale, Christie's, 4–14 June 1860; purchased by the museum.

References: Middeldorf 1934, pp. 159–160; Huntley 1935, pp. 99–100, fig. 72; Venturi 1901–1939, vol. 11, part 1, p. 172; Tolnay 1943–1960, pp. 9, 90; Montini 1957, pp. 310–311; Ward-Jackson 1979–1980, vol. 1, no. 312, pp. 147–148; Blunt 1980, pp. 638–639; Frommel 2001, p. 320; Frommel 2003, p. 335; Bigi Iotti 2008.

Notes
1   On the provenance of the drawing and on Talman's collector's mark, seen here on the inscribed panel, see Ward-Jackson, 1979–1980, vol. 1, p. 147. The other two tomb drawings with Talman's collector's mark are Victoria and Albert Museum, London, 8621

(Ward-Jackson 1979–1980, vol. 1, no. 311, here fig. 2) and a sheet formerly in Weimar (see Huntley 1935, fig. 71). On John Talman as collector and connoisseur see C.M. Sicca, ed., *John Talman: An Eighteenth-Century Connoisseur* (New Haven and London, 2009). See also the John Talman project at the University of Pisa, http://talman.arte.unipi.it/IT/index.html
2   Middeldorf (1934, p. 160) dated the drawing from shortly after Leo's death in December 1521, while Huntley (1935, p. 99) felt that it could be from as late as 1523 and intended for presentation to Pope Clement VII. Ward-Jackson (1979–1980, vol. 1, p. 148) suggested that the drawing was made in an attempt to obtain the commission either during Leo's lifetime or shortly after his death. See also Bigi Iotti 2008, p. 758.
3   Middeldorf and Huntley did not connect the drawing with Talman. On Talman as the probable author of the attribution to Giovanni Antonio Dosio see Ward-Jackson 1979–1980, p. 147.
4   General works on Andrea Sansovino include Huntley 1935; J. Pope-Hennessey, *An Introduction to Italian Sculpture* (New York, 1985), vol. 3, pp. 54, 344–350; C. Avery, *Florentine Renaissance Sculpture* (New York, 1970), pp. 153–160; V.A. Bonito, in *Grove Art Online*, s.v. "Sansovino, Andrea" (with specialized bibliography). See also Vasari-Milanesi 1878–1885, vol. 4, pp. 509–527. On Andrea's work for Leo X at the church of Santa Maria in Domnica see K. Frey, "Zur Baugeschichte des St. Peter. Mitteilungen aus der Reverendissima Fabbrica di S. Pietro," *Jahrbuch der Königlich Preussischen Kunstsammlungen*, Beiheft 31 (1911), pp. 38–43; G. Giovannoni, "La Chiesa della Navicella in Roma nel Cinquecento," *Palladio* 7 (1943), pp. 152–158; C.L. Frommel, "'In pristinam formam': Il rifacimento di Santa Maria in Domnica a opera di Leone X," in C.L. Frommel, *Architettura alla corte papale nel Rinascimento* (Milan, 2003), pp. 317–333. On his work for the Medici popes at the Santa Casa in Loreto see K. Weil-Garris, *The Santa Casa di Loreto: Problems in Cinquecento Sculpture*, Garland Outstanding Dissertations in the Fine Arts (New York, 1977), passim; Pope-Hennessey, *An Introduction to Italian Sculpture*, vol. 3, pp. 347–349. Ward-Jackson (1979–1980, p. 147) suggests that the present drawing is autograph while the other Victoria and Albert Museum tomb project and the one formerly at Weimar may have been by another hand. Blunt (1980, pp. 638–639) questioned the attribution to Sansovino and thought the drawing dated from later in the Cinquecento.
5   Tolnay (1943–1960, p. 90) suggested that Michelangelo's juxtaposition of standing figures on the lower zone with seated figures on the platform of the Julius tomb as envisioned in 1505 inspired Sansovino. For a later design for the Julius tomb that also juxtaposes standing and seated figures see cat. 1, p. 66.
6   Clawed lions' feet are also found in Victoria and Albert Museum, London, 8621, here fig. 24.2. The roundel on the sarcophagus is similar to those on the sarcophagus bases of the Santa Maria del Popolo tombs, which carry Sansovino's signature.
7   This motif has been seen as inspired either by Etruscan and Roman sarcophagi with recumbent effigies or by non-Italian sources, especially Spanish tomb sculpture (particularly the tomb of Martin Vázquez de Arce in the cathedral of Sigüenza) or English examples that Sansovino may have seen in

Portugal. The former idea was first put forth in F. Burger, *Geschichte des florentinischen Grabmals von den ältesten Zeiten bis Michelangelo* (Strasburg, 2004), p. 276. Huntley (1935, p. 60) notes Etruscan and Roman traditions but also proposes Spanish and/or English influences. He also suggests purely functional motivations for the activated, reclining figures. E. Panofsky (*Tomb Sculpture: Four Lectures on Its Changing Aspects from Ancient Egypt to Bernini*, ed. H.W. Janson [London, 1964], p. 82) advocated Spanish inspiration for what he called "demi-giants," while Pope-Hennessey (*An Introduction to Italian Sculpture*, vol. 3, p. 55) mentions the pose but does not address its origins. Recent scholarship has remained divided on the question. C.M. Richardson ("Art and Death," in *Viewing Renaissance Art*, ed. K.W. Woods, C.M. Richardson, and A. Lymberopoulou [New Haven and London, 2007], pp. 235–236) stresses Sansovino's Iberian experience. Y. Ascher ("Form and Content in Some Roman Reclining Effigies from the Early Sixteenth Century," *Gazette des Beaux-Arts*, ser. 6, 139 [2002], pp. 315–330), somewhat misstating Huntley's arguments, discounts Spanish influence and notes that Etruscan influence is more likely – an opinion held by S. Valtieri ("Il 'revival' etrusco nel Rinascimento toscano," *Architettura* 194 [1971], p. 548), Bigi Iotti (2008, p. 758), and the present writer. J. Röll ("'Do We Affect Fashion in the Grave?' Italian and Spanish Tomb Sculptures and the Pose of the Dreamer," in *The Image of the Individual: Portraits in the Renaissance*, ed. N. Mann and L. Syson [London, 1998], pp. 155–157) dismisses both Etruscan/Roman and Iberian influences, proposing instead sources in Renaissance pictorial art. See also J. Imorde, "Träumende Prälaten: Zu einer 'invenzione' Andrea Sansovinos," in *Die Jagiellonen: Kunst und Kultur einer europäischen Dynastie an der Wende zur Neuzeit*, ed. D. Popp and R. Suckale (Nuremberg, 2002), pp. 375–383. It is also debated whether such figures are dreaming or shown in the dreamless sleep of death. It is possible, of course, the idea was Sansovino's own. See Ascher, "Form and Content," p. 318, for similar speculation.

8 On these influential tombs and their setting in the Bramante choir of Santa Maria del Popolo (with frescoes by Pinturricchio and stained glass windows by Guillaume de Marciallat) see E. Lavagnino, *Santa Maria del Popolo* (Rome, 1928); E. Bentivoglio and S. Valtieri, *Santa Maria del Popolo a Roma* (Rome, 1976); S. Valtieri Bentivoglio, "S. Maria del Popolo e il coro detto 'del Rossellino,'" *Mitteilungen des Kunsthistorischen Institutes in Florenz* 20 (1976), pp. 197–204; Pope-Hennessey, *An Introduction to Italian Sculpture*, vol. 3, pp. 54–55, 346–347; N. Riegel, "Capella Ascanii-Coemiterium Julium," *Römisches Jahrbuch der Bibliotheca Hertziana* 30 (1995), pp. 193–219; C.L. Frommel, "Giulio II e il coro di Santa Maria del Popolo," *Bolletino d'arte*, ser. 6, 85 (2000), pp. 1–34; P. Zitzlsperger, "Die ursachen der Sansovinograbmäler in S. Maria del Popolo (Rom)," in *Tod und Verklärung: Grabmalskultur in der Frühen Neuzeit*, ed. A. Karsten and P. Zitzlsperger (Cologne, 2004), pp. 91–113. Frommel ("Giulio II e il coro di Santa Maria del Popolo." p. 14ff.) has recently dated the tombs to 1509–1511, several years later than they have usually been placed.

9 On fifteenth-century tomb sculpture in Rome and the demand for replication, speed, and collaboration of workshops see S. Zuraw, "Mino da Fiesole's Forteguerri Tomb: A 'Florentine' Monument in Rome," in *Artistic Exchange and Cultural Translation in the Italian Renaissance City*, ed. S.J. Campbell and S.J. Milner (Cambridge, U.K., and New York, 2004), esp. pp. 75–76. On late medieval and Renaissance tomb sculpture in Rome, particularly papal and curial examples, see G.S. Davies, *Renascence: The Sculptured Tombs of the Fifteenth Century in Rome, with Chapters on the Previous Centuries from 1100* (London, 1910); H.K. Mann, *Tombs and Portraits of the Popes of the Middle Ages* (London, n.d. [1929]); Gregorovius and Hülsen 1932; J. Gardner, *The Tomb and the Tiara: Curial Tomb Sculpture in Rome and Avignon in the Later Middle Ages* (Oxford, 1992); H. Bredekamp, "Grabmäler der Renaissancepäpste: Die Kunst der Nachwelt," in Bonn 1999, pp. 259–267; M.J. Gill, "The Fourteenth and Fifteenth Centuries," in *Rome*, ed. M.B. Hall (Cambridge, U.K., and New York, 2005), pp. 27–106, passim.

10 I am grateful to Ingo Herklotz and Shelley Zuraw for their discussions with me about the possible functions of the present drawing. In his 1980 review of Ward-Jackson 1979–1980, Blunt (p. 638) noted: "In spite of the inscription this can hardly be a design for the tomb of Leo X since it shows no papal insignia and the coats of arms are covered by bishops' (or possibly cardinals' hats)." Here Blunt errs – the *stemmi* unequivocally show cardinals' hats.

11 Middeldorf's remark (1934, p. 160) that "the lack of arms and other emblems – the deceased does not even wear a tiara – point to an unofficial origin of the drawing" does not really make sense. Andrea Sansovino was in the papal service and would certainly have known how to represent a deceased pontiff. Two papal effigies that did not wear mitres were those of Alexander VI (destroyed) and of Pius III in his original tomb slab ordered when he was still a cardinal and thus mitred; see W.J. Reardon, *The Deaths of the Popes: Comprehensive Accounts, including Funerals, Burial Places and Epitaphs* (Jefferson, N.C., 2004), p. 173.

12 The *stemmi* of Cardinal Giuliano della Rovere (the future Pope Julius II) appear on Antonio del Pollaiuolo's *Tomb of Pope Sixtus IV*, while those of Cardinal Willem van Enckevoirt are seen on the *Tomb of Pope Adrian VI*. The *Tomb of Pope Pius II*, formerly in Old Saint Peter's and now in Sant'Andrea della Valle, displays the *stemmi* of that pontiff's nephew Cardinal Francesco Todeschini Piccolomini (who briefly reigned as Pope Pius III in the autumn of 1503).

13 See note 10, above.

14 Two cardinals particularly close to Leo X who died during his pontificate were Luigi Rossi (d. 1519, buried in Santa Felicita, Florence), best known to art historians because of his presence in Raphael's *Portrait of Pope Leo X with Two Cardinals* in the Uffizi (fig. 46.1), and Cardinal Bernardo Dovizi da Bibbiena (d. 1520, buried in Santa Maria in Aracoeli, Rome).

15 For recent accounts of Michelangelo's plans for Medici papal tombs in San Lorenzo, Florence, see C. Elam in *Michelangelo e il disegno di architettura*, ed. C. Elam, exh. cat. (Venice, 2006), nos. 15, 16. On the vicissitudes of the Medici papal tombs in Rome and the eventual monuments erected in the Minerva see P. Pecchiai, "I lavori fatti nella chiesa della Minerva per collocarvi le sepolture di Leone X e Clemente VII," *Archivi d'Italia*, ser. 2, 17 (1950), pp. 199–208; D. Heikamp, "Die Entwurfszeichnungen für die Grabmäler der Mediceer-Päpste Leo X. und Clemens VII.," *Albertina Studien* 4 (1966), pp. 134–152; V. Goldberg, "Leo X, Clement VII and the Immortality of the Soul," *Simiolus* 8 (1975/1976), pp. 16–25; S. Pasti, "Documenti cinquecenteschi per l'abside della Minerva," in *Atti della IV settimana di studi di storia dell'arte medievale dell'Università di Roma "La Sapienza,"* ed. A.M. Romanini (Rome, 1983), pp. 591–600; U. Kleefisch-Jobst, "Die Errichtung der Grabmäler für Leo X. und Clemens VII. und die Projekte für die Neugestaltung der Hauptchorkapelle von S. Maria sopra Minerva," *Zeitschrift für Kunstgeschichte* 51 (1988), pp. 524–541; Bredekamp, "Grabmäler der Renaissancepäpste," pp. 264–266; Frommel 2001; Frommel 2003; N. Hegener, "Mediceischer Ruhm und künstlerische Selbstinszenierung," in *Tod und Verklärung: Grabmalskultur in der Frühen Neuzeit*, ed. A. Karsten and P. Zitzlsperger (Cologne, 2004), pp. 259–312; Reardon, *The Deaths of the Popes*, pp. 179–180, 182–184; J. Götzmann, "Der Triumph der Medici: Zur Ikonographie der Grabmäler Leos X. und Clemens' VII. in S. Maria sopra Minerva," in *Praemium Virtutis II: Grabmäler und Begräbniszeremoniell in der italienischen Hoch-und Spätrenaissance*, ed. J. Poeschke (Münster, 2005), pp. 171–200; D. Greve, *Status und Statue: Studien zum Leben und Werk des Florentiner Bildhauers Baccio Bandinelli* (Berlin, 2008), chap. 8; N. Hegener, *Divi Iacobi Eqves: Selbstdarstellung im Werk des Florentiner Bildhauers Baccio Bandinelli* (Munich and Berlin, 2008), passim.

25
PIERO BUONACCORSI, CALLED PERINO DEL VAGA
1501–1547
Study for a Wall Decoration
Pen and brown ink, brush with brown wash over underdrawing in black chalk
c. 1522
40.9 × 26.8 cm
The J. Paul Getty Museum, Los Angeles (94.GA.47)

Provenance: Possibly P.-J. Mariette; Commendatore Genevosio (L. 545); "Mercer's Collection" from which purchased by Whitehead; Sir J. C. Robinson, London (L. 1433); John Malcolm of Poltalloch; Given by Malcolm to the Hon. Alfred E. Gathorne-Hardy; By descent to the Hon. Robert Gathorne-Hardy, Donington Hall, Berkshire (sale, Sotheby's, London, 24 November, 1976, lot 13); British Rail Pension Fund.

References: Gathorne-Hardy 1902, p. 28, no. 50 (as Dosso Dossi); Edinburgh 1969, pp. 26–27, no. 57; White and Stock 1971–1972), no. 12; Marabottini 1969, vol. 1, p. 41; Ravelli 1972, pp. 27–28 (as Polidoro); Kultzen 1973, p. 638 (as copy of Perino); Ravelli 1978, pp. 45–46, 111–113 (as Polidoro); Gere 1985–1986, pp. 72–73; Parma Armani 1986, p. 319; Gere 1987, p. 239–241, no. 74; Ravelli 1988, p. 25, n. 30; de Castris 1988, p. 11ff.; Gnann 1996, p. 75ff.; Gnann in Mantua 1999, pp. 304–305, no. 218; Parma 2001, pp. 163–164; Turner et al. 2001, pp. 77–79; Hirst in Monbeig Goguel et al. 2001, pp. 81–84; de Castris, 2001, pp. 78–97.

Notes

1 R. Kutzen, "Der Freskenzyklus in der ehemaligen Kapelle der Schweizergarde in Rom," in *Zeitschrift für Schweizer Archäeologie und Kunstgeeschichte* (1961), p. 19–30.

2 For the best summary see Gnann in Mantua 1999, p. 304.

3 "*... la cappella della Passione che alcuni dicono esser di Polidoro, ma è ... d'un todesco.*" *Considerazioni sulla Pittura*, ed. A. Marucchi and L. Salerno, I, 1956, p. 269, cited by Gere 1987, p. 240. That it might indeed have been painted by a northerner should come as no surprise, given the patron.

4 A. Gnann in Mantua 1999, p. 304, accepts these two at least; de Castris, 2001 (p. 80ff.) proposes a greater involvement.

26
PIERO BUONACCORSI, CALLED PERINO DEL VAGA
1501–1547
The Judgment of Zaleucus
c. 1520–1522
Detached fresco, transferred to canvas
14.8 × 19.7 cm
Galleria degli Uffizi, Florence (P1152)

Provenance: Palazzo Baldassini, Rome (until 1830); Vincenzo and Pietro Cammuccini, Rome; Ministero della Pubblica Istruzione, Florence; Galleria degli Uffizi, Florence (1881).

References: Poggi 1909; Parma Armani 1986, pp. 36–40; Mantua 1999, pp. 186–187, no. 123; Parma 2001, pp. 108–110, no. 14; Wolk-Simon 2002, p. 15.

Notes

1 "La più bella e meglio fatta che sia in Roma" (3 August 1544), quoted in C.L. Frommel, *Der Römische Palastbau der Hochrenaissance* (Tubingen, 1973), vol. 2, p. 23.

2 In my opinion, the 1517–1518 dating proposed by Gnann in Mantua 1999, p. 187, is too early.

3 These three artists and the architect Antonio da Sangallo the Younger, another Raphael collaborator, formed an informal and intermittent association of *compagni* at the Palazzo Baldassini and elsewhere in the years between their master's premature death in 1520 and the Sack of Rome in 1527. See L. Wolk-Simon, "Competition, Collaboration and Specialization in the Roman Art World, 1520–1527," in *The Pontificate of Clement VII: History Politics, Culture*, ed. K. Gouwens and S.E. Reiss (Aldershot, Hampshire, England, and Burlington, Vt., 2005), pp. 253–276.

4 Vasari-Milanesi 1878–1885, vol. 5, pp. 598–599.

5 G.B. Armenini, *De' veri precetti della pittura* (1587; New York, 1971), pp. 177–178.

6 Wolk-Simon 2002, pp. 11–21.

7 Ibid.

8 V. Massimo, *De' fatti e detti degni di memoria della Città di Roma e delle stranie genti*, ed. R. de Visiani (Bologna, 1867), pp. 252, 444.

9 On the iconography of the decorative program, see Wolk-Simon, 2002, pp. 11–21.

10 Vasari-Milanesi 1878–1885, vol. 5, p. 598.

11 Noted, inter alia, by B.F. Davidson, "Early Drawings by Perino del Vaga," part 1, *Master Drawings* 1:3 (1963), p. 20.

27
POLIDORO CALDARA, CALLED POLIDORO DA CARAVAGGIO
c. 1499–c. 1543
A Deathbed Scene (recto)
Seated Woman (verso)
c. 1521–1522
Red chalk
21 × 29 cm
The National Gallery of Art,
Washington, D.C. (1991.9.1.a)
Gift of David E. Rust, in Honour of
the 50th Anniversary of The
National Gallery of Art, 1991.

Provenance: Robert Udny (1722–
1830), England, before 1802
(L. 2248); Sir Thomas Lawrence
(1769–1830), London (L. 2445);
Samuel Woodburn (his posthumous sale, Christie's, London, 7
June 1860, no. 691); purchased by
Evans; Sotheby's, London, 12 March
1963, no. 21; D.E. Rust,
Washington, D.C., 1963–1991; gift
to the National Gallery of Art, 1991.

References: Marabottini 1969,
vol. 1, pp. 310–311, nos. 51–52;
Ravelli 1978, p. 121, nos. 52–53;
Parma Armani 1986, pp. 39–40,
fig. 36; Gere 1987, no. 82; Leone de
Castris 1988, no. 7; Ravelli 1988,
pp. 43–44, figs. 64–65; Leone de
Castris 2001, pp. 74, 76, figs. 82–83,
p. 492, no. 283.

Notes
1   *Nella casa di Baldassino, da
Sant'Agostino, fecero [i.e., Polidoro
and Maturino] graffiti e storie, e nel
cortile alcune teste d'imperadori
sopra le finestre.* Vasari-Milanesi
1878–1885, vol. 5, p. 146.
2   Wolk-Simon 2002, pp. 11–21.
3   L. Wolk, "Studies in Perino del
Vaga's Early Career," Ph.D. diss.,
Ann Arbor, 1987, p. 225, note 117.
4   Wolk-Simon 2002, pp. 13–14.
5   The subject of the present
drawing was so identified in the
1963 Sotheby's sale catalogue and
by Marbottini 1969, vol. 1, no. 51,
who was unaware of the existence
of the corresponding fresco by
Polidoro in the Palazzo Baldassini.
6   Statens Museum fur Kunst,
Copenhagen. See J.D. Draper and
G. Scherf, *Playing with Fire,
European Terracotta Models, 1740–
1840*, exh. cat. (New York, 2004),
under no. 65.
7   See L. Wolk-Simon,
"Naturalism in Lombard Drawing
from Leonardo to Cerano," in
Painters of Reality, exh. cat., ed.
Andrea Bayer (New York, 2004),
pp. 53, 101–102, under nos. 21a and
21b.

28
ATTRIBUTED TO PERINO DEL VAGA
1501–1547
St. Julian Hospitaller (?)
c. 1520–1525
Tempera grassa on panel
127 × 80 cm
Inscriptions: *M Iacomo. F. F*
Galleria Colonna, Rome
The restoration of this painting
was made possible with the gener-
ous support of Alenia North
America, a Finmeccanica Company

Provenance: Fidecommesso
Colonna, 1660

References: Corti 1937, no. 36 (as
Pier Francesco di Sandro); Safarik
1981, no. 142 (as Perino del Vaga);
Rome 1984, no. 43.

Notes
1   Safarik 1981, p. 104. On Jacopo
da Carpi, see G. Martinotti, "Il
Testamento de M.O. Jacopo
Barigazzi, or Berengario, da Carpi,"
in *Lettore de Chirugia nello Studio
de Bologna* (Siena, 1923), pp. 65–73.
2   The painting is now in the
Accademia, Florence.
3   Neither of these Quattrocento
examples showed Saint Julian with a
bird. In Castagno's *Assumption with
Saints Julian and Miniato* altarpiece
(Gemaldegalerie, Berlin), he holds

only a sword. Piero's *Saint Julian*
fresco in Sansepolcro is damaged
and fragmentary, but according to
D. Franklin ("Piero della Francesca's
'St. Julian' at Sansepolcro," in *The
Burlington Magazine*, 141 [August
1999], pp. 473–475), the figure must
have held "his usual attribute of a
sword" (p. 473); there is no suggestion that a bird was part of Piero's
original conception. Of further relevance for this discussion is the
depiction of Saint Julian in an altarpiece of 1444 by Pietro di Giovanni
d'Ambrogio (reproduced in
Franklin, "della Francesca's
'St. Julian,'" fig. 25), once again
represented holding a sword but
absent the bird. On the iconography
of Saint Julian, see G. Kaftal,
*Iconography of the Saints in Tuscan
Painting* (Florence, 1952), pp. 564–
572. I would like to thank Eveline
Baseggio for compiling helpful
material on the imagery and iconography of Saint Julian.
4   Reproduced in Parma Armani
1986, p. 58, fig. 50.

29
GIOVANNI FRANCESCO PENNI, CALLED IL FATTORE
c. 1496–c. 1528
Portrait of a Young Man
c. 1521–1527
Oil on panel
52 × 41 cm
Inscriptions: *G. Franc./Penni*
National Gallery of Ireland, Dublin
(1018)
Provenance: Earl of Lincoln,
London; acquired by Christie's,
London, 11 March 1939, no. 43.

References: Gnann in Mantua 1999,
p. 243, no. 170 (with bibliography);
Joannides 2000, p. 30.

Notes
1   The portrait was in Lucien
Bonaparte's collection from 1802 to
1816 (see *Choix de gravures à l'eau
forte d'après les peintures originales
et les marbres de la Galerie de Lucien
Bonaparte*, London, 1812, p. 6,
no. 132, *stanza* VII, no. 76),
engraved by "testa" and attributed
to Raphael, then passed into the
collection of the king of Holland,
William II (see B. Edelein-Badie, *La
collection de tableaux de Lucien
Bonaparte, prince de Canino. Notes
et documents des musées de France*,
30 [Paris, 1997], pp. 246–247,
no. 200). According to Passavant
1860, II, p. 362, no. 301), on the
paper that the model held in his left
hand was the inscription *Dom.
Fraño Penni Florentiam* (also visible
on the engraving).
2   Curiously, this portrait is classified among the works of Ridolfo
del Ghirlandaio in the Berenson de
la Villa I Tatti photo library in
Florence (Harvard University),
with the note "with Ridolfo."
K. Garas ("Bildnisse der
Renaissance. III. Der junge Raffael
und der alte Tizian," in *Acta
Historiae artium Academiae
Scientiarum Hungaricae*, vol. 21,
Budapest, 1975, pp. 63, 73, n. 22),
through his relations with the
Tuscan school, dates the portrait to
the artist's Florentine period.
3   Shearman (1983, p. 87) thinks
that the young man in the Dublin
portrait is Giovanni Francesco
Penni, painted by Battista Dossi
around 1519–1520. Joannides 2000
concurs about the model's identity,
but attributes the portrait to an
anonymous artist in Raphael's
entourage (p. 30).
4   Inv. 1949-2-12-3; see A. Gnann,
in Oberhuber 1999, p. 226, no. 156
(with bibliography). The drawing, a
preparatory study for the figure
visible behind Constantine in the
L'Aldocutio fresco on the eastern
wall of the Hall of Constantine in
the Vatican palace, served as a reference for Vasari for the frontispiece
of the life of Giovanni Francesco
Penni.

5   This old identification was
picked up by S. Béguin (*Raphaël
dans les collections françaises*, exh.
cat., Paris, 1983, p. 114) and C. Bon
(*Aspetti dell'arte a Roma prima e
dopo Raffaello*), exh. cat. (Rome,
1984), p. 120.
6   Giovanni Francesco Penni's
career has yet to be defined; however, P. de Castris (in P. Giusti and
P. de Castris, *Pittura del
Cinquecento a Napoli: 1510–1540
forastieri e regnicoli*, Naples, 1988,
p. 64) proposes, thanks to Vasari's
text and an analysis of historical
events, that Penni left Rome for
Naples (after a brief stay in
Mantua) between 1527 and 1529.
The only work mentioned by Vasari
during Penni's stay in the south is a
copy of Raphael's *Transfiguration*
that Penni executed in Ischia for
Alfonso d'Avalos, today conserved
at the Prado in Madrid (ibid., p. 66).
7   The name of Franciabigio was
advanced for the first time by
S. Freedberg (*Painting of the High
Renaissance in Rome and Florence*,
2 vols., Cambridge, 1961, p. 482), and
more recently by F. Sricchia Santoro
("Del Franciabigio, dell'Indaco e di
una vecchia questione, I,"
Prospettiva, vol. 70 [1993],
pp. 29–30, 45, n. 26).
8   B. Cellini, book I, chap. 26, *La
vie de Benvenuto Cellini écrite par
lui-même* (1500–71), ed. A. Chastel
(Paris, 1986), pp. 45–46: "One St.
John's morning – ours in Florence –
I was having breakfast with a number of my colleagues, painters,
sculptors, goldsmiths, many of
whom are quite remarkable, such as
the painter Rosso and the student
of Raphael of Urbin,
Gianfrancesco" (our translation).

30
POLIDORO CALDARA, CALLED POLIDORO DA CARAVAGGIO
c. 1499–c. 1543
*Prisoner Brought Before a Judge
(Condemnation of Perillus?)*
early 1520s
Pen and brown ink, brown wash,
heightened with white gouache,
over black chalk, on light brown
paper
16.5 × 23.2 cm
Inscriptions: *Polidoro da
Caravaggio; Crozat, De Tessin,
Queen of Sweden (Ulrica), Count de
Steenbock, Count de Barck.*
The Pierpont Morgan Library,
New York (I, 20)
Purchased by Pierpont Morgan,
1909

Provenance: E. Jabach, Paris;
P. Crozat (?), Paris; C.G. Tessin (?);
Queen Louisa Ulrica of Sweden (?);
Count Gustav Herold Steenbock (?);
Count Nils Barck, Paris and Madrid
(L. 1959); C. Fairfax Murray,
London and Europe; from whom
purchased through Galerie
Alexandre Imbert, Rome, in 1909
by Pierpont Morgan, New York (no
mark, see L. 1509); his son, J.P.
Morgan, Jr. (1867–1943), New York.

References: Fairfax Murray 1905–
1912, vol. 1, no. 20, repr. (Polidoro);
Marabottini 1969, vol. 1, pp. 108–
109, 124, 305, no. 30; vol. 2, fig. 74,1;
Ravelli 1978, pp. 108–109, no. 30
repr.; Gnann 1997, pp. 86–87, 100–
101, fig. 53; Mantua 1999, p. 310,
no. 222, repr. [illus. reversed]; Py
2001, p. 44, no. 54.

Notes
1   The relationship of the
Morgan study to the via dei
Coronari facade was first noted by
Gnann (1997, p. 100).
2   Ovid, *Tristia*, Book 3, chapter
11: 39–54.
3   Marabottini 1969, vol. 1,
pp. 122–123, 356–358, no. 10; vol. 2,
pl. 131, 3.
4   Inv. 1950-8-16-3; Gere and
Pouncey 1983, no. 175, repr.

5   Vasari 1996, vol. 1, pp. 891–
892; compare Vasari- Milanesi
1878–1885, vol. 5, p. 144, *Nella via
che camina all'Imagne di ponte è una
facciata bellissima, con la storia di
Perillo, quando egli è messo nel toro
di bronzo da lui fabbricato; nella
quale si vede la forza di coloro che
mettono in esso toro, ed il terrore di
chi aspetta vedere tal morte inusi-
tata; oltre che vi è a sedere Falari
(come io credo) che comanda con
imperiosità bellissima, che e'si pun-
isca il troppo feroce ingegno che
aveva trovato crudeltà nuova per
ammazzar gli uomini con maggior
pena.*
6   Marabottini 1969, vol. 1,
pp. 123–124, 358–360, no. 11; vol. 2,
pl. 134.
7   Mantua 1999, p. 310.

31
POLIDORO CALDARA, CALLED POLIDORO DA CARAVAGGIO
c. 1499–c. 1543
A Cavalry Battle
c. 1524–1526
Red chalk
20.2 × 28.4 cm
Inscriptions: *d'mà Propria
d'Raffaiel. d' Vr^{no}/ C. 3.* (verso)
Agnes Etherington Art Centre,
Queen's University, Kingston
(41-018.06)
Gift of Bayside Lakeshore
Properties Ltd., Montreal 1998

Provenance: An unidentified
armorial drystamp; Boguslaw Jolles
(L. 381a); sale London, Christie's,
13 December 1984, lot 33; Roberto
Ferretti di Castelferretto.

References: McTavish 1985–1986,
pp. 20–21, no. 2; Gere 1985–1986,
p. 67, pl. 39; Gere 1987, pp. 266–268,
no. 84; Leone de Castris 1988,
pp. 27, 46–47; Düsseldorf 1993,
p. 52; Gnann 1997, p. 211 and note
891; Leone de Castris 2001, pp. 224,
247, 257, 260, 267, 482, D 173;
Cordellier 2007, pp. 68 (under
no. 16) and 69 (under no.19);
McTavish, 2008, p. 391

Notes
1   See Gere 1985–1986, p. 74, note
22.
2   For example, the drawing of
heads and shoulders of eight apostles formerly in the Woodner collection, and now in the National
Gallery of Art, Washington, or of
the standing young man in the
Louvre, Paris (inv. 3854); Joannides
1983, p. 223, no. 358. The comment
by M. Hirst ("Exhibition Review,
Naples, Polidoro da Caravaggio,"
The Burlington Magazine 131 [1989],
pp. 238), that Polidoro was influenced by Raphael's red-chalk drawings from as early as those for the
Massacre of the Innocents (c. 1510)
should also be noted.
3   Goethe-Nationalmuseum,
Weimar, pen and brown ink and
brown wash, heightened with
white; 35.5 × 28 cm (attached to
another sheet at the top); Gnann in
Mantua 1999, p. 213, no. 145, dated
to about 1520.
4   Gere 1985–1986, p. 67.
5   Leone de Castris 2001, p. 482,
no. 173.
6   G.P. Lomazzo, "Idea del Tempo
della Pittura" (in R.P. Ciardi, ed.,
Scritti sulle Arti, 2 vols. [Florence,
1973–1974]), 1, p. 344: *A Polidoro
furono concessi da Marte i moti furi-
osi, empi, fieri, colmi d'ira e di
maestà, talmente che nelle guerre
rappresentate da lui chi vuol notare
et esprimer convenevolmente la gran
furia e prontezza delle sue figure e
dell'altre cose ch'egli ha formate co'l
suo armonic pennello, resta vinto e
confuso solo a pensarvi.*

32
POLIDORO CALDARA, CALLED
POLIDORO DA CARAVAGGIO
c. 1499–c. 1543
Betrayal of Christ
c. 1524–1525
Pen and brown ink, brown and grey
washes, with white heightening on
blue prepared paper
21.2 × 26.3 cm
Annotations: *Benevenuto Garofalo*
The Royal Collection (RL 050)

Provenance: P. Sandby (L.);
T. Lawrence (L.); W. Mayor (L.);
Acquired by the Royal Collection in
1875.

References: Clayton 1999, pp. 202–
203, no. 61; Leone de Castris 2001,
p. 493, no. 287.

Notes
1   Vasari-Milanesi, 1878–1885, V,
p. 380 ["divine cross of crystal"].
2   For the Belli work see
Raffaello in Vaticano, exh. cat.
(Milan, 1984), p. 378, no. 149a–c.

33
ROSSO FIORENTINO
1494–1540
Seated Nude Woman
c. 1524
Red chalk
31.5 × 17.8 cm
Annotations: *Chechino Salviati*
National Gallery of Scotland,
Edinburgh (D4870)

Provenance: Purchased from
H.M. Calmann, London in 1962.

References: Carroll 1987–1988,
no. 6, pp. 66–68. Franklin 1994,
pp. 130–132.

Notes
1   M. Hirst, "Rosso: A Document
and a Drawing," *The Burlington
Magazine* 106 (1964), p. 122.
2   Franklin 1994, pp. 122–133.

34
PIERO BUONACCORSI, CALLED
PERINO DEL VAGA
1501–1547
*Sketch for a Wall Decoration with
the Coat of Arms of a Medici Pope*
c. 1521–1527
Pen and brown ink
45.3 × 29.8 cm
Christ Church Picture Gallery,
Oxford (0966)
By permission of the Governing
Body of Christ Church, Oxford

Provenance: Filippo Baldinucci.
General John Guise; bequeathed by
him to Christ Church, 1765.

References: Byam Shaw 1976, vol. 1,
no. 479, vol. 2, fig. 261; Mantua
1999, p. 324, no. 234; Parma 2001,
p. 124, no. 27.

Notes
1   See L. Wolk-Simon,
"Competition, Collaboration, and
Specialization in the Roman Art
World, 1520–1527," in *The
Pontificate of Clement VII: History,
Politics, Culture*, ed. K. Gouwens
and S.E. Reiss (Aldershot,
Hampshire, England, and
Burlington, Vt., 2005), pp. 253–276.
2   Mantua 1999, p. 324.
3   Vasari-Milanesi 1878–1885,
vol. 5, p. 609; see Wolk-Simon,
"Competition, Collaboration, and
Specialization," pp. 275–276.
4   Giovanni da Udine's stucco
reliefs on the facade of the
destroyed Palazzo Branconio con-
formed to this formula, as did many
of Polidoro da Caravaggio's now-
lost facade paintings (for example,
his design for the Palazzo Gaddi,
which showed the Medici stemma
flanked by two other coats of arms
above the door, as a detailed copy of
that design records; see Ravelli
1978, fig. 611).
5   The Metropolitan Museum of
Art, New York (1998.10). See
L. Wolk-Simon and C. Bambach,
"Towards a Framework and

Chronology for Giulio Romano's
Early Pen Drawings," *Master
Drawings* 37 (1999), p. 176, fig. 10,
demonstrating that the design is
for a three-dimensional structure,
proposing its function, and pointing to a similar invention by
Michelangelo Anselmi.
6   The present author (review of
E. Parma Armani, *Perino del Vaga:
L'anello mancante*, in *The Art
Bulletin* 71 [September 1989],
p. 516) has refuted the flawed con-
tention that the ceiling, with its
specific astrological and biographical references to the horoscope of
Leo X, was finished during the pontificate of Clement VII. First
advanced by M. Brugnoli and
endorsed by Parma Armani, that
improbable chronology is based on
the account offered in Vasari's *Life*
of Giovanni da Udine, which con-
tradicts the testimony he gives in
his *Life* of Perino.
7   Parma 2001, p. 125.
8   Another possibility for the
intended decoration of the walls of
this room is that one of the two
decorative series of tapestries commissioned by Leo X and designed
by Raphael's workshop for
unrecorded locations – either the
Giochi dei Putti or the so-called
Grotesques of Leo X – was intended
for the Sala dei Pontefici. The former of these was suggested in
L. Wolk, "Studies in Perino del
Vaga's Early Career," Ph.D. diss.,
Ann Arbor, 1987, pp. 101–102, note
68; the latter is currently being
investigated by Lorraine Karafel in
her doctoral dissertation on tapestries designed by the Raphael
Workshop. On these two tapestry
projects see T.P. Campbell, *Tapestry
in the Renaissance: Art and
Magnificence*, exh. cat. (New York
and New Haven, 2002), pp. 225–233,
246–256, nos. 26 and 27.
9   For which see Campbell,
Tapestry in the Renaissance,
pp. 241–243.
10   L. Wolk, "Studies in Perino del
Vaga's Early Career," pp. 98–104

35
GIROLAMO FRANCESCO MARIA
MAZZOLA, CALLED
PARMIGIANINO
1503–1540
*The Holy Family with Saint
Elizabeth and the Baby John the
Baptist*
c. 1524–1527
Pen and brown ink and wash, with
white heightening, over black
chalk, on greenish prepared paper
16.2 × 11.9 cm
Agnes Etherington Art Centre,
Queen's University, Kingston (41-
018.13)
Gift of Bayside Lakeshore
Properties Ltd., Montreal. 1998

Provenance: Sir Peter Lely
(L. 2092); William, 2nd Duke of
Devonshire (L. 718); Chatsworth
no. 805; sale London, Christie's, 3
July 1984, lot 33; Roberto Ferretti
di Castelferretto.

References: London 1953, no. 72;
Popham 1961, no. 44; Popham
1962–1963, no. 45; Popham 1969,
no. 45; Popham 1971, p. 212, no. 733,
pl. 249; Ghidiglia Quintavalle 1971,
p. 12; McTavish l985–1986,
pp. 28–29, no.6; Jaffé 1994, vol. 3,
no. 702; Franklin 2002, p. 221, fig. 1;
Gnann in Fornari Schianchi and
Ferino Pagden 2003, pp. 279–280,
no. 2.3.49.

Notes
1   Vasari–Milanesi 1879–1906, V,
p. 222.
2   Ibid., pp. 223–224 *lo spirito del
qual Raffaello si diceva poi passato
nel corpo di Francesco ... e, che è più,
sentendosi quanto egli s'ingegnava
d'imitarlo in tutte le cose, ma sopra
tutto nella pittura.*

3   As preliminary drawings
prove, Parmigianino even explored
the possibility of including the
baby John the Baptist in the
Madonna of the Long Neck; Popham
1971, nos. 359, O.C.25 362.
4   Inv. no. 747E; Popham 1971,
p. 66, no. 72.
5   Popham repeatedly dated the
drawing to the second half of the
1520s, while Gnann in Fornari
Schianchi and Ferino Pagden, 2003,
p. 280, narrowed the years to
1526–1527.
6   Saint Elizabeth is shown here
as being much older than she is
in Parmigianino's drawing of the
Visitation (Galleria Nazionale di
Parma). Popham 1971, p. 212,
no. 733, understandably also
allowed for the possibility that the
figure is Saint Anne, the mother of
the Virgin Mary.
7   For these paintings, see
K. Oberhuber, *Raphael, the
Paintings* (Munich, London, New
York 1999), pp. 241–242; pls. 221–
223. D. Ekserdjian, in *Parmigianino*
(New Haven and London, 2006),
p. 32, noted that "[W]hat may be
the earliest surviving drawing by
Parmigianino, in Turin, is after
Raphael's *Madonna of Divine Love*
in Naples." With regard to the figure in the doorway, Popham 1971,
p. 212, no. 733, compared the
present drawing to Parmigianino's
Mystic Marriage of St. Catherine
(National Gallery, London), which
in turn C. Gould in "Notes on
Parmigianino's 'Mystic Marriage of
St. Catherine,'" *The Burlington
Magazine* 117 (1975), p. 233 and in
Parmigianino (New York, London,
Paris, 1994), p. 102, sees as having
been inspired by Giulio Romano's
Madonna della Gatta.
8   For many of the same observa-
tions, see Gnann in Fornari
Schianchi and Ferino 2003, p. 280.
9   McTavish 1985–1986, p. 28.
10   Gould, *Parmigianino*, p. 75.
Gnann in Fornari Schianchi and
Ferino 2003, 2003, p. 280, also dis-
cerns the influence of
Michelangelo's Ancestors of Christ
in the lunettes of the Sistine
Chapel on Parmigianino's figure of
the Virgin Mary. For
Parmigianino's connections with
Michelangelo, see also
D. Ekserdjian, "Parmigianino and
Michelangelo," *Master Drawings* 31
(1993), pp. 390–394, and more spe-
cifically in "Parmigianino and
Michelangelo," in *Reactions to the
Master, Michelangelo's Effect on Art
and Artists in the Sixteenth Century*,
ed. F. Ames-Lewis and P. Joannides
(Aldershot, 2003), p. 64, and
Ekserdjian in *Parmigianino*, p. 30,
where he endorses the suggestion
that Parmigianino stopped in
Florence in 1524, but is inclined not
to see any influence from the
Medici Tombs.
11   Popham 1971, p. 212, no. 733;
M. Joannides, *Master Drawings
from the De Pass Collection, Royal
Cornwall Museum, Truro*, exh. cat.
(London and Truro, 1994), pp. 26–27,
no. 8.

36
SEBASTIANO DEL PIOMBO
1485–1547
*Portrait of Anton Francesco degli
Albizzi*
c. 1525
Oil on canvas, transferred from
panel
134.6 × 87.7 cm
The Museum of Fine Arts, Houston
Samuel H. Kress Collection (61.79)

Provenance: Albizzi, Florence. By
descent to the Falconieri, Rome by
1664. Thomas Lister Parker,
Broxholme, in 1804; Robert
Heathcote; George, 4th Earl of
Aberdeen, 1805; Charles Cecil
Hope, 3rd Earl of Liverpool, by
c 1829; Richard Sanderson;
Frederick John, Lord Monson,
Gatton Park, by 1857; Viscount

Oxenbridge to 1888 to M. Colnaghi;
Colnaghi's London; Robert H. and
Evelyn Benson, London, by 1895
and to 1927; acquired from Duveen
for the Kress Collection, 1957.

References: Hirst 1981, pp. 102–105.
Contarini in Strinati et al. 2008,
no. 45

Notes
1   For the painting's attribu-
tional history, see C. Wilson,
*Italian Paintings XIV–XVI
Centuries in the Museum of Fine
Arts, Houston* (Houston, 1996),
pp. 344–345.
2   Vasari-Milanesi 1878–1885, V,
p. 575; Vasari 1996, p. 146.
3   P. Barocchi and R. Ristori eds.,
Il Carteggio di Michelangelo
(Florence, 1973), III, p. 156.
4   B. Varchi, *Storia fiorentina*,
ed. G. Milanesi (Florence, 1888), III,
p. 71.
5   E. Howard, "New Evidence on
the Italian Provenance of a Portrait
by Sebastiano del Piombo," *The
Burlington Magazine*, 130 (1988),
pp. 457–459.

37
BALDASSARE PERUZZI
1481–1536
An Allegory of Fortune
c. 1527
Pen and brown ink over black
chalk, pricked for transfer
27.3 × 20.4 cm
Annotations: *Baldassar da Siena*
Christ Church Picture Gallery,
Oxford
By permission of the Governing
Body of Christ Church, Oxford

Provenance: Sir Peter Lely (L. 2092);
William Gibson (L. Suppl. 2885);
General John Guise; bequest to
Christ Church College

References: Bell 1914, p. 74; Von
Hadeln 1926; Tietze and Tietze-
Conrat 1937, p. 87; Eisler 1947, p. 155;
Frommel 1968, pp. 137–138, no. 100;
Byam Shaw 1976, vol. 1, p. 117,
no. 358; C. D'Afflitto in Florence
1980, p. 426, no. 3.11.11; Biondi in
Fanti 1983, p. 20, note 51; Chastel
1983, pp. 87–89; Cox-Rearick 1984,
p. 173; Ernst 1994, p. 640; Johnson
2001, pp. 199, 204, note 3; Thompson
in Bayer 2008, p. 143.

Notes
1   Byam Shaw identified the
hand in the annotation as that of
the British miniature painter
William Gibson (d. 1703).
2   For subsequent questions concerning Peruzzi's authorship see
Biondi in Fanti 1983, p. 20, note 51.
3   The last page states: *Impreso
in la inclita Citta di Venegia per
Agostin da Portese. Nel anno dil vir-
gineo parto .M.D.XXVII. Nel mese di
Genaro, and insta[n]tia di Iacomo
Giunta Merca[n]tate Florentino. Con
il Privilegio di CLEMENTE PAPA VII.
et del Senato Veneto a requistione di
L'AUTORE.* On Fanti's *Triompho di
Fortuna* (and its woodcut illustra-
tions, including the frontispiece)
see L. Baer, "Die Darstellung
Michelangelos in Fanti's 'Triompho
di Fortuna,'" *Frankfurter
Bücherfreund* 6 (1908), pp. 21–27;
Von Hadeln 1926; Eisler 1947;
Tietze and Tietze-Conrat 1937,
p. 87; L. Thorndike, *A History of
Magic and Experimental Science*
(New York, 1923–1958), vol. 5,
pp. 253–254, vol. 6, pp. 469–471;
G. Ernst in Florence 1980, p. 426,
no. 3.11.10; Biondi in Fanti 1983,
pp. 5–20; Chastel 1983, pp. 87–90;
Cox-Rearick 1984, p. 173; O. Niccoli,
"Gioco, divinazione, livelli di cul-
tura: Ill Triompho di Fortuna de
Sigismondo Fanti," *Rivista Storica
italiana* 96 (1984), pp. 591–599;
Ernst 1994, pp. 639–640;
L. Thomson, *All Is But Fortune*
(Seattle, 2000), pp. 84–85, no. 95;
L. Bolzoni, *The Gallery of Memory:
Literary and Iconographic Models*

453

in the Age of the Printing Press, tr. J. Parzen (Toronto, 2001), pp. 110–117; Johnson 2001; Thompson in Bayer 2008, pp. 143–145, no. 63a.
4 On Fanti see Biondi in Fanti 1983, p. 6ff.; Ernst 1994; Bolzoni, *The Gallery of Memory*, p. 110. On his *Theorica et practica del modo scribendi fabricandique omnes literarum species* (Venice, 1514) see Biondi in Fanti 1983, pp. 6–8; Ernst 1994, p. 639; Bolzoni, *The Gallery of Memory*, pp. 110–111.
5 On the opposition of Fortuna and *virtù* in the Renaissance see F. Kiefer, "The Conflation of *Fortuna* and *Occasio* in Renaissance Thought and Iconography," *Journal of Medieval and Renaissance Studies* 9 (1979), pp. 1–27; Thomson, *All Is But Fortune*. The first Italian book of fortune-telling was Lorenzo Spirito's *Libro della ventura*, the first edition of which appeared in 1482. On *libri di sorti* and fortune-telling in the Renaissance see Thorndike, *A History of Magic and Experimental Science*, volumes 5 and 6, passim; Biondi in Fanti 1983, pp. 5–6; Niccoli, "Gioco, divinazione, livelli di cultura"; Bolzoni, *The Gallery of Memory*.
6 G.K. Nagler, *Die Monogrammisten und diejenigen bekannten und unbekannten Künstler aller Schulen, welche sich zur Bezeichnung ihrer Werke eines figürlichen Zeichens, der Initialen des Namens, der Abbreviatur desselben &c. bedient haben ...*, vol. 3 (Munich, 1919), pp. 1089–1090, no. 2809; Eisler 1947, p. 155; Johnson 2001, p. 204, note 3.
7 Eisler 1947, p. 155, note 5; Biondi in Fanti 1983, p. 18, note 14; Johnson 2001, p. 204, note 1. Because of the date printed on the first edition, the book is frequently described as having been published in January 1526, but this is impossible given that papal privilege was granted on 3 July 1526 and the Venetian Senate gave privilege on 9 November of that year (see Fanti 1983, fol. 1v). Some of the rare copies of Fanti's *Triompho di Fortuna* are found in the British Library, the Biblioteca Apostolica Vaticana, the Metropolitan Museum of Art, and the Houghton Library of Harvard University. It is also available in a facsimile edition, printed slightly larger than the original (Fanti 1983).
8 Biondi in Fanti 1983, p. 16. On fol. 3r Fanti praises Clement's "grandezza del animo" and the fame of the Medici house, and implores the pontiff to accept *la servitu mia laquale gia longo tempo con l'animo, et hora con il corpo gli offerisco.*
9 See, for example, Cristoforo Marcello's *De fato* of 1519 (Biblioteca Apostolica Vaticana, Vat. lat. 5800), which contains a *disputa* on the nature of predetermined events vis-à-vis human *virtù* and free will. See also I. Fosi, "Il ms. Vaticano Latino 5800: Un opera inedita di Cristoforo Marcello," in *Le chiavi della memoria: Miscellanea in occasione del I centenario della Scuola Vaticana di Paleografia Diplomatica e Archivistica* (Vatican City, 1984), pp. 441–460. For other works on fortune and prognostication dedicated to Clement see P. Zambelli in Florence 1980, pp. 318–322. and nos. 3.9.38 and 3.9.43 in that catalogue.
10 The same generic figure is used for other pontiffs in subsequent illustrations. Concerning Clement's growth of a beard after the Sack of Rome see cat. 39, p. 175.
11 The figure has been associated with the *Farnese Atlas*, now in the Museo Archeologico Nazionale, Naples.
12 For these identifications see Eisler 1947, p. 157; G. Ernst in Florence 1980, p. 426; Thomson, *All Is But Fortune*, p. 85.
13 For a vivid (if inaccurate) description of the struggle between beneficent and malignant forces in the frontispiece, see C.S. Sherrington. *Man on His Nature* (Cambridge, 1951), p. 53. Cf. Eisler 1947, p. 155.
14 Eisler (1947, pp. 157–159) associated the nude youth with the aphorism of the "weeping philosopher" Heraclitus that Aeon (Time or Eternity) is a boy playing at dice, and the figure has often been identified as Time (see, for example, G. Ernst in Florence 1980, p. 426, and Ernst 1994, p. 640). But the prominent twenty-four-hour clock would seem better to embody the notion of Time. The prominent youth may perhaps signify the randomness and unpredictability of events.
15 Chastel (1983, p. 89) erroneously identifies the clock-tower as the Horologium of Augustus in Rome. The Horologium was an enormous sundial rather than a twenty-four-hour clock such as the recently completed one in Venice, where the *Triompho* was published. I am grateful to Niall Atkinson and Gwen Ajello for discussing this topic with me.
16 On the Pantheon's astrological associations see Eisler 1947, p. 156.
17 Scholars who have associated the pontiff on the frontispiece with Clement include Eisler (1947, p. 157), Ernst (in Florence 1980, p. 426), and Thomson (*All Is But Fortune*, p. 85).
18 On how this striking image may be a premonition of the Sack of Rome see Eisler 1947, p. 157; Chastel 1983, pp. 87–90; G. Ernst in Florence 1980, p. 426; Ernst 1994, p. 640; S.E. Reiss, "Cardinal Giulio de' Medici as a Patron of Art, 1513–1523," Ph.D. diss., Princeton University, 1992, p. viii; S.E. Reiss, "Clemens VII.," in Bonn 1999, p. 63.
19 F. Vettori, *Sommario della istoria d'Italia 1511–1527*, in *Scritti storici e politici*, ed. E. Niccolini (Bari, 1972), p. 207. On Clement, Vettori, and the antipathy of Fortuna see F. Gilbert, *Machiavelli and Guicciardini: Politics and History in Sixteenth-Century Florence* (Princeton, 1965), p. 251. L. von Ranke (*Die römischen Päpste in den letzten vier Jahrhunderten* [Vienna, n.d.], p. 85) described Clement as probably the most unfortunate pontiff to sit on Saint Peter's throne. For recent reassessments of his calamity-ridden papacy see K. Gouwens and S.E. Reiss, ed., *The Pontificate of Clement VI: History, Politics, Culture* (Aldershot, U.K., and Burlington, Vt., 2005).

38
SEBASTIANO DEL PIOMBO
1485–1547
Portrait of Cardinal Giovanni Salviati and Giovanni da Cepperello
c. 1531
Oil on panel
105 × 99 cm
The John and Mable Ringling Museum of Art, Sarasota, Florida
Bequest of John Ringling, 1936 (SN65)

Provenance: Cardinal Antonio Maria Salviati, Rome, 1634; Thomas Erskine, purchased Rome, c. 1847; David Erskine, Linlathen, Scotland; sold Sotheby's London, December 5, 1922 (lot 72) to anonymous buyer; sold Christie's London, July 17, 1925 (lot 70); Colnaghi's London (stock no. A1293); John Ringling, Sarasota, Florida, 1928.

References: Gilbert 1961; Tomory 1976; Hirst 1981; Pope-Hennessy 1985; Costamagna in Monbeig Goguel et al. 2001; Costamagna in Chong et al. 2003

Notes
1 Gilbert 1961, pp. 38–42, identified the main sitter of this portrait and dated the work to c. 1531.
2 See Gilbert 1961 and Costamagna in Monbeig Goguel et al. 2001 for Salviati's biography.
3 The Cardinal commissioned many portraits of his family members from the artist, one of which may be the *Portrait of an Aristocratic Youth* also in the collection of the John and Mable Ringling Museum of Art, SN733.
4 See Costamagna in Monbeig Goguel et al. 2001 for Salviati's collections.
5 Gilbert first made the association between the letter and the portrait.
6 Costamagna in Chong et al. 2003 discusses the reasoning behind the offer of a painting.
7 See Costamagna 2003 for the relationship between Sebastiano and Michelangelo with regard to portrait painting.
8 For the previous attribution see Tomory 1976, p. 106.
9 Gilbert 1961.
10 Hirst 1981, p. 114. See Costamagna in Monbeig Goguel et al. 2001, p. 237 for Benvenuto della Volpaia.
11 Ibid., p. 238.
12 Ibid., pp. 238–239.

39
GIULIANO BUGIARDINI
1475–1554
Portrait of Pope Clement VII
c. 1532
Oil on panel
91.2 × 74.2 cm
Deutsches Historisches Museum, Berlin (Gm 96/19)

Provenance: Cosimo I de' Medici (?). The 12th Duke of Hamilton, Hamilton Palace; Christie's, 1 July 1882 (= 7th day), lot 754, as S. del Piombo (225 gns. to Lesser). with L. Lesser, London. with Sedelmeyer, Paris (as Sebastiano del Piombo). Marczell von Nemes; sale, Mensing, Cassirer and Helbing, Munich, 16 June 1931, lot 29. with Kleinberger Galleries, New York; sale, Parke-Bernet, New York, 24 March 1938, lot 41. with Central Picture Galleries, New York, by 1973. Walter P. Chrysler, Jr., by whom purchased from the above in December 1975; Sotheby's, New York, 1 June 1989, lot 16. In auction of *Old Master Pictures*, Christie's London, July 5, 1996, lot no. 34. Deutsches Historisches Museum, Berlin

References: Vasari-Milanesi 1878–1885, vol. 5, pp. 581–582, vol. 6, pp. 205–206; Waagen 1854, vol. 3, p. 303 (as Sebastiano del Piombo, c. 1523); Crowe and Cavalcaselle 1871, vol. 2, p. 350; Rolfs 1925, p. 125; Dussler 1942, p. 116; Volpe and Lucco 1980, p. 117; Hirst 1981, p. 111, note 90; Langedijk 1981–1987, vol. 2, p. 1364, nos. 8 and 9; Pagnotta 1987, pp. 67–69 and 219–220, no. 65; Zambrano 1991, pp. 84–85; Sotheby's 1989, lot 16; Christie's 1996, lot 34; D. Carr in Ferino-Pagden 1997, p. 102; Pieken in Koschnick 1997, p. 48; S.E. Reiss in Bonn 1999, no. 57, pp. 449–450; R. Contini in Strinati et al. 2008, p. 246.

Notes
1 On the demand for portraits of Clement following his return to Rome from exile and the restoration of the Medici to power in Florence see Hirst 1981, pp. 110–111; R. Contini in Strinati et al. 2008, p. 246. On Bugiardini see Vasari-Milanesi 1878–1885, vol. 6, pp. 201–211; Meloni-Trkulja in *Dizionario biografico degli Italiani* (Rome, 1960–), vol. 15, s.v. "Bugiardini, Giuliano"; Pagnotta 1987; Zambrano 1991, pp. 84–85; Franklin 2005, nos. 27, 28.
2 *Carteggio di Michelangelo*, vol. 3, pp. 303, 318, 332–333. On this correspondence and the vicissitudes of the requests to Sebastiano for likenesses of the pope see Hirst 1981, p. 110; Pagnotta 1987, p. 67, note 26; S.E. Reiss in Bonn 1999, no. 57, pp. 449–450; Contini in Strinati et al. 2008, no. 64, p. 246.
3 *Carteggio di Michelangelo*, vol. 3, p. 318. Sebastiano uses the term "sopra una pietra." On his experimentation with slate and other stone as supports see Vasari-Milanesi 1878–1885, vol. 5, pp. 579–580. For Vittorio Soranzo's letter of 8 June 1530 to Pietro Bembo praising the durability of Sebastiano's painting on marble see Hirst 1981, pp. 123–125. See also Langedijk 1981–1987, vol. 1, p. 54; C.J. Hessler, "The Man on Slate: Sebastiano del Piombo's Portrait of Baccio Valori and Valori the Younger's Speech in Borghini's *Il Riposo*," *Source* 25 (2006), pp. 18–22; Strinati et al. 2008, passim.
4 *Carteggio di Michelangelo*, vol. 3, p. 318. A very beautiful head of Clement in Naples, on slate and shown bearded and bare-headed (see Strinati et al. 2008, no. 64, with bibliography), has sometimes been associated with the version mentioned in this letter, as has the large portrait of Clement on slate in the J. Paul Getty Museum in Los Angeles (see D. Carr in Ferino Pagden 1997, p. 102).
5 *Carteggio di Michelangelo*, vol. 3, p. 332.
6 Ibid. See also Giovan Battista Mini's letter of 8 October 1531 to Baccio Valori (published in *Carteggio di Michelangelo*, vol. 3, pp. 333–335). Concerning the political expediency of Michelangelo's currying favour with Valori see Hirst 1981, pp. 110–111. On Sebastiano and Valori see Hessler, "The Man on Slate." On the Valori family and Florentine politics see M. Jurdjrvic, *Guardians of Republicanism: The Valori Family in the Florentine Renaissance* (Oxford, 2008).
7 *Carteggio di Michelangelo*, vol. 3, p. 332. That the painter alluded to by Sebastiano was Bugiardini is confirmed in Mini's letter to Valori cited in the preceding note.
8 *Carteggio di Michelangelo*, vol. 3, pp. 384, 390, 406. On a now-lost portrait of Clement formerly in the Corsini Gallery that has been associated with the one sent to Florence see Rolfs 1925, pp. 124–125; Dussler 1942, pp. 69, 115, note 58; R. Palluchini, *Sebastian Viniziano (Fra Sebastiano del Piombo)* (Milan, 1944), p. 170; Langedijk 1981–1987, vol. 2, no. 102,24, p. 1368; Pagnotta 1987, p. 68, note 27. Pagnotta was unable to find a reproduction of the Corsini painting. Another possible candidate has come to light recently. This is a portrait of Clement, attributed to Sebastiano, in oil on paper laid down on slate, presently with the Hazlitt, Gooden and Fox Gallery in London and shown in the Sebastiano del Piombo exhibition in Berlin in 2008. See also Contini in Strinati et al. 2008, p. 246. I am most grateful to Paul Joannides for making me aware of this work and to Michael Simpson for providing an image and details. I am also grateful to Peter Humfrey, who kindly shared with me a draft of his catalogue entry on a portrait of Clement VII after Sebastiano in Pollock House, Glasgow.
9 Vasari-Milanesi 1878–1885, vol. 5, p. 581. See also A.M. Bracciante, *Ottaviano de' Medici e gli artisti* (Florence, 1984), p. 63. It should be noted that the Michelangelo correspondence suggests that it was the pope or the other sitters who wanted the portraits and does not indicate that they were the result of Bugiardini's agency.

10 Vasari-Milanesi 1878–1885, vol. 5, pp. 581–582. On Ottaviano de' Medici and his relationship with artists see Bracciante, *Ottaviano de' Medici*.
11 Vasari-Milanesi 1878–1885, vol. 6, pp. 205–206. On 27 June 1550 "uno quadro grande dove era ritratto Papa Clemente et Bartolomeo Valori" is mentioned in the Medici *guardaroba* (Archivio di Stato, Florence, Guardaroba Medicea 23, c. 35). I am grateful to Douglas Dow and Louis Waldman for checking and transcribing this document for me. See also Langedijk 1981–1987, vol. 2, p. 1363, note 7; Pagnotta 1987, p. 220, note 1.
12 Vasari-Milanesi 1878–1885, vol. 6, p. 205. On the later sixteenth-century copy on deposit at the Uffizi (formerly at Poggio Imperiale) see Langedijk 1981–1987, vol. 2, no. 102,2, pp. 1361–1362; Pagnotta 1987, p. 68, tav. XXV. P. Joannides (Strinati et al. 2008, no. 95, p. 312) has associated the seated figure of Clement in the lost Schomberg portrait with the depiction of the Medici pontiff in a drawing now in the Louvre, which he accepts as autograph; see Hirst 1981, p. 111, for a discussion of the sheet as a copy.
13 Pagnotta 1987, pp. 68 and 219–220.
14 Waagen 1854, vol. 3, p. 303.
15 See Pagnotta 1987, fig. 65, for the portrait with Clement seen at full length. It is described thus in Crowe and Cavalcaselle 1871, vol. 2, p. 350, and in Rolfs 1925, p. 125.
16 Concerning Clement's beard see M.J. Zucker, "Raphael and the Beard of Pope Julius II," *The Art Bulletin* 59 (1977), p. 532; Chastel 1983, pp. 186–188.
17 *Carteggio di Michelangelo*, vol. 3, p. 303. See also Hirst 1981, p. 106.
18 On the seasonality of papal attire see B. Davidson, *Raphael's Bible: A Study of the Vatican Logge* (New York, 1985), p. 11; N.H. Minnich, "Raphael's Portrait *Leo X with Cardinals Giulio de' Medici and Luigi de' Rossi*: A Religious Interpretation," *Renaissance Quarterly* 56 (2003), p. 1014; Woods-Marsden in Hall 2005, p. 121; J.M. De Silva, "Ritual Negotiations: Paris de' Grassi and the Office of Ceremonies under Pope Julius II and Leo X (1504–1521)," Ph.D. diss., University of Toronto, 2007, pp. 273–274; O. Mansour, "Prince and Pontiff: Secular and Spiritual Authority in Papal State Portraiture between Raphael's *Julius II* and the Portraits of Pius V and Clement VIII," in *Art and Identity in Early Modern Rome*, ed. J. Burke and M. Bury (Aldershot, U.K., and Burlington, Vt., 2008), p. 215. On the origins and significance of the everyday, non-liturgical *camauro* and *mozzetta* see L. Partridge and R. Starn, *A Renaissance Likeness: Art and Culture in Raphael's Julius II* (Berkeley, 1980), pp. 2, 11, 49, 136; P. Zitzlsperger, *Gianlorenzo Bernini: Die Papst-und Herrscherporträts. Zum Verhältnis von Bildnis und Macht* (Munich, 2002), pp. 48–95; Minnich, "Raphael's Portrait *Leo X*," pp. 1014, 1037; Mansour, "Prince and Pontiff," pp. 210, 212, 215.
19 Many Renaissance papal portraits show the sitters in ermine-trimmed velvet winter attire. Examples include Melozzo da Forlì's frescoed group portrait of Sixtus IV appointing Platina Prefect of the Vatican Library (Pinacoteca Vaticana); Raphael's portraits of Julius II in the National Gallery, London, and in the Stanza d'Eliodoro; his *Pope Leo X with Cardinals Giulio de' Medici and Luigi de' Rossi* in the Uffizi; Sebastiano's portraits of Clement in Naples (Capodimonte) and Los Angeles (J. Paul Getty Museum); and Titian's portraits of Paul III in Naples. On papal summer attire see Mansour, "Prince and Pontiff," p. 227, note 26.
20 See Partridge and Starn, *A Renaissance Likeness*, pp. 55–56, 60–62, on the cloth and rings in Raphael's *Portrait of Pope Julius II* in London. But see also R. Quednau, "Raphael's 'Julius II,'" *The Burlington Magazine* 123 (1981), p. 552, questioning the interpretation of the cloth as *consular mappa*.
21 Recent studies of Raphael's Leo portrait include A. del Serra et al., *Raffaello e il ritratto di papa Leone: Per il restauro del Leone X con due cardinali nella Galleria degli Uffizi* (Milan, 1996); F.P. Di Teodoro, *Ritratto di Leone X di Raffaello Sanzio* (Milan, 1998); R. Zapperi, "Raffaels Bildnis Papst Leos X. mit zwei Kardinälen," in *Re-Visionen: Zur Aktualität von Kunstgeschichte*, ed. B. Hüttel, R. Hüttel, and J. Kohl (Berlin, 2002), pp. 97–105.; M. Rohlmann, "I ritratti di Giulio II and Leone X di Raffaello," in *Rafael i jego spadkobiercy: Portret klasyczny w sztuce nowoóytnej Europ*, ed. S. Dudzik (Torún, 2003) pp. 185–219; Minnich "Raphael's Portrait *Leo X*," pp. 1005–1052.; Woods-Marsden in Hall 2005.
22 Galleria Nazionale d'Arte Antica di Palazzo Barberini, Rome (901; ex-Galleria Corsini). See Vasari-Milanesi 1878–1885, vol. 6, pp. 206–207; Langedijk 1981–1987, vol. 2, no. 103; C.L. Frommel, S. Ray, and M. Tafuri, ed., *Raffaello architetto*, exh. cat. (Milan, 1984), p. 228, no. 2.11.2; Pagnotta 1987, no. 38, pp. 207–208 (with bibliography). On the shipping of Raphael's portrait to Florence in September 1518 see R. Sherr, "A New Document Concerning Raphael's Portrait of Leo X," *The Burlington Magazine* 125 (1983), pp. 31–32; J. Shearman, *Raphael in Early Modern Sources (1483–1602)* (New Haven, 2003) vol. 1, pp. 364–366, docs. 1518/61, 1518/21.
23 Pagnotta (1987, p. 208) dates Bugiardini's painting to late 1518–1519, soon after the arrival of Raphael's original in Florence. Regarding copies of Raphael's painting see *Raffaello a Firenze: Dipinti e disegni delle collezioni fiorentine*, exh. cat. (Florence, 1984), no. 17; A. Nesselrath in Bonn 1999, no. 22. See also Vasari's copy of 1537, here cat. 46.
24 Hirst (1981, p. 111) beautifully characterized the vastly different psychological tenor of the Naples portrait and the canvas version depicting the seated, bearded Clement in Vienna (now held by Hirst and some others to be a copy). His words certainly apply to the other, post-Sack images of the bearded Clement, such as the present work. The Naples portrait on canvas is likely to be the painting Sebastiano described in April 1531 as one he had made before the Sack, "senza barba, che credo non sia al proposito" (*Carteggio di Michelangelo*, vol. 3, p. 303). For bibliography on this painting see Contini in Strinati et al. 2008, p. 210, no. 47.
25 Contemporaries remarked on Clement's transformation after the Sack – see, for example, *I diarii di Marino Sanuto* (Venice, 1879–1903), vol. 47, col. 349. On Clement's illness in 1529 see L. von Pastor, *The History of the Popes from the Close of the Middle Ages, Drawn from the Secret Archives of the Vatican and Other Original Sources*, ed. F.I. Antrobus et al., 3rd. ed. (London, 1901–1933), vol. 10, p. 39ff.; G. Pieraccini, *La stirpe de' Medici di Cafaggiolo: Saggio di ricerche sulla trasmissione ereditaria dei caratteri biologici* (Florence, 1986), vol. 1, p. 295ff. On the decisive importance of Raphael's likeness of Julius II in the history of papal portraiture see C. Gould, *Raphael's Portrait of Pope Julius II: The Re-emergence of the Original* (London, 1970), p. 12; Zitzlsperger, *Gianlorenzo Bernini*, pp. 89–94; C. Plazzotta in H. Chapman, T. Henry, C. Plazzotta, et al., *Raphael: From Urbino to Rome*, exh. cat. (London, 2004), p. 274; Mansour, "Prince and Pontiff," pp. 209–229.

40
MICHELANGELO BUONARROTI, CALLED MICHELANGELO
1475–1564
Studies for the Last Judgment (recto and verso)
c. 1534–1536
Black chalk
27.7 × 41.9 cm
Annotations: *di Bona Roti* (verso)
The Royal Collection (RL 12776)

Provenance: George III (inventory A)

References: Popham and Wilde 1949, pp. 255–256, no. 432; Hirst 1988b, p. 126, no. 52; Joannides 1996, pp. 169–171, nos. 55a-b; Chapman 2005, p. 236.

Notes
1 On the commission see, most recently, *Michelangelo's Last Judgment*, ed. M. Hall, Cambridge, 2005.
2 Hirst 1988b, p. 126.
3 Popham and Wilde 1949, pp. 255–256, relate each figure to the fresco in detail.

41
ANTONIO DA SANGALLO THE YOUNGER
1484–1546
Design for a Freestanding Tomb Seen in Elevation and Plan
c. 1534–1536
Pen and brown ink, brush and brown wash, over extensive compass-incised and stylus-ruled construction with pin-pricked measurements; the elevation drawing is inscribed by the artist with measurements
40.1 × 18.8 cm
The Metropolitan Museum of Art, New York (1998.265)
Edward Pearce Casey Fund, 1998

Provenance: Christie's sale, London, 7 July 1998, lot 51, Kunsthandel Katrin Bellinger, Munich; purchased by The Metropolitan Museum of Art in 1998.

References: Bambach 2007, pp. 81–82, 91 (n. 37), fig. 95; Bambach 2008, p. 128, fig. 3.

Notes
1 As stated in the auction catalogue, Christie's sale, 7 July 1998, lot 51; the other three sheets sold as lots 50, 52, and 53.
2 The auction catalogue, Christie's sale, 7 July 1998, quotes C.L. Frommel who states that lot 50 may have been intended as a design for the chapel and funerary monument of Piero de' Medici at Montecassino, while noting that lots 52 and 53 were perhaps alternative designs for the tomb of Giovanni dalle Bande Nere on Piazza S. Lorenzo, Florence.
3 As calculated, 1 *palmo (romano)* = 0.2234 metres; or alternatively, 1 *piede (romano)* = 0.29 metres. The Uffizi copy (no. 183A recto) after the Metropolitan Museum of Art also exhibits an inscribed measurement "20–10" like the Metropolitan sheet, and it has been said that this unit is in "piedi" which does not seem convincing as it would mean the monument was even more enormous than is calculated here (see U. Kleefisch-Jobst in Jobst in *The Architectural Drawings of Antonio da Sangallo The Younger and His Circle*, ed. C.L. Frommel and N. Adams (New York, 2000), vol. 2, p. 117, no. U 183A, as Giovanni Battista da Sangallo).
4 See, for example, the sheets (Uffizi inv. nos. 73A recto, 79A recto, 83A recto, 185A recto, 1096 recto-verso, Florence).
5 U. Kleefisch-Jobst, "Die Errichtung der Grabmäler für Leo X. und Clemens VII.," *Zeitschrift für Kunstgeschichte*, vol. 51, no. 4 (1988), pp. 524–41.
6 See Vasari 1966–1987, vol. 5 (testo), pp. 253, 255–260.
7 D. Heikamp, "Die Entwurfszeichnungen für die Grabmäler der Mediceer-Päpste Leo X. und Clemens VII.," *Albertina Studien*, vol. 6, no. 3 (1966), pp. 134–152; U. Kleefisch-Jobst, "Die Errichtung der Grabmäler für Leo X. und Clemens VII.," vol. 51, no. 4 (1988), pp. 524–541.
8 The executors of Pope Clement's will being Cardinals Giovanni Cibo, Giovanni Salviati, and Niccolò Ridoli. See copy of this contract dated 25 March 1536, and the list of blocks of marble of late March 1536 for the tomb of Clement VII, as published in L.A. Waldman, *Baccio Bandinelli and Art at the Medici Court: A Corpus of Early Modern Sources* (Philadelphia, 2004), pp. 146–150, nos. 254–255.
9 Compare D. Heikamp, "Die Entwurfszeichnungen," pp. 138, 141–143 (figs. 8, 959), pp. 151 (nn. 10, 13) and R. Ward, *Baccio Bandinelli 1493–1560: Drawings from British Collections*, exh. cat. (Cambridge, 1988), no. 31.
10 D. Heikamp, "Die Entwurfszeichnungen," p. 137.
11 Ibid., pp. 139–140, figs. 5, 6, 7 are identified as redesigns by Sangallo of the choir of Santa Maria sopra Minerva.
12 On this drawing (Graphische Sammlung Abertina inv. 15461, Vienna), some pen and brown ink, brush and brown wash, over black chalk and ruled construction, 55.5 × 41.2 cm; see now the excellent analysis by Waldman in *Baccio Bandinelli*, pp. 148–150 (and nn. 1–5); see also V. Birke and J. Kertész, *Die italienischen Zeichnungen der Albertina: Generalverzeichnis*. 4 vols. Veröffentlichungen der Albertina, 33–36 (Vienna-Cologne-Weimar, 1992–1997), vol. 4, pp. 2103, no. 15461.
13 Statues of prophets and evangelists are mentioned in the document of late March 1536 listing the marble blocks for the tomb of Clement VII to be carved by Baccio Bandinelli, as published in Waldman, *Baccio Bandinelli*, p. 148, no. 255.
14 Uffizi inv. nos. 185A, 1129A, 1559A, Florence.
15 Uffizi inv. No. 183A. See U. Kleefisch-Jobst in *Architectural Drawings*, vol. 2, pp. 117–119, nos. U 183A (Giovanni Battista da Sangallo) and U 185A (Antonio da Sangallo); but with no mention of the drawing in The Metropolitan Museum of Art.
16 Compare D. Heikamp, "Die Entwurfszeichnungen," pp. 135–136, figs. 1, 2; C.L. Frommel and N. Adams, *The Drawings of Antonio da Sangallo the Younger and His Circle* (New York, 1994), p. 45, pls. 39–40; P.N. Pagliara, "Giovanni Battista da Sangallo," in *The Dictionary of Art*, ed. J.S. Turner, vol. 27, pp. 747–749, 642–653. 34 vols. (London, 1996).
17 In the Sacristy Museum, Basilica of Saint Peter's, illustrated and discussed in A. Wright, *The Pollaiuolo Brothers: The Arts of Florence and Rome* (New Haven, CT and London, 2005), pp. 358–387, 528–529, no. 69.
18 D. Heikamp, "Die Entwurfszeichnungen," p. 134.
19 Vasari 1966–1987, vol. 6, pp. 75–86.

42

VINCENZO DE' ROSSI
1525–1587
Purported Design for the Tomb of Pope Clement VII
After 1560
Pen and brown ink over traces of black chalk and more extensive underdrawing with stylus, straight-edge and compass
35.4 × 21.3 cm
Museum of Art, Rhode Island School of Design, Providence (51.507)
Museum Works of Art Fund

References: Goldberg 1975–1976; Ward 1982, no. 378; Hegener 2008, pp. 90–91, 645–646, cat. B106.

Notes
1   Goldberg 1975–1976, pp. 16–25. More recently, the motif of the interceding Virgin has been read as a refutation of Luther's doctrine of intercession through Christ alone, see H. Bredekamp, "Grabmäler der Renaissancepäpste. Die Kunst der Nachwelt," in Bonn 1999, p. 264.
2   The most important study of Vincenzo de' Rossi's work yet published, though focused on the first half of his career, is by R. Schallert, *Studien zu Vincenzo de' Rossi. Die frühen und mittleren Werke (1536–1561)* (Hildesheim, 1998).
3   See esp. D. Heikamp, "Vincenzo de' Rossi disegnatore," *Paragone*, 15, No. 175 (1964), pp. 38–42; and W. Vitzthum. "A Drawing by Vincenzo de' Rossi," *Master Drawings* III (1965), p. 165.
4   Madrid, Academia de San Fernando 163; Stockholm, Nationalmuseum 134/135; Christ Church 1413; Louvre 113.
5   Louvre 84, 85 and 86; Ashmolean P.II.85; Cooper-Hewitt 1938-88-1741.
6   Christ Church 0088.
7   Louvre 92. For another drawing attributed to Rossi for the first time after long oblivion, see the catalogue entry on Herman Posthumus (cat. 45, p. 194).
8   Sold at Christie's, 6 July 1987; see J. Cox-Rearick, *Bronzino's Chapel of Eleonora in the Palazzo Vecchio* (Berkeley, 1993), pp. 158–159; Hegener 2008, pp. 368–369, 623 cat. B45.
9   Waldman 2004, doc. 1424: *Hora sarà tempo, che Vincenzo Rossi sollecitassi la cosa sua … E' mi haveva promesso non so che disegni del Bandinello…* For Borghini's previous interventions on Vincenzo's behalf, see ibid., docs. 1400, 1412, 1417, 1419.

43

FRANCESCO DE ROSSI, CALLED SALVIATI
1510–1563
Virgin and Child with an Angel
c. 1535–1540
Oil on panel
112.3 × 83 cm
National Gallery of Canada, Ottawa (41690)
Purchased 2005 with the support of the Volunteer Circle of the National Gallery of Canada and the National Gallery of Canada Foundation Renaissance Ball Patrons, for the Gallery's 125th Anniversary

Provenance: Private collection, France; Private collection, England; Purchased from Hazlitt, Gooden & Fox, London, in 2005.

References: Costamagna 2005, pp. 67–70.

Notes
1   P. Costamagna, "Une 'Vierge à l'Enfant avec un'ange' de la jeunesse de Francesco Salviati decouverte," *Paragone* LVI, no. 64 (669) (2005), pp. 67–70. Monbeig Goguel et al. 2001, p. 18, note 11, described the painting as a contemporary replica by Salviati – the only published reference to the work

prior to Costamagna's article. There is a copy of the Ottawa painting in the Palazzo Ducale, Urbino.
2   Vasari 1996, p. 563.
3   Whitaker and Clayton 2007, no. 8, pp. 71–73, where the paintings are dated to c. 1538–1540.

44

ATTRIBUTED TO FRANCESCO DE' ROSSI, CALLED SALVIATI
1510–1563
The Council of the Gods
c. 1530s
Red chalk
22 × 44.2 cm
The Phillips Family Collection

Provenance: J. Richardson Sr. collection (L. 2184); W. Roscoe collection (L. 2645); his sale, Winstanley, Liverpool, 24 September 1816, lot 176 (Raphaël's workshop); Christie's, London, 6 July 1977, lot 36, pl. 2 (Raphael school); Colnaghi's, London, November 1977, lot 51 (Raphael's workshop).

References: Byam Shaw 1983, p. 127 (copy); Oberhuber 1986, fig. 26; Harprath 1985, p. 412 (workshop); Monbeig Goguel 2004, p. 207 (Salviati).

Notes
1   Book IV, 28, at VI, 24. See Cordellier and Py 1992, p. 362.
2   J. Shearman, "Die Loggia der Psyche in der Villa Farnesina und die Probleme der letzten Phase von Raffaels graphischem Stil," in *Jahrbuch der Kunsthistorischen Sammlungen in Wien*, vol. 60 (1964), pp. 59–100.
3   These drawings are discussed in the exhibition catalogue *Francesco Salviati ou la bella maniera*. See Monbeig Goguel 1998, nos. 2 and 30.
4   *Siché due casse di disegni comprai da lei tutti fatti a mano, dove erano tutte le fatiche ch'egli giamai fece, e molte ancora di Raffael d'Urbino, già stato suo maestro.* Partially quoted in Monbeig Goguel 2004, p. 205. For the transcription of Strada's preface in which the famous sale is mentioned, see J. Shearman, *Raphael in Early Modern Sources (1483–1602)* (New Haven and London 2003), document 1575/4.
5   On the origins of the decoration, from an organizational point of view, see the excellent article by B. Marocchini and F. Piacentini, "L'organizzazione del cantiere della loggia di Amore e Psiche," in R. Varoli Piazza (ed.), *Raffaello. La loggia di Amore e Psiche alla Farnesina* (Milan, 2002), pp. 71–97; on Raphael's studio in general, see J. Shearman, "The Organization of Raphael's Workshop," *Art Institute of Chicago Museum Studies* 10 (1983), pp. 40–57.
6   Vasari–Milanesi 1879–1906, IV, p. 644.
7   On Penni, see Pouncey and Gere 1962, pp. 50–58; K. Oberhuber, "Penni o Raffaello," in D. Cordellier, *Raffaello e i suoi. Disegni di Raffaello e della sua cerchia* (Rome, 1992), pp. 21–26; A. Gnann, "On a Drawing Attributed to Giovanni Francesco Penni," *Master Drawings* vol. 45, no. 2 (2007), pp. 229–235.
8   See B.XV.89.54.

45

HERMAN POSTHUMUS
c. 1500 – after 1542
Landscape with Antique Ruins
1536
Oil on canvas
96 × 141 cm
Liechtenstein Museum, Vienna (GE740)
Sammlungen des Fürsten von und zu Liechtenstein, Vaduz–Wien

References: New York 1985b, pp. 250–252, no. 158; Dacos 1985; Rubinstein 1985; Dacos 1989; Dacos 2001, pp. 7–15.

Notes
1   Rubinstein 1985, p. 425
2   Ibid. pp. 426–433
3   Dacos 1985, p. 434; Rubinstein 1985, p. 426
4   Dacos 1985, p. 434; Dacos 1989, pp. 63–64
5   Dacos 1985, p. 438.
6   C. Hülsen and H. Egger, *Die römischen Skizzenbücher von Marten van Heemskerck im Königlichen Kupferstichkabinett zu Berlin*, 2 vols. (Berlin, 1913–1916). pp. vii–xviii; Dacos 1985; Dacos 1989; Dacos 2001.
7   Dacos 1985, p. 437; Dacos 1989, p. 64.
8   compare Dacos 1985, p. 436, figs. 13 and 14.

46

GIORGIO VASARI
1511–1574
Pope Leo X with the Cardinals Giulio de' Medici and Luigi de' Rossi (copy after Raphael)
1537
Oil on panel
157.5 × 117 cm
Viscount Coke and the Trustees of the Holkham Estate, Norfolk

References: Passavant 1860, II, pp. 269–274, no. 234; Crowe and Cavacaselle 1885, II, pp. 329–333; Gruyer 1881, II, pp. 333–339; Vasari-Milanesi 1906, IV, p. 352, V, pp. 41–43, VI, S. 206ff., VII, p. 662; Frey 1923, p. 92ff.; Burkhalter 1932, p. 96; Dussler 1966, p. 34, no. 46;

Notes
1   Pinacoteca Nazionale, inv. no. 534.
2   Florence, Uffizi, inv. no. 1578.
3   Uffizi, inv. no. 1563.

47

PIERO BUONACCORSI, CALLED PERINO DEL VAGA
1501–1547
Design for the Decoration of a Chapel Wall (recto)
The Feast of Herod (verso)
c. 1537
Black chalk, pen and brown ink, with brown and grey washes
41.9 × 29 cm
Inscriptions: *paganazo / di viterbo libre 15 / nero di fuma libre 2 / leone batista alberti / le stampe d'alberto* (verso)
Szépmüvészeti Múzeum, Budapest (1838)

Provenance: Esterhazy (L. 1965).

References: Gere 1960, pp. 10–13; Chicago 1985, no. 15, pp. 46–47; Parma Armani 1986, pp. 179, 186, 286; Parma 2001, no. 71, pp. 178–182; Wolk-Simon 2003, p. 51.

Notes
1   As established in a notarial document in the Archivio di Stato, Rome; see K. Oberhuber, "Observations on Perino del Vaga as a Draughtsman," *Master Drawings* 4 (1966), p. 180, note 29. According to Vasari, Perino's patron was Pietro Massimo (Vasari-Milanesi 1878–1885, vol. 5, p. 620). In addition to the Massimi chapel, the artist also painted a frieze in the salone of the Palazzo Pirro Massimo at the end of the 1530s.
2   On the letter see Parma Armani 1986, p. 328; see also Robertson 1992, pp. 36–37. A number of Perino's drawings for Bernardi's six plaques (five of which survive) are known; see Parma 2001, pp. 266–270. This was probably the first commission Perino received from Cardinal Alessandro Farnese.
3   The pre-Massimi decorations are variously mentioned by Vasari in the *Lives* of Marcantonio Raimondi (who engraved some of Giulio and Penni's compositions), Giulio Romano, and Perino. On the chapel's early history and patronage see C.L.L. Whitcombe,

"The Chapel of the Courtesan and the Quarrel of the Magdalens," *The Art Bulletin* 84 (June 2002), pp. 273–292. It has been plausibly suggested that the unnamed "most famous" courtesan referred to by Vasari was Lucrezia Scanatoria, who died before 14 February 1522 and left money to Trinità dei Monti in her will. She may be the unidentified sitter – certainly a courtesan – in Giulio's portrait of a nude woman in the Pushkin Museum, Moscow; see Wolk-Simon in Bayer 2008, pp. 46–47, 185, no. 87. The altarpiece, sometimes ascribed to Giulio's follower Raffaellino del Colle but undoubtedly based on his design if not fully executed by him, is now in the Museo del Prado, Madrid; a replica by Penni is in the Museo Nazionale di Capodimonte, Naples. A previously unidentified partial copy after the lost ceiling, to be published by the present author, shows a blessing God the Father in one of the compartments – a hitherto unrecorded detail of this lost decoration.
4   Bacou (in Bacou and Beguin 1983, pp. 9–10, 134) proposed that two detached frescoes of the Evangelists Matthew and Mark, attributed to Perino by Gere and purportedly from the Trinità dei Monti (now Musée des Beaux-Arts, Chartres) are from the Massimi Chapel. Both the attribution and the conjecture about their original setting were rightly rejected by Parma Armani (1986, p. 285). That author's subsequent suggestion (Parma 2001, p. 182) that these may be two of the Evangelists from the vault, and that they are by Penni, is not persuasive.
5   Parma 2001, under nos. 71–73, pp. 178–183.
6   Chicago 1985, no. 15, pp. 46–47.
7   This attractive hypothesis was first advanced by L. Trezzani (in A. Bacchi et al., "La pittura del Cinquecento a Roma e nel Lazio," in *La pittura in Italia: Il Cinquecento* [Milan, 1987], p. 391), and repeated by Parma (2001, p. 177), both in passing, and elaborated by Wolk-Simon (2003, p. 51).
8   Wolk-Simon 2003, p. 51.
9   "Il reverendissimo cardinal Farnese gli cominciasse a dar provisione e servirsene in molte cose." Vasari-Milanesi 1878–1885, vol. 5, p. 622.

48

PIERO BUONACCORSI, CALLED PERINO DEL VAGA
1501–1547
Juno Visiting Aeolus and Neptune Calming the Tempest
1540
Pen and grey ink, grey wash, with white heightening, over traces of black chalk
22 × 21.5 cm [at maximum]
Inscriptions: QVOS EGO
The Royal Collection (RL 5497)

Provenance: George III.

References: Popham and Wilde 1949, no. 975; Askew 1956, p. 49; Pouncey and Gere 1962, under no. 169, p. 100; Hirst 1965, pp. 569–571; Bacou and Beguin 1983, p. 80; Parma Armani 1986, pp. 126, 272; Jaffe 1994, p. 48; Clayton 1999, no. 55, pp. 188–190; Parma 2001, no. 101, p. 211.

Notes
1   Clayton 1999, no. 55, pp. 188–190.
2   P. Boccardo, *Andrea Doria e le arti* (Rome, 1989), pp. 82–85; T.P. Campbell, *Tapestry in the Renaissance: Art and Magnificence*, exh. cat. (New York and New Haven, 2002), pp. 359–360.
3   B. XIV, 264. See I.H. Shoemaker and E. Broun, *The Engravings of Marcantonio Raimondi*, exh. cat. (Lawrence, Kans., and Chapel Hill, N.C., 1981), no. 32.

4   Musée du Louvre, Paris (636). See B.F. Davidson, *Mostra di disegni di Perino del Vaga e la sua cerchia*, exh. cat. (Florence, 1966), no. 17; Bacou and Beguin 1983, no. 90. For Bonasone's engraving (B.XV.104) see A. Gnann in Parma 2001, p. 210, no. 100.

49
PIERO BUONACCORSI, CALLED PERINO DEL VAGA
1501–1547
Saint Paul Lowered from the Walls of Damascus in a Basket: Study for the Cope of Pope Paul III
c. 1542–1545
Pen and brown ink with brown wash, with white heightening
25.4 × 15.2 cm
Devonshire Collection, Chatsworth (164)

Provenance: Probably Sir Peter Lely; presumably 1st or 2nd Duke of Devonshire.

References: Pouncey and Gere 1962, under no. 172; Parma Armani 1986, p. 335, fig. 360; Jaffé 1987, p. 100, no. 56; Davidson 1990, p. 135, fig. 9; Jaffé 1994, p. 164, no. 372; Parma 2001, p. 277, no. 148.

Notes
1   "Otto storie di San Pietro, tratti delle Atti degli Apostoli," Vasari-Milanesi 1878–1885, vol. 5, pp. 631–632.
2   Davidson 1990, pp. 138, 141, note 30.
3   See Davidson 1990.
4   Suggested by Davidson, ibid., p. 135.

50
PIERO BUONACCORSI, CALLED PERINO DEL VAGA
1501–1547
Alexander the Great Cutting the Gordian Knot
c. 1545
Pen and brown ink, grey wash, with white heightening; squared in black chalk
19 × 11.2 cm
The Metropolitan Museum of Art, New York
Harry G. Sperling Fund, 1984 (1984.413)

Provenance: French private collection; sale, Nouveau Drouot, Paris, 10–11 October 1983, lot 71 (as School of Polidoro da Caravaggio).

References: Turçic in New York 1985c, p. 29; Gere 1987, no. 79; Wolk-Simon 1992, p. 63, fig. 9; Wolk-Simon in Griswold and Wolk-Simon 1994, no. 66; Wolk-Simon in Parma 2001, no. 187, pp. 324–325.

51
PIERO BUONACCORSI, CALLED PERINO DEL VAGA
1501–1547
Various Studies after the Antique
1538–1540
Pen and brown and grey ink on blue paper
Inscriptions: *G . IV LIVS . L . F . CAESAR / STRABO / AED CVR . O . TR . MIL . BIS . X . VIR / ARGDAND . AD TR . IVD . PONTIF,* and *a porta Apostolo.*
Inscribed indistinctly on the verso.
23.7 × 39.8 cm
Agnes Etherington Art Centre, Queen's University, Kingston (41–018.04)
Gift of Bayside Lakeshore Properties Ltd., Montreal, 1998

Provenance: Cassiano dal Pozzo's Museo Cartaceo; Carlo Antonio Pozzo; thence by descent to Cosimo Antonio dal Pozzo; Pope Clement XI; Cardinal Alessandro Albani; King George III; Richard Dalton; John MacGowan; Charles Townley; his sale, London, Sotheby, Wilkinson and Hodge, 10–11 May 1865, lot 406 (to Thorpe for £5.5.0);

William Stirling Maxwell; thence by descent; his sale, London, Phillips Son & Neale, 12 December 1990, lot 294 (as Perino del Vaga); Roberto Ferretti di Castelferretto.

Notes
1   In an annotation on the mount, A.E. Popham attributed the Kingston drawing to Giulio Romano, but this has not received subsequent support. The attribution to Perino del Vaga was evidently first made in the 1990 sale catalogue. From a digital image, Elena Parma (communication to the author of 8 September 2008) is inclined to agree with the attribution to Perino del Vaga. For analogous drawings by Perino, see his pen-and-ink drawing of Saint John the Baptist preaching, used by Jacopino del Conte in a fresco of 1538 (Vienna, Albertina, n. 23751; *Perino del Vaga, tra Raffaello e Michelangelo*, exh. cat. [Mantua, 2001], no. 70), or his pen-and-ink drawing of Christ cleansing the temple, engraved on rock crystal by Giovanni Bernardi in Venice in 1539 (Stockholm, Nationalmuseum, NMH 256/1973; Mantua, *Perino del Vaga, tra Raffaello e Michelangelo,* no. 139).
2   Bober and Rubinstein 1986, pp. 219–220, no. 186.
3   Nationalmuseum, Stockholm, NM 88/1863; P. Bjurström, *Italian Drawings from the Collection of Giorgio Vasari*, exh. cat. (Stockholm 2001), no. 1072R. See also F. Ames-Lewis, *The Intellectual Life of the Early Renaissance Artist* (New Haven and London, 2000), pp. 119–121, fig. 58, where, however, the wreath is mistakenly said to be of laurel rather than oak.
4   I am grateful to Professor Ross Kilpatrick for this suggestion.
5   The best known example is now embedded into the façade of the Rospigliosi Casino, Rome, but the Kingston drawing is much closer to the reversed design of a lost sarcophagus that was in the house of Livia Colonna in the mid-sixteenth-century; for which, see Bober and Rubinstein 1986, pp. 68–69, no. 26, esp. 26b.

52
FOLLOWER OF PERINO DEL VAGA
Design for a Mantlepiece for Pope Paul III
c. 1543–1548
Pen and brown ink, brown and grey washes, over black chalk
26.4 × 21.8 cm
Inscriptions: *PAVLVS III PONT M*
Agnes Etherington Art Centre, Queen's University, Kingston (41–018.20)
Gift of Bayside Lakeshore Properties Ltd., Montreal, 1998

Provenance: Cassiano dal Pozzo's Museo Cartaceo; Carlo Antonio Pozzo; thence by descent to Cosimo Antonio dal Pozzo; Pope Clement XI; Cardinal Alessandro Albani; King George III; Richard Dalton; John MacGowan; Charles Townley; his sale, London, Sotheby, Wilkinson and Hodge, 10–11 May 1865, lot 406 (to Thorpe for £5.5.0);

William Stirling Maxwell; thence by descent; his sale, London, Phillips Son & Neale, 12 December 1990, part of lot 282; Roberto Ferretti di Castelferretto.

Notes
1   For the renovations in the Castel Sant'Angelo, see E. Gaudioso, "I lavori farnesiani a Castel Sant'Angelo – documenti contabili (1544–1548)," *Bollettino d'Arte,* ser. V, LXI, 1976, III–IV, pp. 228–262; and E. Gaudioso "La decorazione dell'appartamento farnesiano a Castel Sant'Angelo," in *Gli Affreschi di Paolo III a Castel Sant'Angelo 1543–1548,* exh. cat., 2 vols. (Rome, 1981–1982), I, pp. 30–37.

2   British Museum, 1946–7–13–452; Pouncey and Gere 1962, pp. 111–112, no. 186; *Gli Affreschi di Paolo III,* 1981–1982, II, p. 36, no.17.
3   For the payments, see Gaudioso, "I lavori farnesiani," pp. 232–234, and Rome 1981–1982, II, pp. 18–21.
4   For a mask, similar in effect though not in detail, to that in the Kingston drawing, see the fresco attributed to Pellegrino Tibaldi in the Sala di Apollo (1546–1548) of the Castel Sant'Angelo, repr. in *Gli Affreschi di Paolo III,* I, p. 239, fig. 206.
5   Parma 2001, pp. 286–289, nos. 156–158.

53
PELLEGRINO TIBALDI
1527–1596
Prudence
c. 1545–1550
Black chalk, brown wash (added by a later hand)
31.7 × 25.7 cm
Inscriptions: *Pellegrino da Bologna*
Staatliche Museen zu Berlin, Kupferstichkabinett (15456)

References: Voss 1913, p. 299, fig. 1; Gere 1971, p. 88, fig. 12; Romani 1990, pp. 54–55, fig. 42; Romani 1997, p. 73, pl. XV

Notes
1   E. Maccari, *Graffiti e chiaroscuri, esistenti nell'esterno delle case riprodotti in rame*, Rome, n.d., repr. In Voss 1913, fig. 2.
2   Vasari-Milanesi VII, p. 417.
3   F. Edler, "The Van der Molen, Commission Merchants of Antwerp: Trade with Italy 1538–44," in J. Lea Cate, ed. *Medieval and Historiographical Essays in Honor of James Westfall Thompson* (Chicago 1938), p. 98.
4   Vasari-Milanesi VII, p. 416.
5   Gere and Pouncey 1983, no. 268, illustrated. Parts of the figure in the Berlin drawing are rather crudely covered with brown wash. This is fairly unusual in a black chalk figure study in the tradition of Michelangelo, or even Perino. One may suspect, therefore, that the wash was added later, presumably to dress up the sheet, and possibly dates from the same time as the inscription in the lower right corner.
6   Vasari-Milanesi 1879–1906, VII, pp. 416–417.

54
MICHELANGELO BUONARROTI, CALLED MICHELANGELO
1475–1564
Annunciation to the Virgin
c. 1547–1550
Black chalk, outlines indented
38.3 × 29.7 cm
Inscriptions: *From Mr. Lawrence-Woodburn colln / sale catalogue no. 103 / J.C. Robinson*
The Pierpont Morgan Library, New York (IV, 7)
Purchased by Pierpont Morgan, 1909

Provenance: Nicholas Lanière, London (L. 2885); Sir Thomas Lawrence, London; Samuel Woodburn, London; his sale, London, Christie's, 4 June 1860, lot 103, as Michelangelo, "Another Study for the Same Picture, More Elaborately Carried Out, and More in Conformity, in Design, with the Painting-*black chalk. Superb. From the Collection of Charles I*," bought by Enson for £8.15.0; [Brooke] sale, London, Sotheby's, 19–20 June 1891, lot 188, as "Michaelangelo. The Annunciation, a study for the celebrated picture by Venusti, painted from the above and other drawings; from the Collection of Charles I"; bought by Murray for £1.12.0; Sir John Charles Robinson, Edinburgh and London; probably

his sale, Christie's, London, 13 May 1902, lot 215, "Michelangelo Buonarroti. Study for 'The Annunciation' – *black chalk. From the Lawrence-Woodburn Collection. Exhibited at the Guildhall,* 1895," bought by Murray for £11.0.0; Charles Fairfax Murray, London and Florence; from whom purchased through Galerie Alexandre Imbert, Rome, in 1909 by Pierpont Morgan, New York (no mark; see L. 1509); his son, J. P. Morgan, Jr., New York.

References: Lawrence Gallery 1853, no. 2 (Michelangelo); Fairfax Murray 1905–1912, vol. 4, no. 7, repr. (Venusti after Michelangelo); Wilde 1959, p. 377, fig. 1 (Michelangelo); Hirst 1988b, no. 55, repr.; Wallace 2003, pp. 140, 143, 145, 153, fig. 7.1

Notes
1   The Michelangelo/Venusti original altarpiece was replaced by Carlo Cesi's (c. 1622 – c. 1682) *Holy Family with Saint Anne*; oil on canvas, 216 × 138 cm; see A. Vannugli in *Pietro da Cortona 1597–1669,* exh. cat. (Rome, 1997–1998), pp. 432–433, no. 93, repr.
2   Inv. 255; Photo: GFN C 6044
3   Oil on panel; 40 × 30 cm; repr. in S. Capelli, "Marcello Venusti: Un Valtellinese pittore a Roma, *Studi di Storia dell'arte,* 12 (2001), p. 40, fig. 6.
4   Inv. A 3443.
5   45 × 30 cm; Tolnay 1943–1960, vol. 5, p. 208, figs. 212, 213; A. Perrig, "Michelangelo und Marcello Venusti: Das Problem der Verkündigungs- und Ölberg-Konzeptionen Michelangelos," *Wallraf-Richartz-Jahrbuch,* vol. 24 (1962), p. 264, fig. 159.
6   Vasari–Milanesi 1878–1885, vol. 7, p. 272: *Ha fatto poi fare messer Tommaso a Michelagnolo molti disegni per amici; come per il cardinale di Cesis la tavola là dov'è la Nostra Donna annunziata dall'Angelo; cosa nuova, che poi fu da Marcello Mantovano colorita, e posta nella cappella di marmo che ha fatto fare quel cardinale nella chiesa della Pace di Roma.*
7   Wallace 2003, p. 139, which is the authoritative discussion of the relationship between Michelangelo and Venusti.
8   Baglione writes of Venusti's *Last Judgment* "lo condusse tanto eccellentemente, che il Buonarotti gli pose grand'affezione, e impose-gli molte altre copie" (Baglione 1642, p. 20).
9   Cod. Vat. 3211, fol. 74r; Tolnay 1943–1960, vol. 5, fig. 205.

55
GIULIO CLOVIO
1498–1578
Pietà
c. 1546–1553
Black chalk
34.8 × 25.7 cm
Victoria and Albert Museum, London (Dyce 218)
Dyce Bequest 1869

Provenance: Count Gelosi (L. 545).

Reference: Ward-Jackson 1979, no. 124, p. 61.

Notes
1   P. Bellini, *L'opera incise di Adamo e Diana Scultori* (Vicenza, 1991), pp. 195–197, no. 20.
2   M. Cionini Visani, "Un itinerario nel manierismo italiano: Giulio Clovio," *Arte Veneta* 25 (1971), pp. 136–137.
3   Ragghianti Collobi 1974, I, p. 157, suggests the identification of the particular drawing owned by Vasari is unresolved.
4   Vasari 1996, p. 854.
5   C. Monbeig Goguel, "Giulio Clovio: 'Nouveau petit Michel-Ange.' A propos des dessins du Louvre," *Revue de l'Art* 80 (1988), p. 41.

56
TADDEO ZUCCARO
1529–1566
Scene from Roman History
c. 1550
Pen and brown ink over black
chalk, brush with brown wash and
white heightening, on blue paper
25.7 × 28 cm
Private collection, New York

Provenance: William Young Ottley;
Sir Thomas Lawrence (L. 2445);
Samuel Woodburn; Lawrence
Gallery, April 1836, no. 26 (as
Polidoro da Caravaggio); Sotheby's
London, 12 March 1963, lot 22 (as
Federico Zuccaro).

References: *Apollo*, February 1963,
p. xlvii; Gere 1969b, pp. 38–39, 179,
214–215, no. 250; Gere 1971, p. 83;
Ravelli 1978, p. 473; Mundy 1989,
p. 70, no. 6; L. Wolk-Simon in
Griswold and Wolk-Simon 1994,
pp. 82–83; Acidini Luchinat 1998–
1999, vol. 1, p. 113; Brooks et al.
2007, pp. 51–52, no. 39.

Notes
1   For a series of drawings made
by Federico Zuccaro, telling his
brother's story, see Brooks et al.
2007. For the drawings relating to
the Palazzo Mattei commission see
ibid, pp. 47–50.
2   It has been suggested (ibid,
p. 68, note 19) that this drawing
could be preparatory for the Mattei
scene of the Battle of Satricum,
where the aging Camillus dis-
mounts from his horse, grabs a
nearby standard, and leads his
troops to victory. In its size and
square shape it is fairly similar to
the other drawings for the panels
on that facade, but the principal
figure does not seem old enough,
nor the standard prominent
enough.
3   First linked in Gere 1969b,
pp. 179, 214–215, no. 250, plate 9,
and no. 143, plates 12 and 14. The
verso of The Metropolitan Museum
of Art drawing no. 41 has a red
chalk study of three soldiers with
tonal effects similar to those of
Rosso Fiorentino. It perhaps relates
to a drawing such as Uffizi, inv.
no. 11216F (Gere 1969b, p. 153,
no. 72, pl. 15).
4   As pointed out by Mundy
1989, p. 70.

57
GIORGIO VASARI
1511–1574
*Design for the Cappella del Monte in
San Pietro in Montorio, Rome*
c. 1550
Black chalk, brown wash, partially
drawn with a ruler and a pair of
compasses; the *Pietà* drawing executed on a separate sheet of paper
in pen and brown ink, brown wash,
over black chalk, with pen and
brown ink framing lines
51.1 × 31.4 cm
Inscriptions: *IVLIVS III P. M* [below
the altarpiece]
Gabinetto Disgni e Stampe degli
Uffizi, Florence (639F)

Provenance: Fondo Mediceo
Lorenese

References: Barocchi 1964b, p. 133,
no. 40; Barrochi in Florence 1964,
no. 15, fig. 9; Monbeig Goguel 1972,
under nos. 200–201; Corti et al.
1981, p. 91, no. 30a/b (cat. entry by
C. Davis); Nova 1984, p. 150, note 1;
Morrogh 1985, no. 10, fig. 11;
Conforti 1993, pp. 133–134, fig. 126

Notes
1   For a discussion of all the
related documents, see Nova 1984.
2   K. and H.-W. Frey, *Der literarische Nachlass: Giorgio Vasari*, vol. 2
(Munich, 1923), p. 283, 1930 and
1940, p. 283.
3   Ibid, p. 869, no. 197. Vasari
mentions the project also in his
autobiography; see Vasari-
Milanesi VII, p. 693.

4   *Der literarische Nachlas*,
pp. 337–339, no. CLXXV. Nova
(1984, p. 152) suggested that Vasari
began with the execution of the
altarpiece in the beginning of 1551.
The scaffolding was erected in
August 1551. The date 1552 is also
inscribed on top of the chapel's
arch, although the sculptural
decoration was possibly completed
only in 1554. This is suggested by a
payment to Ammannati from July
1554; see C. Conforti, "Momenti di
un sodalizio artistico e profes-
sionale; Giorgio Vasari e Bartolomeo
Ammannati," in N. Roselli del Turco
and F. Salvi, eds., *Bartolomeo
Annannati. Scultore e architetto
1511–1592* (Florence, 1995), p. 142.
Nova (1984, p. 153) suggested the
artist may well have finished his
work by December 1552 and that he
received his last payment only in
1554.
5   Vasari wanted to hire first
Simone Mosca and then Raffaello
da Montelupo, but both were
rejected by Michelangelo.
Ammannato was chosen prior to 28
May 1550: see *Der literarische
Nachlas*, vol. I, p. 291, and Nova
1984, p. 151.
6   Vasari-Milanesi VI, p. 308.
7   Vasari-Milanesi VI, p. 478.
8   Inv. 2198 and 2152. Two drawings in the Uffizi (14274F) and the
Louvre (2151) are related to the
decoration as it was eventually executed. Another drawing from the
Louvre (2180), incorrectly identified in the past, is in fact one of
Vasari's few surviving cartoon fragments. It served as the cartoon for
the upper part for the fresco of
Charity in the chapel's vault.
9   Vasari made such drawings
usually in pen and brown ink over a
black chalk sketch. Based on this
relatively unusual technique
Andrew Morrogh has suggested that
Vasari's choice of medium may have
been influenced by Michelangelo's
architectural drawings, which is
not inconceivable.

58
DANIELE DA VOLTERRA
c. 1509–1566
*A Bearded Man Leaning Against
a Wall*
c. 1548 – early 1550s
Black chalk on pale grey paper
37.1 × 22.7 cm.
The British Museum, London
(1946-7-13-114)

References: Popham 1935, p. 113,
no. 1, pl. LIII; Levie 1962, pp. 101,
note 26, and 189; Barolsky 1979,
pp. 82–86, esp. p. 86; Gere and
Pouncey 1983, no. 76; Romani 2003,
pp. 41–44, 108–110 no. 26, Ciardi
and Moreschini 2004, pp. 188–213.

Notes
1   C. Valone, "The Art of
Hearing: Sermons and Images in
the Chapel of Lucrezia della
Rovere," *Sixteenth Century Journal*
21 (Autumn 2000), p. 761.
2   "The Art of Hearing," p. 767,
and C.P. Murphy, *The Pope's
Daughter* (Oxford, 2005), pp. 73–78.
3   Vasari-Milanesi 1878–
1885, VII, pp. 52–56; C. Valone,
"Elena Orsini, Daniele da Volterra,
and the Orsini Chapel," *Artibus et
Historiae* 11 (1990), pp. 79–87;
Ciardi and Moreschini 2004,
pp. 112–114.
4   "The Art of Hearing," p. 761.
5   Vasari-Milanesi 1878–1885,
VII, pp. 59–61.
6   "The Art of Hearing,"
pp. 754–755.
7   F. Bonnard, *Histoire du
Couvent royal de la Trinité du Mont
Pincio à Rome* (Rome and Paris,
1933), pp. 41–42.
8   Vasari-Milanesi 1878–
1885, VII, pp. 60–61 [author's
translation].
9   "The Art of Hearing,"
pp. 771–772.

10   J. Shearman, *Pontormo's
Altarpiece in S. Felicita* (Newcastle
upon Tyne, 1971), p. 22.
11   L.A. Waldman, "New Light on
the Capponi Chapel in S. Felicita,"
Art Bulletin, 84, no. 2 (June 2002),
p. 304.
12   Romani 2003, p. 181.
13   L.A. Waldman, *Baccio
Bandinelli and Art at the Medici
Court: A Corpus of Early Modern
Sources* (Philadelphia, 2004.), doc.
1313 [author's translation].

59
MARCELLO VENUSTI
c. 1512/15–1579
The Purification of the Temple
After 1550
Oil on panel
60 × 38 cm
The National Gallery, London
(1194)

Provenance: Palazzo Borghese until
1798; the French superintendent
Reboul from 1798; Woodburn col-
lection, London, sale, 25 March
1826; Christie's sale, Thomas
Lawrence collection, 15 May 1830;
Christie's sale, Hamilton collection,
1882, bought by Mainwaring;
Denison auction, 1885; Agnew &
Sons, 1885; The National Gallery,
London, 1885.

References: Wilde 1959, p. 378;
Tolnay 1975–1980, vol. III, p. 49;
Chapman 2005, p. 266; Orsini de
Marzo 2006, p. 229.

Notes
1   A. de Rinaldis, "Documenti
inediti per la storia della R. Galleria
Borghese in Roma. III: Un catalogo
della quadreria Borghese nel
palazzo a Campo Marzio, redatto
nel 1760," *Archivia* 4 (1937), fasc.
3–4, 1937, pp. 218–232, 224, no. 67.
2   These sheets, with drawings
on the recto and verso, are numbered PD1860,0616.2/1–3; Tolnay
1978, nos. 385–387, pp. 49–51.

60
FRANCESCO DE' ROSSI, CALLED
SALVIATI
1510–1563
Portrait of Annibale Caro
c. 1550
Oil on marble
Diameter approx. 10 cm
Collection of Mr. and Mrs. Marco
Grassi

Provenance: sale, Sotheby's,
London, 26 October 1988, lot 92;
Marco Grassi, New York

References: Monbeig Goguel 1998,
p. 47, 49.

Notes
1   P. Costamagna, "Il ritrattista,"
in Monbeig Goguel 1998, pp. 47–52.
2   Mortari 1992. Costamagna
lists a good number of original
sources in Monbeig Goguel 1998,
pp. 47–53.
3   On the role of Caro as iconog-
raphist, see C. Robertson, "Annibal
Caro and the Visual Arts," M.A.
thesis, University of London,
Warburg Institute, 1981.
4   Annibale Caro, *Lettere familiari*, Florence, 3 vol., 1957–1962.
Concerning the portraits of
Bronzino and Salviati showing a
young Caro and the painting for the
Accademia Bocchi, without specifi-
cation of the period, see vol. 3,
no. 648 (letter dated January 1562);
for the painting by Del Conte portraying an aging Caro, see vol. 3,
nos. 661, 663 (letters dated late
May and late June 1562).
5   Attribution accepted by
Venturi 1901–1940, vol. IX, p. 212;
J. Alazard, *Le portrait florentin de
Botticelli à Bronzino* (Paris, 1938),
p. 184; and Robertson, *Annibale
Caro*, p. 24ff., no. 42. With regard
to Mortari, she rejects the attribution to Salviati (see *Francesco
Salviati*, no. 137).

6   J. Pope-Hennessy, "Antonio
Calcagni's bust of Annibale Caro,"
in *Scritti di storia dell'arte in onore
di Edoardo Aslan* (Milan, 1966),
pp. 577–579 and ills. 374–376.
7   E. Bassi, "Annibal Caro,
Ranuccio Farnese e il Salviati," in
Critica d'Arte Nuova, vol. 4 (1957),
pp. 131–134, erroneously attributes
the Venetian drawing to Salviati,
dating it around 1547–1548.
Robertson associates it, instead, with
the anonymous artist who made the
painting for the Accademia Bocchi,
dating it around 1555, while Mortari
attributes it to the school of Federico
Zuccari (see no. 551).
8   G. Vasari, *Les vies des meilleurs
peintres, sculpteurs et architectes*,
trans. and ed. A. Chastel (Paris,
1981), vol. 9, p. 63.
9   On decoration of the Farnese
chapel, see P. Rubin, "The Private
Chapel of Cardinal Alessandro
Farnese in the Cancelleria, Rome,"
*Journal of the Warburg and
Courtauld Institutes*, vol. 50 (1987),
pp. 82–112.
10   Caro, *Lettere familiari*, vol. 1,
no. 218 (letter to Salviati, February
1544).
11   A letter from Vittorio Soranzo
to Pietro Bembo (8 June 1530)
lauds the beauty of a *Christ* painted
on marble by del Piombo. Later,
the artist used a preparation of
peperine for the altar of S. Maria
del Popolo, which was completed by
Salviati after Sebastiano's death.
On the technical innovation of del
Piombo, see Hirst 1981, pp. 124–
126. With regard to painting on
stone, see *Pietra dipinta: tesori nas-
costi de '500 e del '600 da una collezi-
one privata milanese*, exh. cat., ed.
M. Bona Castellotti (Milan, 2000),
especially the reflection of F. Zeri.

61
JACOPINO DEL CONTE
1510–1598
Portrait of Bindo Altoviti
early 1550s
Oil on panel (transferred)
128.5 × 103 cm
The Montreal Museum of Fine Arts
(2000.14)
Purchase, Edward Cleghorn
Memorial Fund

Provenance: Altoviti family by 1644
to c. 1940 (recorded in a photograph
dating to the 1880s of the interior
of the *palazzo*); private collection,
Florence; purchased by Wildenstein
Gallery, 1965; acquired by The
Montreal Museum of Fine Arts,
2000.

References: Chong et al. 2003,
no. 18, pp. 400–401; Costamagna
1988, pp. 27, 31, notes, 33, 34;
Costamagna 2002, p. 201; Zeri 1978,
pp. 120–121, note 15;

Notes
1   *Costui, dunque essendo stato in
fin dalla sua giovanezza molto
inclinato a ritrarre di naturale, ha
voluto che questa sia stata sua prin-
cipale professione; ancora che abbia,
secondo l'occasioni, fatto tavole e
lavori in fresco pure assai in Roma e
fuori. Ma de'ritratti, per non dire di
tutti, che sarebbe lunghissima storia,
dirò solamente che egli ha ritratto, da
papa Paulo terzo in qua, tutti i pontefici che sono stati, e tutti i signori ed
ambasciatori d'importanza che sono
stati a quella corte: e similmente cap-
itani d'eserciti e grand'uomini di casa
Colonna e degli Orsini, il signor Piero
Strozzi, ed una infinità di vescovi,
cardinali, ed altri gran prelati e
signori, senza molti letterati ed altri
galantuomini, che gli hanno fatto
acquistare in Roma nome, onore ed
utile; onde si sta in quella città con
sua famiglia molto agiata ed onorata-
mente. Vasari-Milanesi 1879–1906,
vol. 7, p. 576.*

2   Besides the Raphael, Cellini, and Jacopino portraits, another one by an Emilian artist, probably Girolamo da Carpi, exists in a private Swiss collection. See note 4. A further one by Francesco Salviati is lost.
3   See D. Pegazzano, "A Banker as Patron," in Chong et al. 2003, pp. 59–91.
4   Chong et al. 2003, no. 19, pp. 401–404, both faces of the medal are illustrated. The Raphael portrait, no. 8, pp. 378–379; the portrait attributed to Girolamo da Carpi, no. 17, pp. 398–400; the Jacopino, no. 18, pp. 400–401; a portrait by Salviati unconvincingly associated with the lost Bindo portrait, no. 16a, pp. 397–398.
5   F. Zeri, "There is no doubt that Jacopino, the most celebrated portrait painter in Rome around 1550, is the author of this fine work." In a letter to Wildenstein Gallery, 1973.
6   M. Natale, in Art vénitien en Suisse et au Liechtenstein, exh. cat. (Switzerland, 1978) p. 104, no. 65 (as Jacopino). Also S. Morris, "Renaissance Men," Galleries Magazine, XIV, no. 6 (Nov. 1996), p. 15 (as Jacopino).
7   See also Chong et al. 2003, no. 18, pp. 400–401, entry by Costamanga as Jacopino.
8   The Philadelphia and ex-Watney paintings are reproduced in F. Zeri 1976, p. 117, fig. 8, p. 120, fig. 13; the Borghese and Doria portraits reproduced in L. Bellosi, "Intorno a un ritratto fiorentino di Jacopino del Conte," in M. Cammerer, ed., Kunst des Cinquecento in der Toskana (Munich, 1992), p. 217, fig. 8, p. 218, fig. 9.

62
GIROLAMO SELLARI, CALLED GIROLAMO DA CARPI
1501– c. 1556
Portrait of a Man
c. 1550
Oil on canvas
109.2 × 82.6 cm
Seattle Art Museum (61.164)
Gift of the Samuel H. Kress Foundation

Provenance: Earl of Weymyss, Gosford House, Longniddry; Wildenstein, New York; Kress Collection, New York, 1947; gift to the museum.

References: Pattanaro 2000, pp. 80–82, 148–149, no 15 (with bibliography); Costamagna in Chong et al. 2003, p. 398, no 17.

Notes
1   See F. Mozzetti, *Tiziano. Ritratto di Pietro Aretino* (Modena, 1996).
2   London, Sotheby's sale, 3 December 2008, no. 35; for an analysis of the work, see Costamagna in Chong et al. 2003, no. 17.
3   On the ancient paintings copied in Rome by Giralomo, see N.W. Canedy, *The Roman Sketchbook of Girolamo da Carpi* (London, 1976); for those in the collection of Bindo Altoviti, see A. Chong, in Chong et al. 2003, pp. 364–366, nos. 1a–2a.
4   A. Pattanaro's cautious hypothesis (2000, p. 82) that the person portrayed was the humanist Francesco Alunno cannot be taken into consideration unless the painting was executed in the Ferrare court.

63
GIROLAMO SELLARI, CALLED GIROLAMO DA CARPI
1501– c. 1556
Sheet of Studies (recto and verso)
1553
Pen and brown ink
25.8 × 20.6 cm
Inscriptions: *lai 12 hotobre di 1553 in roma*
Szépművészeti Múzeum, Budapest (1952)

Provenance: Paulus Praun; purchased by Prince Miklós Esterházy from the Nuremberg dealer Johann Friedrich Frauenholz, c. 1804 (L. 1965); acquired by the National Picture Gallery, Budapest, 1870.

References: Zentai 1997, pp. 132–134 (with previous literature); Zentai 1998, no. 44; Zentai 2003, no. 9; Dauner 2005, p. 129, note 2.

Notes
1   N.W. Canedy, *The Roman Sketchbook of Girolamo da Carpi* (London, 1976). Canedy acknowledged that the original makeup and organization of the album could not be reconstructed. Serious doubts about the sketchbook hypothesis were raised by A.J. Elen in *Italian Late-Medieval and Renaissance Drawing-Books from Giovanni de' Grassi to Palma Giovane: A Codicological Approach* (Leiden 1995), p. 323.
2   The view of Canedy (*Roman Sketchbook*, pp. 15–23) is not accepted by Gere and Pouncey 1983, vol. 1, p. 96) nor by A.M. Riccomini ("Sul taccuino torinese di Girolamo da Carpi," *Prospettiva* 67 [1992], p. 66–78).
3   See G. Dauner, "A Traveling Cinquecento Artist: Sources for the Drawings of Girolamo da Carpi," *Master Drawings* 43 (2005), pp. 488–499, and Dauner 2005. Although Canedy too had listed other locations outside Rome to which some drawings in the "Roman Sketchbook" could be related (*The Roman Sketchbook*, pp. 7–14), until Dauner's exhaustive studies scholars basically thought of the "Roman Sketchbook" as having been made during Girolamo's brief sojourn in Rome between 1549 and 1553.
4   *Roman Sketchbook*, R35.
5   Zentai 1997, pp. 132–134.
6   See A. Serafini, *Girolamo da Carpi* (Rome, 1915), p. 321, fig. 157.
7   On the marble statue and its Renaissance copies, see Bober and Rubinstein 1986, no. 32.
8   See T. Riggs, *Hieronymus Cock: Printmaker and Publisher* (New York, 1977), vol. 2, no. 148.
9   *Roman Sketchbook*, R42, R72.
10   R. Parma in *Giulio Romano pinxit et delineavit: Opere grafiche autografe di collaborazione e bottega*, exh. cat., ed. S. Massari (Rome, 1993), no. 63. Sotheby's, London, 25 March 1985, lot 5; see Zentai 1998, pp. 116, 118, fig. 21.
11   Zentai 1998, p. 118; Metropolitan Museum of Art, New York (62.247). See Griswold and Wolk-Simon 1994, no. 12.

64
ATTRIBUTED TO ERCOLE SETTI
1530–1617
Cardinal Giovanni de'Medici's Triumphal Re-entry into Florence in 1512 (After Raphael)
c. 1550s
Pen and brown ink and wash
12.6 × 28.3 cm
Private collection, Toronto

Provenance: Commendator Vittorio Genevosio (L. 545)

Notes
1   Shearman 1972, p. 31.
2   Ibid., p. 85.
3   Ibid., p. 88, interprets the giving of the right hands as an attribute of Leo X's pontificate, "apparently a token of *unitas* or *concordia* (as on Roman coins)."
4   Pioneering articles on Setti are by W. Vitzthum, "Drawings by Ercole Setti," *The Burlington Magazine*, 97 (1955), p. 252, and F.Z. Boccazzi, "An unpublished Album of drawings by Ercole Setti" *Master Drawings*, VI (1968), pp. 356–363, pls.1–9.

65
PROSPERO FONTANA
1512–1597
Bacchanalian Feast
c. 1553–1555
Pen and brown ink, brown wash, over black chalk, with white heightening, on blue paper, squared for transfer in pen and brown ink
36.8 × 47 cm
Musée du Louvre, Paris (2214)

Provenance: Evérard Jabach (L. 2959); acquired by the king in 1671

References: Gere 1965, no. 745, p. 200, fig. 42; Gere 1971, p. 90, fig. 25; Härb in Monbeig Goguel et al. 2001, p. 583, n. 24; Faietti in Faietti and Cordellier 2002, no. 57, illustrated (with previous literature)

66
PROSPERO FONTANA
1512–1597
The Marriage Banquet of Peleus and Thetis
c. 1553–1555
Pen and brown ink, brown wash, over black chalk, with white heightening (partly oxidized), on blue paper, squared for transfer
35.4 × 54.2 cm
Inscriptions: *prospero*
The British Museum, London (1875,0710.2631)

Provenance: P. Woutiers, Brussels (Giulio Romano); E. Daniell; purchased 1985.

References: Gere 1965, no. 745, p. 202, fig. 41; Gere and Pouncey 1983, I, no. 103, II, pl. 96; Monbeig Goguel in Gilet 2001–2002, under no. 3

Notes
1   Vasari-Milanesi 1879–1906, VII, p. 107.
2   Ibid., VII, p. 82.
3   Acidini Luchinat 1998–1999, vol. I, pp. 31–38.
4   Three further drawings securely connected with the Villa Giulia decoration are at Windsor (Inv. 5990, see Gere 1965, p. 200, fig. 43), the Uffizi (Inv. 109066, see Di Giampaolo 1989, no. 89, illustrated), and at Tours (Inv. D 1986-1-14, see Tour 2001, no. 3, illustrated).
5   F. Härb, "Prospero Fontana alias Giogio Vasari: Collaboration and the Limits of Authorship," in Monbeig Goguel et al. 2001.
6   Vasari-Milanesi 1879–1906, VII, p. 694.
7   K. and H.-W. Frey, *Giorgio Vasari: Der Literarische Hachlass*, vol. I, pp. 346–356, no. CLXXXIII.
8   For a comprehensive account of Vasari's work in the Villa Giulia see C. Davis, "Per l'attività romana del Vasari nel 1553: Incisioni degli affreschi di Villa Altoviti e la Fontanalia di Villa Giulia," in *Mitteilungen des Kunsthistorischen Institutes in Florenz*, vol. 23 (1979), pp. 197–224
9   A copy of Caro's *invenzione* survives in Vasari's notebook, see A. del Vita, ed., *Lo Zibaldone di Giorgio Vasari* (Rome, 1938), pp. 308–309. "Drunken Bacchus with his company of men and women Bacchantes, satyrs, with Silenus, and Priapus all crowned with ivy, vine leaves and figs, with goatskins and wine goblets, which are being raised and tilted, some holding *thyrsi* topped with ivy, all together making an uproar and falling about."
10   Uffizi (Inv. 620F), Louvre (Inv. 2157); for the drawing in a private collection and an account of the entire project see F. Härb in W.M. Brady and Co., Inc., *Master Drawings 1520–1890*, exh. cat. (New York, 2006), no. 3, illustrated.
11   Inv. 2008,7023.1. Pen and brown ink, with brown wash, heightened with white, over black chalk, on blue paper, squared for transfer 30.9 × 21.6 cm.

12   The identification of the subject is due to Prof. L. Slatkin (see "Kunstkabinett," New York, *Old Master Drawings*, catalogue, 2002, no. 4, illustrated).
13   Fontana was certainly also impressed by Giulio's figure of the drunken Silenus and his companions, which he reused, with some differences, in the *Bacchanalian Feast*.
14   The Solomonic columns and the staircase feature prominently also in two of Vasari's earlier refectory projects. The first is his *Christ in the House of Marta and Mary*, painted in 1539–40 for the refectory of San Michele in Bosco, Bologna, the second his triptych of *Christ and Simon the Pharisee* painted in 1544–1545 for the monastery of Monteoliveto, Naples. While Fontana would have certainly known the former painting extremely well, he may have known the latter from Vasari's drawings, several of which survive in the Rijksmuseum, Amsterdam (inv. 1951.1), and the J. Paul Getty Museum, Los Angeles (inv. 94.GA.33.1 and 94.GA.33.2).
15   See C. Rosini, *Dietro la moda delle grottesche. Prospero Fontana e Paolo Vitelli*, Città di Castello, 1986, fig. 197. A preparatory drawing by Fontana for this fresco was with Jean-Luc Baroni Ltd. in 2008 (*Master Drawings and Paintings*, exh. cat. [New York, 2008], no. 3, illustrated).

67
FRANCESCO DE' ROSSI, CALLED SALVIATI
1510–1563
Victory
c. 1550–1555
Black chalk, with white heightening, on blue paper
29.5 × 25 cm
Annotations: *286* and *Salviati*
National Gallery of Canada, Ottawa (41645)

Provenance: American private collection. Purchased from Hill-Stone, New York in 2005.

Notes
1   Mortari 1992, no. 4.

68
JAN VAN DER STRAET, CALLED STRADANUS
1523–1605
Saint Peter, after Sebastiano del Piombo
c. 1550–1560
Pen and brown ink and brown wash, with white heightening, over black chalk, on blue paper
33.9 × 15.7 cm
Annotations: *Bast. Del Piomb.* On the old mount *Sebastiano del Piombo (Sebastiano Luciano) 1485–1547* and *Collection P. Lely peintre de Charles Ier.*
National Gallery of Canada, Ottawa (41728)

Provenance: P. Lely (L. 2092). L. Deglatigny (L. 1768a). Private Collection, France. Purchased from Mark Brady, New York, in 2005.

Notes
1   In W.M. Brady Co., *Master Drawings, 1520–1890* (New York, 2006), no. 6, the drawing is dated later to the 1580s by A. Baroni Vannucci.
2   Hirst 1981, pp. 49–65. According to Hirst, Pellegrino Tibaldi – a contemporary of Stradanus – also copied this particular figure in a work in Bologna (p. 65, note 68). Another copy drawing after Sebastiano's *Saint Francis* from this chapel in the Royal Collection, Windsor (Inv. 4810) appears unrelated to the Ottawa sheet. See Popham and Wilde 1949, no. 923, pp. 332–333.
3   See, for example, A. Baroni Vannucci, *Jan Van Der Straet detto Giovanni Stradano* (Milan, Rome, 1997), no. 60 for his early copies after Michelangelo's *Last Judgment*.

459

69

DANIELE DA VOLTERRA
c. 1509–1566
David and Goliath
c. 1555
black chalk
33.8 × 40.8 cm
Biblioteca Apostolica Vaticana,
Vatican City (Vat. Lat. 13619, f.2).

Provenance: Rospigliosi collection,
Rome, sixteenth century

References: Barolsky 1979; Romani
2003; Scailliérez et al. 2007.

Notes

1 Scailliérez et al., 2007.
2 Illustrated B.XXVI.10–I (12).
3 P. Barocchi and R. Bettarini,
eds., *Giorgio Vasari: Le Vite nelle
redazioni del 1550 e 1568* (Florence,
1976–87), V, p. 545: *Avendo monsignor Giovanni della Casa, fiorentino ed uomo dottissimo ...
cominciato a scrivere un trattato
delle cose di pittura, e volendo chia-
rirsi d'alcune minuzie e particolari
degli uomini della professione, fece
fare a Daniello, con tutta quella diligenza che fu possibile, il modello d'un
Davit di terra finito; e dopo li fece
dipingere, o vero ritrarre in questo
quadro, il medesimo Davit, che è
bellissimo, da tutte e due le bande,
cioè il dinanzi e il di dietro, che fu
cosa capricciosa; il quale quadro è
oggi appresso messer Annibale
Rucellai.* [author's translation]
4 P. Barocchi, ed., *Trattati d'arte
del cinquecento*, Bari 1960–1962, I,
p. 82: "*Io dico che la pittura mi par
più tenuta buona quanto più va
verso il rilievo ... e però a me soleva
parere che la scultura fussi la
lanterna della pittura ...*"
5 L. Treves, "Daniele da Volterra
and Michelangelo. A Collaborative
Relationship," *Apollo* 154 (2001),
pp. 36–45; Joannides 2007, no. 45;
Di Majo in Romani 2003, prefers an
earlier date during Della Casa's
first Roman sojourn of 1550–51, on
the basis of the stylistic similarity
between Daniele's drawings for
David and Goliath and those for the
della Rovere Chapel in Trinità dei
Monti. For the other paintings in
the group – an *Aeneas Commanded
by Mercury to Abandon Dido*, a
St. John the Baptist, a *Pietà*, and a
St. Jerome – and Daniele's collaborative relationship with
Michelangelo, see Treves, "Daniel da
Volterra and Michelangelo," 2001.
6 G. Morello, "La Sistina tra
copie ed incisioni," *Michelangelo e
la Sistina, La tecnica, il restauro, il
mito*, exh. cat. (Rome, 1990), no. 39,
p. 168.
7 J.P. Richter, ed., *The Literary
Works of Leonardo da Vinci*, 3rd ed.
(New York, 1970), I, p. 93, no. 38: *lo
scultore nel fare una figure tonda fa
solamente due figure, e non infinite
per li infiniti aspetti, d'onde essa po
essere veduta, e di queste due figure
l'una è veduta dinanzi, e l'altra di
dietro.* L.B. Alberti, *On Painting and
On Sculpture*, trans. C. Grayson
(London, 1972), p. 139.
8 Morello, "La Sistina."
9 L. Corti, *The Genius of the
Sculptor in Michelangelo's Work*,
exh. cat. (Montreal, 1992), no. 140,
pp. 440–441; B. Thomas, "'The
Lantern of Painting': Michelangelo,
Daniele da Volterra and the 'paragone'," *Apollo* 154 (2001), p. 49;
Joannides 2007, no. 46; P. Joannides,
"Daniela da Volterra's 'Dido'," *The
Burlington Magazine* 135 (Dec. 1993),
pp. 818, note 3; and also Di Majo in
Romani 2003, no. 32.
10 M. Hirst, "Daniele da Volterra
and the Orsini Chapel – I," *The
Burlington Magazine*, 109 (Sep.
1967), p. 498.

70

TADDEO ZUCCARO
1529–1566
*A Male Figure on Crutches and a
Right Arm* (recto)
A Man Bending Forward (verso)
c. 1556–1559
Black chalk, with white height-
ening, on blue paper
24.5 × 34.8 cm
Inscriptions: [Ta]*ddeo Zuccaro*
(verso)
Private collection

Provenance: Sir Peter Lely (L. 2092);
W. Gibson, his price code '2.3' in pen
on verso; R. Düb (L. 2197b); pur-
chased by the present owner from
Sabrina Förster Gallery, Dusseldorf;
Private collection

Notes

1 I attributed the drawing and
connected it to the Frangipani commission on the basis of a photograph sent to me by S. Förster in the
mid 1990s
2 The Ashmolean drawing is not
illustrated in Karl Parker's 1956
catalogue of the Italian drawings
(no. 761), nor in either Gere or
Acidini Luchinat's monographs.
The only illustration I know of it is
in L. Goldscheider's *Michelangelo
Drawings* (London, 1951), fig. 169
with the corresponding detail of
the Frangipani fresco reproduced
beside it. The cartoon was thought
by Sir Thomas Lawrence to be by
Michelangelo and was acquired as
such by Oxford in 1846. It hangs
above the windows in the Western
Art Print Room.

71

FEDERICO ZUCCARO
c. 1542/43–1609
Vision of Saint Eustace
c. 1558
Brush with brown, grey, green,
yellow and red washes, with white
heightening, pen and brown ink,
over traces of red and black chalk,
squared in black chalk
34.1 × 20.2 cm
The Metropolitan Museum of Art,
New York (62.76)
The Rogers Fund, 1962

Provenance: Jonathan Richardson,
Sr. (L. 2184); Jonathan Richardson,
Jr. (L. 2170); Sir Joshua Reynolds
(L. 2364); Rogers Fund, 1962.

References: Bean 1963, p. 232; Gere
1963, p. 394, n. 12; Bean 1964, no. 26;
Bean and Stampfle 1965, p. 77,
no. 140; Gere 1966a, p. 27; Gere 1971,
no. 18; Smith 1977, p. 30, no. 37;
Olszewski in Cleveland, 1981, pp. 15,
16, 55, no. 81; Bean and Turçic, 1982,
pp. 268–269, no. 273; Gere and
Pouncey, 1983, p. 182; Mundy 1989,
pp. 164–165, no. 48; Fusconi 1992,
pp. 157–160; Acidini Luchinat 1998–
1999, vol. 1, pp. 111, 133 n. 56;
Brooks et al. 2007, p. 52, no. 41.

Notes

1 Baglione records that the two
brothers jointly decorated a facade
in Piazza Colonna with a Pietà in
between Saint Peter and Saint Paul:
Federico painted the figure of Saint
Paul, and Taddeo the rest. Cited in
Gere 1969b, p. 41. Federico's date of
birth has not yet been clearly ascertained, and Federico himself is
inconsistent in legal documents.
2 The commission is fully discussed by Acidini Luchinat 1998–
1999, I, pp. 110–113; see also Mundy
1989, no. 48 and Gere 1969b,
pp. 99–100.
3 The cost of the colours used
would not have been small, and so
the patron must have been involved
in this decision.
4 Chicago, Art Institute, Gift of
Robert B. Harshe, inv. 1928.196; S.F.
McCullagh and L.M. Giles, *Italian
Drawings before 1600 in the Art
Institute of Chicago: A Catalogue of
the Collection* (Chicago, 1997),
pp. 268–270, no. 350, ill. As
observed by Mundy 1989 (166).

5 Florence, Uffizi 11173F;
J. Brooks in Brooks et al. 2007, p. 53,
cat. no. 42; made in pen and brown
ink, with brown wash, and the right
hand parts completed in a grey ink;
squared for transfer to another
sheet, perhaps the modello. It is in
poor condition. In a note on the
MMA curatorial file of May 28,
2003, Mundy points out the existence of a further Uffizi drawing for
one of the lost portions of the
exterior frescoes, the *Baptism of
St. Eustace*, and a drawing for the
figure of Justice on the facade in
the collection of the Kunstmuseum,
Düsseldorf (inv. FP 6505).
6 As observed by Acidini
Luchinat 1998–1999, I, p. 111.
7 Vasari 1878–1885, VII: *Taddeo,
che pure considerava quell'opera
essere in luogo publico, e che import-
ava molto all'onore di Federigo, non
solo andava alcuna volta a vederlo
lavorare, ma anco taluna voleva
alcuna cosa ritoccare e racconciare.
Perche Federigo, avendo un pezzo
avuto pacienzia, finalmente trapor-
tato una volta dalla collera, come
quegli che arebbe voluto fare da se,
prese la martellina, e gitto in terra
non so che aveva fatto [ritocho]
Taddeo, e per isdegno stette alcuni
giorni che non torno a casa. La qual
cosa intendendo gli amici dell'uno e
dell'altro, feciono tanto che si rapat-
tumarono; con questo, che Taddeo
potesse [struck through] correggere
[correggese] e mettere mano nei disegni e cartoni di Federigo a suo piaci-
mento; ma non mai [struck through]
nell' opera che facesse o a fresco o a
olio, o in altro modo.* (The bracketed
insertions reflect Federico's annotations in his copy of this book.),
pp. 90–91.
8 Federico denies little, only soft-
ening the text somewhat (see the
bracketed insertions in the preceding note). Federico's annotations are
most fully discussed by Z. Wazbinski
in "Lo Studio – La Scuola Fiorentina
di Federico Zuccari," in *Mitteilungen
des Kunsthistorischen Institutes in
Florenz*, vol. 29, 1985, pp. 296–309.
9 Taddeo was probably particularly concerned in this case, given
the potential to win the important
commission at Caprarola for
Cardinal Alessandro Farnese, Tizio
Chermandio's master (Acidini
Luchinat 1998–1999, I, p. 112).
10 Note in MMA curatorial file.
Muziano's drawing and print are
discussed J.A. Gere, "Girolamo
Muziano and Taddeo Zuccaro: A
Note on an Early Work by Muziano,"
The Burlington Magazine 108
(August 1966), p. 417.

72

**FRANCESCO DE' ROSSI, CALLED
SALVIATI**
1510–1563
*The Siege of Parma: Design for a
Wall Decoration Flanked by Pilasters*
1557–1558
Pen and brown ink and brush and
brown wash, heightened with
white gouache (oxidized in places)
15.2 × 11.3 cm
Inscriptions: *parma piano*
Private collection, Chicago

References: Bellinger 1991, under
no. 8; Robertson 1992, pp. 224–225;
Mortari 1992, no. 393; Kliemann in
Monbeig Goguel et al. 2001,
pp. 303–304; New York and London
2004, under no. 5.

Provenance: Christie's, London, 9
December 1982, lot 29 (property of
a Continental collector); Duke
Roberto Ferretti di Castelferretto,
Montreal; Yvonne Tan Bunzl,
London; sold to the private col-
lector, Spring 2007.

73

**FRANCESCO DE' ROSSI, CALLED
SALVIATI**
1510–1563
*The Siege of Parma: Design for a
Wall Decoration Flanked by
Pilasters*
1557–1558
Pen and brown ink and brown wash
over black chalk
15.2 × 11.5 cm
National Gallery of Canada, Ottawa
(41557)

Provenance: A continental col-
lector; sold, Christie's, London, 9
December 1982, lot 28; Katrin
Bellinger, Munich; Colnaghi's
London.

References; McTavish 1985,
no. 11.1; Cheney 1992, p. 158, note
18; Mortari 1992, no. 312;
Robertson 1992, p. 222; Kliemann
1993, p. 54; Strinati and Walter
1995, pp. 55–56, 68, note 30.

Notes

1 Cheney 1992, p. 158, note 18.
Although traditionally thought to
have been begun and largely executed between 1549 and 1556,
before the artist's sojourn in France
(February 1556–October 1557), the
decoration has been plausibly
reassigned by J. Kliemann to the
period immediately after, around
1557–1558. In Kliemann's opinion,
it is inconceivable that such a subject would have been considered
for representation before Pope
Julius III's death, in 1555. The
painted decoration must predate
1559, when Ottavio Farnese was
awarded the Order of the Golden
Fleece, as it is not included in his
coat of arms depicted at the top of
the fresco (Kliemann 1993, p. 54.1).
See also Strinati and Walter 1995,
pp. 56, 68, note 30.
2 The two drawings remained
together until 1982 when they were
sold in separate lots at Christie's.
D. McTavish (1985) was the first to
associate these two sheets with the
Siege of Parma. For the history of
the room decoration and four other
drawings, all single-figure chalk
studies, connected with it, see
Cheney 1981. Recently, Ingeborg
Walter proposed that the Canadian
drawing depicts the siege of the
town of Mirandola, a subject
chosen to pay tribute to Orazio
Farnese who successfully staved off
the papal troops (Strinati and
Walter 1995, pp. 55–56, 68, note 30).
He further suggested that the
drawings were pendants.

74

GIOVANNI BATTISTA NALDINI
1537–1591
View of the Colosseum (recto)
*The Rape of the Daughters of
Leucippus* (verso, top)
Two Boars' Heads (verso)
c. 1560–1561
Pen and brown ink over black
chalk; boars' heads in red chalk
(verso)
28 × 44 cm
National Gallery of Scotland,
Edinburgh (D 992 A)

References: Andrews 1968,
pp. 78–79; Bober and Rubinstein
1986, p. 162, no. 126; Cecchi 1998;
Thiem 2002, pp. 42–45, 80–81.

Notes

1 Thiem 2002, pp. 11–12.
2 Ibid., 2002.

75
GIROLAMO MUZIANO
1532–1592
*Christ Washing the Feet of the
Apostles*
1560–1561
Pen and brown ink with brown
wash with white heightening
36 × 49 cm
Private collection

Notes
1   For a summary of the six-
teenth-century renovation of the
cathedral at Orvieto see L. Fumi, *Il
Duomo di Orvieto e i suoi Restauri*
(Rome, 1891); M. Cambereri,
*Ippolito Scalza and the Sixteenth-
Century Renovation Projects at
Orvieto Cathedral*, Ph.D. diss., New
York University, 1998; A. Satolli,
"Documentazione inedita sugli
interventi Cinquecenteschi nel
Duomo scomparso con i restauri del
1877," *Bollettino dell'Istituto Storico
Artistico Orvietano* 34 (1978),
pp. 129–160. None of these focuses
on Muziano's contributions either
in 1555–1558 or later in 1572–1584,
for which see Marciari 2000,
pp. 117–147 and 283–305.
2   U. Procacci, "Una 'Vita' inedita
del Muziano," *Arte Veneta* 8 (1954),
p. 250 (a biographical account that
Muziano narrated to his confessor
around 1585). Baglione (1642, p. 49)
claims that Michelangelo admired
Muziano's *Resurrection of Lazarus*
and used his influence to win him a
place with the Este, but the five- or
six-year gap between the *Lazarus*
and the entrance into the Este
household suggests that Baglione's
account is a confused version of the
story (recorded in the biographical
"confession" published by Procacci)
that Muziano won the Orvieto commission when Raffaello da
Montelupo saw the *Lazarus*.
3   For the documents see
V. Pacifici, *Ippolito II d'Este, cardinale di Ferrara* (Tivoli, 1923). For
further details on the works from
this period, many of which are lost
but are known through Muziano's
drawings and through engravings
by Cornelis Cort, see Marciari
2000, pp. 162–201. The most
important painting that survives
from this period is the *Resurrection
of the Daughter of Jairus* (Escorial),
commissioned by Giovanni Ricci of
Montepulciano and sent as a gift to
King Philip II.
4   Procacci, "Una 'Vita' inedita
del Muziano," p. 251; Borghini 1584,
p. 575.
5   Pacifici, *Ippolito II d'Este*, p. 389.
6   One might compare, for
example, the two compositional
studies of Louvre, Paris, 5095,
which are related to Cornelis Cort's
engravings of 1567. Muziano's wash
manner, however, was adopted and
long used by his primary pupil,
Cesare Nebbia, leading to some
confusion regarding the attribution
of works in this style.
7   See Marciari 2000, pp. 45–51.
8   An additional preparatory
drawing by Muziano for the apostle
removing a sandal is in the
Staatliche Graphische Sammlung,
Munich (2796). For a recent discussion of Tintoretto's painting see
M. Falomir, ed., *Tintoretto*, exh. cat.
(Madrid, 2007), esp. pp. 229–241.
9   It has also been suggested that
Muziano's *Christ Washing the Feet*
relies on Taddeo Zuccaro's fresco in
Santa Maria della Consolazione,
but as I have argued elsewhere, the
case is of a general similarity
between these two artists rather
than of a direct line of influence.
See Marciari 2002, pp. 113–134, esp.
p. 116.
10   Louvre, Paris, 5141, pen and
brown ink and wash, 37.8 × 24.2 cm.
11   Published in C. Fischer, *Italian
Drawings in the J.F. Willumsen
Collection, II*, exh. cat. (Copenhagen,
1988), no. 93.
12   Borghini 1584, p. 575.

13   U. da Como, *Girolamo Muziano,
1528–1592* (Bergamo, 1930), pp. 193–
196. It is possible, however, that
these later designs related not to the
Este paintings but rather to the
Gregorian chapel at Saint Peter's.
Muziano was the supervising artist
there, and he may have had a hand
in the design of the *Christ Washing
the Feet* relief that Taddeo Landini
produced for the chapel (now
Quirinal Palace, Rome).

76
NICCOLÒ TROMETTA
c.1540–1611
*Design For A Ceiling With The Coat
Of Arms Of Pope Pius IV*
c. 1559–1565
Pen and brown ink and brown wash
over black chalk with white height-
ening, on blue paper
55.9 × 36.9 cm
Staatliche Museen zu Berlin,
Kupferstichkabinett (15414)

Provenance: K.E. Hasse (L. 860);
gift to the museum

References: Gere 1971, p. 84, no. 24.

Notes
1   J.A. Gere, "Drawings by
Niccolo Martinelli, Il Trometta,"
Master Drawings 1 (1963), pp. 3–18.
This remains the fundamental arti-
cle on his drawings.

77
FEDERICO BAROCCI
c. 1528–1612
Temperance
c. 1561–1563
Pen and brown ink and brown wash
with white heightening, on blue
paper
22.5 × 10.1 cm
Annotations: in pen and ink, *Baroci*
National Gallery of Canada, Ottawa
(6896)

Provenance: purchased from
P. & D. Colnaghi & Co., 1957.

References: Popham and Fenwick
1965, no. 40; Gere 1969b, p. 182;
Smith 1970, pp. 108–110; Pillsbury
and Richards 1978, pp. 34–35; Smith
1978, p. 333; Cazort 1988, pp. 29–30;
Mundy 1989, pp. 106–108; Goldner
1992, p. 125; Franklin 2003,
pp. 48–49, no. 15.

Notes
1   The life of young artists in
Rome around 1550 is best documented by Giovanni Battista
Armenini, in his *De' veri precetti
della pittura* of 1586 (Armenini had
been a student artist in Rome
around 1550), and by Federico
Zuccaro, in his well-known pictorial biography of his brother Taddeo
(J. Paul Getty Museum, Los
Angeles). On the changes in Roman
art around mid-century see Gere
1969b, pp. 27–28; Gere 1971;
Marciari 2000, pp. 55–68;
J. Marciari, "Girolamo Muziano and
the Dialogue of Drawings in
Cinquecento Rome," *Master
Drawings* 40 (2002), pp. 113–134;
J. Brooks, *Taddeo and Federico
Zuccaro: Artist-Brothers in
Renaissance Rome* (Los Angeles,
2007). On the related development
of competitive collaborative projects
see Marciari 2000, pp. 396–408.
2   Popham and Fenwick 1965,
pp. 31–32.
3   Smith 1970, pp. 108–110.
4   Smith (1978, p. 323) noted,
however, that although the drawing
and fresco seem to be the work of
Barocci, there is no strong *documentary* evidence that Barocci worked
on the upper floor, and "the payments do seem to be quite clear in
assigning the *galleria* to Giovanni da
Cherso and Federico Zuccaro." For a
bibliography regarding the decoration of the Casino see A. Emiliani,
Federico Barocci (Bologna, 1985),
vol. 1, pp. 15–25.

5   See, for example, P. Tosini,
"Gli esordi romani di Federico
Zuccari e Federico Barocci in
Vaticano," in *Federico Zuccari: Le
idee, gli scritti*, ed. B. Cleri (Milan,
1997), p. 127, for another example
of Federico using one of Taddeo's
drawings at the Casino.
6   Pillsbury and Richards 1978,
pp. 34–35.
7   Since Pillsbury's 1978 publication, the attribution to Taddeo has
been supported only by Mundy
(1989, pp. 106–108). The attribution
to Barocci has been endorsed by
McTavish (Cazort 1988, pp. 29–30),
Goldner (1992, p. 125), and Franklin
(2003, pp. 48–49). Gere (1969b,
p. 182) initially published the sheet
as Barocci but later hesitated and
noted on the drawing's mat that it
was "worth considering whether
the traditional attribution may not
be correct." Smith (1978, p. 333)
similarly seemed to retract his earlier strong support for the attribution to Taddeo and noted that the
drawing "may well be by Barocci."
In a review of the Mundy 1989
exhibition, Iris Cheney (*Master
Drawings* 32 [1994], p. 65) did not
reinforce the attribution to Barocci
but noted that the sheet did not fit
among Taddeo's drawings.
8   Pillsbury and Richards 1978,
p. 37; see also the related sheet in
the Louvre, Paris, 2845.
9   See Emiliani, *Federico Barocci*,
vol. 1, pp. 15–25. There is a copy of
the Ottawa drawing, presumably
made by one of Barocci's assistants
at the Casino, at Windsor, formerly
attributed to Giuseppe Porta. See
Popham and Wilde 1949, no. 753.
10   Bellori 1672, p. 174.

78
ORLANDO PARENTINI
active c. 1560 – c. 1590
*Study for the Apartment of Pope
Pius IV in the Vatican*
c. 1559–1565
Pen and brown ink and brown wash
16 × 27.6 cm
Annotations: *Sc[uola]. di Lelio da
Novellara; S.R. no 108* (verso)
S.R. No. 108
National Gallery of Canada, Ottawa
(42301)

Provenance: So-called Sagredo-
Borghese Collection, Scuola
Romana, no 108. Private collection,
France. Purchased from Galerie de
La Scala, Paris, 2008.

References: Galerie de la Scala
2008, no. 3

Notes
1   J.S. Ackerman, *The Cortile del
Belvedere*, Vatican, 1954, pp. 92, 174.
2   B. Davidson, "Pius IV and
Raphael's Logge," *Art Bulletin* 66,
1984, p. 384, n. 13.
3   P. Tosini, "Federico Zuccari,
Pirro Ligorio e Pio IV: la sala del
Buon Governo nell'appartamento di
Belvedere in Vaticano," *Storia
dell'Arte* 86 (1996), pp. 13–38.

79
TIBERIO CALCAGNI
1532–1565
*Project for a Statue Court in Farnese
Palace*
c. 1564
Pen and brown ink and wash
32 × 25 cm
Gabinetto Disegni e Stampe degli
Uffizi, Florence (220A)

Provenance: Gift of Tiberio
Calcagni to Giorgio Vasari, 1564;
Mariette; Séroux d'Agincourt, 1775;
Grand Duke Pietro Leopoldo
de' Medici, 1798

References: Ragghianti Collobi
1973; Ragghianti Collobi 1974,
p. 149, fig. 455; Robertson 1992,
p. 138.

Notes
1   Vasari-Milanesi, VII, pp. 244,
262; H. Hibbard, *Michelangelo*
(Harmondsworth 1978), p. 285.
2   Vasari-Milanesi, VII, 262–264;
J.S. Ackerman, *The Architecture
of Michelangelo* (2nd ed.)
(Harmondsworth 1986), pp. 326–328.
3   For the emblems, see
M. Pastoreau in *Le Palais Farnèse*,
vol. II (Rome, 1981), pp. 443–448.
4   F. Haskell and N. Penny, *Taste
and the Antique* (New Haven and
London 1981), pp. 286–288.
5   C. Riebesell, *Die Sammlung des
Kardinal Alessandro Farnese. Ein
"studio" für Künstler und Gelehrte*
(Weinheim, 1989), p. 45.
6   *Taste and the Antique*,
pp. 169–172.
7   F.-C. Uginet, *Le Palais Farnèse
à travers les documents financiers
(1535–1612)* (Rome, 1980),
pp. 79–85, esp. 83, no. 772.
8   *Taste and the Antique*, pp. 165–
167; Robertson 1992, p. 140.
9   C.L. Frommel in *Le Palais
Farnèse*, vol. I, p. 167ff., and Lotz in
ibid., p. 230ff.; Robertson 1992,
pp. 138–189.

80
**GIUSEPPE PORTA CALLED
GIUSEPPE SALVIATI**
c. 1520–1575
*The Seven Kings Paying Homage to a
Pope*
1565
Pen and brown ink and brown
wash, over black chalk, heightened
with white bodycolour, on blue
paper, squared in black chalk
39 × 50 cm
Inscriptions: *PIVS.IIII/PONT.MA*
Devonshire Collection, Chatsworth
(no. 16)

Provenance: Sir Peter Lely
(L. 2092); William, 2nd Duke of
Devonshire (L. 718)

References: Popham 1960, no. 559;
Popham 1962–1963, no. 53; Popham
1969, no. 53; Gere 1971, p. 85,
pl. xxvii; Smith 1976, pp. 102, 105;
McTavish 1981, pp. 249–251, 320–
321, fig. 227; Alasko 1983, no. 36;
Partridge and Starn 1990, pp. 46,
58; Mortari 1992, p. 174, no. 31;
Jaffé 1993, no. 113; Jaffé 1994,
p. 120, no. 831; Böck 1997, pp. 49,
60–62, 162–163.

Notes
1   R. Lanciani, *Storia degli Scavi,
di Roma e notizie intorno le collezioni romane di antichita* (Rome,
1902–1912), III, p. 228; Smith 1976,
p. 105, n. 10.
2   Vasari-Milanesi, vol. 7, p. 46.
*Essendo chiamato a Roma [...]
[Giuseppe Salviati] finì una delle
maggiori storie che sieno nella detta
sala dei Re, e ne cominciò un'altra; e
dopo, essendo morto papa Pio quarto,
se ne tornò a Venezia.*
3   Partridge and Starn 1990, p. 46
suggest that the subject was
inspired by the Fourth Lateran
Council in 1215, which was
attended by seven ambassadors
representing two emperors and five
kings, and that in the fresco the
ambassadors have been transformed into kings. Böck 1997,
pp. 60–62, suggests that the fresco
represents the seven kings of Anglo
Saxon England before Pope Gregory
the Great.
4   For the renovations see
R.O. Rubinstein, "Pius II's Piazza
S. Pietro and St. Andrew's Head,"
*Essays in the History of Architecture
Presented to Rudolf Wittkower*
(London, 1967), pp. 22–33. For the
debate about the proper location of
images of saints Peter and Paul, see
Shearman 1972, pp. 38–41.
5   For example, see Jaffé, 1994a,
p. 120.
6   Inv. 1938.44. Pen and brown
ink and wash. For the connections
between the drawing and the frescoes in the Sala Regia, see McTavish
1981, pp. 250–251.

461

81

GIROLAMO SICIOLANTE DA
SERMONETA
1521–1575
*Pepin the Short Taking Captive
Aistulf, King of the Lombards, and
Returning the Exarchate of Ravenna
to the Church*
c. 1565
Black chalk and pen and brown ink,
with brown wash and white heightening, on yellow prepared paper,
squared in black chalk
45.5 × 42.8 cm
Inscriptions: *1, 2, 3,... 9*
Annotations: *324; trois cent vingt
quatre*
Musée du Louvre, Paris (1960)

Provenance: Giorgio
Vasari. Everhard Jabach (L. 2959);
sold to Louis XIV, 1671; transferred
to the Musée du Louvre (L. 1899
and L. 2207).

References: Coulanges-Rosenberg
1965, no. 127; Gere and Pouncey
1983, p. 161; Hunter 1988, p. 25;
Hunter 1996, pp. 69, 76, n. 19,
pp. 268–269, 280, D-19; Böck 1997,
p. 152, n. 192.

Notes
1   Annotation on the backing
paper, published in Coulanges-
Rosenberg 1965, no. 127; Gere 1971,
pl. 28; Stock and Scrase 1985, no. 57.
2   P. Perali, "I fasti del pontificato
nella Sala Regia," *L'Illustrazione
vaticana* 2:4 (1931), p. 38.
3   Hunter 1996, pp. 68, 112.
4   Ibid., pp. 69–70, 110.
5   Vasari-Milanesi 1878–1885,
vol. 7, pp. 93–94, 573.
6   *The Battle of Lepanto, The Fleet
of the League off Messina*, or *Coligny
Wounded*. See Hunter 1996, pp. 111,
115–116, n. 25.
7   Hunter 1996, p. 110.
8   Ibid., pp. 303–305.
9   "Il disegno di propria mano di
Girolamo ... storia, che fu molto
lodata ... Pepino re de' Franchi dona
Ravenna alla chiesa romana,
e mena prigione Astulfo re de'
Lombardi." Vasari-Milanesi 1878–
1885, vol. 7, p. 573.
10   Coulanges-Rosenberg 1965,
no. 127; L. Ragghianti Collobi 1974,
vol. 1, p. 157; vol. 2, p. 284, fig. 485;
C. Monbeig Goguel in *Collections de
Louis XI: Dessins, albums, manu-
scrits*, exh. cat., ed. R. Bacou and
M.-R. Séguy (Paris, 1977), no. 69;
C. Monbeig Goguel in *Vasari illus-
tré: Du texte à l'image, dessins du
Libro*, vol. 12 of *Giorgio Vasari: Les
vies des meilleurs peintres, sculpteurs et architectes*, ed. A. Chastel
(Paris, 1989), pp. 406–407.
11   Hunter 1988, p. 25; Hunter
1996, pp. 69, 268–269.
12   Hunter 1996, p. 75, n. 9.
13   Böck 1997, p. 34.
14   Vasari-Milanesi 1878–1885,
vol. 4, p. 361, vol. 5, p. 524.
15   Davidson 1966, under no. 47,
pp. 48–49; D. Redig de Campos,
*Raphaël dans les chambres du
Vatican*, tr. J. Humbert (Milan,
1971), p. 80, n. 2; Parma Armani
1986, p. 287.
16   J.W. Jacoby, *Den Päpsten zu
Diensten Raffaels Herrscherzyklus in
der Stanza dell'Incendio im vatikan-
sichen Palast* (Hildesheim, 1987).
17   Böck 1997, p. 34.
18   Coulanges-Rosenberg 1965,
no. 127.
19   Notably the *modello* for the
altarpiece in San Martino Maggiore
in Bologna (Louvre, Paris, Cabinet
des Dessins, 10055). See Hunter
1988, p. 25; Hunter 1996, p. 269.
20   Gabinetto Nazionale delle
Stampe e Disegni, Rome, FC124183;
Hunter 1988, pp. 7–12, 25, plate 6.
See Hunter 1996, p. 269.
21   Respectively in *Fire in the
Borgo, The Expulsion of Heliodorus
from the Temple*, and *The Battle of
Ostia*. See Hunter 1996, p. 68.

22   Monbeig Goguel, *Giorgio
Vasari*, p. 406; Hunter 1996, p. 68,
indicates that this fresco by Peruzzi
had already served as Siciolante's
model in his *Presentation of the
Virgin in the Temple* at Santa Maria
dell'Anima, as suggested by Perali in
"I fasti del pontificato nella Sala
Regia," vol. 2, no. 4 (1931), pp. 33–38.
23   Hunter 1996, p. 68.

82

CIRCLE OF GUGLIELMO DELLA
PORTA
active 1532–1577
Project for the Tomb of Pius IV Medici
c. 1565?
Pen and ink and wash
38.7 × 21.2 cm
Victoria and Albert Museum,
London (2261)

Provenance: John Talman
(L. 2884A); Sir Thomas Lawrence
(L. 2445); Woodburn sale,
Christie's, London, 4–10 June 1860,
acquired by the museum

References: Gregorovius and
Hülsen 1932, n. 76, p. 148, and
pl. LXX; Siebenhüner 1962, p. 251
and fig. 13; Ward-Jackson 1979–
1980, vol. 1, no. 320, pp. 152–153.

83

BARTOLOMEO PASSAROTTI AND
WORKSHOP
1529–1592
Portrait of Pope Pius V
c. 1566
Oil on canvas
129 × 94.5 cm
Inscriptions: *PIUS V GHISLERIUS.
P.[ontifex] M.[AXIMUS] CRE.[ATUS]:
ID[IBIS]: FEB[RUARIS]: MDLXVI.
OB[IIT].K[ALENDIIS].MAII[S]
MDLXXII VIX[IT]: AN[NOS]:
LXVII.M[ENSES]. III.D[IES]. XIV*
The Walters Art Museum,
Baltimore, Maryland (37.453)

Provenance: Hercolani collection,
Bologna, by 1780; Don Marcello
Massarenti, Rome, by 1881; Henry
Walters, 1902, with the Massarenti
collection.

References: Zeri 1976; Höper 1987;
Ghirardi 1986; Ghirardi 1990;
Hanson in Hanson and Spicer 2005,
no. 29; Petrucci 2005.

Notes
1   Höper 1987 (G 207), replica,
suggesting that the first version
could be that formerly in the
Sacchetti collection in Rome;
Petrucci 2005, in the literature as
the original; Hanson, in Hanson
and Spicer 2005, original or a replica. Unless the painting is located,
further speculation is difficult.
2   The date of the addition is
unknown. The pope was elected in
January, not February.
3   Höper 1987 calls it a bible;
Petrucci 2005, gospels (under
no. XI) and breviary (p. 31). My
thanks to Will Noel, Curator of
Manuscripts and Rare Books,
Walters Art Museum, for con-
firming a description of the book.
The breviary contains everything
necessary for saying the canonical
office. The open book featured in
Scipio Pulzone's *Portrait of Pope
Pius V with an Ivory Crucifix*, oil on
canvas, 136 × 105 cm (London,
Sotheby's, sale 16.2.1983, lot 44)
features passages in red, thus the
sections of the office to be sung.
The characterization of Pius indicates that the painting was based
on a lost composition by Passarotti.
4   Calvi, J.A. *Versi e prose sopra
une serie di eccellenti pitture pos-
sedute dal signor Marchese Filippo
Heercolani Principe del S.R.I.*
(Bologna, 1780), p. 90, as cited by
Ghirardi 1990, p. 154.
5   Ghirardi 1986.

6   Höper 1987. Borghini 1584,
pp. 565–566. He links the portrait
of Pius with one of his successor
Gregory XIII; and there was a portrait by Passarotti of that pope as
well in the Sacchetti collection. It
was discovered and published by
Ghirardi (1990); the execution is
close to that of the bust-length portrait illustrated here (fig. 83.1).
7   Zeri 1976, under no. 258, as
"not long after the election," but
more probably after the coronation.
8   For his biography, see Ghirardi
1990 and Höper 1987.
9   *Madonna and Child with Saints
and Giulia Brigola and her Husband*
Ghirardi 1990, no. 1.
10   The first dated portrait is
Portrait of a Gentleman, 1566,
Marseille, Musée des Beaux Arts,
Ghirardi 1990, no. 4.
11   Besides the versions attributed to Passarotti cited in old
inventories and listed by Höper
(G 207, 146, 168, 205), there is a version called "El Greco" (Paris, private
collection; http://en.wikipedia.org/
wiki/Image: El _ Greco _ 050.jpg
[accessed 03.30.2009]); portraits
signed by Scipio Pulzone (1544–
1598) that are surely derived from
Passarotti's portraits (Dern 2003,
nos. 13–15); portraits apparently of
the older Pius, said to be signed by
Giulio Clovio, 112 × 84 cm (Milan,
Koelliker collection; Petrucci 2005,
no. XIII) and a similar piece, as
attributed to Lavinia Fortano
(Imola, Palazzo Tozzini; *Pittura
bolognese del '500*, 1986, p. 773).
Petrucci 2005, p. 33 (n. 10), notes
further portraits of Pius V in
Vatican storerooms.
12   *Bust-length Portrait of Pope
Pius V*, probably 1566, oil on canvas,
56 × 42 cm. (Rome, private collection, acquired from a Bolognese
collection), first published Petrucci
(2005), no. XII). Another bust-
length portrait, oil on canvas,
46 × 34 cm. (Modena, Seminario) is
cited by Ghirardi 1990, no. 5a, ill.,
as an autograph replica of the
Baltimore painting.
13   In contrast, the sleeve is confused suggesting, perhaps, that
areas away from the face were
worked up later. An X-ray would be
valuable.
14   Ghirardi 1990 found the
expression "ironic and grotesque,"
the eyes "suspicious."
15   For an overview of sixteenth-
century papal portraits, see
Petrucci 2005, pp. 27–33. See also
C. Denker Nesselrath, "The
Likeness of Peter's Successors: 2000
Years of Papal Portraits," in Allen
Duston and Roberto Zagnoli, eds.,
*Saint Peter and the Vatican, The
Legacy of the Popes* (Alexandria,
2003), pp. 109–133.
16   Petrucci 2005, under no. XI.
Raphael depicted Leo X (Florence,
Galleria degli Uffizi) as an art lover
examining an illuminated manuscript with a magnifying glass. The
composition (which must go back to
Passarotti) combining a breviary
with a crucifix (n. 3) is a closely
related example of Pius's assertion
of the role of private spirituality.

84

TADDEO ZUCCARO
1529–1566
Marine Deities in a Cartouche
c. 1566
Pen and brown ink, brown wash,
over black chalk
11.9 × 24.7 cm
National Gallery of Canada, Ottawa
(42297)

Provenance: John Thane, London
(L. 1544); Thomas Lawrence
(L. 2445); David Lachenmann,
Zurich; Purchased from La Tâche
Fine Arts, Zurich in 2008.

References: Gere 1995, no. 134-A,
fig. 52

Notes
1   Gere 1995. The other drawing
is illustrated in Robertson 1992,
p. 113, figs. 101–2.
2   Bober and Rubinstein 1986,
nos. 99–104.
3   For his work at Caprarola see
C. Acidini Luchinat 1998–1999,
vol. 1, pp. 156–226.

85

FEDERICO ZUCCARO
c. 1542/43–1609
Saint John the Baptist
c. 1566–1567
Pen and brown ink and brown wash
over traces of black chalk on light
brown paper; repair at lower left
23.1 × 17.5 cm
Inscriptions: *.gb*. [by "Pseudo-Resta"]
Private collection

Provenance: The Pseudo-Resta;
Jonathan Richardson, Sr. (L. 2184),
mount with shelfmarks 'V.44/Zg.
15/LL.26'; anonymous sale,
Christie's, London, 8 December
1981, lot 36; Roberto Ferretti di
Castelferretto; Christie's, London,
7 July 1992, lot 130; private collection, Montreal.

References: Mundy 1989, pp. 144–
145, no. 40; Acidini Luchinat 1998–
1999, II, pp. 16, 19, 40, note 25;
Partridge in Winner and Heikamp
1999, p. 173

Notes
1   In a letter of 19 October 1970,
cited in Mundy 1989, p. 144. For the
date, see Partridge 1999, pp. 169–170.
2   Mundy 1989, p. 144.
3   Florence, Gabinetto Disegni
e Stampe degli Uffizi, n. 821 S; pen
and brown and wash, heightened
with white, on brown tinted paper;
17.1 × 23.5 cm. Gere 1966a, p. 40,
no. 52. Partridge in Winner and
Heikamp, 1999, p. 169, argues that
the related ceiling fresco is also by
Federico.
4   Ibid. Berlin,
Kupferstichkabinett, KdZ inv. n.
21806; Stockholm,
Nationalmuseum, NM 448/1863.
P. Bjurström and B. Magnusson,
*Italian Drawings, Umbria, Rome,
Naples* (Stockholm, 1998), no. 578.
5   Florence, Gabinetto Disegni e
Stampe degli Uffizi, n. 1132F. It is
possible that the drawing is a copy
after a lost original sheet by
Federico. In the eighteenth century
Stevano Mulinari published a facsimile engraving after this drawing; it is numbered at the upper
fight: *N. XXVII*, and inscribed lower
left: *Federigo Zuccheri inv: e del:*
and at the lower right: *Mulinari
inci*. In addition, on the basis of a
Gernsheim photograph (110900),
Hugo Chapman has tentatively
attributed a drawing of John the
Baptist in the Ambrosiana, Milan,
to Federico Zuccaro. Currently
attributed to Procaccini (no first
name given), the drawing (F269
INF N.10-10 verso) is in black and
red chalk and shows the saint
three-quarter length. On the recto,
there is a Judgment of Paris in pen
and ink wash that is not by either
Taddeo or Federico Zuccaro.

86

ATTRIBUTED TO FEDERICO
ZUCCARO
c. 1542/43–1609
Conversion of Saint Paul
c. 1566
Oil on canvas
68 × 47 cm
Galleria Doria Pamphili, Rome
(168)
Not in exhibition

References: Galleria Doria Pamphilj
1823, pp. 15–16, 147; Sestieri 1942,
p. 370, no. 370; Acidini Luchinat
1998–1999, I, pp. 70, 77 no. 59; Balass
2001, p. 197 no. 11.

87
GIOVANNI ANTONIO DOSIO
1533–1609
Design for the Tomb of Paul IV
1566
Pen and brown wash with underdrawing in leadpoint
34.9 × 33.5 cm
Inscriptions: *Jul: Romano, GIOVANANTONIO DOSIO DA SANGIMIGNANO SCVLTOR FIORENTINO*
The British Museum, London (1861-8-10-34)

References: Vallone 1977, p. 254; Gere and Pouncey 1983, no. 94.

Notes
1 See Vallone 1977.

88
TIZIANO VECCELLIO, CALLED TITIAN
c. 1488/90–1576
Saint Mary Magdalene in Penitence
1567
Inscriptions: *TITIANUS P.*
Oil on canvas
128 × 103 cm
Museo Nazionale di Capodimonte, Naples (136)

Provenance: Cardinal Alessandro Farnese, Rome, 1567; Farnese Collection, Palazzo del Giardino, Parma, 1680; Naples, mid-eighteenth century; French took possession, 1799; Rome, 1800; Palazzo Francavilla, Naples, 1800; Palermo, 1806; Naples, 1815.

References: Wethey 1969, I, pp. 145–146; Valcanover 1990, p. 336; Goffen 1997, pp. 186–187; Gentili 2008, pp. 282–284.

Notes
1 On the development of the legend of the Magdalene, which was based on a conflation of different figures in the Bible and apocryphal accounts, see K.L. Jansen, *The Making of the Magdalene: Preaching and Popular Devotion in the Later Middle Ages* (Princeton, 2000). On the iconography of the Magdalene, see M. Ingenhoff-Dannhäuser, *Maria Magdalena: Heilige und Sünderin in der Italienischen Renaissance: Studien zur Ikonographie der Heiligen von Leonardo bis Titian* (Tübingen, 1984) and S. Haskins, *Mary Magdalene: Myth and Metaphor* (New York, San Diego, and London, 1993).
2 Wethey 1969, pp. 145–146, no. 122. On Cardinal Farnese as a patron, see Robertson 1992.
3 C. Hope, "A Neglected Document about Titian's 'Danae' in Naples," *Arte Veneta,* XXXI (1977), pp. 188–189.
4 On Giovanni della Casa's career and connections with Titian, see, with further bibliography, U. D'Elia, *The Poetics of Titian's Religious Paintings* (Cambridge, 2005), p. 171.
5 R. de Maio, "Il mito della Maddalena nella Controriforma," *La Maddalena tra sacro e profano,* exh. cat. (Milan, 1986), pp. 82–83.
6 As quoted in Robert Williams, "The Façade of the *Palazzo dei 'Visacci',*" *I Tatti Studies,* V (1993), p. 213.
7 See D'Elia, *Titian's Religious Paintings,* pp. 88–91, 103–104.
8 Ibid, pp. 84–106.
9 The most famous example, which was much imitated in painting and sculpture, is Donatello's wooden statue, now in the Museo dell'Opera del Duomo, Florence.
10 F.M. Molza, quoted in D'Elia, *Titian's Religious Paintings,* p. 99.
11 For an opposing view, in which these changes in the later versions are seen as radically altering the interpretation of the image, see Goffen 1997, p. 187.
12 D'Elia, *Titian's Religious Paintings,* pp. 148–150.
13 On the making of replicas in Titian's shop in this period, including this painting, which Hope considers a "good example," see C. Hope, *Titian* (London, 1980), p. 154. Often deemed inferior to the Hermitage version, most scholars agree that the work is partly by the workshop and partly by the master. See, with further references, Valcanover 1990, p. 336 and Gentili 2008, p. 282.
14 Gentili 2008, pp. 241, 279–284.
15 D'Elia, *Titian's Religious Paintings,* pp. 2–5.

89
ATTRIBUTED TO VENTURA DI VINCENZIO ULIVIERI
active in Florence, c. 1565–c. 1600
The Conversion of Saint Paul
c. 1567
Oil on panel
60 × 43·5 cm
Bob Jones University Museum and Gallery, Greenville, South Carolina

Provenance: Vincenzo Borghini; sale by the Ospedale degli Innocenti to the Panciatichi family in December 1833; sale by Marchese Ferdinando Panciatichi Ximenes d'Aragona, April 1902; Havemeyer Collection, New York, until 1927; Julius Weitzner, New York, from c. 1952–1958; Bob Jones University Museum and Gallery from 1959

References: Baltimore 1961, no. 74 (as Vasari); Barocchi 1964a, p. 142 (as Morandini); New York 1967, no. 32 (as Vasari); Milkovich and Porter 1970, no. P21 (as Vasari); Charlotte 1982, no. 20 (as Vasari); Pepper 1984, p. 79, no. 80.1 (as Morandini); Townsend 1994, pp. 114–115, no. 3 (attributed to Morandini); Giovannetti 1995, p. 218 (not by Morandini); Nolan 2001, no. 15 (attributed to Morandini); Scorza 2003, pp. 87–93 (attributed to Ventura di Vincenzio Ulivieri)

Notes
1 Most were likely tokens of friendship and gratitude from the artist, not least for the years of iconographic advice Borghini had given him. See further Scorza 2003, pp. 87–104. Borghini's replica of the *Adoration of the Magi* of 1566–1567, commissioned by Pius V for his burial chapel in Santa Croce, Bosco Marengo, was exhibited recently at the National Gallery of Canada. See my catalogue entry in Franklin 2005, pp. 314–317, no 115. It is now in the National Gallery of Scotland, Edinburgh.
2 It hung alongside its companion piece, *Christ Carrying the Cross* in the Spencer Museum of Art, Kansas (Scorza 2003, pp. 87–94 and Appendix II, nos. 10–11). The inventory was compiled by the notary, Raffaello Eschini, who described the Kansas picture as "uno quadro simile di uno Cristo che porta la croce." Eschini's description of the *Conversion* as "uno quadro grande" is in no way disconcerting; it simply differentiates this painting from the many "quadretti" and "quadrettini" that he recorded in Borghini's collection.
3 It was sold by the Ospedale with an attribution to Vasari. See Scorza 2003, pp. 87–88, and the inventory of sale as published by A. Piccini, "Ricordi documentari inediti o poco noti sulla costruzione dell'Ospedale degli Innocenti e su opere d'arte ad esso appartenenti o appartenute," in *Il Museo dello Spedale degli Innocenti a Firenze,* ed. L. Bellosi (Florence 1977), p. 26: *"36 – Uno detto Come Sopra rappresentante S. Paolo che si presenta ad Anania – del sudetto [i.e. Vasari]. L 300. 1833, 7 Dicembre. Al Sig. March. Panciatichi."* In the Panciatichi-Ximenes d'Aragona auction catalogue, the subject was given as Paul's conversion after the recovery of his sight. It is illustrated in what appears to be its original frame (Galardelli e Mazzoni, Florence, 3 April 1902, lot 31).
4 This has only recently been contested. L. Corti's suggestion (*Vasari. Catalogo completo dei dipinti* [Florence, 1989], pp. 82–83) that the painting is a replica of Vasari's Del Monte altarpiece was rejected by Townsend (1994, p. 114). Following Barocchi 1964a, p. 142, he maintained it shows *Abraham and Melchisedek*. In his review of Townsend's catalogue (*The Burlington Magazine* 137 [1995], pp. 345–347), R. Ward identified the subject correctly, observing that the presence of the Holy Spirit suggests a New Testament episode. Nolan 2001 (no. 15) supported this view.
5 Now in the Musée Calvet, Avignon. See Barocchi 1964a, pp. 118–119, pl. 32.
6 The bread and wine with which Melchisadech pronounced his blessing on Abraham, and the tithe of spoils he received in return, are prominent in the foreground of the Avignon painting (Genesis, XIV, 18–20).
7 *"... per variare da quello che avea fatto il Buonarruoto nella Paulina, feci S. Paulo, come egli scrive, giovane, che già cascato da cavallo è condotto dai soldati ad Anania cieco, dal quale per imposizione delle mani riceve il lume degl'occhi perduto et è battezzato"* (Vasari 1568, II, p. 1001). He even varied his composition to the extent of representing Saul as a beardless youth.
8 *"... et inponens ei manus dixit Saule frater Dominus misit me Iesus qui apparuit tibi in via qua veniebas ut videas et implearis Spiritu Sancto"* (Acts, IX, 17).
9 The house of Judas, to be precise (Acts IX, 11).
10 "... vas electionis est mihi" (Acts, IX, 15). Ananias had been fearful of obeying the divine instruction to seek out Paul, who prior to his blindness was "breathing murderous threats against the disciples of the Lord" (Acts IX, 1).
11 To give Paul "strength" after his baptism, as observed by Nolan 2001 (no. 15), with reference to Acts IX, 18–19.
12 Executed in 1539–40 for the refectory of San Michele in Bosco, Bologna. See Barocchi 1964b, pp. 17–18, 114, pl. IV; L. Corti, *Vasari,* pp. 24–27, no. 11. The staircase in the Greenville painting is closer to that in Vasari's preparatory drawing in the Louvre (Monbeig Goguel 1972, p. 147, no. 190), which may have been Borghini's point of reference.
13 "... quoniam unus panis unum corpus multi sumus omnes quidem de uno pane participamur" (I Corinthians, X, 17).
14 I Corinthians XIII, 1–13. The concept of charity had a specific resonance for the Cassinese Congregation, on of the constituent congregations of the Benedictine Confederation, of which Borghini was a member. Its writers consistently expounded a doctrine on salvation drawn from Pauline theology. See further B. Collett, *Italian Benedictine Scholars and the Reformation. The Congregation of Santa Giustina of Padua* (Oxford 1985), pp. 172–173, 183.
15 Scorza 2003, p. 89, and Appendix III, no. 16. The drawing is described as "della medesima misura" as the preceding item in the list, which measured *"uno braccio in circa"* in height (c. 58.4 cm).
16 Barocchi's attribution to Morandini (Barocchi 1964a, p. 142) was accepted with caution by Townsend, but rejected by Giovannetti 1995 (p. 218, under no. D27).
17 Livo was one of the artists in residence, or "Pittori di casa," that Cosimo I allowed Borghini to employ at the Ospedale. He contributed further works to Borghini's collection, including a female "testa," and possibly a copy after Michelangelo's *Jeremiah*. See further Scorza 2003, pp. 66–67, 70–71, pp. 78–80.
18 Borghini recorded *"Ulivo delli Innocenti"* among the artists working for Vasari during the preparations for the 1565 *Apparato,* celebrating Francesco de' Medici's wedding. See E. Pilliod, *Pontormo, Bronzino, Allori. A Genealogy of Florentine Art* (New Haven and London 2001), pp. 208–209, fig. 167, Scorza 2003, p. 66, and esp. P. Gavitt, "An experimental Culture: the Art of the Economy and the Economy of Art under Cosimo I and Francesco I," in *The Cultural Politics of Duke Cosimo I de' Medici,* ed. K. Eisenbichler (Aldershot 2001), pp. 205–221. Livo was evidently too young to feature in Vasari's section of the *Vite* dedicated to the *Accademici del Disegno.*
19 The painting, now in the Duomo, was originally commissioned by Borghini for the high altar of the abbey of San Salvatore a Spugna (Giovannetti 1995, pp. 75–76, no. 2, fig. 2).
20 The cast, features and handling of Charity, for example, are particularly close to those of the kneeling female at the lower right of his Livo's *Lamentation*; compare also the incisive contours of the younger centurion's head with that of John the Evangelist to the left of Morandini's *Crucifixion with Saints,* where Livo was responsible for the subsidiary figures. Both works are in the Museum of the Ospedale degli Innocenti (Giovannetti 1995, pp. 101–102, no. 48, fig. 62; L. Cavazzini, "Dipinti e sculture nelle chiese dell'Ospedale," in *Gli Innocenti e Firenze nei secoli. Un Ospedale, un archivio, una città,* ed. Lucia Sandri [Florence 1996], pp. 128–130, figs 82–83). The proportions, facial types and handling of the figures on the steps and balustrade of the *Conversion* correspond especially well with those in the background of the copy after Bronzino's *Banquet of Joseph* in the Walters Art Museum, Baltimore, which appears to have been another collaborative work by Livo and Morandini. See further Scorza 2003, pp. 111–112, fig. 124.
21 P. & D. Colnaghi & Co, *Old Master Paintings and Drawings* (London 1979), no. 47 ascribed to Vasari. The lost profile in the drawing is transformed into a full profile in the painting, showing a boy in his early teens.
22 It brought him into close contact with Michelangelo, who negotiated the price and closely monitored the project. See further Monbeig Goguel 1972, pp. 154–156, nos 200–201.
23 Florence, Gabinetto disegni e stampe degli Uffizi, 11138F. As in Vasari's altarpiece, the younger centurion supports Paul by his shoulder while the older gently lifts his left hand. John Gere initially thought this represented an abandoned idea by Federico Zuccaro for the Cappella Paolina, but later accepted it as by his brother Taddeo (J.A. Gere, *Taddeo Zuccari nel Gabinetto delle Stampe e dei Disegni della Galleria degli Uffizi,* exh. cat. [Sanseverino 1992], pp. 104–107, nos. 50–51, and Gere 1995, pp. 246–247, no. 59A, fig. 21). The drawing appears to date from around 1563–1565, since the topmost section of the composition is repeated on the verso of a study for the altarpiece in San Lorenzo in Damaso.

24 St John Chrysostom was central to the education of the monks of Borghini's congregation, who defined faith and salvation along the lines of Chrysostom's exegeses of Saint Paul, promoting charity and good works. Borghini owned at least five early editions of Paul's Letters, one of them in manuscript, and two copies of Chrysostom's commentaries. He frequently travelled with Pauline works in his baggage, and devised pressmarks for his books, inspired by a passage in the First Letter to the Thessalonians, promoting open-mindedness. See further Scorza 2003, p. 91.
25 *"... et in una di quelle persone, che vi sono, fece il ritratto di sè medesimo,"* (Baglione 1642, p. 12).

90
JACOPO ZANGUIDI, CALLED BERTOIA
1544–c. 1572/74
The Entry of Christ into Jerusalem
c. 1568
Oil on canvas
49 × 38.5 cm
Galleria Nazionale di Parma (32)

Provenance: Ducal Guardamobile; moved to the Galleria Nazionale in 1820.

References: De Grazia 1991, pp. 87–88; Muzii in Fornari Schianchi and Spinosa 1995, p. 141; Sricchia Santoro in Dacos 1995, pp. 76–77; Frattarolo in Fornari Schianchi 1998, pp. 118–119 (with previous literature); Venturelli 1999, p. 148; Bernardini 2002, pp. 61–65; Chiusa 2005, p. 68.

91
FEDERICO ZUCCARO
c. 1542/43–1609
Calumny of Apelles
c. 1569
Oil on canvas
144 × 237 cm
Inscriptions: *INPAVIDUM FERIENT* (originally *IMPAVIDUM FERIENT*)
The Royal Collection (RCIN 405695)

Provenance: Possibly Francesco Maria II Duke of Urbino; Kensington Palace, London; Hampton Court, London.

References: Shearman 1983, pp. 299–303, no. 328; Massing 1990, pp. 363–364, no. 26D; Acidini Luchinat 1998–1999, II, pp. 35–36; Whitaker-Clayton 2007, pp. 76–79, no. 10

Notes
1 Lucian of Samosata, "Slander," in *Lucian with an English Translation, Eight Volumes*, vol. 5 (London, New York, 1913–1967), I, pp. 361–393, see pp. 365–367.
2 See Shearman 1983.

92
ALESSANDRO ALLORI
1535–1607
Laocoön
c. 1570
Oil on panel
73.7 × 57.2 cm
Private collection, United States

Provenance: Sotheby's, New York, 14 October 1992, lot 179; Private Collection, United States

Notes
1 S. Lecchini Giovannoni, *Alessandro Allori* (Torino, 1991), nos. 12 and 36; figs. 13 and 72
2 Ibid., nos. 28 and 29; figs. 56, 57, and 60.

93
DOMENIKOS THEOTOKOPOULOS, CALLED EL GRECO
1541–1614
A Boy Blowing on an Ember to Light a Candle ('El Soplón')
c. 1570–1572
Oil on canvas
60.5 × 50.5 cm.
Museo Nazionale di Capodimonte, Naples (Q192)

Provenance: Recorded in the *Stanza dei Quadri* in the Palazzo Farnese, Rome, 1644; sent by the Farnese to Parma in 1662 and hung first in the Palazzo del Giardino and then from at least 1680 (when it was attributed to Guilio Clovio) in the ducal gallery of the Palazzo della Pilotta; transferred to Naples in 1734, first to the Palazzo Reale and then to the Palazzo di Capodimonte before 1776; in 1799 taken to Rome by the French but returned to Naples in 1800.

References: Alvarez Lopera 2005–2007, II, pp. 106–107, no. 39 (with previous literature).

Notes
1 H.E. Wethey, *El Greco and His School*, 2 vols. (Princeton, 1962), vol. 1, pp. 7, 81, note 32; Alvarez Lopera 2006–2007, vol. I, pp. 83–84.
2 X. De Salas, "Un Exemplaire des "Vies" de Vasari annoté par El Greco," *Gazette des Beaux-Arts*, 69 (1967), pp. 176–180; X. De Salas, "Las notas del Greco a la 'Vida de Tiziano,' de Vasari," in *El Greco: Italy and Spain*, ed. J. Brown and J.M. Pita Andrade, *Studies in the History of Art*, 13 (1984), pp. 161–169; X. De Salas and F. Marías, *El Greco y el arte de su tiempo: Las notas de El Greco a Vasari* (Madrid, 1992).
3 For effective descriptions, see D. Davies and G. Finaldi in *El Greco*, exh. cat. (New York and London 2003–2004), respectively pp. 221 and 226.
4 Alvarez Lopera 2006–2007, vol. II, p. 43, no. 10. El Greco then painted a much larger version on canvas, now in the collection of the Duke of Buccleuch and Queensberry at Kettering, Northamptonshire; Ibid, II, pp. 47–48, no. 14.
5 J. Bialostocki, "Puer Sufflans Ignes," in *Arte in Europa, Scritti di Storia dell'Art in Onore di Edoardo Arslan*, 2 vols. (Milan, 1966), I, p. 592.
6 Pliny the Elder, *Natural History* (Loeb ed.), 10. vols. (Cambridge, MA. and London, 1938–1962), 9:138, pp. 361, 363.
7 K. and H.-W. Frey, eds., *Der literarische Nachlass Giorgio Vasari*, 3 vols. (Munich/Berlin, 1923–1940), II, p. 101, letter dated 14 August 1564: *Scrive Plinio (eccovi la dottrina in campo), che fu molto celebrato dun' pittore un fanciullo che soffiava nel fuoco, che quello splendore gli ribatteva nella bocca et per certi vugli del casa, come la vostra notte di Camaldolj ...*
8 In particular, see N. Hadjinicolaou, ed., in *El Greco in Italy and Italian Art*, exh. cat. (Athens 1995) pp. 354–359, 530–534.
9 Alvarez Lopera 2006–2007, vol. II, pp. 103–107.
10 D. Davies, ed., *El Greco: Mystery and Illumination*, exh. cat. (Edinburgh, 1989), pp. 11–32; and Ibid., pp. 221–225.
11 J. Bialostocki, "Puer Sufflans Ignes," vol. I, pp. 591–595.

94
GIORGIO VASARI
1511–1574
Saint Peter Martyr Staving off the Devil on the Piazza del Mercato Vecchio, Florence
c. 1570–1571
Pen and brown ink, brown wash, over black chalk, partially drawn with a ruler and a pair of compasses; the drawing of the main composition mounted on a larger sheet containing the architectural frame and the figure of Christ in a lunette
45.4 × 35.2 cm
Private collection, New York

Provenance: Edward Fairfax Murray (?); Hans Calmann, London; Loriano Bertini, Calenzano (Florence) c. 1972; Private collection, Zurich, 1982; with Artemis Fine Art, London, 1985; with Trinity Fine Art, London, New York, 1994, no. 6, illustrated; Saul Steinberg, New York; with Richard Feigen, New York

References: Cecchi 1976, p. 157; Cecchi 1978, p. 58; Corti et al. 1981, pp. 96–97, no. IV/37f; Fairbairn 1998, vol. II, p. 519

Notes
1 K. and H.-W. Frey, eds. *Der literarische Nachlass: Giorgio Vasari*. 3 vols. (Munich, 1923, 1930 and 1940), vol. II, pp. 471–73, no. DCXCV.
2 Ibid., II, pp. 573.
3 The others are: *Saint Peter Martyr Unmasking the Devil Appearing in Guise of the Madonna and Child with the Help of a Host* (for a preparatory drawing, formerly in the collection of Juan de Beistegui, Paris, and acquired in 2004 for the Musée des Beaux-Arts, Marseille, see D. Cordellier, *Da la Renaissance à l'Age baroque. Une collection de dessins italiens pour les musées de France*, exh. cat. (Paris, 2005), no. 28, illustrated); *Saint Peter Martyr Adoring the Crucifix*, and *Saint Peter Martyr Presenting the Banners to the Families Well Proven in the Fight against the Heretics*.
4 Frey *Der literarische Nachlass*, II, p. 552.
5 Ibid, pp. 558–559, no. 773 (1 January 1571, Vasari to Francesco de' Medici): "... and already in this short period of time, a month today, I have not only made all the drawings for the three chapels but also painted two of the altarpieces, not just sketched, but finished, and the third will be like the others by the day of Epiphany (6 January), something, my Lord, that has amazed our Holy Father, who shows his great contentment with it."
6 Fairbairn 1998, vol. II, p. 519. It should be noted that the architectural drawing does not appear to be the work of Vasari's pupil Jacopo Zucchi, who is known to have made ornamental frames of this kind for his master. Zucchi's hand is clearly discernible in the altar architecture and predella scenes in Vasari's large drawing of the *Last Judgment* in the Louvre (2153; Monbeig Goguel 1972, no. 198), for his altarpiece of 1569–1570 in church of Bosco Marengo. In particular, the figures of Charit, Hope, and Faith on top of the altar are characteristic of Zucchi's figure style. Zucchi also drew several ornamental borders for Vasari's *Libro de'disegni*.

95
PIRRO LIGORIO
c. 1513/14–1583
Sheet of Studies with Mythological Subjects ("Effects of Drunkeness")
c. 1570
Red chalk
37.2 × 24.3 cm
Inscriptions: *P 80; 11, 13*; *Giulio Romano* (verso)
Szépmüvészeti Múzeum, Budapest (K.67.4)

Provenance: Praun; Esterházy (L. 1965).

References: Zentai 1998, p. 112 ff.; Zentai 1997, pp. 131–132.

Notes
1 State Archives, Turin, Ja.II.17, vol. 30.
2 See C. Volpi, ed., *Disegni di Pirro Ligorio all'Archivio di Stato di Torino* (Rome, 1994), p. 95, n. 12.
3 Ibid., p. 94.
4 *"Me diedi alle cose matematiche, al disegno, ... non per farme nell'arte della pittura profittevole, ma per possere esprimere le cose antiche o d'edificij in prospettiva, ... et per potere cavare gli essempli delle cose delle medaglie, et dell'altre sculture."* State Archives, Turin, MS. a.III.3, vol. 1, fol. 6r; see A. Schreurs, *Antikenbild und Kunstanschauungen des neapolitanischen Malers, Architekten und Antiquars Pirro Ligorio (1513–1583)* (Cologne, 2000), p. 338, no. 24. In retrospect, he described his work as an architect and painter in Rome as a burdensome means of earning a livelihood (Schreurs, Ibid., p. 338, no. 21) and regretted that he was left with too little time for his antiquarian pursuits, "after the fatigue of painting" (Bodleian Library, Oxford, MS. Canon Ital. 138, fol. 43r; Schreurs, *Antikenbild und Kunstanschauungen*, p. 337, no. 20).
5 State Archives, Turin, MS. a.III., volumes 1–18.
6 See E. Mandowsky and C. Mitchell, *Pirro Ligorio's Roman Antiquities: The Drawings in MS XIII.B.7 in the National Library in Naples* (London, 1963), p. 62ff., no. 15.
7 Mandowsky and Mitchell ("Some Observations on Pirro Ligorio's Drawings of Roman Monuments," *Rendiconti della Pontifica Accademia Romana de Archeologia* 27:24 [1952–1954], p. 342) sought to rehabilitate Ligorio's reputation by arguing that his main objective had been "to show the monument in all its magnificence, as it was described by ancient authors. ... In order to renew the glory of a splendid past, he felt obliged to restore the statuary to its former completeness."
8 See Schreurs, *Antikenbild und Kunstanschauungen*, pp. 68–74.
9 Biblioteca Nazionale, Naples, MS. XIII, fol. 492; see Mandowsky and Mitchell, *Pirro Ligorio's Roman Antiquities*, p. 118, no. 130, fig. 71c.
10 M. Winner, "Pirro Ligorio Disegnatore," in Volpi, *Disegni di Pirro Ligorio*, p. 25.

96
GIORGIO VASARI
1511–1574
Pope Gregory XI Returning from Avignon
1572–1573
Pen and brown ink, brown wash, over black chalk, squared in black chalk
37.3 × 48.3 cm
Musée du Louvre, Paris (2163)

Provenance: Evérard Jabach (L. 2959)

References: Egger 1911, p. 25, fig. 12; Barocchi 1964b, p. 73; Monbeig Goguel 1972, no. 221, illustrated; Corti et al. 1981, p. 98, no. IV/39g (entry by J. Kliemann)

Notes

1 K. and H.-W. Frey, eds., *Der literarische Nachlass: Giorgio Vasari*, 3 vols. (Munich, 1923, 1930 and 1940), vol. II, p. 618, no. DCCCXXXII (10 November 1571, Cardinal Cesi to Vasari).
2 Ibid., p. 685, no. DCCCIIIC (14 June 1572, Cardinal Cesi to Vasari).
3 Ibid., pp. 729–731, no. CMXLV (Vasari to Borghini): *Vorrej bene dj questj Gregorij ponteficj trovar qualche cosa notabile, come quel Gregorio che ricondusse d' Avignione la Siede Apostoljca, et quello che levo via l autorita al inpero.*
4 Ibid., pp. 744–747, no. CMLVIII (10 or 17 January 1573, Borghini to Vasari).
5 Ibid., pp. 744–747, no. CMLVIII (Borghini to Vasari): *Quando s' intramettesse in qualche buon modo la persona della santa, mi piacerebbe, ma con gravita et da non dar che far beffe a malevoli et alle cicale.*
6 A thus far unidentified sketch for the group of Tiber with putti in the lower left is in the Uffizi (Fig. 2, Inv. 987S). Traditionally attributed to Vasari, this small but vigorous sketch, possibly cut down from a larger sheet, was ascribed to Francesco Morandini by Barocchi, unaware of its connection with the fresco, in 1964 (Florence 1964, no. 101, fig. 58). In a note on the mount Petrioli Tofani later correctly returned to the old attribution. It is in fact a study for the group on the far left in the fresco, including most of the details that Vasari then fully worked up in the present sheet.
7 See F. Haskell and N. Penny, *Taste and the Antique. The Lure of Classical Sculpture, 1500–1900* (New Haven/London, 1981), p. 257.
8 H. Egger, "Giorgio Vasaris Darstellung des Einzuges Gregors XI. in Rom," in *Zeitschrift für Kunstwissenschaft* 2 (3–4) (1948), pp. 43–48.
9 The pope sat to Vasari on 8 April 1573 for two hours (*Der literarische Nachlass*, II, pp. 769, 772); the portrait was finished the next day.
10 Vasari seems to have first entertained this idea in a letter to Borghini of 5 February 1573, *Der literarische Nachlass*, II, pp. 571–572, no. CMLXIII; see further ibid., pp. 769–771, no. CMLXXX (8 April 1573, Vasari to Borghini); pp. 776–777, no. CMLXXXVI (23 April 1573, Vasari to Borghini); pp. 780–783, no. CMLXXXIX (2 May 1573, Borghini to Vasari).
11 Ibid., pp. 784–785, no. CMXCI (Vasari to Francesco de' Medici). The final inscription, which does not mention Vasari's name, is on the wall opposite the entrance to the Cappella Paolina and has been reprinted on p. 782.
12 Ibid., pp. 786–788, no. CMXCIII (22 May 1573, Vasari to Borghini): *la sala e finita et jermattina si scoperse con molta mia laude et honore....*

97
SCIPIONE PULZONE
c. 1550–1598
Portrait of Jacopo Boncompagni
1574
Oil on canvas
121 × 98.8 cm
Inscriptions: *Scipio. Caietano faciebat. 1574; Ill.mo et Ecc.s.mo S.or Jaco.*
Private collection, Washington

Provenance: Haskard Collection; Agnew & Sons, London (1899); W.C. Whitney; Smith Sale, American Art Collection, New York (18–22 January 1910); Hazlitt, Gooden & Fox, London.

References: Venturi 1901–1940, IX.7, p. 780; Vannugli 1991, pp. 54–66; Vannugli in Volpi 2002, pp. 280, 282; Dern 2003, pp. 32, 110–111, no. 19.

Notes

1 R. Preimesberger in *Rom in Bayern. Kunst und Spiritualität der ersten Jesuiten*, exh. cat. (Munich, 1997) pp. 275–280, no. 8.
2 See Vannugli 1991, pp 60–61.
3 See Dern 2003, p. 32.

98
GIULIO MAZZONI
c. 1525–c. 1618
Saint Jerome
c. 1570–1575
Oil on panel transferred to canvas
147 × 98 cm
Pinacoteca Vaticana, Vatican City (40369)

Provenance: from the church of Santa Marta in Vaticano (destroyed 1930).

References: Mack 1972, pp. 360–361; Vatican 1983, pp. 215–219; Tosini 1997, pp. 71–73; Marciari 2000, p. 495; Romani 2003, pp. 144–146.

Notes

1 The picture was transferred to canvas in a 1981 restoration. See Vatican 1983, pp. 215–219.
2 The three most important and complete early biographies of Muziano are U. Procacci, "Una 'Vita' inedita del Muziano," *Arte Veneta* 8 (1954), pp. 242–264 (a biographical account that Muziano narrated to his confessor around 1585); Borghini 1584, *Il riposo de Raffaello Borghini, in cui della pittura, e della scultura si favella, de' più illustri pittori, e scultori, e delle più famose opere loro si fa mentione; e le cose principali appartenenti a dette arti s'insegnano*, pp. 574–578; and Baglione 1995, vol. 1, pp. 49–52. Vasari, Van Mander and Mancini also give notes on Muziano, but none mentions this painting.
3 G. Celio, *Memorie delli nomi dell'artifici delle pitture che sono in alcune chiese, facciate, e palazzi di Roma* [1638], ed. E. Zocca (Milan, 1967), pp. 27, 75; Baglione 1995, p. 67. The church is identified by Celio as "S. Maria," no doubt a printer's error.
4 The papal privilege related to the work similarly describes the engraving as "from a model and invention of Daniele da Volterra." See E. Lincoln, *The Invention of the Italian Renaissance Printmaker* (New Haven and London, 2000), p. 124.
5 G. Alvieri, *Della Roma in ogni Stato* (Rome, 1670), vol. 2, p. 221; Titi 1674–1763, p. 17. The only writers to reject the attribution have been Mack 1972, pp. 360–361, and Marciari 2000, p. 495, no. RP50.
6 On Santa Marta see G. Bossi, *La Chiesa di Santa Marta al Vaticano* (Rome, 1883); M.J. Lewine, *The Roman Church Interior 1527–1580*, Ph.D. diss., Columbia University, 1960, pp. 419–428; J. Wasserman, "Una chiesa scomparsa: S. Marta in Vaticano," *Capitolium* 36 (1961), pp. 23–27; C. Pietrangeli, "Ricordo di una chiesa distrutta: Santa Marta al Vaticano," *Bollettino: Monumenti Musei e Gallerie Pontificie* 5 (1984), pp. 91–111.
7 V. Forcella, *Iscrizioni delle chiese e d'altri edificii di Roma dal secolo XI fino ai giorni nostri* (Rome, 1875), vol. 6, nos. 1038–1039.
8 B. Moreschini, "La «maniera» grafica di Daniele da Volterra," in *Dopo il Rosso: Artisti a Volterra e Pomarance*, exh. cat. (Florence and Venice, 1987), pp. 83–86; Lincoln, *The Italian Renaissance Printmaker*, pp. 124–127; and esp. A. Bisceglia in Romani 2003, pp. 144–146, no. 42.
9 Tosini 1997, pp. 71–73.
10 Procacci, "Una 'Vita' inedita del Muziano." There has been a tendency to date the Vatican painting to the last years of Muziano's career because it is absent from the biography, but the print would seem to give a *terminus ante quem*. There is, moreover, little reason to think that Muziano, in the busy last years of his career, would have painted a panel following a design by the long-dead Daniele.
11 On Mazzoni see P. Dreyer, "Giulio Mazzoni as a Draughtsman," *Master Drawings* 6 (1968), pp. 21–24; C. Strinati, "Giulio Mazzoni da Piacenza nella Roma di Metà Cinquecento," *Bollettino d'Arte* 64 (1979), pp. 27–36; and esp. T. Pugliatti, *Giulio Mazzoni e la decorazione a Roma nella cerchia di Daniele da Volterra* (Rome, 1984).
12 R. Lanciani, *Storia degli scavi di Roma*, vol. 4, *Pius V–Clement VIII* (Rome, 1913), p. 14, for example, records Mazzoni at work in 1565 in the "capella nuper constructa in Santiis habitionis custodiae Helvetiorum."
13 Pugliatti, *Giulio Mazzoni*, pp. 199–202.
14 The Vatican *Saint Jerome* might be contrasted, for example, with Muziano's *Saint Jerome* in the Pinacoteca Nazionale, Bologna.
15 A. Bisceglia in Romani 2003, pp. 144–146, notes the similarity of Mazzoni's work to the Vatican painting, but does not go so far as to suggest that the latter is by Mazzoni. Bisceglia also mentions that Vasari included a *Penitent Saint Jerome* "grande quanto il naturale" in his life of Daniele, and that paintings of Saint Jerome attributed to Daniele appeared in the 1564 inventory of Rodolfo Pio da Carpi and in the 1638 inventory of Vincenzo Giustiniani. There is also a copy, signed Lavinia Fontana and dated 1580, in a private collection, published in C. Murphy, *Lavinia Fontana: A Painter and Her Patrons in Sixteenth-Century Bologna* (New Haven and London, 2003), p. 20. The Giustiniani version remained in the collection until at least 1673 and cannot be the Santa Marta painting.

99
FOLLOWER OF GIROLAMO MUZIANO
1532–1592
Landscape with Saint Onuphrius
After 1574
Oil on copper
39.7 × 28.6 cm
National Gallery of Canada, Ottawa (15679)

Provenance: Joan Booth, Cambridge, UK; donated to Westminster Memorial Trust, London, by 1967; their sale (Sotheby's, London, 22 Feb. 1967, lot #173); purchased by G. Nehmad, Milan; sold to Yvonne Tan Bunzl, London, by 1968; 1968/08/22, purchased by the National Gallery of Canada from Yvonne Tan Bunzl.

References: Marciari 2000, p. 488.

Notes

1 Baglione 1995, vol. 1, p. 49.
2 For further discussion of Muziano's landscapes see Marciari 2000, esp. chapters 3 and 5.
3 For the best summary of the project see M. Bury, *The Print in Italy 1550–1620* (London, 2001), pp. 94–96. Drawings survive for four of the prints: studies for *Saint Onuphrius* (fig. 2) and *Saint Mary Magdalene* are in the Frits Lugt Collection at the Institut Néerlandais, Paris (4482A and 4482B); the study for *Saint Eustache* is in the École des Beaux-Arts, Paris (M2355); *Saint Jerome Translating the Bible* is in the Kunsthalle, Bremen (37/118). The additional sheets by Muziano that seem to be part of the set, although they were never engraved, include a *Saint Benedict* (Rijksmuseum, Amsterdam, 1954:144) and a *Saint Roch* (Smith College Museum of Art, Northampton, Mass., 1999:1). A *Penitent Saint Jerome* (Musée des Beaux-Arts, Rennes, 794.1.2981) might also be by Muziano and for the set, but it appears to have been reworked by a later hand and the attribution is difficult to confirm. O. Rossi (*Elogi storici di Bresciani illustri* [Brescia, 1620], p. 505) suggests that some of the drawings for Cort's engravings were executed by Pietro Maria Bagnadore rather than by Muziano himself, but the surviving sheets are unquestionably Muziano's own; see Marciari 2000, pp. 309–311, for further details.
4 Bury, *The Print in Italy*, pp. 94–96.
5 Some of Cort's prints were later engraved, in a smaller format, by Jan Sadeler; these copies again reverse the compositions, so that they return to the direction of the original drawings. Sadeler's *Saint Onuphrius* print, however, lacks many details found in the drawing – the books to the saint's left, for example – and cannot be considered a source for the painting.

100
RAFFAELLINO MOTTA, CALLED RAFFAELLINO DA REGGIO
1550?–1578
Tobias and the Angel
After 1575
Oil on panel
107 × 69 cm
Galleria Borghese, Rome (298)

References: Faldi 1951; Winkelmann in Nobili and Ciroldi 1988, pp. 65–66; Sricchia Santoro in Dacos 1995, p. 159, no. 231; Bernardini 2002, p. 91; Bigi Iotti and Zavatta 2008.

Notes

1 Fantini 1616 in Bigi Iotti and Zavatta 2008, p. 88.
2 Faldi 1951, pp. 328, 333, no. 29.
3 J. Manilli, *Villa Borghese fuori Porta Pinciana* (Rome, 1650), p. 83.
4 Della Pergola 1955, pp. 63–64.
5 L. Gambara, M. Pellegri, and M. De Grazia, *Palazzi e Casate di Parma* (Parma, 1971), pp. 358–373.
6 Fantini, op cit., p. 88.
7 The sheet of high technical quality and intense pictorial impact, has a considerable "lacuna" in the centre, which Raffaellino seems to have left consciously in the lower part of the two figures. The drawing in Reggio Emilia (for which we have only seen in photographs) does not have this. On the Uffizi drawing, see Venturi 1893, p. 153, no. 298; Voss 1920, p. 557; F. Bologna and R. Causa, *Fontainebleau e la Maniera Italiana*, exh. cat. Napoli (Florence, 1952), p. 44, no. 78; Gere 1966a, p. 52, no. 82. For the modern bibliography on the drawing, see M. Di Giampaolo, *Disegni emiliani del Rinascimento* (Modena and Milano 1989), p. 266, no. 131.
8 The drawing in Reggio Emilia (pen and brown ink, brown wash, 26.5 × 38 cm), was exhibited in a gallery in Milan in 1977; see J. Winkelmann, *Disegni dal XV al XVIII secolo. Gabinetto delle Stampe* (Milan 1977), p. 5; and Winkelmann in in Nobili and Ciroldi, pp. 65–66. Glued to the back is a print of Raffaellino's *Tobias and the Angel* by Matthias Greuter.
9 On the engravings of Raffaellino's *Tobias and the Angel*, see S. Beretta, "Raffaellino da Reggio e i suoi incisori," in *Rassegna di Studi e Notizie*, XII (Milan 1984–1985), pp. 22–28.
10 According to Winkelmann, the Carracci engraving should not be considered original but a copy with variants of the print by Greuter, which is considered original as it is derived directly from the drawing by Raffaellino: see J. Winkelmann, *Una decorazione cinquecentesca a Reggio Emilia: le "Fatiche di Ercole" di Palazzo Vicedomini*, in J. Bentini (a cura di), *Lelio Orsi e la cultura del*

suo tempo, atti del convegno internazionale di studi, Reggio Emilia – Novellara, 28–29 gennaio 1988, Bologna 1990, p. 66.
11 Louvre, Département des Arts Graphiques, inv. 11210.
12 This sheet is inv. 794.1.2523, for which see Gere and Pouncey 1983, p. 146; see also *Les Dessins italiens du Musèe de Rennes*, Rennes 1990, pp. 120–121, no. 54.
13 J.-P. Huys, "Raffaellino da Reggio (1550–1578). La personnalité d'un jeune artiste maniériste," *Annales d'histoire de l'art et d'archéologie* 21 (1999), pp. 54–55.
14 Sricchia Santoro in Dacos 1995, p. 159, no. 231.
15 See L. Collobi, "Raffaellino Motta detto Raffaellino da Reggio," in *Rivista del Regio Istituto d'Archeologia e Storia dell'Arte* VI, file III (Rome, 1938), pp. 272–273. The author also offers a very low opinion of the painting, which he considers "student-like."
16 D. de Grazia, ed., *Correggio e il suo lascito. Disegni del cinquecento emiliano,* exh. cat. (Parma 1984), p. 362.
17 Bernardini 2002, p. 91.
18 B.L. Wollesen Wisch, *The Archiconfraternite del Gonfalone and its Oratory in Rome: Art and Counter Reformation Spiritual Values* (Berkeley 1985).
19 Gabinetto Disegni e Stampe degli Uffizi, inv. 477 S; the drawing, in V. Romani, *Tibaldi "d'intorno" a Perino* (Padova, 1990), fig. 24, was first attributed to Tibaldi by Gere 1960 (pp. 9–19), who also pointed out the existence of an engraving executed in 1575 by Cherubino Alberti that derives from Tibaldi's sheet.
20 S.J. Freedberg, *La pittura in Italia dal 1550 al 1600* (Bologna 1988), p. 789. [trans.]

101
ATTRIBUTED TO CESARE NEBBIA
c. 1536–1614
The Emperor Charlemagne
c. 1572–1582
Pen and brown ink and brown wash, with white heightening, over black chalk
30.6 × 16 cm
National Gallery of Canada, Ottawa (6861)

Provenance: purchased from P. & D. Colnaghi & Co., through Paul Oppé.

References: Mack 1972, pp. 319–320; Marciari 2000, pp. 204–206.

Notes
1 For the *Solomon* drawing see Eitel-Porter 1997b, p. 455; for the Orvieto tribune drawings, and on Nebbia's drawings more generally, see R. Eitel-Porter, *Disegni per Orvieto dell'"... Illustre concittadino Cesare Nebbia"* (Orvieto, 2004).
2 Borghini 1584, pp. 575–576.
3 For the sale of the picture see A. Bertolotti, *Artisti Lombardi a Roma nel secolo XV, XVI, XVII* (Bologna, 1881), vol. 1, p. 121. The composition is recorded in prints by Jacques Callot and Giovanni Maggi and in a painted copy at the parochial church of Anguillara Sabazia. The sale of the completed high altarpiece must have been provoked by some exceptional circumstances. According to Baglione, "perche non restò d'accordo, altrove fu collocato" (1995, vol. 1, p. 50), a statement that might be variously interpreted. It is my suspicion that payment for the altarpiece and for the still-incomplete chapel decorations were somehow tied together, a question that I hope to resolve in a forthcoming article. See also Marciari 2000, pp. 201–210. It should be noted that the *Assumption of the Virgin* sold at Sotheby's, London, 8 July 2004, lot 155, as a *bozzetto* or *ricordo* of the lost San Luigi altarpiece has, in fact, no relationship whatsoever to Muziano's painting.

4 See C.E. Gilbert, *Caravaggio and His Two Cardinals* (University Park, PA., 1995), chapter 3, for arguments in favour of Celio's particular accuracy.
5 J. Marciari, "Girolamo Muziano and the Dialogue of Drawings in Cinquecento Rome," *Master Drawings* 40 (2002), pp. 113–134.

102
LIVIO AGRESTI
c. 1530/31–1579
Christ Healing the Paralytic
c. 1573–1575
Pen and ink, wash, with white heightening, traces of black chalk, squared with black chalk on prepared blue washed paper
42.9 × 29.2 cm
Gabinetto Disegni e Stampe degli Uffizi, Florence (1885F)

Provenance: first mention Pelli Bencivenni [before 1793], vol. II, Vol. XXII dei Piccoli, no. 31.

References: Pelli Bencivenni 1793, vol. II, Vol. XXII dei Piccoli, no. 31; Ferri 1890, p. 273; da Como 1930, p. 92; Gere 1971, plate 29; Spazzoli 1972, p. 80; Bross 1994, p. 341–342, fig. 218, Petrioli Tofani 2005 , p. 400.

Notes
1 The identification of the sheet as an autograph of Livio Agresti and the discovery of its function are owed to A.E. Popham (Gere 1971, table 29); the drawing had been previously considered as the work of Girolamo Muziano (Pelli [ante 1793] vol. II, Vol. XXII dei Piccoli, no. 31; Ferri 1890, p. 273; da Como 1930, p. 92). As for the dating of the decoration in the chapel, reference is made to S. Alloisi and L. Cardilli, *Santo Spirito in Saxia* (Le chiese di Roma illustrate, nuova serie, 34) (Rome, 2002), p. 97; Bross, 1994, p. 25.
2 C. Strinati, "La tavola Pelucchi," in *Prospettiva* 9 (1977), pp. 70–71.
3 While until the 1940s it was customary to date the outset of the artistic career of Livio Agresti to the sixth decade of the 16th century, in 1951 some documents were published regarding a certain "magister Livius quondam Silvestri ab agresta pictor de Forolivio," dating back to 1539–1541 and referring to the payment of two panels painted for the church of Santa Maria dei Servi in Forlì. Following this revelation, critics pre-dated the artist's chronology and significantly extended his *corpus*, going so far as to assume that he was born between 1505 and 1510. More recently, M. Daly Davis maintained that the said historical reconstruction of the life of Agresti and, consequently, the critical interpretation of his opus, had been compromised by a misunderstanding concerning a namesake. The scholar, in fact, publicized some new documents that refer to the Livio Agresti who made this drawing: not only do these place his date of birth between 1530 and 1531, they also lead to the assumption that the aforementioned payments, discovered in 1951, actually relate to another painter by the name of Livio (known as "Il Riccio"), also from Forlì. On this subject see M. Daly Davis, "Precisazioni sulla vita di Livio Agresti da Forlì, 'vittima di equivoci,'" in *Antichità viva*, 23 (1994), p. 35, note 5.
4 Vasari 1966–1987, vol. 6, pp. 150–151.
5 L.S. Bross, "New Documents for Livio Agresti's Saint Stephen Chapel in the Church of S. Spirito in Sassia, Rome," *The Burlington Magazine* 135 (May 1993), pp. 338–345.

103
RAFFAELLINO MOTTA, CALLED RAFFAELLINO DA REGGIO
1550?–1578
Design for the Decoration of a Chapel
mid-1570s
Pen and brown ink and wash over black chalk, laid down
26.6 × 17.8 cm
Annotations: ~~Zuccaro~~
National Gallery of Scotland, Edinburgh (D1475)

Provenance: David Laing; his bequest to the Royal Scottish Academy, 1879 (L. 2188); transferred to the National Gallery, 1910.

References: Andrews 1968, vol. 1, p. 102; Andrews 1976, no. 64; Alasko 1983, no. 38; Stock and Scrase 1985, no. 54; Edinburgh 1999, no. 9.

104
JACOPO ZUCCHI
c. 1541–c. 1589/90
Design for the Decoration of a Chapel
mid-1570s
Pen and brown ink and brown wash over black chalk
36 × 27.7 cm
Inscriptions: see note 5 below
Annotations: *Boscolie f.*
Christ Church Picture Gallery, Oxford (0983)
By permission of the Governing Body of Christ Church, Oxford

Provenance: General John Guise; by whom bequeathed to Christ Church, 1765.

References: Pillsbury 1974a, pp. 21–22, 32, note 82; Pillsbury 1974b, pp. 442–443; Byam Shaw 1976, vol. 1, p. 86; Alasko 1983, under no. 38; Stock and Scrase 1985, no. 62; Edinburgh 1999, under no. 9.

Notes
1 The link between the two drawings was first noted by Andrews (1976) and explored further by Alasko (1983) and especially by the present writer (in Edinburgh 1999, from which this current entry is developed).
2 See Stock and Scrase 1985, nos. 54 and 62.
3 Pillsbury 1974a, p. 21.
4 It has been suggested (M.G. Aurigemma, "Un corpus perduto? Sui disegni di Jacopo Zucchi," *Studiolo* 5 [2007], pp. 134, 143, note 164) that the Christ Church drawing might be identical with one described as "a drawing of a chapel arch with two prophets, with touches of wash" ("un disegnio di unarco di una cappella con due profeti tochi di aquarello") in a recently discovered list of hundreds of drawings and prints from Zucchi's estate. This is an attractive idea, although since the descriptions in this inventory are for the most part quite detailed, one might have expected the subject of the altarpiece to have been mentioned in addition to the prophets. Aurigemma tentatively connects the Christ Church design with a project for a chapel in the Roman church of San Giovanni dei Fiorentini, documented but unrealized due to Zucchi's death.
5 The extensive Latin inscriptions by the artist are transcribed and their scriptural sources identified in Pillsbury 1974a, p. 32, n. 82.
6 Andrews (1968, vol. 1, p. 102) was the first to make this connection and to set out some of the arguments for and against. Stock and Scrase (1985, no. 54) argued against the connection. For the chapel and its history see A. Negro, *Guide rionali di Roma: Rione II – Trevi. Parte seconda, fascicolo II* (Rome, 1985), pp. 38–40.
7 What is probably Raffaellino's initial design for this fresco, which includes musician angels, was sold at Sotheby's, New York, 11 January 1990 (lot 45).

8 Raffaellino's preparatory drawing for the *Dream of Saint Joseph*, formerly in the Mond Collection, was sold at Sotheby's, London, 4 July 1988 (lot 17); see De Grazia 1984, no. 114.
9 This latter fresco in fact appears to be by Gianfrancesco Romanelli or another artist from the circle of Pietro da Cortona, and presumably replaced one by Raffaellino.
10 Gere and Pouncey (1983, p. 145) noted that the *Annunciation* was destroyed during a restoration of the chapel in 1641.
11 Concerning Venusti's altarpiece see S. Capelli, "Marcello Venusti: Un valtellinese pittore a Roma," *Studi di storia dell'arte* 12 (2001), p. 30 and fig. 23, where it is dated to the mid-1570s.
12 Negro, *Guide rionali di Roma*, p. 38.
13 For this and the following information about Francesca Baglioni Orsini see M.R. Dunn, "Spiritual Philanthropists: Women as Convent Patrons in Seicento Rome," in *Women and Art in Early Modern Europe: Patrons, Collectors and Connoisseurs*, ed. C. Lawrence (University Park, PA., 1997), pp. 157–163. I am indebted to John Marciari for this reference.
14 San Silvestro al Quirinale was given by Paul IV in 1555 to the Theatines, who rebuilt it, and it was reconsecrated in 1584; see A. Blunt, *Guide to Baroque Rome* (London, 1982), p. 145.
15 Dunn, "Spiritual Philanthropists," pp. 159–161.
16 C. Strinati ("Note sur Jacopo et Francesco Zucchi," in *La Villa Médicis: Volume II, Études*, ed. A. Chastel and P. Morel [Rome, 1991], p. 556) and A. Vannugli ("Per Jacopo Zucchi: Un 'Annunciazione' a Bagnoregio ed altre opere," *Prospettiva* 75–76 [1994], p. 173, note 73) argued that it was a collaborative venture dating from early in the Roman careers of the two artists, around 1570–1572. Faldi 1951(p. 328) suggested c. 1575, while Marciari 2006 (p. 191, note 27) proposed 1575–1577. A. Coliva ("Raffaellismo o michelangelismo: Il dibattito di metà secolo," in *Pittura in Italia: Il Cinquecento*, ed. G. Briganti [Milan, 1988], vol. 2, pp. 454–456, 816), Morel in Hochmann 1999 (p. 123), and Bigi Iotti and Zavatta 2008, pp. 75–79, all prefer the theory that the project was begun by Raffaellino around 1578 but interrupted by his death that year and only then transferred jointly to Zucchi and Venusti.
17 This is the view shared by Gere and Pouncey (1983, vol. 1, p. 145), Dunn ("Spiritual Philanthropists," p. 161) and J.-P. Huys ("Raffaellino da Reggio (1550–1578): La personnalité d'un jeune artiste maniériste," *Annales d'histoire de l'art et d'archéologie* 21 [1999], p. 55).
18 See F. Sricchia Santoro, "Jacopo Zucchi (e Raffaellino da Reggio?) a Palazzo Firenze," in *Kunst des Cinquecento in der Toskana*, ed. M. Cämmerer (Florence, 1992), pp. 375–381.
19 Ibid., figures 2 and 5.
20 This idea was put forward by John Marciari in an email to the present writer, 12 August 2008.

105

DURANTE ALBERTI
1538–1613
Scene from Roman History (recto)
Study of Saint Matthew and the Angel, a Standing Bishop and other Studies (verso)
c. 1575
Pen and grey and brown ink, brown wash, over black chalk (recto); pen and brown ink, red wash, and black chalk (verso)
23.2 × 28.2 cm
Annotations: *Durante del Borgo* (recto); *Durante del Borgo* and *Consolo...* [illegible words] (verso)
National Gallery of Canada, Ottawa (42024)

Provenance: Sold Sotheby's, New York, 25 January 2006, lot 56; purchased from La Tâche Fine Arts, Zurich in 2007.

106

RAFFAELLINO MOTTA DA REGGIO
1550?–1578
The Apparition of the Angel to Saint Joseph
c. 1575
Pen and brown ink and wash over red chalk
38.1 × 28.2 cm
Inscriptions: *Zuchero.*
The Pierpont Morgan Library, New York (2007.80)
Purchased in honour of Charles E. Pierce, Jr.'s tenure as director by the Visiting Committee to the Department of Drawings and Prints through the generosity of Ildiko Butler, Diane A. Nixon, Andrea Woodner, Hamilton Robinson, Jr., Joan Taub Ades, Clement C. Moore II, Jayne Wrightsman, David M. Tobey, Eugene V. Thaw, George L.K. Frelinghuysen, Seymour and Helen Mae Askin, Catherine G. Curran, Melvin R. Seiden, Hubert and Mireille Goldschmidt, and Wheelock Whitney III.

Provenance: Sir Robert Ludwig Mond, London (L. Suppl. 2813a); possibly by descent to W.D. Austin; sale, Sotheby's, London, 4 July 1988, lot 17; Yvonne Tan Bunzl (dealer); London; private collection; Yvonne Tan Bunzl (dealer), London; from whom acquired.

References: Borenius and Wittkower 1937, no. 275, pl. XLIX (as Federico Zuccaro); Collobi 1939, pp. 13–14, fig. 2 (as Raffaellino); Gere and Pouncey 1983, p. 145; De Grazia 1984, no. 114, p. 341, repr. (study for the fresco); London 1996, no. 6, repr.; Marciari 2006, p. 190, and note 12 (final preparatory study).

Notes

1 Fresco described by Baglione 1642, p. 26, "e l'angelo, che apparisce in sogno a S. Gioseppe."
2 Information on the Orsini/Ghisleri patronym taken from T.M. di Blasio, *San Silvestro al Quirinale*, n.d. (2006) [brochure on the church provided in the church itself, based on di Blasio's archival research] n. p. and oral communication between Eveline Baseggio, Research Assistant, Morgan Library & Museum and Dr. di Blasio in 2008. Dr. di Blasio's brochure was based on her own archival research which she kindly shared with us.
3 Baglione 1642, p. 26; Faldi, p. 332, note 5; Gere and Pouncey 1983, p. 145.
4 Gere and Pouncey 1983, p. 145; transcription in J.-P. Huys, "Raffaellino da Reggio (1550–1578). La personnalité d'un jeune artiste maniériste," *Annales d'histoire de l'art et d'archéologie* 21 (1999), p. 55, note 46.
5 Recognized as such in De Grazia 1984, pp. 341 and 342, note 5; A. Weston-Lewis in Edinburgh 1999, p. 173, note 4; and Marciari 2006, p. 190.

107

GIROLAMO MUZIANO
1532–1592
Pentecost
c. 1576
Pen and brown ink and black chalk
28 × 54.5 cm
Musée du Louvre, Paris (5104)

References: Marciari 2000, p. 513.

Notes

1 For records of payments from 24 November 1576 to 11 January 1578 see Mack 1972, p. 191.
2 Marciari 2006, pp. 187–191.
3 This important but damaged altarpiece is not well known and has been the subject of conflicting and incomplete references, so a brief account of its history is useful here. It was probably not originally made for Santa Marta, although it was there until 1673, when, following the renovation of the church, it no longer fit on the high altar and was sold to Queen Christina of Sweden; see M.R. Dunn, "Nuns as Art Patrons: The Decoration of S. Marta al Collegio Romano," *Art Bulletin* 70 (1988), p. 459. It remained in Queen Christina's collection and was part of the bequest that passed to Cardinal Azzolino before it was purchased by Prince Odescalchi. In 1720 the picture was bought by the Duke of Orleans, whose collection was brought to London in 1790 and sold at Bryan's Gallery (14 February 1800, lot 28). It was acquired by the Earl of Suffolk and Berkshire, whose heirs gave the picture to Malmesbury Abbey towards the end of nineteenth century. Sold by Malmesbury (Sotheby's, London, 10 July 1974), the large canvas was acquired by Nardo Peretti, who in 1975 sold it to the Birmingham City Art Gallery. Muziano's biography (U. Procacci, "Una 'Vita' inedita del Muziano," *Arte Veneta* 8 [1954], pp. 242–264) mentions only one *Lazarus* among the works from the 1570s, a painting "donata come preziosa cosa all'Illustrissimo Cardinale Maffeo." The reference is probably to this painting, but it does not explain the circumstances of its creation.
4 For several examples see Marciari 2002, pp. 113–134.
5 For a good example see Joannides 1996, no. 49.
6 Borghini 1584, p. 576; Baglione 1995, vol. 1, p. 51.
7 C. Valone, "The Pentecost: Image and Experience in Late Sixteenth-Century Rome," *Sixteenth Century Journal* 24 (1993), p. 803.
8 Ibid., pp. 806–812.
9 Marciari 2002, pp. 125–130. Another drawing of the subject, Uffizi 11874F, was published in da Como 1930, p. 117, as a study by Muziano for the Vatican canvas, but the drawing is in fact related to Stefano Molinari's eighteenth-century reproductive print after Muziano's painting.
10 S. Prosperi Valenti Rodinò, ed., *Disegni Romani dal XVI al XVIII secolo*, exh. cat. (Rome, 1995), no. 8.

108

CESARE NEBBIA
c. 1536–1614
Noli me tangere
1579
Pen and brown ink, brown wash, with white heightening, over red chalk
30 × 19.2 cm
Private collection, Toronto

Provenance: Sir John Charles Robinson, Edinburgh and London (L. 1433); unknown collector, who assembled an album of 51 drawings in the years after 1859 (according to 1963 Sotheby's sale catalogue); sale, Sotheby's, London, 12 March 1963, lot 43 (as Cesare Nebbia); Felton L. Gibbons, Princeton; Galerie François Baroni, Paris; private collection, Toronto.

References: Gere and Pouncey 1983, vol. 1, p. 132 (as study for painting in Santa Maria degli Angeli); Eitel-Porter 1997a, ch. V.4, repr.; Marciari 2002, p. 125, fig. 20.

Notes

1 J. von Henneberg, *L'Oratorio dell'Arciconfraternità del Santissimo Crocifisso di San Marcello* (Rome, 1974), p. 19. Alverio's name appears for instance in a list dated 12 August 1578 (ASV, Fondo della Arciconfraternità del Santissimo Crocifisso di San Marcello, P-I-58, [Congregazioni e Decreti dal 1576 a tutto il 1587], fol. 37). For Nebbia's contribution to the Oratory decorations see R. Eitel-Porter, "The Oratorio of SS. Crocifisso in Rome revisited," *The Burlington Magazine*, 142 (October 2000), pp. 613–623.
2 See T. Amayden, *La storia delle famiglie Romane, con note ed aggiunte del Comm. Carlo Augusto Bertini*, 2 vols. (Rome, 1910–1914), 1, pp. 5–7, who also makes mention of the burial chapel in Santa Maria degli Angeli.
3 Baglione 1642, p. 77.
4 M.V. Brugnoli in *Mostra Antologica dell'Attività delle Soprintendenze. IX Settimana dei Musei*, exh. cat., *Sala di Marte* (Rome, 1966), p. 146ff.
5 See the dedicatory inscription on the right wall of the chapel, in V. Forcella, *Iscrizioni delle chiese e d'àltri edificii di Roma dal secolo XI fino ai giorni nostri*, 14 vols. (Rome, 1869–1884), vol. 9, p. 156, no. 305: *Consalvus Alberus io f sacellum hoc situ et ruinis deforme a Cartusianis huius monasterii monachis / optatum acceptumq in hanc speciem exornavit / divae Mariae Magdalenae recte poenitentum exemplari / eius solennitatis die in lucem editus dedicavit / vasa vestes perpetuos ad sacra sumptus attribuit / monumentumq subterraneum medio sacello extruxit / sibi et suius omnibus gentilibus posterisq. eorum anno Christianae salutis MCLXXIX.* [author's emphasis].
6 The landscape background, with a prominent, overgrown rock at left and a smallish vista opening up at right, is most similar to the Dresden painting *Rest on the Flight into Egypt*, long given to Muziano, though more recently doubted. Gemäldegalerie Dresden, inv. 91, oil on canvas, 125 × 105 cm. Once thought to be by Francesco Vanni, the painting was attributed to Girolamo Muziano by Voss 1920 (vol. 2, pp. 565 and 567, fig. 229). Marciari 2000, however, does not accept the attribution (p. 486), and P. Tosini in *Girolamo Muziano 1532–1592, dalla Maniera alla Natura* (Rome, 2009) recently suggested it was possibly by Lavinia Fontana working under Muziano's influence (pp. 301, 304, 500, fig. 277, no. E 170).
7 The contract transcribed in Eitel-Porter 1997a, Dokumentenanhang. I am grateful to Lothar Sickel, Rome, who recently reexamined the contract, and noted that it specified "Et sia obligato detto ms. Cesare assistere nel mettere li detti quadri, et far far' la colla et altre cose necessarie della qualità che si suol fare il Mutiano."
8 Marciari 2002, p. 134, note 39.
9 E. Mâle, *L'art religieux de la fin du XVe siècle, du XVIe siècle et du XVIIIe siècle. Étude sur l'iconographie après le Concile de Trente* (Paris, 1952), pp. 294–295.
10 Gabinetto Disegni e Stampe degli Uffizi, inv. 102866 (placed as Bachiacca); M. Chiarini, G. Dillon and A. Petrioli Tofani, *Philip Pouncey per gli Uffizi. Disegni italiani di tre secoli*, exh. cat. (Florence, 1994), pp. 74–75, no. 77 (as Muziano); Eitel-Porter 1997a, chapter V.4 (as Nebbia); Marciari 2002, p. 135, fig. 21 (as Muziano).

109

FEDERICO ZUCCARO
c. 1542/43–1609
Design for Quarant'Ore Decoration
c. 1580
Pen and brown ink with brown wash with white heightening over black chalk
38.9 × 28.5 cm
Inscriptions: *Federigo Zuccaro*
The Metropolitan Museum of Art, New York (1993.120)

Provenance: Sir Thomas Lawrence (L. 2445); Samuel Woodburn; Christie's, London, 4 June 1860, part of lot 1074; Sir Thomas Phillipps; T. Fitzroy Fenwick; A.S.W. Rosenbach; Philip H. and A.S.W. Rosenbach Foundation; British Rail Pension Fund; Sotheby's, New York, 11 January 1990, lot 39; acquired for the Metropolitan Museum of Art from W.M. Brady and Co. in 1993.

References: Gere 1970, p. 131, no. 19; Griswold in Griswold and Wolk-Simon 1994, pp. 96–97, no. 86; Acidini Luchinat 1998–1999, II, p. 123; Mundy in Winner and Heikamp 1999, pp. 34–36.

Notes

1 Gere 1970, pp. 123–140.
2 J. Imorde, *Präsenz und Repräsentanz: oder: die Kunst, den Leib Christi auszustellen; (das vierzigstündige Gebet von den Anfängen bis in das Pontifikat Innocenz X.)* [Emsdetten, 1997].

110

FEDERICO ZUCCARO
c. 1542/43–1609
Porta Virtutis (Gate of Virtue) or *Minerva Triumphant Over Ignorance and Calumny*
1581
Pen and brown ink, brown wash, with some corrections in white gouache; squared for transfer in red chalk.
37.8 × 27.6 cm
Inscriptions: *fama, porta virtus; fama; gloria; disegnio; colorito; inventione; inteligentia; decoro; faticha; diligenzia; studio; inteligenzia; sic semper; spirito; adulatione; ignioranzia crasa; persuasione; presumptione; inscitia; ministro de la invidia; parto di maldicenzia; detratio; prospetiva; architectura; invidia comites; ingniorantia crassa; rifugio di maligno; serva delli dapochi.*
Christ Church Picture Gallery, Oxford (0213)
By permission of the Governing Body of Christ Church, Oxford

Provenance: General John Guise, by whom bequeathed in 1765.

References: Heikamp 1958, pp. 46, 49, fig. 1; Bean and Stampfle 1965, under no. 41; Byam Shaw 1976, vo. 1, p. 155, no. 544, repr.; Cavazzini 1989, pp. 169–170, fig. 1; Acidini Luchinat 1998–1999, vol. 2, pp. 129, 149 note 53, fig. 17.

Notes

1 Inv. 1319; D. Heikamp, "Vicende de Federico Zuccari," Rivista d'Arte 32 (1957) [pp. 175–232], p. 192, fig. 6.
2 For a recent discussion of the painting commissioned by Ghiselli and the ensuing porta virtutis scandal see Acidini Luchinat 1998–1999, vol. 2, pp. 127–132.
3 See Acidini Luchinat 1998–1999, vol. 2, p. 130, fig. 19 for a painted copy of the lost cartoon.
4 Acc. no. 1983.67.

7   Berlin, Kunstbibliothek, inv. HdZ 6685; Jacob 1975, p. 40, no. 109; Parma Armani in Parma Armani et al., *Libri di immagini, disegni e incisioni di Giovanni Guerra (Modena 1544– Roma 1618)*, exh. cat. (Modena, 1978); pp. 23 and 34, notes 20–21; Morello in Madonna 1993, p. 366, no. 27 and fig. 44.

8   Nebbia's drawings for this project include: a study for the *Pasce oves meas* identified by B. Haas in the Louvre, inv. 5092; a design in the Prado, inv. D-1744 (FD 2019), for the *Donation of Constantine*, attributed to Nebbia by K. Oberhuber and connected with the fresco by A. Zuccari; a study in Lisbon, inv. 2575, for the *Coronation of the Virgin;* the *Saint Andrew* in the collection of R. Scorza, London; and Siena, Biblioteca Comunale degli Intronati, inv. S.III.8, 7r(b), *A Prophet Seated on Clouds.* Uffizi, inv. 1713S, *Church Father*, is probably a copy after the related spandrel fresco.

123
CESARE NEBBIA
c. 1536–1614
Daniel Slays the Serpent of Babylon (Daniel 14:22–26)
c. 1588
Pen and brown ink, grey-brown wash
26.7 × 19.1 cm
Szépmüvészeti Múzeum, Budapest (1917)

Provenance: Prince Nikolaus Esterházy (L. 1965).

References: Eitel-Porter 1997a, ch 8, repr.; Zentai 1998, pp. 152–153, no. 60, repr.; Zuccari 2005, p. 9, fig. 19.

Notes
1   Zentai 1998, p. 152.
2   Sotheby's, London, 3 July 1989, lot 62 (as Nebbia); pen and brown ink, brown wash, over black chalk, with traces of white heightening, squared in red chalk. Zuccari 1992, p. 137, fig. 109; Morello in Madonna 1993, p. 364, no. 24, repr.; Zentai 1998, p. 153, fig. 27.
3   Alessandro Zuccari, in discussion with the author, 1992.
4   The serpent in the drawing resembles, among other emblems, the dragon from the coat of arms of Sixtus V's predecessor, Gregory XIII Boncompagni.
5   B. Haas in Madonna 1993, pp. 56–58.
6   Zuccari 1992, pp. 136–137.
7   Zuccari 2005, p. 21, note 38.
8   For the Lateran Palace see P. Lauer, *Le Palais de Latran* (Paris, 1911). For its fresco decorations see C. Mandel in Madonna 1993, pp. 94–119 and C. Mandel, *Sixtus V and the Lateran Palace* (Rome, 1994). For a plan with the sequence of rooms, see Madonna 1993, pp. 107–111.
9   A document of 28 February 1588 records frescoes with the scenes from the story of Solomon, David and Samuel – all rooms situated in the north-west of the building (A. Bertolotti. *Artisti modenesi, parmensi e della Lunigiana in Roma nei secoli XV–XVII.* [Modena, 1882], p. 35). From an Avviso of 29 August 1589, one may deduce that the work was complete at that time: '*Si è dato fine al gran palazzo fatto nella piazza Lateranense da Sisto V*' cited according to L. Freiherr von Pastor. *Geschichte der Päpste seit dem Ausgang des Mittelalters. Mit Benutzung des päpstlichen Geheim-Archives und vieler anderer Archive, 1. bis 4. Auflage.* 16 vols. (Freiburg i. Br., [1899–1939]), vol.10 (1926), p. 609, no. 62. Furthermore, inscriptions at various locations refer to the fourth pontifical year, which ended on 23 April 1585.

124
CESARE NEBBIA
c. 1536–1614
Emperor Augustus in the Palatine Library
c. 1588
Pen and brown ink, brown wash over black chalk, with paper correction over pasted
26.4 × 20.4 cm
Inscriptions: *August Cæs Palatina Biblioth. magnifice / ornata viros literatos fovet; Ces. Nebbia*
Private collection, Chicago

Provenance: Padre Sebastiano Resta (?); John, Lord Somers (L. 2981); British Library, London, Resta-Somers inventory, Lansdowne Ms. 802, fol. 45 as Nebbia "Augustus Cesar in his Library. GG. 41," from 1710 until at least 1716; his sale, London, 1717 (?); Ingeborg Tremmel, Germany; sale, Ketterer Kunst, Munich, 5–6 May 2003, lot 363, repr. (as Nebbia); Artemis Ltd, London, 2003; with Nissman and Abromson Ltd., Brookline MA.; private collection.

References: Eitel-Porter 1997a, chapter 8; Turner 2009, forthcoming.

Notes
1   On the subject of the Vatican Library see J. Hess, "La Biblioteca Vaticana: Storia della costruzione," in J. Hess, *Kunstgeschichtliche Studien zu Renaissance und Barock,* 2 vols. (Rome, 1967), pp. 143–152, and J. Hess, "Some notes on paintings in the Vatican Library," in J. Hess, Ibid., pp. 163–179. Essential for the interpretation of the iconography is A. Böck, *Das Dekorationsprogramm des Lesesaals der Vatikanischen Bibliothek* (Munich, 1988), *passim*, and A. Böck, "La Biblioteca Vaticana," in Madonna 1993, pp. 77–83. For a plan of the series of rooms and a compilation of the subjects of the frescoes, see Ibid., pp. 84–90.
2   Noted in an avviso of 13 May 1587; L.F. Pastor, *Geschichte der Päpste seit dem Ausgang des Mittelalters. Mit Benutzung des päpstlichen Geheim-Archives und vieler anderer Archive,* editions 1–4, 16 vols. (Freiburg, 1899–1939), vol. 10 (1926), p. 604, note 27; Hess, "Notes," p. 164.
3   A. Rocca, *Biblioteca Apostolica Vaticana a Sisto V. Pont. Max. in splendidiorem, commodioremq. locum translata ...* (Rome, 1591).
4   ASV, Arch. Bibli. I, fol. 40–50, Constitutioni e leggi per la Vaticana Cardinali Bibliotecar. Custodi Scrittori; Böck, *Das Dekorationsprogramm*, pp. 21–22, 131.
5   Rocca 1591, p. 272: *Caesar enim Urbevetanus arte pollens pictoria ... Bibliothecarum, Conciliorumq. historias, litterarumq. Inventores, ceterasq. imagines ad historiam pertinentes delineavit*' and '*Ionnes vero Mutinensis ingenio praestans, & ex arte non ignobilis Emblemata omnia, necnon cetera Bibliothecae ornamenta ad pictoris arbitrium facta adinvenit, ac delineavit, & ab aliis item pictoribus ad unguem absoluenda studuit*; Böck, *Das Dekorationsprogramm*, p. 19, and Böck, "La Biblioteca Vaticana," p. 77.
6   Eitel-Porter 1997a, ch. 8. At least thirteen drawings directly connected to the Sistine Library have been identified. Six of these are certainly by Nebbia, a seventh probably so, and an eighth one seems to be a copy after a drawing by Nebbia. Two drawings clearly by the same hand for the *Second Lateran Council* are probably by Andrea Lilio, see Eitel-Porter 1998, pp. 17–22. Furthermore, in the Crocker Art Gallery, Sacramento, there is a drawing by Giovanni Baglione for the fresco *Tarquinius*

Superbus buys the three books of the Sibyl (inv. 319); L. Hopwood, "Tarquinius Superbus Buying the Three Books of the Sibyl," in *Classical Narratives in Master Drawings Selected from the Collections of the E.B. Crocker Art Gallery*, exh. cat., ed., S. Howard (Sacramento, 1972), no. 6, pp. 15–16; Smith O'Neil, "Cavaliere Giovanni Baglione: Il Modo Eccellente di Disegnare," *Master Drawings* 36 (1998), p. 376, note 23, and a drawing in Haarlem possibly by Baglione (see cat. 129, p. 392). A thirteenth study in the Louvre has been attributed to Giovanni Battista Pozzo by A. Zuccari.
7   A. Böck, "La Biblioteca Vaticana," p. 77.
8   Zuccari 1992, p. 87.

125
PASQUALE CATI
c. 1550–c. 1620
Death of the Virgin
c. 1588–1590
Pen and brown ink and brown wash over black chalk, squared for transfer in red chalk
28.4 × 19.7 cm
Annotations: *Mutiani;* ~~Luccarno~~ *Mutiani* (verso)
National Gallery of Canada, Ottawa (42194)

Provenance: European private collection; purchased from La Tâche Fine Arts, Zurich, 2007.

References: Romalli 2009, pp. 90–91, fig. 9.

Notes
1   Concerning the chapel see esp. H. Friedel, "Die Cappella Altemps in S. Maria in Trastevere," *Romisches Jahrbuch fur Kunstgeschichte* 17 (1978), pp. 89–123.
2   See Gere and Pouncey 1983, no. 58, p. 47.

126
GIOVANNI DE' VECCHI
1537–1615
Virgin and Child with Two Saints
c. 1589?
Pen and brown ink
29.8 × 22.5 cm
Gabinetto Disegni e Stampe degli Uffizi, Florence (7369F)

References: Roli 1965, p. 332, no. 9; Pinelli 1977, p. 58ff.; Robertson 1992, p. 200; Robertson 2008.

Notes
1   F. Zeri, *Pittura e Controriforma. Alle origini dell'arte 'senza tempo'*" (Turin, 1957), esp. pp. 55–61.
2   For Farnese, see Robertson 1992.
3   For the Abbey's history, see C. D'Onofrio and C. Pietrangeli, *Abbazie del Lazio* (Rome 1971), pp. 177–195; K. Schwager, "Santa Maria Scala Coeli in Tre Fontanebei Rom," in *Praestant Interna. Festschrift für Ulrich Hausmann* (Tübingen, 1982), pp. 394–417; Robertson 2008, pp. 95–111; X.F. Salomon, *The Religious Artistic and Architectural Patronage of Cardinal Pietro Aldobrandini (1571–1621)*, Ph.D. diss., University of London, Courtauld Institute of Art, 2005, p. 68ff.
4   Robertson 1992, p. 200.
5   Robertson 1992, pp. 116–121, 195–196.

127
GIUSEPPE CESARI, CALLED IL CAVALIERE D'ARPINO
1568–1640
Pope Sixtus V Kneeling in Prayer
1589
Black and red chalk on light tan paper, frame lining in pencil, top corners cut
38.6 × 23.5 cm
Inscription: *Aquino* (verso)
Teylers Museum, Haarlem

Provenance: Acquired in 1790 from Odescalchi collection in Rome (L. 2392).

References: Van Regteren Altena 1966, p. 110; van Tuyll van Serooskerken in Meijer and van Tuyll van Serooskerken 1983, pp. 174–175, no. 76; Morello in Madonna 1993, pp. 351–352, no. 4; van Tuyll van Serooskerken 2000, pp. 185–186, no. 120; Röttgen 2002, pp. 15–16, 512.

Notes
1   Röttgen 2002, pp. 237–239, no. 19.
2   G. Mancini, *Considerazioni sulla Pittura (1617–1621)*, ed. A Marucchi and L. Salernono, 2 vols. (Rome 1956–1957), pp. 110, 238.

128
CESARE NEBBIA
c. 1536–1614
Pope Pius V Crowns Cosimo I de' Medici Grand Duke of Tuscany
late 1580s
Pen and brown ink, brown wash, heightened with white gouache over black chalk
60.7 × 52.9 cm
Inscriptions: *iLo^{tt}.; Paolo Veronese*, and *Ventura Salimbeni*
Museum of Art, Rhode Island School of Design, Providence (49.390)
Gift of Mrs. Murray F. Danforth

Provenance: The Collector's Corner, New York; purchased 1949 by Mrs. Murray S. Danforth, Providence, and donated by her to RISD that same year.

References: Schwarz 1953, pp. 336–340, fig. 1 (as Passignano); Johnson 1983, pp. 21–25, no. 5 (as Nebbia); Morello in Madonna 1993, pp. 352–353; under no. 5b, fig. 9.

Notes
1   Inv. 34910, formerly as Cristofaro Roncalli; pen and brown ink and wash, over black chalk, 27.2 × 20.6 cm; unpublished.
2   Inv. 735; pen and brown ink, brown-grey wash, over black chalk, heightened with white gouache; 40 × 34.5 cm; Schwarz 1953, pp. 336–340 and Johnson 1983, pp. 21–25.
3   As noted by Schwarz 1953, pp. 337 and 339, who also observed that if reversed, the *Last Judgment* would, however, have appeared in the wrong direction.
4   Morello in Madonna 1993, p. 352, under no. 5b.
5   For Cosimo I's catafalque see the drawing by Jacopo Zucchi in the Morgan Library and Museum, New York, inv. 1965.5; for the Ligozzi painting, L. Conigliello, *Jacopo Ligozzi. Le vedute del Sacro Monte della Verna. I dipinti di Poppi e Bibbiena* (Poppi, 1992), p. 147, fig. 19.
6   L.F. Pastor, *Geschichte der Päpste seit dem Ausgang des Mittelalters. Mit Benutzung des päpstlichen Geheim-Archives und vieler anderer Archive*, editions 1–4, 16 vols. (Freiburg, 1899–1939), vol. 10 (1926), pp. 32–33.
7   Ibid., vol. 10, (1926), p. 35, n. 5.
8   Morello in Madonna 1993, p. 352 suggested the drawings could have been early designs for the tomb, which I think unlikely.

9   Pastor, *Geschichte der Päpste*, vol. 10 (1926), pp. 424–425. On the topic of their friendship see also G. Leti, *Vita di Sisto V. Pontefice Romano* (Amsterdam, 1698), vol. 1, pp. 365 and 427–428.
10   V. Massimo, *Notizie istoriche della Villa Massimo alle Terme Diocleziane con un'appendice di documenti* (Rome, 1836), p. 38 and S.F. Ostrow, *The Sistine Chapel at S. Maria Maggiore: Sixtus V and the Art of the Counter Reformation*, Ph.D. diss. Princeton University, 1987, p. 119, n. 48; S.F. Ostrow, *Art and Spirituality in Counter-Reformation Rome. The Sistine and Pauline Chapels in S. Maria Maggiore* (Cambridge University Press), 1996, p. 11.
11   Chappell et al. 1979, pp. 115–117.

129
GIOVANNI BAGLIONE
c. 1566–1643
Study for the Babylonian Library
c. 1588–1589
Black chalk on blue paper
36.7 × 29.2 cm
Teylers Museum, Haarlem (K III 11)

Provenance: Collection of Queen Christina of Sweden; Odescalchi dukes of Bracciano; purchased by Willem A. Lestevenon for the Teylers Museum, 1790.

References: van Tuyll van Seerooskerken in Meijer and van Tuyll van Seerooskerken 1983, p. 178; Zuccari 1992, pp. 81–83; Morello in Madonna 1993, p. 355; van Tuyll van Seerooskerken 2000, p. 190.

Notes
1   C. van Tuyll van Seerooskerken, "Giovanni Baglione, La Biblioteca babilonica," in Meijer and van Tuyll van Seerooskerken 1983, p. 178.
2   Zuccari 1992, pp. 75–100.
3   C. Guglielmi, "Intorno all'opera pittorica di Giovanni Baglione," in *Bollettino d'Arte* 39 (October-December 1954), pp. 311–313.
4   Baglione 1642, p. 401.
5   A. Zuccari 1992, p. 75 and note 1.
6   C. Bon, "Precisazioni sulla biografia di Giovanni Baglione," in *Paragone* 347 (January 1979), pp. 88–93.
7   C. Bon, "Una proposta per la cronologia delle opere giovanili di Giovanni Baglione," in *Paragone* 373 (March 1981), pp. 18–21; Zuccari 1992, pp. 81–83.
8   A. Zuccari, "La Biblioteca Vaticana e i pittori sistini," in Madonna 1993, p. 63.
9   Morello, "La biblioteca di Babilonia," in Madonna 1993, p. 355; S. Macioce, "Per una introduzione a Giovanni Baglione," in *Giovanni Baglione (1566–1644). Pittore e biografo di artisti*, ed. S. Macioce (Rome 2002), p. 16; van Tuyll van Seerooskerken 2000, p. 190.
10   C. Strinati, "Il Ritrovamento di Mosè di Giovanni Baglione," in *Giovanni Baglione (1566–1644)*, p. 14, note 1.
11   A. Zuccari, *Progretti grafica per gli affreschi della Biblioteca Vaticana*, Rome, forthcoming.
12   A. Zuccari, "I disegni per gli affreschi della Scala Santa: Nebbia, Guerra, Fenzoni, Bril e le strategie progettuali di un cantiere sistino," in *En blanc et noir. Studi in onore di Silvana Macchioni*, ed. F. Sorce (Rome 2007), pp. 38–39.
13   Eitel-Porter 1997b, pp. 452–462.

131
HENDRICK GOLTZIUS
1558–1617
Study after the Flora Farnese
1591
Red chalk
41.8 × 22 cm
Teylers Museum, Haarlem (29)

Provenance: Emperor Rudolph II, Prague; Queen Christina of Sweden, Stockholm-Antwerp-Rome; Prince Livio Odescalchi, Rome; in 1790 acquired from his heirs for the Teyler's Stichting (L. 2392).

130
LUDOVICO CARDI, CALLED IL CIGOLI
1559–1613
The Dove of the Holy Ghost Appearing to Pope Sixtus V, Seated at a Table, Assisted by Two Angels
c. 1590–1593
Pen and black and brown ink and watercolour, heightened with touches of lead white, over black chalk, squared
26.6 × 22.8 cm
Private collection, Chicago

Provenance: J. Richardson junior (L. 1921, 2170); anonymous collector (sale, Sotheby's, New York, 8 January 1991, lot 16); with K. Bellinger, at Harari & Johns, London, *Drawing in Florence, 1500–1650*, June–July 1991, no. 18a; Katrin Bellinger, 1991; private collection, Chicago.

References: Chappell 1992, under nos. 22, 23; Chappell 2006, pp. 356–357, note 4.

Notes
1   *Al cardinal Montalto [fece] molti disegni per far panni di arazzi tocchi con acquarelli, nei quali facendo storie sacre conforme all'ordine ricevuto, attorno ad essi per ornamento andò scherzando con poetica invenzione secondo che la storia richiedeva.* Giovan Battista Cardi, *Vita di Lodovico Cardi Cigoli (1559–1613)* [1628], ed. Guido Battelli and Kurt Heinrich Busse (San Miniato, 1913) pp. 36–37. The tapestry's narrative is in fact not a biblical story but rather a glorification of Pope Sixtus V as a religious leader.
2   The drawing, formerly in the collection of Dr. and Mrs. Malcolm Bick, was sold at Christie's, New York, 12 January 1995, lot 17, and is now in a private collection, New York. The verso studies are illustrated in both the Christie's sale catalogue. Signed and dated 1593, they are sketches for Cigoli's altarpiece of the *Virgin and Child with Saints Michael and Peter* in San Michele Arcangelo, Pianezzole; see F. Faranda, *Ludovico Cardi detto il Cigoli* (De Luca, 1986), p. 123, no. 14.
3   His revised version of the Vulgate Bible, the so-called 'Editio Sixtina,' was published in 1589.
4   Turner 2009.
5   The fragment was stolen from Katrin Bellinger. It is reproduced in Bellinger 1991, no. 18b.
6   F. Viatte, *Dessins toscans, XVIᵉ– XVIIIᵉ siècles: 1560–1640*, vol. 1 of *Inventaire général des dessins italiens*, ed. R. Bacou (Paris, 1988), p. 77, no. 131.
7   M.L. Chappell et al., *Disegni dei toscani a Roma, 1580–1620* (Florence, 1979), p. 117, under no. 74.
8   Uffizi, Florence, 124 Orn. and 14022F. See Chappell's comprehensive discussion of the drawings, and of the Cardinal Montalto commission in general, in *Disegni dei toscani a Roma*, nos. 73 and 74, and Chappell 1992, nos. 22 and 23, respectively).
9   Gabinetto Nazionale delle Stampe, Rome, 130678. This was first identified by A. Forlani Tempesti, and is cited by Chappell in *Disegni dei toscani a Roma*, p. 117, under no. 74.
10   See Chappell 2006, pp. 354–356, fig. 1.

References: Reznicek 1961, pp. 93, 338–339, no. 229; Miedema 1969, pp. 76–77; Stolzenburg 2000, p. 440, no. 177; Leeflang 2003, pp. 136–137, no. 43.

132
ANNIBALE CARRACCI
1560–1609
Hercules Resting
c. 1596–1597 (1599?)
Black chalk, with white heightening on blue paper, partly squared in black chalk, laid down
35.5 × 52.4 cm
The Cleveland Museum of Art (1997.52)
Leonard C. Hanna Jr. Fund

Provenance: Bertrand Talabardon, Paris; acquired by the Cleveland Museum in 1997.

References: De Grazia 1998, pp. 296–297; van Tuyll van Seerooskerken in Benati et al. 1999, pp. 136–138, no. 34; De Grazia and Foster 2000, pp. 46–47, no. 13; Robertson 2000, pp. 64–65.

Notes
1   S. Ginzburg, *Annibale Carracci a Roma. Gli affreschi di Palazzo Farnese* (Rome, 2000), pp. 35–77; and Ginzburg in Benati and Riccòmini 2006, pp. 294–297, 300–311, 449–451.
2   C. Volpi, "Odoardo al bivio: l'invenzione del Camerino Farnese tra encomio e filosofia," *Bollettino d'Arte* 83 (1999), pp. 87–95, 105–106.
3   Martin 1965, pp. 240–249.
4   In Benati and Riccòmini 2006, pp. 300–311.
5   See van Tuyll van Seerooskerken in Benati et al. 1999

133
ANNIBALE CARRACCI
1560–1609
Study for a Bacchante
c. 1598
Black chalk, pen and brown ink, with white heightening on blue paper
47.8 × 27.9 cm
Inscriptions: *h. m.*
Szépmüvészeti Múzeum, Budapest (inv. 1812)

Provenance: Jonathan Richardson (L. 2184); Antonio Cesare Poggi (L. 617); Nicholas Esterházy (L. 1965); Orzágos Képtár (L. 2000); acquired for the National Picture Gallery in 1870.

References: Martin 1965, p. 255, no. 64; Czére 1989, pp. 36–37, no. 14; Loisel in Borea 2000, p. 240, no. 13; Grasselli in Benati et al. 1999, p. 169; Czére 2004, pp. 84–85, no. 71.

Notes
1   Martin 1965, pp. 249–277.

134
ANNIBALE CARRACCI
1560–1609
Holy Family with Infant Saint John the Baptist ("The Montalto Madonna")
c. 1597–1598
Oil on copper
35 × 27.5 cm
Inscriptions: *591 Annibale Carracci* and *77*
The National Gallery, London (6597)
Bought with funds from generous legacies and recent donations, 2004

Provenance: Cardinal Alessandro Peretti Montalto, Rome; Principe Michele Peretti Montalto, Rome; Cardinal Francesco Peretti Montalto, Rome; Monsignor Lorenzo Salviati, Rome; Francesco Maria Salviati, Rome; Anton Maria Salviati, Rome; Caterina Maria Zefferina Salviati, Rome; Principe Fabrizio Colonna, Rome; Principe Filippo III Colonna, Rome; Sir Archibald Campbell of Succoth,

Garscube House; Sir George Campbell of Succoth, Garscube House; Christie's, London, 27 February 1948, no. 153; Mr. und Mrs. Pavica Mauthner; Sotheby's, London, 11 July 2003, no. 35; acquired by the National Gallery in 2004.

References: Bellori 1672, p. 95; Waagen 1854, III, p. 292; Martinelli 1969, pp. 323, 326; Posner 1971, I, p. 86, II, pp. 43–44, no. 100; Costamagna 2000, pp. 179, 194, no. 161, p. 225 no. 237; catalogue Sotheby's, London 11 July 2003, pp. 84–91, no. 35; Schütze in Bonn 2005, pp. 227–228, no. 121; Benati in Benati and Riccòmini 2006, pp. 284–285, no. VI.4.

Notes
1   Bellori 2005, p. 101.
2   See Posner 1971.

135
ANNIBALE CARRACCI
1560–1609
Vision of Saint Francis
c. 1597–1598
Oil on copper, two copper strips of 2.5 cm added on each side
46.8 × 37.2 cm
National Gallery of Canada, Ottawa (18905)

Provenance: Monsignor Lorenzo Salviati, Rome; Nicolas de Launay, Paris; Louis Duc d'Orleans, Paris; Louis-Philippe Duc d'Orléans, Paris; Louis-Philippe-Joseph Duc d'Orleans, Paris; Edouard Vicomte Walquers, Brussels; Francois-Louis-Joseph Comte Laborde de Méreville, Paris; Francis Egerton 3rd Duke of Bridgewater, London; George Granville Leveson-Gower 2nd Marquess of Stafford and 1st Duke of Sutherland; Lord Francis Egerton 1st Earl of Ellesmere; Francis Charles Granville Egerton 3rd Earl of Ellesmere; 5th Earl of Ellesmere, Bridgewater House; Christie's, London, 18 October 1946, no. 66; Dent Collection, London; Sir John Pope-Hennessy, London; with Colnaghi, London, 1977; purchased 1977.

References: Bellori 1672, p. 95; Bologna 1956, pp. 213–214, no. 91; Posner 1971, I, pp. 85–86, II, p. 43, no. 99; Lehmann 1980, p. 77; Johnston, in Johnston 1986, pp. 52–53, no. 2; Laskin and Pantazzi 1987, pp. 60–61; B.L. Brown 1997, pp. 188–190; Costamagna 2000, pp. 183, 212–213 n. 65.

Notes
1   Bellori 2005, p. 101.
2   Johnston in Ottawa 1986, pp. 52–53, no. 2
3   R. Wittkower, *The Drawings of the Carracci in the Collection of Her Majesty the Queen at Windsor Castle* (London, 1952), p. 155, no. 415.
4   A. Brogi, *Ludovico Carracci (1555–1619)*, 2 vols. (Ozzano Emilia, 2001), pp. 117–119, no. 13.

136
ANNIBALE CARRACCI
1560–1609
Vision of Saint Francis (recto)
Study of a Door or Tabernacle Frame (verso)
c. 1597–1598
Pen and brown ink with brown wash; pen and brown ink and black chalk (verso)
20.9 × 22.6 cm
National Gallery of Canada, Ottawa (26531)

Provenance: J. Richardson; T. Hudson (L. 2432); Shickman Gallery, New York; purchased in 1981 from David Rust, Washington.

References: Posner 1971, I, p. 86, II, p. 43; Cazort and Johnston 1982, no. 30; Johnston, in Cazort 1988, pp. 39–43, no. 9; Franklin 2003, no. 19.

471

137
PAUL BRIL
1554–1626
Landscape with Roman Ruins
Overlooking a Bay
c. 1594
Pen and brown ink over black chalk
13.7 × 20.7 cm
Annotations: *27* (encircled): *258870*
Private Collection, Toronto

Provenance: J.H.J. Mellaart; Einar Perman, Stockholm; sale, Sotheby's, Amsterdam, 9 June 75, lot 23; sale, Sotheby's, Amsterdam, 21 Nov. 89, lot 24, illus.

References: Ruby 1999, p. 80, no. 9, pl. 10 [as "Extensive Landscape with Ruins by a Waterfall"]; Boon 1992, pp. 49–50, n. 6.; Spicer 2004, pp. 68–69, no. 24.

Notes
1   Posner 1971, p. 78, and M. Abromson, *Painting in Rome During the Papacy of Clement VIII (1592–1605): A Documented Study* (New York, 1981), p. 287. That Bril was hired for a large section of the more prestigious commission could suggest that at that time he held a higher position in the Roman artistic hierarchy than did Annibale Carracci, who ultimately executed the Gallery Farnese frescos.
2   J. Freiberg, *The Lateran in 1600: Christian Concord in Reformation Rome* (Cambridge and New York, 1995), pp. 82, 301. Bril's hand can be seen particularly in Bernardino Cesari's *Triumphal Entry of Constantine* and Paris Nogeri's *Discovery of Pope Sylvester.*

138
PAUL BRIL
1554–1626
Fantastic Landscape
1598
Oil on copper: 21.3 × 29.2 cm.
Inscriptions: *PA. BRIL. ROMAE. 1598.*
National Gallery of Scotland, Edinburgh (NG 1492)

Provenance: James Fenton, Norton Hall, Gloucestershire; Sale London (Christie's) 27 February 1880 (L. 39936), no. 224 (13.5 Gns, to Waters); Mrs Nisbet Hamilton Ogilvy of Biel; bequest 1921.

References: Faggin 1965, no. 26, p. 32; Thompson and Brigstocke 1978, p. 12; Brown 1986, no. 1; Phoenix 1999, no. 6; Essen and Vienna 2003, no. 43 Cappelletti 2006, no. 48, p. 237.

Notes
1   Biography based on L. Pijl, "Bril, Paul," in: *Saur. Allgemeines Künstlerlexikon. Die Bildenden Künstler aller Zeiten und Völker*, vol. 14 (Munich/Leipzig 1996), pp. 228–230 (with further literature). On Bril's mural paintings see Carla Hendriks, *Northern Landscapes on Roman Walls. The Frescoes of Matthijs and Paul Bril* (Florence 2003); on his drawings see L.W. Ruby, *Paul Bril. The Drawings* [Pictura Nova. Studies in 16th- and 17th-Century Flemish Painting and Drawing, vol. IV] (Turnhout 1999).
2   L. Pijl, "Paintings by Paul Bril in Collaboration with Rottenhammer, Elsheimer and Rubens," *The Burlington Magazine* 140 (1998), pp. 660–667.
3   Ruby 1999, nos. 47–49, pl. 51–53.
4   Copper, 22 × 30 cm, inv. no. 859. Hans Ebert, *Kriegsverluste der Dresdener Gemäldegalerie: Vernichtete und vermisste Kunstwerke* (Dresden 1963), p. 72, illus. Judging from the old photograph the painting seems to be slightly weaker than the one in the National Gallery. The delicate sunrays for example seem to miss. With thanks to Luuk Pijl who however confirmed the painting to be an autograph version.

5   Copper, 21.5 × 29.5 cm, signed and dated: "P. Bril. 1600.", inv. no. 858. Gemäldegalerie Dresden. Alte Meister: *Katalog der ausgestellten Werke* (Dresden 1992), p. 131, ill. [A. Meyer-Meintschel].
6   *Roman Landscape with Waterfall,* canvas, 84 × 112 cm, signed and dated: "Paolo Brill 16[..]," and *Roman Landscape with Ruins of the Roman Forum*, canvas, 84 × 112 cm, signed with the rebus "glasses," Brunswick, Herzog Anton Ulrich-Museum (inv. nos. 60, 61). R. Klessmann, *Die flämischen Gemälde des 17. und 18. Jahrhunderts,* exh. cat. (München 2003), pp. 21–22, nos. 60, 61.

139
HANS ROTTENHAMMER
1564–1625
Diana and Actaeon
1595
Black and red chalk
18.1 × 22.6 cm
Inscriptions: *HRottenhammer/1595 Roma*
Private collection

Provenance: Norbert L.H. Roesler (sale, Christie's New York, 31 May 1990, lot 117); Haboldt and Company, Paris and New York (sale catalogue 1991, no. 29); sale, Sotheby's New York, 23 January 2001, lot 130; Private collection Zurich.

References: Schlichtenmaier 1988, Z II 8; Bischoff 2007, pp. 74–75, 84–84; Czére 2007, no. 20; Borggrefe et al. 2008, pp. 54, 97, no. 3.

Notes
1   Louvre, Inv. Nr. R. F. 11.992; illustrated in Borggrefe et al. 2008, p. 12, fig. 4.
2   Bischoff 2007, p. 75; Bischoff also mentions the poses of the female figure seen from the back, which he suggests might have been taken from Raimondi's *Judgment of Paris* after Raphael, although this reliance on this print is stronger in the Louvre version, and this particular borrowing may also have been taken from a print of the same theme by Ägidius Sadeler after Paolo Fiammingo.
3   T. Kaufmann and H. Borggrefe, "Hans Rottenhammer als Zeichner," in Borggrefe 2008, p. 53.
4   See J. Zimmer, *Joseph Heintz der Ältere.Zeichnungen und Dokumente* (Munich 1988), esp. p. 77.
5   Ibid., p. 142 A66/67, figs. 108, 109; T. Kaufmann, *The School of Prague. Painting at the Court of Rudolf II* (Chicago and London 1988), p. 189, cat. no. 7.20, ill; Bischoff 2007, pp. 82–86.
6   Bischoff 2007; Borggrefe et al. 2008, p. 97, no. 3.

140
FEDERICO ZUCCARO
c. 1542/43–1609
An Allegory of Medicine
c. 1596–1597
Pen and brown ink and wash over traces of black chalk
17.6 × 23.2 cm. oval
Inscriptions: *APOLLINI / medicina / SALVTARI*
Agnes Etherington Art Centre, Queen's University, Kingston (44–013)
Purchase, George Taylor Richardson Memorial Fund, Walter and Duncan Gordon Foundation, Gallery Association, 2001

Provenance: Private collection, Oxford; sale, Bucknall and Ballard, Oxford, 7 December1981; private collection, England; sale Christie's, London, 6 July 1987, lot 30; Day and Faber, London, 2001.

References; Day and Faber 2001, p. 4, no. 1; Herrmann Fiore 2001, pp. 71, fig. 69.

Notes
1   The fundamental study on the Palazzo Zuccaro is in W. Körte, *Der Palazzo Zuccari in Rom: Sein Freskenschmuck und seine Geschichte* (Leipzig, 1935). For a recent discussion, see Acidini Luchinat 1998–1999, pp. 199–231.
2   K. Herrmann Fiore, "Disegno and Giuditio, Allegorical Drawings by Federico Zuccaro and Cherubino Alberti." *Master Drawings* 20 (Fall, 1982), p. 247. According to Day and Faber, 2001, p. 4, note 1, J. Merz was the first to connect the drawing with the Sala del Disegno in a letter dated 8 July 1987. Körte, in *Der Palazzo Zuccaro in Rom*, pp. 68–70, proposed that Federico's series of oil paintings on leather about the life of his brother Taddeo (Rome, Galleria Nazionale d'Arte Antica) was to be hung on the walls of this room. See also C. Strunck, "The Original Setting of the Early Life of Taddeo Series: A New Reading of the Pictorial Program in the Palazzo Zuccari, Rome," in Acidini Luchinat 1998–1999, pp. 113–125.
3   K. Demirsoy, "Disegno speculativo, amor divino ed arte: Das Ganymed-Fresko des römischen Palazzo Zuccari im Lichte der thomasischen Kontemplationslehre," in *Federico Zuccaro, Kunst zwischen Ideal und Reform*, vol. 27 (Basel, 2000), pp. 110–114
4   Alberti, 1604, p. 28, cited in Acidini Luchinat 1998–1999, p. 230, note 144. See also Herrmann Fiore 2001.
5   For a related drawing by Federico Zuccaro of *Father Disegno and the Three Arts* (Urbino, Palazzo Ducale, Viviani collection, Inv. no. 1820), see Herrmann Fiore, *Allegorical Drawings*, pp. 247–256, pl. 4. It seems not to have been noted that in 1948 Federico Zuccaro's oval drawing in pen and ink and wash for *Science* on the ceiling of the Sala del Disegno was on the London art market (photograph in the Witt Library, Courtauld Institute of Art, London).
6   Herrmann Fiore, p. 248.

141
CHERUBINO ALBERTI
1553–1615
Study of a Male Nude and Leg Studies
c. 1596–1600
Red chalk and black chalk
26.3 × 19.7 cm
Annotations: *b.r.c.* and *41*
National Gallery of Canada, Ottawa (42151)

Provenance: Hans Calmann, London by 1969. Herbert List, Munich, before 1975; bought 1975 (?) by Wolfgang Ratjen, Vaduz, Lichtenstein; bequeathed to the Ratjen Foundation, Vaduz, Lichtenstein, 1997; La Tâche Fine Arts, Zurich; from whom purchased by the Gallery in 2007.

Notes
1   K. Herrmann Fiore, "Studi sui disegni di figure di Giovanni e Cherubino Alberti," *Bollettino d'Arte* 65, 1980, pp. 47–48, 52, fig. 24. On this commission see also M.C. Abromson, "Clement VIII's Patronage of the Brothers Alberti," *The Art Bulletin* 60 (1978), pp. 531–547.
2   Herrmann Fiore, ibid., fig. 23.
3   See Franklin 2003, no. 46.

142
GIOVANNI ALBERTI
1558–1601
Study of a Male Nude
Study of a Male Nude (verso)
c. 1596–1600
Black and red chalk
25.2 × 12.3 cm
Annotations: *HL*
Watermark: *M* surmounted by a crown
National Gallery of Canada, Ottawa (42150)

Provenance: G. Vallardi (L. 1223); Kurt Meissner, Zurich by 1969; Herbert List, Munich; Ratjen Foundation; Purchased from La Tâche Fine Arts, Zurich in 2007.

Notes
1   K. Herrmann Fiore, "Studi sui disegni di figure di Giovanni e Cherubino Alberti," *Bollettino d'Arte*, 65 1980, p. 51, fig. 20. For the attribution to Giovanni see her p. 217, under no. 143. See also her catalogue: *Disegni degli Alberti*, ll volume 2503, exh. cat. (Rome, 1983), under nos. 20 and 143.

143
CRISTOFORO RONCALLI, CALLED IL POMARANCIO
c. 1553–1626
Diana Killing the Children of Niobe
c. 1595–1610
Black chalk with white heightening on blue paper
27.1 × 42 cm
Inscriptions: *67*
Teylers Museum, Haarlem (inv. I, 43)

Provenance: Prince Livio Odescalchi, Rome; acquired in 1790 from his heirs (L. 2392) for the Teylers Stichting in Haarlem.

References: Van Regteren Altena 1966, p. 104, no. 82; Vitzthum 1966, p. 300; van Tuyll van Serooskerken in Meijer and van Tuyll van Serooskerken 1983, no. 74; Meijer 1985, no. 42; van Tuyll van Serooskerken 2000, p. 295, no. 281.

144
CRISTOFORO RONCALLI, CALLED IL POMARANCIO
c. 1553–1626
Saint Domitilla between Saints Nereo and Achilleo
c. 1596–1597
Black chalk, squared in black chalk
41.4 × 26.2 cm
Inscriptions: *B.*
The Courtauld Gallery, London
The Samuel Courtauld Trust

Provenance: Benjamin West (L. 419); Sir Robert Witt (L. 2228b).

References: Pouncey 1952, p. 356; Blunt 1956, p. 86, no. 4370; Kirwin 1978, pp. 38–40; Chiappini di Sorio 1983, p. 122; Stock and Scrase 1985, no. 55.

145
CRISTOFORO RONCALLI, CALLED IL POMARANCIO
c. 1553–1626
Death of Sapphira
c. 1599–1603
Oil on canvas
124.5 × 85 cm
Inscriptions: *Pietro da Cortona; 578* (verso)
National Gallery of Canada (42019)

Provenance: Charles Chatfield (?) , London by 1816; anonymous sale, Sotheby's, New York, 2 Dec 1976, lot 139; British Rail Pension Fund by 1991; sale, Sotheby's, London, 7 Dec 1994, lot 29; purchased by Richard L. Feigen & Company, New York; sale, Christie's, New York, 25 May 2005; purchased by W.M. Brady & Co., New York; purchased 2007.

References: Pouncey 1977, p. 225, fig. 108; Kirwin 1978, p. 59, n. 126; Chiappini di Sorio 1983, no. 17, no. 3, no. 45.

Notes

1   For further details and bibliography, see Ileana Chiappini di Sorio. "Roncalli, Cristoforo." In *Grove Art Online. Oxford Art Online*, http://www.oxfordartonline.com/subscriber/article/grove/art/T073762 (accessed 12 November 2008).
2   For instance, Giovanni Baglione notes that the work was painted "with many figures, well made, and giving much satisfaction" ("con molte figure, ben fatto, c dicdc assai soddisfattione") in Baglione 1642, p. 290.
3   The documents are published, and the drawings extensively described, in M. Chappell and W.C. Kirwin, "A Petrine Triumph: The Decoration of the Navi Piccolc in San Pietro under Clement VIII," *Storia dell'arte* 21 (1974), pp. 119–170.
4   There are similar oil *bozzetti* by Roncalli in other collections, including those at the British Museum and Christ Church, Oxford.
5   A. Bartsch, *The Illustrated Bartsch, Vol. 48, Formerly Volume 12, Italian Chiaroscuro Woodcuts* (New York, 1983), Diogenes (B.XII.100.10), illus. p. 155.
6   See the biography of Mancini in the *Grove Dictionary of Art*. Philip Sohm, "Mancini, Giulio," in *Grove Art Online. Oxford Art Online*, http://www.oxfordartonline.com/subscriber/article/grove/art/T053690 (accessed 13 November 2008).

146
GIUSEPPE CESARI, CALLED IL CAVALIERE D'ARPINO
1568–1640
Rest on the Flight to Egypt
c. 1596–1597
Oil on copper
43.2 × 31.7 cm
Inscriptions: *F 22*
Museum of Fine Arts, Boston
(1983.301)
Gift of John Goelet

Provenance: Cardinal Francesco Barberini Junior, Rome; Barberini collection, Rome; Colnaghi's, London.

References: Florence 1922, p. 126, no. 664; Longhi 1928, p. 344, no. 231; Cappelletti in Brown 2001, pp. 182–183, no. 63; Kottgen 2002, pp. 48–49, 312, no. 71.

Notes

1   Röttgen 2002, p. 286, no. 56.

147
GIUSEPPE CESARI, CALLED IL CAVALIERE D'ARPINO
1568–1640
David with the Head of Goliath
1598
Oil on canvas
100 × 76.5 cm
Inscriptions: *Di mano del Cavalier Giuseppe d'Arpino del no 255*
Annotations: *1598 IOSEF.A.*
Koelliker Collection (LK0092)

Provenance: Cardinal Pietro Aldobrandini, Villa a Magnanapoli, Rome; Cardinal Ippolito Aldobrandini, Villa a Magnanapoli, Rome; Olimpia Aldobrandini Junior, Villa a Magnanapoli, Rome; Vincenzo Camuccini, Rome; acquired in Milan from Carlo Orsi in 2000.

References: Ramdohr 1787, I, p. 182; Röttgen 2002, pp. 67, 73, 317–318, no. 79; Terzaghi in Volpi 2002, pp. 327–334.

Notes

1   C. D'Onofrio, "Inventario dei dipinti del cardinal Pietro Aldobrandini compilato da G.B. Agucchi nel 1603." *Palatino* VIII (1964), p. 207.
2   See Röttgen 2002 and Terzaghi in Volpi 2002.
3   Ibid.

148
GIUSEPPE CESARI, CALLED IL CAVALIERE D'ARPINO
1568–1640
An Angel in Flight
1599–1600
Black and red chalk
38 × 35.7 cm
Inscriptions: *Joseppo d'Arpinas* and *16.10.*
Private collection, New York

Provenance: Lambert Hermandsz. ten Kate (1674–1731); Antoni Rutgers (1695–1778); Cornelis Ploos van Amstel (1726–1798); Baron Roger Portalis († 1912), Paris (L. 2232); Léon Voillemont (L. 789d); Private collection, Brussels; W.M. Brady and Co., Inc., New York.

References: De Bisschop 1671, pl. 9 (etched in reverse and inscribed, *Jos. Arp. inv.d.*); Weigel 1865, p. 9, no. 98; Van Gelder and Jost 1985, pp. 234–235 (as considered lost); F. Härb in Brady and Co. 2006, no. 8, illus.

Notes

1   G. Baglione, *Le vite de' pittori, scultori et architetti. Dal Pontificato di Gregorio XIII fino a tutto quello d'Urbano Ottavo* (Rome, 1649), p. 371.
2   H.A. Noë, *Carel van Mander en Italië* (The Hague, 1954), p. 283.
3   Röttgen 2002, p. 327.
4   Ibid., pp. 325–326, nos. 89a and 89b, illus.
5   Van Gelder and Jost 1985, pp. 234–235, nos. 7 and 10, respectively, both illustrated. For the Louvre drawing see Röttgen 2002, pp. 307–308, fig. 670, and for that at Chatsworth, Jaffé 1994, p. 47, illus.

149
GIOVANNI BAGLIONE
c. 1566–1643
Saint Peter Baptizing Saint Prisca
c. 1599–1600
Pen and ink, brown wash, red chalk with white heightening on blue paper
37.7 × 26.6 cm
The British Museum, London
(1895.9.15.666)

Provenance: P. Crozat; Marquis de Lagoy (L. 1710); Malcolm.

References: Gere 1971, pp. 21, 86; Gere and Pouncey 1983, pp. 35–36, no. 36; Zuccari 2001, pp. 81–82; Smith O'Neil 2002, p. 245, no. 32.

Notes

1   Danesi Squarzina, "The Inventories of Benedetto Giustiniani," Part I, *The Burlington Magazine* 139 (1997), nos. 24, 38, 54, 138, 139, pp. 766–791; Part II, *The Burlington Magazine* 140 (1998), pp. 102–118.
2   The British Museum, London inv. 1978.5.20.4.
3   Zuccari 2001.

150
CARLO SARACENI
c. 1579–1620
Mars and Venus
c. 1600
Oil on copper
39.5 × 55 cm
Carmen Thyssen-Bornemisza Collection on loan at the Thyssen-Bornemisza Museum, Madrid
(CTB 1982.32)

Provenance: William Suida, New York; Silvano Lodi, Campione d'Italia; acquired in 1982.

References: Ottani Cavina, in New York 1985a, pp. 188–190, no. 56; Cappelletti, in Brown 2001, pp. 198, 384, no. 70; Contini 2002, pp. 26–29, no. 5; Contini, in Museo Thyssen-Bornemisza 2004, I, pp. 62–63;

Notes

1   Ottani Cavina, in New York 1985, pp. 188–190, no. 56.
2   See Cappelletti in Brown 2001, pp. 198, 384.

151
ADAM ELSHEIMER
1578–1610
The Flight into Egypt
c. 1604
Oil on silvered copper
9.8 × 7.6 cm (oval)
Kimbell Art Museum, Fort Worth, Texas

Provenance: (?) Chevalier de Quérelles, Paris; sold, Martin, Paris, 6 November 1820, lot 94; Gustave Rothan, Paris, by 1883; sold, Galerie Georges Petit, Paris, 29–31 May 1890, lot 246; Eugène Féral, Paris, until 1901 (?); Jules Féral, Paris, until c. 1920; Mme. Paule Andral, Paris, before 1956; sold, Sotheby's, Monte Carlo, 22 February 1986, lot 249; Bob P. Haboldt & Co., New York; Peter Jay Sharp, New York, 1986; sold, Sotheby's, London, 13 January 1994, lot 67; Bob P. Haboldt & Co., New York; Kimbell Art Foundation, Fort Worth, 1994.

References: Bode 1883, p. 289; Weizsäcker 1952 p. 102; Andrews 1986, pp. 795–797; Bob P. Haboldt & Co. 1989, p. 5; R. Klessmann in Pessach 2000, no. 18; Cappelletti in Brown 2001, no. 68; Potts 2003, p. 56; Klessmann 2006, no. 23; Cappelletti in Di Lorenzo and Frangi 2007, no. 65.

Notes

1   On the Venetian influences in this picture, see Klessmann 2006, no. 8.
2   The earliest document for Elsheimer in Rome is a dedicatory inscription dated 21 April 1600 appearing on a leaf in an *album amicorum* now in the Bayerisches Nationalmuseum, Munich. See K. Andrews, *Adam Elsheimer: Paintings, Drawings, Prints* (Oxford, 1977), p. 47, doc. 2.
3   For the collaborations between Bril and Rottenhammer, see L. Pijl, "Paintings by Paul Bril in Collaboration with Rottenhammer, Elsheimer and Rubens," in *The Burlington Magazine* 140 (1998), pp. 660–662.
4   For the document of the wedding, see K. Andrews, "The Elsheimer Inventory and Other Documents" in *The Burlington Magazine* 114 (1972), p. 598, doc. 1. As a sign of Bril's admiration for Elsheimer, he is known to have owned at least two paintings by his friend. See Klessmann 2006, nos. 15, 19. The relevant inventories are published by D. Bodart in "Les tableaux de la succession de Paul Bril," *Mélanges d'archéologie et d'histoire de l'art offerts au Professeur Jacques Lavalleye* (Louvain, 1970), pp. 10–14.
5   Andrews 1986, p. 796. Another panel from the series is at the Musée Fabre, Montpellier.
6   K. Andrews, *Adam Elsheimer: Paintings, Drawings, Prints* (Oxford, 1977), p. 148. For early references to Teniers as Elsheimer's student, see C. De Bie, *Het Gulden Cabinet* (Antwerp, 1661), pp. 140–142; and J. von Sandrart, *Academie der Bau-, Bild- und Mahlery-Künste von 1675*, A.R. Peltzer, ed. (Munich, 1925), p. 181.
7   For the *Stoning of St. Stephen*, see Klessmann 2006, no. 19.
8   Good discussions of the intellectual milieu in which Elsheimer moved include F. Huemer, *Rubens and the Roman Circle: Studies of the First Decade* (New York and London, 1996), pp. 3–17; D. Freedberg, *The Eye of the Lynx: Galileo, His Friends, and the Beginnings of Modern Natural History* (Chicago, 2002), and Klessmann 2006, pp. 21–23, 34.
9   For example, D. Howard, "Elsheimer's Flight into Egypt and the Night Sky in the Renaissance," in *Zeithschrift für Kunstgeschichte* 55 (1992): 212–224, and Klessmann 2006, p. 34.
10   For these copies, see Klessmann 2006, p. 126, n. 5, and Cappelletti in Di Lorenzo and Frangi 2007, p. 166. The painting by Lastman is his *Flight into Egypt* in the Museum Boijmans van Beuningen, Rotterdam. See Andrews 1986, p. 797. The painting by Cigoli is his *Flight into Egypt* in the Musée Fabre, Montpellier (the best of several versions). See Cappelletti in Brown 2001, no. 64.

473

ACIDINI LUCHINAT 1998–1999
C. Acidini Luchinat. *Taddeo e
Federico Zuccari, fratelli pittori del
Cinquecento*, 2 vols. Milan and
Rome, 1998–1999.

ACIDINI LUCHINAT ET AL. 2002
C. Acidini Luchinat et al. *The
Medici, Michelangelo, and the Art of
Late Renaissance Florence.* New
Haven, 2002.

ALASKO 1983   R. Alasko, ed.
*Religious Narrative in Sixteenth-
century Rome* (exh. cat.). Notre
Dame, Indiana, 1983.

ALVAREZ LOPERA 2005–2007
J.Alvarez Lopera. *El Greco. Estudio
y Catálogo.* 2 vols. Madrid,
2005–2007.

AMES-LEWIS 1986   F. Ames-Lewis.
The Draftsman Raphael. New
Haven and London, 1986.

ANDREWS 1968   K. Andrews.
Catalogue of Italian Drawings.
2 vols. Cambridge, 1968.

ANDREWS 1976   K. Andrews, ed.
*Old Master Drawings from the
David Laing Bequest* (exh. cat.).
Edinburgh, 1976.

ANDREWS 1986   K. Andrews. "A
Rediscovered Elsheimer." *The
Burlington Magazine* 128 (1986),
pp. 795–797.

ASKEW 1956   P. Askew. "Perino del
Vaga's Decorations for the Palazzo
Doria, Genoa." *The Burlington
Magazine* 98 (1956), pp. 45–53.

AVIGNON 1998   *Disegni della
Donazione Marcel Puech al Museo
Calvet di Avignone*, eds., S. Béguin,
Mario Di Giampaolo and
P. Malgouyres, 2 vols. Naples, 1998.

BACCHESCHI AND CALVESI 1978
E. Baccheschi and M. Calvesi.
"Simone Peterzano." In *I Pittori
Bergamaschi. Il Cinquecento* IV.
Bergamo 1978, pp. 471–557.

BACOU AND BÉGUIN 1983   R. Bacou
and S. Béguin. *Autour de Raphaël:
Dessins et peintures du Musée du
Louvre*, exh. cat. Paris, 1983.

BAGLIONE 1639   G. Baglione. *Le
nove chiese di Roma*. Rome, 1639
(reprinted, L. Barroero, ed., Rome,
1990).

BAGLIONE 1642   G. Baglione. *Le
vite de' pittori, scultori et architetti.
Dal pontificato di Gregorio XIII. In
fino a' tempi di Papa Urbano VIII nel
1642*. Rome, 1642.

BAGLIONE 1995   G. Baglione. *Le
vite de' pittori, scultori et architetti.
Dal pontificato di Gregorio XIII. In
fino a' tempi di Papa Urbano VIII nel
1642*. [Rome, 1642]. 2 vols., ed.
J. Hess and H. Röttgen. Vatican
City, 1995.

BALASS 2001   G. Balass. "Taddeo
Zuccari's decoration for the
Frangipani Chapel in S. Marcello al
Corso, Rome." *Assaph* 6 (2001),
pp. 177–204.

BALTIMORE 1961   *Bacchiacca and
his Friends. Florentine Paintings
and Drawings of the Sixteenth
Century* (exh. cat.). Baltimore 1961.

BAMBACH 1997   C.C. Bambach. A
Review of A. Perrig, 'Michelangelo's
Drawings: The Science of Attribution.' In *Master Drawings* 35 (1997),
pp. 67–72.

BAMBACH 1998   C.C. Bambach.
"Recent Acquisitions: A Selection:
1997–1998." *The Metropolitan
Museum of Art Bulletin* 56 (Fall
1998).

BAMBACH 2007   C.C. Bambach.
"Disegni toscani al Metropolitan
Museum of Art." In *Invisibile agli
occhi: Atti della giornata di studio in
ricordo di Lisa Venturini (Firenze,
Fondazione Roberto Longhi, 15
dicembre 2005)*, ed. N. Baldini.
Florence, 2007.

BAMBACH 2008   C.C. Bambach.
"Drawings in Dresden: Further
Newly Identified works by Italian
Masters." *Apollo Magazine* 167
(2008).

BAROCCHI 1964a   P. Barocchi.
"Appunti su Francesco Morandini
da Poppi." *Mitteilungen des kunsthistorischen Institutes in Florenz.*
XI (1964), pp. 117–148.

BAROCCHI 1964b   P. Barocchi.
Vasari pittore. Milan, 1964.

BAROLSKY 1979   P. Barolsky.
*Daniele da Volterra: A Catalogue
Raisonné.* New York and London,
1979.

BAYER 2008   A. Bayer, ed. *Art and
Love in Renaissance Italy* (exh. cat.).
New York, New Haven, and London,
2008.

BEAN 1963   J. Bean. "Form and
Function in Italian Drawings:
Observations on Several New
Acquisitions." *The Bulletin of The
Metropolitan Museum of Art,*
vol. 21, 1963.

BEAN 1964   J. Bean. *100 European
Drawings in the Metropolitan
Museum of Art.* New York, 1964.

BEAN AND STAMPFLE 1965   J. Bean
and F. Stampfle. *Drawings from
New York Collections, Vol. I: The
Italian Renaissance* (exh. cat.). New
York, 1965.

BEAN AND TURÇIC 1982   J. Bean
and L. Turçic. *15th and 16th Century
Italian Drawings in the
Metropolitan Museum of Art.* New
York, 1982.

BELL 1914   C.F. Bell. *Drawings
by the Old Masters in the Library
of Christ Church, Oxford: An
Alphabetical List of the Artists
Represented in the Collection
(Mounted Series).* Oxford, 1914.

BELLINGER 1991   K. Bellinger, ed.
*Die Zeichnung in Florenz / Drawing
in Florence, 1500–1650.* Munich and
London, 1991.

BELLINGER 2005   K. Bellinger.
Master Drawings: 1985–2005.
London, 2005.

BELLINI 2007   F. Bellini. "Lorenzo
Lotto San Girolamo." In *Dürer e
l'Italia* (exh. cat.), ed. K. Herrmann
Fiore, p. 295. Milan, 2007.

BELLINI 2008   F. Bellini. "Lorenzo
Lotto, San Girolamo." In
*Rinascimento e passione per l'antico:
Andrea Riccio e il suo tempo* (exh.
cat.), ed. A. Bacchi and L. Giacomelli,
pp. 294–295. Trento, 2008.

BELLORI 1672   G.P. Bellori. *Le Vite
de' Pittori, Scultori e Architetti
Moderni* (1672), ed. E. Borea. Turin,
1976.

BELLORI 2005   G.P. Bellori. *The
Lives of the Modern Painters,
Sculptors and Architects* (1672),
English ed., ed. A. Sedwick Wohl,
H. Wohl, and T. Montanari.
Cambridge 2005.

BENATI AND RICCÒMINI 2006
D. Benati and E. Riccòmini, eds.
Annibale Carracci (exh. cat.).
Bologna-Rome 2006.

BENATI ET AL. 1999   D. Benati,
D. De Grazia and G. Feigenbaum,
eds. *The Drawings of Annibale
Carracci* (exh. cat.). Washington,
1999.

BERENSON 1903   B. Berenson. *The
Drawings of the Florentine Painters:
Classified, Criticised and Studied as
Documents in the History and
Appreciation of Tuscan Art; with a
Copious Catalogue Raisonné.* 2 vols.
London, 1903.

BERENSON 1938   B. Berenson. *The
Drawings of the Florentine Painters*
3 vols. Chicago, 1938.

BERENSON 1961   B. Berenson.
I disegni dei pittori fiorentini, trans.
L. Vertova. Milan, 1961.

BERNARDINI 2002   M.G. Bernardini,
ed. *L'Oratorio del Gonfalone a Roma.*
Milan, 2002.

BIGI IOTTI 2008   A. Bigi Iotti.
"Andrea Sansovino and the Design
for a Funerary Monument for
Leo X." *The Burlington Magazine*
150 (2008), pp. 757–759.

BIGI IOTTI AND ZAVATTA 2008
A. Bigi Iotti and G. Zavatta.
*Raffaellino da Reggio Tracce di una
biografia artistica.* Reggio Emilia,
2008.

BISCHOFF 2007   M. Bischoff.
"Diana und Aktäon: eine ikonog-
raphische Erfolgsgeschichte in
Venedig, Rom und Prag." In *Hans
Rottenhammer (1564–1625).
Ergebnisse des in Kooperation mit
dem Institut für Kunstgeschichte mit
der Tschechischen Akademie der
Wissenschaften durchgeführten
internationalen Symposions am
Weserrenaissance-Museum Schloß
Brake (17–18 February 2007)*, ed.
H. Borggrefe, V. Lüpkes, and
L. Konecný. Marburg, 2007.

BISSELL 1993   G. Bissell.
"Beobachtungen zum Werden des
Juliusgrabs bis 1513." In *Musis et
Litteris: Festschrift für Bernhard
Rupprecht zum 65. Geburtstag*, ed.
V. Greiselmayer. Munich, 1993.

BLUNT 1956   A. Blunt. *Hand-List of
the Drawings in the Witt Collection.*
London, 1956.

BLUNT 1980   A. Blunt. Review of
Ward-Jackson 1979–1980, vol. 1.
The Burlington Magazine 122
(1980), pp. 638–639.

BOB P. HABOLDT & CO. 1989
Old Master Paintings and Drawings.
New York, 1989.

BOBER AND RUBINSTEIN 1986
P.P. Bober and R. Rubinstein.
*Renaissance Artists and Antique
Sculpture: A Handbook of Sources.*
London and Oxford, 1986.

BÖCK 1997   A. Böck. *Die Sala Regia
im Vatikan als Beispiel der
Selbstarstellung des Papsttums in
der zweiten Hälfte des 16.
Jahrhunderts.* Hildesheim, 1997.

BODE 1883   W. von Bode. *Studien
zur Geschichte der holländischen
Malerei.* Braunschweig, 1883.

BOLOGNA 1956   G. P. Bellori.
Mostra dei Carracci (exh. cat.).
Bologna, 1956.

BOLOGNA 1975   *Mostra di Federico
Barocci (Urbino 1535–1612)* (exh.
cat). Bologna, 1975.

BONN 1999   *Hochrenaissance im
Vatikan: Kunst und Kultur im Rom
der Päpste I, 1503–1534* (exh. cat.).
Bonn, 1999.

BONN 2005   *Barock im Vatikan.
Kunst und Kultur der Päpste 1572–
1676* (exh. cat.). Bonn, 2005.

BOON 1992   K.G. Boon. *The
Netherlandish and German
Drawings of the XVth and XVIth
Centuries of the Frits Lugt
Collection.* 3 vols. Paris, 1992.

BOREA 2000   E. Borea, ed. *L'Idea
del Bello: Viaggio per Roma nel
Seicento con Giovan Pietro Bellori*
(exh. cat.). Rome, 2000.

BORENIUS AND WITTKOWER 1937
T. Borenius and R. Wittkower.
*Catalogue of the Collection of
Drawings by the Old Masters formed
by Sir Robert Mond.* London, 1937.

BORGGREFE ET AL. 2008
H. Borggrefe et al. eds. *Hans
Rottenhammer begehrt – vergessen –
neu entdeckt* (exh.cat.). Munich,
2008.

BORGHINI 1584   R. Borghini. *Il
Riposo di Raffaello Borghini in cui
della pittura, e della scultura si
favella, de' più illustri pittori e scultori e delle più famose opere loro si
fa mentione; e le cose principali
appartenanti a dette arti
s'insegnano.* Florence, 1584.

BRADY AND CO. 2006 W.M. Brady and Co., Inc. *Master Drawings 1520–1890* (ex. cat.). New York, 2006.

BRAUER AND WITTKOWER 1931 H. Brauer and R. Wittkower. *Die Zeichnungen des Gianlorenzo Bernini*. 2 vols. Berlin, 1931.

BRIGSTOCKE 1982 H. Brigstocke. *William Buchanan and the 19th Century Art Trade: 100 Letters to His Agents in London and Italy.* London, 1982.

BRINCKMANN 1925 A.E. Brinckmann. *Michelangelo Zeichnungen.* Munich, 1925.

BROOKS ET AL. 2007 J. Brooks et al. *Taddeo and Federico Zuccaro: Artist-Brothers in Renaissance Rome* (exh. cat.). Los Angeles, 2007.

BROSS 1994 L.S. Bross. *The Church of Santo Spirito in Sassia: A Study in the Development of Art, Architecture and Patronage in Counter-Reformation Rome*, Ph.D Diss. University of Chicago, 1994.

BROWN 1986 C. Brown. *Dutch Landscape, The Early Years*, Haarlem and Amsterdam 1590–1650 (exh. cat.). London, 1986.

BROWN 1997 B.L. Brown. "Annibale Carracci's 'Coronation of St. Stephen'." *The Burlington Magazine* 139 (1997), pp. 188–193.

BROWN ET AL. 1997 D.A. Brown, P. Humfrey, and M. Lucco. *Lorenzo Lotto: Rediscovered Master of the Renaissance* (exh. cat.). Washington, 1997.

BROWN 2001 B.L. Brown, ed. *The Genius of Rome* (exh. cat.). London, 2001.

BRUGNOLI 1973 M.V. Brugnoli. "Baldassare Peruzzi nella chiesa di S. Maria della Pace e nella "Uccelliera" di Giulio II." *Bollettino d'Arte* 58 (1973), pp. 115–116.

BUCHANAN 1824 W. Buchanan. *Memoirs of Paintings, with a Chronological History of the Importation of Pictures by the Great Masters into England since the French Revolution*. 2 vols. London, 1824.

BURKHALTER 1932 M. Burkhalter. *Die Bildnisse Raffaels.* Laupen, 1932.

BURROUGHS 1925 B. Burroughs. "Drawings by Michelangelo for the Libyan Sibyl." *The Metropolitan Museum of Art Bulletin* 20 (January 1925), pp. 6–14.

BYAM SHAW 1976 J. Byam Shaw. *Drawings by Old Masters at Christ Church, Oxford*. 2 vols. Oxford, 1976.

BYAM SHAW 1983 J. Byam Shaw. *The Italian Drawings of the Frits Lugt Collection.*

CALVESI 1954 M. Calvesi. "Simone Peterzano maestro del Caravaggio." *Bollettino d'Arte* 39 (1954), pp. 114–133.

CALVESI 1990 M. Calvesi. *La Realtà del Caravaggio.* Turin 1990.

CANNATÀ AND GIAVARIANA GHISETTI 1991 R. Cannatà and A. Giavarina Ghisetti. *Cola dell'Amatrice.* Florence, 1991.

CAPPELLETTI 2006 F. Cappelletti. *Paul Bril e la pittura di paesaggio a Roma 1580–1630.* Rome, 2006.

CARROLL 1987–1988 E.A. Carroll. *Rosso Fiorentino: Drawings, Prints, and Decorative Arts* (exh. cat.). Washington, 1987–1988.

CAVAZZINI 1989 P. Cavazzini. "The Porta Virtutis and Federico Zuccari's Expulsion from the Papal State. An Unjust Conviction." *Römisches Jahrbuch der Biblioteca Hertziana* 25 (1989), pp. 167–177.

CAZORT 1988 M. Cazort, ed. *Master Drawings from the National Gallery of Canada* (exh. cat.). Ottawa, 1988.

CAZORT AND JOHNSTON 1982 M. Cazort and C. Johnston, eds. *Bolognese Drawings in North American Collections* (exh. cat.). Ottawa, 1982.

CECCHI 1976 A. Cecchi. "Qualche contributo al corpus grafico del Vasari e del suo ambiente." In *Il Vasari storiografo e artista.* Florence, 1976.

CECCHI 1978 A. Cecchi. "Nuove acquisizioni per un catalogo dei disegni di Giorgio Vasari." In *Antichità viva.* XVII (1978), I, pp. 52–61.

CECCHI 1998 A. Cecchi. "Alcuni disegni del soggiorno romano di Battista Naldini." In *Gedenkschrift für Richard Harprath*, ed. Wolfgang Liebenwein and Anchise Tempestini. Munich, 1998. pp. 53–58.

CECCHI AND NATALI 1996 A. Cecchi and A. Natali, eds. *L'officina della maniera: Varietà e fierezza nell'arte fiorentina del Cinquecento fra le due repubbliche, 1494–1530* (exh. cat.). Florence and Venice, 1996.

CHAPMAN 2005 H. Chapman. *Michelangelo Drawings: Closer to the Master.* New Haven, 2005.

CHAPMAN ET AL. 2004 H. Chapman, T. Henry, and C. Plazzotta, et al. *Raphael from Urbino to Rome* (exh. cat.). London, 2004.

CHAPPELL 1992 M.L. Chappell. *Disegni di Lodovico Cigoli (1559–1613),* [exh. cat.]. Florence, 1992.

CHAPPELL 2006 M.L. Chappell. "Three New Drawings by Cigoli." *Master Drawings* 44 (2006), pp. 354–357.

CHARLOTTE 1982 *Italian Renaissance Paintings from Southern Museums* (exh. cat.). North Carolina, 1982.

CHASTEL 1983 A. Chastel. *The Sack of Rome, 1527,* trans. B. Archer. Princeton, 1983.

CHENEY 1992 I. Cheney. "Comment: The Date of Francesco Salviati's French Journey." *Art Bulletin* 74:1 (1992), pp. 157–158.

CHIAPPINI DI SORIO 1983 I. Chiappini di Sorio. *Cristoforo Roncalli detto il Pomarancio.* Bergamo, 1983.

CHICAGO 1985 *Leonardo to Van Gogh: Master Drawings from Budapest* (exh. cat.). Chicago, 1985.

CHIUSA 2005 M.C. Chiusa. "Per un catalogo ragionato di Bertoja: Un nuovo disegno." In *Saggi di Storia e di Stile.* Milan, 2005.

CHONG ET AL. 2003 A. Chong, D. Pegazzano, and D. Zikos, eds. *Raphael, Cellini and a Renaissance Banker: The Patronage of Bindo Altoviti* (exh. cat.). Boston and Florence, 2003.

CIARDI AND MORESCHINI 2004 R.P. Ciardi and B. Moreschini. *Daniele Ricciarelli. Da Volterra a Roma,* Milan, 2004.

CLAYTON 1999 M. Clayton. *Raphael and His Circle: Drawings from Windsor Castle* (exh. cat.). London, 1999.

CLAYTON 2004 M. Clayton. *Holbein to Hockney: Drawings from the Royal Collection.* London, 2004.

COLLOBI 1939 L. Collobi. "Disegni di Raffaellino da Reggio." *Critica d'Arte* 4 (April–December 1939), pp. 13–14.

CONFORTI 1993 C. Conforti. *Vasari architetto.* Milan, 1993.

CONTARDI AND GENTILI 1983 B. Contardi and A. Gentili, eds. *Il S. Girolamo di Lorenzo Lotto a Castel S. Angelo.* Rome, 1983.

CONTINI 2002 R. Contini. *Seventeenth and Eighteenth Century Italian Painting: The Thyssen-Bornemisza Collection.* London, 2002.

CORDELLIER 1991 D. Cordellier. "Fragments de jeunesse: deux feuilles inédites de Michel-Ange au Louvre." *Revue du Louvre* (1991), pp. 43–55.

CORDELLIER 2007 D. Cordellier, *Polidoro da Caravaggio* (exh. cat.). Paris, 2007.

CORDELLIER AND PY 1992 D. Cordellier and B. Py. *Musée du Louvre, Musée d'Orsay, Département des Arts graphiques: Inventaire général des dessins. Italiens, V. Raphaël, son atelier, ses copistes.* Paris, 1992.

CORTI 1937 G. Corti. *Galleria Colonna.* Rome, 1937.

CORTI ET AL. 1981 L. Corti et al. *Giorgio Vasari, principi, letterati e artisti nelle carte di Giorgio Vasari. Pittura vasariana dal 1532 al 1554* (exh. cat.). Arezzo, 1981.

COSTAMAGNA 1988 P. Costamagna. "Osservazioni sull'attività giovanile di Alessandro Allori: seconda parte, i ritratti." *Antichità Viva* 27 (1988), pp. 27, 31.

COSTAMAGNA 2000 P. Costamagna. "La collection de peintures d'un famille Florentine établie à Rome : l'inventaire après décès du Duc Anton Maria Salviati dressé 1704." *Nuovi Studi* 5 (2000), pp. 177–233.

COSTAMAGNA 2002 P. Costamagna. "De l'idéal de beauté aux problèmes d'attribution:Vingt ans de recherche sur le portrait florentin au XVIᵉ siècle." *Studiolo: Revue d'histoire de l'art de l'Académie de France à Rome* I (2002).

COSTAMAGNA 2005 P. Costamagna. "Une 'Vierge á l'Enfant avec un ange' de la jeunesse de Francesco Salviati découverte." *Paragone* LVI no. 64 (669), 2005, pp. 67–70.

COULANGES-ROSENBERG 1965 F. Coulanges-Rosenberg. *Le XVIᵉ siècle européen: Dessin du Louvre* (exh. cat.). Paris, 1965.

COX-REARICK 1984 J. Cox-Rearick. *Dynasty and Destiny in Medici Art: Pontormo, Leo X, and the Two Cosimos.* Princeton, 1984.

CROWE AND CAVALCASELLE 1871 J.A. Crowe and G.B. Cavalcaselle. *A History of Painting in North Italy: Venice, Padua, Vicenza, Ferrara, Milan, Friuli, Brescia from the Fourteenth to the Sixteenth Century.* 2 vols. London, 1871.

CROWE AND CAVACASELLE 1885 J.A. Crowe and G.B. Cavacaselle. *Raphael Sein Leben und seine Werke.* Leipzig, 1885.

CROWE AND CAVALCASELLE 1882–1885 J.A. Crowe and G.B. Cavalcaselle. *Raphael, His Life and Works: With particular reference to Recently Discovered Records, and an Exhaustive Study of Extant Drawings and Pictures.* 2 vols. London, 1882–1885.

CZÉRE 1989 A. Czére. *Disegni di artisti bolognesi nel Museo delle Belle Arti di Budapest* (exh. cat.). Bologna, 1989.

CZÉRE 2004 A. Czére. *17th Century Italian Drawings in the Budapest Museum of Fine Arts.* Budapest, 2004.

CZÉRE 2007 A. Czére, ed. *In arte Venustas: Studies on Drawings in Honour of Teréz Gerszi, Presented on Her Eightieth Birthday.* Budapest, 2007.

DA COMO 1930 U. da Como. *Girolamo Muziano 1528–1592.* Bergamo, 1930.

DACOS 1977 N. Dacos. *Le Logge di Raffaello: Maestro e bottega di fronte all'antico.* Rome, 1977.

DACOS 1985 N. Dacos. "Hermannus Posthumus. Rome, Mantua, Landshut." *The Burlington Magazine* 127 (July 1985), pp. 433–438.

DACOS 1989 N. Dacos. "L'Anonyme A de Berlin: Hermannus Posthumus." In *Antikenzeichnung und Antikenstudium in Renaissance und Frühbarock. Akten des internationalen Symposions 8.–10. September 1986 in Coburg.* Mainz, 1989, pp. 61–80.

DACOS 1993 N. Dacos. "Entre Bruxelles et Séville. Peter de Kempeneer en Italie." In *Nederlands Kunsthistorisch Jaarboek (XLIV)*, 1993, pp. 143–164.

DACOS 1995 N. Dacos, ed. *Fiamminghi a Roma, 1508–1608: Artisti dei Paesi Bassi e del Principato di Liegi a Roma durante il Rinascimento* (exh. cat.). Brussels and Milan, 1995.

DACOS 2001 N. Dacos. *Roma quanta fuit. Tre pittori fiamminghi nella Domus Aurea,* 2nd ed., trans. Maria Baiocchi. Rome, 2001.

DAUNER 2005 G. Dauner. *Drawn Together: Two Albums of Renaissance Drawings by Girolamo da Carpi* (exh. cat.). Philadelphia, 2005.

DAVANZATI 1725 B. Davanzati. *Notizie al Pellegrino della Basilica di Santa Prassede.* Rome, 1725.

DAVIDSON 1966 B.F. Davidson. *Mostra di disegni di Perino del Vaga e la sua cerchia* (exh. cat.). Florence, 1966.

DAVIDSON 1990 B.F. Davidson. "The Cope Embroideries Designed for Paul III by Perino del Vaga." *Master Drawings* 28 (1990), pp. 123–141.

DAY AND FABER 2001 R. Day and J. Faber. *European Drawings 1570–1870.* London, 2001.

DE BISSCHOP 1671 J. de Bisschop. *Paradigmata graphices variorum artificum: voor-beelden der tekenkonst van verscheyde meesters.* The Hague, 1671.

DE GRAZIA 1984 D. De Grazia, ed. *Correggio and His Legacy: Sixteenth-Century Emilian Drawings.* Washington and Parma, 1984.

DE GRAZIA 1991 D. De Grazia. *Bertoja, Mirola and the Farnese Court.* Milan, 1991.

DE GRAZIA 1998 D. De Grazia. "Carracci Drawings in Britain and the State of Carracci Studies." *Master Drawings* 36 (1998), pp. 292–304.

DE GRAZIA AND FOSTER 2000 D. De Grazia and C.E. Foster, eds. *Master Drawings from the Cleveland Museum of Art* (exh. cat.). Cleveland and New York, 2000.

TOLNAY 1943–1960 C. de Tolnay. *Michelangelo.* 5 vols. Princeton, 1943–1960.

TOLNAY 1969 C. de Tolnay. *Michelangelo.* Princeton, 1969.

TOLNAY 1975–1980 C. de Tolnay. *Corpus dei disegni di Michelangelo.* 4 vols. Novara, 1975–1980.

DELLA PERGOLA 1955–1959 P. della Pergola. *Galleria Borghese. I dipinti,* 2 vols. Rome, 1955–1959.

DERN 2003 A. Dern. *Scipione Pulzone (c. 1546–1598).*Weimar, 2003.

DI LORENZO AND FRANGI 2007
A. Di Lorenzo and F. Frangi, eds. *La raccolta Mario Scaglia: Dipinti e sculture, medaglie e placchette da Pisanello a Ceruti.* Milan, 2007.

DREYER 1979 P. Dreyer. *I grandi disegni italiani del Kupferstich-kabinett di Berlino.* Milan, 1979.

DÜSSELDORF 1993 *Sammlung Pieter de Boer* (exh. cat.). Düsseldorf, 1993.

DUSSLER 1942 L. Dussler. *Sebastiano del Piombo.* Basel, 1942.

DUSSLER 1959 L. Dussler. *Die Zeichnungen des Michelangelo.* Berlin, 1959.

DUSSLER 1966 L. Dussler. *Raffael. Kritishes Verzeichnis der Gemälde, Wandbilder und Bildteppiche.* Munich, 1966.

ECHINGER-MAURACH 1991
C. Echinger-Maurach. *Studien zu Michelangelos Julius Grabmal.* 2 vols. Hildesheim and New York, 1991.

ECHINGER-MAURACH 1998
C. Echinger-Maurach. "Ein Entwurf Michelangelos für den Tondo Pitti und seine Beziehungen zu Leonardo da Vinci, zu antiken Werken und zu Raffael." In *Mitteilungen des Kunsthistorischen Institutes in Florenz* 42 (1998), pp. 274–310.

ECHINGER-MAURACH 2002
C. Echinger-Maurach. *Praemium Virtutis: Grabmonumente und Begräbniszermoniell im Zeichen des Humanismus: Zwischen Quattrocento und Barock: Michelangelos Entwurf für das Juliusgrabmal in New York.* Münster, 2002.

EDINBURGH 1969 *Italian 16th-Century Drawings from British Private Collections* (exh. cat.). Edinburgh, 1969.

EDINBURGH 1999 National Gallery of Scotland. *The Draughtsman's Art: Master Drawings from the National Gallery of Scotland* (exh. cat.). Edinburgh, 1999.

EGGER 1911 H. Egger. *Römische Veduten,* 2 vols. Vienna, 1911.

EISLER 1947 R. Eisler. "The Frontispiece to Sigismondo Fanti's *Triompho di Fortuna.*" *Journal of the Warburg and Courtauld Institutes* 10 (1947), pp. 155–159.

EITEL-PORTER 1997a R. Eitel-Porter. *Das Graphische Oeuvre des Cesare Nebbia 1536–1614. Mit einem Katalog der Zeichnungen.* 2 vols, Ph.D diss., University of Vienna, 1997.

EITEL-PORTER 1997b R. Eitel-Porter. "Artistic co-operation in late sixteenth-century Rome: the Sistine Chapel in S. Maria Maggiore and the Scala Santa." *The Burlington Magazine* 139 (1997), pp. 452–462.

EITEL-PORTER 1998 R. Eitel-Porter. "Andrea Lilio's Early Years in Rome. Some Newly Proposed Attributions." *Apollo* 441 (November 1998), pp. 17–22.

ELIASSON AND ELIASSON 1997
G. Eliasson and U. Eliasson. *Företagandets konst, Om Konstproduktionen i renässansens Florens.* Stockholm, 1997.

EMILYANI 1985 A. Emiliani. *Federico Barocci (Urbino 1535–1612).* 2 vols. Pesaro, 1985.

ERNST 1994 G. Ernst. "Fanti, Sigismondo." In *Dizionario biografico degli Italiani* 44. Rome, 1960–.

ESSEN AND VIENNA 2003 *Die Flämische Landschaft 1520–1700* (exh. cat.). Essen and Vienna, 2003.

FAGGIN 1965 G.T. Faggin. "Per Paolo Bril." *Paragone* 16 (July 1965), pp. 21–35.

FAIETTI 1989 M. Faietti. "A New Preparatory Drawing by Marcantonio Raimondi for His 'Kneeling Venus.'" *Print Quarterly* 6 (1989), pp. 308–321.

FAIETTI 2003 M. Faietti. "Marcantonio Raimondi e la grande stagione del bulino in Italia." In *Le tecniche calcografiche d'incisione diretta: Bulino puntasecca maniera nera,* ed. G. Mariani. Rome, 2003. pp. 55–66.

FAIETTI 2004a M. Faietti. "A Paradigm of Harmony and Disharmony: Antiquity in Bologna between the Fifteenth and Sixteenth Century." In *In the Light of Apollo: Italian Renaissance and Greece* (exh. cat.), ed. M. Gregori. Milan, 2004. pp. 444–454.

FAIETTI 2004b M. Faietti. "Paradigma di regole e di sregolatezze: L'antico a Bologna tra Quattrocento e Cinquecento." *Schede Umanistiche* 1 (2004), pp. 123–157.

FAIETTI 2005 M. Faietti. "... carte belle, più che oneste ..." In *Mythologica et Erotica: Arte e Cultura dall'antichità al XVIII secolo* (exh. cat.), ed. O. Casazza and R. Gennaioli. Livorno, 2005. pp. 90–107.

FAIETTI AND CORDELLIER 2002
M. Faietti and D. Cordellier. *Il Cinquecento a Bologna. Disegni dal Louvre e dipinti a confronto* (exh. cat.). Bologna, 2002.

FAIETTI AND OBERHUBER 1988
M. Faietti and K. Oberhuber, eds. *Bologna e l'Umanesimo 1490–1510* (exh. cat.). Bologna, 1988. Also published in German as *Humanismus in Bologna 1490–1510.*

FAIRBAIRN 1998 L. Fairbairn. *Italian Renaissance Drawings from the Collection of Sir John Soane's Museum,* 2 vols. London, 1998.

FAIRFAX MURRAY 1905–1912
C. Fairfax Murray. *Collection of Drawings by the Old Masters formed by C. Fairfax Murray (J. Pierpont Morgan Collection),* 4 vols., London, 1905–1912.

FALDI 1951 I. Faldi. "Contributi a Raffaellino da Reggio." *Bollettino d'Arte* 36 (1951).

FANTI 1983 S. Fanti. *Triompho di Fortuna* (1527). Facsimile edition. Modena, 1983.

FERINO PAGDEN 1997 S. Ferino Pagden, ed. *Vittoria Colonna: Dichterin und Muse Michelangelos* (exh. cat). Vienna and Geneva, 1997.

FERRI 1890 P.N. Ferri. *Catalogo riassuntivo della raccolta di disegni antichi e moderni posseduta dalla R. Galleria degli Uffizi di Firenze.* Rome, 1890.

FIAMMINGHI A ROMA 1995
Fiamminghi a Roma 1508–1608 (exh. cat.). Milan, 1995.

FISCHEL 1898 O. Fischel. *Raphaels Zeichnungen Versuch einer Kritik der bisher veröffentlichen Blätter.* Strasbourg, 1898.

FISCHEL 1925a O. Fischel, "An Unknown Drawing for Raphael's Disputa." *The Burlington Magazine* 47 (October 1925), pp. 174–179.

FISCHEL 1925b O. Fischel. *Raphaels Zeichnungen,* vol. 6. Berlin, 1925.

FISCHEL 1935 O. Fischel. "Un cartone per il ritratto di Leone X, nella sala di Costantino in Vaticano." *Bollettino d'arte* 28 (1935), pp. 484–486.

FLORENCE 1922 *Mostra della pittura italiana del Sei e Settecento* (exh. cat.). Florence, 1922.

FLORENCE 1964 P. Barocchi. *Mostra di disegni del Vasari e della sua cerchia* (exh. cat.). Florence, 1964.

FLORENCE 1980 *La corte il mare i mercanti: La rinascita della scienza; Editoria e societa; Astrologia, magia e alchimia* (exh. cat.). Milan and Florence, 1980.

FORNARI SCHIANCHI 1998
L. Fornari Schianchi, ed. *Galleria Nazionale di Parma: Catalogo delle opere. Il Cinquecento.* Milan, 1998.

FORNARI SCHIANCHI AND FERINO PAGDEN 2003 L. Fornari Schianchi and S. Ferino Pagden, eds. *Parmigianino e il Manierismo europeo* (exh. cat.). Milan, 2003.

FORNARI SCHIANCHI AND SPINOSA 1995 L. Fornari Schianchi and N. Spinosa, eds. *I Farnese: Arte e collezionismo* Milan, 1995.

FRANKLIN 1994 D. Franklin. *Rosso in Italy.* New Haven and London, 1994.

FRANKLIN 2002 D. Franklin. "Drawings by Parmigianino in Canadian Collections." In *Parmigianino e il manierismo europeo,* ed. L. Fornari Schianchi. Parma, 2002.

FRANKLIN 2003 D. Franklin. *Italian Drawings from the National Gallery of Canada.* Ottawa, 2003.

FRANKLIN 2005 D. Franklin. *Leonardo da Vinci, Michelangelo, and the Renaissance in Florence.* Ottawa, 2005.

FREY 1909 K. Frey. *Die Handzeichnungen Michelangelo Buonarroti,* 3 vols. Berlin, 1909.

FREY 1923 K. Frey. *Il Carteggio di Giorgio Vasari.* 2 vols. Munich, 1923–1930.

FROMMEL 1968 C.L. Frommel. *Baldassare Peruzzi als Maler und Zeichner.* Vienna, 1967.

FROMMEL 2001 C.L. Frommel. "Unbekannte Entwürfe Sangallos für die Gräber Leos X und Clemens' VII." In *Italia et Germania: Liber amicorum Arnold Esch,* ed. H. Heller, W. Paravacini, and W. Schieder, pp. 319–358. Tübingen, 2001.

FROMMEL 2003 C.L. Frommel. "Disegni sconosciuti di Sangallo per le tombe di Leone X e Clemente VII." In C.L. Frommel, *Architettura alla corte papale nel Rinascimento,* pp. 335–357. Milan, 2003.

FROMMEL ET AL. 1984
C.L. Frommel, et al. *Raffaello Architetto.* Rome, 1984.

FUSCONI 1992 G. Fusconi. *Les dessin: Les grands collectionneurs – Sir Joshua Reynolds.* Turin, 1992, pp. 157–160.

GALERIE DE LA SCALA
2008 *Dessins et Tableaux du 16ème au 20ème siecle.* Paris, 2008.

GALLERIA DORIA PAMPHILJ
1823 *Descrizione ragionata della Galleria Doria.* Rome, 1823. Galleria Doria Pamphilj, 1823.

GATHORNE-HARDY 1902
A.E. Gathorne-Hardy. *Descriptive Catalogue of Drawings in the Possession of A. E. Gathorne-Hardy.* London, 1902.

GENTILI 2008 A. Gentili. *Late Titian and the Sensuality of Painting,* ed. S. Ferino Pagden (exh. cat.). Venice, 2008.

GERE 1949 J.A. Gere. "Some Italian Drawings in the Chatsworth Exhibition." *The Burlington Magazine* 91 (1949), pp. 169–173.

GERE 1960 J.A. Gere. "Two Late Fresco Cycles by Perino del Vaga: The Massimi Chapel and the Sala Paolina." *The Burlington Magazine* 102 (January 1960).

GERE 1963 J. Gere. "Two panel-pictures by Taddeo Zuccaro." *The Burlington Magazine,* 105 (September 1963), pp. 390–395.

GERE 1965 J.A. Gere. "The Decoration of the Villa Giulia." *The Burlington Magazine,* 107 (1965), pp. 199–207.

GERE 1966a J. Gere. *Mostra di disegni degli Zuccari (Taddeo e Federico Zuccari, e Raffaellino da Reggio)* (exh. cat.). Florence, 1966.

GERE 1966b J.A. Gere. "Two of Taddeo Zuccaro's last commissions, completed by Federico Zuccaro. I. The Pucci Chapel in S. Trinità dei Monti." *The Burlington Magazine* 108 (1966), pp. 286–293.

GERE 1969a J. Gere. *Dessins de Taddeo et Federico Zuccaro* (exh. cat.). Paris, 1969.

GERE 1969b J.A. Gere. *Taddeo Zuccaro, His Development Studied in His Drawings,* Chicago, 1969.

GERE 1970 J. Gere. "The Lawrence-Phillipps-Rosenbach'Zuccaro Album'." *Master Drawings* 8 (1970), pp. 123–140.

GERE 1971 J. Gere. *Il Manierismo a Roma (I Disegni dei Maestri).* Vol. 10. Milan, 1971.

GERE 1985–1986 J.A. Gere. "Review of Lanfranco Ravelli, *Polidoro Caldara da Caravaggio: I Disegni di Polidoro; Copie da Polidoro.*" *Master Drawings,* 23–24 (1985–1986), pp. 61–74.

GERE 1987 J.A. Gere. *Drawings by Raphael and His Circle from British and North American Collections* (exh. cat.). New York, 1987.

GERE 1995 J.A. Gere. "Taddeo Zuccaro: Addenda and Corrigenda." *Master Drawings* 38 (1995), p. 275.

GERE AND POUNCEY 1983 J. Gere and P. Pouncey. *Italian Drawings in the Department of Prints and Drawings in the British Museum. Artists Working in Rome c. 1550 to c. 1640.* London, 1983.

GERE AND TURNER 1983 J.A. Gere and N. Turner. *Drawings by Raphael from the Royal Library, the Ashmolean, the British Museum, Chatsworth and Other English Collections* (exh. cat.). London, 1983.

GETTY MUSEUM 1996
"Acquisitions / 1995." *The J. Paul Getty Museum Journal* 24 (1996), p. 111.

GETTY MUSEUM 1997 *Masterpieces of the J. Paul Getty Museum: Paintings.* Los Angeles, 1997.

GHIDIGLIA QUINTAVALLE 1971
A. Ghidiglia Quintavalle. *Parmigianino, Disegni.* Florence, 1971.

GHIRARDI 1986 A. Ghirardi. "Batololomeo Passerotti." In *Pittura Bolognese del '500,* ed. V.F. Fortunati Pietrantonio. 2 vols. Bologna, 1986.

GHIRARDI 1990 A. Ghirardi. *Bartolomeo Passerotti.* Rimini, 1990.

GILBERT 1961 C. Gilbert. "A Sarasota Notebook." *Arte veneta* 15 (1961), pp. 38–42.

GILET 2001–2002 A. Gilet et al. *Dessins XVe–XXe siècles. La collection du Musée de Tours* (exh. cat.). Tours, 2001–2002.

GIOVANNETTI 1995 A. Giovannetti. *Francesco Morandini detto il Poppi.* Florence, 1995.

GNANN 1996 A. Gnann. "Zur Beteilungen des Polidoro da Caravaggio an der Ausmalung der Salone der Villa Lante." In *Ianiculum-Gianicolo: Storia, topographia, monumenti, leggende dall'antichità al rinascimento,* ed. E.M. Steinby, pp. 237–259. *Acta Instituti Romani Finlandiae* 16 (Rome, 1996), p. 75ff.

GNANN 1997   A. Gnann. *Polidoro da Caravaggio (um 1499–1543): die römischen Innendekorationen.* Munich, 1997.

GOFFEN 1997   R. Goffen. *Titian's Women.* New Haven and London, 1997.

GOLDBERG 1975–1976   V.L. Goldberg. "Leo X, Clement VII and the Immortality of the Soul." *Simiolus* 8 (1975–76), pp. 16–25.

GOLDFARB 1995   H. Goldfarb. *The Isabella Stewart Gardner Museum: A Companion Guide and History.* New Haven, 1995.

GOLDNER ET AL. 1988   G.R. Goldner et al. *European Drawings: Catalogue of the Collections, Volume 1.* Malibu, 1988.

GOLDNER 1992   G. Goldner. Review of Mundy 1989. *The Burlington Magazine* 134 (1992), pp. 124–125.

GOLDSCHEIDER 1966   L. Goldscheider. *Michelangelo Drawings.* Greenwich, CT and New York, 1966.

GOMBRICH ET AL. 1989   E.H. Gombrich et al. *Giulio Romano* (exh. cat.). Milan, 1989.

GRAMBERG 1984   W. Gramberg. "Guglielmo della Portas Grabmal für Paul III. Farnese in San Pietro in Vaticano." In *Römisches Jahrbuch für Kunstgeschichte* 21 (1984), pp. 253–364.

GRASSELLI 1995   M.M. Grasselli, ed. *The Touch of the Artist: Master Drawings from the Woodner Collection* (exh. cat.). Washington, 1995.

GREGORI AND HEIKAMP 1997   M. Gregori and D. Heikamp, eds. *Magnificenza alla corte dei Medici: Arte a Firenze alla fine del Cinquecento* (exh. cat.). Milan, 1997.

GREGOROVIUS AND HÜLSEN 1932   F. Gregorovius and C. Hülsen. *Le tombe dei papi.* Second edition revised and expanded by C. Hülsen. 2 vols. Rome, 1932.

GRIBBON 1997   D. Gribbon. "Selected Acquisitions Made by the J. Paul Getty Museum, 1995–97." *The Burlington Magazine* 139:1136 (November 1997), pp. 821–832.

GRIBBON 2001   *The J. Paul Getty Museum: Handbook of the Collections.* Introduction by D. Gribbon. Los Angeles, 2001.

GRISWOLD AND WOLK-SIMON 1994   W. Griswold and L. Wolk-Simon. *Sixteenth-Century Italian Drawings in New York Collections* (exh. cat.). New York, 1994.

GROSVENOR GALLERY 1877–1878   *Winter Exhibition of Drawings by the Old Masters and Water-colour Drawings by Deceased Artists of the British school, 1877–78* (exh. cat.). London, 1877–1878.

GRUYER 1881   F.-A. Gruyer. *Raphael – Peintre de Portraits.* Paris 1881.

HADLEY 1968   R. van N. Hadley, ed. *Drawings: Isabella Stewart Gardner Museum.* Boston, 1968.

HALL 2005   M.B. Hall, ed. *The Cambridge Companion to Raphael.* Cambridge and New York, 2005.

HAMBURG AND COLOGNE 1963–1964   *Italienische Meisterzeichnungen vom 14. bis zum 18. Jahrhundert aus amerikanischem Besitz: Die Sammlung Janos Scholz, New York* (exh. cat.). Hamburger and Cologne, 1963–1964.

HANSON AND SPICER 2005   M. Hanson and Spicer, eds. *Masterpieces of Italian Painting in the Walters Art Museum.* Baltimore, 2005.

HARPRATH 1985   R. Harprath. Raffaels Zeichnung " 'Merkur und Psyche': aus Chatsworth neuerworben für München." *Zeitschrift für Kunstgeschichte* 48 (1985), pp. 407–433.

HARTT 1944   F. Hartt. "Raphael and Giulio Romano with Notes on Raphael's School." *The Art Bulletin* 26 (1944), pp. 67–94.

HARTT 1958   F. Hartt. *Giulio Romano.* 2 vols. New Haven, 1958.

HARTT 1970   F. Hartt. *Michelangelo Drawings.* New York, 1970.

HEGENER 2008   N. Hegener. *Divi Iacobi Eques. Selbstdarstellung im Werk des Florentiner Bildhauer Baccio Bandinelli.* Munich and Berlin, 2008.

HEIKAMP 1958   D. Heikamp. "Ancora su Federico Zuccari." *Rivista d'Arte* 33 (1958), pp. 45–50.

HERRMANN FIORE 2001   K. Herrmann Fiore. "Un dipinto inventato da Federico Zuccari: la lezione di anatomia degli artisti." In *Federico Zuccari: la "Pietà degli angeli." il prototipo riscoperto del fratello Taddeo e un' "Anatomia degli artisti."* (exh. cat.). Rome, 2001.

HESS 1947   J. Hess. "On Raphael and Giulio Romano." *Gazette des Beaux-Arts* 6:32 (1947), pp. 73–106.

HIRST 1965   M. Hirst. "Tibaldi around Perino." *The Burlington Magazine* 107 (1965), pp. 569–571.

HIRST 1976   M. Hirst. "A Project of Michelangelo's for the Tomb of Julius II." *Master Drawings* 14 (1976), pp. 375–382.

HIRST 1981   M. Hirst. *Sebastiano del Piombo.* Oxford, 1981.

HIRST 1988a   M. Hirst. *Michelangelo and His Drawings.* New Haven and London, 1988.

HIRST 1988b   M. Hirst. *Michelangelo Draftsman* (exh. cat.). Washington, 1988.

HOCHMANN 1999   M. Hochmann, ed. *Villa Medici: il sogno di un cardinale. Collezioni e artisti di Ferdinando de' Medici* (exh. cat.). Rome 1999.

HÖPER 1987   C. Höper. *Bartolomeo Passerotti (1529–1592).* Worms, 1987.

HOUSTON 1966   *Builders and Humanists: The Renaissance Popes as Patrons of the Arts* (exh. cat.). Houston, 1966.

HUNTER 1988   J. Hunter. "The Drawings and Draughtsmanship of Girolamo Siciolante da Sermoneta." *Master Drawings* 26 (Spring 1988), pp. 3–35.

HUNTER 1996   J. Hunter. *Girolamo Siciolante, pittore da Sermoneta (1521–1575).* Rome, 1996.

HUNTLEY 1935   G.H. Huntley. *Andrea Sansovino, Sculptor and Architect of the Italian Renaissance.* Cambridge, MA., 1935.

JAFFÉ 1987   M. Jaffé. *Old Master Drawings from Chatsworth, A Loan Exhibition from the Devonshire Collections* (exh. cat.). Pittsburgh, 1987.

JAFFÉ 1993   M. Jaffé. *Old Master Drawings from Chatsworth* (exh. cat.). London, 1993.

JAFFÉ 1994   M. Jaffé. *The Devonshire Collection of Italian Drawings.* 4 vols. London, 1994.

JAFFE 1994   D. Jaffe. "Drawings for Renaissance Medals." In *Designs on Posterity*, ed. M. Jones. London, 1994.

JAFFÉ 1995   M. Jaffé. *A Great Heritage: Renaissance and Baroque Drawings from Chatsworth* (exh. cat.). Washington, DC, 1995.

JAFFÉ 1997   M. Jaffé. *Summary of European Paintings in the J. Paul Getty Museum.* Los Angeles, 1997.

JOANNIDES 1981   P. Joannides. Review of Charles de Tolnay, *Corpus dei Disegni di Michelangelo, The Art Bulletin* 63 (1981).

JOANNIDES 1982   P. Joannides. "Letter." *The Burlington Magazine* 124 (October 1982), p. 634.

JOANNIDES 1983   P. Joannides. *The Drawings of Raphael: With a Complete Catalogue.* Oxford, 1983.

JOANNIDES 1985   P. Joannides. "The Early Easel Paintings of Giulio Romano." *Paragone* 425 (1985), pp. 17–46.

JOANNIDES 1991   P. Joannides. "La Chronologie du tombeau de Jules II à propos d'un dessin de Michel-Ange decouvert." *Revue du Louvre* (1991), pp. 33–42.

JOANNIDES 1996   P. Joannides. *Michelangelo and His Influence: Drawings from Windsor Castle* (exh. cat.). Washington and London, 1996.

JOANNIDES 2000   P. Joannides. "Raphael and His Circle." *Paragone* 30 (March 2000), pp. 3–42.

JOANNIDES ET AL. 2003   P. Joannides, et al. *Musée du Louvre, Musée D'Orsay, Departement Des Arts Graphiques, Inventaire General Des Dessins Italiens VI: Michel-Ange, Eleves et Copistes.* Paris, 2003.

JOANNIDES 2007   P. Joannides. *The Drawings of Michelangelo and His Followers in the Ashmolean Museum.* Cambridge, New York, Melbourne, 2007.

JOANNIDES AND YOUNG 1995   P. Joannides and P. Young. "Giulio Romano's Madonna at Apsley House." *The Burlington Magazine* 137 (November 1995), pp. 728–736.

JOHNSON 1983   D.J. Johnson. *Old Master Drawings from the Museum of Art, Rhode Island School of Design* (exh. cat.). Providence, RI, 1983.

JOHNSON 2001   G.A. Johnson. "Michelangelo, Fortunetelling and the Formation of Artistic Canons in Fanti's *Triompho di Fortuna.*" In *Coming About ...: A Festschrift for John Shearman*, ed. L.R. Jones and L.C. Matthew, pp. 199–205. Cambridge, MA, 2001.

JOHNSTON 1986   C. Johnston. *Vatican Splendour. Masterpieces of Baroque Art* (exh. cat.). Ottawa, 1986.

KIRWIN 1978   C.W. Kirwin. "The Life and Drawing Style of Cristoforo Roncalli." *Paragone* 335 (January 1978).

KLESSMANN 2006   R. Klessmann. *Adam Elsheimer, 1578–1610* (exh. cat.). Edinburgh and London, 2006.

KLIEMANN 1993   J. Kliemann. *Gesta dipinte: La grande decorazione nelle dimore italiane dal Quattrocentro al Seicento.* Milan, 1993.

KNAB ET AL. 1983a   E. Knab, E. Mitsch, and K. Oberhuber. *Raphael: Die Zeichnungen.* Stuttgart, 1983.

KNAB ET AL. 1983b   E. Knab, E. Mitsch, and K. Oberhuber. *Raffaello: I disegni.* Florence, 1983.

KORNELL 1992   M.N. Kornell. *Artists and the Study of Anatomy in Sixteenth-Century Italy*, London, 1992.

KOSCHNICK 1997   L. Koschnick, ed. *Bilder und Zeugnisse der deutschen Geschichte: Aus den Sammlungen Deutschen Historischen Museums.* 2 vols. Berlin, 1997.

KULTZEN 1973   R. Kultzen. "Review of Polidoro da Caravaggio by Alessandro Marabottini (Rome, 1969, 2 vols.)" *The Art Bulletin* 55 (1973), pp. 637–639.

LANDAU AND PARSHALL 1994   D. Landau and P. Parshall. *The Renaissance Print.* London and New Haven, 1994.

LANGEDIJK 1981–1987   K. Langedijk. *The Portraits of the Medici: 15th–18th Centuries.* 3 vols. Florence, 1981–1987.

LASKIN AND PANTAZZI 1987   M. Laskin, Jr. and M. Pantazzi. *European and American Painting, Sculpture, and Decorative Arts* (exh. cat.) Vol. I 1300–1800. Ottawa, 1987.

LAWRENCE GALLERY 1853   *Lawrence Gallery. A Series of facsimiles of Original Drawings by M. Angelo Buonarotti, selected from the matchless collection formed by Sir Thomas Lawrence ... published by S. and A. Woodburn.* London, 1853.

LEEFLANG 2003   H. Leeflang, ed. *Hendrick Goltzius (1558–1617): Drawings, Prints and Paintings* (exh. cat.). New York and Toledo, 2003.

LEHMANN 1980   J.M. Lehmann. *Italienische, Französische und Spanische Gemälde des 16. bis 18. Jahrhunderts* (exh. cat.). Fridingen, 1980.

LEONE DE CASTRIS 1988   P. Leone de Castris. *Polidoro da Caravaggio fra Napoli e Messina* (ex. cat.). Naples, 1988.

LEONE DE CASTRIS 2001   P. Leone de Castris. *Polidoro da Caravaggio, L'opera completa*, Naples 2001.

LEVIE 1962   S.H. Levie. *Der Maler Daniele da Volterra, 1509–1566*, Ph.D. diss., Cologne, 1962.

LOGAN AND PLOMP 2005   A.M. Logan and M.C. Plomp. *Peter Paul Rubens: The Drawings* (exh. cat.). New York, 2005.

LONDON 1953   *Drawings by Old Masters* (exh. cat.). London, 1953.

LONDON 1996   Y. Tan Bunzl. *Mast Drawings* (dealer's cat.). London, 1996.

LONGHI 1928   R. Longhi. "Precisazioni sulle Gallerie Italiane: La Galleria Borghese" (1928). Reprinted in R. Longhi, *Saggi e Ricerche 1925–1928.* Florence, 1967.

LONGHI 1928   R. Longhi. *Precisioni nelle Gallerie italiane, I. La Galleria Borghese.* Rome, 1928.

MILLER 1990   M. Miller. "A Michelangelo Drawing." CMA Bulletin 77 (1990), pp. 146–174.

MACK 1972   R. Mack. *Girolamo Muziano.* Ph.D. diss., Harvard University, 1972.

MADONNA 1993   M.L. Madonna, ed. *Roma di Sisto V. Le arti e la cultura* (exh. cat.). Rome, 1993.

MANTUA 1999   K. Oberhuber and A. Gnann. *Roma e lo stile classico di Raffaello: 1515–1527* (exh. cat.). Mantua, 1999.

MARABOTTINI 1969   A. Marabottini. *Polidoro da Caravaggio*, 2 vols, Rome, 1969.

MARCIARI 2000   J. Marciari. *Girolamo Muziano and Art in Rome, ca. 1550–1600.* Ph.D. diss., Yale University, 2000.

MARCIARI 2002   J. Marciari. "Girolamo Muziano and the Dialogue of Drawings in Cinquecento Rome." *Master Drawings* 40 (2002), pp. 113–134.

MARCIARI 2006   J. Marciari. "Raffaellino da Reggio in the Vatican." *The Burlington Magazine* 148 (March 2006), pp.187–191.

478

MARIETTE 1851–1860
P.-J. Mariette. *Abecedario de P.-J. Mariette et autres notes inédites sur les arts et les artistes*, vol. 2. Archives de l'Art Français, ed. Philippe de Chennevières and Anatole de Montaiglon. Paris, 1851–1860.

MARMUGI 1984   C. Marmugi, ed. *Raffaello a Firenze: Dipinti e disegni delle collezioni fiorentine* (exh. cat.). Florence, 1984.

MARTIN 1965   J. R. Martin. *The Farnese Gallery*. Princeton, 1965.

MARTINELLI 1969   F. Martinelli. "Roma ornata dall'Architettura, Pittura e Scoltura." In *Roma nel Seicento*, ed. C. D'Onofrio. Rome, 1969.

MASSARI 1993   S. Massari, ed. *Giulio Romano pinxit et delineavit: Opere grafiche autografe di collaborazione e bottega* (exh. cat.) Mantua, 1993.

MASSING 1990   J.M. Massing. *Du texte à l'image: la calomnie d'Apelle et son iconographie*. Strasbourg, 1990.

MATZ 1969   F. Matz. *Die dionysischen Sarkophage,* vol. 3. Berlin, 1969.

MCGRATH 1994   T.H. McGrath. "*Disegno, colore* and the *disegno colorito: The Use and Significance of Color in Italian Renaissance Drawings*. Ph.D. diss., Harvard University, 1994.

MCGRATH 1998   T.H. McGrath. "Federico Barocci and the History of *pastelli* in Central Italy. *Apollo* 148 (1998), pp. 3–9.

MCTAVISH 1981   D. McTavish. *Giuseppe Porta called Giuseppe Salviati*, New York/London, 1981.

MCTAVISH 1985–1986
D. McTavish. *Italian Drawings from the Collection of Duke Roberto Ferretti* (exh. cat.). Toronto and New York, 1985–1986.

MCTAVISH 2008   D. McTavish. "Review of Dominique Cordellier, *Polidoro da Caravaggio*"(exh. cat.). Paris, 2007. *Master Drawings* 46 (2008), pp. 386–392.

MEIJER 1985   B.W. Meijer. *I Grandi Disegni Italiani del Teylers Museum di Haarlem*. Milan, 1985.

MEIJER AND VAN TUYLL VAN SEROOSKERKEN 1983   B.W. Meijer and C. van Tuyll van Serooskerken, eds. *Disegni Italiani del Teyler Museum Haarlem provenienti dalle collezioni di Cristina di Svezia e dei principi Odescalchi* (exh.cat.). Florence, 1983.

MELLER 1976   P. Meller. "Riccio's Satyress Triumphant: Its Source, Its Meaning." *The Bulletin of the Cleveland Museum of Art* 63 (1976), pp. 324–334.

MEYER ZUR CAPELLEN 2005
J. Meyer zur Capellen. *Raphael: A Critical Catalogue of His Paintings. Volume II: The Roman Religious Paintings ca. 1509–1520*. Landshut, Germany, 2005.

MIDDELDORF 1934   U. Middeldorf. "Two Sansovino Drawings." *The Burlington Magazine* 64 (1934), pp. 159–164.

MIEDEMA 1969   H. Miedema. "Het voorbeheld niet te bij te hebben: over Hendrick Goltzius' tekeningen naar de antieken." In *Miscellanea I. Q. van Regteren Altena*. Amsterdam 1969, pp. 74–78.

MILKOVICH AND PORTER 1970
M. Milkovich and D. Porter, eds. *The Age of Vasari. A Loan Exhibition under the High Patronage of His Excellency, Egidio Ortona, the Ambassador of Italy to the United States* (exh. cat.). Notre Dame, Indiana 1970

MILLER 1990   M. Miller, "A Michelangelo Drawing." *CMA Bulletin* 77 (1990), pp. 146–174.

MONBEIG GOGUEL 1972
C. Monbeig Goguel. *Vasari et son temps: maîtres toscans nés après 1500, morts avant 1600*. Paris, 1972.

MONBEIG GOGUEL 1998
C. Monbeig Goguel, ed. *Francesco Salviati (1510–1563), o la Bella Maniera* (exh.cat.). Rome and Paris, 1998.

MONBEIG GOGUEL 1999
C. Monbeig-Goguel. "Drawings by Raphael and His Circle: Mantua, Vienna and London." *The Burlington Magazine* 141 (1999), pp. 495–499.

MONBEIG GOGUEL 2004
C. Monbeig Goguel. "Attualità della ricerca su Francesco Salviati, dieci anni dopo la monografia di Luisa Mortari." In *Per la storia dell'arte in Italia e in Europa. Studi l omore di Luisa Mortari*, M. Pasculli Ferrera, ed., pp. 203–211. Rome, 2004.

MONBEIG GOGUEL ET AL. 2001
C. Monbeig Goguel, P. Costamagna, and M. Hochmann, eds. *Francesco Salviati et la Bella Maniera: actes des colloques de Rome et de Paris (1998)*. Rome, 2001.

MONTINI 1957   R.U. Montini. *Le tombe dei papi*. Rome, 1957.

MORROGH 1985   A. Morrogh. *Disegni di architetti fiorentini 1540–1640* (exh. cat.). Florence, 1985.

MORTARI 1992   L. Mortari. *Francesco Salviati*, Rome, 1993.

MUNDY 1989   E.J. Mundy. *Renaissance into Baroque, Italian Master Drawings by the Zuccari, 1550–1600* (exh. cat.). Milwaukee, 1989.

MUSEO THYSSEN-BORNEMISZA 2004
J. Arnaldo, ed. *Carmen Thyssen-Bornemisza Collection*. 2 vols. Madrid, 2004.

NEW YORK 1967   *The Italian Heritage. An Exhibition of Works of Art Lent from American Collections for the Benefit of the Committee to Rescue Italian Art* (exh. cat.). Providence, 1967.

NEW YORK 1985a   *The Age of Caravaggio* (exh. cat.). New York, 1985.

NEW YORK 1985b   *Liechtenstein: The Princely Collections* (exh. cat.). New York, 1985.

NEW YORK 1985c
The Metropolitan Museum of Art. *Notable Acquisitions 1984–1985*. New York, 1985.

NEW YORK AND LONDON 2004
Master Drawings 2004 (exh. cat.). New York and London 2004.

NOBILI AND CIROLDI 1988
U. Nobili and S. Ciroldi. *Allievi e collaboratori di Lelio Orsi: la lezione di un maestro* (exh. cat.). Reggio Emilia, 1988.

NOLAN 2001   J. Nolan. *Selected Masterworks from the Bob Jones University Museum and Gallery*. Greenville, North Carolina 2001.

NOVA 1984   A. Nova. "The Chronology of the De Monte Chapel in S. Pietro in Montorio in Rome." *The Art Bulletin* 66:1 (1984) pp. 150–154.

OBERHUBER 1962   K. Oberhuber. "Vorzeichnungen zu Raffaels 'Transfiguration'." *Jahrbuch der Berliner Museen* 4 (1962), pp. 116–149.

OBERHUBER 1966   K. Oberhuber. "Observations on Perino del Vaga as a Draughtsman." *Master Drawings* 4 (1966), pp. 170–182.

OBERHUBER 1972   K. Oberhuber. *Raphael's Zeichnungen. Abteilung IX. Entwürfe zu Werken Raphaels und seiner Schule im Vatikan, 1511–1512 bis 1520*. Berlin, 1972.

OBERHUBER 1982   K. Oberhuber. *Raphaels "Transfiguration": Stil und Bedeutung*. Stuttgart, 1982.

OBERHUBER 1986   K. Oberhuber. "Raphael's Drawings for the Loggia of Psyche in the Farnesina." In *Raffaello a Roma: il convegno del 1983*. pp. 189–207. Rome, 1986.

OBERHUBER 1999   K. Oberhuber. *Raphaël*. Paris, 1999.

OBERHUBER AND WALKER 1973
K. Oberhuber and D. Walker. *Sixteenth Century Italian Drawings from the Collection of Janos Scholz* (exh. cat.). New York, 1973.

OLSZEWSKI 1981   E.J. Olszewski. *The Draftsman's Eye: Late Italian Renaissance Schools and Styles* (exh. cat.). Cleveland, 1981.

ORSINI DE MARZO 2006   N. Orsini de Marzo. "From the Gallery: Dalla Galleria Borghese di Roma a una casa Borghese Romana." *Bollettino della Società Storica Valtellinese* 59 (2006), pp. 227–250.

PAGNOTTA 1987   L. Pagnotta. *Giuliano Bugiardini*. Turin, 1987.

PARIS 1992   *L'oeil du connaisseur: Hommage à Philip Pouncey* (exh. cat.). Paris, 1992.

PARKER 1956   K.T. Parker. *Catalogue of the Collection of Drawings in the Ashmolean Museum, vol. 2. Italian Schools*. Oxford, 1956.

PARMA 2001   E. Parma. *Perino del Vaga tra Raffaello e Michelangelo* (exh. cat.). Milan, 2001.

PARMA ARMANI 1986   E. Parma Armani. *Perin del Vaga: L'anello mancante*. Genoa, 1986.

PARTRIDGE AND STARN 1990
L. Partridge and R. Starn. "Triumphalism and the Sala Regia in the Vatican." In *"All the World's a Stage...": Art and Pageantry in the Renaissance and Baroque*. Part 1, *Triumphal Celebrations and the Rituals of Statecraft*. Papers in Art History from The Pennsylvania State University. University Park, PA, 1990, pp. 22–81.

PASSAVANT 1836   J.D. Passavant. *Tour of a German Artist in England: With Notices of Private Galleries, and Remarks on the State of Art*. 2 vols. London, 1836.

PASSAVANT 1860   J.D. Passavant. *Raphaël d'Urbin et son père Giovanni Santi*. 2 vols. Paris 1860.

PATTANARO 2000   A. Pattanaro. *Girolamo da Carpi: Ritratti*. Cittadella, 2000.

PELLI BENCIVENNI 1793   G. Pelli Bencivenni. *Inventario dei Disegni, ante 1793*. Gabinetto Disegni e Stampe degli Uffizi, ms. 102. Florence, 1793.

PEPPER 1984   D.S. Pepper. *Bob Jones University Collection of Religious Art: Italian Paintings*. Greenville, South Carolina, 1984.

PERRIG 1976   A. Perrig. *Michelangelo Studien*, Frankfurt, 1976.

PERRIG 1991   A. Perrig. *Michelangelo's Drawings: The Science of Attribution*, trans. M. Joyce. New Haven and London, 1991.

PESSACH 2000   G. Pessach, ed. *Landscapes of the Bible: Sacred Scenes in European Master Paintings* (exh. cat.). Jerusalem, 2000.

PETRIOLI TOFANI 1986   A. Petrioli Tofani, ed. *Gabinetto Disegni e Stampe degli Uffizi, Inventario 1: Disegni esposti*. Florence, 1986.

PETRIOLI TOFANI 2005   A. Petroli Tofani, ed. *Inventario: Gabinetto disegni e stampe degli Uffizi*. Florence, 2005.

PETRIOLI TOFANI AND DE VECCHI 1982   A. Petrioli Tofani and P. De Vecchi. *I disegni di Raffaello nel Gabinetto dei disegni e delle stampe degli Uffizi*. Milan, 1982.

PETRUCCI 2005   F. Petrucci. *Papi in Posa, 500 Years of Papal Portraiture* (exh. cat.). Washington, 2005.

PHOENIX 1999   *Copper as Canvas. Two Centuries of Masterpiece Paintings on Copper 1575–1775* (exh. cat.). Phoenix, 1999.

PILLSBURY 1974a   E. Pillsbury. "Drawings by Jacopo Zucchi." *Master Drawings* 12 (1974), pp. 3–33.

PILLSBURY 1974b   E. Pillsbury. "Jacopo Zucchi in S. Spirito in Sassia." *The Burlington Magazine* 116 (1974), pp. 434–444.

PILLSBURY 1980   E.P. Pillsbury. "The Cabinet Paintings of Jacopo Zucchi: their Meaning and Function." In *Monuments et mémoires publiés par l'Académie des inscriptions et belles-lettres*. 63 (1980), pp. 187–226.

PILLSBURY AND RICHARDS 1978
E.P. Pillsbury and L.S. Richards. *The Graphic Art of Federico Barocci*. Cleveland and New Haven, 1978.

PINELLI 1977   A. Pinelli. "Pittura e Controriforma. 'Convenienza' e misticismo in Giovanni de' Vecchi. Note e schede." *Ricerche di storia dell'arte*, 6 (1977), pp. 49–85.

POGGI 1909   G. Poggi. "Due affreschi di Perino del Vaga nella Galleria degli Uffizi." *Bollettino d'arte* 3 (1909).

PON 2004   L. Pon. *Raphael, Dürer, and Marcantonio Raimondi: Copying and Italian Renaissance Print*. New Haven and London, 2004.

POPE-HENNESSY 1985   J. Pope-Hennessy. *Cellini*. London, 1985.

POPHAM 1931   E. Popham. *Italian Drawings Exhibited at the Royal Academy Burlington House London*, 1930. London, 1931.

POPHAM 1935   A.E. Popham. *Catalogue of Drawings in the Collection Formed by Sir Thomas Phillipps, Bart., F.R.S., Now in the Possession of His Grandson, T. Fitzroy Phillipps Fenwick of Thirlestaine House, Cheltenham*, vol. I. London, 1935.

POPHAM 1960   A.E. Popham. *Italian Art and Britain* (exh. cat.). London, 1960.

POPHAM 1961   A.E. Popham, ed. *Old Master Drawings from Chatsworth* (exh. cat.). Manchester, 1961.

POPHAM 1962–1963   A.E. Popham. *Old Master Drawings from Chatsworth* (exh. cat.). Washington, 1962–1963.

POPHAM 1969   A.E. Popham, ed. *Old Master Drawings from Chatsworth* (exh. cat. reprinted from Washington 1962–1963). London, 1969.

POPHAM 1971   A.E. Popham. *Catalogue of the Drawings of Parmigianino*. 3 vols. New Haven and London, 1971.

POPHAM AND FENWICK 1965
A.E. Popham and K.M. Fenwick. *European Drawings in the Collection of the National Gallery of Canada*. Toronto, 1965.

POPHAM AND WILDE 1949
A.E. Popham and J. Wilde. *The Italian Drawings of the XV and XVI Centuries in the Collection of His Majesty the King at Windsor Castle*. London, 1949.

POSNER 1971 D. Posner. *Annibale Carracci. A Study in the Reform of Italian Painting around 1590*. 2 vols. London, 1971.

POTTS 2003 T. Potts. *Kimbell Art Museum: Handbook of the Collection*. New Haven, 2003.

POUNCEY 1952 P. Pouncey. "Two Drawings by Cristofano Roncalli." *The Burlington Magazine* 94 (1952), p. 356.

POUNCEY 1977 P. Pouncey. "A 'Bozzetto' by Roncalli for his Altarpiece in St. Peter's." *The Burlington Magazine* 119 (March, 1977).

POUNCEY AND GERE 1962 P. Pouncey and J. Gere. *Italian Drawings in the Department of Prints and Drawings in the British Museum: Raphael and His Circle*. London, 1962.

PRATT 1966 R.E. Pratt [Rosamond Mack]. "An Unpublished Drawing for the Sala di Costantino in the Isabella Stewart Gardner Museum, Boston." Unpublished paper submitted to the Department of Fine Arts, Harvard University, in partial fullfilment of requirements for the Ph.D. diss., August 1966.

PULINI 2003 M. Pullini. *Andrea Lilio*. Milan, 2003.

PY 2001 B. Py. *Everhard Jabach Collectioneur (1618–1695): les dessins de l'inventaire de 1695*. Paris, 2001.

QUEDNAU 1979 R. Quednau. *Die Sala di Costantino im Vatikanischen Palast: Zur Dekoration der beiden Medici-Päpste Leo X. und Clemens VII*. Hildesheim and New York, 1979.

RAGGHIANTI COLLOBI 1973 L. Ragghianti Collobi. "Nuove precisazioni sui disegni di architettura del "Libro" del Vasari." *Critica d'arte* 38 (1973), 55–71.

RAGGHIANTI COLLOBI 1974 L. Ragghianti Collobi. *Il libro de' disegni del Vasari*. Florence, 1974.

RAMDOHR 1787 F.W.B. Ramdohr. *Über Mahlerei und Bildhauerarbeit für Liebhaber des Schönen in der Kunst*, 3 vols. Leipzig, 1787.

RAVELLI 1972 L. Ravelli. "Gli affreschi della Cappella della Passione in S. Maria della Pietà in Camposanto a Roma." *Bergamo Arte* 12 (1972), pp. 27–28.

RAVELLI 1978 L. Ravelli. *Polidoro Caldara da Caravaggio*, Bergamo 1978.

RAVELLI 1988 L. Ravelli. *Un Fregio di Polidoro a Palazzo Baldassini in Roma*. Bergamo, 1988.

REDFORD 1878 G. Redford. *Descriptive Catalogue of Works of Art at Overstone Park*. Lockinge House and Carlton Gardens, 1878.

REDFORD 1888 G. Redford. *Art Sales. A History of Sales of Pictures and other Works of Art*, 2 vols. London, 1888.

REVELEY 1820 H. Reveley. *Notices Illustrative of the Drawings and Sketches of the Most Distinguished Masters in All the Principal Schools of Design*. London, 1820.

REZNICEK 1961 E.K.J. Reznicek. *Die Zeichnungen von Hendrik Goltzius. Mit einem beschreibenden Katalog*, 2 vols. Utrecht, 1961.

ROBERTSON 1992 C. Robertson. *'Il Gran Cardinale.' Alessandro Farnese, Patron of the Arts*. New Haven and London, 1992.

ROBERTSON 2000 C. Robertson. "Washington: Drawings by Annibale Carracci." *The Burlington Magazine* 142 (2000), pp. 63–65.

ROBERTSON 2001–2002 C. Robertson. "New Documents for the tomb of Paul III." In *Römisches Jahrbuch der Bibliotheca Hertziana*, 34 (2001/2002), pp. 201–220.

ROBERTSON 2008 Clare Robertson. "Patronage Rivalries: Cardinals Odoardo Farnese and Pietro Aldobrandini." In *Art and Identity in Early Modern Rome*, ed. J. Burke and M. Bury. Aldershot, 2008.

ROHLMANN 1994 M. Rohlmann. "Leoninische Siegverheissung und clementinische Heilserfüllung in der Sala di Costantino." *Zeitschrift für Kunstgeschichte* 57 (1994), pp. 153–169.

ROLFS 1925 W. Rolfs. "Klemens VII. und Peter Carnesecchi." *Repertorium für Kunstwissenschaft* 45 (1925), pp. 117–140.

ROLI 1965 R. Roli. "Giovanni de' Vecchi." *Arte antica e moderna* 29 (1965), pp. 45–56 and 324–334.

ROMALLI 2009 C. Romalli. "New Proposals for Some Late Mannerist Drawings and Frescoes in Rome." *Master Drawings* 47 (2009), pp. 85–93.

ROMANI 1990 V. Romani. *Tibaldi "d'intorno" a Perino (quaderni del seminario di storia dell'arte moderna, 3)*. Padua, 1990.

ROMANI 1997 V. Romani. *Primaticcio, Tibaldi, e la questione delle "cose del cielo."* Cittadella (Padua), 1997.

ROMANI 2003 V. Romani, ed. *Daniele da Volterra: Amico di Michelangelo*, ed. Vittoria Romani (exh. cat.). Florence, 2003.

ROME 1984 *Aspetti dell'arte a Roma prima e dopo Raffaello* (exh. cat.). Rome, 1984.

ROSAND 1988 D. Rosand. "Raphael Drawings Revisited." *Master Drawings* 26 (1988).

ROSENBERG 1997 P. Rosenberg, ed. *La donation Jacques Petithory au Musée Bonnat: objets d'art, sculptures, dessins*. Paris, 1997.

RÖTTGEN 2002 H. Röttgen. *Il Cavalier Giuseppe Cesari D'Arpino. Un grande pittore nello splendore della fama e nell'inconsistenza della fortuna*. Rome, 2002.

RUBINSTEIN 1985 R.O. Rubinstein. "'Tempus edax rerum': A Newly Discovered Painting by Hermannus Posthumus." *The Burlington Magazine* 127 (July 1985), pp. 425–433.

RUBY 1999 L.W. Ruby. *Paul Bril: The Drawings*. Turnhout, 1999.

RUIZ MANERO 1996 J.M. Ruiz Manero. "Raphael y su escuela." In *Pintura italiana del siglo XVI en España*, vol. 2, pp. 69–71. Madrid, 1996.

RULAND 1876 C. Ruland. *The Works of Raphael Santi da Urbino as Represented in the Raphael Collection in the Royal Library at Windsor Castle Formed by H.R.H. The Prince Consort, 1853–1861 and Completed by Her Majesty Queen Victoria*. Weimar, 1876, 59 vols. Venice, 1879–1903.

RUSSELL 1924 A.G.B. Russell. Notice in *The Vasari Society*. 2nd ser., pt. 5. Oxford, 1924.

RUSSELL 1982a F. Russell. "The Spinola *Holy Family* of Giulio Romano." *The Burlington Magazine* 124 (May 1982), pp. 297–298.

RUSSELL 1982b F. Russell. "Letter." *The Burlington Magazine* 124 (October 1982), p. 634.

SAFARIK 1981 E.A. Safarik. *Catalogo Sommario della Galleria Colonna in Roma: Depinti*. Busto Arsizio, 1981.

SCAILLIÉREZ ET AL. 2007 C. Scailliérez, C. Sindaco-Domas, C. Mouterde et al. "L'ardoise double-face de Daniele da Volterra figurant David et Goliath: étude et restauration d'une oeuvre d'exception." *Techné: Science et conservation* 25 (2007), pp. 5–11.

SCAVIZZI 1960 G. Scavizzi. "Gli affreschi della Scala Santa ed alcune aggiunte per il tardo manierismo romano." *Bollettino d'arte* 45 (1960), pp. 111–122 and 325–335.

SCAVIZZI AND SCHWED 2006 G. Savizzi and N. Schwed. *Ferraù Fenzoni. Pittore/Disegnatore, as a Painter/as a Draughtsman*. Todi, 2006.

SCHLICHTENMAIER 1988 H. Schlichtenmaier. "Studien zum Werk Hans Rottenhammers des Älteren Maler und Zeichner." Ph.D. diss., Tübingen, 1988.

SCHWARZ 1953 Heinrich Schwarz. "Two Drawings attributed to Domenico Passignano." *The Art Quarterly* 16 (1953), pp. 336–340.

SCHWED 2000 N. Schwed. "New Drawings by Ferraù Fenzoni." *Master Drawings* 38 (2000), pp. 29–54.

SCHWED 2007 N. Schwed. "Commentaires et additions au catalogue d'Andrea Lilli, dit Andrea d'Ancona." *Bulletin de l'Association des Historiens de l'Art Italian*, no. 13 (2007), pp. 57–70.

SCHWEIKHART 1986 G. Schweikhart. *Der Codex Wolfegg: Zeichnungen nach der Antike von Amico Aspertini*. London, 1986.

SCORZA 2003 R. Scorza. "Vincenzo Borghini's Collection of Paintings, Drawings and Wax Models. New Evidence from Manuscript Sources." *Journal of the Warburg and Courtauld Institutes*. 66 (2003), pp. 63–122.

SCRASE 2006 D. Scrase, ed. *A Touch of the Divine: Drawings by Federico Barocci in British Collections* (exh. cat.). Cambridge, 2006.

SESTIERI 1942 E. Sestieri. *Catalogo della Galleria ex-fidecommissaria Doria-Pamphilj*. Rome 1942.

SHEARMAN 1972 J. Shearman. *Raphael's Cartoons in the Collection of Her Majesty the Queen and the Tapestries for the Sistine Chapel*, London 1972.

SHEARMAN 1983 J. Shearman. *The Early Italian Pictures in the Collection of Her Majesty the Queen*. Cambridge, 1983.

SHEARMAN 2007 J. Shearman. *Studi su Raffaello*, ed. B. Agosti and V. Romani. Rome, 2007.

SIEBENHÜNER 1962 H. Siebenhüner. "Umrisse zur Geschichte der Ausstattung von St. Peter in Rom von Paul III bis Paul V (1547–1606)." In *Festschrift für Hans Sedlmayr*. Munich, 1962.

SMITH 1970 G. Smith. "A Drawing for the Interior Decoration of the Casino of Pius IV." *The Burlington Magazine* 112 (1970), pp. 83–91.

SMITH 1976 G. Smith. "A Drawing for the Sala Regia." *The Burlington Magazine*, 118 (1976), pp. 102–106.

SMITH 1977 G. Smith. *The Casino of Pius IV*. Princeton, 1977.

SMITH 1978 G. Smith. "Review of Pillsbury and Richards 1978." *The Burlington Magazine* 120 (1978), pp. 330–333.

SMITH O'NEIL 2002 M. Smith O'Neil. *Giovanni Baglione. Artistic Reputation in Baroque Rome*. Cambridge, 2002.

SPAZZOLI 1972 Franco Spazzoli. "Livio Agresti, attualità di un piccolo maestro." *Studi romagnoli* 23 (1972), pp. 63–96.

SPICER 2004 J. Spicer. *Dutch and Flemish Drawings from the National Gallery of Ottawa*. Ottawa, 2004.

STOCK 1984 J. Stock. "A Drawing by Raphael of *Lucretia*." *The Burlington Magazine*, 126 (July 1984). pp. 423–424.

STOCK AND SCRASE 1985 J. Stock and D. Scrase, eds. *The Achievement of a Connoisseur: Philip Pouncey* (exh. cat.). Cambridge, 1985.

STOLZENBURG 2000 A. Stolzenburg. "An Inventory of Goltzius Drawings from the Collection of Queen Christina." *Master Drawings* 38 (2000), pp. 424–442.

STRINATI ET AL. 2008 C.M. Strinati, B.W. Lindemann, and R. Contini, eds. *Sebastiano del Piombo, 1485–1547* (exh. cat.). Rome and Berlin, 2008.

STRINATI AND WALTER 1995 C. Strinati and I. Walter, eds. *La Dignità del Casato: Il salotto dipinto di Palazzo Farnese* Rome, 1995.

TALVACCHIA 2007 B. Talvacchia. *Raphael*. London, 2007.

THIEM 2002 C. Thiem. *Das römische Reiseskizzenbuch des Florentiners Giovanni Battista Naldini, 1560/61*. Munich and Berlin, 2002.

THODE 1908 H. Thode. *Michelangelo: Kritische Untersuchungen über seine Werke*, vol. 1. Berlin, 1908.

THOMPSON AND BRIGSTOCKE 1978 C. Thompson and H. Brigstocke. *National Gallery of Scotland: Shorter Catalogue*. 2nd rev. ed. Edinburgh, 1978.

TIETZE AND TIETZE-CONRAT 1937 H. Tietze and E. Tietze-Conrat. "Contributi critici allo studio organico dei disegni veneziani del cinquecento." *Critica d'arte* 8 (1937), pp. 77–88.

TITI 1674–1763 F. Titi. *Studio di Pittura, Scoltura, et Architettura, nelle Chiese di Roma (1674–1763)*, ed. B. Contardi and S. Romano, 2 vols. Florence 1987.

TOESCA 1966 I. Toesca. "La Flagellazione in Santa Prassede." *Paragone* 193 (1966), pp. 79–85.

TOMORY 1976 P. Tomory. *Catalogue of the Italian Paintings before 1800: The John and Mable Ringling Museum of Art, Sarasota* (Sarasota, 1976), p. 106.

TOSINI 1994 P. Tosini, "Rivedendo Giovanni de' Vecchi." *Storia dell'Arte* 82 (1994), pp. 303–347.

TOSINI 1997 P. Tosini. "Un Muziano ritrovato: la 'Visitazione' della cappella Altoviti a Loreto (e alcune annotazioni in margine al catalogo dell'artista)." *Paragone* 48 (1997), pp. 66–80.

TOTTI 1638 P. Totti. *Ritratto di Roma Moderna*. Rome 1638.

TOWNSEND 1994 R.P. Townsend, ed. *Botticelli to Tiepolo: Three Centuries of Italian Painting from Bob Jones University* (exh. cat.). Washington 1994.

TURNER 2009 N. Turner. *Drawn to Italian Drawings: The Goldman Collection*. Chicago, 2009 (forthcoming).

TURNER ET AL. 2001 N. Turner et al. *European Drawings 4: Catalogue of the Collections*. Los Angeles, 2001.

UTRILLO 1907 M. Utrillo. "De la colección Beruete" *Forma* 2. Barcelona, 1907.

480